All recipes that appear in *Southern Living* are tested, tasted, and reviewed by home economists in our test kitchens.

All three kitchens open off a dining area with the garden kitchen (right) designed as an extension of the dining space. The country kitchen is to the left, the gourmet kitchen at center.

Above: Martha Hinrichs, Test Kitchens Director

Right: Foods Editor, Jean Wickstrom Liles

Southern Living®
1979 ANNUAL RECIPES

Oxmoor House, Inc., Birmingham

Copyright © 1979 by Oxmoor House, Inc.
Book Division of The Progressive Farmer Company
Publisher of *Southern Living*®, *Progressive Farmer*®, and
Decorating & Craft Ideas® magazines.
P.O. Box 2463, Birmingham, Alabama 35201

Eugene Butler	Chairman of the Board
Emory Cunningham	President and Publisher
Vernon Owens, Jr.	Senior Executive Vice President

Conceived, edited and published by Oxmoor House, Inc., under the
direction of:

Don Logan	Vice President and General Manager
Gary McCalla	Editor, *Southern Living*
John Logue	Editor-in-Chief
Jean Wickstrom Liles	Foods Editor, *Southern Living*
Ann H. Harvey	Managing Editor
Jerry Higdon	Production Manager
Mary Jean Haddin	Editor

Southern Living® *1979 Annual Recipes*

Designer and Illustrator: Carol Middleton
Food Art: *Southern Living* Art Staff
Photography: *Southern Living* Photographic Staff

Production Assistant: Joan Denman
Production Manager, *Southern Living*: Clay Nordan
Editorial Assistants: Annette Thompson, Rebecca Morton,
  Nita Robinson, Jo Voce, Cecilia Robinson
Assistant Foods Editors: Margaret Chason, Jane Elliott, Linda Welch
Foods Assistants: Martha Hinrichs, Diane Hogan, Ann Lewis,
  Karen Parker, Susan Payne, Peggy Smith

Southern Living® and *Progressive Farmer*® are federally registered trade-
marks belonging to The Progressive Farmer Company. *Decorating &
Craft Ideas*® is a federally registered trademark belonging to Southern
Living, Inc. *Southern Breakfasts*™, *Summer Suppers*®, and *Holiday
Dinners*™ are trademarks of The Progressive Farmer Company.

Library of Congress Catalog Number: 79-88364
ISBN: 0-8487-0513-0

Manufactured in the United States of America
First Printing 1979

*Page i: Celebrate summer with an old-
fashioned vegetable dinner. Recipes,
plus tips on selection and storage, begin on
page 122.*

Table of Contents

Introduction

At *Southern Living* each morning's mail brings continuing evidence that our readers are using and enjoying our recipes. Not only do readers furnish us their favorite recipes for possible publication, but also a significant portion of the daily mail contains reader requests for recipes previously published in *Southern Living*. A common theme of these letters is that through the years a favorite recipe has been misplaced or possibly loaned to a friend who has forgotten to return it.

Another comment frequent in our letters is that many of our readers clip and save each month's recipes. Not only is this a time-consuming task, but we believe most *Southern Living* readers would really enjoy keeping each issue intact.

From these letters came the idea for *Southern Living's 1979 Annual Recipes*. This cookbook contains every recipe published in *Southern Living* during 1979 (over 1300 recipes). A major goal of our book is to make every recipe easy to find.

At the beginning of our book, you will find a table of contents listing the month and name of every *Southern Living* food article in the order in which it appears in the cookbook. This table of contents gives a broad overview of the contents of the book which includes our food features plus bonus articles. These are the food columns that we run in different state issues in different months. By referring to the table of contents you can easily determine where in the book a specific article appears.

To assist you in finding specific recipes, three detailed indexes are included at the end of the book. First, there is a title index where every recipe is alphabetized according to the first word of the title. Second, there is a month-by-month index which lists every article and the recipes contained in that article. Finally, there is an extensive, cross-referenced general index. If you only remember the basic ingredient of a recipe, you can quickly find the recipe you are looking for.

We believe that the combination of the table of contents and the three indexes makes *1979 Annual Recipes* a ready source of your favorite recipes. But this is more than just a recipe book. For instance, you will find in the Appendices an invaluable and extensive kitchen reference guide. There is a spice and herb chart; timetables for cooking meat, fish, and poultry; equivalent weights and measures table; and many more cooking aids. An added bonus of this cookbook is more than 30 pages of color photographs illustrating many of the recipes and menus.

One thing that we have always felt set the *Southern Living* food section apart from those in other publications is that virtually every recipe we publish comes to us from our readers. Each month our readers favor us with literally thousands of their family's favorite recipes. Before we even receive these recipes they have passed a taste test in homes throughout the South. But before these recipes are published, they are tested, tasted, and eva-

luated by our staff of experienced home economists. Several factors are considered in recipe evaluation: taste, appearance, ease of preparation, and cost of dish.

While the taste of a recipe is, of course, important, the appearance of a dish adds much to its overall appeal. In view of the active pace of most people's lives and the increased cost of living, ease of preparation and cost of preparing a recipe are important factors to consider in reviewing our recipes.

And our staff of home economists test each recipe in kitchens much like yours. In 1978 we completely redesigned our testing facilities to make them as much like your home kitchen as possible. We sincerely believe that you would feel just as comfortable in our kitchens as you do in yours.

Beyond the testing of these recipes, a number of talented journalists, editors, photographers, and artists have contributed their considerable skills to each month's food section. The care which goes into each issue of *Southern Living* has been incorporated in *Southern Living's 1979 Annual Recipes*.

But this cookbook is not just for those familiar with the magazine. It is for cooks everywhere who are searching for new ways to please the appetites of family and friends. Therefore, we believe you will find this book to be the most practical, usable cookbook in your kitchen.

Jean Wickstrom Liles

January

Southern custom calls for eating black-eyed peas on New Year's Day to ensure good luck throughout the year. Whether you prefer to serve the traditional Hopping John or want to try a newer dish such as Pickled Black-Eyed Peas, you will find some delicious ways to start the New Year off right.

After the holiday feasting, you often think of serving meals that have a lighter touch. Citrus fruits are a perfect solution, as they brighten snacks, salads, and desserts without adding excess calories. And you should not pass by spinach and cabbage, two wintertime vegetables that are at the height of their season.

For a delightful main dish, serve boiled shrimp, or barbecue ribs in the oven. On a cold winter evening, nothing could be more welcome than a steaming dish of pasta.

Fresh Citrus Gems That Sparkle And Please

One of the bright spots of winter is that citrus fruits are at their juicy best. Since they are so abundant, you'll want to enjoy them to the fullest—as snacks, in salads and dressings, and as the basis for delectable, nutritious desserts.

When buying fresh citrus, look for fruits that have smooth, blemish-free skin. Indications of high juice content are that fruits feel firm and are heavy for their size. Store citrus fruits in the refrigerator until ready to use.

Leftover citrus rind can be grated and frozen in plastic bags. When needed, use the same as freshly grated rind. Fresh citrus juice can be frozen and stored as long as four months. It's especially handy to freeze the juice in ice cube trays. Measure a specific amount of juice, such as 1 or 2 tablespoonfuls, into each ice compartment; then when a recipe calls for a few tablespoonfuls of fresh citrus juice, you'll be prepared.

SNOWBALL CITRUS CUP

4 oranges, peeled, seeded, and sectioned
2 grapefruit, peeled, seeded, and sectioned
1 (15½-ounce) can pineapple chunks
1 pint lemon sherbet

Combine first 3 ingredients; cover and chill. Spoon into sherbet glasses, and top each with a small scoop of sherbet. Yield: 8 servings.
Mrs. Margaret L. Hunter,
Princeton, Kentucky.

LIME DRESSING

1 cup sugar
¼ cup water
Juice of 2 limes
1 teaspoon grated lime rind

Combine sugar and water in a saucepan; bring to a boil, stirring occasionally. Remove from heat; stir in lime juice and rind. Cool. Refrigerate several hours before serving. Serve over citrus or other fruit salads. Yield: 1 cup.
Mrs. Robert B. James, Jr.,
Marion, Ohio.

LIME SQUARES

1 cup all-purpose flour
½ cup butter, softened
½ cup chopped pecans
¼ cup sugar
2 eggs
2 tablespoons lime juice
1 to 1½ tablespoons grated lime rind
1 cup sugar
2 tablespoons all-purpose flour
½ teaspoon baking powder
Powdered sugar (optional)

Combine 1 cup flour, butter, pecans, and ¼ cup sugar; mix until crumbly, using a pastry blender. Press into a greased and floured 12- x 8-inch baking pan. Bake at 350° for 15 minutes.

Beat eggs with a fork, adding lime juice, rind, 1 cup sugar, 2 tablespoons flour, and baking powder. Pour mixture over crust. Bake an additional 25 minutes. Cool. Sprinkle with powdered sugar, if desired. Yield: about 3½ dozen.
Mrs. E. L. McMath,
Jacksonville, Florida.

ORANGE RUM CAKE

1 cup butter or margarine
1 cup sugar
2 eggs
¼ cup grated orange rind
2 tablespoons grated lemon rind
2½ cups all-purpose flour
2 teaspoons baking powder
1 teaspoon soda
½ teaspoon salt
1 cup buttermilk
1 cup chopped pecans
Orange Glaze

Combine butter and sugar, creaming until light and fluffy; add eggs and citrus rind, beating well. Combine dry ingredients; add to creamed mixture alternately with buttermilk, beginning and ending with dry ingredients. Beat well after each addition. Stir in pecans.

Spoon batter into a well-greased 10-inch tube pan. Bake at 350° for 1 hour or until cake tests done. Leave in pan, and pour glaze over hot cake. Yield: one 10-inch cake.

Orange Glaze:

Juice of 2 large oranges
Juice of 1 lemon
1 cup sugar
2 tablespoons rum extract

Combine all ingredients in a saucepan; bring to a boil, stirring to dissolve sugar. Pour over hot cake. Yield: about ¾ cup.
Susan Bell,
Ashburn, Virginia.

LEMON-CHEESE TARTS

¼ cup lemon juice
Grated rind of 1½ lemons
½ cup plus 1 tablespoon sugar
2 eggs, beaten
¼ cup butter or margarine
Cream Cheese Shells
Whipped cream (optional)

Combine lemon juice, rind, and sugar in top of a double boiler; stir in eggs and butter. Cook over boiling water, stirring constantly, until thickened. (Filling will thicken more when cool.)

Spoon filling into Cream Cheese Shells; garnish with whipped cream, if desired. Yield: about 2 dozen.

Cream Cheese Shells:

½ cup butter or margarine, softened
1 (3-ounce) package cream cheese, softened
1 cup all-purpose flour

Combine butter and cream cheese, mixing until smooth; add flour, mixing well. Chill 1 hour.

Shape dough into 1-inch balls; place each in a well-greased miniature muffin cup, shaping into a shell. Bake at 350° for 25 minutes. Allow to cool before filling. Yield: about 2 dozen.
Mrs. Vivian Gregory,
Naples, Florida.

This Shrimp Is Something Special

Shrimp lovers think nothing could be better than boiled shrimp served with a tangy sauce. Everyone seems to have a favorite recipe for boiling shrimp: Some prefer to use a commercial shrimp or crab boil for flavoring; others use a stock made with salted water, lemon, onion, and seasonings.

Shrimp may be peeled either before or after boiling. Some connoisseurs insist that shrimp is more flavorful when cooked with the shell on. In addition, this method results in the shrimp having a richer pink color. Depending on the size of the shrimp, let boil for 3 to 5 minutes. Avoid overcooking, or the shrimp will be tough and dry.

In addition to boiling, this favorite seafood can be prepared hundreds of ways, and some of the best recipes are the simplest to prepare. Try, for example, our Sautéed Shrimp, quickly cooked with garlic, butter, lemon juice, vermouth, and seasonings; or Broiled

Shrimp Supreme, in which the shrimp are marinated, then broiled in a portion of the marinade.

When deciding on the amount of shrimp to buy for your favorite recipe, remember that small shrimp yield 35 or more shrimp per pound; medium, 26 to 35 per pound; large, 21 to 25 per pound; jumbo, less than 20 per pound. From approximately 1½ pounds of fresh unpeeled shrimp you will get ¾ pound or 2 cups of cooked, peeled, and deveined shrimp.

BOILED SHRIMP

4 large bay leaves
20 peppercorns
1 teaspoon mustard seeds
½ teaspoon whole basil leaves
12 whole cloves
⅛ teaspoon cumin seeds
1 teaspoon crushed red pepper
⅛ teaspoon celery seeds
⅛ teaspoon light fennel seeds
⅛ teaspoon caraway seeds
¼ teaspoon ground marjoram
¼ teaspoon whole thyme
1 teaspoon salt
1 lemon, cut in half
2 cloves garlic
2 teaspoons dehydrated onion flakes
5 pounds medium or large shrimp
Lettuce leaves (optional)
Lemon slices (optional)

Combine first 12 ingredients in a doubled cheesecloth bag; tie securely with string.

Bring 4 to 5 quarts of water to a boil. Add salt, lemon halves, garlic, onion flakes, and herb bag; return to a boil, and cook 2 to 3 minutes. Stir in shrimp; return to a boil, and cook 3 to 5 minutes. Drain well; chill. Peel shrimp. Serve on lettuce leaves and garnish with lemon slices, if desired. (Would be good served with Seafood Sauce or Seafood Dip.) Yield: 8 to 10 servings.
Dave Shuppert,
Dallas, Texas.

SEAFOOD SAUCE

1½ to 2 cups catsup
½ teaspoon garlic powder
½ teaspoon onion powder
1 teaspoon prepared horseradish
2 tablespoons lemon juice
⅛ teaspoon Worcestershire sauce
2 drops hot sauce
⅛ teaspoon salt
Dash of pepper

Combine all ingredients; stir well and chill. Serve with boiled shrimp. Yield: 1½ to 2 cups.
Pat Andrus,
Scott, Louisiana.

SEAFOOD DIP

1½ cups mayonnaise
1 cup catsup
¼ to ½ cup grated Parmesan cheese
1 tablespoon parsley flakes

Combine all ingredients; stir well and chill. Serve with boiled shrimp. Yield: about 3 cups.
Pat Andrus,
Scott, Louisiana.

SAUTEED SHRIMP

4 cloves garlic, minced
½ cup butter, melted
⅓ cup lemon juice
¼ cup dry vermouth
2 tablespoons soy sauce
1 tablespoon Worcestershire sauce
1 tablespoon tarragon vinegar
¼ teaspoon salt
4 drops hot sauce
2 pounds shrimp, peeled and deveined
Hot cooked rice

Sauté garlic in butter in a skillet; combine the next 7 ingredients, and gradually add mixture to skillet. Add shrimp; cook 5 minutes, or until shrimp are done, stirring frequently. Serve over rice. Yield: 4 to 6 servings.
Marcia T. Meyer,
Frogmore, South Carolina.

BROILED SHRIMP SUPREME

2 cups vegetable oil
¼ cup catsup
1 small clove garlic, minced
1 teaspoon salt
1 teaspoon paprika
2 pounds shrimp, peeled and deveined

Combine first 5 ingredients in a bowl; stir well. Add shrimp, and refrigerate at least 2 hours.

Remove shrimp from marinade; place shrimp in a 15- x 10- x 1-inch baking pan. Pour enough marinade over shrimp to coat but not cover (about 1 cup). Broil 3 minutes; turn shrimp over, and broil 3 minutes or until done. Serve hot. Yield: 4 to 6 servings.
Estelle Geno,
Waco, Texas.

POLYNESIAN SHRIMP

1 green pepper, chopped
2 tablespoons margarine, melted
2 tablespoons cornstarch
1 (10½-ounce) can beef broth
½ cup pineapple juice
¼ cup water
1 tablespoon soy sauce
1 teaspoon lemon juice
½ cup pineapple chunks
1½ to 2 cups peeled, deveined, cooked shrimp
Hot cooked rice

Sauté green pepper in margarine until tender; remove pepper, and set aside. Add cornstarch to pan drippings; cook until smooth and bubbly, stirring constantly. Gradually stir in broth, pineapple juice, water, soy sauce, and lemon juice. Cook until smooth and slightly thickened. Add green pepper, pineapple chunks, and shrimp; heat thoroughly. Serve over rice. Yield: 4 to 6 servings.
Mrs. George Sellers,
Albany, Georgia.

PICKLED SHRIMP

2½ pounds shrimp
½ cup celery leaves
4 teaspoons salt
¼ cup pickling spice
2 large onions, thinly sliced
3 to 5 bay leaves
1¼ cups vegetable oil
¾ cup vinegar
1½ teaspoons salt
2½ teaspoons celery seeds
2½ tablespoons capers, undrained
3 drops hot sauce

Place shrimp, celery leaves, salt, and pickling spice in boiling water to cover; cook 3 to 5 minutes, and drain well. Rinse shrimp with cold water; peel and devein.

Place half the shrimp in a large shallow dish; top with half the onion. Repeat layers; place 3 to 5 bay leaves over top, and set aside.

Combine remaining ingredients, mixing well, and pour over layered shrimp and onion; cover and chill 24 hours. Yield: 5 to 6 servings.
Mrs. Paul Newberry,
Macon, Georgia.

SHRIMP ETOUFFEE

2 pounds fresh shrimp, peeled and
    deveined
Salt and pepper
Red pepper
1 cup finely chopped onion
½ cup finely chopped celery
4 cloves garlic, crushed
½ cup melted butter or margarine
½ cup sherry
Hot cooked rice

Season the shrimp to taste with salt, pepper, and red pepper; then set aside.

Sauté onion, celery, and garlic in melted butter until tender. Add seasoned shrimp; cook over medium heat 10 minutes, stirring occasionally. Stir in sherry, and continue cooking 10 to 15 minutes. Serve over hot cooked rice. Yield: 4 to 6 servings. *Becky Givens, Houma, Louisiana.*

PUFFY FRIED SHRIMP

1 cup all-purpose flour
¾ cup water
2 teaspoons shortening, melted
½ teaspoon salt
⅛ teaspoon pepper
2 egg whites, stiffly beaten
1½ pounds medium or large fresh shrimp,
    peeled and deveined
Hot vegetable oil

Fold flour, water, shortening, salt, and pepper into egg whites. Dip shrimp in mixture, and fry in deep hot oil until golden. Yield: 3 to 4 servings. *Carolyn Freeman, Beaumont, Texas.*

FRENCH-FRIED SHRIMP

2 pounds medium or large fresh shrimp
1 cup all-purpose flour
½ teaspoon sugar
½ teaspoon salt
1 egg, slightly beaten
1 cup cold water
2 tablespoons vegetable oil
Hot vegetable oil

Peel shrimp, leaving the last section of shell and tail intact. Butterfly shrimp by cutting along outside curve almost through; remove vein. Flatten shrimp, and set aside.

Combine flour, sugar, salt, egg, water, and 2 tablespoons oil; beat until smooth.

Dip shrimp into batter, and fry in deep hot oil until golden. Yield: 4 to 6 servings. *Mrs. Debra Lancaster, Hawkinsville, Georgia.*

CREAMY SHRIMP SHELLS

1½ pounds shrimp, cooked, peeled, and
    deveined
¼ cup chopped green onion
1 clove garlic, pressed
2 tablespoons melted butter or margarine
¼ cup all-purpose flour
½ teaspoon salt
1½ cups half-and-half
½ cup dry white wine
¼ cup soft breadcrumbs
2 tablespoons grated Parmesan cheese
2 teaspoons chopped parsley
¼ teaspoon paprika
1½ tablespoons melted butter or
    margarine

Reserve 6 whole shrimp; cut remainder in half lengthwise, and set aside.

Sauté onion and garlic in 2 tablespoons butter until tender. Stir in flour and salt; remove from heat, and gradually add half-and-half, stirring constantly. Bring to a boil, and cook 1 minute, stirring constantly, until very thick. Stir in wine and shrimp.

Spoon shrimp mixture evenly into 6 buttered (5-inch) baking seashells. Set aside.

Combine breadcrumbs, cheese, parsley, paprika, and 1½ tablespoons butter; stir until crumbly. Sprinkle over shrimp mixture; bake at 350° for 15 to 20 minutes or until heated thoroughly. Garnish with whole shrimp. Yield: 6 servings. *Mrs. Charles R. Lee III, Clearwater, Florida.*

Cabbage Made Supreme And Cheesy

Our readers have discovered some new ways with that most versatile of vegetables—the cabbage. Green cabbage is featured raw, cooked crisp-tender, and fully cooked in such dishes as Cabbage Supreme, Overnight Slaw, and Cheesy Cabbage Casserole. Sweet-Sour Red Cabbage demonstrates the flavor of red cabbage.

When selecting fresh cabbage, choose heads that are solid and heavy in relation to their size. Cabbage leaves should be fresh, crisp, and free from bruises and disease.

CABBAGE SUPREME

1 beef bouillon cube
¼ cup hot water
5 cups shredded cabbage
1 cup shredded carrots
½ cup chopped green onion
½ teaspoon salt
½ teaspoon pepper
¼ cup butter or margarine
1 teaspoon prepared mustard
⅓ cup chopped pecans
¼ teaspoon paprika

Dissolve bouillon cube in water. Combine bouillon, cabbage, carrots, onion, salt, and pepper in a heavy saucepan; toss lightly. Cover and cook over low heat 5 minutes, stirring occasionally. Drain and set aside.

Melt butter in a small saucepan; stir in mustard and pecans, and continue cooking 1 to 2 minutes, stirring constantly. Pour over vegetables, and mix well; sprinkle top with paprika. Yield: 6 servings. *Mrs. Loren D. Martin, Knoxville, Tennessee.*

CHEESY CABBAGE CASSEROLE

1 medium head cabbage
1 (10¾-ounce) can cream of chicken soup,
    undiluted
1 (5-ounce) jar process American cheese
    spread
Pepper
¼ cup soft breadcrumbs
2 tablespoons butter or margarine

Break leaves from cabbage head, and place in cold water to cover for 5 to 10 minutes. Drain well; cut into ½-inch strips, removing ribs. Place in boiling salted water to cover; return to a boil, and cook 5 minutes. Remove from heat; let stand 2 to 3 minutes, and drain well.

Place half the cabbage in a greased 1½-quart casserole; spread with half the soup and half the cheese. Sprinkle lightly with pepper; repeat layers. Top with breadcrumbs, and dot with butter. Bake at 350° for 25 to 30 minutes. Yield: 6 servings. *Audrey Bledsoe, Atlanta, Georgia.*

CREAMED CABBAGE WITH ALMONDS

1 medium head cabbage, coarsely chopped
¼ cup milk
2 tablespoons all-purpose flour
¾ teaspoon salt
Dash of pepper
6 tablespoons milk
⅓ cup slivered almonds

Cabbage Supreme, a hot slaw, preserves the crispy texture of shredded cabbage and carrots.

bring to a boil. Pour dressing over vegetables, tossing lightly; chill overnight. Yield: 6 to 8 servings.

Mrs. Byron Schisler,
Jonesboro, Arkansas.

Pasta Dishes To Warm You Up

Take the chill off a cold winter evening with a steaming dish of pasta. The spirited entrées included here are made with a wide selection of noodles and shells: Manicotti shells and jumbo macaroni seashells are stuffed and baked; lasagna noodles are filled and rolled into pinwheels; and macaroni is folded into a rich cheese sauce and baked into a handsome soufflé-like puff.

Italians prefer their pasta cooked *al dente*, which means it is cooked until tender yet is still firm to the bite. Overcooking results in a soft, shapeless mass. If cooked pasta has to be left standing while you are preparing other parts of the recipe, let it stand in cold water to keep the sections of pasta from sticking together.

Combine cabbage and ¼ cup milk in a large skillet; cover and cook over medium heat 5 to 8 minutes or until crisp-tender. Combine flour, salt, and pepper; sprinkle over cabbage, and mix well. Cook 2 to 3 minutes over low heat, stirring constantly. Stir in 6 tablespoons milk; then cook, stirring constantly, until cabbage is lightly coated with white sauce. Spoon into serving dish; sprinkle almonds over top. Yield: 4 to 5 servings. *Mrs. Janet Tingdale, Dothan, Alabama.*

SWEET-SOUR RED CABBAGE

1 medium onion, thinly sliced
2 medium apples, peeled, cored, and diced
2 tablespoons vegetable oil
1 medium head (about 2½ pounds) red cabbage, shredded
1 (6-ounce) can frozen orange juice concentrate, undiluted
½ cup water
1 tablespoon lemon juice
¾ teaspoon salt
½ teaspoon ground cinnamon
Dash of ground cloves
1 orange, cut into ¼-inch slices (optional)

Sauté onion and apple in oil until just tender. Add cabbage, tossing lightly. Stir in orange juice concentrate, water, lemon juice, salt, cinnamon, and cloves; bring to a boil. Reduce heat; cover and simmer 15 minutes or until cabbage is tender, stirring occasionally. Spoon into a serving dish and garnish with orange slices, if desired. Yield: 6 to 8 servings.

Mrs. Bruce Fowler,
Woodruff, South Carolina.

OVERNIGHT SLAW

1 medium head cabbage, finely chopped
½ cup green pepper, finely chopped
1 medium onion, finely chopped
8 to 10 pimiento-stuffed olives, sliced
½ teaspoon salt
½ cup vinegar
½ cup vegetable oil
1 tablespoon prepared mustard
½ cup sugar
1 teaspoon celery seeds

Combine cabbage, green pepper, onion, olives, and salt in a large bowl; mix well and set aside.

Combine vinegar, oil, mustard, sugar, and celery seeds in a small saucepan;

MACARONI AND CHEESE PUFF

½ cup uncooked elbow macaroni
1½ cups scalded milk
2 cups (½ pound) shredded sharp Cheddar cheese, divided
1 cup soft breadcrumbs
¼ cup chopped pimiento
3 tablespoons melted butter or margarine
1 tablespoon chopped parsley
1 tablespoon grated onion
½ teaspoon salt
3 eggs, separated
¼ teaspoon cream of tartar

Cook macaroni according to package directions; drain and set aside.

Combine milk and 1½ cups cheese, stirring until cheese melts. Add macaroni, breadcrumbs, pimiento, butter, parsley, onion, and salt. Beat egg yolks, and stir into mixture.

Beat egg whites and cream of tartar until stiff but not dry; fold into macaroni mixture. Spoon into a lightly greased 2-quart baking dish. Bake at 325° about 50 minutes or until set. Sprinkle with remaining cheese; return to oven, and bake 5 additional minutes or until cheese melts. Yield: 6 servings.

Mrs. John A. Shoemaker,
Louisville, Kentucky.

QUICK MANICOTTI

8 manicotti shells
1 pound ground beef
1 clove garlic, crushed
1 cup cottage cheese
1 cup (¼ pound) shredded mozzarella
    cheese
½ teaspoon salt
¼ cup mayonnaise
1 (15½-ounce) jar spaghetti sauce
½ teaspoon whole oregano
About ⅓ cup grated Parmesan cheese

Cook manicotti shells according to package directions; drain. Rinse in cold water; drain and set aside.

Sauté ground beef and garlic, stirring to crumble beef, until beef is no longer pink; drain off pan drippings. Add cottage cheese, mozzarella cheese, salt, and mayonnaise to skillet; stir well.

Stuff manicotti shells with meat mixture; arrange shells in a lightly greased 13- x 9- x 2-inch baking dish. Combine spaghetti sauce and oregano; pour over manicotti. Sprinkle with Parmesan cheese. Cover and bake at 350° for 15 minutes. Uncover and bake 10 additional minutes. Yield: 8 servings.

Jaynie Lamb,
Dallas, Texas.

JUMBO SEASHELLS FLORENTINE

12 jumbo macaroni seashells
1 (10-ounce) package chopped spinach,
    thawed and uncooked
1 small onion, minced
1 egg, beaten
½ teaspoon salt
⅛ teaspoon pepper
1 cup well-drained cottage cheese
1 (10¾-ounce) can cream of mushroom
    soup, undiluted
⅓ cup water

Cook macaroni according to package directions; drain.

Combine spinach, onion, egg, salt, pepper, and cottage cheese; stir gently. Spoon spinach mixture into macaroni shells, and place shells in a shallow baking dish. Combine soup and water; pour over macaroni shells. Cover and bake at 350° for 25 minutes. Spoon sauce over macaroni, and bake 20 additional minutes. Yield: 6 servings.

Jenni Rogers Ford,
Atlanta, Georgia.

Tip: Use baking soda on a damp cloth to shine up your kitchen appliances.

The manicotti shells are stuffed with a beef and cheese mixture, topped with a tomato sauce and Parmesan cheese, then baked.

LASAGNA SAUSAGE PINWHEELS

1 pound hot Italian link sausage, cut into
    1-inch pieces
¾ cup chopped onion
1 clove garlic, minced
3 cups tomato juice
1 (6-ounce) can tomato paste
½ cup water
2 teaspoons sugar
½ teaspoon salt
1 bay leaf
1 (12-ounce) carton cottage cheese
1 egg, beaten
½ cup grated Parmesan cheese, divided
2 cups shredded mozzarella cheese,
    divided
Salt and pepper to taste
½ (16-ounce) package lasagna noodles

Brown sausage over low heat in a large heavy skillet; drain sausage on paper towels, reserving ¼ cup drippings. Sauté onion and garlic in drippings until crisp-tender.

Return sausage to skillet; stir in tomato juice, tomato paste, water, sugar, ½ teaspoon salt, and bay leaf. Simmer, uncovered, 1 hour; stir occasionally. Discard bay leaf.

Combine cottage cheese, egg, ¼ cup Parmesan cheese, 1 cup mozzarella cheese, and salt and pepper to taste; set aside.

Cook noodles according to package directions; drain. Spread about 1 tablespoon cheese mixture on each noodle. Roll each noodle, jellyroll fashion, beginning at narrow end.

Spread 1 cup sausage sauce in a 13- x 9- x 2-inch baking dish. Arrange rolls, seam side down, in sauce. Spoon remaining sauce over rolls. Sprinkle with remaining mozzarella and Parmesan. Bake at 350° for 30 to 40 minutes or until bubbly. Yield: 8 servings.

Mrs. Barbara Dotson,
McDonough, Georgia.

Bake A Batch Of Muffins

A warm, sweet muffin generously spread with butter is enough to start tastebuds tingling. And our readers have graciously shared some of their extra special recipes.

Refrigerator Bran Muffins can be mixed ahead and baked up to six weeks later at a busy moment's notice. Yam Muffins are great for snacks, and any child would be delighted to taste his favorite jam mixed directly into the batter of Jam Muffins.

The secret to good muffins is in the mixing. Combine all the dry ingredients in a bowl, and form a well in the center of mixture. Add the liquid all at once, and stir only enough to moisten the dry ingredients. The mixture will be lumpy, but further mixing will make the muffins tough and produces a peaked surface and tunnels inside.

For easy removal, let the muffins remain in the pan a few minutes after baking. Then tip them to one side of the tin to allow steam to escape and prevent them from becoming soggy.

REFRIGERATOR BRAN MUFFINS

1 (15-ounce) box wheat bran flakes cereal
    with raisins
5 cups all-purpose flour
3 cups sugar
5 teaspoons soda
2 teaspoons salt
4 eggs, beaten
1 quart buttermilk
1 cup shortening, melted

Combine first 5 ingredients in a large bowl; make a well in center of mixture. Add eggs, buttermilk, and shortening; stir just enough to moisten dry ingredients. Cover and store in refrigerator until ready to bake, as long as five to six weeks.

When ready to bake, spoon batter into greased muffin tins, filling two-thirds full. Bake at 350° for 20 minutes. Yield: about 5½ dozen.
Mrs. H. S. Wright,
Leesville, South Carolina.

JAM MUFFINS

2¼ cups all-purpose flour
½ cup firmly packed brown sugar
1 tablespoon baking powder
½ teaspoon ground cinnamon
1 cup milk
1 cup fruit jam
½ cup raisins
¼ cup margarine, softened
2 eggs, beaten

Combine flour, sugar, baking powder, and cinnamon; stir well, and make a well in center of mixture.

Combine milk, jam, raisins, margarine, and eggs, stirring well. Add to dry ingredients, stirring just until moistened. Fill greased muffin tins two-thirds full. Bake at 350° for 25 minutes or until golden brown. Yield: about 2 dozen.
Mrs. William Bell,
Chattanooga, Tennessee.

BLUEBERRY-LEMON MUFFINS

1¾ cups all-purpose flour
½ cup sugar
2½ teaspoons baking powder
¾ teaspoon salt
¾ cup milk
⅓ cup vegetable oil
1 egg, beaten
1 cup blueberries
2 tablespoons sugar
1 teaspoon grated lemon rind
Melted butter (optional)
Sugar (optional)

Combine flour, ½ cup sugar, baking powder, and salt in a large mixing bowl; make a well in center of mixture. Combine milk, oil, and egg; add to dry ingredients, stirring just until moistened. Toss blueberries with 2 tablespoons sugar and lemon rind; gently fold into batter. Spoon into greased muffin tins, filling two-thirds full. Bake at 400° for 25 minutes or until muffins are golden brown. While muffins are still warm, dip tops in melted butter and then in sugar, if desired. Yield: 1 dozen.
Mrs. June Johnson,
Mocksville, North Carolina.

YAM MUFFINS

1¾ cups all-purpose flour
½ cup chopped pecans
¼ cup firmly packaged brown sugar
1 tablespoon baking powder
2 teaspoons ground cinnamon
1 teaspoon salt
2 eggs, beaten
1½ cups mashed yams
¾ cup milk
¼ cup butter or margarine, melted
Ground cinnamon
Sugar

Combine first 6 ingredients; make a well in center of mixture. Combine eggs, yams, milk, and butter; add to dry ingredients, stirring just until moistened. Spoon into greased muffin tins, filling two-thirds full; sprinkle with cinnamon and sugar. Bake at 425° for 35 minutes. Yield: 1½ dozen.
Mrs. W. Snellgrove,
La Grange, Georgia.

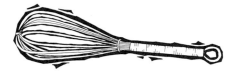

COFFEE CAKE MUFFINS

½ cup firmly packed brown sugar
½ cup chopped walnuts or pecans
2 tablespoons all-purpose flour
2 tablespoons butter or margarine, melted
2 teaspoons ground cinnamon
1½ cups all-purpose flour
½ cup sugar
2 teaspoons baking powder
½ teaspoon salt
¼ cup shortening
½ cup milk
1 egg, beaten

Combine brown sugar, walnuts, 2 tablespoons flour, butter, and cinnamon; stir well, and set aside.

Combine 1½ cups flour, sugar, baking powder, and salt in a large bowl; cut in shortening until mixture resembles coarse crumbs.

Combine milk and egg; add to flour mixture, stirring just until moistened. Place paper liners in muffin tins. Spoon 1 tablespoon of batter into each cup; sprinkle with 1 tablespoon brown sugar mixture; spoon in remaining batter, and top with remaining brown sugar mixture. Bake at 375° for 25 minutes. Yield: 1 dozen.
Mrs. Parke LaGourgue Cory,
Neosho, Missouri.

Ice Cream Torte For Dessert

This Chocolate-Strawberry Ice Cream Torte looks and tastes as if it requires many hours to prepare, while, in fact, it's easy and quick to assemble. Split a layer of your favorite chocolate cake, fill with alternating layers of chocolate and strawberry ice cream and strawberry preserves, and top with powdered sugar. Pass a bowl of chocolate syrup with slices of this inviting torte.

CHOCOLATE-STRAWBERRY ICE CREAM TORTE

1 (9-inch) chocolate or devil's food cake layer
1½ pints strawberry ice cream, softened
1½ pints chocolate ice cream, softened
½ cup strawberry preserves, divided
Powdered sugar
Chocolate syrup

Split cake layer in half crosswise; set aside.

Line an 8-inch round cakepan with plastic wrap, allowing wrap to extend about 1 inch over edge of pan. Spoon strawberry ice cream evenly into pan, pressing to pack; freeze until firm. Spoon chocolate ice cream over frozen strawbery ice cream, pressing to pack; freeze until firm.

Place bottom half of cake layer, cut side up, on a cake plate; spread evenly with ¼ cup strawberry preserves. Remove ice cream from plastic wrap in cakepan, and place on top of preserves. Spread remaining ¼ cup preserves on ice cream. Top with remaining half of cake layer, cut side down. Sprinkle with powdered sugar. Serve with chocolate syrup. Yield: one 9-inch torte.

Note: To form a design, place a paper doily over top of cake, and sift lightly with powdered sugar. *Freddie Bowen,*
Americus, Georgia.

Tip: It's a good idea to learn as much as you can about the metric system of measuring since these measurements are now appearing on some canned foods. To give you an idea of some new measurements: 1 cup flour equals 140 grams; 1 cup butter equals 200 grams; and 1 cup sugar equals 190 grams.

Enjoy The Best Of Fresh Spinach

The moist and tender greens of spinach can be enjoyed so many ways—and particularly so now that the fresh leaves are abundant.

One of the grandest ways to serve spinach is in a soufflé, and our version, Spinach Soufflé Deluxe, makes a light and airy entrée for brunch and dinner. As a side dish, serve spinach scalloped or baked in a ring. As a salad, serve it fresh in French Spinach Salad tossed with a lemony dressing.

SPINACH SOUFFLE DELUXE

2 tablespoons butter, melted
1 tablespoon all-purpose flour
1 cup milk
½ teaspoon salt
Dash of pepper
4 eggs, separated
1 cup cooked, chopped spinach, pressed dry
⅓ cup grated Parmesan cheese

Melt butter in a heavy saucepan over low heat; blend in flour, stirring until smooth. Cook 3 to 4 minutes, stirring constantly. Gradually stir in milk; cook over low heat, stirring constantly, about 6 to 8 minutes or until thickened. Stir in salt and pepper.

Beat egg yolks. Add a small amount of hot white sauce to yolks, stirring well; stir yolk mixture into white sauce. Add spinach and cheese; stir well.

Beat egg whites until stiff; fold into spinach mixture. Spoon into a lightly greased 1-quart soufflé dish. Bake at 325° for 50 minutes or until firm. Serve immediately. Yield: 4 to 5 servings.

Mrs. George Sellers,
Albany, Georgia.

SCALLOPED SPINACH WITH CHEESE

1½ pounds fresh spinach, washed and drained
2 tablespoons butter or margarine
2 tablespoons all-purpose flour
1 cup milk
½ cup shredded Cheddar cheese
½ teaspoon salt
Dash of pepper
2 tablespoons grated onion
½ cup soft breadcrumbs
2 tablespoons butter or margarine, melted

Cook spinach in a small amount of salted water 8 to 10 minutes or until tender. Drain, and spoon into a lightly greased 1-quart casserole; set aside.

Melt 2 tablespoons butter in a heavy saucepan over low heat; blend in flour, stirring until smooth. Cook 3 to 4 minutes, stirring constantly. Gradually stir in milk; cook over low heat, stirring constantly, about 6 to 8 minutes or until sauce is thickened.

Add cheese, salt, pepper, and onion, stirring until cheese melts. Spoon sauce over spinach. Combine breadcrumbs and remaining butter; sprinkle over cheese sauce.

Bake at 375° for 20 minutes or until bubbly. Yield: 4 to 5 servings.

Dora Farrar,
Gadsden, Alabama.

SPINACH RING AU FROMAGE

3 tablespoons butter or margarine, melted
3 tablespoons all-purpose flour
1 cup milk
2 cups (½ pound) shredded Cheddar cheese
1½ cups uncooked finely chopped spinach
1½ cups breadcrumbs
½ teaspoon salt
½ teaspoon pepper
3 eggs, beaten

Melt butter in a heavy saucepan over low heat; blend in flour, stirring until smooth. Cook 3 to 4 minutes, stirring constantly. Gradually stir in milk; cook over low heat, stirring constantly, about 6 to 8 minutes or until thickened.

Stir in remaining ingredients in order given. Spoon mixture into a well-greased 8-inch ring mold or 1½-quart casserole. Bake at 325° for 50 minutes or until firm. Unmold on heated plate. Yield: 6 servings.

Mrs. Althea D. Loughlin,
Winter Park, Florida.

VINAIGRETTE SPINACH

2½ to 3 cups unsalted cooked spinach, drained
1 teaspoon minced onion
⅓ cup butter or margarine, melted
½ teaspoon prepared mustard
2 tablespoons vinegar
½ teaspoon salt
¼ teaspoon pepper
2 hard-cooked eggs, chopped

Place spinach in a 1-quart casserole; keep warm.

Sauté onion in butter until tender. Add remaining ingredients except eggs. Heat thoroughly. Pour mixture over spinach; sprinkle with chopped egg. Serve immediately. Yield: 4 servings.

Betty Ruth Holtum,
Vienna, Virginia.

FRENCH SPINACH SALAD

½ pound fresh spinach, torn
1 medium onion, minced
¼ cup diced celery
4 hard-cooked eggs, sliced
Lemon Salad Dressing

Combine all ingredients except dressing; toss and chill. Serve with Lemon Salad Dressing. Yield: about 8 servings.

Lemon Salad Dressing:
9 tablespoons salad oil, divided
2 tablespoons all-purpose flour
½ cup water
1 egg yolk
½ teaspoon dry mustard
½ teaspoon salt
Paprika
2 tablespoons lemon juice

Combine 1 tablespoon salad oil and flour in a saucepan; gradually add water, stirring until smooth. Cook over low heat until thickened, stirring constantly. Combine 8 tablespoons oil and remaining ingredients; add to cooked mixture, beating rapidly until smooth. Yield: about 1¼ cups.

Mrs. Paul A. Robertson,
Knoxville, Tennessee.

Potato Pie, Light And Sweet

If you haven't had homemade sweet potato pie lately, you'll see what you've been missing when you taste Old-Fashioned Sweet Potato Pie. It combines sweet potatoes, butter, brown sugar, and spices with stiffly beaten egg whites to create a pie with a light texture.

Also included are recipes for other sweet potato dishes that will accent any meal. Try them stuffed with a hint of marshmallows, beer battered and deep fried until golden brown, or gently basted with a sweetly spiced glaze.

When buying sweet potatoes, select well-shaped, firm potatoes with smooth, bright colored skins. Avoid those with cuts or holes. To prevent spoilage, store in a dry place and use promptly; or try cooking the potatoes, then freezing them for later use.

OLD-FASHIONED SWEET POTATO PIE

2 cups cooked, mashed sweet potatoes
1 cup firmly packed brown sugar
½ cup butter or margarine, softened
2 eggs, separated
½ teaspoon ground ginger
½ teaspoon ground cinnamon
½ teaspoon ground nutmeg
¼ teaspoon salt
½ cup evaporated milk
¼ cup sugar
1 unbaked 10-inch pastry shell
Whipped topping (optional)

Combine sweet potatoes, brown sugar, butter, egg yolks, spices, and salt in a large mixing bowl; beat until light and fluffy. Add evaporated milk; mix just until combined.

Beat egg whites until foamy; gradually add sugar, beating until stiff. Fold into potato mixture. Pour filling into pastry shell. Bake at 400° for 10 minutes; reduce heat to 350°, and bake an additional 45 to 50 minutes or until set. Cool. Top with whipped topping, if desired. Yield: one 10-inch pie.

Mrs. Byron Schisler,
Jonesboro, Arkansas.

Old-Fashioned Sweet Potato Pie and Fluffy Stuffed Sweet Potatoes are two delicious ways to enjoy the season's bounty.

FLUFFY STUFFED SWEET POTATOES

4 medium-size sweet potatoes
½ cup marshmallow cream
¼ cup melted margarine
1 tablespoon brown sugar
½ teaspoon salt
Dash of pepper
4 large marshmallows, quartered (optional)

Wash potatoes well; place on a greased baking sheet. Bake at 450° for 40 minutes or until tender.

Allow potatoes to cool to touch. Slice skin away from top of each potato. Carefully scoop out pulp, leaving shells intact. Combine pulp, marshmallow cream, margarine, sugar, salt, and pepper in a bowl. Beat with electric mixer until light and fluffy.

Spoon potato mixture into shells; top each with a quartered marshmallow, if

desired. Bake at 350° for 20 minutes or until well heated. Yield: 4 servings.

Miss Patricia Chapman,
Huntsville, Alabama.

CANDIED SWEET POTATOES

8 medium-size sweet potatoes
1⅓ cups firmly packed brown sugar
⅔ cup water
¼ cup sugar
⅓ cup butter or margarine, melted
½ teaspoon molasses
¼ teaspoon salt
¼ teaspoon ground ginger
Dash of pepper

Cook potatoes in boiling water until tender. Drain, peel, and cut potatoes in half lengthwise. Place cut side up in a greased shallow baking pan. Set aside.

Combine remaining ingredients in a saucepan; bring to a boil. Boil 6 minutes, stirring frequently. Pour over potatoes; bake at 375° for 30 minutes, basting frequently. Yield: 8 servings.

Mrs. John B. Holloway, Jr.,
Tallahassee, Florida.

GOLDEN SWEET POTATO FRITTERS

1⅓ cups beer
3 eggs, separated
1 tablespoon vegetable oil
Salt
2⅔ cups all-purpose flour
6 medium-size sweet potatoes
Hot vegetable oil

Open beer, and let stand at room temperature until warm and flat (about 4 to 5 hours).

Combine beer, egg yolks, 1 tablespoon oil, and 1 teaspoon salt; beat with electric mixer until frothy. Gradually add flour, beating until smooth and stiff (batter will be thick). Let batter stand 30 minutes.

Wash potatoes; cover with water, and cook just until fork tender. Drain and let cool to touch. Peel potatoes, and cut into ¼-inch slices. Set aside.

Beat egg whites until stiff; fold into batter. Dip potato slices into batter to coat lightly; fry in hot oil 3 to 4 minutes on each side or until golden brown. Drain; sprinkle with salt. Yield: 8 to 10 servings.

Mrs. Elizabeth L. Pasch,
Miami, Florida.

Skillet Hopping John, made with rice and black-eyed peas, will highlight your New Year's Day good luck meal.

Good Luck Peas Make Good Eating

Most Southerners are devoted to the tradition of eating black-eyed peas on New Year's Day for good luck all year long. Many serve black-eyed peas cooked with tomatoes, and others enjoy adding a bit of spiciness with chili powder or hot peppers.

In this selection of recipes we offer a variation of a black-eyed pea favorite—hopping John, a combination of black-eyed peas and rice.

For some newer ways to prepare black-eyed peas, serve Pickled Black-eyed Peas, a chilled dish made with oil and wine vinegar and flavored with onion. Or try Black-eyed Peas Mexicano, a delicious alternative to soup or chili on a cold winter day.

PICKLED BLACK-EYED PEAS

2 (16-ounce) cans black-eyed peas, drained
½ to ¾ cup vegetable oil
¼ cup wine vinegar
1 clove garlic
¼ cup thinly sliced onion
½ teaspoon salt
⅛ teaspoon pepper

Combine all ingredients; cover and chill 24 hours. Remove garlic. Chill 2 days to 2 weeks before serving. Yield: 6 to 8 servings.

Mrs. Ted M. Robertson,
Canton, Texas.

BLACK-EYED PEAS MEXICANO

1 pound bulk pork sausage
1 medium onion, chopped
1 clove garlic, minced
2 (16-ounce) cans black-eyed peas, drained, or 1 (16-ounce) package frozen black-eyed peas
1 (16-ounce) can tomatoes
¼ cup water
1 teaspoon chili powder
¼ teaspoon pepper

Crumble sausage in a skillet, and cook until done. Drain well. Stir in onion and garlic; sauté 3 to 5 minutes.

Stir in the remaining ingredients; simmer mixture 1 hour, stirring occasionally. Yield: about 6 servings.

Dean D. Piercy,
Memphis, Tennessee.

SKILLET HOPPING JOHN

1 large onion, chopped
2 large cloves garlic, pressed
2 tablespoons butter or margarine, melted
2 (16-ounce) cans black-eyed peas, drained and rinsed
2 cups chicken or vegetable bouillon
1 cup uncooked regular rice
1 teaspoon salt
Crushed red pepper

Sauté onion and garlic in butter until onion is tender. Stir in black-eyed peas, chicken bouillon, rice, salt, and ½ teaspoon crushed red pepper.

Bring mixture to a boil; cover and simmer 20 minutes or until liquid is absorbed and rice is tender. Serve with additional crushed red pepper, if desired. Yield: 6 servings.

Jennifer Fowler,
Woodruff, South Carolina.

Salads That Hold Their Shape

In textures that range from creamy to crunchy and flavors equally as varied, there's nothing quite like congealed salads for adding flair to a menu. What's more, they are easy to master and fun to make. Here are some pointers to help you get started.

—Before you begin, lightly oil the gelatin mold; this will make the salad easier to unmold.

—To prevent ingredients from settling to the bottom of the salad, first chill the gelatin mixture until slightly thickened or about the consistency of unbeaten egg white. Then fold in fruit, vegetables, and other solid ingredients.

—When making a layered gelatin salad, chill each layer until set before adding the next layer. And make sure the ingredients for the layer being added are well chilled; this prevents softening the layer that is already set.

Unmolding a congealed salad correctly is essential to the attractiveness of your masterpiece. Here are two ways it can be done.

—Using the tip of a knife, loosen the edges of the gelatin from the mold. Dip the mold in lukewarm water about 5 seconds. Lift from the water, and shake the mold gently. Moisten a serving plate with cold water, and place it over the top of the mold. Then, holding firmly, quickly invert the mold and plate. Shake the mold gently, and lift it off. Since the plate is moist, you can easily slide the salad to center it on the plate.

—The alternative method is to first invert the gelatin mold on a plate that has been moistened with cold water, and then wrap a warm towel around the mold for about 30 seconds. Remove the towel, and firmly hold the plate and mold together. Shake gently, and slowly lift off the mold. Center the salad on the plate by carefully sliding it over the moist surface.

CRUNCHY VEGETABLE SALAD

2 envelopes unflavored gelatin
1¾ cups water, divided
¼ teaspoon salt
¼ teaspoon white pepper
⅓ cup vinegar
¾ cup sugar
1 cup shredded cabbage
2 cups chopped celery
1 (7-ounce) jar pimiento, diced
1 cup grated carrots
1 (8-ounce) can green peas, drained
1 cup chopped pecans
Salad greens
Cherry tomatoes
Carrot curls
½ cup mayonnaise
1 tablespoon half-and-half

Soften gelatin in 1 cup water, and set aside. Combine ¾ cup water, salt, pepper, vinegar, and sugar in a saucepan; bring to a boil. Remove from heat. Add softened gelatin mixture, stirring until dissolved; chill until slightly thickened.

Stir cabbage, celery, pimiento, carrots, peas, and nuts into thickened gelatin. Spoon mixture into a lightly oiled 6-cup mold or individual molds. Chill salad until firm. Unmold on salad greens, and garnish with cherry tomatoes and carrot curls.

Combine mayonnaise and half-and-half, mixing well; serve with salad. Yield: 8 to 10 servings.

Mrs. Earl L. Faulkenberry,
Lancaster, South Carolina.

The crunch in Crunchy Vegetable Salad comes from nuts and a variety of vegetables.

PEACH PINWHEEL SALAD

2 (3-ounce) packages peach-flavored
  gelatin
2 cups boiling water
¾ cup cold water
1 pint vanilla ice cream
1 (8¾-ounce) can sliced peaches, drained

Dissolve 1 package of gelatin in 1 cup boiling water. Add ¾ cup cold water, and chill until slightly thickened.

Dissolve remaining gelatin in 1 cup boiling water. Add ice cream, stirring until melted. Pour ice cream mixture into an 8-inch pieplate; chill until firm. Arrange peaches in pinwheel fashion over ice cream mixture; top with thickened gelatin. Chill until firm. Yield: 6 to 8 servings.
Billie Taylor,
Afton, Virginia.

HIDDEN TREASURE STRAWBERRY SALAD

2 (3-ounce) packages strawberry-flavored
  gelatin
1 cup boiling water
2 (10-ounce) packages frozen sliced
  strawberries, partially thawed
1 (20-ounce) can crushed pineapple,
  drained
3 medium bananas, mashed
½ cup walnuts or pecans, coarsely
  chopped
1 (10½-ounce) package unbaked
  cheesecake mix

Dissolve gelatin in boiling water; stir in fruit and nuts. Pour half of gelatin mixture into a 13- x 9- x 2-inch pan; chill until firm. Store remaining gelatin mixture at room temperature.

Prepare cheesecake filling according to package directions; reserve graham cracker crumbs for other uses. Spoon cheesecake filling over congealed fruit mixture. Spoon remaining gelatin mixture over filling, and chill until firm. Yield: about 18 servings.
Gailya Godfrey,
Charlotte, North Carolina.

Tip: Check newspaper food ads for weekly specials and menu ideas. You can save money on sale items, but don't buy something just because it's on sale; it's no bargain if your family won't eat it. Clip discount coupons in newspapers and magazines; remember to cash them when you purchase that item.

CUCUMBER MOUSSE

3 to 4 cucumbers, peeled, seeded, and
  finely chopped
1 tablespoon vinegar
½ teaspoon sugar
½ tablespoon unflavored gelatin
½ cup cold water
1 (3-ounce) package lime-flavored gelatin
1 cup boiling water
1 (8-ounce) package cream cheese,
  softened
½ cup mayonnaise
Juice of 1 lemon
3 dashes of hot sauce
½ teaspoon Worcestershire sauce
½ teaspoon salt
½ teaspoon seasoned pepper
3 to 5 green onions, minced
Salad greens
Mayonnaise (optional)

Sprinkle cucumber with vinegar and sugar; cover with ice water, and soak 30 minutes. Drain well.

Soften unflavored gelatin in ½ cup cold water. Dissolve lime-flavored gelatin in boiling water. Add enough water to unflavored gelatin to make 2 cups liquid; stir in lime-flavored gelatin mixture. Chill until slightly thickened.

Combine cream cheese and ½ cup mayonnaise, beating until smooth. Stir in lemon juice, hot sauce, Worcestershire sauce, salt, pepper, and thickened gelatin mixture. Fold in cucumber and green onion. Pour into a lightly oiled 6-cup mold or individual molds. Chill until firm. Unmold on salad greens; serve with mayonnaise, if desired. Yield: 10 servings.
Mrs. Henry DeBlieux, Sr.,
Natchitoches, Louisiana.

ORANGE SURPRISE SALAD

1 (3-ounce) package orange-flavored gelatin
2 tablespoons orange-flavored instant breakfast drink
1¾ cups boiling water
1 (9-ounce) container frozen whipped topping, thawed
1 (8-ounce) can crushed pineapple, drained
1 cup shredded Cheddar cheese

Dissolve gelatin and breakfast drink in boiling water; chill until slightly thickened. Fold in remaining ingredients. Pour into lightly oiled 5-cup mold, and chill until firm. Yield: 6 servings. *Mrs. V. O. Walker, Pennington, Texas.*

Cardamom, A Sweet Accent

Cardamom is a member of the ginger family but tastes sweeter than ginger, more like anise. It's a flavor most often associated with Indian curries and Danish pastries. In these recipes, it lends a pleasing accent to Apple-Nut Bread, cookies, glazed carrots, and a curry dish called Bengalese Chicken.

You can buy ground cardamom, whole seeds, or whole pods. In recipes calling for the ground form, you can easily grind the whole seeds to a powder with a mortar and pestle or by placing them between sheets of waxed paper and crushing them with a mallet; to use pods, simply discard the soft shell, and grind the whole seeds.

Like many spices, a little cardamom goes a long way. So when experimenting, use it sparingly.

CARDAMOM COOKIES

1 cup butter or margarine, softened
1 cup all-purpose flour
1 teaspoon ground cardamom
½ cup powdered sugar
½ cup cornstarch

Cream butter until light and fluffy. Combine flour and cardamom; add to butter, beating well. Add sugar and cornstarch, beating until smooth. Divide dough into 2 portions; cover and refrigerate several hours or overnight.

Remove 1 portion of dough at a time from refrigerator. Shape dough into 1-inch balls, and place on ungreased cookie sheets. Flatten balls with tines of a fork dipped into flour. Bake at 325° for 12 to 15 minutes or until lightly browned. Cool on wire racks. Yield: about 3 dozen. *Lillian Rendak, Chicago, Illinois.*

BENGALESE CHICKEN

3 cups water
2 teaspoons salt
3 whole chicken breasts
4 stalks celery, sliced
4 large onions, sliced
¼ cup olive oil
1 (8-ounce) can tomato sauce
6 bay leaves
1½ teaspoons garlic salt
1½ teaspoons ground cardamom
1 teaspoon ground cinnamon
1 teaspoon curry powder
1 teaspoon ground ginger
2 (10-ounce) packages frozen green peas
¼ cup raisins
Hot cooked rice

Bring water and salt to boil; add chicken, and cook until tender. Drain, reserving stock. Remove chicken from bones, and cut into large cubes; set chicken aside.

Sauté celery and onion in oil in a large Dutch oven for 4 minutes. Add tomato sauce, seasonings, and 2 cups reserved chicken stock. Bring to a boil; add green peas, raisins, and chicken. Reduce heat, and simmer 15 to 20 minutes. Serve over rice. Yield: 10 to 12 servings. *Mrs. George Sellers, Albany, Georgia.*

CARDAMOM POT ROAST

1 (4- to 5-pound) beef pot roast
¼ cup vegetable oil
2 cups water
1 cup red wine vinegar
1 cup Chablis or other dry white wine
1 cup chopped onion
½ cup firmly packed brown sugar
2 tablespoons mixed pickling spices
2 tablespoons ground cardamom
⅓ cup all-purpose flour
⅓ cup water
Hot cooked buttered noodles (optional)

Brown roast on all sides in hot oil in a Dutch oven; remove from heat. Drain off excess fat. Add 2 cups water, vinegar, Chablis, onion, sugar, and spices to roast. Cover and cook over low heat 3 to 4 hours or until tender. Remove meat from pan.

Combine flour and ⅓ cup water in a jar; shake until well mixed. Slowly add to pan juices; cook until smooth and thickened, stirring constantly. Serve roast and gravy with hot buttered noodles, if desired. Yield: about 8 to 10 servings. *Mrs. G. Thompson, Highland, Maryland.*

ORANGE-GLAZED CARROTS

2 pounds carrots
1½ cups water
1 teaspoon salt
1 teaspoon grated orange rind
¼ cup butter or margarine
¼ cup firmly packed brown sugar
½ teaspoon ground cardamom

Peel carrots; cut in quarters lengthwise and in half crosswise. Bring water and salt to a boil; add carrots. Cover and cook 10 to 15 minutes or until tender; drain.

Add remaining ingredients to carrots. Gently stir over low heat until butter is melted and carrots are glazed. Yield: 8 servings. *Mrs. C. D. Marshall, Culpeper, Virginia.*

APPLE-NUT BREAD

½ cup shortening
⅔ cup sugar
2 eggs
2¼ cups all-purpose flour, divided
1 teaspoon baking powder
1 teaspoon soda
¾ teaspoon salt
¼ teaspoon ground cardamom
2 cups coarsely shredded peeled apple
Grated rind of 1 lemon
½ cup chopped walnuts

Cream shortening and sugar until light and fluffy; add eggs, one at a time, beating well after each addition.

Combine 2 cups flour, baking powder, soda, salt, and cardamom; add to creamed mixture gradually, mixing well.

Toss apples with remaining ¼ cup flour until coated; stir into batter along with lemon rind and walnuts.

Spoon batter into a greased and floured 9- x 5- x 3-inch loafpan. Bake at 350° for 45 to 55 minutes or until a toothpick inserted 1 inch from edge comes out clean. Yield: 1 loaf.

Eleanor Brandt, Arlington, Texas.

Pick A Cake, Any Cake

Stir up some excitement with one of these taste-tempting cakes. Whether you're a chocolate lover or a fruit and spice fanatic, there's a cake here that's just right for you.

Plantation Poppy Seed Cake starts with cake and pudding mixes for ease of preparation, with sour cream and cream sherry added for texture and flavor. Buttermilk Chocolate Cake is topped with a chocolate frosting that is rich with coconut and pecans. Fruit and spice lovers will delight in Dried-Apple Cake—full of raisins, pecans, and a variety of spices.

PLANTATION POPPY SEED CAKE

1 (18.5-ounce) package regular yellow cake mix
1 (3¾-ounce) instant vanilla pudding and pie filling mix
4 eggs
½ cup commercial sour cream
½ cup cream sherry
½ cup salad oil
¼ cup poppy seeds

Combine all ingredients, stirring until just blended. Beat at medium speed of electric mixer exactly 2 minutes. Pour batter into a well-greased 10-inch Bundt pan or tube pan. Bake at 350° for 50 minutes or until cake tests done. Serve warm or cool. If desired, serve with fruit preserves, applesauce, or ice cream. Yield: one 10-inch cake.

Mrs. Ashley Newmyer III,
Washington, D.C.

BUTTERMILK CHOCOLATE CAKE

2 cups all-purpose flour
2 cups sugar
1 teaspoon soda
1 cup water
½ cup butter or margarine
¼ cup cocoa
2 eggs
½ cup buttermilk
Coconut Chocolate Frosting

Sift together flour, sugar, and soda into a large mixing bowl. Combine water, butter, and cocoa in a small saucepan; cook over low heat until mixture comes to a boil; remove from heat and pour over dry ingredients, mixing thoroughly. Add eggs and buttermilk; beat well.

Spoon batter into a well-greased 13- x 9- x 2-inch pan. Bake at 350° for 30 minutes or until cake tests done. Cool. Frost with Coconut Chocolate Frosting. Yield: 15 to 18 servings.

Coconut Chocolate Frosting:

1 (16-ounce) package powdered sugar
1 cup chopped pecans
1 cup shredded coconut
⅓ cup plus 2 teaspoons milk
½ cup butter or margarine
3 tablespoons cocoa

Combine powdered sugar, pecans, and coconut in a large mixing bowl; set aside. Combine milk, butter, and cocoa in a small saucepan; cook over low heat until mixture comes to a boil. Add chocolate mixture to sugar mixture; beat with electric mixer until frosting is fluffy. Yield: enough frosting for one 13- x 9- x 2-inch cake.

Mrs. Michael R. Woods,
Independence, Kansas.

GRAHAM CRACKER CAKE

¾ cup shortening
1½ cups sugar
5 eggs, separated
¼ cup plus 2 tablespoons all-purpose flour
2 teaspoons baking powder
¼ teaspoon salt
3 cups graham cracker crumbs
1¼ cups milk
1 teaspoon vanilla extract
Filling (recipe follows)
Brown Sugar Frosting

Cream shortening and sugar until light and fluffy. Add egg yolks, beating well. Sift together flour, baking powder, and salt; combine with graham cracker crumbs. Add to creamed mixture alternately with milk, beating well after each addition. Stir in vanilla. Beat egg whites until stiff; fold into batter.

Pour the batter into 3 greased and floured 9-inch cakepans; bake at 350° for 30 minutes or until done. Cool completely. Spread filling between layers. Frost top and sides of cake with Brown Sugar Frosting. Store in refrigerator. Yield: one 3-layer cake.

Filling:

¼ cup plus 1 tablespoon all-purpose flour
½ cup sugar
½ teaspoon salt
2 cups milk, scalded
2 egg yolks, slightly beaten
1 teaspoon vanilla extract

Combine flour, sugar, and salt in a saucepan. Slowly stir in milk; cook over low heat 15 minutes or until thick, stirring constantly. Add a small amount of hot mixture to yolks. Stir yolk mixture into hot mixture, and cook 3 minutes longer. Remove from heat, and stir in vanilla. Cool. Yield: enough for one 3-layer cake.

Brown Sugar Frosting:

1 cup firmly packed brown sugar
¼ cup water
2 egg whites

Combine sugar and water in a heavy saucepan; cook over low heat to soft ball stage (234° to 240°).

Beat egg whites until soft peaks form. Continue to beat egg whites, gradually adding syrup mixture; beat well. Yield: enough for a 3-layer cake.

Karen Grubaugh,
San Antonio, Texas.

DRIED-APPLE CAKE

2 (6-ounce) packages dried apples
1¾ cups water
4 to 5 tablespoons sugar
2 cups firmly packed brown sugar
1 cup melted butter or margarine
2 eggs
4 cups all-purpose flour
1 tablespoon soda
1 tablespoon ground nutmeg
1 tablespoon ground cloves
1 tablespoon ground cinnamon
1 cup cold water
1 (15-ounce) box raisins
1 cup chopped pecans

Combine apples and 1¾ cups water. Cover and cook until water is absorbed. Cool slightly; mash. Add 4 to 5 tablespoons sugar, and set aside.

Combine brown sugar, butter, and eggs in a large mixing bowl; beat well. Stir in apples. Combine dry ingredients; add to apple mixture alternately with 1 cup water, beating well after each addition. Stir in raisins and pecans.

Pour batter into a greased 13- x 9- x 2-inch pan. Bake at 350° for 1 hour or until done. Yield: about 15 servings.

Mrs. E. G. Pillow,
Fairdale, Kentucky.

Mouth-Watering Ribs

When you taste Saucy Barbecued Spareribs, you'll think they've been cooked over an open fire instead of in the oven. And you'll get that same outdoor flavor with shortribs when you simmer them in a savory tomato sauce for Beef Shortribs Supreme.

Besides barbecued, try other flavors with ribs: a cinnamon-flavored fruit stuffing between layers of spareribs, or carrots and small whole onions simmered with shortribs.

SAUCY BARBECUED SPARERIBS

3 cloves garlic, pressed
1¼ cups catsup
⅓ cup soy sauce
2 tablespoons gin
1 teaspoon hot sauce
1 teaspoon Worcestershire sauce
¼ cup sugar
2½ pounds spareribs
Salt and pepper

Combine first 7 ingredients. Mix well, and set aside.

Cut ribs into serving-size pieces; sprinkle with salt and pepper, and place in a 13- x 9- x 2-inch baking pan. Bake at 350° for 20 minutes; turn and bake an additional 20 minutes. Pour sauce over ribs, and bake 20 more minutes or until tender. Yield: 4 to 5 servings.

Mrs. Bobby G. Boyd,
Shreveport, Louisiana.

BEEF SHORTRIBS SUPREME

3 pounds beef shortribs
2 teaspoons salt
½ cup water
½ cup chopped onion
1 clove garlic, minced
1 (6-ounce) can tomato paste
1 cup catsup
¾ cup firmly packed brown sugar
½ cup vinegar
2 tablespoons prepared mustard

Brown ribs on all sides in a large skillet (do not add oil or shortening). Cover and cook over low heat 1 hour. Drain off pan drippings.

Combine remaining ingredients; pour over ribs. Cover tightly, and cook over low heat 1½ hours or until meat is tender. Yield: 4 to 6 servings.

Mrs. James W. Bachus,
Austin, Texas.

HEARTY BEEF SHORTRIBS

3 tablespoons all-purpose flour
2 tablespoons brown sugar
1½ teaspoons salt
⅛ teaspoon coarsely ground pepper
3 pounds beef shortribs
2 tablespoons shortening
½ cup coarsely chopped onion
¼ teaspoon whole allspice
1 small bay leaf
¾ cup water
8 medium carrots
8 small whole onions
Prepared horseradish sauce (optional)

Combine flour, sugar, salt, and pepper; dredge ribs in flour mixture. Reserve remaining flour mixture.

Melt shortening in a large Dutch oven; add ribs, and cook over medium heat until well browned. Turn meat frequently to brown evenly. Stir in remaining flour mixture, onion, seasonings, and water.

Reduce heat; cover and simmer 1½ hours or until meat is fork tender. Add carrots and whole onions; cover and cook 30 minutes or until vegetables are tender. Serve with prepared horseradish sauce, if desired. Yield: 4 servings.

Mrs. Evelyn Short,
Maryville, Tennessee.

FRUIT-STUFFED SPARERIBS

1 cup diced pineapple
4 medium cooking apples, peeled and each cut into 8 wedges
3 tablespoons all-purpose flour, divided
2 tablespoons sugar
⅛ teaspoon ground cinnamon
3½ pounds spareribs
Salt and pepper to taste

Combine pineapple, apples, 2 tablespoons flour, sugar, and cinnamon; stir well, and set aside.

Cut slab of meat in half, slicing between ribs. Place half of ribs, meaty side up, in a baking pan; season with salt and pepper. Spoon fruit mixture over ribs. Top with remaining half of ribs, meaty side up; season with salt and pepper.

Tie string securely around spareribs; sprinkle with remaining 1 tablespoon flour. Bake at 425° for 30 minutes; reduce heat to 350° and bake 1½ hours. Yield: 4 to 6 servings.

Mrs. James S. Tiffany,
Dallas, Texas.

Sandwich With A Flair

For an interesting sandwich idea, try Oriental Stuffed Pockets: Mideastern pocket bread and a filling with an Oriental flavor.

For the filling, strips of cooked chicken and Chinese vegetables are heated in a sauce flavored with brown sugar, teriyaki sauce, garlic, and catsup. The hot mixture is spooned into the hollow halves of pocket bread, and the sandwich is finished with a crisp topping of lettuce.

ORIENTAL STUFFED POCKETS

1 tablespoon brown sugar
1 tablespoon cornstarch
¾ cup water
¼ cup teriyaki sauce
1 tablespoon catsup
1 tablespoon lemon juice
1 clove garlic, minced
⅛ teaspoon ground ginger
2 cups cooked chicken, cut into strips
1 (16-ounce) can mixed Chinese vegetables, drained
2 tablespoons sliced green onion
3 (7- to 8-inch) pocket bread rounds
Shredded lettuce

Combine first 8 ingredients in a medium saucepan; cook over medium heat, stirring constantly, until thickened. Stir in chicken, Chinese vegetables, and onion; cook, stirring often, until thoroughly heated.

Cut bread rounds in half, and spoon chicken mixture into hollows. Top with lettuce. Yield: 3 servings.

Mrs. Anne Ringer,
Warner Robins, Georgia.

Tip: Keep butter, margarine, and fat drippings tightly covered in the refrigerator. Vegetable shortening can be kept covered at room temperature. Homemade salad dressing should be kept in the refrigerator; mayonnaise and commercial salad dressings should be refrigerated after opening. Foods mixed with mayonnaise, such as potato salad or egg salad, should be refrigerated and used within a couple of days.

February

As the weather is still nippy outside, February is the perfect month to enjoy a potful of steaming chowder. You can make this hearty soup from a variety of ingredients—cheese, broccoli, mushrooms, or the ever-popular fish. Choose your favorite chowder or try them all for casual family dining.

Another cool weather choice is pot roast. Because the meat and vegetables simmer together, meal preparation is easy on the cook. And we show you how versatile pot roast can be with six flavorful combinations.

End dinner on an elegant note with a flaming dessert, such as Cherries Jubilee. We even give you step-by-step directions with photographs.

Chowder—It Isn't Just For Clams

What better way to warm up on a chilly winter evening than by bringing out a potful of simmering chowder. The heartiest of the soup family, chowder isn't reserved just for clams. A variety of ingredients can bring about the same result—a rich, satisfying meal-in-a-bowl.

For instance, Hearty Cheddar Chowder is thick with vegetables and Cheddar cheese and sparked with pimiento. Ham and Swiss cheese enrich Broccoli Chowder, while potatoes, carrots, and mushrooms combine for Mushroom Chowder. Creamy Fish Chowder—made with fish fillets and potatoes—should satisfy those who prefer a fish chowder.

BROCCOLI CHOWDER

2 pounds fresh broccoli
2 (13¾-ounce) cans chicken broth
3 cups milk
1 cup chopped cooked ham
2 teaspoons salt
¼ teaspoon pepper
1 cup half-and-half
2 cups (½ pound) shredded Swiss cheese
¼ cup butter or margarine

Combine broccoli and 1 can chicken broth in a Dutch oven; cover and cook 7 minutes or until broccoli is crisp-tender. Remove broccoli from broth; cool, and chop coarsely.

Add remaining can of chicken broth, milk, ham, salt, and pepper to Dutch oven; bring to a boil over medium heat, stirring occasionally. Stir in broccoli and remaining ingredients. Cook over low heat until thoroughly heated (do not boil). Yield: 6 to 8 servings.
Johanna Lawler,
Virginia Beach, Virginia.

HEARTY CHEDDAR CHOWDER

3 cups water
3 chicken bouillon cubes
4 medium potatoes, peeled and diced
1 medium onion, sliced
1 cup thinly sliced carrots
½ cup diced green pepper
⅓ cup butter or margarine
⅓ cup all-purpose flour
3½ cups milk
4 cups (1 pound) shredded sharp Cheddar cheese
1 (2-ounce) jar diced pimiento, drained
¼ teaspoon hot sauce (optional)

Combine water and bouillon cubes in a Dutch oven; bring to a boil. Add vegetables; cover and simmer 12 minutes or until vegetables are tender.

Melt butter in a heavy saucepan; blend in flour, and cook 1 minute. Gradually add milk; cook over medium heat until thickened, stirring constantly. Add cheese, stirring until melted.

Stir cheese sauce, pimiento, and hot sauce (if desired) into vegetable mixture. Cook over low heat until thoroughly heated (do not boil). Yield: 8 to 10 servings. *Mrs. Sandra Souther,*
Gainesville, Georgia.

HAM AND CORN CHOWDER

½ cup onion slices
½ cup melted butter or margarine
1 (20-ounce) can cream-style corn
½ cup half-and-half
1 cup chopped ham
½ teaspoon salt
⅛ teaspoon pepper
Celery Croutons

Sauté onion in butter in a Dutch oven until tender. Add remaining ingredients except Celery Croutons. Cook over low heat until thoroughly heated (do not boil). Garnish each serving with Celery Croutons. Yield: 6 to 8 servings.

Celery Croutons:

1½ cups of ¼-inch bread cubes
2½ tablespoons melted butter or margarine
Celery salt

Sauté bread cubes in butter, tossing frequently, until golden brown. Sprinkle with celery salt. Yield: 1½ cups.
Mrs. R. E. Gentry,
Memphis, Tennessee.

CREAMY FISH CHOWDER

1 cup diced potatoes
1 cup boiling water
3 slices bacon, chopped
1 medium onion, chopped
¾ pound fish fillets, cubed
1 cup milk
½ teaspoon salt
⅛ teaspoon pepper
2 tablespoons chopped fresh parsley

Place potatoes in boiling water in a Dutch oven; cover and cook 10 to 15 minutes. Fry bacon until transparent; add onion, and cook until onion is soft and bacon is lightly browned. Add bacon, onion, bacon drippings, and fish fillets to potatoes. Simmer 10 minutes or until potatoes and fish are done. Stir in milk, salt, and pepper; simmer 5 minutes. Sprinkle with parsley. Yield: 2 to 3 servings. *Myra Schisler,*
Jonesboro, Arkansas.

MUSHROOM CHOWDER

½ cup chopped onion
½ cup melted butter or margarine
1 pound fresh mushrooms, sliced
1 cup diced potatoes
1 cup finely chopped celery
½ cup diced carrots
1 teaspoon salt
¼ teaspoon pepper
1 tablespoon all-purpose flour
2 tablespoons water
3 cups chicken stock
1 cup milk
Grated Parmesan cheese

Sauté onion in butter in a Dutch oven until tender. Add vegetables, salt, and pepper; cover and simmer 15 to 20 minutes or until vegetables are tender.

Combine flour and water, mixing until smooth; stir into vegetable mixture. Add chicken stock, and simmer 10 minutes. Stir in milk and ¼ cup Parmesan cheese. Cook over low heat until thoroughly heated (do not boil). Sprinkle each serving with additional Parmesan cheese. Yield: 6 to 8 servings.
Mrs. Mary Andrew,
Winston-Salem, North Carolina.

Give Pot Roast A Flavor Lift

A pinch of this and a dash of that can turn pot roast into a dining delight for the whole family. Braised with vegetables in a well-seasoned liquid, pot roast can take on an infinite variety of tastes according to the seasonings and vegetables used.

For instance, Barbecued Pot Roast is simmered in a tangy catsup-based sauce; the leftovers will disappear in a hurry when sliced and served on buns as hearty sandwiches.

Regal Pot Roast owes its name to the subtle flavoring it receives from wine and brandy. Caraway seeds and vinegar give a German accent to Bavarian-Style Pot Roast. And for a south-of-the-border flavor, try Beef Diablo.

REGAL POT ROAST

1 (4- to 5-pound) boneless chuck roast
2 teaspoons salt
Freshly ground pepper
1 carrot, sliced
1 rib celery, cut into 1-inch pieces
1 medium onion, sliced
2 whole cloves
1 clove garlic, minced
1 teaspoon thyme
2 bay leaves
3 sprigs parsley, minced
1 cup Burgundy
¼ cup brandy
1 tablespoon tomato sauce

Place roast in a shallow pan; broil 3 inches from heat for 2 to 3 minutes on each side or until browned. Sprinkle roast with salt and pepper, and place in a large oven browning bag. Set aside.

Place carrot, celery, and onion in pan in which roast was browned; broil 3 inches from heat 2 to 3 minutes or until edges begin to brown. Spoon vegetables on top of roast in browning bag; add remaining ingredients. Seal bag according to package directions, cutting slits in top of bag. Place bag on a 15- x 10- x 1-inch jellyroll pan; bake at 300° for 3 hours. Yield: 8 servings.

Note: If gravy is desired, strain cooking liquid. For 1 cup gravy, combine 1 tablespoon cornstarch and 1 tablespoon wine; mix well. Gradually stir mixture into 1 cup hot cooking liquid and cook, stirring constantly, until thickened.

Mrs. Bruce Weilbacher,
San Antonio, Texas.

BAVARIAN-STYLE POT ROAST

2 tablespoons all-purpose flour
2 teaspoons salt
¼ teaspoon pepper
1 (3- to 4-pound) blade-cut chuck roast
2 tablespoons vegetable oil
1 medium onion, quartered
1 bay leaf
½ teaspoon caraway seeds
2 tablespoons vinegar
¼ cup water

Combine flour, salt, and pepper; mix well. Dredge roast in seasoned flour, reserving any excess flour. Brown roast on all sides in hot oil in a large Dutch oven; drain off drippings. Add remaining ingredients to roast; cover and simmer 3 hours or until meat is tender.

If gravy is desired, thicken pan liquid with reserved seasoned flour. Yield: about 6 servings. *Mrs. Ray Harp,*
Shawnee, Oklahoma.

BARBECUED POT ROAST

1 (4- to 5-pound) beef shoulder or chuck roast
2 tablespoons vegetable oil
2 medium onions, sliced
2 cloves garlic, minced
½ cup catsup
½ cup water
¼ cup red wine vinegar
2 tablespoons Worcestershire sauce
1 teaspoon rosemary leaves
1 teaspoon salt
1½ pounds small potatoes, peeled

Brown roast on all sides in hot oil in a large Dutch oven; add onion and garlic. Combine remaining ingredients except potatoes; mix well, and pour over roast. Cover and simmer 2 hours; add potatoes, and cook an additional 30 minutes. Yield: 8 servings.

Susan S. Lombardo,
Greensboro, North Carolina.

MUSHROOM POT ROAST

1 (3- to 4-pound) boneless pot roast (bottom round, chuck, rump, or sirloin tip)
½ cup all-purpose flour
Hot salad oil
Salt and pepper to taste
2 medium onions, sliced
⅓ cup cooking sherry
½ cup water
¼ cup catsup
1 clove garlic, minced
¼ teaspoon dry mustard
¼ teaspoon marjoram
¼ teaspoon rosemary
¼ teaspoon thyme
1 small bay leaf
2 (8-ounce) cans sliced mushrooms, undrained
½ cup cold water
¼ cup all-purpose flour

Dredge roast in ½ cup flour; brown on all sides in a small amount of oil. Sprinkle with salt and pepper; add onion. Combine sherry, ½ cup water, catsup, and seasonings; add to roast. Cover and simmer 2½ to 3 hours. Add mushrooms, and heat well.

Remove roast from cooking liquid; skim fat from liquid. Combine ½ cup cold water and ¼ cup flour, blending until smooth; stir into liquid. Cook, stirring constantly, until thickened. Discard bay leaf. Serve gravy with roast. Yield: 6 to 8 servings.

Mildred Morrow,
Porterdale, Georgia.

POT ROAST WITH SOUR CREAM GRAVY

1 (2½-pound) boneless chuck roast
2 tablespoons vegetable oil
½ cup water
3 medium potatoes, peeled and quartered
3 medium carrots, cut into 2-inch pieces
3 medium onions, quartered
1 tablespoon all-purpose flour
1 (8-ounce) carton commercial sour cream

Brown roast on all sides in hot oil in a large Dutch oven; add water. Reduce heat; cover and simmer 2½ hours. Add potatoes, carrots, and onions. Cover and simmer 30 minutes or until vegetables are tender.

Remove roast and vegetables to a serving dish. Drain off drippings, leaving 1 tablespoons in pan; reserve remainder. Stir flour into drippings in pan; cook over medium heat until browned, stirring constantly. Add water to reserved drippings to make 1 cup; stir into flour and cook, stirring constantly, until smooth and slightly thickened. Add sour cream and cook, stirring constantly, until thoroughly heated. Serve gravy with roast. Yield: 5 to 6 servings. *Mrs. Anne Mann,*
Woodlawn, Tennessee.

BEEF DIABLO

1 (3- to 4-pound) blade-cut chuck roast
3 tablespoons vegetable oil
¼ cup finely chopped onion
½ cup beef stock, divided
2 teaspoons salt
¼ teaspoon pepper
¼ cup chili sauce
2 tablespoons all-purpose flour
1 tablespoon sugar
2 tablespoons prepared mustard
1 tablespoon Worcestershire sauce
1 tablespoon vinegar
¼ cup water

Brown roast on all sides in hot oil in a large Dutch oven; remove roast and pour off drippings, leaving 1 tablespoon in pan. Return roast to pan; add onion, ¼ cup beef stock, salt, and pepper. Cover and simmer 2½ hours or until meat is tender.

Combine chili sauce, flour, sugar, mustard, Worcestershire sauce, and vinegar; stir in water, and pour over roast. Simmer an additional 30 minutes or until tender; remove roast to serving dish. Stir remaining ¼ cup beef stock into pan. Simmer 5 minutes; strain and serve with roast. Yield: 6 to 8 servings.
Ruth E. Cunliffe,
Lake Placid, Florida.

Flame A Dessert For Show And Taste

Dazzle your guests by flaming and serving Cherries Jubilee at the table as a dramatic finale to a special dinner. Showmanship is an obvious motive for serving a flaming dessert, but the most important reason is, of course, flavor.

Both kirsch, a colorless brandy made from the fermented juice of cherries, and Cognac (also a brandy) produce the rich flaming sauce for Cherries Jubilee. Once the alcohol has escaped in the flame, the essence of the brandy remains to delicately flavor the dark sweet cherries, which are then spooned over vanilla ice cream.

As spectacular as Cherries Jubilee is, it isn't difficult to master. Just use the recipe included here, and follow the step-by-step procedure illustrated. Some of these same techniques also apply to other flamed desserts, including Bananas Foster and Cherry Crêpes Flambé.

Bananas Foster, which originated at Brennan's in New Orleans, combines the delectable flavors of bananas and rum in a sauce that is flamed and served over vanilla ice cream. There are many recipes for Bananas Foster, but the one included here is a good choice for your first attempt at flaming a dessert.

In Cherry Crêpes Flambé, basic crêpes are sauced with orange marmalade, currant jelly, and sweet cherries. Then brandy sets the dessert aglow, creating a warm, romantic flavor. The crêpes may be prepared in advance and refrigerated or frozen until needed, making this an impressive, yet easy, dessert for that last minute dinner party.

To ensure your success with flamed desserts, here are some points you'll need to know.

—Brandies, liquors, and liqueurs with a high alcoholic content are best for flaming, since the flammability of the spirit is based on the amount of alcohol it contains.

—Sweet liqueurs, such as the banana-flavored liqueur used in Bananas Foster, will produce a higher flame and burn slightly longer than will liqueurs containing less sugar but the same percentage of alcohol.

—To produce enough fumes to ignite, the liquid must be heated quickly; it's the fumes that burn, not the liquid.

—Follow this procedure when flaming: Warm the spirit, ignite it, and pour the flames evenly over the food. An alternate method is to warm the spirit, pour it over the food, and then ignite. The first method is preferred; in testing the alternate method, we found that the alcohol dispersed and diluted when poured over the food, making it difficult to ignite.

—Cooking with flames is not dangerous if common sense and caution are used during the flaming process; the flame itself is not very hot. One caution: If you are heating the spirit over a flame (gas range or tabletop burner) prior to igniting, do not allow it to boil, as it can self-ignite.

—In flaming desserts, the alcohol vanishes completely as it burns; since only the flavor of the liquid remains, persons who do not care for alcohol may still enjoy flamed desserts.

CHERRIES JUBILEE

2 (16-ounce) cans pitted dark sweet cherries
¼ cup red currant jelly
⅓ cup kirsch
⅔ cup Cognac
2 pints vanilla ice cream

Drain cherries, reserving ¼ cup liquid; set both aside.

Melt jelly over low heat; add cherries, reserved cherry liquid, and kirsch. Thoroughly heat cherry mixture, stirring gently. Transfer mixture to chafing dish or flambé pan, and keep warm.

Rapidly heat Cognac in a small saucepan to produce fumes (do not boil). Pour into a decorative container. Ignite Cognac, and pour over cherries. After flames die down, immediately spoon cherries over individual servings of ice cream. Yield: 6 servings.

Frances R. Dickson,
Tucker, Georgia.

BANANAS FOSTER

6 tablespoons butter
½ cup firmly packed brown sugar
½ teaspoon ground cinnamon
4 bananas, halved lengthwise
½ cup banana-flavored liqueur
¾ cup rum
1 pint vanilla ice cream

Melt butter in a chafing dish. Add sugar and cinnamon; cook syrup over medium heat until bubbly. Add bananas; heat 3 to 4 minutes, basting constantly with syrup.

Combine liqueur and rum in a small, long-handled pan; heat just until warm. Ignite with a long match, and pour over bananas. Baste bananas with sauce until flames die down. Serve immediately over ice cream. Yield: 4 servings.

CHERRY CREPES FLAMBE

3 eggs
1 cup all-purpose flour
½ teaspoon salt
1½ cups milk
3 tablespoons melted margarine
Vegetable oil
Powdered sugar
1 cup currant or apple jelly
2 tablespoons orange marmalade
1 cup pitted dark sweet cherries
¼ cup brandy

Combine eggs, flour, and salt; mix well. Add milk and margarine, beating until mixture is smooth. Refrigerate batter at least 2 hours (this allows flour particles to swell and soften so crêpes are light in texture).

Brush crêpe pan with oil; place over medium heat until just hot but not smoking. Pour in 3 tablespoons batter, and quickly tilt pan to cover the entire bottom thinly and evenly.

Cook crêpe about 1 minute. Lift edge of crêpe to test for doneness. When lightly browned, flip crêpe over and cook about ½ minute on other side. Stack crêpes between layers of waxed paper to prevent sticking.

Fold crêpes in half, then into quarters. Sprinkle with powdered sugar, and arrange in a chafing dish.

Combine jelly and marmalade in a saucepan; place over low heat until melted. Add cherries, and heat thoroughly. Pour over crêpes.

Heat brandy in a small saucepan over medium heat. (Do not boil.) Ignite with a long match, and pour over crêpes. After flames die down, serve immediately. Yield: 6 servings.

Note: Crêpes can be made in advance, wrapped in foil, and stored in refrigerator or freezer. When needed, remove waxed paper and place in covered dish or wrap in foil; heat at 300° about 10 minutes. *Ruth E. Cunliffe,*
Lake Placid, Florida.

Step 1—*To make Cherries Jubilee, first melt jelly over low heat; then add cherries, reserved cherry liquid, and kirsch. Stir gently until cherry mixture is thoroughly heated. Transfer to chafing dish or flambé pan, and keep warm.*

Step 2—*Rapidly heat Cognac in a small saucepan to produce fumes (do not boil). Pour into a decorative container.*

Step 3—*Ignite Cognac, and pour over cherries. The warm Cognac may be poured over the cherries before igniting; however, we found igniting to be difficult with this method.*

Step 4—*When the flame dies down, spoon cherries over individual servings of ice cream. To make sure the ice cream is frozen hard before adding the warm cherry sauce, spoon into individual serving dishes in advance and keep frozen until ready to serve.*

Salads That Improve With Time

If your salad repertoire could use a lift, try marinated vegetable salads. Besides being a nice change of pace from salad greens, these salads offer another advantage: They can (and should) be prepared in advance and chilled until you are ready to serve—a bonus for the busy cook.

Almost any vegetable can be used in a marinated salad. These recipes offer a wide selection, including Chilled Corn Salad, Cauliflower-Broccoli Salad, and Medley Marinade.

Chilled Corn Salad is a marinated combination that's as colorful as it is delicious.

CHILLED CORN SALAD

1 (12-ounce) can whole kernel corn, drained
1 small onion, chopped
½ cup chopped green pepper
2 tablespoons minced parsley
2 tablespoons cider vinegar
1 tablespoon oil
¼ teaspoon salt
¼ teaspoon pepper
Lettuce leaves (optional)

Combine all ingredients except lettuce leaves. Chill several hours or overnight. Serve on lettuce leaves, if desired. Yield: 4 to 6 servings.

Mrs. Bettina Hambrick,
Muskogee, Oklahoma.

MEDLEY MARINADE

1 (17-ounce) can whole kernel corn, drained
1 (16-ounce) can French-style green beans, drained
1 (17-ounce) can small early peas, drained
1 (4-ounce) jar pimiento, diced
1 onion, chopped
1 carrot, grated
1 green pepper, chopped
1 stalk celery, chopped
1 cucumber, chopped
1 cup vinegar
1 cup sugar
½ cup vegetable oil

Combine all vegetables, mixing well. Combine remaining ingredients; mix well, and pour over vegetables. Chill 24 hours. Drain before serving. Yield: 10 to 12 servings. *Mrs. Roger Walden, Macon, Georgia.*

FOUR-BEAN SALAD

1 (16-ounce) can green beans, rinsed and drained
1 (16-ounce) can wax beans, rinsed and drained
1 (16-ounce) can kidney beans, rinsed and drained
1 (16-ounce) can lima beans, rinsed and drained
1 medium-size green pepper, thinly sliced
1 medium onion, thinly sliced and separated into rings
¾ cup sugar
½ cup vinegar
½ cup salad oil
½ teaspoon salt
½ teaspoon pepper
1 tablespoon minced parsley

Combine first 6 ingredients, tossing gently. Combine remaining ingredients; heat, stirring constantly, until sugar dissolves. Pour hot mixture over vegetables; cover and chill several hours. Yield: 12 servings.

Miss Charlotte Pierce,
Greensburg, Kentucky.

Tip: Sprinkle freshly cut avocados, bananas, apples, and peaches with lemon juice to prevent darkening.

CAULIFLOWER-BROCCOLI SALAD

2½ cups chopped fresh broccoli
2½ cups chopped fresh cauliflower
1 cup chopped green or purple onion
⅔ cup salad dressing or mayonnaise
⅓ cup buttermilk
2 teaspoons celery seeds

Combine vegetables in a large bowl; add remaining ingredients, tossing well. Chill. Yield: 5 to 6 servings.

Mrs. F. A. Schad,
Burleson, Texas.

MARINATED ASPARAGUS SALAD

1 (0.7-ounce) package garlic salad dressing mix
1 (15-ounce) can asparagus, drained
1 (8½-ounce) can small early peas, drained
3 hard-cooked eggs, chopped
Shredded lettuce (optional)

Prepare salad dressing mix according to package directions; set aside. Combine asparagus, peas, and eggs; pour dressing over mixture. Stir gently. Cover and chill several hours. Drain well; serve on shredded lettuce, if desired. Yield: 4 servings.

Mrs. Donly Ray,
Birmingham, Alabama.

Vegetables In Savory Combinations

No matter what your vegetable likes may be, you can mix them and match them, add a variety of seasonings, and develop an extra special dish for color and flavor. These vegetable combinations are suitable for a variety of meals.

For an Oriental Touch, you might serve Snow Peas Piquant. Tomato wedges, pineapple chunks, and water chestnuts are stir-fried with snow peas in a tangy sauce. Spanish Eggplant is baked with green peppers, tomatoes, onions, and Parmesan cheese. And brussels sprouts and celery are combined in a cream sauce.

CAULIFLOWER GOLDENROD

1 hard-cooked egg
1 medium head cauliflower
¼ cup milk
1½ cups water
5 tablespoons melted butter or margarine, divided
Salt
Freshly ground pepper
2 tablespoons finely chopped parsley

Press egg through a fine sieve, and set aside.

Wash cauliflower, and remove green leaves. Break into flowerets. Combine milk and water in a saucepan; bring to a boil. Add cauliflower; cover and cook 10 minutes. Drain well. Toss cauliflower and 1 tablespoon melted butter until thoroughly coated. Transfer to a serving dish.

Combine remaining 4 tablespoons butter, egg, salt, and pepper. Pour over cauliflower. Sprinkle with chopped parsley. Yield: 4 servings.
Mrs. J. John Stearman,
Louisville, Kentucky.

BRUSSELS SPROUTS AND CELERY

1½ cups chopped celery
3 tablespoons melted butter or margarine
3 tablespoons all-purpose flour
1½ cups scalded milk
4 cups cooked brussels sprouts
½ teaspoon salt
⅛ teaspoon pepper
½ cup dry breadcrumbs
1 tablespoon butter or margarine

Sauté celery in 3 tablespoons butter 2 minutes. Stir in flour; cook, stirring, until bubbly. Gradually add milk; cook over medium heat, stirring constantly, until mixture boils. Add brussels sprouts, salt, and pepper; toss lightly.

Spoon into a greased, shallow 2-quart casserole. Sprinkle breadcrumbs over top, and dot with 1 tablespoon butter. Bake at 400° for 20 minutes. Yield: 6 to 8 servings. *Mrs. Charles H. Lilly,*
Jacksonville, Florida.

SPANISH-STYLE CAULIFLOWER

1 head cauliflower
¼ cup melted butter or margarine
1 tablespoon sugar
½ teaspoon salt
½ teaspoon pepper
¾ cup cracker crumbs
½ cup diced green pepper
1 (16-ounce) can tomatoes
1 medium onion, chopped
1½ cups shredded Cheddar cheese, divided

Wash cauliflower, and remove green leaves. Break into flowerets. Cover and cook in small amount of boiling salted water 5 minutes; drain.

Combine butter, sugar, salt, pepper, and cracker crumbs. Stir in green pepper, tomatoes, onion, 1¼ cups cheese, and cauliflower. Pour into a 2-quart casserole; sprinkle remaining cheese on top. Bake at 350° for 1 hour. Yield: 6 to 8 servings. *Mrs. M. M. Fillingame,*
Jackson, Mississippi.

SPANISH EGGPLANT

1 medium eggplant, peeled and cut into ½-inch slices
½ cup chopped onion
½ cup chopped green pepper
¼ cup bacon drippings
1 (16-ounce) can whole tomatoes, cut into quarters
1½ teaspoons salt
2 tablespoons sugar
½ cup dry breadcrumbs
½ cup grated Parmesan cheese

Combine eggplant, onion, green pepper, and bacon drippings; mix well, and let stand 10 minutes. Stir in tomatoes, salt, and sugar. Place in a medium saucepan; cover and cook 5 to 10 minutes over low heat.

Spoon mixture into a greased, shallow 2-quart casserole; sprinkle with breadcrumbs and cheese. Bake at 350° for 20 minutes. Yield: 6 to 8 servings.
Marsha Wren,
Batesville, Mississippi.

Snow Peas Piquant combines tomato wedges, pineapple chunks, water chestnuts, and green onions in a tangy sauce.

SNOW PEAS PIQUANT

1 (20-ounce) can pineapple chunks
3 tablespoons cornstarch
½ teaspoon curry powder
¼ cup melted butter or margarine
½ cup sliced green onion
4 cups fresh snow peas or 2 (6-ounce) packages frozen snow peas, thawed
1 cup beef broth
¼ cup red wine vinegar
2 tablespoons brown sugar
1 tablespoon soy sauce
1 (8½-ounce) can water chestnuts, drained and sliced
2 medium tomatoes, each cut into 8 wedges

Drain pineapple, reserving ½ cup syrup; set pineapple aside. Combine ½ cup pineapple syrup and cornstarch, stirring until cornstarch is dissolved; set mixture aside.

Stir curry powder into butter; cook over low heat 2 to 3 minutes. Add green onion and snow peas, stirring well. Cook over medium heat until snow peas begin to wilt. Stir in broth, wine vinegar, brown sugar, and cornstarch mixture; cook, stirring constantly, until thickened. Add soy sauce, pineapple chunks, water chestnuts, and tomatoes; stir gently. Cook over medium heat 5 minutes. Yield: 8 servings.
Edna Chadsey,
Corpus Christi, Texas.

Tip: Keep bacon drippings in a covered container in the refrigerator; use for browning meats or seasoning vegetables.

For a special breakfast, crêpes are filled with a hearty portion of Country-Style Scrambled Eggs.

Fill Some Crêpes For Breakfast

For a special family breakfast, Mrs. Victor Seine of Austin, Texas, serves these egg-filled crêpes, topped with her simple-to-prepare cheese sauce.

The filling of Country-Style Scrambled Eggs is what makes these crêpes really different: A mixture of sautéed vegetables—grated potato, onion, and green pepper—is scrambled with eggs and mixed with a generous amount of crisply fried bits of bacon.

COUNTRY-STYLE BREAKFAST CREPES

1 cup all-purpose flour
¼ teaspoon salt
2 eggs
½ cup milk
½ cup water
2 tablespoons butter or margarine, melted
Vegetable oil
Country-Style Scrambled Eggs
Easy Cheese Sauce

Combine flour, salt, and eggs; mix well. Add milk, water, and butter; beat until smooth. Refrigerate batter at least 2 hours. (This allows flour particles to swell and soften so the crêpes are light in texture.)

Brush the bottom of a 6- or 7-inch crêpe pan or heavy skillet with vegetable oil; place pan over medium heat until oil is just hot, not smoking.

Pour 2 to 3 tablespoons batter into pan; quickly tilt pan in all directions so batter covers the pan in a thin film. Cook about 1 minute.

Lift edge of crêpe to test for doneness. Crêpe is ready for flipping when it can be shaken loose from pan. Flip the crêpe, and cook about 30 seconds on the other side. (This side is rarely more than spotty brown and is the side on which the filling is placed.)

When crêpes are done, place on a towel to cool. Stack them between layers of waxed paper to prevent sticking.

Spoon ⅓ cup Country-Style Scrambled Eggs in center of each crêpe; do not spread. Roll up crêpes, leaving ends open. Place crêpes seam side down in a serving dish.

Spoon Easy Cheese Sauce over filled crêpes, and serve immediately. Yield: 8 servings.

Country-Style Scrambled Eggs:

1 large onion, finely chopped
1 large green pepper, finely chopped
1 medium potato, peeled and grated
2 tablespoons butter or margarine, melted
6 to 8 eggs
1 teaspoon salt
½ teaspoon whole basil leaves
¼ teaspoon pepper
15 slices bacon, cooked and crumbled

Sauté vegetables in butter 15 to 20 minutes or until tender but not brown. Beat eggs slightly; add seasonings, and beat until frothy. Stir eggs into vegetable mixture; cook over low heat until eggs are set but still moist. Stir in bacon. Yield: about 5 cups.

Note: If desired, 1 pound ground cooked ham or 1 pound cooked and crumbled bulk sausage may be substituted for bacon.

Easy Cheese Sauce:

1 (11-ounce) can Cheddar cheese soup, undiluted
⅔ cup milk

Combine soup and milk in a saucepan; cook over low heat until thoroughly heated. Keep mixture warm until it is needed, stirring occasionally. Yield: about 2 cups.

A Hint Of Cinnamon Flavors These Dishes

The warm, spicy aroma of cinnamon is a sure sign that good things are in the making. In these recipes, cinnamon lends its flavor to a variety of dishes.

Ground cinnamon is a staple in most kitchens, but it's a good idea also to have stick cinnamon on hand to use as stirrers in beverages and for dishes like Pickled Pineapple and Spiced Fruit.

SPICED BEETS

1 (16-ounce) jar tiny whole beets, drained
1 small onion, sliced
½ cup water
⅓ cup tarragon-flavored vinegar
1½ tablespoons sugar
5 whole cloves
1 (1½-inch) stick cinnamon
⅛ teaspoon salt

Combine beets and onion; set aside. Combine remaining ingredients in a saucepan; simmer 10 minutes. Stir in beets and onion; simmer 5 to 10 minutes. Yield: 4 to 6 servings.

Mrs. Gordon Gray,
Clemson, South Carolina.

CINNAMON BALLS

1 cup butter
⅓ cup sugar
2 teaspoons vanilla extract
2 cups sifted cake flour
1 teaspoon ground cinnamon
2 cups corn flakes, crushed
1 cup chopped pecans
Powdered sugar

Combine butter, sugar, and vanilla; cream until light and fluffy. Sift together flour and cinnamon; add to creamed mixture, mixing well. Stir in corn flakes and pecans.

Shape dough into small balls, and place on lightly greased cookie sheets. Bake at 350° for 20 to 25 minutes. Cool slightly; remove from pan. Sprinkle with powdered sugar while warm. Yield: about 4 dozen. *Joan W. Rodriguez,*
Falls Church, Virginia.

The aroma of cinnamon is surpassed only by its flavor in such treats as Cinnamon Balls and Cinnamon Swirl Loaf.

CINNAMON SWIRL LOAF

1 package dry yeast
¼ cup warm water (105° to 115°)
2 cups milk, scalded
½ cup sugar
½ cup shortening
2 teaspoons salt
7½ to 8 cups all-purpose flour
2 eggs
1½ tablespoons ground cinnamon
¾ cup sugar
2 tablespoons melted butter or margarine

Dissolve yeast in warm water; set aside. Combine milk, ½ cup sugar, shortening and salt; stir until sugar dissolves. Cool to lukewarm. Add 3 cups flour, mixing well. Beat in yeast mixture and eggs. Add enough remaining flour to make a soft dough.

Turn dough out on a lightly floured board; cover and let rest 10 minutes. Knead until smooth and elastic (about 8 to 10 minutes). Place in a greased bowl, turning once to grease top. Cover and let rise in a warm place (85°) until doubled in bulk (about 2 hours). Punch dough down; let rise 1 hour.

Punch dough down, and divide in half; cover and let rest 10 minutes. On a lightly floured surface, roll each half into a 15- x 7-inch rectangle about ½ inch thick. Combine cinnamon and ¾ cup sugar; reserve 2 tablespoons, and sprinkle remainder over rectangles of dough. Roll up jellyroll fashion.

Place each roll, seam side down, in a greased 9- x 5- x 3-inch loafpan. Cover and let rise 1 hour. Brush dough with butter; sprinkle with reserved cinnamon-sugar mixture. Bake at 375° for 35 to 40 minutes. Yield: 2 loaves.

Mrs. Pat Fitz,
Lewisburg, Tennessee.

SPICED FRUIT

2 oranges
2 (1-pound 13-ounce) cans pear halves, drained
2 (1-pound 14-ounce) cans apricots halves, drained
1½ cups orange juice
¼ cup sugar
2 to 3 (2-inch) sticks cinnamon
12 whole cloves
½ teaspoon salt

Peel oranges, reserving 1 peel; cut oranges into 1-inch pieces. Combine orange pieces, peel, pears, and apricots in a large bowl. Combine remaining ingredients in a medium saucepan; simmer 5 minutes. Pour over fruit; cover and chill several hours. Yield: 10 to 12 servings.
Mrs. Sue-Sue Hartstern,
Louisville, Kentucky.

DRIED FRUIT SOUP

6 prunes
8 dried apricot halves
½ cup seedless raisins
1 quart boiling water
½ teaspoon salt
½ cup honey
1½ tablespoons quick-cooking tapioca
1 (2-inch) stick cinnamon

Combine fruits in a medium saucepan. Pour boiling water over fruit; let stand until fruit is plump. Add remaining ingredients; cover and cook over low heat about 1 hour or until fruit is tender and tapioca is clear. Yield: 4 servings. *Mrs. George M. Wheaton,*
West Palm Beach, Florida.

APPLE KUCHEN

½ cup butter or margarine, softened
1 (18.5-ounce) package yellow cake mix
1 (21-ounce) can pie-sliced apples, drained
½ cup sugar
1 teaspoon ground cinnamon
1 cup commercial sour cream
1 egg

Cut butter into cake mix until mixture resembles coarse meal. Press mixture lightly in bottom and 1 inch up sides of a greased 13- x 9- x 2-inch pan. Bake at 350° for 10 minutes.

Arrange apple slices on warm crust. Combine sugar and cinnamon; sprinkle over apples. Combine sour cream and egg, beating lightly; spoon over apples. Bake an additional 15 to 20 minutes. To serve, cut into squares. Yield: about 15 servings.

Mrs. James F. Crowell,
Princeton, Kentucky.

PICKLED PINEAPPLE

1 (20-ounce) can pineapple chunks
1 (8¼-ounce) can pineapple chunks
¾ cup vinegar
1¼ cups sugar
Pinch of salt
6 to 8 whole cloves
1 (3-inch) stick cinnamon

Drain pineapple, reserving juice. Combine pineapple juice, vinegar, sugar, salt, and spices in a large saucepan; bring to a boil. Simmer 10 minutes, uncovered. Add pineapple, and bring to a boil. Cool; cover and refrigerate 1 week. Yield: 12 to 16 servings.
Mrs. Richard P. Rose,
Winston-Salem, North Carolina.

ZUCCHINI CAKE

3 eggs, beaten
1 cup vegetable oil
2 cups sugar
2 teaspoons vanilla extract
2 cups all-purpose flour
3 teaspoons ground cinnamon
2 teaspoons soda
1 teaspoon salt
½ teaspoon baking powder
2 cups peeled, coarsely grated zucchini
Powdered Sugar Glaze (optional)

Combine eggs, oil, sugar, and vanilla; mix well. Combine dry ingredients; add to oil mixture, mixing well. Stir in grated zucchini.

Pour batter into a greased and floured 10-inch Bundt pan. Bake at 350° for 55 to 60 minutes. Allow to cool 20 minutes before removing from pan. If desired, spoon glaze over cake. Yield: one 10-inch cake.

Powdered Sugar Glaze:

½ cup powdered sugar
2 teaspoons milk

Combine ingredients, mixing until smooth. Yield: about ½ cup.
Mrs. Lloyd M. Mordy,
Independence, Kansas.

Fruit Breads Make Sweet Offerings

Send your Valentine greetings in a personal way by giving a loaf of quick bread. Wrap up one of these breads with a ribbon, and attach the recipe on a gift card for a long remembered gift.

Your friends will enjoy Lemon-Nut Bread, topped with a lemony glaze, or Strawberry-Nut Bread, full of sliced strawberries and pecans. A quick bread that features more than fruit and nuts, Butternut-Raisin Bread has a bonus of mashed butternut squash.

STRAWBERRY-NUT BREAD

2 cups all-purpose flour
1 teaspoon baking soda
1 teaspoon salt
1 tablespoon ground cinnamon
2 cups sugar
4 eggs, beaten
1¼ cups vegetable oil
2 cups thawed sliced frozen strawberries
1¼ cups chopped pecans

Combine dry ingredients. Add eggs, oil, strawberries, and pecans; stir just until all the ingredients are moistened.

Spoon batter into 2 well-greased 9- x 5- x 3-inch loafpans. Bake at 350° for 60 to 70 minutes or until bread tests done. Cool in pans 5 minutes; remove to wire rack to cool. Yield: 2 loaves.
Mrs. Christine S. Jarreau,
Baton Rouge, Louisiana.

LEMON-NUT BREAD

¾ cup butter or margarine, softened
1½ cups sugar
3 eggs
2¼ cups all-purpose flour
¼ teaspoon salt
¼ teaspoon soda
¼ cup buttermilk
Grated rind of 1 lemon
¾ cup chopped pecans
Juice of 2 lemons
¾ cup powdered sugar

Combine butter and sugar, creaming until light and fluffy; add eggs, beating well. Combine dry ingredients. Add buttermilk and dry ingredients alternately to creamed mixture, beginning and ending with buttermilk; stir just until all ingredients are moistened. Stir in lemon rind and pecans.

Spoon batter into a greased and floured 9- x 5- x 3-inch loafpan. Bake at 325° for 1 hour and 15 minutes or until bread tests done. Cool 15 minutes, and remove from pan.

Combine lemon juice and powdered sugar; stir well. Punch holes in top of warm bread with a toothpick; pour on glaze. Cool on wire rack. Yield: 1 loaf.
Vicky H. Nelson,
Murrells Inlet, South Carolina.

APRICOT-NUT BREAD

1 (16-ounce) can apricot halves
½ cup sugar
⅓ cup shortening
2 eggs
1¾ cups all-purpose flour
1 teaspoon baking powder
½ teaspoon soda
½ teaspoon salt
½ cup chopped walnuts

Drain apricots, reserving syrup; press apricots through a sieve or food mill. Add enough reserved syrup to apricots to make 1 cup; set aside.

Combine sugar and shortening; cream until fluffy. Add eggs, one at a time, beating well after each addition.

Combine dry ingredients. Add dry ingredients and apricots alternately to creamed mixture, beginning and ending with dry ingredients; stir just until all ingredients are moistened. Stir in walnuts. Spoon batter into a well-greased 9- x 5- x 3-inch loafpan. Bake at 350° for 50 minutes or until bread tests done. Remove from pan; cool on a wire rack. Yield: 1 loaf.
Elizabeth Moore,
Huntsville, Alabama.

BUTTERNUT-RAISIN BREAD

3½ cups unbleached flour
2 teaspoons soda
1 cup raisins
1 cup vegetable oil
2 cups sugar
4 eggs
1½ cups cooked mashed butternut squash
½ cup honey
1 cup water
1½ teaspoons ground nutmeg
1½ teaspoons ground cinnamon
1 teaspoon ground mace
1½ teaspoons salt

Combine flour, soda, and raisins; stir well, and set aside.

Combine oil, sugar, and eggs in large mixing bowl; beat well. Stir in squash, honey, water, spices, and salt. Add flour mixture; stir just until all ingredients are moistened.

Pour batter into 3 greased 9- x 5- x 3-inch loafpans. Bake at 350° for 1 hour. Cool. Yield: 3 loaves.

Note: Batter may be baked in 3 greased 1-pound coffee cans. Bake at 350° for 1 hour and 20 minutes.

Linda Clark,
Charlottesville, Virginia.

Make It Meatless

Spinach Lasagna, Artichoke Pie, and Cheesy Sour Cream Enchiladas—as different as they sound, they have one thing in common: All are satisfying, meatless main dishes. That means a saving on your food budget; it doesn't mean less nutrition, for each of these dishes is made with lots of cheese or eggs or vitamin-rich vegetables.

CHEESY SOUR CREAM ENCHILADAS

2 (10¾-ounce) cans cream of mushroom soup, undiluted
1 (8-ounce) carton commercial sour cream
1 (4-ounce) can chopped green chiles
¼ teaspoon salt
¼ teaspoon pepper
½ teaspoon garlic powder
2 cups shredded Cheddar cheese
1 cup chopped green onion
1 (8-ounce) package or 1 dozen corn tortillas
Hot salad oil

Combine soup, sour cream, green chiles, salt, pepper, and garlic powder

Cheesy Sour Cream Enchiladas is one of those meatless main dishes that stretch your food dollar without sacrificing nutrition.

in a medium saucepan; mix well. Cook over medium heat, stirring often, just until hot. Combine cheese and onion, mixing well.

Cook each tortilla in hot oil for a few seconds or just until softened; drain on paper towels. Immediately spoon about 1½ tablespoons cheese mixture and 2 tablespoons soup mixture onto center of each. Roll up tightly, and place in a greased 13- x 9- x 2-inch baking dish.

Spoon remaining soup mixture over top of enchiladas, and sprinkle with remaining cheese mixture. Bake at 350° for 20 to 30 minutes. Yield: 6 servings. *Mrs. William F. Smith,*
Lampasas, Texas.

SPINACH LASAGNA

1 (16-ounce) carton ricotta or small-curd cottage cheese
1½ cups shredded mozzarella cheese, divided
1 egg
1 (10-ounce) package frozen chopped spinach, thawed and drained
1 teaspoon salt
⅛ teaspoon pepper
¾ teaspoon whole oregano
2 (15½-ounce) jars spaghetti sauce
1 (8-ounce) package lasagna noodles, uncooked
1 cup water

Combine ricotta cheese, 1 cup mozzarella cheese, egg, spinach, salt, pepper, and oregano in a large mixing bowl; stir well.

Spread ½ cup spaghetti sauce in a greased 13- x 9- x 2-inch baking dish. Place one-third of the lasagna noodles over sauce, and spread with half the cheese mixture. Repeat layers. Top with remaining noodles, spaghetti sauce, and ½ cup mozzarella cheese; pour water around edges.

Cover securely with aluminum foil, and bake at 350° for 1 hour and 15 minutes. Let stand 15 minutes before serving. Yield: 8 servings.

John Wahl,
Landrum, South Carolina.

ARTICHOKE PIE

2 large cloves garlic
1 (10-ounce) package frozen artichoke hearts, thawed
1 tablespoon hot salad oil
¼ cup shredded mozzarella cheese
1 tablespoon grated Parmesan cheese
4 eggs, slightly beaten
½ teaspoon salt
⅛ teaspoon pepper
Dash of ground oregano
Pastry for double crust 9-inch pie
1 egg, beaten
1 tablespoon whipping cream

Sauté garlic and artichoke hearts in oil until lightly browned; cool. Combine sautéed vegetables, mozzarella, Parmesan, 4 eggs, salt, pepper, and oregano; mix well.

Line a 9-inch pieplate with half of pastry rolled to ⅛-inch thickness. Pour filling into shell. Roll remaining pastry to ⅛-inch thickness, and carefully place over filling. Trim the edges; then seal and flute.

Make several slits in top pastry near center to allow steam to escape. Combine 1 egg and whipping cream, mixing well. Brush over pie. Bake at 350° for 1 hour or until pie is golden. Yield: 6 to 8 servings. *Mrs. Pat M. Ritch,*
Cos Cob, Connecticut.

Tip: Wash most vegetables; trim any wilted parts or excess leaves before storing in crisper compartment of refrigerator. Keep potatoes and onions in a cool, dark place with plenty of air circulation to prevent sprouting.

THREE-CHEESE RAMEKINS

5 eggs, separated
¼ teaspoon dry mustard
Pinch of thyme
Pinch of ground nutmeg
Pinch of cayenne
¼ teaspoon salt
⅛ teaspoon pepper
2 tablespoons brandy (optional)
½ cup ricotta cheese
¾ cup grated Romano cheese
¾ cup shredded Gruyère cheese
Breadcrumbs

Combine egg yolks and seasonings; add brandy, if desired. Beat until light and lemon colored. Stir in cheese.

Beat egg whites until stiff but not dry; stir about one-fourth of egg whites into egg yolk mixture. Then fold in remaining egg whites.

Coat 4 buttered 6-ounce ramekins with breadcrumbs. Spoon mixture evenly into each. Bake at 400° for 20 minutes or until puffed and brown. Yield: 4 servings.   *Emmy Hessberg, Charlotte, North Carolina.*

Sausage-Cheddar Quiche slices into moist, meat-filled wedges. Just add a green salad and beverage for a complete meal.

Sample A Slice Of Meat-Filled Quiche

Meat-filled quiche is easily a favorite entrée for a light meal. And we offer two choices; both have lots of cheese and are meaty with either ham or sausage. To avoid last-minute preparation, make the filling in advance and place it in the refrigerator; when ready to bake, just pour the filling into the pastry shell.

SAUSAGE-CHEDDAR QUICHE

Pastry for 9-inch quiche dish or piepan
1 pound hot bulk pork sausage
1 (4-ounce) can sliced mushrooms, drained
½ cup chopped onion
¼ cup chopped green pepper
1 teaspoon minced parsley
½ teaspoon whole basil leaves
Dash of granulated garlic
⅛ teaspoon salt
1½ cups (⅜ pound) shredded Cheddar cheese
1 cup milk
2 eggs
Paprika

Line a 9-inch quiche dish or piepan with pastry; trim excess pastry around edges. Place a piece of buttered aluminum foil, buttered side down, over pastry; press into pastry shell. (This keeps sides of shell from collapsing.)

Cover foil with a layer of dried peas or beans. Bake at 400° for 10 minutes; remove peas and foil. Prick shell, and bake 3 to 5 additional minutes or until lightly browned. Cool.

Cook sausage until browned; drain. Combine sausage with next 7 ingredients, mixing well. Spoon into quiche shell; top with cheese.

Combine milk and eggs, beating just until foamy. Pour evenly over cheese; sprinkle with paprika. Bake at 325° for 50 minutes or until cheese is lightly browned and quiche is set. Yield: one 9-inch quiche.   *Mrs. B. N. Brown, Germantown, Tennessee.*

HAM-CHEESE QUICHE

Pastry for 9-inch quiche dish or piepan
½ cup milk
½ cup mayonnaise
2 eggs, slightly beaten
1 tablespoon cornstarch
1½ cups diced cooked ham
1½ cups cubed Swiss cheese
⅓ cup chopped green pepper
⅓ cup sliced green onion
Dash of pepper

Line a 9-inch quiche dish or piepan with pastry; trim off excess pastry around edges. Place a piece of buttered aluminum foil, buttered side down, over pastry; gently press into pastry shell. (This will keep the sides of pastry shell from collapsing.)

Cover foil with a layer of dried peas or beans. Bake at 400° for 10 minutes; remove peas and foil. Prick shell, and bake 3 to 5 minutes or until lightly browned. Cool.

Combine milk, mayonnaise, eggs, and cornstarch; mix until smooth. Stir in remaining ingredients. Pour mixture into quiche shell; bake at 350° for 40 to 45 minutes or until set. Yield: one 9-inch quiche.   *Mrs. Leslie Villeneuve, Atlantic Beach, Florida.*

Lime Dressing (page 2) brings out the best in citrus or other fruit salads. At a special dinner, serve it in small pitchers for guests to help themselves.

Overleaf: Once the flames die down, the essence of the brandy remains to delicately flavor the dark sweet cherries of Cherries Jubilee (page 18).

March

With spring in full bloom, Southerners look for fresh new ways to entertain family and friends. To help you make the most of the season, we offer a *Southern Breakfasts* section with recipes and entertaining ideas for breakfast and brunch. Included in this special March feature are recipes for everything from classic egg dishes to beverages for toasting the occasion.

In this chapter we also bring you the traditional cooking of North Carolina's tiny Ocracoke Island. Read how the islanders have preserved their unique way with food, and then prepare some of their favorites at your house.

Because pork is such a versatile meat, it is a perfect choice for any occasion. In addition to a collection of mouth-watering recipes, we present basic cooking instructions and guidelines for selection and storage.

The Special Flavor Of Ocracoke

Ocracoke is a "tight" little island. The residents will proudly tell you so, but even if they don't, it's easy to see it in the first few minutes on this remote, unspoiled island. Ocracokers delight in telling the colorful history of what was once the home of the pirate Blackbeard and about the development of their unusual traditional food.

Because of its isolation on the Outer Banks of North Carolina, the islanders historically depended upon the seafood bounty and what they could grow on the island for their food. Virtually every family had a milk cow, chickens, and a garden. Crabapples, beach plums, wild grapes, and blueberries were utilized for jams, jellies, and desserts. Neighbors shared the food they grew, their seafood catches, and the work of the annual penning of the wild animals. This comradeship contributed to the remarkable love the residents have for their island and their reluctance to live anywhere else.

"No one ever leaves Ocracoke; they just go away for a while," said Larry Williams, who recently returned to the island after teaching on the mainland for 28 years. "There was never any question that I would come back; it just took me longer than I thought. Some people get involved and don't make it back, and then they are brought back in a box. But everyone plans to come back.

"When I was young, everyone had to go away to make a living," he continued. "From the 1900's until very recently everyone had to go away; they couldn't support themselves as commercial fishermen," he explained.

However, prices for fish have increased, and a fish house recently opened—making commercial fishing profitable again, according to Edward Carson O'Neal, Jr., who retired recently from the U.S. Coast Guard to return to commercial fishing. Jimmy Creech, the local Methodist minister, remarked that the return of the fishing industry, plus the tourist trade and the National Park Service, has created many jobs, thus allowing the young people to stay on the island.

Because the natives have stayed on the island, the traditional cooking remains popular. "Ocracoke cooking is not Southern cooking as you usually think of it," Williams said. "There is not nearly as much frying—especially of seafood. More of the fish here is stewed or baked than in any other area of the South."

The drum "ceremony" is the traditional method for preparing drum, a large, strong-flavored fish. The boiled fish is mixed with hard-cooked eggs, potatoes, onions, and cracklings at the table. The added ingredients give the dish a milder flavor than if the drum were served alone.

"The islanders are sweets eaters," said Williams. "We eat sweet potato pudding along with the meal, rather than as a dessert. We also used to drink molasses water, which was just water sweetened with molasses. Before the water system was installed in 1977, the water tasted so bad that they were always coming up with something to put in it," he added.

Collards, She-Crab Soup with Marigold, and Baked Flounder are typical Ocracoke dishes.

Molasses and other supplies coming to the island before the ferry system was installed in the 1950's were shipped by freight boat from Washington, North Carolina, according to Williams. The supplies such as flour, snuff, and molasses came in bulk. "Everyone had a molasses jar. They would take the jar to the store and put it under the spigot to get their molasses," he explained. Molasses is also used in the local pone bread, making the bread quite unlike that found in other areas of the South. The bread has a creamy texture and sweet taste, making it more like cake than bread. It is traditionally served on all holidays and special occasions.

Leaves from the yaupon hollies growing all along the narrow, winding streets of the village are still dried and used for tea. The hot tea was once believed to be a healer, according to Williams. Today it is also enjoyed iced by many islanders and visitors. Packages of the strong-flavored tea leaves can be purchased in many of the small shops dotting the village. The green branches from the yaupon with their festive red berries are still used for decorating at Christmas. In earlier times, they were also used at funerals during the winter since fresh flowers were unavailable.

Some natives snip the leaves of marigolds and use them in place of parsley or other mainland garnishes, Williams said. "My mother loved to garnish food with marigold leaves. She also mixed them with scrambled eggs," he added.

Although the island is no longer isolated, growth has been restricted to the small village nestled around Silver Lake on the south end of the island. The remainder of the fragile island is protected as part of the Cape Hatteras National Seashore, leaving tranquil, unspoiled beaches. Residents, numbering about 550, still buy all their groceries and supplies in small general stores located around the island.

The number of tourists to the island is limited by the 150 rooms available in small inns scattered around the island. The visitors have made few changes on Ocracoke. Small curio shops are found dotting the village, but they are locally owned and managed. The proprietors explain the local crafts with a charming British accent that is shared by all the native Ocracokers.

Sarah Ellen O'Neal Gaskill, who recently celebrated her 99th birthday, reflected on her life on the island with a distinct pride in her voice. "I remember when everyone on this island was born and I've seen a lot of changes, but they've been good changes. We have a lot of visitors now, but they don't hurt anything," she said.

Miss Sarah Ellen, as she is called by the islanders, said that although she has traveled off the island a few times, she's never seen a place as pretty as Ocracoke. "I was 10 years old when I first left the island. I went to Washington, North Carolina, with my aunt and I've been to Elizabeth City," she continued, "but I like Ocracoke best—it's my home and I've never wanted to live anywhere else."

This attitude expressed by Miss Sarah Ellen radiates from all the residents of Ocracoke. This is a comforting thought, for as long as the islanders cherish their home and life style, Ocracoke is sure to retain its rare beauty and special way with food.

Cooking In The Ocracoke Style

The food of Ocracoke Island is as unique as the life-style that characterizes the tiny insular community. The residents have shared their traditional recipes so that you can enjoy the flavor of the island at home.

■ These delicious crisp-fried fritters will delight even those who aren't oyster lovers.

OYSTER FRITTERS

1 cup pancake mix
1 teaspoon baking powder
1 pint oysters, undrained
1 egg
2 tablespoons finely chopped onion
Salt and pepper
¼ cup vegetable oil

Combine first 5 ingredients, mixing well; add salt and pepper to taste.

Drop mixture by tablespoonfuls into hot oil. Fry until brown on one side; turn and fry until done. Drain well on paper towels. Serve fritters hot. Yield: about 20 fritters.

■ Onions, potatoes, and salt pork flavor this delicate seafood dish.

BAKED FLOUNDER

1 cup water
6 medium potatoes, peeled and sliced ¼ inch thick
2 pounds flounder fillets, cut into 4-inch pieces
1 large onion, cut into ¼-inch slices and separated into rings
Salt and pepper to taste
½ cup chopped green onion
¼ cup coarsely chopped salt pork

Pour water in a greased 13- x 9- x 2-inch baking pan. Layer one-third of potatoes, flounder, and onion rings in pan; sprinkle with salt, pepper, and one-third of green onion. Repeat layers twice, and sprinkle with salt pork.

Cover with foil, and bake at 350° for 1 hour; uncover and bake until potatoes are tender, about 30 minutes. Yield: 4 to 6 servings.

■ Ocracokers prefer their chowder with a water base and a strong clam flavor.

OCRACOKE CLAM CHOWDER

1 (1-inch-thick) slice salt pork
2½ pounds potatoes, peeled and diced
1½ pints fresh minced clams
1 onion, chopped
3 quarts water
2¼ teaspoons salt

Fry salt pork over medium heat in a large Dutch oven until done. Remove pork, reserving drippings in pan.

Dice pork; combine with potatoes, clams, onion, water, and salt in Dutch oven. Bring to a boil, and reduce heat; cover and simmer 2 hours and 15 minutes or until potatoes are tender. Yield: 8 to 12 servings.

■ This is a delicious shrimp pie flavored with onions and potatoes, then baked with a biscuit topping.

STEWED SHRIMP WITH DUMPLINGS

2 pounds shrimp, cooked, peeled, and deveined
2 cups diced cooked potatoes
1 small onion, chopped
¼ cup butter or margarine
2 hard-cooked eggs, chopped
3 cups water
2 tablespoons cornstarch
¼ cup cold water
Salt and pepper
5 or 6 (2-inch) unbaked biscuits

Combine shrimp, potatoes, onion, butter, chopped eggs, and 3 cups water. Cook over medium heat 5 minutes.

Combine cornstarch and ¼ cup cold water, stirring until smooth. Stir cornstarch mixture into shrimp mixture. Cook, stirring constantly, until thickened and bubbly. Season to taste with salt and pepper.

Pour shrimp mixture into a 2-quart casserole. Top with biscuits, and bake at 450° for 15 to 20 minutes or until biscuits are lightly browned. Yield: 5 to 6 servings.

Tip: As a rule, thawed fish should not be held longer than a day before cooking; the flavor is better if it is cooked immediately after thawing.

■ Young, small leaves of yaupon holly are dried to make this strong tea. It was once used for medicinal purposes.

YAUPON TEA

1 (½-ounce) package yaupon leaves
1 quart water
Sugar (optional)
Lemon juice (optional)

Combine yaupon leaves and water in a saucepan; bring to a boil, and boil 10 minutes. Strain tea; do not dilute. Serve hot or over ice cubes. May be served with sugar and lemon juice, if desired. Yield: about 1 quart.

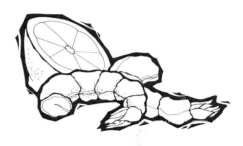

■ This modern version of the traditional dish is simplified with the use of cream of chicken soup.

SHRIMP AND CHICKEN ARIOSTO

1 (3-pound) broiler-fryer, cooked
½ cup butter or margarine
1 pound fresh shrimp, cooked, peeled, and deveined
½ head cabbage, shredded
1 onion, sliced and separated into rings
2 (10¾-ounce) cans cream of chicken soup, undiluted
1 (2-ounce) jar diced pimiento, undrained
1 teaspoon soy sauce
¼ teaspoon granulated garlic
2 drops liquid smoke
Salt and pepper
¼ cup dry white wine
Lettuce leaves
Chopped tomatoes
½ cup chopped salted peanuts

Remove chicken from bones, and flake with a fork. Melt butter in a large Dutch oven; add chicken, shrimp, cabbage, and onion. Cook over medium heat until onion is tender.

Stir soup, pimiento, soy sauce, garlic, and liquid smoke into meat mixture. Season to taste with salt and pepper. Simmer 15 minutes. Stir in wine, and cook 2 additional minutes over low heat. Remove from heat.

Serve meat mixture on a lettuce-lined platter; top with chopped tomatoes and salted peanuts. Yield: 6 to 8 servings.

■ Mashed potatoes are flavored with prepared mustard for a quick side dish.

MUSTARD POTATOES

8 medium potatoes, cooked and mashed
¼ cup butter or margarine, softened
¼ cup prepared mustard
2 tablespoons mayonnaise
1 teaspoon salt
Diced onion (optional)
Parsley sprigs (optional)

Combine all ingredients except parsley, stirring well. Garnish with parsley, if desired. Yield: 10 to 12 servings.

■ Chopped dates may be substituted for fig preserves in this moist cake.

FIG CAKE

3 eggs
1½ cups sugar
1 cup vegetable oil
½ cup buttermilk
1 teaspoon soda, dissolved in 2 teaspoons
   hot water
2 cups all-purpose flour
1 teaspoon salt
1 teaspoon ground cinnamon
1 teaspoon ground nutmeg
1 teaspoon ground allspice
1 teaspoon vanilla extract
1 cup fig preserves with juice, chopped
1 cup chopped nuts
Powdered sugar

Beat eggs with electric mixer until thick and lemon colored; add sugar and oil, beating well.

Combine buttermilk and soda mixture. Sift next 5 ingredients together; add to egg mixture alternately with buttermilk mixture, mixing well after each addition. Stir in vanilla, figs, and nuts.

Pour batter into a greased and floured 10-inch tube pan. Bake at 350° for 1 hour and 10 to 15 minutes. Cool 20 to 30 minutes. Remove from pan, and sprinkle with powdered sugar. Yield: one 10-inch cake.

■ Collards are plentiful on the island and are commonly served with potatoes and salt pork.

COLLARDS

2 pounds collards
½ pound salt pork, coarsely chopped
1 gallon water
4 medium potatoes, peeled
Salt

Cut off and discard tough stems and discolored leaves from collards. Wash thoroughly.

Combine salt pork and water in a Dutch oven; bring to a boil, and cook 15 to 30 minutes. Add collards; cover and cook at low boil for 1½ hours. Add potatoes, and cook 30 minutes or until potatoes are tender. Season to taste with salt. Yield: 6 to 8 servings.

■ An island favorite, this pie has a soft center and a delicate lemon flavor.

LEMON CHESS PIE

2 cups sugar
1 tablespoon all-purpose flour
1 tablespoon cornmeal
Pinch of salt
¼ cup melted butter or margarine
¼ cup milk
Juice and grated rind of 2 lemons
4 eggs, beaten
1 unbaked 9-inch pastry shell

Combine sugar, flour, cornmeal, and salt; mix well. Add butter and milk, mixing well. Add lemon juice, lemon rind, and eggs; beat well.

Broil unbaked pastry shell 1 minute; remove from oven, and pour in filling. Bake at 350° for 30 to 35 minutes or until slightly firm in center. Yield: one 9-inch pie.

■ Snipped marigold leaves are used to garnish a simplified version of the classic she-crab soup.

SHE-CRAB SOUP WITH MARIGOLD

2 (10¾-ounce) cans cream of celery soup,
   undiluted
3 cups milk
1 cup half-and-half
½ cup butter or margarine
2 hard-cooked eggs, chopped
½ teaspoon Old Bay Seasoning
½ teaspoon Worcestershire sauce
¼ teaspoon garlic salt
¼ teaspoon white pepper
1 cup crabmeat, drained and flaked
¼ cup dry sherry
Chopped marigold leaves (optional)

Combine first 9 ingredients in a large Dutch oven; bring to a boil. Add crabmeat; cook over medium heat, stirring occasionally, until thoroughly heated. Stir in sherry. Sprinkle each serving with marigold leaves, if desired. Yield: about 2 quarts.

■ Wild muscadines grow in abundance all along Ocracoke's beaches. The jelly is a delicious accompaniment for meat or wild fowl.

WILD MUSCADINE JELLY

Remove stems from muscadines; wash and drain thoroughly. Mash grapes, a small amount at a time; bring to a boil, and boil 30 minutes. Remove from heat, and strain through jelly bag.

Measure juice, then measure an equal amount of sugar. Return juice to a boil, and boil 5 minutes. Add sugar, stirring until dissolved. Cook rapidly until mixture sheets off a metal spoon.

Ladle jelly into hot sterilized glasses. Seal with a ⅛-inch layer of melted paraffin. When paraffin has cooled, top with another ⅛-inch layer.

■ A dried fish with a chewy texture, corned fish is an old favorite on the island.

CORNED FISH

The oily types of fish, such as shad, mullet, mackerel, and bluefish, are best for this method of preparation.

Clean and wash fish thoroughly; fillet. Sprinkle both sides of fillets generously with salt; cover and let stand 30 to 40 minutes. Wash all salt off.

Make a small hole in the tail end of each fillet; thread twine or string through hole. Hang in a dry place where air can circulate. Dry fillets until they no longer feel moist or sticky (2 or 3 days).

To pan fry, melt enough butter to coat skillet; sauté fillets 5 to 10 minutes on each side, depending on size of pieces, or until browned. Sprinkle fillets with pepper, if desired.

To broil, place fillets on a broiler pan; dot with butter, and sprinkle with pepper. Broil until lightly browned; turn and broil until done.

Serve with pan drippings and lemon slices, if desired.

Southern Breakfasts

Fresh Ideas For Breakfast Or Brunch

In the South, good food is as essential to the beginning of each day as the sunrise itself. Whether starting your day with an old-fashioned Southern breakfast, a relaxing brunch, or a quick breakfast on-the-run, the morning meal should be as appealing as any other.

With that in mind, we are presenting a special section on Southern breakfasts and brunches, offering you a useful collection of recipes, menus, and entertaining ideas. In these pages, you'll find recipes that range from the classic eggs Benedict and quiche Lorraine to new breakfast creations like Sausage-Filled Crêpes and Pep Shake.

Since many Southerners see midmorning as an ideal time to entertain, there's good reason for the popularity of the leisurely brunch. Such is the case with Martha Lou and Buddy Derrick of Lexington, Virginia, and their special springtime brunch is an occasion their friends look forward to.

The party begins on the Derrick's sunny, glassed-in porch, which sets the mood for the warm, friendly gathering. As guests arrive, they're greeted with Bloody Marys and Screwdrivers flavored and garnished with lots of limes, a favorite serving idea of the host.

For appetizers, Martha Lou chooses bacon and eggs: Bacon Rollups and Frosted Egg Mound, an egg spread seasoned with green onion and curry powder and frosted with sour cream.

The main course is centered around foods traditional in the Old Dominion—Virginia-cured country ham and fresh oysters from the Chesapeake Bay. In a dish called Oysters Casino on Cornbread, squares of cornbread are split and served as the base for thin slices of country ham and oysters.

Martha Lou's unique way of including a green vegetable on the menu is Florentine Crêpe Pie. This delectable offering is a mound of crêpes layered with spinach and mushroom fillings, then covered with cheese sauce. Buddy makes the crêpes for this delicacy and for other specialties of the Derricks.

Complementing the hot dishes is the cool, tart taste of Raspberry Fruit Mounds, a congealed salad garnished with colorful fruit. Of course, the meal ends as distinctively as it began, with a luscious dessert of Lemon Bars Deluxe.

As impressive as the Derricks' brunch is, Martha Lou can relax and enjoy the occasion. The secret lies in her menu; it's a careful composition of complementing flavors and dishes that can be prepared in advance. The complete menu and her recipes follow.

**Bloody Marys   Screwdrivers
Frosted Egg Mound   Bacon Rollups
Oysters Casino on Cornbread
Florentine Crêpe Pie
Raspberry Fruit Mounds
Lemon Bars Deluxe
Coffee**

BLOODY MARYS

3 quarts tomato juice
3 cups vodka
⅓ cup steak sauce
¼ cup Worcestershire sauce
2½ tablespoons salt
1 tablespoon sugar
¼ teaspoon hot sauce
Juice of 12 limes
Lime slices (optional)
Celery sticks

Combine first 8 ingredients, stirring well; pour into punch bowl. Float lime slices on top, if desired.

To serve, pour Bloody Marys into ice-filled glasses; garnish with celery sticks. Yield: about 4 quarts.

SCREWDRIVERS

3 quarts orange juice
3 cups vodka
¼ cup lime juice
Lime slices (optional)

Combine orange juice, vodka, and lime juice; mix well, and pour into punch bowl. Float lime slices on top, if desired. To serve, pour into ice-filled glasses. Yield: about 4 quarts.

FROSTED EGG MOUND

11 hard-cooked eggs
½ cup melted butter or margarine
½ teaspoon minced green onion
½ to ¾ teaspoon salt
⅛ teaspoon pepper
⅛ teaspoon curry powder
⅓ cup commercial sour cream
Chopped chives
Parsley

Line a small round mixing bowl with a large piece of plastic wrap; set aside.

Finely chop 8 eggs; add butter, onion, salt, pepper, and curry powder. Mix well, and spoon into mixing bowl; cover and chill at least 3 hours.

Unmold egg mixture onto a serving dish, and spread evenly with sour cream; sprinkle with chives.

Cut remaining 3 eggs in half, and place around mound; garnish with parsley. Serve with crackers. Yield: 3 cups.

BACON ROLLUPS

2 (3-ounce) packages cream cheese with
  chives, softened
1 tablespoon milk or mayonnaise
25 slices mixed-grain sandwich bread,
  crusts removed and cut in half
25 slices bacon, cut in half
Parsley sprigs (optional)

Combine cream cheese and milk, stirring until spreading consistency.

Spread 1 scant teaspoon of cream
cheese mixture on each slice of bread,
and roll tightly. Wrap each rollup with
bacon, securing with a toothpick.

Place rollups on a broiler pan; bake
at 350° for 30 minutes, turning if necessary to prevent overbrowning. Garnish
with parsley, if desired. Yield: about 4
dozen.

Note: Bacon Rollups may be assembled ahead and frozen. To serve, thaw
overnight in refrigerator; bake at 350°
for 30 to 40 minutes.

OYSTERS CASINO ON
CORNBREAD

24 slices bacon, chopped
2 cups chopped onion
1 cup chopped green pepper
1 cup chopped celery
1 tablespoon salt
⅛ teaspoon pepper
3 tablespoons lemon juice
1 tablespoon plus 1 teaspoon
  Worcestershire sauce
⅛ teaspoon hot sauce
4 (12- or 16-ounce) cans fresh Select
  oysters, drained
Chopped parsley (optional)
Buttermilk cornbread (recipe follows)
Cooked country ham slices

Fry bacon in a large skillet until
transparent. Add vegetables; sauté until
vegetables are tender and bacon is
crisp. Stir in salt, pepper, lemon juice,
Worcestershire sauce, and hot sauce.

Place oysters in a single layer in 2
lightly greased 13- x 9- x 2-inch baking
dishes; spread bacon mixture over oysters. Bake at 400° for 10 to 12 minutes.
Serve oysters in a chafing dish; sprinkle
with parsley, if desired.

To serve, slice cornbread squares in
half horizontally; top one half with a
country ham slice, and spoon oyster
mixture over other half. Yield: 12 to 16
servings.

Buttermilk Cornbread:

2 cups plain cornmeal
⅔ cup all-purpose flour
2 teaspoons baking powder
1 teaspoon salt
½ teaspoon soda
2 eggs, beaten
2 cups buttermilk

Combine dry ingredients; add eggs
and buttermilk, mixing well. Pour batter
into 2 greased 8-inch square pans. Bake
at 400° for 20 minutes or until lightly
browned. Cut into squares. Yield: 16 to
18 squares.

FLORENTINE CREPE PIE

2 cups sifted cake flour
2½ cups milk
4 egg yolks
2 egg whites
½ teaspoon sugar
½ cup plus 2 tablespoons butter, melted
2 egg whites
Spinach Filling
Mushroom Filling
Swiss Cheese Sauce
¼ cup shredded Swiss cheese
1 teaspoon paprika
Chopped parsley (optional)
Parsley sprigs (optional)

Combine flour and milk, beating until
smooth. Add egg yolks and 2 egg
whites; beat until well blended. Stir
sugar and melted butter into batter. Refrigerate batter 1 hour. (This allows
flour particles to swell and soften so the
crepes are light in texture.)

Beat remaining 2 egg whites to soft-
peak stage; fold into batter.

Brush the bottom of a 6- or 6½-inch
crêpe pan with melted butter; place pan
over medium heat until butter is just
hot, not smoking.

Pour 1½ to 2 tablespoons batter into
pan; quickly tilt pan in all directions so
batter covers the pan in a thin film.
Cook about 1 minute.

Lift edge of crêpe to test for doneness. Crêpe is ready for flipping when it
can be shaken loose from pan. Flip the
crêpe, and cook about 30 seconds on
the other side. (This side is rarely more
than spotty brown.)

When the crêpes are done, place on a
towel to cool. Stack between layers of
waxed paper to prevent sticking.

Place 2 crêpes side by side in a 13- x
9- x 2-inch buttered baking dish.

Spoon 2 tablespoons Spinach Filling
over each crêpe, spreading evenly. Top
each with another crêpe; then spoon 2
tablespoons Mushroom Filling over
each, and spread evenly.

Repeat procedure with remaining
crêpes, Spinach Filling, and Mushroom
Filling, ending with crêpes.

Spoon Swiss Cheese Sauce over the 2
stacks of crêpes. Top with shredded
Swiss cheese and paprika.

Bake at 375° for 20 to 25 minutes or
until sauce is bubbly and top is lightly
browned. If desired, garnish with
chopped parsley and parsley sprigs. To
serve, cut into wedges. Yield: 16 to 20
servings.

Spinach Filling:

2 (10-ounce) packages frozen chopped
  spinach
¼ cup plus 2 tablespoons Swiss Cheese
  Sauce

Cook spinach according to package
directions; drain. Combine spinach and
sauce, mixing well. Yield: about 3 cups.

Note: 3 cups cooked fresh spinach
may be substituted for frozen spinach.

Mushroom Filling:

2 cups diced fresh mushrooms
¼ cup minced green onion
2 tablespoons butter or margarine, melted
2 (8-ounce) packages cream cheese
2 eggs, beaten
1 cup Swiss Cheese Sauce

Sauté mushrooms and onion in butter until tender.

Combine cream cheese and eggs; beat with electric mixer until thoroughly blended. Add mushroom mixture and cheese sauce; mix well. Yield: about 3½ cups.

Swiss Cheese Sauce:

½ cup butter or margarine
½ cup plus 2 tablespoons all-purpose
    flour
5½ cups milk
1 teaspoon salt
¼ teaspoon pepper
½ teaspoon nutmeg
½ cup whipping cream
2 cups shredded Swiss cheese
3 tablespoons grated Parmesan cheese

Melt butter in a heavy saucepan over low heat; blend in flour, and cook 1 minute. Gradually add milk; cook over medium heat, stirring constantly, until thickened and bubbly.

Add seasonings to white sauce; then add cream, stirring constantly. Add cheese, stirring until cheese melts. Yield: about 6 cups.

The hot dishes on the menu are complemented by the tart, cool flavor of Raspberry Fruit Mounds, a congealed salad garnished with colorful fruit.

RASPBERRY FRUIT MOUNDS

1 (6-ounce) package raspberry-flavored
    gelatin
2 cups boiling water
2 (10-ounce) packages frozen raspberries,
    thawed
1 teaspoon lemon juice
1 cup applesauce
Lettuce leaves
Peeled orange slices (optional)
Maraschino cherries (optional)
Fresh pineapple wedges (optional)

Combine gelatin and water, stirring until gelatin dissolves. Stir in raspberries with juice, lemon juice, and applesauce.

Pour gelatin mixture into a 13- x 9- x 2-inch baking dish or individual molds. Chill mixture until firm, and cut into squares.

To serve, place gelatin squares on lettuce leaves. If desired, garnish each serving with 1 orange slice, 1 maraschino cherry, and 1 pineapple wedge. Yield: 12 to 16 servings.

LEMON BARS DELUXE

2½ cups all-purpose flour, divided
¾ cup powdered sugar, divided
1 cup butter or margarine
½ teaspoon baking powder
4 eggs, beaten
2 cups sugar
⅓ cup lemon juice
1 slice lemon (optional)
Fresh mint (optional)

Combine 2 cups flour and ½ cup powdered sugar. Cut butter into flour mixture with a pastry blender until mixture resembles cornmeal.

Spoon flour mixture into a 13- x 9- x 2-inch baking pan; press into pan evenly and firmly using fingertips. Bake at 350° for 20 to 25 minutes or until lightly browned.

Combine ½ cup flour and baking powder; set aside. Combine eggs, 2 cups sugar, and lemon juice; beat well. Stir dry ingredients into egg mixture, and pour over baked crust.

Bake at 350° for 25 minutes or until lightly brown and set. Cool on a wire rack. Sprinkle with ¼ cup powdered sugar, and cut into bars. Garnish with lemon slice and mint, if desired. Yield: about 2 dozen.

Tip: To use a griddle or frypan, preheat on medium or medium-high heat before adding the food. It is properly preheated when a few drops of water spatter when they hit the surface. Add food and reduce heat so that it cooks without spattering and smoking.

More Than Just Toast

Plain white toast can get mighty mundane, but that needn't be the case—not with this selection of tempting toast ideas. For something really different, try Orange Praline Toast. It's thick slices of toasted French bread topped with an orange-flavored mixture of pecans and brown sugar. Or treat yourself to Toasted Cheese Delights, English muffins layered with cheese, tomato slices, and crumbled bacon.

Even plain white toast is anything but ordinary when spread with a fruit- or maple-flavored butter. Better still, mix and match the butters with different kinds of bread, slices of pound cake, rolls, English muffins, and toaster waffles.

ORANGE PRALINE TOAST

12 slices French bread
⅓ cup butter or margarine, softened
⅔ cup firmly packed brown sugar
¼ cup orange juice
2 tablespoons grated orange rind
½ cup finely chopped pecans

Toast bread on both sides, and spread with butter.

Combine remaining ingredients, mixing well. Spread about 1 tablespoon sugar mixture on each slice of toast. Place on baking sheet, and bake at 350° about 5 to 8 minutes or until sugar melts. Yield: 12 servings.
Mrs. Elizabeth Moore,
Huntsville, Alabama.

ORANGE TOAST TOPPER

1 tablespoon butter or margarine, softened
3 tablespoons powdered sugar
1 teaspoon grated orange rind
1 teaspoon orange juice
4 slices toast

Combine first 4 ingredients, beating until smooth. Spread on hot toast. Yield: 3 to 4 servings. *Pam Norton, San Angelo, Texas.*

HONEY-ORANGE BUTTER

½ cup butter or margarine, softened
3 tablespoons honey
1 tablespoon grated orange rind
1 tablespoon orange juice

Combine all ingredients in a small mixing bowl, beating until light and fluffy. Store in a covered container in refrigerator until ready to use. Spread on toast or toasted slices of pound cake. Yield: about 1 cup.
Mrs. John F. Woods,
Memphis, Tennessee.

STRAWBERRY BUTTER

1 cup powdered sugar
¼ cup butter, softened
1 egg yolk
1 cup sliced strawberries, pureed

Combine sugar, butter, and egg yolk; cream until fluffy. Add strawberries, 1 tablespoon at a time, beating well after each addition.

Store in a covered container in refrigerator until serving time. Serve on toasted pound cake slices, toast, or bread. Yield: 1¼ cups.
Note: Plums or pears may be substituted for strawberries, if desired.
Mrs. Shirley Hastings,
Stillwater, Oklahoma.

BUTTERY SKILLET CINNAMON TOAST

¼ cup powdered sugar
1 tablespoon ground cinnamon
½ cup butter, divided
4 (1-inch-thick) slices bread, quartered

Combine sugar and cinnamon; set aside. Melt ¼ cup butter in a skillet; add 8 bread sections and cook until browned. Remove bread from skillet, and roll each piece in sugar mixture. Repeat procedure with remaining bread and butter. Yield: 4 servings.
Mrs. John Haven,
Jonesboro, Arkansas.

WHIPPED MAPLE-FLAVORED BUTTER

½ cup butter, softened
⅛ teaspoon salt
1 cup maple-flavored syrup, warmed

Combine butter and salt in a small mixing bowl, creaming until light and fluffy. Add syrup, about ¼ cup at a time, beating well after each addition. Continue beating until fluffy and well blended. Serve on toast, toasted pound cake slices, pancakes, or waffles.

Store leftover butter mixture in a covered container in refrigerator; soften at room temperature or beat until fluffy before serving. Yield: 1½ cups.
Mrs. Edna A. Peavy,
Atlanta, Georgia.

BACON-CHEESE TOAST BARS

1 egg, beaten
⅓ cup mayonnaise
1 cup (¼ pound) shredded sharp Cheddar cheese
½ teaspoon Worcestershire sauce
⅛ teaspoon dry mustard
Dash of pepper
5 to 6 drops hot sauce
8 slices bacon, cooked and crumbled
8 slices bread
Paprika

Combine first 7 ingredients; mix well, and stir in bacon. Set aside.

Remove crusts from bread; reserve crusts for another use. Toast bread slices lightly on both sides. Spread toast evenly with cheese mixture. Cut each slice into 3 strips, and sprinkle lightly with paprika. Place on cookie sheet; bake at 350° for 12 to 15 minutes or until lightly browned. Yield: 24 bars.
Note: May be assembled several hours before baking, if desired; cover and place in refrigerator. Let stand at room temperature 30 minutes; then bake as directed above. *Nancy Sloan, Lake Village, Arkansas.*

Southern Breakfasts

TOASTED CHEESE DELIGHTS

3 English muffins, split and toasted
½ pound Cheddar cheese, cut into 6 slices
6 (½-inch-thick) slices tomato
12 slices bacon, cooked and crumbled

Place each muffin half, cut side up, on a baking sheet. Top each with a cheese slice, tomato slice, and crumbled bacon. Bake at 350° for 10 to 15 minutes or until cheese melts. Yield: 6 servings. *Mary P. Taylor, Kings Mountain, North Carolina.*

Reach For The Granola

Nutritious granola can be eaten as a snack or as a breakfast cereal. Either way, homemade granola is easy to prepare; you simply combine the various ingredients and then bake.

Sunshine Granola and Toasty Granola are two crunchy blends you'll want to try. Both rely on honey for their old-fashioned sweetness and vegetable oil for improved color. Sunshine Granola contains a variety of dried fruits, while Toasty Granola enjoys the warm, spicy flavor of cinnamon and nutmeg.

TOASTY GRANOLA

6 cups regular oats, uncooked
1½ cups chopped pecans
1½ cups coconut
1 cup wheat germ
¾ cup honey
¼ cup water
½ cup vegetable oil
1 tablespoon vanilla extract
1 teaspoon ground cinnamon
1 teaspoon ground nutmeg
½ teaspoon salt

Combine oats, pecans, coconut, and wheat germ; set aside.

Combine honey and water in a small saucepan; heat, stirring frequently, until mixture thins and is thoroughly heated. Stir in oil and vanilla; pour over oat mixture and mix well. Add spices and salt, mixing well. Pour into 2 greased 13- x 9- x 2-inch pans. Bake at 250° for 1 hour, stirring every 20 minutes. Store in an airtight container. Yield: 10 cups. *Ann Greer, San Antonio, Texas.*

SUNSHINE GRANOLA

3 cups regular oats, uncooked
1 (1½-ounce) package sesame seeds
1 cup sunflower seeds
1 cup wheat germ
½ cup vegetable oil
½ cup honey
1 cup golden seedless raisins
1 cup dried apricots, diced
1 cup dates, chopped
1 cup flaked coconut
1 cup sliced almonds

Combine first 4 ingredients. Stir oil and honey together; pour over dry mixture, stirring well. Spread mixture on a lightly greased cookie sheet; bake at 250° for 45 to 50 minutes. Allow mixture to cool; break into large pieces. Combine pieces with remaining ingredients. Store in an airtight container. Yield: about 12 cups. *Mrs. Edward K. Beckes, Franklin, Tennessee.*

Wake Up To A Southern Breakfast

To most Southerners, a classic breakfast means country ham with red-eye gravy, eggs, grits, and homemade biscuits. When Kathleen D. Stone of Houston serves this hearty combination, she begins her menu with a creamy version of ambrosia. Along with the country ham and red-eye gravy, she serves a special version of grits baked into a light and fluffy spoonbread. And for biscuits, her Benne Seed Biscuits are baked full of toasted sesame seeds and served drenched with butter.

Kathleen's complete menu and recipes follow.

Orange Ambrosia Supreme
Country Ham With Red-Eye Gravy
Sunny-Side-Up Eggs
Grits Spoonbread   Benne Seed Biscuits
Milk   Coffee

ORANGE AMBROSIA SUPREME

4 large oranges, peeled and cut into ¼-inch slices
½ cup flaked coconut
½ cup commercial sour cream
1 tablespoon brown sugar
½ teaspoon grated orange rind
Pinch of salt
¼ cup coarsely chopped pecans

Place a third of the orange slices in a medium-size serving bowl. Top with about one-third of the coconut; repeat layers twice. Cover and refrigerate at least 1 hour.

Combine sour cream and sugar; mix well. Stir in rind and salt; cover and refrigerate dressing at least 1 hour. Top fruit with dressing and pecans before serving. Yield: 6 servings.

COUNTRY HAM WITH RED-EYE GRAVY

6 (¼-inch-thick) slices country ham
¼ cup margarine
¼ cup firmly packed brown sugar
½ cup strong black coffee
Sprig of fresh mint (optional)

Cut gashes in fat to keep ham from curling. Sauté ham in margarine in a heavy skillet over low heat until light brown, turning several times. Remove ham from skillet, and keep warm.

Stir sugar into pan drippings; cook over low heat until sugar dissolves, stirring constantly. Add coffee to pan drippings, stirring well. Simmer gravy 5 minutes, and keep warm.

Garnish ham slices with fresh mint, if desired. Serve gravy over ham. Yield: 6 servings.

Tip: Small amounts of jelly left in jars may be combined, melted, and used to glaze a ham.

SUNNY-SIDE-UP EGGS

2 to 3 tablespoons margarine
6 eggs
Salt and pepper
Lemon verbena (optional)

Melt margarine in a heavy skillet, and heat until hot enough to sizzle a drop of water. Break each egg into a saucer; carefully slip each egg one at a time into skillet. Cook eggs over low heat until whites are firm and yolks are soft, or cook to desired degree of doneness; season with salt and pepper. Garnish eggs with lemon verbena, if desired. Yield: 6 servings.

GRITS SPOONBREAD

2 cups milk
⅓ cup quick grits
1 teaspoon sugar
½ to ¾ teaspoon salt
3 eggs, separated
3 tablespoons melted butter or margarine

Scald milk in a heavy 2-quart saucepan. Combine grits, sugar, and salt; stir into milk. Bring to a boil; reduce heat, and cook, stirring constantly, 4 to 5 minutes or until very thick. Let cool; beat egg yolks, and stir into mixture. Beat egg whites until stiff peaks form; fold into mixture.

Place butter in a 1½-quart casserole; spoon in grits mixture. Bake at 375° for 35 to 40 minutes or until lightly browned. Serve hot with Red-Eye Gravy. Yield: 6 servings.

BENNE SEED BISCUITS

½ cup plus 1 tablespoon sesame seeds
2 cups all-purpose flour
1 tablespoon baking powder
¾ teaspoon salt
¼ cup shortening
¾ cup milk
1 tablespoon sesame seeds

Place ½ cup sesame seeds in a heavy skillet; cook over medium heat, stirring constantly, until lightly browned.

Combine flour, baking powder, salt, and toasted seeds in a large mixing bowl; cut in shortening until mixture resembles coarse cornmeal. Add milk; stir

well. Turn dough out on a floured surface; knead lightly 10 to 12 times.

Roll dough to ½-inch thickness; cut with a 2-inch biscuit cutter. Sprinkle 1 tablespoon sesame seeds over biscuit tops, pressing in slightly. Place on ungreased baking sheet; bake at 450° for 12 to 15 minutes. Yield: about 1½ dozen.

Eye-Opening Breakfast Beverages

Breakfast is even more appealing when it begins with a refreshing beverage like Three-Fruit Drink.

Or you may opt to soothe anxious appetites with a Pep Shake, a creamy, nutritious blend of peaches, eggs, and ice cream.

For a special breakfast or brunch that calls for spirit-laced eye openers, take your pick from Bloody Marys, nose-tingling Orange-Champagne Cocktail, and Milk Punch.

FRENCH CHOCOLATE MILK

⅓ cup semisweet chocolate morsels
¼ cup light corn syrup
3 tablespoons water
½ teaspoon vanilla extract
1 cup whipping cream
1 quart milk, scalded

Combine chocolate morsels, corn syrup, and water in a small heavy saucepan; cook over low heat, stirring constantly, until chocolate is melted and mixture is smooth. Stir in vanilla. Cover mixture, and chill 30 to 45 minutes, stirring occasionally.

Gradually add chocolate mixture to whipping cream, beating with electric mixer until stiff (mixture will mound when dropped from a spoon). Cover and chill.

To serve, place ½ cup chocolate cream in each cup. Add milk, stirring well. Yield: about 7 cups.
Linda H. Sutton,
Winston-Salem, North Carolina.

BLOODY MARYS

1½ cups tomato-clam juice
½ cup vodka
1 tablespoon plus 1 teaspoon Worcestershire sauce
Juice of 1 lime
3 to 4 dashes hot sauce
Celery salt
Salt and pepper
2 celery stalks (optional)

Combine first 5 ingredients in a pitcher, mixing well. Pour over ice cubes; sprinkle each serving with celery salt, salt, and pepper. Garnish each with a celery stalk, if desired. Yield: 2 servings.
Mrs. Susan Houston,
Tucker, Georgia.

PEP SHAKE

1 (16-ounce) can sliced peaches
1 cup vanilla ice cream
2 eggs
Fresh mint sprigs (optional)

Combine all ingredients except mint sprigs in container of electric blender; process until smooth. Pour into chilled glasses; garnish each with a sprig of mint, if desired. Yield: 3¼ cups.
Mrs. James L. Twilley,
Macon, Georgia.

MILK PUNCH

1½ cups half-and-half
¼ cup light rum
¼ cup bourbon
1 tablespoon plus 1 teaspoon sugar

Combine all ingredients in a cocktail shaker or jar; tighten lid securely, and shake well. Serve over crushed ice. Yield: 2 cups.
Jeanne Owen,
Lewisville, Texas.

THREE-FRUIT DRINK

1 banana, cut into 2-inch slices
1 (17-ounce) can apricot halves, undrained
1 cup orange juice
½ cup milk

Combine all ingredients in container of electric blender; process until smooth. Yield: 4 cups. *Susan Leftwich, DeSoto, Texas.*

ORANGE-CHAMPAGNE COCKTAIL

3½ cups champagne, chilled
1 (28-ounce) bottle ginger ale, chilled
2 cups orange juice, chilled

Combine champagne, ginger ale, and orange juice in a pitcher or punch bowl; stir gently. Garnish with fresh fruit, if desired. Yield: 9 cups.

*Carla C. Hunter,
Norcross, Georgia.*

Start The Day With A Classic

The popularity of entertaining informally with a special breakfast or brunch has prompted a renewed interest in the classic egg dishes and the creation of some new ones.

Besides enjoying poached eggs in the well-known eggs Benedict, delight brunch guests with a variation called Eggs Florentine. The poached eggs are layered with spinach, ham, and tomato slices on onion-flavored buns. The topping is the traditional hollandaise sauce.

Even scrambled eggs are spectacular in Scrambled Eggs Supreme, a combination of eggs, sour cream, and cheese spread cooked with crisp bits of bacon. As an accompaniment, we suggest Sausage-Filled Crêpes and have included the recipe here.

SCRAMBLED EGGS SUPREME

6 slices bacon, cut into small pieces
8 eggs
¼ cup commercial sour cream
¼ cup pasteurized process cheese spread
¾ teaspoon seasoned salt
Dash of pepper

Fry bacon in a large skillet; drain off all but 3 tablespoons drippings.

Combine remaining ingredients in container of electric blender; process on low speed until light and fluffy. Pour into skillet with bacon and hot drippings. Cook over low heat, stirring gently until done. Serve immediately. Yield: about 6 servings.

*Mrs. Timothy J. Mutter,
St. Joseph, Missouri.*

SAUSAGE-FILLED CREPES

⅔ cup all-purpose flour
½ teaspoon salt
2 eggs, beaten
1 tablespoon vegetable oil
⅔ cup milk
Sausage Filling
Topping (recipe follows)

Combine flour, salt, and eggs; mix well. Blend in oil and milk, beating until smooth. Refrigerate batter at least 2 hours. (This allows flour particles to swell and soften so crêpes are light in texture.)

Brush the bottom of a 6-inch crêpe pan or heavy skillet with vegetable oil; place over medium heat until just hot, not smoking.

Pour 2 tablespoons batter in pan; quickly tilt pan in all directions so batter covers pan in a thin film. Cook about 1 minute.

Lift edge of crêpe to test for doneness. Crêpe is ready for flipping when it can be shaken loose from pan. Flip crêpe, and cook about 30 seconds on the other side. (This side is rarely more than spotty brown and is the side on which the filling should be placed.)

Remove crêpe from pan, and repeat procedure until all batter is used.

Place 2 tablespoons Sausage Filling off-center on each crêpe. Roll crêpe over filling. Place, seam side down, in a 13- x 9- x 2-inch baking dish. Bake at 375° for 25 to 30 minutes. Remove from oven, and spoon topping over crêpes. Return to oven for an additional 5 minutes. Yield: about 1 dozen.

Note: Crêpes may be made in advance. Stack crêpes between layers of waxed paper, and cover tightly with plastic wrap or foil; store in refrigerator or freeze until needed.

Sausage Filling:

1 pound bulk pork sausage
¼ cup chopped onion
½ cup shredded Cheddar cheese
1 (3-ounce) package cream cheese, softened
½ teaspoon ground marjoram

Sauté sausage and onion until brown; drain well. Stir in remaining ingredients. Yield: about 2 cups.

Topping:

½ cup commercial sour cream
¼ cup butter, softened

Combine ingredients, beating well. Yield: ½ cup. *Jennifer Kimmel, Nashville, Tennessee.*

EGGS FLORENTINE

2 onion-flavored buns
Softened butter
1 (10-ounce) package frozen leaf spinach, thawed and well drained
2 tablespoons melted butter
4 slices boiled ham
4 slices tomato
4 poached eggs
Blender Hollandaise Sauce

Cut onion buns in half, and spread cut side with butter; broil until lightly browned.

Sauté spinach 2 minutes in 2 tablespoons melted butter. Place a slice of ham and a slice of tomato on each bun half; top with a small amount of spinach and a poached egg. Spoon hollandaise sauce over each. Yield: 2 servings.

Blender Hollandaise Sauce:

3 egg yolks
1 tablespoon lemon juice
¼ teaspoon tarragon leaves
¼ teaspoon salt
½ cup hot melted butter

Combine all ingredients except butter in container of electric blender; blend until thick and lemon-colored. Add melted butter in a slow, steady stream, and continue to process until thick. Yield: about ½ cup.

*Mrs. W. A. Shannon,
Dallas, Texas.*

EGGS BENEDICT

2 English muffins, halved and buttered
4 slices boiled ham
4 poached eggs
Hollandaise sauce (recipe follows)

Broil muffins until lightly browned. Cut ham slices in round pieces to fit muffins; fry and place on muffin halves. Top with poached egg and cover with hollandaise sauce. Yield: 2 servings.

Hollandaise Sauce:

2 tablespoons vinegar
¼ teaspoon white pepper
¼ cup water
4 egg yolks
2½ teaspoons lemon juice
1 cup butter, divided into thirds
¼ teaspoon salt

Combine vinegar, pepper, and water; boil until liquid is reduced by half.

Combine egg yolks, lemon juice, and ⅓ cup butter in top of double boiler. Cook over hot (not boiling) water, stirring constantly, until butter melts.

Add another third of butter, stirring constantly; as sauce thickens, stir in remaining butter. Add vinegar mixture by ½ teaspoonfuls, stirring constantly to keep sauce from curdling. Add salt, and cook until thickened. Yield: about 1½ cups.   *Mrs. Elizabeth Moore, Huntsville, Alabama.*

QUICHE LORRAINE

1 unbaked 9-inch quiche shell or pastry shell
1 pound bacon, cut into ½-inch pieces
¼ cup chopped green onion
2 cups (½ pound) shredded Swiss cheese, divided
6 eggs, beaten
1 cup whipping cream
½ teaspoon salt
Dash of cayenne pepper
Dash of white pepper
⅛ teaspoon ground nutmeg
Ground nutmeg

Prick bottom and sides of quiche shell with a fork; bake at 425° for 6 to 8 minutes. Set aside.

Sauté bacon and onion in a skillet until browned; drain well, and sprinkle evenly in pastry shell. Sprinkle with 1 cup cheese, and set aside.

Combine eggs, whipping cream, salt, pepper, and ⅛ teaspoon nutmeg; mix well. Pour over cheese layer, and top with remaining cheese. Sprinkle lightly with nutmeg. Bake at 350° for 45 to 55 minutes or until set. Yield: about 6 to 8 servings.   *Mrs. Carter Scott, Roswell, Georgia.*

On Cooking With Eggs

Did you ever stop to think what makes an angel food cake or a soufflé rise to spectacular heights or why custards and sauces will thicken when stirred? There is only one food that does all this and much more—the versatile, economical, and nutritious egg. To make the most of cooking with eggs, here are some tips.

■ If egg yolks are to be added to a hot mixture, first stir a small amount of the hot mixture into the yolks to warm them; then stir the warmed egg yolk mixture into the remaining hot mixture.

■ When bits of shell fall into a broken egg, remove the broken bits by using half of the shell as a scoop. This works much better than a spoon.

■ Eggs separate better when cold, but beat faster and to a larger volume at room temperature. Remove from refrigerator 30 minutes before beating.

■ For best results when beating egg whites, use either a metal or glass bowl. All bowls and beaters must be free of traces of oil or grease to ensure maximum volume. A bowl with a rounded bottom that is not too wide works best as the entire mass of egg white can be in motion at once.

■ Buy eggs from a refrigerated case, and always refrigerate them promptly at home. Variations in storage temperature cause eggs to lose quality, as the whites become thin.

To maintain quality, eggs should always be stored large end up and in their original container. This allows the yolk to stay centered, which is important when deviling eggs or using sliced hard-cooked eggs as a garnish. Do not store eggs near any strong-flavored foods since their shells are very porous and will absorb odors.

Eggs maintained under these conditions may be kept approximately five weeks with no appreciable loss in their quality.

■ Remove scrambled eggs and omelets from the pan when thickened throughout but still moist. The heat retained in the eggs completes the cooking and makes for a more desirable taste. Because eggs are a delicate high-protein food, high temperatures and overcooking will toughen them.

■ Eggs should never be boiled. To hard-cook, put eggs in a saucepan with enough water to come at least 1 inch above the eggs. Cover and bring rapidly just to boiling. Turn off heat and, if necessary, remove pan from heat to prevent further boiling.

Let eggs stand in the hot water about 15 minutes for large eggs, adjusting the time up or down by approximately 3 minutes for each size larger or smaller. Cool immediately under cold running water. The shell will be much easier to remove and you are less likely to have a dark area around the yolk when this method is used.

For soft-cooked eggs, follow the same method but allow eggs to stand in the hot water only 1 to 4 minutes, depending on desired degree of doneness.

■ Hard-cooked eggs are sometimes hard to peel; this is usually due to the freshness of the eggs. Eggs lose carbon dioxide and are easier to peel when stored for several days. This makes them better for hard-cooking.

Adding about a teaspoon of salt to the cooking water or punching a hole in the large end of the shell with an egg pick or thumb tack will help make the shells of even the freshest eggs easier to remove.

To peel a hard-cooked egg, crack by gently tapping all over; then roll between hands or on countertop to loosen shell. Peel, starting at large end, holding egg under cold water to help ease off shell.

■ For a golden-brown crust on bread and pastry, brush dough with unbeaten egg white before baking. This will keep a pastry shell from becoming soggy when filled with a juicy filling.

Spring Calls For Pork

Usher out winter and welcome spring with the fresh and flavorful taste of pork. The endless variety of cuts—ribs, chops, steaks, roasts, ham, sausage, tenderloin—provide a multitude of ways to brighten your menus.

Fruits and vegetables are natural complements for the lively flavor of pork. Brushed on as a glaze, served as an accompaniment, or simmered in for extra flavor, they accent that pleasing pork taste. Pineapple Pork Roast is a good example. The rolled pork loin roast is baked along with onion, celery, and carrots, then topped with a pineapple-apricot glaze. Ham-Asparagus Rolls combines the fresh flavor of asparagus with ham and a cheese sauce.

You can't think of pork without thinking of ribs, and country-style ones are the meatiest cut of ribs. Our Country-Style Barbecued Ribs are baked in a tangy barbecue sauce.

If a sweet-and-sour flavor is your preference with pork, you'll enjoy the recipe included here. Cubes of pork are battered and deep fried, covered with a pineapple-vegetable sauce, and spooned over rice.

Ground pork gives a whole new taste to burgers in a dish called Swedish Porkburgers. And in the version of jambalaya that we've included here, smoked sausage lends its flavor to this old Southern favorite.

To get the most from pork, it must be bought wisely, then properly stored. Here are some pointers.

—Buy by cost per serving, not cost per pound. One pound of boneless pork will serve three to four. Pork with little bone, such as chops, will yield two to three servings per pound. Pork with a lot of bone, such as spareribs, will serve about one person per pound.

—Select fresh, pink cuts of pork with some marbling. Take pork directly home after purchasing, and refrigerate or freeze immediately. Fresh pork can be stored in the refrigerator for two days. If you plan to keep it longer, wrap it in freezer paper or foil and freeze immediately. Smoked pork can be stored in the refrigerator for one to two weeks. Canned hams should be stored according to package directions.

—When freezing, label pork with name of cut, weight, and date frozen. Ground pork can be frozen for one to three months. Other fresh cuts can be frozen for three to six months, and most smoked pork for one to two months. Meat should be thawed in refrigerator.

Cooking Pork

Pork can be prepared in a variety of ways. Use the methods that follow, depending on the cut.

Roasting: (Use for roasts, ham, picnic shoulder, tenderloin, ribs, Canadian-style bacon, Boston shoulder, shoulder roll, and pork loaf.) Place pork, fat side up, on rack in a roasting pan. Season with salt and pepper, if desired. Insert meat thermometer, being sure it does not touch bone or fat. Roast at 325° to recommended internal temperature. (See chart in Appendix.)

Broiling: (Use for ham slice, chops, sliced Canadian-style bacon, pork patties, bacon, and blade steaks.) Place pork on a broiling pan. Broil at moderate temperature 3 to 5 inches from heat until pork is brown on one side. Season with salt and pepper, if desired. Turn and cook until done.

Pan broiling: (Use for same cuts as broiling.) Place pork in a skillet with no added oil or water. Cook slowly, pouring off all pan drippings as they accumulate. Turn meat occasionally, and cook until done.

Pan frying: (Use for bacon, ham slice, sliced Canadian-style bacon, and pork patties.) Place pork in a skillet; add a small amount of vegetable oil or shortening, if desired. Brown meat on all sides. Season with salt and pepper, if desired. Cook at moderate temperature, turning occasionally, until done.

Braising: (Use for chops, ribs, tenderloin, blade steaks, and pork cubes.) Place pork in a heavy skillet or Dutch oven. Brown meat on all sides. Season with salt and pepper, if desired. Add a small amount of liquid, and cover tightly. Cook over low heat until tender.

PINEAPPLE PORK ROAST

1 small onion, sliced
¼ cup sliced celery
¼ cup sliced carrots
1 (3-pound) pork loin roast, boned, rolled, and tied
Salt and pepper
1 small bay leaf, crumbled
½ cup pineapple juice
¼ cup soy sauce
¼ cup apricot jam
1 teaspoon cornstarch

Arrange vegetables in a greased roasting pan. Season roast with salt and pepper; place roast over vegetables, fat side up, and sprinkle bay leaf on top.

Insert meat thermometer horizontally into one end of roast. Bake at 325° for 45 minutes or until browned; turn roast over, and bake 30 minutes to brown bottom side. Turn roast over again, and drain off drippings.

Combine pineapple juice and soy sauce; pour over roast, and bake 15 to 25 minutes or until meat thermometer registers 170°.

Remove roast from oven; strain the drippings from vegetables, and sprinkle vegetables over roast.

Combine jam and cornstarch; add to strained drippings. Cook over medium heat until slightly thickened, stirring constantly with a whisk or wooden spoon. Spoon some of the glaze over roast; let stand 10 minutes before slicing. Spoon remaining glaze over slices. Yield: about 10 servings.

Mrs. Daniel Cross,
Porter, Texas.

HAM-ASPARAGUS ROLLS

16 fresh or frozen asparagus spears, cooked
4 thin slices cooked ham
Toast points
Creamy Sauce

Place 4 stalks asparagus on each slice of ham; roll up, and secure with a wooden pick. Broil 3 minutes or until ham is browned.

Remove pick, and place rolls on toast points. Pour Creamy Sauce over each roll. Yield: 4 servings.

Creamy Sauce:

2 tablespoons butter or margarine
2 tablespoons all-purpose flour
1 cup milk
½ teaspoon salt
⅛ teaspoon white pepper
½ cup shredded sharp Cheddar cheese

Melt butter in a heavy saucepan over low heat; add flour, stirring until smooth. Cook 1 minute, stirring constantly. Gradually stir in milk; cook over medium heat, stirring constantly, until thickened and bubbly. Add salt, pepper, and cheese; stir until cheese melts. Yield: about 1 cup.

Mrs. Paul Nelson,
Chesapeake, Virginia.

SWEET-AND-SOUR PORK

1 egg, beaten
¼ cup all-purpose flour
½ teaspoon salt
¼ cup cornstarch
1 (13¾-ounce) can chicken broth, divided
1 to 1½ pounds boneless pork, trimmed
    of fat and cut into ½- to 1-inch cubes
Vegetable oil
1 medium-size green pepper, chopped
½ cup thinly sliced carrots
1 clove garlic, minced
¾ cup sugar
½ cup red wine vinegar
3 teaspoons soy sauce
¼ cup cold water
3 tablespoons cornstarch
1 (8-ounce) can pineapple chunks, drained
2 small tomatoes, cut into wedges
Hot cooked rice

Combine egg, flour, salt, ¼ cup corn-starch, and ¼ cup chicken broth in a medium mixing bowl; beat until smooth. Dip pork cubes in batter, coating well; deep fry in hot oil (375°) for 5 to 6 minutes. Drain.

Heat 2 tablespoons oil in a wok or large skillet; add green pepper, carrots, and garlic. Cook until vegetables are tender but not browned. Stir in remaining broth, sugar, vinegar, and soy sauce; boil rapidly 1 minute.

Slowly add ¼ cup water to 3 table-spoons cornstarch, stirring until smooth. Stir cornstarch mixture into vegetable mixture; cook until thickened and bubbly. Add pork, pineapple, and tomato; cook just until well heated. Serve over rice. Yield: 4 to 6 servings.
*Lynn Young,
Knoxville, Tennessee.*

COUNTRY-STYLE
BARBECUED RIBS

4 pounds country-style ribs or spareribs
1 clove garlic, minced
1 tablespoon butter or margarine
½ cup catsup
⅓ cup chili sauce
2 tablespoons brown sugar
2 tablespoons chopped onion
1 tablespoon Worcestershire sauce
1 tablespoon prepared mustard
1 teaspoon celery seeds
½ teaspoon salt
½ teaspoon hot sauce
3 thin slices lemon

Cut ribs into serving-size pieces (3 to 4 ribs per person). Place ribs in a large

Dutch oven; cover with water, and simmer 1 hour.

Sauté garlic in butter in a medium saucepan about 5 minutes. Add remaining ingredients. Bring sauce to a boil, and simmer 5 minutes.

Place half of ribs, meaty side up, in a 13- x 9- x 2-inch baking pan; spoon half of sauce evenly over ribs. Repeat procedure with remaining ribs and sauce. Bake at 325° for 20 minutes. Yield: 4 to 6 servings.
*Virginia Vance,
Lexington Park, Maryland.*

SWEDISH PORKBURGERS

⅓ cup dry breadcrumbs
¾ teaspoon salt
½ teaspoon paprika
¼ teaspoon pepper
1½ cups half-and-half, divided
½ cup water
1 pound lean ground pork
1 egg
2 tablespoons minced parsley
¼ cup butter or margarine
1 medium onion, sliced and separated into
    rings
1 tablespoon all-purpose flour

Combine breadcrumbs, salt, paprika, and pepper; stir in ½ cup half-and-half and water. Add pork, egg, and parsley; mix well, and shape into 8 patties.

Heat butter in a large skillet; add patties, and cook over medium heat 8 to 12 minutes or until done; turn once. Remove burgers to a warm platter, and set aside.

Sauté onion in skillet drippings until tender. Sprinkle onion with flour; stir in remaining half-and-half. Cook mixture over low heat, stirring constantly, until thickened and bubbly; spoon over pork-burgers. Yield: 8 servings.
*Mrs. Marion Dome,
New Braunfels, Texas.*

TENDERLOIN PLATTER

2 tablespoons butter or margarine
8 (¼-pound) pork tenderloins
1 (10¾-ounce) can condensed cream of
    asparagus soup, undiluted
¼ cup milk
½ cup chopped onion
1 (3-ounce) can sliced mushrooms,
    undrained
¼ teaspoon curry powder

Melt butter in a skillet; add pork, and brown on all sides. Remove pork, reserving drippings in skillet.

Combine soup and milk, and add to drippings in skillet; add remaining ingredients, stirring well. Return pork to skillet. Cover and simmer mixture 40 to 45 minutes. Serve sauce over pork. Yield: 8 servings.
*Mrs. Billie Taylor,
Afton, Virginia.*

SMOKED SAUSAGE JAMBALAYA

1 pound smoked sausage, cut into ½-inch
    slices
1 pound ground beef
1 medium-size green pepper, chopped
½ cup chopped green onion
5 cloves garlic, minced
1 (28-ounce) can tomatoes
½ teaspoon salt
¼ teaspoon pepper
1 cup uncooked regular rice
1½ cups water

Cook sausage in Dutch oven until browned; remove from skillet, and discard drippings.

Combine ground beef, green pepper, onion, and garlic; cook until beef is browned. Add tomatoes, salt, pepper, and sausage. Cover; simmer 20 minutes.

Add rice and water to meat-vegetable mixture; cover and cook 25 minutes or until the rice is tender. Yield: 4 to 6 servings.
*Mrs. C. R. LeCroy,
Hattiesburg, Mississippi.*

Tip: When buying meats, consider the cost per serving rather than the cost per pound. Don't ignore the cheaper or less-tender cuts of meat; learn to serve them. Think twice about bypassing boneless meat because of its higher price. Even though a boneless roast is more expensive per pound than a bone-in roast, it has no excess fat and no bones, thus yielding more servings.

Reach For The Rice

The assortment of savory side dishes that can be made with white rice is endless: combine it with spicy jalapeño pepper, spinach and cheese, saffron, or orange juice.

For these recipes long-grain rice is recommended because it is fluffier and drier after cooking than short-grain rice. Some recipes call for instant rice, for when you're in a hurry.

Jalapeño Rice has just enough jalapeño pepper in it to make it spicy. Made with instant rice, it's ready in a hurry.

JALAPENO RICE

1 tablespoon melted butter or margarine
¼ cup thinly sliced celery
2 scallions, thinly sliced
½ to 1 jalapeño pepper, seeded and diced
½ teaspoon salt
⅔ cup chicken broth
⅔ cup instant rice
1 tablespoon diced pimiento

Combine butter, celery, scallions, and jalapeño pepper in a medium skillet; sauté until tender but not brown. Add salt and broth; bring to a boil. Stir in rice and pimiento; cover and remove from heat. Allow to stand 5 minutes before serving. Yield: 2 to 3 servings.
Mrs. Frank O. Appel,
Wimberley, Texas.

GREEN RICE BAKE

1 (10-ounce) package frozen chopped
  spinach
2 eggs, slightly beaten
2 cups milk
¾ cup instant rice
1 cup shredded process American cheese
½ teaspoon salt
⅛ teaspoon pepper
½ teaspoon garlic salt
¼ cup toasted slivered almonds

Cook spinach according to package directions; drain, removing as much liquid as possible.

Combine eggs and milk in a large mixing bowl, stirring well. Add spinach and remaining ingredients; mix well. Pour into a lightly greased 10- x 6- x 1¾-inch glass baking dish; bake at 325° for 35 to 40 minutes or until firm. Yield: 6 servings.   *Mrs. Gene Crow,*
Dallas, Texas.

ORANGE RICE

1 tablespoon butter or margarine
⅔ cup chopped celery
2 tablespoons chopped onion
1 cup orange juice
2 tablespoons grated orange rind
1½ cups water
1¼ teaspoons salt
1 cup regular rice, uncooked

Melt butter in a large skillet; sauté celery and onion until tender but not brown. Add juice, rind, water, and salt; bring to a boil. Stir in rice. Cover and simmer for 25 to 30 minutes or until rice is tender. Yield: 6 servings.
Mrs. B. L. Thomas,
Knoxville, Tennessee.

SAFFRON RICE

1 onion, chopped
¼ cup butter or margarine, melted
1 teaspoon salt
5 whole cloves
1 teaspoon ground ginger
¼ teaspoon saffron
3½ cups chicken bouillon
1¾ cups regular rice, uncooked

Sauté onion in butter until tender. Add salt, spices, bouillon, and rice; mix well. Simmer, covered, for 20 to 25 minutes or until rice is tender. Yield: 6 to 8 servings.   *Ginger Barker,*
Mesquite, Texas.

CHILI-CHEESY RICE

1 cup chopped onion
¼ cup melted butter or margarine
1 cup cream-style cottage cheese
½ teaspoon salt
⅛ teaspoon pepper
3 (4-ounce) cans green chiles, drained,
  seeded, and chopped
4 cups cooked regular rice
2 cups commercial sour cream
2 cups shredded sharp Cheddar cheese

Sauté onion in butter. Remove from heat and add remaining ingredients except Cheddar cheese. Spoon half the rice mixture into a greased 2-quart casserole; top with half the cheese. Repeat with remaining rice mixture and cheese. Bake at 375° for 25 minutes. Yield: 8 servings.   *Ann Elizabeth Harrington,*
Little Rock, Arkansas.

Add Variety And Flavor To Cottage Cheese

Cottage cheese is great for dieters, but its delicate texture and mild flavor also make it the perfect ingredient for a whole range of combinations, from appetizers to desserts.

Combine cottage cheese with Roquefort, Cheddar, and cream cheese, and it becomes Festive Cheese Ball. Adding cottage cheese to main dishes like Cheesy Ground Beef Casserole stretches the number of servings and provides high-quality protein at low cost. For dessert, try Lemon-Cottage Cheese Pie, a delightful blend of ingredients baked in a graham cracker crust and topped with nutmeg-flavored graham cracker crumbs.

The mild flavor and delicate texture of cottage cheese add a special touch to Festive Cheese Ball.

FESTIVE CHEESE BALL

1 cup small-curd cottage cheese
2 (8-ounce) packages cream cheese, softened
¼ cup finely grated sharp Cheddar cheese
1 ounce Roquefort cheese, crumbled
1 medium onion, finely grated
2 tablespoons Worcestershire sauce
Dash of seasoned salt
½ cup chopped pecans
½ cup chopped parsley

Combine first 7 ingredients; mix well. Shape mixture into 2 balls; roll each ball in pecans, then in parsley. Chill thoroughly. Serve with crackers. Yield: 2 cheese balls. *Rebecca Maher, Richardson, Texas.*

CHEESY GROUND BEEF CASSEROLE

1 (5-ounce) package medium egg noodles
½ cup chopped green onion, divided
2 tablespoons butter or margarine
1½ pounds ground beef
2 (8-ounce) cans tomato sauce
1 teaspoon salt
⅛ teaspoon pepper
1 cup small-curd cottage cheese
1 (8-ounce) carton commercial sour cream
¾ cup (3 ounces) shredded sharp process American cheese

Cook noodles according to package directions; rinse well and set aside.

Sauté ¼ cup onion in butter in a large skillet until tender. Add beef, and cook until lightly browned; drain well. Add tomato sauce, salt, and pepper; stir well, and simmer 20 minutes.

Combine cottage cheese, sour cream, and remaining onion; stir well and set aside.

Place noodles in a lightly greased 2½-quart casserole; spoon cottage cheese mixture over noodles. Spoon meat mixture over cheese mixture, and sprinkle with shredded cheese. Bake at 350° for 25 minutes. Yield: 4 to 6 servings. *Mrs. Gilbert P. Levy, Killen, Alabama.*

OUT-OF-THIS-WORLD COTTAGE CHEESE SALAD

1 (6-ounce) package lime-flavored gelatin
2 cups boiling water
5 cups miniature marshmallows
1 (15¼-ounce) can crushed pineapple, drained
15 maraschino cherries, chopped
1 cup chopped pecans
1 (12-ounce) carton small-curd cottage cheese
1 cup whipping cream, whipped

Dissolve gelatin in boiling water; add marshmallows, stirring until melted. Stir in pineapple. Chill until thick, but not firm. Add cherries, pecans, and cottage cheese; fold in whipped cream. Pour into an oiled 2-quart mold; chill until firm. Yield: 8 servings. *Sandy Dyer, Roanoke, Virginia.*

ORANGE-COTTAGE CHEESE SALAD

1 (12-ounce) carton small-curd cottage cheese
1 (4½-ounce) carton frozen whipped topping, thawed
1 (11-ounce) can mandarin oranges, drained
1 (20-ounce) can crushed pineapple, drained
½ cup chopped nuts
1 (3-ounce) package orange-flavored gelatin

Combine cottage cheese and whipped topping in a large mixing bowl; stir well. Add oranges, pineapple, and nuts; mix well. Add gelatin, and stir well. Chill thoroughly. Yield: 6 to 8 servings. *Mrs. Doyle Brown, Oak Ridge, Tennessee.*

LEMON-COTTAGE CHEESE PIE

1 (12-ounce) carton dry-curd cottage cheese
1¼ cups sugar
½ cup milk
½ cup all-purpose flour
3 eggs, beaten
2 tablespoons butter or margarine, melted
1½ tablespoons lemon juice
1 tablespoon grated lemon rind
1 teaspoon vanilla extract
½ teaspoon salt
Graham cracker crust (recipe follows)
¾ cup graham cracker crumbs
½ teaspoon ground nutmeg

Combine first 10 ingredients; beat thoroughly with an electric mixer. Pour into unbaked graham cracker crust.

Combine ¾ cup graham cracker crumbs and nutmeg; sprinkle evenly over filling. Bake at 350° for 1 hour or until firm. Store pie in refrigerator. Yield: one 10-inch pie.

Graham Cracker Crust:

1½ cups graham cracker crumbs
¼ cup sugar
6 tablespoons butter or margarine, melted

Combine graham cracker crumbs and sugar; stir in butter, mixing well. Press mixture firmly into a 10-inch pieplate. Yield: one 10-inch pie shell.

Benn-Macdonald Boelt,
Toano, Virginia.

Carrots Make The Cake

One of the best things that you can do to carrots is to grate them and bake them into a rich, moist, three-layer cake. In addition to this delicious version of the carrot cake, we offer other great ways with the familiar carrot, both in desserts and vegetable dishes.

Partisans of sweet potato or pumpkin pie are sure to be pleased with Carrot Custard Pie. On the carrot-as-vegetable side is Carrot Combo—carrots and celery simmered and flavored with lemon and butter; or Carrots Polynesian, with orange juice, brown sugar, and almonds.

CARROT CAKE

3 cups grated carrots
2 cups all-purpose flour
2 cups sugar
2 teaspoons soda
1 teaspoon baking powder
½ teaspoon salt
1 teaspoon ground cinnamon
4 eggs, well beaten
1½ cups vegetable oil
1 teaspoon vanilla extract
Cream Cheese Frosting

Combine first 7 ingredients; stir in eggs, oil, and vanilla, mixing well. Spoon batter into 3 greased and floured 9-inch cakepans; bake at 350° for 30 minutes or until cake tests done. Spread Cream Cheese Frosting between layers and on top of cake while still warm. Yield: one 3-layer cake.

Cream Cheese Frosting:

1 (16-ounce) package powdered sugar
1 (8-ounce) package cream cheese, softened
½ cup butter or margarine, softened
1 teaspoon vanilla extract
1 cup chopped pecans

Cream first 4 ingredients until well blended; stir in pecans. Yield: enough for one 3-layer cake.

Mrs. Paul B. Keith,
McAllen, Texas.

CARROT COMBO

1 pound carrots, peeled and sliced
1 cup diced celery
1 cup lemon-lime carbonated beverage
1 teaspoon salt
⅛ teaspoon pepper
½ teaspoon grated lemon rind
1 to 2 tablespoons butter or margarine

Combine first 5 ingredients in a saucepan; cover and simmer 15 minutes or until vegetables are tender. Remove from heat, and stir in lemon rind and butter. Yield: 4 servings.

Kate Woolbright,
Quanah, Texas.

CARROTS POLYNESIAN

1 pound carrots, thinly sliced
½ cup orange juice
½ teaspoon salt
1 teaspoon grated orange rind
2 tablespoons brown sugar
2 tablespoons sliced almonds
1 tablespoon butter or margarine
½ teaspoon parsley flakes

Combine carrots, orange juice, and salt in a pressure cooker. Adjust cooker according to manufacturer's directions; cook at 15 pounds pressure for 3 minutes. Before opening, reduce pressure according to manufacturer's directions; open pressure cooker. Add orange rind, sugar, almonds, and butter, stirring over low heat until butter melts; sprinkle with parsley flakes. Yield: 4 servings.

Note: If preferred, carrots, orange juice, and salt may be cooked in a covered saucepan over medium heat 12 to 15 minutes. *Dorothy W. Schneider,*
Ocala, Florida.

Three cups of grated carrots and a rich cream cheese frosting make Carrot Cake extra moist.

CARROT CUSTARD PIE

¾ cup sugar
3 tablespoons butter or margarine, softened
2 tablespoons all-purpose flour
3 eggs
1¼ cups evaporated milk
1¼ cups grated carrots
½ teaspoon ground cinnamon
1 unbaked 9-inch pastry shell

Combine sugar and butter; cream until light and fluffy. Stir in flour. Add eggs, one at a time, beating well after each addition. Add milk, carrots, and cinnamon, stirring well. Spoon batter into pastry shell. Bake at 425° for 15 minutes; reduce heat to 350° and bake 30 minutes or until firm. Yield: one 9-inch pie. *Mrs. Judy Cunningham,*
Roanoke, Virginia.

Tip: Read labels to learn the weight, quality, and size of food products. Don't be afraid to experiment with new brands. Store brands can be equally good in quality and nutritional value, yet lower in price. Lower grades of canned fruits and vegetables are as nutritious as higher grades. Whenever possible, buy most foods by weight or cost per serving rather than by volume or package size.

Plain Potatoes Make Fancy Dishes

With a little imagination and these recipes you can serve a potato side dish that is the star of the whole meal. Just imagine a baked potato filled with blue cheese and sour cream and topped with bacon. Or maybe you'd like sesame seed-topped scalloped potatoes. Or perhaps you'd prefer Cheesy Chive Potatoes, an exceptional dish made with potatoes, sour cream, cottage cheese, and Cheddar cheese.

When using potatoes, remember these hints on selection and storage. Good potatoes should be smooth, firm, and have few eyes, cracks, or bruises. You should never wash potatoes before storing them, since the moisture will speed decay. The best storage area for potatoes is in a cool, but not cold, dark place.

BACON-TOPPED BLUE CHEESE POTATOES

4 medium baking potatoes
Shortening
½ cup commercial sour cream
¼ cup milk
¼ cup butter or margarine
¼ cup crumbled blue cheese
¾ teaspoon salt
Dash of pepper
4 slices bacon, cooked and crumbled

Wash potatoes and rub skins with shortening. Bake at 400° for 1 hour or until done. Allow potatoes to cool to touch; slice skin away from top of each potato. Carefully scoop out pulp, leaving shells intact.

Combine potato pulp and remaining ingredients except bacon in a medium mixing bowl. Beat until light and fluffy; stuff shells with potato mixture. Bake at 400° for 15 minutes; top with crumbled bacon. Serve hot. Yield: 4 servings.
Mrs. R. B. Graves,
Florissant, Missouri.

SAUCY POTATO-TOMATO CASSEROLE

5 to 6 medium potatoes, peeled and quartered
1 (16-ounce) can stewed tomatoes
1 small onion, thinly sliced
¼ cup chopped green pepper
½ teaspoon salt
½ teaspoon pepper
¼ teaspoon granulated garlic
¼ teaspoon cayenne pepper
Cheese sauce (recipe follows)
½ cup round buttery cracker crumbs
1 tablespoon butter or margarine

Cook potatoes in boiling salted water until tender. Drain.

Drain tomatoes, reserving ⅓ cup juice. Combine tomatoes, reserved juice, potatoes, onion, green pepper, and seasonings in a large bowl. Spoon into a greased 2-quart casserole. Top with cheese sauce. Sprinkle casserole with cracker crumbs, and dot with butter.

Cover, and bake at 350° for 25 minutes. Remove cover; bake 5 additional minutes. Yield: 6 to 8 servings.

Cheese Sauce:
2 tablespoons butter or margarine
2 tablespoons all-purpose flour
½ cup milk
½ cup shredded Cheddar cheese
2 tablespoons mayonnaise
½ teaspoon salt

Melt butter in a small saucepan; blend in flour, and cook over low heat, stirring constantly, until smooth. Gradually add milk; cook over medium heat, stirring constantly, until thickened. Add cheese; cook, stirring, until melted. Add remaining ingredients; remove from heat. Yield: about 1 cup.
Susan Settlemyre,
Carrboro, North Carolina.

CHEESY CHIVE POTATOES

6 medium potatoes, boiled
1 (8-ounce) carton commercial sour cream
1 cup cottage cheese
1 tablespoon chopped chives
½ teaspoon granulated garlic
½ teaspoon salt
⅛ teaspoon pepper
⅓ cup shredded sharp Cheddar cheese
Paprika

Peel and dice potatoes; place in a medium bowl. Combine sour cream, cottage cheese, chives, garlic, salt, and pepper; add to potatoes.

Spoon mixture into a greased 1½-quart casserole. Top with cheese; sprinkle with paprika. Bake at 350° for 45 minutes. Yield: 6 to 8 servings.
Mrs. George Sellers,
Albany, Georgia.

BASQUE-STYLE POTATOES

2 pounds potatoes, peeled
1 tablespoon butter or margarine
½ cup chopped onion
½ cup chopped celery
½ cup grated carrot
1 clove garlic, finely minced
2 beef-flavored bouillon cubes
2 cups boiling water
1 teaspoon salt
2 tablespoons chopped parsley

Cut potatoes into 1-inch cubes; cover with water and set aside.

Melt butter in a 10-inch skillet. Add onion, celery, carrot, and garlic; cook over low heat until vegetables are tender. Drain potatoes, and stir into vegetable mixture.

Dissolve bouillon cubes in boiling water. Add bouillon to potato mixture; add salt and bring to a boil. Reduce heat; cover and simmer 25 minutes or until potatoes are tender. Remove from heat; top with parsley. Serve hot. Yield: 6 servings. *Mrs. Eunice M. Davies,*
Sarasota, Florida.

SKILLET SCALLOPED POTATOES

2 tablespoons butter or margarine
4 cups thinly sliced, peeled potatoes
⅓ cup water
1 (1⅜-ounce) envelope onion soup mix
1 cup evaporated milk
¼ cup water
1 cup shredded process American cheese
2 tablespoons chopped parsley
2 tablespoons toasted sesame seeds
Paprika

Melt butter in a 10-inch skillet. Add potatoes and ⅓ cup water; cover and cook over low heat 25 to 30 minutes or until the potatoes are tender.

Combine soup mix, evaporated milk, ¼ cup water, cheese, and parsley; stir well. Pour over potatoes; cook 3 to 5 minutes or until cheese is melted. Remove from heat; sprinkle with sesame seeds and paprika. Yield: about 4 to 6 servings.
Opal M. Rogers,
Tempe, Arizona.

A Non-Cook Shares His Recipes

Texas native Phil Shook took up wok cooking while living in San Francisco after graduation from the University of Texas. "It's like Mexican food in Texas," Phil says. "Everyone cooks Chinese food in San Francisco."

Phil brought his special talent to Birmingham, where he is an editorial writer for the *Birmingham News*. Although Phil admits he doesn't cook unless it's in the wok, he enjoys preparing his specialties when he and his wife entertain a small group of friends.

"Cooking in the wok is really fun. I'm a non-cook, and this is so simple," Phil says, adding that he likes to experiment with a variety of meats and vegetables by just "throwing them together and stirring them up."

The wok cooks foods rapidly, sealing in the flavor of meats, he explains. The fast cooking occurs in the bottom of the wok, while food that is being kept warm is pushed up the sloping sides.

Phil shares two of his stir-fry specialties with us here. These are followed by favorite recipes of other men cooks.

HAM AND ZUCCHINI STIR-FRY

1 (10¾-ounce) can chicken broth,
   undiluted
½ cup soy sauce
2 tablespoons sugar
2 teaspoons grated fresh ginger or ¼
   teaspoon ground ginger
½ teaspoon salt
4 cloves garlic, minced or crushed
4 teaspoons cornstarch
Vegetable oil
1 pound fully cooked ham, cut into 3- x
   ¼-inch strips
2 large carrots, thinly sliced
2 large zucchini, thinly sliced
2 large onions, thinly sliced
Hot cooked rice (optional)

Combine broth, soy sauce, sugar, ginger, salt, and garlic; stir well. Gradually add to cornstarch; mix well. Set aside.

Pour oil around top of hot wok, coating sides until bottom is covered with oil. Add ham; stir-fry until lightly browned. Add vegetables; stir-fry 2 minutes or until crisp-tender. Add broth mixture; cook, stirring, until thickened and bubbly. Serve with rice, if desired. Yield: about 4 servings.

STIR-FRY BEEF AND BROCCOLI

4 pounds round steak
2 bunches broccoli
¾ cup soy sauce
2 tablespoons cornstarch
Vegetable oil
½ teaspoon salt
1 clove garlic, finely minced
1 (4-ounce) can mushroom stems and
   pieces, drained
½ teaspoon salt
1 (10½-ounce) can condensed beef broth,
   undiluted
Hot cooked rice (optional)

Partially freeze steak; slice across the grain into 3- x ¼-inch strips. Set aside.

Cut broccoli stems from buds; separate buds into small sections, and slice stems diagonally into ¼-inch pieces. Set broccoli aside.

Gradually add soy sauce to cornstarch in a large bowl, stirring until blended. Add beef, stirring to coat with soy sauce mixture. Set aside.

Pour oil around top of hot wok, coating sides until bottom is covered with oil. Add ½ teaspoon salt and garlic. Stir-fry briefly. Add beef; stir-fry to desired doneness; remove and set aside.

Add broccoli, mushrooms, ½ teaspoon salt, and broth to wok; bring to boil. Reduce heat and cook, covered, about 4 minutes. Return beef to wok and cook, uncovered, until thoroughly heated. Serve with rice, if desired. Yield: about 8 servings.

CREAMY VEGETABLE SALAD

1 (10¾-ounce) can tomato soup, undiluted
1 (3-ounce) package cream cheese,
   softened
1 (3-ounce) package lemon gelatin
½ cup cold water
1 cup mayonnaise
½ cup finely chopped celery
½ cup minced onion
½ cup chopped pimiento-stuffed olives
½ cup finely chopped green pepper
½ cup chopped cucumber

Place soup in a medium saucepan; bring to a boil. Add cream cheese, stirring until melted. Soften gelatin in cold water; stir into soup mixture. Let mixture cool.

Add mayonnaise and vegetables to gelatin mixture, mixing well. Pour into an oiled 6-cup mold; chill until firm. Yield: 8 to 10 servings.
James T. Mays,
Covington, Virginia.

PORK CHOPS ITALIAN

6 center-cut pork chops
½ cup all-purpose flour
1 egg, well beaten
¼ cup water
¾ cup Italian breadcrumbs
¼ cup olive oil
1 (8-ounce) can tomato sauce
6 slices mozzarella cheese

Remove bone from each pork chop; place each chop on a sheet of waxed paper. Flatten to ¼-inch thickness, using a meat mallet or rolling pin; dredge in flour.

Combine egg and water; dip each pork chop in egg mixture, and dredge in breadcrumbs.

Sauté chops in olive oil on both sides in a large skillet until browned. Place in a 13- x 9- x 2-inch baking dish; spoon half of tomato sauce over chops. Place a slice of cheese on each chop; spoon remaining tomato sauce over cheese. Bake at 325° for 45 minutes or until pork chops are done. Yield: 6 servings.
James Buckley,
Ormond Beach, Florida.

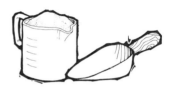

CHAMPIGNONS AU VIN
(Mushrooms and Bacon in Wine Sauce)

4 slices bacon
2 tablespoons butter or margarine
Pinch of dried rosemary or dried thyme
½ pound sliced fresh mushrooms
1 tablespoon all-purpose flour
½ cup dry white wine
2 slices toast

Fry bacon in a skillet until brown. Drain on paper towels, reserving drippings; crumble bacon. Add butter and rosemary to bacon drippings in pan, and heat until bubbly. Add mushrooms and reduce heat; cook, stirring, until mushrooms are tender and begin to darken (about 4 minutes). Add crumbled bacon, and cook 1 minute more. Remove mushrooms and bacon from skillet, and set aside.

Add flour to skillet, stirring constantly until flour begins to brown (about 1 minute). Gradually add wine; cook, stirring constantly, until sauce is smooth and thickened (about 1 minute). Remove from heat; stir in mushrooms and bacon. Serve over toast. Yield: 2 servings.
Arthur Scharff,
Charlottesville, Virginia.

CREAMY ONION SQUARES

3 cups biscuit mix
1 cup beer
¾ cup commercial sour cream
1 (0.56-ounce) package green onion dip
   mix
1 egg, slightly beaten

Combine biscuit mix and beer; stir well. Spoon dough into a greased 9-inch square baking dish.

Combine sour cream, onion dip mix, and egg; spread mixture over biscuit dough. Bake at 450° for 20 minutes or until done. Cut into 3-inch squares. Yield: 9 servings. *Frank E. Holmes, De Bary, Florida.*

CHICKEN-BROCCOLI CASSEROLE

2 (10-ounce) packages frozen chopped
   broccoli
4 whole chicken breasts, cooked and
   chopped
1 (10¾-ounce) can cream of chicken or
   mushroom soup, undiluted
⅔ cup mayonnaise
½ cup evaporated milk
½ cup shredded Cheddar cheese
1 tablespoon lemon juice
1½ teaspoons curry powder
1 cup buttered breadcrumbs

Cook broccoli according to package directions; drain well. Place in a lightly greased 1½-quart casserole; top with chicken. Combine remaining ingredients except breadcrumbs, stirring well. Spoon mixture over chicken; top with breadcrumbs. Bake at 350° for 30 minutes or until bubbly. Yield: 6 servings. *Allen A. Cocks, Milton, Florida.*

DEEP SOUTH OKRA GUMBO

3 slices bacon
4 cups diced okra
1 onion, finely chopped
1 clove garlic, finely chopped
1 green pepper, finely chopped
6 pimiento-stuffed olives, sliced
1 teaspoon salt
¼ teaspoon pepper
3 tomatoes, peeled and finely chopped
Hot cooked rice or toast
Chopped fresh parsley

Cook bacon until crisp; drain, reserving bacon drippings. Crumble bacon, and set aside.

Cook okra, onion, garlic, green pepper, olives, salt, and pepper in reserved bacon drippings until lightly browned. Stir in tomatoes, and cook over low heat about 30 minutes. Serve gumbo over rice or toast; garnish with crumbled bacon and parsley. Yield: about 6 servings. *Thomas Hugh Poole, Conyers, Georgia.*

ORANGE BLOSSOM SPECIAL

2 cups sugar
4 teaspoons all-purpose flour
4 teaspoons yellow cornmeal
¼ teaspoon salt
¼ cup melted butter or margarine
½ cup strained orange juice
Grated rind of 2 medium-size oranges
¼ cup milk
4 eggs (at room temperature)
1 unbaked 9-inch deep-dish pastry shell

Combine sugar, flour, cornmeal, and salt, mixing well. Add butter, orange juice, rind, and milk; stir well. Add eggs, one at a time, beating well after each addition.

Pour mixture into pastry shell. Bake at 350° for 50 to 60 minutes or until set. Cool. Yield: one 9-inch pie.
Lewyn M. Oppenheim, Fairfax, Virginia.

Light Soups Start The Meal

A light soup served as the first course adds such a nice touch to a special dinner. These recipes offer you several delightful choices.

Both the Pumpkin Soup and Almond Soup lend themselves to being served in mugs for guests to sip in the den or garden room while you put the finishing touches on dinner. But the Consommé aux Champignons should be served in handsome soup bowls at the table.

CONSOMME AUX CHAMPIGNONS

½ cup sliced mushrooms
2 teaspoons butter, melted
1 (10½-ounce) can consommé
1⅓ cups water
¼ cup sliced ripe olives
Dash of sherry

Sauté mushrooms in butter; stir in consommé, water, and olives. Heat thoroughly. Just before serving, add sherry. Yield: 4 servings.
Mrs. G. Grogaard, Baltimore, Maryland.

■ For a richer soup, add more half-and-half to this recipe; for a thinner version, add more broth.

PUMPKIN SOUP

1 large onion, chopped
¼ cup butter or margarine
½ teaspoon curry powder
1 (16-ounce) can pumpkin
1½ teaspoons salt
2 cups half-and-half
2½ cups chicken broth
Chopped parsley, commercial sour cream,
   or ground cinnamon (optional)

Sauté onion in butter until tender; sprinkle with curry powder, and sauté an additional 2 minutes. Stir in pumpkin and salt; add half-and-half, stirring constantly. Stir in broth, and heat thoroughly. If desired, garnish with parsley, sour cream, or ground cinnamon. Yield: 8 servings. *Joan Brom, Mountain Lakes, New Jersey.*

ALMOND SOUP

1 cup chopped onion
3 tablespoons butter or margarine, melted
8 cups chicken broth
½ cup uncooked regular rice
1 teaspoon salt
½ teaspoon pepper
½ teaspoon saffron
1 cup finely ground blanched almonds
3 hard-cooked egg yolks, finely chopped
3 tablespoons minced parsley

Sauté onion in butter until golden; stir in broth, and bring to a boil. Cover and simmer 10 minutes. Stir in rice, salt, pepper, and saffron; simmer 20 additional minutes. Add almonds, egg yolks, and parsley; cook 10 minutes longer. Yield: 10 servings.
Eleanor Brandt, Arlington, Texas.

Select A Sensational Onion Soup

When the menu calls for something light, yet warm and satisfying, you can't go wrong with steaming bowls of onion soup. As you might expect, we have three versions of onion soup that are particularly tempting.

Double Cheese-Topped Onion Soup combines mozzarella and Parmesan in its crouton topping, while Oven-Browned Onion Soup has a crust of toasted French bread sprinkled with Parmesan and Swiss cheese. French bread is also used in French Onion Soup—the bread is toasted and the brandy-flavored broth ladled over it.

DOUBLE CHEESE-TOPPED ONION SOUP

½ cup butter or margarine
4 large onions, thinly sliced and separated
   into rings
1 tablespoon all-purpose flour
2 cups chicken broth
1 (10¾-ounce) can beef broth
1 cup water
¼ cup dry white wine
¾ teaspoon salt
⅛ to ¼ teaspoon pepper
Onion- and garlic-flavored croutons
1 (6-ounce) package mozzarella cheese
   slices, cut in half
½ cup grated Parmesan cheese

Melt butter in a 5-quart Dutch oven; add onion, and cook over medium heat until tender. Blend in flour, stirring until smooth.

Stir chicken broth, beef broth, water, and wine into onion mixture. Bring to a boil; reduce heat, and simmer 15 minutes. Add salt and pepper.

Ladle soup into 8 individual baking dishes. Top each with 6 to 8 croutons and a cheese slice; sprinkle with Parmesan cheese. Bake at 350° for 10 minutes or until cheese melts. Yield: 8 servings.

Shirley Waller,
Birmingham, Alabama.

OVEN-BROWNED ONION SOUP

¼ cup butter or margarine
4 cups onion rings
6 cups consommé
½ cup cooking sherry
1 teaspoon salt
1 teaspoon sugar
Dash of ground nutmeg
3 to 4 slices French bread, toasted
1 cup (¼ pound) shredded Swiss cheese
Grated Parmesan cheese

Melt butter in a large Dutch oven; add onion, and sauté until tender. Stir in consommé, sherry, salt, sugar, and nutmeg. Bring to a boil; reduce heat, and simmer 30 minutes.

Ladle soup into individual baking dishes; top each with half a slice of bread. Sprinkle with 2 tablespoons Swiss cheese and Parmesan cheese.

Bake at 350° for 10 to 20 minutes or until cheese melts. Place under broiler to brown top. Yield: 6 to 8 servings.

Ilze Brannon,
Birmingham, Alabama.

FRENCH ONION SOUP

¼ cup olive oil
¼ cup butter or margarine
8 medium onions, thinly sliced and
   separated into rings
6 cups beef broth
2 tablespoons sugar
¾ teaspoon salt
¼ teaspoon pepper
¼ cup brandy
4 to 5 slices French bread, halved and
   toasted
Grated Parmesan cheese

Combine oil and butter in a large Dutch oven; heat until butter melts. Add onion, and sauté until tender. Add broth, sugar, salt, and pepper; bring to a boil. Reduce heat, and simmer soup mixture 20 minutes.

Add brandy to soup mixture, and cook 2 to 3 minutes. Place toasted bread in individual soup bowls; add soup, and top with Parmesan cheese. Yield: 8 to 10 servings.

Mrs. Sue-Sue Hartstern,
Louisville, Kentucky.

Tip: Make croutons from stale bread. Cut bread into cubes and toast at 250° until golden; then toss lightly in melted butter.

Luscious Is The Word For These Desserts

Our test kitchen staff agrees that these three luscious desserts, which substitute preserved, frozen, and canned strawberries or cherries for the flavor of the fresh, are some of the most delicious we've ever had.

Strawberry Cheese Delight is a rich layered dessert made with strawberry preserves, coconut, pecans, cream cheese, and whipped cream. Cherry Cheesecake calls for cream cheese and whipped topping in the filling; canned cherry pie filling is spooned over the top. And Strawberry Cake Roll is a rolled-up confection, filled with a mixture of frozen strawberries and gelatin.

STRAWBERRY CAKE ROLL

4 eggs
1 teaspoon vanilla extract
¾ cup sugar
¾ cup all-purpose flour
¾ teaspoon baking powder
¼ teaspoon salt
Powdered sugar
1 (3-ounce) package strawberry-flavored
   gelatin
1 cup boiling water
1 (10-ounce) package frozen strawberries
Frozen whipped topping, thawed

Beat eggs and vanilla until well blended; gradually add sugar, beating until light and fluffy.

Combine flour, baking powder, and salt; stir into batter. Pour into a greased 15- x 10- x 1-inch jellyroll pan. Bake at 400° for 10 minutes.

Immediately turn cake out on towel sprinkled with powdered sugar. Starting with long end, roll up cake and towel, jellyroll fashion. Let cool 30 minutes; then chill.

Dissolve gelatin in boiling water; add strawberries, stirring until thawed. Chill until gelatin is partially set.

Unroll cake, and spread with gelatin mixture; return to refrigerator, and chill until set. Carefully reroll cake; chill well. Slice and serve with whipped topping. Yield: 10 to 12 servings.

Jack R. Criswell,
Birmingham, Alabama.

STRAWBERRY CHEESE DELIGHT

2 cups flaked coconut
2 tablespoons sugar
1 tablespoon all-purpose flour
2 tablespoons margarine, melted
1 (10-ounce) jar strawberry preserves
1 (8-ounce) package cream cheese,
  softened
½ cup powdered sugar
½ cup chopped pecans
1 tablespoon milk
1 teaspoon almond extract
1 cup whipping cream
¼ cup powdered sugar

Combine coconut, sugar, flour, and margarine; blend well. Press mixture into a greased 8-inch springform pan or 8-inch square pan. Bake at 350° for 10 minutes; chill.

Spread half of preserves over crust. Combine cream cheese, ½ cup powdered sugar, pecans, milk, and almond extract; mix well, and spread evenly over preserves.

Combine whipping cream and ¼ cup powdered sugar, beating until fluffy; spoon over cream cheese layer. Freeze until firm. Let sit at room temperature 15 minutes before serving; garnish with remaining preserves. Yield: 8 servings.
Mrs. Henry DeBlieux, Sr.,
Natchitoches, Louisiana.

CHERRY CHEESECAKE

2 cups all-purpose flour
½ cup firmly packed brown sugar
1 cup chopped pecans
1 cup butter or margarine, softened
2 (1.5-ounce) envelopes whipped topping
  mix
1 cup cold milk
1 (8-ounce) package cream cheese,
  softened
1 cup powdered sugar
1 teaspoon vanilla extract
2 (21-ounce) cans cherry pie filling

Combine flour, brown sugar, pecans, and butter; mix well. Press into a 13- x 9- x 2-inch baking pan. Bake at 400° for 15 minutes; cool. Crumble crust, and firmly press back into pan.

Combine whipped topping mix and milk; beat until fluffy, and set aside.

Combine cream cheese, powdered sugar, and vanilla; mix well, and fold in whipped topping. Spread mixture over crust, and top with pie filling. Chill 12 hours. Yield: 15 servings.
Mrs. Leo Scherle,
Louisville, Kentucky.

Peanut Butter From Soup To Dessert

If you think that peanut butter is good only on bread and crackers, then you're in for a real surprise when you try soup and desserts that are made with peanut butter.

The pleasing aroma, creamy texture, and delightful flavor of Creamy Peanut Soup make it great by itself or as a start to a full-course dinner. On the other hand, Peanut Butter Cream Pie combines the rich flavors of cream cheese and peanut butter in a peanut-graham cracker crust. Topped with a whipped topping and sprinkled with chopped peanuts, this dessert is as attractive as it is tasty.

CREAMY PEANUT SOUP

½ cup butter or margarine
1 small onion, diced
2 stalks celery, diced
3 tablespoons all-purpose flour
2 quarts hot chicken broth
1 (8-ounce) jar creamy peanut butter
1 teaspoon salt
¼ teaspoon celery salt
1 tablespoon lemon juice
½ cup skinless peanuts, ground

Melt butter in a Dutch oven; add onion and celery, and sauté for 5 minutes or until limp. Stir in flour; cook, stirring, until bubbly. Stir in chicken broth, and simmer 30 minutes.

Remove from heat; strain soup, and discard vegetables. Add peanut butter, salt, celery salt, and lemon juice; stir well. Simmer an additional 5 minutes; sprinkle each serving with ground peanuts. Yield: 12 to 15 servings.
Mrs. Allen Cook,
Dallas, Texas.

PEANUT BUTTER CRISPS

1 cup butter or margarine, softened
½ cup creamy peanut butter
½ cup sugar
½ cup firmly packed brown sugar
1 egg
1 teaspoon vanilla extract
1⅓ cups all-purpose flour
3½ cups corn flakes, finely crushed, or 1
  cup corn flake crumbs
Salted peanuts

Combine butter and peanut butter in a large mixing bowl, creaming well. Add sugar, and beat well; add egg and vanilla, mixing well. Gradually add flour, and beat well.

Cover dough tightly, and refrigerate several hours or overnight.

Shape dough into 1-inch balls; roll each in corn flake crumbs. Press one peanut in center of each. Place on a greased cookie sheet; bake at 350° for 12 minutes or until cookies are lightly browned. Yield: about 5 dozen.
Mrs. W. S. Barbery,
Madison, North Carolina.

PEANUT BUTTER CREAM PIE

2 (3-ounce) packages cream cheese,
  softened
¾ cup powdered sugar
½ cup crunchy peanut butter
2 tablespoons milk
2 (1.5-ounce) envelopes whipped topping
  mix
1 cup cold milk, divided
1 teaspoon vanilla extract, divided
Peanut-Graham Cracker Crust
Chopped roasted peanuts

Combine cream cheese and powdered sugar in a large mixing bowl; beat until light and fluffy. Add peanut butter and 2 tablespoons milk; beat well.

Prepare one envelope whipped topping mix according to package directions, using ½ cup milk and ½ teaspoon vanilla; fold into peanut butter mixture, and spoon into baked crust.

Prepare remaining envelope whipped topping mix according to package directions, using remaining ½ cup milk and ½ teaspoon vanilla. Spread evenly over peanut butter mixture. Garnish with peanuts. Chill at least 5 hours before serving. Yield: one 9-inch pie.

Peanut-Graham Cracker Crust:
1¼ cups graham cracker crumbs
1 tablespoon brown sugar
2 tablespoons ground peanuts
¼ cup margarine, melted

Combine graham cracker crumbs, sugar, and peanuts; stir in margarine, and mix well. Press mixture firmly and evenly into a 9-inch pieplate. Bake at 350° for 8 minutes. Yield: one 9-inch pie shell.
Mrs. E. L. Chason,
Tallahassee, Florida.

PEANUT BUTTER CAKE

¾ cup butter
¾ cup creamy peanut butter
2 cups firmly packed brown sugar
1 teaspoon vanilla extract
3 eggs
2 cups all-purpose flour
1 tablespoon baking powder
½ teaspoon salt
1 cup milk
Chocolate frosting (recipe follows)
½ cup chopped peanuts

Combine butter and peanut butter in a large mixing bowl; cream well. Add sugar, and beat well. Add vanilla, and mix well. Add eggs, one at a time, beating well after each addition.

Stir together flour, baking powder, and salt; gradually add to creamed mixture alternately with milk, beating well. Spoon into a greased 13- x 9- x 2-inch baking pan. Bake at 350° for 45 to 50 minutes or until cake tests done. When cool, spread with chocolate frosting, and sprinkle with peanuts. Cut into squares. Yield: 15 to 20 servings.

Chocolate Frosting:

1 (6-ounce) package semisweet chocolate morsels
⅓ cup evaporated milk
1½ cups powdered sugar

Combine chocolate morsels and milk in a medium saucepan; place over low heat, stirring, until melted. Stir in sugar; beat until smooth. Yield: about 1 cup.
Mrs. Howard D. Utter, Louisville, Kentucky.

Bake Some Cookies To Snack On

A fresh batch of cookies is just the right thing to have on hand for after-school snacks or as the perfect accompaniment to coffee. The very best cookies are often the simplest, too, as this selection of recipes illustrates. We feature coconut macaroons, sugar cookies, and two butter-type cookies that have new twists—lemon and almonds. And don't forget brownies; this rich version features chocolate swirled with a cream cheese filling.

CREAM CHEESE SWIRL BROWNIES

1 (4-ounce) package sweet chocolate
5 tablespoons butter or margarine, divided
1 (3-ounce) package cream cheese, softened
1 cup sugar, divided
3 eggs
½ cup plus 1 tablespoon all-purpose flour, divided
1½ teaspoons vanilla extract, divided
½ teaspoon baking powder
¼ teaspoon salt
½ cup coarsely chopped nuts
¼ teaspoon almond extract

Melt chocolate and 3 tablespoons butter over low heat, stirring constantly. Set aside to cool. Combine remaining 2 tablespoons butter and cream cheese; cream well. Gradually add ¼ cup sugar, beating until light and fluffy. Add 1 egg, 1 tablespoon flour, and ½ teaspoon vanilla; beat well. Set aside.

Beat remaining 2 eggs until thick and light colored. Gradually add remaining ¾ cup sugar, beating until thickened. Stir in baking powder, salt, and remaining ½ cup flour. Add chocolate mixture, remaining 1 teaspoon vanilla, nuts, and almond extract; stir batter well, and set aside.

Set aside 1 cup chocolate batter; spread remaining batter in a greased 9-inch baking pan. Top with cream cheese mixture. Drop remaining chocolate batter by tablespoonfuls on cheese layer; swirl to create marbled effect. Bake at 350° for 30 to 35 minutes or until done. Cool and cut into 1½-inch squares. Cover and store in refrigerator. Yield: 3 dozen 1½-inch squares.
Mrs. Roland P. Guest, Jr., Jackson, Mississippi.

LEMONADE COOKIES

1 cup butter or margarine
1 cup sugar
2 eggs
3 cups all-purpose flour
1 teaspoon soda
1 (6-ounce) can frozen lemonade concentrate, thawed, undiluted, and divided
Sugar

Cream butter and 1 cup sugar until light and fluffy. Add eggs, one at a time, beating well after each addition. Combine flour and soda; stir into butter mixture alternately with ½ cup lemonade concentrate.

Drop dough by rounded teaspoonfuls on ungreased cookie sheets. Bake at 400° for 7 to 8 minutes or just until edges of cookies are lightly browned. Remove from oven; brush each cookie lightly with reserved lemonade, and sprinkle each with sugar. Cool on a wire rack. Yield: 6 to 7 dozen.
Evelyn L. Beall, Annapolis, Maryland.

MINCEMEAT COOKIES

1 cup shortening
1½ cups firmly packed brown sugar
3 eggs, beaten
1 teaspoon soda
1 tablespoon hot water
1 (9-ounce) package dry mincemeat, broken into pieces
4 cups all-purpose flour

Cream shortening and sugar until light and fluffy. Add eggs, beating well. Dissolve soda in water, and add to creamed mixture. Stir in mincemeat and flour, mixing well. Chill.

Roll dough on a heavily floured surface to ¼-inch thickness.

Cut out cookies with a 2-inch cutter, and place on lightly greased cookie sheets. Bake at 375° for 10 to 12 minutes or until lightly browned. Yield: about 2½ dozen.

SOUR CREAM SUGAR COOKIES

½ cup shortening
1 cup sugar
1 egg
1 teaspoon vanilla extract
3 cups all-purpose flour
1 teaspoon soda
½ teaspoon salt
½ cup commercial sour cream
Sugar

Combine shortening, 1 cup sugar, egg, and vanilla; cream until light and fluffy. Combine flour, soda, and salt; blend into creamed mixture. Stir in sour cream, mixing well.

Roll dough into 1-inch balls, and place on a lightly greased cookie sheet. Flatten with a fork, and sprinkle with sugar. Bake at 350° for 10 to 12 minutes. Yield: about 5½ dozen.
Mrs. W. D. Floyd, Charlotte, North Carolina.

ALMOND BUTTER COOKIES

1 cup butter or margarine, softened
1 cup sugar
2 egg yolks
½ teaspoon lemon extract
¾ teaspoon vanilla extract
¾ teaspoon almond extract
2 cups all-purpose flour
1 teaspoon baking powder
⅛ teaspoon salt
1 (4-ounce) package whole blanched
   almonds, toasted

Cream butter and sugar until light and fluffy. Add egg yolks, one at a time, beating well after each addition. Stir in flavorings. Add dry ingredients, mixing well. Shape dough into 1-inch balls. Place about 2 inches apart on ungreased cookie sheets. Press an almond in the center of each cookie. Bake at 300° for 15 to 20 minutes or until edges begin to brown. Cool 5 minutes before removing from cookie sheet. Yield: about 4½ dozen. *Jeannine Allen, McAllen, Texas.*

COCONUT MACAROONS

1⅓ cups coconut
⅓ cup sugar
2 egg whites
2 tablespoons all-purpose flour
½ teaspoon vanilla extract
⅛ teaspoon salt

Combine all ingredients, mixing well. Drop by level tablespoonfuls onto greased cookie sheet. Bake at 350° for 20 minutes. Yield: 1½ dozen.
Mrs. Margaret Scruggs, Gaffney, South Carolina.

Tip: If baked foods consistently undercook or overcook at the temperatures and cooking times specified in recipes, have the thermostat of your oven checked. Home service advisors of the gas or electric company will usually do this for you. However, you can check it yourself with a dependable oven thermometer. Place the thermometer in the center of the oven, and set the oven on the desired temperature. Allow enough time for the oven to heat, and compare the thermometer reading with the oven setting.

Explore Some Chive Possibilities

The fresh, tender leaves of chives may be used in any food that can be improved by the addition of a delicate onion flavor. Chives are most often teamed up with salads, eggs, sauces, cheese, potatoes, or vegetables.

You can grow your own chives year-round in a sunny window. All that is required is a pot filled with soil and plenty of sunlight. You'll soon be able to snip a few chive leaves and add them to Cucumbers in Sour Cream or your own homemade Italian dressing.

RICE SALAD WITH BACON

8 slices bacon, cooked and crumbled
3 cups cooked rice
1 cup cooked green peas
1 cup thinly sliced celery
½ cup mayonnaise
¼ cup diced pimiento
¼ cup minced fresh chives
¼ teaspoon salt
¼ teaspoon pepper
Pimiento-stuffed olives (optional)

Combine all ingredients except olives; toss. Garnish with olives, if desired. Chill. Yield: 5 to 6 servings.
Maybelle Pinkston, Corryton, Tennessee.

CHIVE-STUFFED BAKED POTATOES

6 medium baking potatoes
½ cup commercial sour cream
¾ cup cubed American cheese
2 tablespoons butter or margarine
1 tablespoon minced fresh chives
1 tablespoon minced onion
1 teaspoon salt
½ teaspoon pepper

Wash potatoes; bake at 425° for 45 minutes or until done. Allow potatoes to cool to touch.

When cool, slice skin away from top of each potato. Carefully scoop out pulp, leaving shells intact; mash pulp.

Place sour cream over low heat until warm. Remove from heat; add potato pulp and remaining ingredients, mixing well. Stuff shells with potato mixture. Bake at 425° for 15 minutes. Serve hot. Yield: 6 servings. *Thelma Wofford, New Castle, Delaware.*

ITALIAN DRESSING

¾ cup olive oil
¼ cup wine vinegar
2 teaspoons minced fresh chives
1 teaspoon salt
1 teaspoon minced parsley
⅛ teaspoon black pepper
⅛ teaspoon cayenne pepper
⅛ teaspoon dillseeds
1 clove garlic

Combine all ingredients in a jar. Cover tightly, and shake vigorously. Chill several hours. Remove garlic clove before serving. Serve dressing over salad greens. Yield: about 1 cup.
Carole Garner, Little Rock, Arkansas.

CUCUMBERS IN SOUR CREAM

1 cup commercial sour cream
3 tablespoons minced fresh chives
2 tablespoons lemon juice
1½ teaspoons salt
¼ teaspoon pepper
3 cucumbers, peeled and sliced

Combine first 5 ingredients, stirring well; stir in cucumbers. Chill. Yield: 4 to 6 servings. *Jane Zimmerman, Marble Falls, Texas.*

VEGETABLE DIP

1 cup mayonnaise
½ cup whipping cream, whipped
½ cup chopped fresh parsley
2 tablespoons minced fresh chives
1 tablespoon grated onion
1½ teaspoons lemon juice
¼ teaspoon salt
¼ teaspoon paprika
⅛ teaspoon curry powder
1 clove garlic, minced

Combine all ingredients; mix well. Chill 3 hours. Serve as a dip for fresh vegetables. Yield: about 2 cups.
Mrs. Martha Ann Edminster, East Freetown, Massachusetts.

Look What's Cooking In The Blender

You'll be amazed at the number of ways your blender can save you time. Our readers find that their blenders are the beginning for countless creative dishes from first courses to desserts to refreshing beverages. Start your day with Sunshine Shake and crisp Perfect Blender Popovers, and enjoy Magic Coconut Pie in the evening. For in between, we've included other blender recipes for you to enjoy.

To help you get the most from your blender, here are some tips.

—Put liquid portions of recipes into the blender container first unless otherwise specified in the recipe.

—For even blending, fill blender only three-fourths full for liquids and one-fourth full for solids.

—Cut fruits, vegetables, and cooked meats into cubes no larger than 1 inch; cut cheese into ½-inch pieces.

—Do not crush whole ice cubes by themselves; instead, place them in liquid before blending.

—For easy cleanup, fill blender container with warm water, add a few drops of liquid detergent, and blend 30 seconds; rinse.

—Ingredients at room temperature blend faster than cold ones.

—To flash-blend, cover and turn switch quickly from low to off several times until food is chopped.

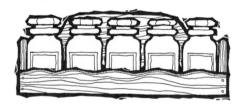

PERFECT BLENDER POPOVERS

2 eggs
1 cup milk
1 cup all-purpose flour
¼ teaspoon salt

Place eggs and milk in container of electric blender; blend until bubbly. Add flour and salt; blend until smooth. Fill well-greased muffin cups half full. Bake at 450° for 20 minutes; reduce heat to 350°, and bake an additional 10 to 12 minutes or until golden brown. Yield: 9 to 10 popovers.

James H. Crowder,
Durham, North Carolina.

Pea Soup Elegante is ready in seconds when prepared in your electric blender.

SUNSHINE SHAKE

2 cups orange juice, chilled
¼ cup instant nonfat dry milk solids
½ teaspoon honey
½ teaspoon vanilla extract
½ cup undrained crushed pineapple
1 banana, cut into chunks
1 egg

Combine all ingredients in container of electric blender; blend until smooth, holding container cover down firmly. Serve immediately. Yield: 1 quart.

Mrs. J. A. Tuthill,
Virginia Beach, Virginia.

MAGIC COCONUT PIE

½ cup biscuit mix
½ cup sugar
4 eggs
2 cups milk
1 cup flaked coconut
1 teaspoon vanilla extract
3 tablespoons melted butter

Combine all ingredients in container of electric blender; blend on low speed 1 minute. Pour mixture into a buttered 9-inch pieplate. Bake at 400° for 20 to 25 minutes or until pie is set. Yield: 6 to 8 servings. *Mrs. Mildred Sherrer,*
Bay City, Texas.

PEA SOUP ELEGANTE

2 teaspoons instant beef bouillon
1 cup hot water
2 (17-ounce) cans small early peas, undrained
1 (8-ounce) carton commercial sour cream
½ teaspoon onion salt
½ teaspoon salt
Dash of pepper
Paprika

Dissolve bouillon in water; set aside.
Place peas in container of electric blender; blend until smooth. Add bouillon; blend well. Pour half of mixture into a large bowl. Add sour cream, onion salt, salt, and pepper to mixture in blender; blend until smooth. Stir into mixture in bowl; chill for 1 to 2 hours. Sprinkle each serving with paprika. Yield: about 6 cups. *Susanne L. Webb,*
Roanoke, Virginia.

CHEESY BROCCOLI FRITTERS

1 egg
1 cup milk
2 cups all-purpose flour
2 teaspoons baking powder
¾ teaspoon salt
1½ cups chopped (1-inch pieces) fresh broccoli
Vegetable oil
Cheese sauce (recipe follows)

Combine all ingredients except vegetable oil and cheese sauce in container of electric blender; blend until broccoli is finely chopped. (Stop blender and scrape sides of container with a rubber spatula when necessary.)

Heat 3 to 4 inches vegetable oil to 375° in deep fat fryer or large saucepan. Drop batter by tablespoonfuls into hot oil; cook about 3 to 4 minutes or until golden brown. Drain on paper towels. Serve cheese sauce over fritters. Yield: about 1½ dozen.

Cheese Sauce:

1 cup milk
3 slices process American cheese, cubed
2 slices process Swiss cheese, cubed
2 tablespoons butter or margarine, softened
2 tablespoons all-purpose flour

Combine all ingredients in container of electric blender; blend until cheese is coarsely chopped. Pour into medium saucepan; cook over low heat, stirring constantly, until smooth and thickened. Yield: about 1 cup.
Mrs. Randy Throneberry,
Shelbyville, Tennessee.

Budget Entrées To Boast About

Spiraling food costs increase the challenge of preparing nutritious and satisfying meals while staying within a budget. However, the careful cook can combine the lower priced meats with a variety of inexpensive items for some exciting, money-saving entrées.

For instance, canned corned beef and fresh cabbage go together well in a quick main dish that's high in vitamin C. Also good is Liver Stroganoff, beef liver combined with sour cream and served on a bed of noodles.

We've also included recipes for other tasty budget entrées calling for chicken, ground beef, and frankfurters. And for an added bonus, you'll find that not only are these dishes economical, they're quick to prepare as well.

Quick Corned Beef and Cabbage makes a fast one-dish meal that's easy on the pocketbook.

QUICK CORNED BEEF AND CABBAGE

3 tablespoons melted margarine
1 small head cabbage, shredded (about 10 cups)
1 teaspoon salt
⅛ teaspoon pepper
1 teaspoon celery seeds
1 (12-ounce) can corned beef, diced

Combine margarine, cabbage, salt, pepper, and celery seeds in a large skillet; cover and cook over medium heat 10 minutes, stirring occasionally. Add corned beef; cover, and cook 5 minutes or until meat is thoroughly heated. Yield: 4 servings. *Mrs. Laura Murphy, Marshall, Texas.*

CHILI-RICE CASSEROLE

1 cup chopped onion
2 tablespoons melted butter or margarine
3 cups hot cooked rice
¾ cup commercial sour cream
Salt and pepper to taste
1 (15-ounce) can chili without beans

Sauté onion in butter in a small skillet. Combine onion, rice, and sour cream in a 1½-quart casserole; stir well. Season to taste with salt and pepper. Spoon chili over rice mixture. Bake at 350° for 15 minutes or until bubbly. Yield: 4 servings. *Karen Grubaugh, San Antonio, Texas.*

LIVER STROGANOFF

1½ pounds calf's or beef liver
All-purpose flour
2 tablespoons melted butter or margarine
2 tablespoons chopped fresh parsley
½ cup chopped onion
⅓ cup chopped green onion tops
1 cup sliced fresh mushrooms
2 cloves garlic, minced
¼ cup melted butter or margarine
3 tablespoons all-purpose flour
1 (10½-ounce) can consommé
1 teaspoon salt
½ teaspoon freshly ground pepper
6 drops hot sauce
1 (8-ounce) carton commercial sour cream
Hot cooked noodles or rice

Dredge liver in flour. Cook in 2 tablespoons melted butter in a large skillet just until it loses its pink color and is lightly browned. Remove and set aside to cool. Cut into narrow strips.

Sauté parsley, onion, onion tops, mushrooms, and garlic in ¼ cup melted butter. Blend in 3 tablespoons flour; cook 1 minute, stirring constantly. Gradually stir in consommé; add salt, pepper, and hot sauce. Cook over medium heat, stirring constantly, until thickened and bubbly.

Add liver to sauce, and simmer 10 minutes. Remove from heat, and add sour cream. Heat thoroughly, but do not boil. Serve over noodles or rice. Yield: about 4 to 6 servings. *Mrs. Michael Champagne, Covington, Louisiana.*

FAMILY-STYLE FRANKS

1 (16-ounce) package franks
½ cup chopped onion
2 tablespoons melted margarine
1 (11-ounce) can Cheddar cheese soup, undiluted
⅓ cup water
4 cups sliced cooked potatoes
Salt and pepper to taste

Diagonally slash partially through each frank in two places.

Sauté onion in margarine until tender; add soup and water, stirring well.

Place half of potatoes in a greased 10- x 6- x 2-inch baking dish; sprinkle with salt and pepper. Top with half of cheese sauce. Repeat with remaining potatoes and cheese sauce. Place franks on casserole; bake at 350° for 30 minutes or until bubbly. Yield: 4 servings. *Mrs. B. L. Nester, Charleston, West Virginia.*

Tip: In comparison shopping, use the cost-per-serving rather than the cost-per-pound comparison. For example, a boneless smoked ham will yield five servings per pound, while a bone-in ham yields only three servings. If the boneless ham is selling for $2.09 per pound (about 42 cents per serving), it is a better buy than the bone-in ham selling for $1.49 per pound (about 50 cents per serving).

OLD-FASHIONED CHICKEN AND DUMPLINGS

1 (3-pound) broiler-fryer, cut up
1 medium onion, halved
1 tablespoon salt
¼ teaspoon pepper
About 6 cups water
2 cups self-rising flour
¼ teaspoon ground thyme
About ½ cup ice water

Combine chicken, onion, salt, pepper, and about 6 cups water in a Dutch oven. Bring to a boil; cover, and simmer 2 hours or until chicken is tender. Remove chicken from broth; cool. Bone chicken. If necessary, add additional water to broth to measure 6 cups. Return chicken to broth, and bring to a boil.

Combine flour and thyme. Add about ½ cup ice water to make a soft dough; stir well. Turn dough out on a lightly floured surface; knead gently 30 seconds. Roll dough to ⅛-inch thickness; cut into ½- x 4-inch strips. Drop strips into boiling broth. Cover and reduce heat; simmer 30 to 40 minutes. Yield: 6 to 8 servings.   *Mrs. Alex B. Snyder, Monroe, North Carolina.*

SOUR CREAM-NOODLE BAKE

1 (8-ounce) package medium egg noodles
1 cup cottage cheese
1 (8-ounce) carton commercial sour cream
½ cup minced onion
1 pound lean ground beef
1 (8-ounce) can tomato sauce
1 teaspoon salt
½ teaspoon garlic salt
¾ cup cubed Cheddar cheese

Cook noodles according to package directions. Drain noodles; fold in cottage cheese, sour cream, and onion. Set aside.

Cook meat until no longer pink; drain. Add tomato sauce and seasonings; simmer 10 minutes.

Spoon half of noodle mixture into a lightly greased 2-quart casserole; top with half the meat mixture. Repeat layers, and bake at 350° for 30 minutes. Remove from oven; sprinkle with cheese, and bake an additional 5 minutes or until cheese melts. Yield: about 8 servings.   *Mrs. Delores Townley, Marietta, Georgia.*

Tip: Crush leftover potato chips or pretzels, and use to top casseroles.

MEXICAN GRITS SOUFFLE

1 cup uncooked grits
4 cups boiling water
1 teaspoon salt
2 cups (½ pound) shredded sharp Cheddar cheese
½ cup chopped onion
1 clove garlic, crushed
2 tablespoons melted butter or margarine
⅓ cup finely chopped jalapeño peppers
4 eggs, separated

Stir grits into boiling water; add salt. Cook 10 to 20 minutes, stirring frequently, until grits are thickened. Remove from heat. Add cheese, stirring until melted.

Sauté onion and garlic in butter; add to grits. Stir in peppers. Add a small amount of hot grits to egg yolks, stirring well; add egg yolk mixture to grits, mixing well.

Beat egg whites until stiff; fold into grits. Spoon mixture into a greased 2-quart casserole; bake at 350° for 45 to 50 minutes. Yield: 6 to 8 servings.
Mrs. Hilda Klier, New Hyde Park, New York.

Make A Meal Of Salad

Main dish salads are perfect for a spur-of-the-moment lunch or supper and are an appealing way to use leftovers as well. Start with meat or fish, add fruits or vegetables, and perhaps cheese and eggs, and you have the makings for a simple, attractive, and nutritious meal. Add crackers or bread and a beverage to complete the menu.

Fancy Chicken Salad makes a traditional chicken salad into a complete meal with the addition of several garnishes. A delicious sour cream dressing tops Ham and Cheese Toss, which features a variety of mixed salad greens. Try combinations of Bibb, romaine, iceberg, leaf lettuce, spinach, and endive for variations on this salad.

Seafood Slaw has several variations, too, since shrimp or crab may be substituted for the tuna. The seafood is combined with shredded cabbage and a tangy sauce for a main dish that is light yet filling.

FANCY CHICKEN SALAD

1 (10-ounce) package frozen French-style green beans
¼ cup commercial Italian dressing
3 large chicken breast halves, cooked
½ cup mayonnaise or salad dressing
¼ cup whipping cream, whipped
1 cup diced celery
½ teaspoon salt
Dash of pepper
3 large outer lettuce leaves
Mayonnaise or salad dressing
2 teaspoons capers
6 slices tomato
6 ripe olives
2 hard-cooked eggs, quartered

Cook beans according to package directions; drain well. Combine beans and Italian dressing; toss well and chill.

Cut a thin slice from each chicken breast; set aside. Remove remaining chicken from bone, and cut meat into small cubes.

Fold ½ cup mayonnaise into whipped cream; fold cubed chicken, celery, salt, and pepper into mayonnaise mixture; chill well.

To serve, place lettuce leaves on serving platter; spoon chicken salad over lettuce leaves. Place a chicken slice on top of each serving; top each with a dollop of mayonnaise; then sprinkle with capers.

Drain green beans, and arrange on platter between lettuce leaves. Garnish with tomato, olives, and eggs. Yield: 3 servings.   *Mrs. Natalie Wyatt, Borger, Texas.*

HAM AND CHEESE TOSS

8 cups mixed salad greens
2 cups cooked ham strips
1½ cups sliced zucchini
1½ cups cauliflower flowerets
1 cup Swiss cheese strips
Russian Sour Cream Dressing

Combine all ingredients except dressing in a large bowl, and toss well. Serve with Russian Sour Cream Dressing. Yield: 6 to 8 servings.

Russian Sour Cream Dressing:

1 (1¼-ounce) envelope sour cream sauce mix
⅔ cup milk
¼ cup chili sauce
Dash of cayenne pepper

Combine all ingredients, mixing well. Let stand 10 minutes before serving. Yield: 1 cup.   *Kathleen D. Stone, Houston, Texas.*

SEAFOOD SLAW

2 cups flaked tuna
4 cups finely shredded cabbage
¼ cup chopped green onion
½ cup mayonnaise
¼ cup lemon juice
2 teaspoons sugar
1 teaspoon seasoned salt
1 teaspoon prepared mustard
¼ teaspoon Worcestershire sauce
¼ teaspoon hot pepper sauce

Combine tuna, cabbage, and onion; set aside. Combine remaining ingredients, and stir well. Pour dressing over tuna mixture and toss. Chill thoroughly. Yield: 6 to 8 servings.

Note: Cooked flaked crab or cooked chopped shrimp may be substituted for the tuna. *Mrs. Harvey Kidd, Hernando, Mississippi.*

ZESTY BEEF SALAD

½ cup salad dressing or mayonnaise
1 tablespoon chili sauce
1 tablespoon sweet relish
¼ teaspoon salt
2 cups cubed cooked beef
1 cup drained red kidney beans
1 cup chopped celery
⅓ cup chopped onion
2 hard-cooked eggs, chopped

Combine first 4 ingredients, and mix well; add remaining ingredients, and toss well. Refrigerate 24 hours before serving. Yield: 4 to 6 servings.
Mrs. Walter Stewart, Mountain Home, Arkansas.

CREAMY SHRIMP SALAD

2 to 3 pounds fresh shrimp, peeled and deveined
1 large bay leaf
2 hard-cooked eggs, diced
1 stalk celery, sliced
2 tablespoons minced onion
¼ cup diced green pepper
⅓ cup mayonnaise
2 to 3 tablespoons commercial sour cream
½ teaspoon salt
¼ teaspoon cayenne pepper
¼ teaspoon basil leaves
Lettuce leaves

Cook shrimp and bay leaf in boiling water 4 to 5 minutes or until done; drain and cool. Combine shrimp, eggs, celery, onion, and green pepper; set aside.

Combine mayonnaise, sour cream, salt, pepper, and basil; add dressing to shrimp, and toss well. Refrigerate salad overnight; serve on lettuce leaves. Yield: 6 to 8 servings.

Susan Settlemyre, Carrboro, North Carolina.

TURKEY-FRUIT SALAD

4 cups cooked diced turkey
1½ cups diced celery
1 (15¼-ounce) can pineapple chunks, drained and cubed
1½ cups mayonnaise
1 cup chopped apple
1 cup chopped pecans

Combine all ingredients, mixing well. Chill 2 hours before serving. Yield: 8 to 10 servings. *Mrs. William S. Bell, Chattanooga, Tennessee.*

TACO SALAD

½ pound ground beef
½ teaspoon seasoned salt
½ teaspoon ground cumin
Dash of granulated garlic
½ medium onion, chopped
½ medium head of lettuce, shredded
2 to 3 tomatoes, chopped
1 medium avocado, chopped (optional)
½ (8½-ounce) package tortilla chips, broken into small pieces
1 cup (¼ pound) shredded Cheddar cheese
3 tablespoons commercial sour cream (optional)

Brown meat with salt, cumin, garlic, and onion; drain well. Combine meat mixture with remaining ingredients, and toss well. Yield: 3 to 4 servings.

Sheri Sweet, Edmond, Oklahoma.

Chicken salad takes on a new look when combined with French-style green beans and garnished with wedges of hard-cooked eggs, tomato slices, and ripe olives.

Canned Shrimp, So Convenient

Have you ever discovered at the last moment that you need shrimp to make that perfect dish? Then next time, reach for a can of shrimp. A 4½- or 5-ounce can holds 1 cup fully cooked shrimp—enough for a casserole or salad for four to five people, or enough to dress up a cracker spread or baked potatoes.

Although it isn't necessary to store canned shrimp in the refrigerator, chilling does improve the shape and texture.

Canned shrimp is available with or without the vein. A can labeled simply "shrimp" will contain shrimp that has not been deveined. However, it will be a bit more economical than shrimp that has been deveined.

POLYNESIAN SEAFOOD SALAD

1 (4½-ounce) can broken shrimp, drained
1 (4½-ounce) can large shrimp, drained
1 (7-ounce) can chunk light tuna, drained and flaked
1 (6-ounce) package frozen crabmeat, thawed and flaked, or 1 (6½-ounce) can flaked crabmeat, drained
1 (8½-ounce) can bamboo shoots, drained
1 (16-ounce) can bean sprouts, drained
1 cup sliced almonds
1 (4-ounce) can sliced mushrooms, drained
1 (5-ounce) can water chestnuts, drained and sliced
1 (5-ounce) can chow mein noodles
½ cup mayonnaise
½ cup commercial sour cream

Combine all ingredients; toss lightly, but thoroughly. Serve immediately. Yield: 8 servings.
Mrs. George M. Shell,
Austin, Texas.

TEMPTING SHRIMP SPREAD

½ cup butter or margarine, softened
1 (8-ounce) package cream cheese, softened
2 teaspoons mayonnaise
Dash of garlic salt
⅛ teaspoon pepper
⅛ teaspoon Worcestershire sauce
2 teaspoons lemon juice
1 small onion, finely chopped
½ cup finely chopped celery
2 (4½-ounce) cans small shrimp, drained

Combine butter, cream cheese, mayonnaise, garlic salt, pepper, Worcestershire sauce, and lemon juice; mix well. Stir in onion, celery, and shrimp. Serve with crackers or party rye bread. Yield: about 2¼ cups. *Eleanor Brandt, Arlington, Texas.*

SNOW PEA-SHRIMP COMBO

1 (6-ounce) package frozen snow peas
1 tablespoon salad oil
¾ cup chicken broth
1 (5-ounce) can water chestnuts, drained and sliced
½ teaspoon monosodium glutamate
¼ teaspoon salt
1 tablespoon cornstarch
2 tablespoons water
1 (5-ounce) can medium shrimp, drained

Sauté snow peas in hot oil until thawed. Stir in broth, water chestnuts, monosodium glutamate, and salt. Cover and cook 2 minutes, stirring twice. Dissolve cornstarch in water; add to snow pea mixture. Cook 2 minutes over low heat, stirring constantly, until thickened. Add shrimp; toss gently, and cook only until shrimp is heated through. Yield: 2 to 3 servings.
Doris Garton,
Shenandoah, Virginia.

SHRIMP BOATS

6 medium potatoes
½ cup butter or margarine
1 cup shredded sharp Cheddar cheese
Dash of cayenne
½ teaspoon salt
2 tablespoons minced onion
¾ cup half-and-half
2 (4½-ounce) cans broken shrimp, drained
Paprika

Bake potatoes at 425° for 45 minutes or until done; cool slightly. Cut in half lengthwise, and carefully scoop out pulp; leave shells intact.

Combine potato pulp, butter, cheese, cayenne, salt, onion, and half-and-half in a large mixing bowl; beat until smooth. Stir in shrimp. Stuff potato shells with mixture; sprinkle with paprika. Bake at 450° for 15 minutes. Yield: 12 servings.

Note: Shrimp Boats may be wrapped in foil and frozen before baking. To serve, unwrap and bake at 450° for 30 minutes.
Miss Lucile Freese,
Nashville, Tennessee.

SHRIMP MOUSSE

2 envelopes unflavored gelatin
½ cup cold water
1 (10¾-ounce) can tomato soup, undiluted
3 (3-ounce) packages cream cheese
1 cup mayonnaise
2 tablespoons lemon juice
2 tablespoons Worcestershire sauce
1 to 2 tablespoons hot sauce
2 (4½-ounce) cans small shrimp, drained
½ cup finely chopped onion
½ cup finely chopped green pepper
½ cup finely chopped celery
1 cup chopped ripe olives
1 cup chopped parsley

Soften gelatin in cold water; set aside.

Heat soup in a medium saucepan; add the cream cheese. Cook over medium heat, stirring constantly, until mixture is smooth. Stir in softened gelatin, mayonnaise, lemon juice, Worcestershire sauce, and hot sauce. Add remaining ingredients, mixing well. Spoon into a 7-cup mold, and chill until firm. Unmold and garnish as desired. Yield: 10 to 12 servings. *Mrs. John Sherman, Dallas, Texas.*

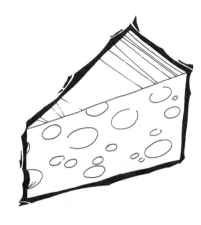

SHRIMP-CRAB PUFF

12 slices white bread, crusts removed
3 cups milk
4 eggs, beaten
1 teaspoon salt
⅛ teaspoon pepper
1 (4½-ounce) can small shrimp, drained
1 (7-ounce) package frozen crabmeat, thawed and flaked
1 cup finely chopped celery
1 (10¾-ounce) can cream of mushroom soup, undiluted
1½ cups shredded Cheddar cheese

Cut bread slices in half. Arrange half the bread in a greased 13- x 9- x 2-inch baking pan.

Combine milk, eggs, salt, and pepper; beat with a fork until mixed well. Pour over bread in baking pan. Combine shrimp, crabmeat, and celery; toss well, and spoon evenly over bread-egg mixture. Top with remaining bread. Cover casserole, and refrigerate overnight.

Spoon soup over bread, and bake at 350° for 1 hour and 15 minutes or until puffy and golden brown. Sprinkle cheese over casserole, and bake an additional 15 minutes. Let stand a few minutes before cutting into squares. Yield: 12 servings. *Mrs. Carl Ramay, Plano, Texas.*

Sandwich Fixings To Mix And Match

Sandwiches are fun to make and eat, especially when you keep the varieties of bread and fillings interesting. So we are offering a selection of fillings and breads that you can mix and match.

We found these combinations particularly good: barbecued lamb tucked in Pocket Bread, and Ham-and-Egg Spread between slices of Coffee Can Lightbread. Even pimiento cheese takes on a whole new appeal when seasoned with garlic and mustard and spread on homemade Whole Wheat Bran Bread.

BARBECUED LAMB

1 teaspoon minced onion
1½ teaspoons butter or margarine
½ cup catsup
½ teaspoon Worcestershire sauce
½ teaspoon chili powder
¼ teaspoon salt
¼ cup Madeira wine
1 pound cubed lamb
2 tablespoons butter or margarine

Sauté onion in 1½ teaspoons butter until tender; stir in next 5 ingredients. Simmer, uncovered, 5 minutes. Pour over lamb; cover and marinate in refrigerator 2 hours.

Place lamb and marinade on aluminum foil, and dot with 2 tablespoons butter; turn up edges of foil to retain juices. Cook over hot coals 20 minutes; turn and cook an additional 20 minutes, basting frequently with marinade. Yield: about 4 servings. *Mrs. Mary Garner, St. Petersburg, Florida.*

■ The procedure for making this bread is involved, but it's worth the effort.

POCKET BREAD

1 package dry yeast
1 tablespoon sugar
3 cups warm water (105° to 115°)
9 cups all-purpose flour
1 tablespoon salt
1 tablespoon salad oil

Combine yeast, sugar, and water; set aside 5 minutes.

Make a well in center of flour; add salt, salad oil, and half of yeast mixture.

Beat well. Add remaining yeast mixture, beating well.

Turn dough out on a well-floured surface. Divide dough in half; cover half, and set aside.

Divide other half of dough into 10 equal pieces; knead each piece 2½ minutes or until smooth and elastic. Form each piece into a ball, and place seam side down on towels. Cover with dry towel; place damp towel on top. Repeat process with remaining half of dough.

Let balls of dough rise in a warm place (85°), free from drafts, 1 to 1½ hours or until slightly puffy.

Place each ball of dough on a well-floured surface; roll into a 6-inch circle. Shake off excess flour, and place on dry towels; cover with dry towel, then damp towel. Place plastic wrap on top. Let rise in a warm place (85°), free from drafts, 1 hour or until slightly puffy.

Lift circles carefully, and place ½ inch apart on lightly greased cookie sheets; do not stretch dough. Place oven rack 2 inches from bottom heating element. Bake bread at 475° for 4 to 6 minutes or until bottom is lightly browned (it will puff, forming a pocket). Immediately turn oven to broil. Broil bread 4 inches from broiler element 30 to 60 seconds or until lightly browned (watch carefully to prevent overbrowning). Place on towels. When cool to touch, flatten each piece by gently pressing down with fingertips.

Repeat baking process with remaining bread. Package bread in airtight containers, and store in refrigerator. Yield: 20 servings.

Note: Bread may be frozen. Thaw and reheat at 300° for 5 minutes. *Anne Ringer, Warner Robins, Georgia.*

WHOLE WHEAT BRAN BREAD

1 package dry yeast
¼ cup warm water (105° to 115°)
½ cup milk
3 tablespoons butter or margarine
2 tablespoons molasses
1 tablespoon brown sugar
1 teaspoon salt
1 cup 100% bran cereal
1 cup whole wheat flour, divided
1 egg
1 cup all-purpose flour
Melted butter or margarine

Combine yeast and water in a small bowl; set aside 5 minutes.

Combine milk, 3 tablespoons butter, molasses, brown sugar, and salt in a saucepan. Place over medium-low heat until steaming. Pour into a large mixing bowl; immediately stir in cereal. Cool to lukewarm (105° to 115°).

Add ½ cup whole wheat flour to cereal mixture; beat well. Add yeast mixture and egg, beating well. Stir in remaining whole wheat flour and all-purpose flour.

Turn dough out on a floured surface, and knead 5 to 8 minutes or until smooth and elastic. Place in a well-greased bowl, turning to grease top. Cover and let rise in a warm place (85°), free from drafts, 1½ to 2 hours or until doubled in bulk.

Punch dough down, and shape into a smooth ball. Place on a greased cookie sheet, and lightly press to flatten bottom. Cover; let rise in a warm place, free from drafts, until doubled in bulk. Bake at 350° for 25 minutes or until loaf sounds hollow when tapped. Brush hot loaf with melted butter. Remove from cookie sheet; cool on wire rack. Yield: 1 loaf. *Mrs. James A. Tuthill, Virginia Beach, Virginia.*

GARLIC PIMIENTO CHEESE SPREAD

4 (4-ounce) jars diced pimientos, drained
½ cup plus 2 tablespoons sandwich and salad sauce
1 pint salad dressing or mayonnaise
2 tablespoons lemon juice
1 teaspoon prepared mustard
½ teaspoon Worcestershire sauce
½ teaspoon red pepper
3 cloves garlic, crushed
2 pounds sharp Cheddar cheese, shredded

Combine all ingredients except cheese in a large mixing bowl; mix until smooth. Add cheese, beating well; chill thoroughly. Yield: about 2 quarts. *Mrs. James S. Tiffany, Dallas, Texas.*

When Pocket Bread is filled with barbecued lamb, chopped tomatoes, and shredded lettuce, it's a meal in itself.

COFFEE CAN LIGHTBREAD

4 cups all-purpose flour, divided
1 package dry yeast
½ cup water
½ cup milk
½ cup salad oil
¼ cup sugar
1 teaspoon salt
2 eggs, beaten

Combine 1½ cups flour and yeast in a large bowl; stir well, and set aside.

Combine water, milk, salad oil, sugar, and salt in a saucepan; mix well. Place over medium heat until mixture reaches 105° to 115°; pour into yeast mixture, and beat with electric mixer until smooth. Add eggs, mixing well.

Add remaining flour to yeast mixture; beat with electric mixer until smooth and elastic. (Batter will be very stiff.)

Spoon batter into 2 well-greased 1-pound coffee cans. Cover with coffee can lids. Let rise in a warm place (85°), free from drafts, 35 to 45 minutes or until batter rises to within 1½ to 2 inches from top of can.

Uncover cans and bake bread at 375° for 30 to 35 minutes or until golden brown; loaf should sound hollow when tapped. Cool in cans 10 minutes. Remove from cans, and cool on wire racks. Yield: 2 loaves.

Diane E. France,
Bel Air, Maryland.

HAM-AND-EGG SPREAD

3 cups ground cooked ham
¼ cup chopped pickle
1½ teaspoons finely chopped pimiento
4 hard-cooked eggs, minced
½ cup mayonnaise

Combine all ingredients, mixing well; chill. Yield: about 3½ cups.

Mrs. Parke LaGourgue Cory,
Neosho, Missouri.

Bread: The Fragrant Dinner Bell

No dinner bell is more effective than the aroma of freshly baked bread. In fact, your family will probably beat you to the table. Our readers have shared their bread specialties, and there's one to match the skill of any baker.

When properly stored, leftover bread can't be distinguished from freshly baked. Refrigeration only hastens staling, but freezing in airtight freezer wrap preserves the freshness of bread for as long as two months. To serve, thaw wrapped bread at room temperature. If the original wrapper is unsuited to oven heat, transfer bread to foil; bake at 300° for 12 minutes or until hot.

SOUR CREAM BREAD

1 package dry yeast
3 tablespoons sugar
¼ cup warm water (105° to 115°)
1 (16-ounce) carton commercial sour cream
1 tablespoon salt
¼ teaspoon soda
4½ cups all-purpose flour

Dissolve yeast and sugar in warm water in a small mixing bowl; let stand 5 minutes. Combine sour cream, salt, and soda in a large mixing bowl; add yeast mixture, mixing well. Gradually add flour, and mix well.

Turn dough out on a lightly floured surface, and knead 1 to 2 minutes or until smooth and elastic. Shape into a ball; place in a greased bowl, turning to grease top. Cover and let rise in a warm place (85°), free from drafts, 1½ hours or until doubled in bulk.

Punch dough down, and divide in half. Place each half in a greased 9- x 5- x 3-inch loafpan. Cover and let rise until doubled in bulk (about 1 hour). Bake at 375° for 35 to 40 minutes. Yield: 2 loaves.

Mrs. Sue-Sue Hartstern,
Louisville, Kentucky.

BUTTERMILK YEAST ROLLS

1 package dry yeast
¼ cup warm water (105° to 115°)
1½ cups warm buttermilk (105° to 115°)
3 tablespoons sugar
½ cup melted shortening
About 4½ cups all-purpose flour
½ teaspoon soda
1 teaspoon salt

Dissolve yeast in warm water in a mixing bowl. Add buttermilk, sugar, and shortening; mix well. Combine flour, soda, and salt; gradually add to yeast mixture, mixing well.

Turn dough out onto a lightly floured surface; knead until smooth and elastic (about 7 minutes). Let rest 10 minutes.

Shape dough into 1½-inch balls, and place in 2 greased 9-inch round pans. Let rise in a warm place (85°), free from drafts, about 1 hour or until doubled in bulk. Bake at 400° for 15 to 20 minutes. Yield: about 1½ dozen.

Mrs. Charles Davis, Jr.,
Birmingham, Alabama.

EASY CRESCENT ROLLS

1 cup milk, scalded
¼ cup sugar
⅓ cup vegetable oil
1 tablespoon salt
2 packages dry yeast
¼ cup warm water (105° to 115°)
2 eggs, beaten
5 cups all-purpose flour
Melted butter or margarine

Combine milk, sugar, vegetable oil, and salt in a large mixing bowl; stir until sugar and salt are dissolved. Cool to 105° to 115°.

Dissolve yeast in warm water. Add yeast mixture and eggs to milk mixture; mix well. Gradually add flour, mixing well. Place dough in a greased bowl, turning to grease top; cover and let rise in a warm place (85°), free from drafts, about 1½ hours or until doubled in bulk.

Punch dough down and divide into 5 portions. Turn each portion out on a lightly floured surface, and knead 4 or 5 times. Roll into a 12-inch circle, and cut into 8 wedges. Roll up each wedge, beginning at wide end. Dip in melted butter, and place on baking sheets.

Let rise 1 hour in a warm place (85°). Bake at 375° for 10 minutes. Yield: 3¼ dozen.
Deanne Anthony,
Benton, Arkansas.

SWISS CHEESE BREAD

½ cup water
2 tablespoons sugar
1 tablespoon salt
2 tablespoons butter or margarine
8 ounces process Swiss cheese, cubed
1 (12-ounce) can beer
2 packages dry yeast
5 cups all-purpose flour, divided
Melted butter or margarine

Combine first 6 ingredients in a medium saucepan. Place over medium heat until cheese melts, stirring constantly. Remove from heat, and let cool to 120° to 130°.

Combine yeast and 2 cups flour in a large mixing bowl; add cheese mixture, mixing well. Beat at medium speed of electric mixer 3 minutes. Gradually add remaining flour, mixing well. Dough will be sticky.

Turn dough out on a lightly floured surface; knead until smooth and elastic (about 5 to 8 minutes). Place in a greased bowl, turning to grease top. Cover and let rise in a warm place (85°), free from drafts, 1 hour.

Punch dough down, and divide in half. Roll each half into an 11- x 5-inch rectangle; cut lengthwise into 3 equal pieces. Place on a greased 13- x 9- x 2-inch baking pan, and firmly pinch pieces together at one end to seal. Braid pieces together, and pinch loose ends together to seal.

Cover and let rise in a warm place (85°), free from drafts, 1 hour. Bake at 350° for 40 to 45 minutes. Brush with melted butter. Yield: 2 loaves.
Mrs. Shirley Crowell,
Princeton, Kentucky.

SPICED APPLE MUFFINS

2 cups all-purpose flour
¾ cup finely chopped apple
⅓ cup sugar
4 teaspoons baking powder
¾ teaspoon salt
1 teaspoon ground cinnamon
¼ teaspoon ground nutmeg
1 cup milk
¼ cup shortening, melted
1 egg, beaten

Combine first 7 ingredients; make a well in center of mixture. Combine milk, shortening, and egg; add to flour mixture, stirring just until moistened. Spoon batter into greased muffin tins, filling two-thirds full. Bake at 400° for 25 minutes or until golden brown. Yield: about 15 muffins.
Mrs. Harvey Kidd,
Hernando, Mississippi.

Tip: To make good yeast breads, it is essential to learn the "feel" of the dough. This takes experience. You will note that most recipes state "about" followed by the number of cups of flour. Some flours absorb more liquid than others, and it is difficult to give an exact measurement. Too much flour results in a heavy loaf, crumbliness, and dryness with an off-flavor. Keep the dough on the soft side, but still easy to handle.

SWISS CHEESE CORNBREAD

2 eggs, slightly beaten
1 (7½-ounce) package corn muffin mix
1 (8¾-ounce) can cream-style corn
1 (7-ounce) can whole kernel corn, drained
1 (8-ounce) carton commercial sour cream
⅓ cup melted butter or margarine
1 cup (¼ pound) shredded Swiss cheese

Combine all ingredients except cheese in a medium mixing bowl, mixing well. Pour into a greased 12- x 7½- x 1½-inch baking pan.

Bake at 350° for 35 minutes. Sprinkle cheese over top; continue baking for 10 to 15 minutes. Yield: 12 servings.
Eunice Beeman,
Fort Lauderdale, Florida.

CORNMEAL ROLLS

1½ cups all-purpose flour
¾ cup cornmeal
4 teaspoons baking powder
¼ teaspoon baking soda
1 teaspoon salt
¼ cup shortening
1 egg, slightly beaten
¾ cup buttermilk
Butter or margarine

Combine first 5 ingredients; cut in shortening until mixture resembles coarse meal. Stir egg into buttermilk; add to dry ingredients, mixing well.

Turn dough out on a lightly floured board, and knead 1 to 2 minutes. Roll dough to ½-inch thickness, and cut into 2½-inch rounds with a biscuit cutter.

With dull edge of knife, make a crease just off-center on each round; brush with melted butter. Fold rounds over so top overlaps slightly; press edges together. Place rolls on a greased baking sheet; bake at 475° for 12 minutes. Yield: about 1½ dozen.
Mrs. J. N. Richardson,
Nashville, Tennessee.

A typical Southern breakfast with country ham and all the trimmings will get your family off to a good start. Menu and recipes begin on page 37.

Above: Delight brunch guests with Eggs Florentine (page 39): poached eggs layered with spinach, ham, and tomato slices on onion-flavored buns, then topped with hollandaise.

Left: For a special breakfast or brunch serv one of these eye openers: Bloody Marys, Orange-Champagne Cocktail, or Pep Shake Recipes begin on page 38.

Appetizers Served Piping Hot

Give your guests a warm welcome by offering them a tempting assortment of hot appetizers—Cocktail Meatballs simmered in sweet-and-sour sauce, Parmesan-flavored Asparagus Rollups, and Crab Crisps broiled to a golden brown.

To keep the appetizers appealingly hot—and you out of the kitchen—plan to use your chafing dish and warming tray for serving.

COCKTAIL MEATBALLS

1 (12-ounce) bottle chili sauce
1 (18-ounce) jar grape jelly
¼ cup water
1½ pounds ground chuck
2 tablespoons chopped parsley
½ teaspoon salt
¼ teaspoon pepper
1 teaspoon prepared mustard
2 teaspoons chili powder
1 clove garlic, finely chopped

Combine chili sauce, grape jelly, and water in a saucepan or chafing dish; heat, stirring until well blended.

Combine remaining ingredients in a small bowl, mixing well; shape into 1-inch balls, and place in jelly sauce. Simmer over low heat 30 minutes or until done. Serve with toothpicks. Yield: about 3 dozen.

Mrs. Robert W. Thomas,
Madison, Mississippi.

BACON-WRAPPED WATER CHESTNUTS

1 (8-ounce) can water chestnuts, drained
¼ cup soy sauce
¼ cup sugar
8 slices bacon, cut in half crosswise

Marinate water chestnuts in soy sauce at least 30 minutes; drain and roll each in sugar. Wrap each water chestnut with a piece of bacon, securing with a toothpick; arrange on cake rack in a shallow baking pan. Bake at 400° for 30 minutes or until golden brown. Drain on paper towels. Keep hot on warming tray. Yield: about 16 appetizers.

Note: This appetizer may be prepared ahead of time and stored in refrigerator until ready to bake.

Mrs. Janet C. Kasper,
Fort Worth, Texas.

CRAB CRISPS

1 (6½-ounce) can crabmeat, drained and flaked, or 1 (6-ounce) package frozen crabmeat, thawed, drained, and flaked
1 (8-ounce) carton commercial sour cream
½ cup shredded Swiss cheese
2 tablespoons dry onion soup mix
3 dozen melba toast rounds or crackers

Combine first 4 ingredients, mixing well. Spread on toast rounds or crackers. Broil 4 to 5 inches from heat 2 to 3 minutes. Yield: 3 dozen.

Mrs. Marvin Reavis,
Austin, Texas.

CHEESE AND MUSHROOM BALLS

1 (4-ounce) package blue cheese, crumbled
3 cups fresh breadcrumbs, divided
1 (2½-ounce) jar sliced mushrooms, drained and finely chopped
2 tablespoons chopped green onion
½ teaspoon ground savory
¼ teaspoon pepper
2 eggs, slightly beaten
Vegetable oil

Combine cheese, 2 cups breadcrumbs, mushrooms, onion, savory, pepper, and eggs in a medium mixing bowl; mix well. Let stand 10 minutes, and shape into 1-inch balls. Roll cheese balls in remaining breadcrumbs.

Heat vegetable oil to 350°. Add cheese balls, and fry until golden brown. Drain well on paper towels. Yield: about 2 dozen.

Mrs. Grace L. Grogaard,
Baltimore, Maryland.

ASPARAGUS ROLLUPS

12 slices white bread, crusts removed
1 (8-ounce) container whipped cream cheese
2 tablespoons chopped chives
8 slices bacon, cooked and crumbled
24 fresh asparagus spears, partially cooked
¼ cup melted butter or margarine
Parmesan cheese

Use a rolling pin to flatten each slice of bread.

Combine cream cheese, chives, and bacon, stirring well. Spread bread with cheese mixture, covering to edges. Place 2 asparagus spears on each slice of bread; roll up, and place seam side down on a greased baking sheet. Brush each with butter, and sprinkle with Parmesan cheese. Bake at 400° for 12 minutes. Yield: 12 servings.

Mrs. Phil Higgins,
Corrigan, Texas.

Franks In And Out Of The Bun

Versatile, simple-to-prepare frankfurters are often the answer to balancing the meat budget. And if you think you've fixed them in every way possible, you'll welcome the opportunity to try Split Pea and Frankfurter Soup. This flavorful and creamy soup is seasoned with franks rather than ham.

Following are some other new ways with frankfurters, including franks in a tangy barbecue sauce and franks in a layered casserole.

TANGY FRANK BARBECUE

2 tablespoons prepared mustard
2 (8-ounce) cans tomato sauce
½ cup dark corn syrup
⅓ cup minced onion
2 tablespoons Worcestershire sauce
½ teaspoon celery seeds
¼ to ½ teaspoon hot sauce
⅓ cup vinegar
1 (16-ounce) package frankfurters, scored diagonally
Warm buns or hot cooked rice

Combine first 8 ingredients in a skillet; bring to a boil, stirring constantly. Reduce heat, and simmer 30 minutes; stir occasionally.

Add frankfurters to skillet, and simmer an additional 10 minutes or until frankfurters are thoroughly heated. Serve in warm buns or over rice. Yield: 8 to 10 servings.

Mrs. Peggy A. Hankins,
Columbia, South Carolina.

SPLIT PEA AND FRANKFURTER SOUP

1 cup split peas
1 quart water
1½ teaspoons salt
1 small onion, sliced
½ cup chopped celery
3 frankfurters, cut into ¼-inch slices
2 tablespoons melted butter or margarine
Croutons (optional)

Sort peas, and wash thoroughly; set peas aside.

Combine water and salt in a large Dutch oven; bring to a boil. Add peas, and allow water to return to a boil. Cover and cook over low heat 1 hour, stirring often. Add onion and celery, and continue cooking over low heat 30 minutes, stirring often.

Sauté frankfurter slices in butter until lightly browned; set aside.

Place pea mixture in container of electric blender, and process until smooth. Return pea mixture to Dutch oven. Add frankfurter slices, and simmer 10 to 15 minutes, stirring often. Serve with croutons, if desired. Yield: 4 servings.   *Mrs. R. W. McGrath,*
Orlando, Florida.

LAYERED FRANKFURTER CASSEROLE

⅛ teaspoon salt
Dash of pepper
1 (11-ounce) can Cheddar cheese soup, undiluted
1½ cups hot cooked rice
½ cup chopped onion
¼ cup chopped green pepper
1 cup (¼ pound) shredded Cheddar cheese
5 frankfurters, cut into ½-inch slices
½ cup commercial barbecue sauce

Stir salt and pepper into soup. Layer rice, onion, green pepper, soup, and cheese in a greased 1½-quart casserole; arrange frankfurter slices evenly over cheese layer, and pour barbecue sauce on top. Bake casserole at 350° for 35 to 40 minutes or until lightly browned. Yield: 4 servings.   *Mrs. B. N. Brown,*
Germantown, Tennessee.

BEANY KRAUT AND FRANKS

1 (16-ounce) package frankfurters
1 (28-ounce) can pork and beans
1 (16-ounce) can sauerkraut, drained
½ cup catsup
1 teaspoon chili powder

Set aside 6 frankfurters; cut remainder into ¼-inch slices. Combine frankfurter slices and remaining ingredients in a large mixing bowl; mix well. Spoon into a well-greased, shallow 2-quart casserole; bake at 350° for 30 minutes. Arrange reserved frankfurters on top, and bake an additional 15 minutes. Yield: 6 servings.   *Lee Roy Perdue,*
Wrens, Georgia.

Basic Rice Goes Three Ways

If you're searching for new ways to serve rice, these recipes created by Louis and Gaye Joyner of Birmingham offer variations to suit any menu. All begin with a basic rice recipe that is flavored with chicken or beef bouillon cubes.

One variation, Rice with Vegetables, can be enjoyed as a side dish with all of the vegetables called for, or a combination of some of them. Shrimp and Sausage Rice and Indian Rice transform the basic recipe into an economical main dish and offer a way to use leftover shrimp or chicken.

BASIC RICE

½ cup regular rice
1 tablespoon melted butter or margarine
1 or 2 chicken or beef bouillon cubes
1 cup hot water

Sauté rice in butter over low heat in a stove-top, ovenproof casserole until golden brown. Dissolve bouillon cube in water; add to rice, and bring to a boil. Remove from heat; cover, and bake at 350° for 20 to 25 minutes or until all liquid is absorbed. Yield: 2 servings.

Tip: Shop alone and after you have eaten. Studies show that people tend to buy more when hungry or when accompanied by others.

RICE WITH VEGETABLES

1 Basic Rice recipe
1 small onion, chopped
½ green pepper, chopped
¼ cup chopped celery
½ cup sliced fresh mushrooms

Prepare rice according to Basic Rice recipe, sautéing vegetables in butter along with rice. Yield: 2 servings.
Note: Any combination of the vegetables may be used.

SHRIMP AND SAUSAGE RICE

1 Basic Rice recipe
¼ pound medium shrimp, cooked, peeled, and deveined
⅓ pound Polish sausage or smoked sausage, cut into ¼-inch slices
2 medium tomatoes, peeled and chopped
⅛ teaspoon pepper
¼ teaspoon paprika

Prepare rice according to Basic Rice recipe, except stir in remaining ingredients before baking. Cover and bake at 350° for 20 to 25 minutes or until liquid is absorbed. Yield: 2 servings.

INDIAN RICE

1 Basic Rice recipe
2 to 3 tablespoons seedless raisins
1 tablespoon toasted sliced almonds
¼ teaspoon curry powder
1 to 1½ cups chopped cooked chicken

Prepare rice according to Basic Rice recipe except for baking. Stir in all ingredients except chicken. Cover and bake at 350° for 10 minutes. Remove rice from oven, and stir in chicken. Return to oven and bake an additional 10 minutes or until liquid is absorbed. Yield: 2 servings.

Tip: Buy quantities you can store and use. Large quantities are usually bargains, but they may not be bargains for small families if they spoil before being used or if leftovers have to be thrown out. Staples (flour, sugar, etc.) generally cost less per pound if purchased in large quantities.

April

O ne of the delights of April is
the abundance of fresh asparagus. Enjoy its delicate flavor
in a variety of dishes from plain to
fancy. Or if a special luncheon or
dinner is on your entertaining calendar, select one of our elegant desserts. They range from dazzling
Double-Chocolate Torte to a lemon-filled cake roll.

Add a special touch to your favorite fruit or vegetable salad with a
homemade dressing. But if a tossed
salad doesn't fit the menu, prepare
one of our tempting alternatives.
Freshly baked breadsticks are a flavorful accompaniment to any salad.

If the thought of baking a soufflé
leaves you skeptical, read our test
kitchen tips and then try your hand at
one of the four variations. You will
find it easier than you thought! And
on those days when you run short of
time, select one of our quick and easy
recipes. They are designed to save
you time and satisfy the family.

Capture The Flavor Of Fresh Asparagus

Spring is the time for bright green fresh asparagus spears to be brought to the table in a delightful array of dishes. An ideal way to enjoy the delicate flavor of asparagus is to serve it cold on a bed of lettuce with a tart yogurt dressing. Asparagus Goldenrod calls for asparagus on toast points, topped with a rich white sauce and hard-cooked eggs. Other choices include Asparagus Soufflé, French-Fried Asparagus, and Sautéed Asparagus.

When buying fresh asparagus, always select stalks that are green and tender; tips should be well formed and tightly closed. One pound usually contains 16 to 20 stalks, which is enough for 3 or 4 servings. To help retain freshness, cut a thin slice from the base of each stalk and wrap a moist paper towel around the bottom of the stalks before placing in the refrigerator.

To prepare fresh asparagus, snap off tough ends by bending the stalk gently until it breaks. Wash spears thoroughly in warm water, and remove scales from stalks with a vegetable peeler or knife. To cook, tie spears with string in serving-size bundles. Stand the bundles in the bottom of a double boiler; cover only the stalks with boiling salted water. Invert the top of the double boiler over the spears, and cook until crisp-tender (10 to 12 minutes).

ASPARAGUS GOLDENROD

¼ cup butter or margarine
¼ cup all-purpose flour
2 cups milk
½ teaspoon salt
Dash of pepper
1 cup cottage cheese
1½ to 2 pounds fresh asparagus, cooked
3 slices toast, cut in half
3 hard-cooked eggs, finely chopped

Melt butter in a heavy saucepan over low heat; blend in flour, and cook 1 minute, stirring constantly. Gradually add milk; cook over medium heat, stirring constantly, until thickened. Stir in salt and pepper. Fold in cottage cheese; cook over low heat 1 minute.

Place asparagus on toast on a serving platter, and top with sauce; sprinkle with egg. Yield: 6 servings.
Eleanor Brandt,
Arlington, Texas.

ASPARAGUS WITH YOGURT DRESSING

1 pound fresh asparagus
½ cup plain yogurt
1 small clove garlic, crushed
1 tablespoon chopped parsley
¼ teaspoon salt
1 small head Boston or Bibb lettuce
1 hard-cooked egg yolk, sieved

Snap off tough ends of asparagus. Remove scales with knife or vegetable peeler.

Cook asparagus in boiling water about 10 minutes or until crisp-tender; drain. Cool, and place in refrigerator to chill.

Combine yogurt, garlic, parsley, and salt; stir well. Chill.

Place asparagus on bed of lettuce; top with yogurt dressing, and sprinkle with egg yolk. Yield: 4 servings.
Mrs. Bruce Fowler,
Woodruff, South Carolina.

FRENCH-FRIED ASPARAGUS

2 pounds fresh asparagus spears
1 egg
¼ cup water
¼ cup soy sauce
½ cup all-purpose flour
Vegetable oil

Snap off tough ends of asparagus. Remove scales from stalks with knife or vegetable peeler.

Combine egg, water, soy sauce, and flour; beat until smooth. Heat vegetable oil to 375°. Dip asparagus in batter, and fry in oil until golden brown. Drain on paper towels. Yield: 6 to 8 servings.
Carol Forcum,
Marion, Illinois.

ASPARAGUS SOUFFLE

3 tablespoons butter or margarine
3 tablespoons all-purpose flour
1 cup milk
3 eggs, separated
Salt and pepper to taste
Dash of ground nutmeg
¼ teaspoon whole basil leaves
1 cup finely chopped cooked asparagus
3 tablespoons grated Parmesan cheese

Melt butter in a heavy saucepan over low heat; blend in flour, and cook 1 minute, stirring constantly. Gradually add milk; cook over medium heat, stirring constantly, until thickened.

Beat egg yolks. Add a small amount of hot white sauce to yolks, and mix well; stir yolk mixture into the remaining white sauce. Stir in seasonings, asparagus, and cheese.

Beat egg whites until stiff; fold into asparagus mixture. Spoon into a lightly greased 1½-quart soufflé or casserole dish. Bake at 375° about 45 minutes. Serve soufflé immediately. Yield: 4 to 5 servings.
Susie Hunter,
Gainesville, Florida.

SAUTEED ASPARAGUS

1 pound asparagus
⅛ to ¼ teaspoon salt
Dash of garlic powder
2 to 3 tablespoons melted butter or margarine

Snap off tough ends of asparagus. Remove scales with knife or vegetable peeler; cut each spear into thin strips. Place asparagus, salt, garlic powder, and butter in a medium skillet; cover and cook over medium heat, stirring occasionally, for 3 to 5 minutes or until crisp-tender. Yield: 3 to 4 servings.
Bobbi Getz,
Sarasota, Florida.

Tip: To make successful white sauce, follow this procedure: Melt butter in a saucepan; then remove from heat to blend in flour and add liquid. Use cold milk; add it gradually, stirring constantly. Return to heat; cook, stirring constantly, until mixture thickens and bubbles. Add seasonings; cook at least 5 minutes, stirring occasionally.

Looking For An Elegant Dessert?

One of the most delightful ways to celebrate a special occasion is to indulge your guests with an elegant dessert. Choose from cream-topped Double-Chocolate Torte, picture-perfect Pear-Glazed Cheesecake, or fruit-filled velvety Peach Charlotte. Other captivating concoctions include a tart Daiquiri Pie and a beautiful meringue-covered lemon cake roll.

These elegant offerings will be even more appealing if you keep a few basic menu-planning guidelines in mind. To complete a hearty satisfying meal, serve a light dessert. A richer finish is in order after a less-filling meal or for a coffee-and-dessert get-together.

DOUBLE-CHOCOLATE TORTE

1¾ cups all-purpose flour
1¾ cups sugar
¼ teaspoon baking powder
1¼ teaspoons soda
1 teaspoon salt
⅔ cup margarine, softened
4 (1-ounce) squares unsweetened chocolate, melted
1¼ cups water
1 teaspoon vanilla extract
3 eggs
Chocolate filling (recipe follows)
Whipped cream (recipe follows)
Grated sweet chocolate

Combine first 9 ingredients in a large mixing bowl, mixing well; then beat 2 minutes at medium speed of electric mixer. Add eggs, and beat an additional 2 minutes.

Spoon one-fourth of batter into each of 4 greased and floured 9-inch cakepans. Bake at 350° for 15 to 18 minutes or until cake tests done. Let cool in pans 10 minutes; remove cake and let cool completely.

Place 1 layer on cake platter; spread with half the chocolate filling. Place another cake layer on top; spread with half the whipped cream. Repeat layers; garnish with grated chocolate. Refrigerate until served. Yield: one 4-layer cake.

Chocolate Filling:

1½ (4-ounce) bars sweet chocolate
¾ cup margarine, softened
½ cup chopped, toasted almonds

Melt chocolate in top of a double boiler; let cool. Add margarine, beating at low speed of electric mixer until smooth. Stir in almonds. Yield: enough for two 9-inch layers.

Whipped Cream:

2 cups whipping cream
1 teaspoon sugar
1 teaspoon vanilla extract

Combine all ingredients in a medium mixing bowl; beat until stiff peaks form. Yield: enough for two 9-inch layers.
Mrs. Nikki Vaughns,
Decatur, Georgia.

PEAR-GLAZED CHEESECAKE

1½ cups graham cracker crumbs
3 tablespoons sugar
¼ cup butter or margarine, melted
2 (8-ounce) packages cream cheese, softened
¾ cup sugar
3 eggs
Grated rind of 1 lemon
1 tablespoon lemon juice
1 teaspoon vanilla extract
¼ teaspoon almond extract
1 (8-ounce) carton commercial sour cream
1 (16-ounce) can pear halves
½ cup strawberries, halved
1 tablespoon lemon juice
Few drops of red food coloring (optional)
1 tablespoon cornstarch

Combine graham cracker crumbs, 3 tablespoons sugar, and butter; mix well. Press mixture into bottom and 1½ inches up sides of a 9-inch springform pan; set aside.

Beat cream cheese with electric mixer until light and fluffy. Gradually add ¾ cup sugar, mixing well. Add eggs, one at a time, beating well after each addition.

Stir in lemon rind, 1 tablespoon lemon juice, flavorings, and sour cream; spoon into crust. Bake at 325° for 50 minutes or until set. Cool thoroughly; chill. Remove sides of springform pan.

Drain pears, reserving ¾ cup liquid; slice each pear half into 4 wedges. Arrange pear slices and strawberry halves on chilled cheesecake as desired.

Combine reserved pear liquid, 1 tablespoon lemon juice, and food coloring, if desired, in a small saucepan; add cornstarch, stirring until dissolved. Cook over low heat until thickened, stirring constantly. Cool slightly, and spoon over cheesecake. Yield: 10 to 12 servings.
Doris Glance,
Union Mills, North Carolina.

CHOCOLATE RUM CAKE

2 (1-ounce) squares unsweetened chocolate
½ cup water
½ cup butter, softened
1½ cups firmly packed light brown sugar
3 eggs
1¾ cups sifted cake flour
1½ teaspoons baking powder
½ teaspoon soda
¼ teaspoon salt
¼ cup rum
Chocolate Rum Frosting

Grease two 9-inch cakepans; line with waxed paper, and grease again. Set aside.

Combine chocolate and water in a small saucepan; place over very low heat. Cook, stirring often, until chocolate melts. Let cool.

Combine butter and sugar; cream until light and fluffy. Add eggs, one at a time, beating well after each addition.

Combine dry ingredients; add to creamed mixture alternately with chocolate, mixing well after each addition. Stir in rum.

Spoon batter into prepared cakepans; bake at 350° for 20 to 25 minutes or until cake tests done. Let cool 5 minutes in pans; remove from pans, peel off waxed paper, and let cool completely.

Spread Chocolate Rum Frosting between layers and on top of cake. Yield: one 9-inch cake.

Chocolate Rum Frosting:

1½ (1-ounce) squares unsweetened chocolate
3 tablespoons semisweet chocolate pieces
1 tablespoon butter
1 cup powdered sugar
1 egg
2 tablespoons milk
2 tablespoons rum

Combine chocolate and butter in top of a double boiler; place over hot water until melted. Set aside.

Combine sugar, egg, milk, and rum; mix until smooth. Stir in chocolate mixture. Place bowl in a larger bowl of ice water; beat until thick and fluffy. Yield: enough for two 9-inch layers.
Bobbie Hathaway,
Clarkston, Georgia.

Tip: All-purpose flour can be substituted for cake flour: 1 cup minus 2 tablespoons of all-purpose flour equals 1 cup cake flour.

SNOW-CAPPED LEMON ROLL

4 eggs, separated
⅓ cup sugar
½ teaspoon grated lemon rind
1 tablespoon lemon juice
⅓ cup sugar
⅔ cup sifted cake flour
¼ teaspoon salt
Powdered sugar
Lemon-Cheese Filling
2 egg whites
¼ cup sugar

Beat 4 egg yolks until light and lemon colored. Gradually add ⅓ cup sugar; continue beating until sugar is dissolved. Stir in lemon rind and juice; set aside.

Beat 4 egg whites until soft peaks form; gradually add ⅓ cup sugar. Continue beating until stiff peaks form and sugar is dissolved; fold into yolks.

Sift together flour and salt, and fold half into egg mixture; then fold in remainder. Spread evenly in a well-greased 15- x 10- x 1-inch jellyroll pan; bake at 350° for 15 minutes. Turn out immediately onto a towel heavily sprinkled with powdered sugar. Starting on short side, roll up cake and towel; let cool.

Unroll cake, and spread with Lemon-Cheese Filling; roll up again, and place on a baking sheet.

Beat remaining 2 egg whites until soft peaks form. Gradually add ¼ cup sugar, beating until stiff peaks form. Spread on sides and top of cake roll; bake at 400° for 8 to 10 minutes or until lightly browned. Yield: one 10-inch cake roll.

Lemon-Cheese Filling:

¾ cup sugar
2 tablespoons cornstarch
Dash of salt
¾ cup cold water
2 egg yolks, slightly beaten
3 tablespoons lemon juice
1 teaspoon butter or margarine
1 (3-ounce) package cream cheese, softened
2 tablespoons whipping cream

Combine sugar, cornstarch, and salt in a medium saucepan; gradually add water, egg yolks, and lemon juice. Stir until smooth. Bring to a boil; cook, stirring constantly, 1 minute. Remove from heat, and stir in butter; cool mixture slightly.

Combine cream cheese and whipping cream, stirring until smooth; add to lemon mixture, and beat until smooth. Yield: about 1¼ cups.

Susan Settlemyre,
Chapel Hill, North Carolina.

DAIQUIRI PIE

1 (8-ounce) package cream cheese, softened
1 (14-ounce) can sweetened condensed milk
1 tablespoon grated lime rind
½ cup fresh lime juice
⅓ cup light rum
1 (9-inch) graham cracker crust
1 tablespoon light rum
1 cup whipping cream
1 teaspoon grated lime rind

Beat cream cheese until smooth and fluffy. Gradually add condensed milk, beating until well blended. Add 1 tablespoon lime rind, lime juice, and ⅓ cup rum; mix well. Pour mixture into piecrust; refrigerate 3 to 4 hours or overnight.

Gradually add 1 tablespoon rum to whipping cream, beating until stiff. Spread over pie, and sprinkle with 1 teaspoon lime rind. Yield: 8 servings.

Edna Chadsey,
Corpus Christi, Texas.

SUGAR COOKIE TORTE

½ cup butter or margarine, softened
½ cup shortening
1½ cups firmly packed light brown sugar
2 eggs, slightly beaten
¼ cup commercial sour cream
1 teaspoon vanilla extract
4 cups all-purpose flour
1 teaspoon soda
1 teaspoon salt
Rich Chocolate Filling
Pecan or walnut halves
Whipped cream (optional)

Cream butter and shortening in a large mixing bowl; add sugar gradually, beating until light and fluffy. Add eggs, sour cream, and vanilla; mix well.

Combine flour, soda, and salt; add to creamed mixture, mixing well. Chill 2 to 3 hours.

Divide dough into 6 equal portions. Roll each portion to ¼-inch thickness on a lightly floured surface; cut into a

9-inch circle. Bake each on a greased cookie sheet at 375° for 12 to 15 minutes; remove from pan while warm, and allow to cool.

Spread Rich Chocolate Filling between layers and on top of torte. Garnish with pecan halves; serve with whipped cream, if desired. Yield: one 9-inch torte.

Rich Chocolate Filling:

4 (1-ounce) squares unsweetened chocolate
½ cup milk
⅓ cup sugar
2 tablespoons cornstarch
¼ teaspoon salt
6 eggs, separated
1½ teaspoons vanilla extract
½ cup butter or margarine, softened
2 cups powdered sugar
½ cup sugar
⅔ cup finely chopped pecans or walnuts

Melt chocolate in a heavy saucepan over low heat; add milk, stirring until mixture is smooth.

Combine ⅓ cup sugar, cornstarch, and salt; add to chocolate, stirring until well blended. Cook over medium heat, stirring constantly, until thickened. Remove from heat, and stir in egg yolks. Place over medium heat; cook, stirring constantly, 1 additional minute. Stir in vanilla, and let cool completely.

Combine butter and powdered sugar; cream until light and fluffy. Add to chocolate mixture, mixing well; chill 1 hour.

Beat egg whites until soft peaks form; gradually add ½ cup sugar. Continue beating until stiff peaks form and sugar is dissolved. Fold into chocolate mixture; stir in pecans. Yield: enough for one 6-layer torte. *Mrs. Dora Miller,*
Canton, North Carolina.

PEACH CHARLOTTE

1 (29-ounce) can cling peach halves
2 tablespoons lemon juice
1½ tablespoons unflavored gelatin
3 eggs, separated
⅛ teaspoon salt
½ cup sugar
1 cup whipping cream, whipped
¼ teaspoon almond extract
1 (3-ounce) package or 8 ladyfingers, split lengthwise

Drain peaches, reserving ¼ cup juice. Combine peach juice and lemon juice; soften gelatin in juices. Mash peaches; measure 1½ cups, and set aside.

Beat egg yolks until thick and lemon colored. Add mashed peaches; cook in top of a double boiler, stirring constantly, until thickened. Stir in gelatin mixture; cool.

Combine egg whites and salt in a large bowl; beat until foamy. Gradually add sugar, and continue to beat until stiff peaks form; fold in gelatin mixture, whipped cream, and almond extract.

Arrange ladyfingers around sides of a 1½-quart mold; spoon in peach mixture. Cover and chill 4 to 5 hours or until firm. Yield: 8 servings.

Mrs. T. E. Cromer,
Anderson, South Carolina.

Pour On A Fresh Dressing

To achieve an outstanding salad, start with fresh ingredients, and add a complementary dressing. These salad dressings provide several new topping ideas for both fruit and vegetable salads. There's a creamy Buttermilk Salad Dressing that's equally good on slaw or salad greens, and a Blue Cheese Dressing that's flavored with port wine. Fruit lovers will especially like Fruit Salad dressing—its sweet flavor will dress up fruit for a salad or a dessert.

YOGURT SALAD DRESSING

1 (8-ounce) carton plain yogurt
¾ cup catsup
1 tablespoon vinegar
Pinch of ground oregano

Combine all ingredients in a small mixing bowl, and mix well. Chill. Serve over tossed salad. Yield: 1½ cups.

Mary Sue Wright,
Blytheville, Arkansas.

FLUFFY FRUIT DRESSING

½ cup mayonnaise
¼ cup dark corn syrup
1 teaspoon lemon juice
Dash of nutmeg
½ cup whipping cream, whipped

Freshen up your favorite fruit or vegetable salad with a new dressing. The flavor can range from sweet to tangy.

Combine first 4 ingredients, mixing well. Fold in whipped cream. Serve over fruit. Yield: 1½ cups.

Mrs. T. J. Compton,
Austin, Texas.

CREAMY ITALIAN-AMERICAN SALAD DRESSING

2 tablespoons olive oil
2 tablespoons vinegar
1 cup mayonnaise
¼ cup catsup
½ teaspoon ground oregano
½ teaspoon garlic powder
3 tablespoons milk

Combine all ingredients, mixing well. Serve over tossed salad. Yield: 2 cups.

Randall DeTrinis,
Brevard, North Carolina.

BUTTERMILK SALAD DRESSING

2 cups buttermilk
2 cups mayonnaise
½ teaspoon garlic powder
1 teaspoon onion powder
2¼ tablespoons parsley flakes
1¾ teaspoons salt
½ teaspoon monosodium glutamate
½ teaspoon white pepper

Combine all ingredients, mixing well. Chill at least 4 hours. Serve with coleslaw or tossed salad. Yield: 4 cups.

Note: Dressing will keep up to 2 weeks in refrigerator.

Mrs. Michael Champagne,
Covington, Louisiana.

PEPPERY SALAD DRESSING

1 medium onion, finely chopped
1½ teaspoons garlic salt
Juice of 1 lemon
2 tablespoons water
1 tablespoon Worcestershire sauce
2 to 3 teaspoons pepper
1½ teaspoons paprika
Dash of hot sauce
½ cup catsup
½ cup vegetable oil
1 cup mayonnaise

Combine all ingredients, mixing well. Serve over tossed salad. Yield: about 2½ cups.

Margaret Connelly,
Fort Worth, Texas.

BLUE CHEESE DRESSING

½ cup wine vinegar with garlic
¼ cup port wine
2 tablespoons vegetable oil
2 tablespoons sugar
2 tablespoons catsup
1 clove garlic, pressed
1 teaspoon paprika
1 teaspoon steak or meat sauce
1 teaspoon Worcestershire sauce
1 teaspoon prepared mustard
¼ cup crumbled blue cheese

Combine all ingredients, mixing well. Serve over tossed salad. Yield: 1 cup.

Mrs. W. Harold Groce,
Arden, North Carolina.

FRUIT SALAD DRESSING

1 cup pineapple juice
2 egg yolks, beaten
Juice of 1 lemon
½ cup sugar
1 tablespoon prepared mustard
Dash of salt
1 cup whipping cream, whipped

Combine all ingredients except whipped cream in a small saucepan. Cook over low heat, stirring occasionally, until smooth and thickened (about 30 minutes). Cool; fold in whipped cream just before serving. Serve over fruit. Yield: about 2 cups.

Mrs. Nancy McKinney,
Elizabethton, Tennessee.

Slice And Season Some Breadsticks

Why buy breadsticks when you can make fresh ones at home? Simply use a loaf of unsliced bread, available in most grocery stores with bakeries. Slice the bread into sticks, season it with garlic, top it with sesame seeds, and bake until toasty brown. Garlic Breadsticks are delicious served with a salad or meat, and you'll particularly enjoy their flavor and texture.

GARLIC BREADSTICKS

1 (9-inch) loaf unsliced bread
½ cup butter or margarine, softened
2 cloves garlic, minced
3 to 4 tablespoons sesame seeds, toasted

Trim crust from bread. Cut loaf in half lengthwise, then in 8 equal crosswise slices.

Combine butter and garlic, mixing well; spread on all sides of bread slices. Arrange on a 15- x 12-inch baking sheet, and sprinkle with sesame seeds. Bake at 400° for 10 minutes or until lightly browned. Yield: 16 sticks.
Mary Lou Vaughn,
Dallas, Texas.

Make Celery The Main Crunch

Celery is considered an essential item in most Southern kitchens as its crunchy texture adds a certain dimension to numerous sauces, stews, salads, and casseroles. However, celery need not be limited to a subordinate role as it acts well as the main ingredient in a great variety of dishes.

Stuff it with a snappy jalapeño cheese mixture for an appetizer or snack, simmer it in a rich broth for Cream of Celery Soup, or cover it with orange glaze for a deliciously different side dish. A simple salad of celery and carrots tossed with a flavorful dressing makes a great substitute for your usual green salad.

Enjoy the crunch of celery in Celery in Orange Sauce.

CELERY SALAD

⅓ cup commercial sour cream
2 tablespoons vegetable oil
1 tablespoon wine vinegar
1 tablespoon sugar
½ teaspoon salt
¼ teaspoon paprika
⅛ teaspoon pepper
3 cups thinly sliced celery
½ cup shredded carrots

Combine first 7 ingredients, mixing well. Add celery and carrots; toss lightly until well mixed. Store in refrigerator. Yield: 4 servings.
Jeannine Allen,
McAllen, Texas.

CELERY IN ORANGE SAUCE

2 chicken bouillon cubes
2 cups boiling water
2 large bunches of celery, cut into 4-inch pieces
4 teaspoons cornstarch
1 (6-ounce) can frozen orange juice concentrate, thawed
2 tablespoons minced onion
2 tablespoons butter or margarine, melted
Orange slices

Dissolve bouillon cubes in boiling water in a large skillet. Add celery; cover and simmer 10 minutes or until tender-crisp. Remove celery, and arrange on a serving platter; set aside, and keep warm.

Combine cornstarch and orange juice, stirring until cornstarch is dissolved; add mixture to broth in skillet, stirring well.

Sauté onion in butter in a small skillet; add to orange juice mixture. Cook over low heat until slightly thickened, stirring constantly. Pour over celery, and garnish with orange slices. Yield: 6 to 8 servings. *Mrs. John R. Armstrong,*
Farwell, Texas.

JALAPENO STUFFED CELERY

1½ cups shredded Cheddar cheese
2 tablespoons mayonnaise
1 tablespoon minced onion
2 teaspoons jalapeño relish or salsa jalapeño
6 to 8 celery stalks, cut into 3-inch pieces
Ripe olive slices (optional)
Vienna sausages, quartered (optional)
Anchovies (optional)
Chili powder to taste

Combine first 4 ingredients, mixing well. Stuff celery pieces with cheese mixture. If desired, top with olive slices, sausages, or anchovies. Sprinkle with chili powder. Yield: 18 to 20 celery sticks. *Mrs. Norman Brown, Jr.,*
Germantown, Tennessee.

CREAM OF CELERY SOUP

6 stalks celery, coarsely chopped
6 green onions, coarsely chopped
3 medium potatoes, coarsely chopped
1 quart milk
½ teaspoon salt
⅛ teaspoon pepper
3 tablespoons whipping cream
1 tablespoon butter or margarine

Combine vegetables, milk, salt, and pepper in a large saucepan. Heat milk mixture to just below the boiling point; simmer 30 minutes or until vegetables are tender, stirring occasionally (do not allow milk to boil).

Pour half of milk mixture into container of electric blender, and process 30 seconds; strain mixture through a sieve into a saucepan. Repeat blending and straining process with remaining half of milk mixture.

Stir whipping cream and butter into soup; heat thoroughly. Serve hot or cold. Yield: 6 to 8 servings.

Maria Frallic,
Hattiesburg, Mississippi.

Mix Up A Special Meat Loaf

There are definitely some secrets to preparing a moist, mouth-watering meat loaf. First, there are no set rules about what types of meats should be used. Our recipes rely on ground ham, ground beef, and bulk sausage for their good flavor and texture.

Another secret for turning plain meat loaf into something special is to add extra ingredients to liven it up. Spicy Meat Loaf is brightened with the addition of vegetable soup. Hawaiian Ham Loaf gains its Polynesian flavor from crushed pineapple, green pepper, and brown sugar. Mozzarella-Layered Meat Loaf is filled with a layer of mozzarella cheese. And for special shape, there's the rolled Stuffed Beef Log, flavored with ground beef, sausage, potatoes, and onion.

Tip: Plan your menus for the week, but stay flexible enough to substitute good buys when you spot them. By planning ahead, you can use leftovers in another day's meal.

STUFFED BEEF LOG

2 pounds ground beef
½ cup quick-cooking oats, uncooked
½ cup finely chopped onion
½ cup milk
1 egg, beaten
2 teaspoons salt
⅛ teaspoon pepper
½ pound mildly seasoned bulk sausage
1 medium potato, peeled and grated
1 cup breadcrumbs
1 egg, beaten
¼ cup finely chopped onion
½ teaspoon salt

Combine first 7 ingredients; mix well. Shape into a 16- x 10-inch rectangle on aluminum foil or waxed paper.

Combine the remaining ingredients; spread evenly over beef mixture. Roll jellyroll fashion, beginning at short side, lifting paper to help roll. Place seam side down on a shallow baking pan. Bake at 300° for 1 hour and 30 minutes. Yield: 10 to 12 servings.

Mrs. Ray Harp,
Shawnee, Oklahoma.

MOZZARELLA-LAYERED MEAT LOAF

1 pound ground beef
½ pound highly seasoned bulk sausage
1 cup breadcrumbs
½ cup finely chopped onion
½ cup grated Parmesan cheese
½ cup milk
1 egg, beaten
2 tablespoons chopped fresh parsley
2 teaspoons salt
½ teaspoon Ac'cent
¼ teaspoon pepper
1 (8-ounce) package mozzarella cheese, sliced

Combine all ingredients except mozzarella cheese; mix well. Spoon half of mixture into a lightly greased 9- x 5- x 3-inch loafpan. Place cheese on top of meat mixture, leaving a 1-inch border on all sides. Spoon remaining meat mixture over cheese, covering cheese layer and pressing lightly on sides to seal. Bake at 350° for 1 hour. Remove from pan before slicing. Yield: 6 servings.

Mrs. Glenna Scherle,
Louisville, Kentucky.

SPICY MEAT LOAF

2 pounds ground chuck
1 (10½-ounce) can vegetable soup, undiluted
½ cup commercial sour cream
¼ cup regular oats, uncooked
¼ cup chopped green pepper
¼ cup chopped onion
1 (1.5-ounce) package spaghetti sauce mix
1 tablespoon minced fresh parsley
1 teaspoon prepared mustard
½ cup catsup

Combine all ingredients except catsup. Spoon mixture into a well-greased 9- x 5- x 3-inch loafpan. Spoon catsup over meat mixture. Bake at 350° for 1½ hours. Let stand 10 minutes before removing from pan. Yield: 6 to 8 servings.
Susan Settlemyre,
Carrboro, North Carolina.

HAWAIIAN HAM LOAF

1 (8-ounce) can crushed pineapple
2 tablespoons brown sugar
1½ cups quick-cooking oats, uncooked
⅓ cup tomato juice
4 cups ground cooked ham
½ pound highly seasoned bulk sausage
⅓ cup diced green pepper
2 eggs, slightly beaten
½ teaspoon salt
Parsley (optional)

Drain pineapple, reserving juice. Combine pineapple juice and sugar in a small saucepan; cook over low heat until sugar dissolves. Pour pineapple juice mixture over uncooked oats; add tomato juice.

Combine remaining ingredients; mix well. Stir in oats mixture. Spoon into a 9- x 5- x 3-inch loafpan or shape into a loaf and place on a shallow baking pan. Bake at 350° for 1½ hours. Garnish with parsley, if desired. Yield: 6 to 8 servings.
Eva G. Key,
Isle of Palms, South Carolina.

Tip: During the week, keep a shopping list handy to write down items as you need them. This will eliminate unnecessary trips to the store. Before your weekly shopping trip, make a complete shopping list. If the list is arranged according to the layout of the store, you'll save time and steps.

Old Favorites With Buttermilk

If anyone knows more than mothers, it must be grandmothers, and that is surely the reason so many old family recipes call for that rich flavor enhancer, buttermilk. Because buttermilk has long been a Southern staple, you still hear many older Southerners specify "sweet milk" or "buttermilk" when they ask for their milk.

A 200-year-old recipe for brown bread, made with buttermilk, comes from Mrs. D. W. Proffitt of Maryville, Tennessee. The recipe first came to the states from Manchester, England, around 1830. We especially like it warm with butter or cream cheese.

A Texas reader shares her recipe for buttermilk pie. She says her secret is to beat the egg mixture until very fluffy.

EIGHTEENTH-CENTURY BROWN BREAD

2 cups whole wheat flour
1 cup cornmeal
2 teaspoons soda
1 teaspoon salt
2½ cups buttermilk
½ cup molasses

Combine dry ingredients in a large bowl; add buttermilk and molasses, stirring well.

Spoon batter into a greased 2-pound coffee can. Cover with foil, and tie securely with string. Place can on rack in a 5-quart Dutch oven. Add enough hot water to cover lower half of can. Bring water to a boil. Cover Dutch oven and steam on medium heat 4 hours.

Remove can from water and foil from top. Let stand 10 minutes. Turn bread out onto rack. Yield: 1 loaf.
Mrs. D. W. Proffitt,
Maryville, Tennessee.

BUTTERMILK CRUMB CAKE

3 cups all-purpose flour
2 cups firmly packed brown sugar
1 cup butter or margarine, softened
2 teaspoons ground nutmeg
1 teaspoon ground cinnamon
2 eggs, lightly beaten
1 cup buttermilk
1 teaspoon baking powder
½ teaspoon soda
¼ cup chopped nuts (optional)

Combine flour, sugar, butter, and spices; mix thoroughly until mixture resembles crumbs. Reserve 1 cup crumb mixture for topping.

Add eggs, buttermilk, baking powder, and soda to remaining crumb mixture; beat well. Pour into a well-greased and floured 13- x 9- x 2-inch baking pan. Top with reserved crumbs. Sprinkle with nuts, if desired.

Bake at 350° for 45 minutes or until cake tests done. Cut into squares, and serve warm or cold. Yield: 15 servings. *Mrs. Donald C. Vanhoy,*
Salisbury, North Carolina.

OLD-FASHIONED BUTTERMILK PIE

½ cup butter or margarine, softened
2 cups sugar
3 eggs
¼ cup all-purpose flour
1 cup buttermilk
Dash of ground nutmeg
1 unbaked 10-inch pastry shell

Combine butter and sugar, creaming well. Add eggs and flour; beat until fluffy (about 2 minutes). Fold in buttermilk and nutmeg.

Pour filling into pastry shell. Bake at 350° for 50 minutes. Cool. Yield: one 10-inch pie. *Mrs. T. J. Compton,*
Austin, Texas.

BUTTERMILK SCRAMBLED EGGS

4 eggs
¼ cup buttermilk
¼ teaspoon paprika
¼ teaspoon salt
Dash of pepper
1 tablespoon butter or margarine
⅓ cup shredded process American cheese
1 green onion, chopped

Combine eggs, buttermilk, paprika, salt, and pepper; beat well with a fork.

Melt butter in a 9-inch skillet. When hot, add egg mixture. Cook over low heat until eggs are partially set, lifting edges gently to allow uncooked eggs to flow underneath. Add cheese and onion. Cover and cook 1 minute or until cheese melts and eggs are set. Yield: 2 to 3 servings. *Ella Stivers,*
Abilene, Texas.

Tip: Lightly oil the cup or spoon used to measure honey or molasses. No-stick cooking spray works well for this.

About Making That Soufflé Rise

Want to try your hand at a dessert soufflé, a vegetable soufflé, or a cheese soufflé? Then keep in mind that one of the secrets of producing a perfect soufflé is in the timing. Your serving schedule should be planned so that the soufflé will be done as close as possible to the moment of serving, because it will sink rapidly soon after being removed from the oven.

To help a soufflé rise as it should, use a straight-sided, flat-bottomed soufflé dish, and butter it lightly. Make a collar for the dish from aluminum foil or brown paper bag. Cut the collar wide enough so that you can fold it in thirds lengthwise and still have it extend 3 inches above the rim when tied in place. Be sure to butter the collar.

CHEESE SOUFFLE

3 tablespoons butter or margarine
3 tablespoons all-purpose flour
1 cup milk
¼ cup plus 1 tablespoon grated Parmesan cheese
¼ cup plus 1 tablespoon shredded Cheddar cheese
3 egg yolks, beaten
4 egg whites, stiffly beaten

Lightly butter a 1½-quart soufflé dish. Cut a piece of aluminum foil long enough to circle the dish, allowing a 1-inch overlap. Fold foil lengthwise into thirds, and lightly butter one side. Wrap foil, buttered side against the dish, so it extends 3 inches above the rim. Securely attach foil with string.

Melt butter in saucepan; gradually stir in flour; cook, stirring constantly, until bubbly. Gradually add milk; bring to a boil, stirring constantly. Remove from heat. Add cheese; stir until melted. Gradually stir in egg yolks; cool. Fold egg whites into cheese mixture. Spoon into prepared soufflé dish. Bake at 350° for 25 to 30 minutes. Remove collar before serving. Yield: 5 to 6 servings.
Mary Bryan Winibrow,
San Marcos, Texas.

CARROT SOUFFLE

1½ cups cooked sliced carrots
1 cup milk
3 tablespoons butter, melted
½ teaspoon salt
⅛ teaspoon paprika
¼ teaspoon onion salt
¼ cup all-purpose flour
¼ cup grated Parmesan cheese
4 eggs, separated

Lightly butter a 1½-quart soufflé dish. Cut a piece of aluminum foil long enough to circle the dish, allowing a 1-inch overlap. Fold foil lengthwise into thirds, and lightly butter one side. Wrap foil, buttered side against the dish, so it extends 3 inches above the rim. Securely attach foil with string.

Combine all ingredients except egg whites in container of electric blender; blend on high speed for 1 minute (mixture will be thick). Pour into a saucepan, and cook over low heat, stirring constantly, until heated thoroughly.

Beat egg whites (at room temperature) until stiff but not dry; gently fold into carrot mixture. Spoon into prepared soufflé dish. Bake at 350° for 45 or 50 minutes or until golden brown. Remove collar before serving. Yield: 4 servings.
Diane Brownlee,
Starkville, Mississippi.

SPINACH SOUFFLE

1 (10-ounce) package frozen chopped
    spinach
¼ cup all-purpose flour
¼ cup butter, softened
1 teaspoon salt
⅛ teaspoon pepper
¾ cup hot milk
5 eggs, separated

Lightly butter a 1½-quart soufflé dish. Cut a piece of aluminum foil long enough to circle the dish, allowing a 1-inch overlap. Fold foil lengthwise into thirds, and lightly butter one side. Wrap foil, buttered side against the dish, so it extends 3 inches above the rim. Securely attach foil with string.

Cook spinach according to package directions; drain well.

Combine spinach and remaining ingredients except egg whites in container of electric blender; blend on high speed for 15 seconds. Pour mixture into a saucepan; cook over low heat, stirring constantly, until thickened. Remove from heat, and allow to cool.

Beat egg whites (at room temperature) until stiff but not dry; gently fold into spinach mixture. Spoon into prepared soufflé dish. Bake at 375° for 30 minutes or until golden brown. Remove collar before serving. Yield 4 servings.
Lilly S. Bradley,
Salem, Virginia.

COCONUT SOUFFLE

2 tablespoons butter
3 tablespoons all-purpose flour
¾ cup scalded milk
3 egg yolks, well beaten
¼ cup sugar
⅛ teaspoon salt
1 teaspoon vanilla extract
1½ cups flaked coconut
4 egg whites
2 tablespoons flaked coconut

Lightly butter a 1-quart soufflé dish. Cut a piece of aluminum foil long enough to circle the dish, allowing a 1-inch overlap. Fold foil lengthwise into thirds, and lightly butter one side. Wrap foil, buttered side against the dish, so it extends 3 inches above the rim. Securely attach foil with string.

Melt butter in top of a double boiler; stir in flour. Cook over boiling water until bubbly. Gradually stir in milk; cook, stirring constantly, until mixture is smooth and thickened.

Combine egg yolks, sugar, and salt; add a small amount of hot white sauce, stirring well. Stir yolk mixture into white sauce, mixing well. Add vanilla and 1½ cups coconut; stir well.

Beat egg whites (at room temperature) until stiff but not dry; gently fold into coconut mixture. Spoon into prepared soufflé dish. Sprinkle with 2 tablespoons coconut. Place in a pan with a small amount of warm water, and bake at 375° for 40 to 45 minutes or until puffy and golden brown. Remove collar before serving. Yield: 6 servings.
Note: If desired, whipped cream may be served with soufflé.
Mrs. Charles R. Simms,
Palestine, Illinois.

Don't Toss That Salad

A meal just isn't complete without a salad, but tossed salad night after night can get tiring. So break the routine and give your salad course a new look. Reach for a mold, put a dressing on rice, or create a hot vegetable salad.

We've selected an array of gelatin, fruit, and vegetable salads to give your meals a change. A Tennessee reader contributes an unusual rice salad full of onion, celery, cucumber, radishes, bacon, and hard-cooked egg. Hot Pole Bean-Potato Salad is topped with a garlic-flavored mayonnaise dressing. For a fruit salad, try Tropical Ambrosia, featuring pineapple, oranges, and sherbet.

CREAMY ROQUEFORT SALAD

1 envelope unflavored gelatin
½ cup water
1 (3-ounce) package cream cheese,
    softened
4 ounces Roquefort cheese, crumbled (at
    room temperature)
2 tablespoons vinegar
2 tablespoons dried parsley flakes
2 teaspoons onion salt
1 cup shredded unpeeled cucumber,
    drained well
2 tablespoons chopped pimiento
1 cup whipping cream, whipped
Lettuce leaves
Cucumber slices (optional)
Tomato wedges (optional)

Combine gelatin and water in top of a double boiler, stirring well. Cook over medium heat until gelatin dissolves; cool mixture.

Combine cream cheese, Roquefort, vinegar, parsley flakes, and onion salt; beat well. Stir in gelatin mixture, cucumber, and pimiento; gently fold in whipped cream.

Spoon mixture into a 4-cup mold, and chill until firm. Unmold on lettuce leaves. Garnish with cucumber slices and tomato wedges, if desired. Yield: 6 servings.
Mrs. James E. Meacham,
Little Rock, Arkansas.

Tip: Freshen wilted vegetables by letting them stand about 10 minutes in cold water to which a few drops of lemon juice have been added; drain well, and store in a plastic bag in the refrigerator.

TANGY TOMATO MOLD

4 cups tomato juice, divided
⅓ cup chopped onion
¼ cup chopped celery leaves
2 tablespoons brown sugar
1 teaspoon salt
2 bay leaves
4 whole cloves
2 envelopes unflavored gelatin
3 tablespoons lemon juice

Combine 2 cups tomato juice, onion, celery leaves, sugar, salt, bay leaves, and cloves. Simmer, uncovered, 5 minutes. Strain.

Soften gelatin in 1 cup tomato juice; add gelatin mixture to hot mixture, stirring until gelatin is dissolved. Add remaining tomato juice and lemon juice. Pour into a lightly oiled 4-cup mold; chill until firm. Yield: about 6 servings.
Doris Garton,
Shenandoah, Virginia.

RICE SALAD

3½ cups cooked rice, chilled
1½ to 2 cups mayonnaise
½ medium onion, finely chopped
1½ cups sliced celery
3 to 4 teaspoons prepared mustard
½ teaspoon salt
½ cup crumbled cooked bacon
1 hard-cooked egg, chopped
3 radishes, sliced
1 medium cucumber, diced
Lettuce
1 medium tomato, cut in wedges

Combine rice, mayonnaise, onion, celery, mustard, and salt, mixing well; chill. Just before serving, stir in bacon, egg, radishes, and cucumber. Line a serving platter with lettuce, and spoon salad on top. Place tomato wedges around side. Yield: 6 to 8 servings.
Mrs. R. L. Bradley,
Sparta, Tennessee.

Tip: The reason some hard-cooked eggs have discolored yolks is that the eggs have been cooked at too high a temperature, or they have not been cooled rapidly following cooking. The greenish color comes from sulfur and iron compounds in the eggs. These compounds form at the surface of the yolks when they have been overcooked. This does not interfere with the taste or nutritional value of the eggs, however.

HOT POLE BEAN-POTATO SALAD

1 pound new potatoes, peeled and cut into ¾-inch cubes
1 pound fresh pole beans, cut in 1½-inch pieces
6 slices bacon
½ cup finely chopped onion
¼ cup mayonnaise or salad dressing
1 tablespoon vinegar
1 teaspoon salt
¼ teaspoon garlic powder
⅛ teaspoon white pepper

Cook potatoes and beans, covered, in boiling salted water in a small Dutch oven 10 to 15 minutes or until tender; drain.

Fry bacon until crisp; remove from skillet and drain, reserving 2 tablespoons drippings in pan. Crumble bacon. Sauté onion in drippings; stir into vegetables. Combine remaining ingredients; pour over vegetables, stirring well. Add bacon; toss gently. Serve warm. Yield: 6 to 8 servings.
Dorothy Kole Mucklo,
Berea, Ohio.

BEET-NUT SALAD

1 (20-ounce) can crushed pineapple
1 (16-ounce) can julienne beets
½ cup water
¼ cup vinegar
2 tablespoons sugar
3 tablespoons lemon juice
2 (3-ounce) packages black raspberry-flavored gelatin
½ cup chopped pecans
1 (8-ounce) carton commercial sour cream (optional)
3 tablespoons mayonnaise (optional)
1 tablespoon commercial blue cheese dressing (optional)

Drain pineapple and beets, reserving juice. Combine juice, water, vinegar, sugar, and lemon juice; bring to a boil. Dissolve gelatin in hot liquid. Chill until mixture is the consistency of unbeaten egg whites.

Stir pineapple, beets, and nuts into thickened gelatin. Pour into a lightly oiled 6-cup mold; chill until firm.

If a dressing is desired, combine sour cream, mayonnaise, and blue cheese dressing; mix well, and serve with salad. Yield: 10 servings.
Note: Sliced beets may be cut into narrow strips and substituted for julienne beets. Black cherry- or blackberry-flavored gelatin may be substituted for the black raspberry gelatin.
Mrs. W. Harold Groce,
Arden, North Carolina.

CHERRY-ORANGE SALAD

1 (6-ounce) can frozen orange juice concentrate, thawed and undiluted
1¼ cups water
1 (3-ounce) package cherry-flavored gelatin
1 (3-ounce) package orange-flavored gelatin
2 carrots, grated
2 cups crushed pineapple, drained
3 medium apples, grated
1 cup chopped pecans
2 cups miniature marshmallows
1 cup whipping cream, whipped

Combine orange juice concentrate and water in a saucepan; stir well, and bring to a boil. Combine cherry- and orange-flavored gelatin in a mixing bowl; add hot orange juice, stirring until gelatin dissolves. Stir in carrots and fruit. Chill until mixture is the consistency of unbeaten egg whites.

Fold remaining ingredients into gelatin. Spoon into two 5-cup molds or one 10-cup mold. Chill until firm. Yield: 20 servings.
Mrs. D. W. Hicks,
Bandera, Texas.

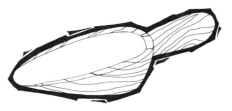

TROPICAL AMBROSIA

2 (15¼-ounce) cans pineapple chunks, divided
1 (11-ounce) can mandarin oranges
1 (6-ounce) package orange-pineapple-flavored gelatin
1 pint orange sherbet
1 (8-ounce) carton commercial sour cream
1 cup flaked coconut
1 cup miniature marshmallows

Drain pineapple and oranges, reserving liquid. Add enough water to liquid to make 2 cups. Bring liquid to a boil in a medium saucepan; add gelatin, and stir until dissolved. Remove from heat.

Add sherbet, oranges, and half the pineapple, stirring until sherbet is melted. Pour into a 6-cup ring mold and chill until firm. Unmold onto serving platter.

Combine sour cream, coconut, marshmallows, and remaining pineapple; spoon into center of gelatin ring. Yield: 10 to 12 servings. *Mrs. E. C. Daniels,*
Winter Haven, Florida.

Bake Your Fish To Perfection

Everybody knows how good fish tastes and how good it is for you. What you might not know is how to vary the flavor of baked fish with the addition of sauces and seasonings.

French dressing and cheese cracker crumbs form a crisp coating for Festive Mullet. For Baked Flounder Supreme, the rolled fillets are baked with Swiss cheese and tomato slices in a sherry-flavored sauce. Saucy Fish Bake is based on a well-seasoned tomato sauce and is versatile enough to use with your own choice of fish.

For fish to be good, it must be fresh. So when buying, choose those with firm, elastic flesh, a fresh odor, bright eyes, red gills, and shiny skin.

FESTIVE MULLET

2 pounds mullet fillets
½ cup commercial French salad dressing
1½ cups crushed cheese crackers
2 tablespoons melted butter or margarine
Paprika

Dip fillets in dressing, and coat with cracker crumbs. Place on a well-greased baking sheet; drizzle with butter, and sprinkle with paprika. Bake at 500° for 10 to 12 minutes. Yield: 6 to 7 servings.
Mrs. Anna May Simmons,
Gainesville, Florida.

OVEN-FRIED FISH FILLETS

1 pound sole or flounder fillets
¼ cup mayonnaise
Breadcrumbs
Paprika
½ teaspoon salt
¼ teaspoon pepper
Lemon wedges

Thinly coat fish fillets with mayonnaise; dredge in breadcrumbs. Arrange in a greased 13- x 9- x 2-inch baking pan. Sprinkle with paprika, salt, and pepper.

Bake at 450° about 12 minutes or until fish flakes easily when tested with a fork. Garnish with lemon wedges. Yield: 3 to 4 servings. *Helen Dill,*
Oklahoma City, Oklahoma.

SAUCY FISH BAKE

1 cup chopped onion
½ cup chopped celery
½ cup chopped parsley
2 pounds fish fillets
1 teaspoon salt
¼ teaspoon pepper
¼ cup vegetable oil
½ to ¾ teaspoon paprika or cayenne pepper
2 (8-ounce) cans tomato sauce

Combine onion, celery, and parsley; mix well. Spoon into a greased 13- x 9- x 2-inch baking pan.

Sprinkle each fillet with salt and pepper; arrange over vegetables. Pour oil over fish, and sprinkle with paprika. Bake at 375° for 10 minutes.

Pour tomato sauce over fish, and bake 30 minutes longer or until fish flakes easily when tested with a fork. Yield: about 6 servings.
Barbara Sullivan,
Ocala, Florida.

BAKED FLOUNDER SUPREME

1 (4-ounce) can sliced mushrooms
6 large flounder fillets, skinned
Seasoned salt
6 slices Swiss cheese, folded in half
1 large tomato, peeled and cut into 6 slices
2 small onions, sliced
2 tablespoons melted butter or margarine
1½ tablespoons all-purpose flour
1 cup half-and-half
¼ cup plus 2 tablespoons dry sherry
Hot cooked rice

Drain mushrooms, reserving liquid. Add enough water to liquid to make ½ cup; set aside.

Sprinkle fillets on all sides with seasoned salt; starting at wide end, roll up each fillet. Place, seam side down, in a greased 13- x 9- x 2-inch baking dish. Place a cheese slice topped with a tomato slice between each roll; set aside.

Sauté onion and mushrooms in butter until golden. Stir in flour, 1½ teaspoons seasoned salt, half-and-half, mushroom liquid, and sherry. Bring to a boil, and pour over fish. Bake at 400° for 20 minutes or until fish flakes easily when tested with a fork. Serve with hot cooked rice. Yield: 6 servings.
Mrs. E. L. Donohue,
Warner Robins, Georgia.

Try Shortcut Cooking

Here is a selection of quick and easy recipes for those busy days when you have little time to cook. Some can be prepared ahead, most use convenience foods or mixes, and all are designed to save you time and please the family.

Easy Chocolate Dessert uses cake and pudding mixes and frozen whipped topping for a quickly assembled dessert. Sweet Cabbage Slaw can be mixed at the last minute or made ahead and refrigerated until serving time. And our two tasty casseroles are extra fast; they require only 20 minutes to bake.

EASY CHOCOLATE DESSERT

1 (9-ounce) package cake mix
1 (8-ounce) package cream cheese, softened
2 cups milk, divided
1 (4-ounce) package instant chocolate pudding
1 (8-ounce) carton whipping cream
2 to 4 tablespoons sugar
½ teaspoon vanilla extract
2 to 4 tablespoons toasted slivered almonds

Prepare cake mix according to package directions; pour into a greased and floured 13- x 9- x 2-inch baking pan. Bake at 350° for 15 minutes or until cake tests done; let cool in pan.

Place cream cheese in a large mixing bowl; gradually add 1 cup milk, beating constantly. Add pudding mix, and remaining 1 cup milk; beat until smooth and thickened. Spread evenly on cake, and set aside.

Combine whipping cream, sugar, and vanilla; beat until stiff peaks form. Spread over pudding layer, and sprinkle almonds evenly on top. Chill. Yield: 15 servings. *Mrs. James S. Tiffany,*
Dallas, Texas.

Tip: Save lemon and orange rinds.
Store in the freezer, and grate as needed for pies, cakes, breads, and cookies. Or the rinds can be candied for holiday uses.

TUNA BISQUE

2½ cups milk, divided
1 (10¾-ounce) can cream of asparagus
    soup, undiluted
1 (10¾-ounce) can cream of mushroom
    soup, undiluted
5 tablespoons sherry
1 (7-ounce) can tuna, drained and flaked
Lemon slices (optional)

Combine 1 cup of milk, soup, and sherry in the container of an electric blender; puree until smooth. Pour mixture into a heavy saucepan; add remaining milk and tuna. Heat thoroughly, stirring constantly. Garnish each serving with a lemon slice, if desired. Yield: 6 servings.   *Jessie S. Grigg,*
Farmville, Virginia.

GREEN ENCHILADA CASSEROLE

12 (6-inch) corn tortillas, broken in pieces
1 (10¾-ounce) can cream of mushroom
    soup, undiluted
1 (10¾-ounce) can cream of chicken soup,
    undiluted
1 (5.33-ounce) can evaporated milk
1 (5-ounce) can chunk white chicken,
    drained
1 (4-ounce) can chopped green chiles,
    drained
1 small onion, chopped
1 cup (¼ pound) shredded Cheddar
    cheese

Arrange tortillas in bottom of a 2-quart shallow casserole; set aside.
Combine soup, milk, chicken, chiles, and onion in a large saucepan; bring to a boil over medium heat, stirring often. Pour chicken mixture over tortillas; sprinkle with cheese. Bake at 350° for 20 minutes. Yield: 6 to 8 servings.
Mrs. Ethleen S. Mayfield,
La Porte, Texas.

SWEET CABBAGE SLAW

1 large head cabbage, shredded
1 (8-ounce) can crushed pineapple,
    drained
1 cup slivered almonds, toasted
1 cup frozen whipped topping, thawed
1 cup mayonnaise
Salt and pepper to taste

Combine all ingredients; toss well and chill. Yield: 8 to 10 servings.
Mrs. Gerald S. May,
Stanford, Kentucky.

SUNDAY SUPPER SUPREME

1 (7¼-ounce) package macaroni and
    cheese dinner
½ cup milk
¼ cup chopped green pepper
¼ cup sliced green onion
1 tablespoon melted margarine
1 (10¾-ounce) can cream of celery soup,
    undiluted
8 slices Canadian bacon

Prepare macaroni dinner according to package directions, using ½ cup milk. Sauté green pepper and onion in margarine until tender.
Combine prepared macaroni dinner, vegetables, and soup. Spoon into a greased 10- x 6- x 2-inch baking dish. Arrange bacon slices on top. Bake at 350° for 20 minutes. Yield: 4 servings.
Mrs. Margaret L. Hunter,
Princeton, Kentucky.

Artichokes Were Made For Stuffing

The artichoke is in the height of its season this month. While artichokes are always delicious served simply with melted butter or a sauce, they're also perfect for stuffing. In this recipe they are filled with a mixture of pepperoni or ham, breadcrumbs, and tomatoes, flavored with garlic and olive oil.

When selecting fresh artichokes, be sure to look for an even color and tightly closed leaves.

STUFFED ARTICHOKES

6 large artichokes
⅓ pound sliced pepperoni or chopped
    cooked ham
1 teaspoon olive oil
1½ cups soft breadcrumbs
2 tablespoons chopped fresh parsley
2 cloves garlic, minced
3 eggs
¼ cup milk
2 tablespoons olive oil
¼ teaspoon salt
⅛ teaspoon pepper
4 cups water
2 cloves garlic
½ teaspoon salt
½ cup peeled and chopped tomatoes
4 tablespoons olive oil

Wash artichokes well, and trim stem even with base. Slice about ¾ inch off top of artichoke, and remove discolored leaves at base. Trim off thorny leaf tips. Spread leaves apart; pull out center leaves, and scrape off the fuzzy thistle center (choke) with a spoon. (If not cooking immediately, place artichokes in a bowl containing a solution of 1 tablespoon lemon juice to 1 quart water to prevent discoloration.)

Sauté meat in 1 teaspoon oil until thoroughly heated; drain. Combine meat, breadcrumbs, parsley, and minced garlic; mix well. Combine eggs, milk, 2 tablespoons olive oil, ¼ teaspoon salt, and pepper; stir into meat mixture.

Spoon meat mixture into center of each artichoke. Pour 4 cups water into a Dutch oven; add whole garlic cloves and ½ teaspoon salt. Tightly pack artichokes into Dutch oven. Sprinkle chopped tomatoes and 4 tablespoons olive oil over artichokes.

Cover tightly, and bring to a boil; reduce heat and simmer 35 to 55 minutes or until leaves pull out easily. Remove artichokes from water, and arrange them on a serving platter. Serve hot. Yield: 6 servings.   *Pauline Vann,*
Fort Oglethorpe, Georgia.

Chicken, Other Than Fried

Probably nothing exemplifies Southern cooking quite like fried chicken, but Southerners like their chicken prepared other ways, too. And we've gathered some mouth-watering recipes from our readers to prove the point.

Like Chicken Breasts With Orange Sauce, for example: The chicken is filled with an herb-butter mixture, simmered in an orange-flavored sauce, and served over hot cooked noodles. For a new casserole idea, try Chicken-Wild Rice Supreme. Rice, chicken, and parsley are baked in a cream sauce for a delicious one-dish meal.

If fried chicken remains your favorite, you'll find two recipes for oven frying that give that crispy crunch with less trouble.

OVEN-FRIED SESAME CHICKEN

½ cup melted butter or margarine
1 egg, well beaten
⅓ cup milk
¾ cup all-purpose flour
1 teaspoon baking powder
1 teaspoon salt
2 teaspoons paprika
⅛ teaspoon pepper
½ cup finely chopped pecans
2 tablespoons sesame seeds
1 (2½- to 3-pound) broiler-fryer, cut up
   or 3 whole chicken breasts, split

Pour butter into a 15- x 10- x 1-inch jellyroll pan, spreading evenly; set aside.

Combine egg and milk, mixing well. Combine flour, baking powder, salt, paprika, pepper, chopped pecans, and sesame seeds.

Rinse chicken, and pat dry. Dip chicken in egg mixture, and dredge in flour mixture. Place chicken, skin side down, in prepared jellyroll pan. Bake at 325° for 40 minutes; turn chicken, and bake an additional 40 minutes or until tender. Yield: 4 to 6 servings.
Judith Roth,
Merritt Island, Florida.

CHICKEN PEACH DINNER

3 whole chicken breasts, split
Salt and pepper
1 (10-ounce) package frozen sliced
   peaches, thawed
1 (6-ounce) can frozen apple juice
   concentrate, undiluted
3 tablespoons lemon juice
¼ cup honey
¼ cup melted butter or margarine
Parsley (optional)

Sprinkle chicken with salt and pepper; place skin side up in a greased 13- x 9- x 2-inch baking dish. Set chicken aside.

Drain peaches, reserving liquid; set peaches aside.

Combine apple juice concentrate, lemon juice, honey, butter, and reserved peach liquid; stir well. Brush chicken with mixture; bake at 350° for 1 hour or until tender, brushing with additional mixture every 10 minutes. Add peaches during last 5 minutes. To serve, spoon pan drippings and peaches over chicken. Garnish with parsley, if desired. Yield: 6 servings.
Mrs. Earl L. Faulkenberry,
Lancaster, South Carolina.

CHICKEN BREASTS WITH ORANGE SAUCE

6 whole chicken breasts, boned
Salt
2 tablespoons butter or margarine,
   softened
2 tablespoons minced fresh parsley
2 tablespoons minced onion
1 to 2 teaspoons dried tarragon leaves
Paprika
2 tablespoons melted butter or margarine
1 cup orange juice
¼ cup plus 2 tablespoons currant jelly
1 tablespoon grated orange rind
¼ teaspoon dry mustard
2 tablespoons cold water
1 tablespoon cornstarch
Hot cooked noodles (optional)

Rinse chicken breasts, and pat dry. Sprinkle inside of chicken breasts with 1 teaspoon salt.

Combine 2 tablespoons softened butter, parsley, onion, and tarragon; mix well. Spread about 1 teaspoon butter mixture over inside of each chicken breast. Fold long sides of chicken over butter, and secure with toothpicks. Sprinkle chicken with ½ teaspoon salt and paprika.

Sauté chicken in 2 tablespoons melted butter over medium heat in a large skillet until golden brown on both sides, turning once.

Combine orange juice, jelly, orange rind, and mustard; pour over chicken. Cover and simmer 20 to 30 minutes or until tender. Remove chicken from skillet and keep warm.

Combine water and cornstarch; stir until smooth, and pour into orange sauce. Cook over medium heat, stirring constantly, until thickened and bubbly. Serve sauce over chicken and noodles, if desired. Yield: 6 servings.
Mrs. John H. Yardley,
Baltimore, Maryland.

LEMON-FRIED CHICKEN

1 (2½- to 3-pound) broiler-fryer, cut up
½ teaspoon salt
¼ teaspoon pepper
¼ cup melted shortening
⅓ cup lemon juice
¼ cup vegetable oil
½ teaspoon sugar
½ teaspoon salt
½ teaspoon pepper
¼ teaspoon paprika
¼ teaspoon prepared mustard
⅛ teaspoon garlic powder

Rinse chicken and pat dry. Season with ½ teaspoon salt and ¼ teaspoon pepper. Brown chicken on both sides in shortening in a large skillet.

Combine remaining ingredients in a jar; tighten lid, and shake well. Pour lemon sauce over chicken; cover and simmer 40 to 50 minutes or until tender. Yield: 4 to 6 servings. *Vivian Carter,*
Pisgah, Alabama.

CHICKEN-WILD RICE SUPREME

1 (6-ounce) package long grain and wild
   rice mix
¼ cup butter or margarine
⅓ cup chopped onion
⅓ cup all-purpose flour
1 cup half-and-half
1 cup chicken broth
1 teaspoon salt
Dash of pepper
2 cups cubed cooked chicken
1 teaspoon chopped parsley

Prepare rice according to package directions.

Melt butter in a heavy saucepan; add onion and cook until transparent. Blend in flour, and cook 1 minute. Gradually add half-and-half and broth; cook, stirring constantly, until thickened. Stir in salt and pepper. Add rice, chicken, and parsley. Spoon mixture into a lightly greased 2-quart casserole. Bake at 425° for 30 minutes or until bubbly. Yield: 6 servings.
Peggy Kettell,
Spanish Fort, Alabama.

CRUSTY OVEN-FRIED CHICKEN

1 cup breadcrumbs
¼ cup grated Parmesan cheese
1 teaspoon salt
¼ teaspoon garlic powder
¼ teaspoon pepper
2 tablespoons chopped fresh parsley
   (optional)
1 (2½- to 3-pound) broiler-fryer, cut up
½ cup melted butter or margarine

Combine breadcrumbs, cheese, salt, garlic powder, and pepper. Add parsley, if desired.

Rinse chicken, and pat dry. Dip chicken in butter, and dredge in breadcrumb mixture. Place chicken, skin side up, in a 15- x 10- x 1-inch jellyroll pan. Bake at 350° for 1 hour or until tender. Yield: 4 to 6 servings.
JoAnn B. Mischke,
Dyersburg, Tennessee.

Serve The Potato Salad Hot

Break away from the old tradition of serving cold potato salad. Served hot, potato salad will add new interest to your meals.

These potato salad recipes offer some unusual flavors as well as preparation methods. Hot Potato Salad Supreme is baked with sour cream, Cheddar cheese, and chicken soup, while Hot Parmesan Potato Salad is flavored with Parmesan cheese and Italian dressing. The Hot German Potato Salad is baked in aluminum foil and brightened with radishes and parsley.

HOT POTATO SALAD

10 medium potatoes
2 teaspoons salt
½ teaspoon celery seeds
⅛ teaspoon pepper
6 slices bacon, cut into 1-inch pieces
1 cup chopped onion
½ cup vinegar
2 tablespoons sugar
1 tablespoon water
1 egg, beaten
2 tablespoons minced fresh parsley

Cook potatoes in boiling salted water about 30 minutes or until tender. Drain well, and cool slightly. Peel and thinly slice potatoes; add salt, celery seeds, and pepper.

Fry bacon until crisp; remove from pan, and drain on paper towels. Sauté onion in bacon drippings; remove from pan, and add to potatoes, reserving drippings. Add vinegar, sugar, and water to drippings; simmer 2 minutes. Add vinegar mixture to egg slowly, stirring constantly; pour dressing over potatoes. Add bacon and parsley; toss. Serve warm. Yield: 8 to 10 servings.

Mrs. Karl Koenig,
Dallas, Texas.

HOT POTATO SALAD SUPREME

5 medium potatoes
1 (8-ounce) carton commercial sour cream
1 (10¾-ounce) can cream of chicken soup
1 cup (¼-pound) shredded Cheddar cheese
5 hard-cooked eggs, chopped
1 medium onion, finely chopped
1 tablespoon chopped fresh parsley

Cook potatoes in boiling salted water about 30 minutes or until tender. Drain well, and cool slightly. Peel and cut potatoes into ¾-inch cubes.

Combine sour cream, soup, and cheese. Add potatoes, eggs, onion, and parsley to sour cream mixture; stir well. Spread in a 13- x 9- x 2-inch baking dish. Bake at 350° for 30 minutes. Serve warm. Yield: 8 servings.

Note: Dish can be assembled ahead and refrigerated. Bake as directed.

Arlene Kummer,
Arlington, Texas.

HOT DILL POTATO SALAD

1 tablespoon butter or margarine
1 tablespoon all-purpose flour
1 cup milk
1 teaspoon salt
¼ teaspoon dried dillweed
⅛ teaspoon pepper
½ cup mayonnaise or salad dressing
2 tablespoons finely chopped onion
4 cups diced cooked potatoes
Paprika

Melt butter in a heavy saucepan over low heat; blend in flour, and cook 1 minute. Gradually add milk; cook over medium heat, stirring constantly, until thickened and bubbly. Stir in salt, dillweed, and pepper; add mayonnaise, stirring well. Stir in onion and potatoes. Sprinkle with paprika. Serve warm. Yield: 4 to 6 servings.

Jan M. Gardner,
Warrenton, North Carolina.

POTATO SALAD IN PEPPER CUPS

5 medium-size red potatoes
¼ pound bacon, cut into 1-inch pieces
⅓ cup vinegar
¼ cup sugar
½ teaspoon salt
⅛ teaspoon pepper
½ cup chopped celery
3 tablespoons chopped green pepper
¼ cup chopped green onion
2 tablespoons pimiento, cut into small strips
3 large green peppers

Cook potatoes in boiling salted water about 30 minutes or until tender. Drain well, and cool slightly. Peel and dice potatoes; set aside.

Fry bacon until crisp; remove from pan, and drain on paper towels. Drain off bacon drippings, reserving 2 tablespoons in skillet; add vinegar, sugar, salt, and pepper to skillet; cook over medium heat, stirring until sugar is dissolved. Remove from heat.

Combine potatoes, bacon, celery, chopped green pepper, onion, and pimiento; add dressing, stirring to coat evenly.

Cut green peppers in half; remove membrane and seeds. Cook peppers in boiling salted water just until crisp-tender (about 3 minutes). Remove from water, and drain on paper towels. Place peppers in serving dish, and fill with potato mixture. Serve warm. Yield: 6 servings.

Mrs. Marie H. Webb,
Roanoke, Virginia.

HOT GERMAN POTATO SALAD

3 medium potatoes
1 tablespoon instant minced onion
1½ teaspoons all-purpose flour
1½ teaspoons sugar
¾ teaspoon salt
½ teaspoon freshly ground pepper
½ teaspoon celery seeds
3 slices bacon
¼ cup vinegar
2 tablespoons sliced radishes
1 tablespoon chopped fresh parsley

Cook potatoes in boiling salted water about 30 minutes or until tender. Drain well, and cool slightly. Peel and cut potatoes into ½-inch cubes; place in the center of heavy-duty foil.

Combine onion, flour, sugar, salt, pepper, and celery seeds. Then sprinkle over potatoes.

Fry bacon until crisp; remove from pan, and drain on paper towels. Drain off bacon drippings, reserving 2 tablespoons in pan. Stir vinegar into drippings, and pour over potatoes. Crumble bacon; sprinkle over potatoes.

Wrap foil tightly, and place on a cookie sheet. Bake at 425° for 1 hour. Add radishes and parsley; toss. Serve warm. Yield: 4 servings.

Mrs. R. M. Lancaster,
Brentwood, Tennessee.

HOT PARMESAN POTATO SALAD

8 slices bacon
4 cups sliced cooked potatoes
½ cup sliced green onion
⅓ cup commercial Italian dressing
½ cup grated Parmesan cheese

Fry bacon until crisp; remove from pan, and drain on paper towels. Crumble bacon.

Combine bacon with potatoes, onion, and Italian dressing in a medium saucepan. Cook over low heat until thoroughly heated, stirring occasionally. Remove from heat, and stir in cheese. Serve warm. Yield: 4 to 6 servings.

Lynn Nelson,
Biloxi, Mississippi.

Ice Cream Parlor Sauces

Those glorious ice cream parlor desserts are yours for the making, with Heavenly Chocolate Sauce or Caramel Sauce and scoops of your favorite flavor of ice cream. Both are easy to make and particularly delicious served warm.

HEAVENLY CHOCOLATE SAUCE

½ cup butter or margarine
4 (1-ounce) squares unsweetened chocolate
3 cups sugar
½ teaspoon salt
1 (13-ounce) can evaporated milk

Melt butter and chocolate in top of double boiler; stir in remaining ingredients. Cook, stirring constantly, until sugar is dissolved and sauce is smooth. Serve warm or cold over ice cream. Yield: about 4 cups.

Mrs. John A. Andrew,
Winston Salem, North Carolina

CARAMEL SAUCE

1½ cups firmly packed brown sugar
⅔ cup light corn syrup
¼ cup butter or margarine
⅛ teaspoon salt
1 (5.33-ounce) can evaporated milk

Combine sugar, corn syrup, and butter in a medium saucepan; cook over medium heat to soft ball stage (234° to 240°), stirring constantly. Remove from heat; stir in salt and milk. Serve warm over ice cream. Yield: 2¼ cups.

Mrs. J. L. Pleasants, Jr.,
Lynchburg, Virginia.

Crust Worthy Of The Filling

If you're about to use a store-bought crust for that special homemade pie filling, here are three good reasons not to. One is an oatmeal crust that wholegrain buffs will love. Another, Deluxe Piecrust, features a crunchy mixture of graham crackers and ground pecans. Never Fail Pastry will yield enough for five pies and may be stored conveniently in the refrigerator.

OATMEAL PIECRUST

1 cup all-purpose flour
1 teaspoon salt
¼ cup sugar
½ cup shortening
½ cup regular oats, uncooked
3 to 4 tablespoons water

Combine flour, salt, and sugar in a mixing bowl; cut in shortening until mixture resembles coarse meal. Stir in oats. Sprinkle water evenly over surface; stir with a fork until all ingredients are moistened.

Shape dough into a ball; chill. Roll to fit a 9-inch piepan. Yield: one 9-inch pastry shell. *Mrs. Robert Collins,*
Fairfax, Missouri.

DELUXE PIECRUST

2½ cups graham cracker crumbs
2 tablespoons light brown sugar
¼ cup ground pecans
½ cup margarine, softened

Combine graham cracker crumbs, sugar, and pecans; stir in margarine, and mix well. Press mixture firmly and evenly into a 9-inch pieplate. Bake at 350° for 12 to 15 minutes. Yield: one 9-inch pie shell. *Mrs. William S. Bell,*
Chattanooga, Tennessee.

NEVER FAIL PASTRY

4 cups all-purpose flour
1 teaspoon baking powder
1 teaspoon salt
1 tablespoon sugar
1¾ cups shortening
1 egg, beaten
1 tablespoon vinegar
½ cup cold water

Combine dry ingredients; cut in shortening until mixture resembles coarse meal. Stir in remaining ingredients. Divide dough into 5 equal parts; shape each into a ball and wrap tightly. Chill. May be stored up to 2 weeks in refrigerator. Yield: pastry for five 9-inch pies.

Mary Ann Owens,
Winston-Salem, North Carolina.

Quick Vegetable Fix-Ups

The season of fresh vegetables has finally arrived. So make the best of the bounty with quick fix-ups that add extra flavor and eye appeal.

If you like vegetables with a crunch, you're sure to enjoy the topping recipe included here. It's a favorite of Byrda Martin of Knoxville, Tennessee, and is especially good sprinkled on cauliflower, broccoli, and asparagus.

Here are some other quick ideas.

—Mix and match herbs and vegetables to suit your taste. Some standard combinations include dill with peas, potatoes, tomatoes, green beans, and broccoli; basil as an accent for squash, eggplant, and tomatoes; chives with potatoes and green beans; tomatoes enhanced with oregano.

—Combine an appropriate herb with 2 parts vinegar and 1 part vegetable oil; mix well, and use it as a marinade for a cold vegetable.

—Experiment with the variety of sauce mixes on the market. They can be prepared in a jiffy and complement a multitude of fresh vegetables.

VEGETABLE TOPPING

1 (2-ounce) jar diced pimientos
½ cup cracker crumbs
½ cup grated Parmesan cheese
½ cup finely chopped unsalted peanuts
½ cup chopped fresh mushrooms
½ cup melted butter or margarine
Hot cooked cauliflower, broccoli, or
  asparagus

Combine first 5 ingredients; add melted butter, and toss well. Place cooked vegetable in a shallow casserole dish; sprinkle with topping, and broil until golden brown. Spoon excess topping into an airtight container; store in refrigerator. Yield: 2 cups topping.

Sweet Roll Dough gives you double eating pleasure with Honey Twist and Cinnamon Rolls.

Divide The Dough For Two Treats

The buttery flavor and fresh, delicate aroma of homemade sweet rolls and coffee cake have long been a special morning treat in the South. Mrs. V. O. Walker of Pennington, Texas, makes it twice as nice and easy by using one yeast dough, Sweet Roll Dough, as the basis for both.

Once the basic dough is prepared, she makes half into Cinnamon Rolls and half into Honey Twist, a coffee cake that is coated with honey and pecans. The coffee cake is baked on top of a honey and pecan mixture in a heavy skillet.

Whether you use the dough to make both treats or just make one large batch of one of them, be sure to store the bread in an airtight container.

Tip: Freshen dry, crusty rolls or French bread by sprinkling with a few drops of water, wrapping in aluminum foil, and reheating at 350° about 10 minutes.

SWEET ROLL DOUGH

⅔ cup milk
½ cup sugar
⅓ cup shortening
1¼ teaspoons salt
⅔ cup warm water (105° to 115°)
2 packages dry yeast
2 tablespoons sugar
3 eggs, beaten
About 6 cups all-purpose flour

Scald milk; add ½ cup sugar, shortening, and salt, stirring until sugar dissolves and shortening melts. Cool mixture to lukewarm.

Combine water, yeast, and 2 tablespoons sugar in a large bowl; let stand 5 minutes. Stir in milk mixture, eggs, and 3 cups flour; beat until mixture is smooth. Add remaining flour, 1 cup at a time, stirring well until a soft dough is formed.

Turn dough out on a floured surface, and knead until smooth and elastic (5 to 8 minutes). Place in a well-greased bowl, turning to grease top. Cover tightly, and let rise in a warm place (85°), free of drafts, 1½ hours or until doubled in bulk.

Punch dough down and divide in half. Proceed with directions for Honey Twist or Cinnamon Rolls. Yield: 2 coffee cakes or 3 dozen rolls.

HONEY TWIST

½ cup chopped pecans
¼ cup sugar
¼ cup all-purpose flour
¼ cup melted butter or margarine
¼ cup honey
½ recipe Sweet Roll Dough

Combine all ingredients except Sweet Roll Dough in a heavy ovenproof 9- or 10-inch skillet; stir well and set aside.

Turn dough out on a floured surface; shape dough into a long rope 1 inch in diameter. Coil rope in prepared skillet, beginning at center and working outward; leave a small space between sections of rope. Cover; let rise in a warm place (85°), free of drafts, about 45 minutes or until doubled in bulk.

Bake at 375° for 30 to 35 minutes or until loaf sounds hollow when tapped with finger. Invert coffee cake immediately onto a serving plate. Store cooled cake in an airtight container. Yield: 1 coffee cake.

Tip: Do not wash eggs before storing; washing removes the coating that prevents the entrance of bacteria. Wash just before using, if desired.

CINNAMON ROLLS

½ recipe Sweet Roll Dough
1½ tablespoons butter or margarine, softened
½ cup sugar
2 teaspoons ground cinnamon
Raisins (optional)
Chopped pecans (optional)

Turn dough out on a floured surface; roll dough into a rectangle ½-inch thick. Spread butter over dough, leaving a narrow margin on all sides. Combine sugar and cinnamon; sprinkle over butter. Sprinkle dough with raisins and nuts, if desired. Tightly roll up jellyroll fashion, beginning at long side. Pinch edge and ends to seal. Cut roll into 1-inch slices. Place slices, cut side down, in a greased 9-inch cakepan (fit will be tight).

Cover; let rise in a warm place (85°), free of drafts, 45 minutes or until doubled in bulk. Bake at 375° for 25 to 30 minutes. Store rolls in an airtight container. Yield: 1½ dozen.

Cooking For Two With Half The Trouble

Serving appetizing and nutritious meals for two doesn't have to mean lots of leftovers or too much trouble.

Today, more and more manufacturers are packaging foods designed for couples and singles, recipes are being developed to yield a small number of servings, and kitchen appliances designed to prepare small servings are on the market. These helps, coupled with a few commonsense rules, can have you well on your way to exciting meals.

—Plan menus and shopping lists for a week at a time. Consider which recipes require only partial packages or containers for a specific food and then plan another use for the remaining food if it will spoil before the next week.

—When buying produce, select small-size items. Produce is the one area where smaller items don't usually cost more per serving than larger ones.

—Locate a handy bakery that sells individual rolls, pastries, and small loaves of bread. If you have bread left over, you can transform it into breadcrumbs or croutons.

—Invest in airtight containers and freezer materials, as proper storage materials will preserve the freshness of foods for days longer.

And to avoid the problem of leftovers altogether, here are some of our readers' best recipes designed just for serving two.

BACON-WRAPPED MEATBALLS

½ pound ground beef
¼ cup cold water
2 teaspoons instant minced onion
½ teaspoon salt
¼ teaspoon seasoned pepper
4 slices bacon, cut in half crosswise

Combine first 5 ingredients, mixing well; shape into 8 meatballs. Roll bacon pieces around meatballs, and secure with toothpicks. Sauté over medium heat until bacon is crisp and brown; drain off fat. If meatballs are not done, cover and simmer an additional 5 to 7 minutes. Yield: 2 servings.
Mrs. Marian Jenkins,
Savannah, Georgia.

SHRIMP STROGANOFF

1 medium onion, minced
1 clove garlic, minced
¼ cup minced green pepper
1 cup thinly sliced mushrooms
2 tablespoons minced parsley
¼ cup melted butter or margarine
¼ cup all-purpose flour
1 cup beef bouillon
1 teaspoon salt
½ teaspoon freshly ground pepper
6 drops of hot sauce
2 cups medium shrimp, peeled and deveined
½ to ¾ cup commercial sour cream
Hot cooked noodles

Sauté onion, garlic, green pepper, mushrooms, and parsley in butter until tender; blend in flour, and cook 1 minute. Gradually add bouillon; cook over medium heat, stirring constantly, until thickened. Stir in salt, pepper, and hot sauce, mixing well. Add shrimp and simmer 10 minutes, stirring occasionally. Stir in sour cream; cook over low heat, stirring constantly, until thoroughly heated. Serve over hot cooked noodles. Yield: 2 servings.
Mrs. Michael Champagne,
Covington, Louisiana.

PORK CHOP SPECIAL

2 (½-inch-thick) pork chops
1 tablespoon all-purpose flour
1 tablespoon vegetable oil
2½ tablespoons grated Parmesan cheese
¼ teaspoon salt
⅛ teaspoon pepper
2 cups thinly sliced potatoes
1 medium onion, thinly sliced
2 beef bouillon cubes
¼ cup plus 2 tablespoons hot water
1½ teaspoons lemon juice

Dredge pork chops in flour; brown in hot oil in a medium skillet. Combine cheese, salt, and pepper; sprinkle 1 tablespoon cheese mixture over pork chops. Arrange potatoes over meat; sprinkle 1 tablespoon cheese mixture over potatoes. Arrange onion on top.

Dissolve bouillon cubes in hot water; stir in lemon juice, and pour over vegetables. Sprinkle remaining cheese mixture on top. Cover and simmer 40 minutes or until pork chops are done. Yield: 2 servings.
Jeannette Milstead,
Nacogdoches, Texas.

The Filling Makes The Sandwich

Sandwiches need never be routine when you make them with one of these delicious fillings. Chicken Filling Luau perks up any kind of bread with an exciting crunch, as it's filled with toasted almonds, chopped celery, crushed pineapple, and chunks of chicken. Rich and creamy fillings like Shrimp-Cucumber Spread and German Cheese Spread can be served on bite-size sandwiches for parties, while Braunschweiger-Onion Spread makes a hearty filling for a man-size sandwich.

CHICKEN FILLING LUAU

2 cups finely chopped cooked chicken
⅔ cup drained crushed pineapple
½ cup finely chopped celery
⅓ cup mayonnaise
⅓ cup finely chopped toasted almonds
1½ teaspoons sugar
1½ teaspoons vinegar
¼ teaspoon salt
⅛ teaspoon pepper

Combine all ingredients; stir well. Chill to allow flavors to blend. Serve on bread or, if desired, in patty shells. Yield: about 2½ cups. *Dorsella Utter,*
Middletown, Kentucky.

SHRIMP-CUCUMBER SPREAD

2 tablespoons mayonnaise
1 (3-ounce) package cream cheese, softened
1 tablespoon catsup
1 teaspoon dry mustard
Dash of garlic powder
1 (4½-ounce) can broken shrimp, drained
¼ cup minced cucumber
1 teaspoon minced onion

Combine mayonnaise, cream cheese, catsup, mustard, and garlic powder in a medium bowl; mix until smooth. Add shrimp, cucumber, and onion; stir well. Serve on rye bread. Yield: about ¾ cup.
Jaynie Lamb,
Dallas, Texas.

CRABMEAT SPREAD

1 (3-ounce) package cream cheese, softened
¼ cup mayonnaise
1 tablespoon catsup
1 (6½-ounce) can crabmeat, drained and flaked
1 tablespoon grated onion

Combine cream cheese, mayonnaise, and catsup; mix until smooth. Stir in crabmeat and onion. Yield: 1 cup.
Mrs. Robert B. Coomer,
Louisville, Kentucky.

DEVILED HAM SPREAD

1 (8-ounce) package cream cheese, softened
1 (2¼-ounce) can deviled ham
¼ cup chili sauce
2 tablespoons sweet pickle relish
1 tablespoon prepared mustard

Combine all ingredients; stir well. Chill thoroughly. Yield: about 1½ cups. *Mrs. Margaret L. Hunter,*
Princeton, Kentucky.

GERMAN CHEESE SPREAD

⅔ cup margarine, softened
1 (8-ounce) package cream cheese,
    softened
2 anchovy fillets, chopped
1 teaspoon dry mustard
1 teaspoon paprika
1 teaspoon minced onion
1 teaspoon chopped parsley
1 teaspoon chopped chives
1 teaspoon capers
½ teaspoon caraway seeds
½ teaspoon salt
½ teaspoon pepper

Combine margarine and cream cheese
in a medium bowl; mix until smooth.
Add remaining ingredients; stir well.
Chill. Serve on bread or crackers.
Yield: 1½ cups.   *Bill Lowenberg,*
              Birmingham, Alabama.

BRAUNSCHWEIGER-ONION
SPREAD

1 (8-ounce) carton commercial sour cream
1 (1⅜-ounce) envelope dry onion soup mix
1 (3-ounce) package cream cheese,
    softened
1 teaspoon steak sauce
2 drops hot sauce
1 (8-ounce) package sliced
    braunschweiger, cut into small cubes

Combine sour cream and soup mix;
stir well and set aside for 15 minutes.
Beat cream cheese until fluffy in a
medium bowl. Add sour cream mixture,
steak sauce, and hot sauce; mix well.
Add braunschweiger; stir gently. Chill.
Serve with rye bread, crackers, or chips.
Yield: 2⅓ cups.   *Barbara Sullivan,*
                   Ocala, Florida.

CHEESE-OLIVE SPREAD

1 (3-ounce) package cream cheese,
    softened
¼ cup crumbled blue cheese, at room
    temperature
2 tablespoons mayonnaise
¾ cup coarsely chopped pitted ripe olives
¼ cup minced celery

Combine cream cheese, blue cheese,
and mayonnaise in a medium bowl; mix
until smooth. Stir in olives and celery.
Yield: about 1 cup.   *Charlotte Pierce,*
                 Greensburg, Kentucky.

A Delightful
Watercress Soup

Growing wild in brooks and streams
in some areas is a crisp, peppery green
called watercress. Its delicious leaves
make it a pretty garnish, and its pungent flavor makes it delicious in salads
or soups. You can buy watercress by
the bunch in almost any well-stocked
produce market.

Since the green is very perishable,
you must store it properly. Rinse the
bunch, place the stems in a glass of cold
water, and cover the leaves loosely with
a plastic bag. Secure the bag to the jar
with a rubber band or tape, and store in
the refrigerator up to one week.

To prepare watercress for cooking,
discard yellow leaves and any stems
over ¼ inch thick. Use both the bright-
green leaves and tender stems.

WATERCRESS SOUP

2½ cups (about 2 bunches) watercress
2 (½-inch-thick) slices onion
1 (3-inch) slice celery
1 tablespoon sugar
1 tablespoon cornstarch
3 cups chicken bouillon, divided
1 (13-ounce) can evaporated milk
1 tablespoon butter or margarine
1 teaspoon salt
Watercress leaves (optional)

Combine watercress, onion, celery,
sugar, cornstarch, and 2 cups bouillon
in container of electric blender; process
until smooth. Pour watercress mixture
into a saucepan; add remaining 1 cup
bouillon, and stir well. Bring to a boil.
Reduce heat, and simmer 10 minutes,
stirring constantly. Stir in evaporated
milk, butter, and salt; simmer 3 to 5
minutes, stirring occasionally. Garnish
individual servings with watercress
leaves, if desired. Yield: 8 to 10
servings.   *Mrs. R. V. Forrester,*
                Springfield, Virginia.

*Tip: For efficient refrigerator storage,
most foods should be wrapped or covered to protect against loss of flavor and
moisture, absorption of moisture, and
transfer of odors. An assortment of
food wraps—aluminum foil, plastic film
and bags, and waxed paper—is available
for refrigerator storage.*

Brighten The Flavor
With Dry Mustard

Dry mustard adds a tangy flavor to a
variety of foods. Here, it adds zest to
the marinade for Overnight Cabbage
Salad, Extra-Special Mustard Sauce,
and Crab Imperial. Dry mustard also
perks up Deviled Eggs Surprise and
Sherried Baked Chicken Breasts. Small
wonder that it is one of the most popular spices.

EXTRA-SPECIAL MUSTARD
SAUCE

½ cup sugar
2 tablespoons dry mustard
1 teaspoon salt
2 egg yolks, beaten
1 (13-ounce) can evaporated milk, divided
½ cup vinegar

Combine sugar, mustard, and salt;
stir into egg yolks. Add ¼ cup evaporated milk, and stir until smooth.

Heat remaining milk in the top of a
double boiler until hot (do not boil).
Add a small amount of hot milk to egg
mixture, stirring constantly. Add egg
mixture to remaining hot milk; cook
until smooth and thickened, stirring
constantly.

Remove from heat; stir in vinegar.
Cook 5 additional minutes or until
creamy and thickened. Serve hot over
ham slices, or chill and serve as a sandwich spread. Yield: 2 cups.
                   Mrs. T. J. Compton,
                     Austin, Texas.

CRAB IMPERIAL

½ cup butter or margarine, divided
1½ cups breadcrumbs, divided
¾ cup half-and-half
2 eggs, beaten
1 tablespoon chopped fresh parsley
1½ teaspoons dry mustard
½ teaspoon salt
⅛ teaspoon pepper
1 pound fresh crabmeat

Melt 6 tablespoons butter in a medium saucepan. Add 1 cup breadcrumbs
and half-and-half; cook until slightly
thickened, stirring constantly. Add eggs,
parsley, mustard, salt, and pepper; remove from heat. Stir in crabmeat.

Pour mixture into a greased 1½-quart
casserole. Melt remaining 2 tablespoons

butter, and stir in remaining bread-crumbs; sprinkle over casserole. Bake at 350° for 30 minutes. Yield: about 6 servings.   *Mrs. Mariel Fails,*
Temple Hills, Maryland.

SHERRIED BAKED CHICKEN BREASTS

4 to 6 chicken breasts
¼ cup vegetable oil
¾ cup cooking sherry
¾ cup water
¼ cup butter or margarine, melted
½ teaspoon dry mustard
½ teaspoon whole basil leaves
1 small onion, chopped
1 clove garlic, minced
½ teaspoon salt
⅛ teaspoon pepper
2 tablespoons all-purpose flour

Lightly brown chicken breasts in hot vegetable oil, place in a 9-inch baking dish. Combine remaining ingredients except flour; pour over chicken. Bake at 350° for 1 hour.

Place chicken on a serving platter. Pour pan drippings into a small saucepan. Make a paste with flour and a small amount of water; add to pan drippings and cook until thickened, stirring constantly. Strain gravy, and serve hot over chicken breasts. Yield: 4 to 6 servings.   *Mrs. Berry S. Hedrick,*
Clarksville, Tennessee.

OVERNIGHT CABBAGE SALAD

1 large head cabbage, shredded
5 stalks celery, sliced
6 green onions, chopped
1 green pepper, chopped
2 tablespoons diced pimiento
¾ cup vinegar
⅔ cup vegetable oil
½ cup sugar
2 tablespoons honey
1 tablespoon salt
1 teaspoon dry mustard
1 teaspoon celery seeds

Combine cabbage, celery, onion, green pepper, and pimento in a large bowl. Stir together remaining ingredients in a small saucepan; bring to a boil. Pour over cabbage mixture (do not stir). Cover and refrigerate 24 hours. Stir well, and serve cold. Yield: 10 to 12 servings.   *Betty Jane Morrison,*
Lakewood, Colorado.

DEVILED EGGS SURPRISE

6 hard-cooked eggs
1 (2¼-ounce) can deviled ham
⅓ cup grated carrot
2 tablespoons salad dressing
¼ teaspoon dry mustard
Paprika
Fresh parsley

Cut eggs in half lengthwise; remove yolks. Mash yolks; add ham, carrot, salad dressing, and mustard. Stir well.

Fill egg halves with mixture; chill. Sprinkle with paprika, or garnish with fresh parsley. Yield: 6 servings.
Mrs. Thomas Lee Adams,
Kingsport, Tennessee.

The Best Of Bar Cookies

When you bite into rich chewy squares of chocolate and caramel or moist chocolate brownies covered with a frosting of honey and chocolate, you'll delight in their divine taste and texture. These luscious bar cookies are quick and easy to prepare, easy to serve, great for brown bagging—and they store well.

You'd never guess that the marvelous rich flavor of Chocolate-Caramel Layer Squares all begins with a German chocolate cake mix. The chewy center is due to melted caramel candy and chocolate morsels. And you'll find that Heavenly Honey Brownies are well named.

CHOCOLATE-CARAMEL LAYER SQUARES

1 (14-ounce) bag caramels
⅔ cup evaporated milk, divided
1 (18½-ounce) package regular German
**   chocolate cake mix**
¾ cup butter or margarine, softened
1 cup chopped nuts
1 (6-ounce) package semisweet chocolate
**   morsels**

Combine caramels and ⅓ cup evaporated milk in top of a double boiler; cook, stirring constantly, until caramels are completely melted. Remove double boiler from heat.

Combine dry cake mix, remaining ⅓ cup milk, butter, and nuts; stir until dough holds together. Press ½ of cake mixture into a greased 13- x 9- x 2-inch baking pan. Bake at 350° for 6 minutes.

Sprinkle chocolate morsels over crust. Pour caramel mixture over chocolate morsels, spreading evenly. Crumble remaining cake mixture over caramel mixture. Return to oven, and bake 15 to 18 minutes; cool. Chill 30 minutes; cut into small bars. Yield: about 5 dozen.
Susan Settlemyre,
Carrboro, North Carolina.

HEAVENLY HONEY BROWNIES

⅓ cup margarine, softened
¾ cup sugar
½ cup honey
2 teaspoons vanilla extract
2 eggs
½ cup all-purpose flour
½ teaspoon salt
⅓ cup cocoa
1 cup chopped pecans
Honey Chocolate Frosting

Combine margarine and sugar; cream until light and fluffy. Add honey and vanilla; mix well. Add eggs one at a time, beating well after each addition. Combine flour, salt, and cocoa; add to creamed mixture, mixing well. Stir in pecans.

Spoon batter into a greased 8-inch square pan; bake at 350° for 30 to 35 minutes or until done. Let cool; spread Honey Chocolate Frosting over top of layer. Yield: about 3 dozen (1¼-inch) squares.

Honey Chocolate Frosting:

3 tablespoons margarine, softened
3 tablespoons cocoa
¾ teaspoon vanilla extract
1 cup powdered sugar
1 tablespoon milk
1 tablespoon honey

Combine margarine and cocoa; cream well. Add remaining ingredients, and beat until smooth. Yield: enough for 1 (8-inch) layer.   *Mrs. Shirley Doran,*
Fort Worth, Texas.

Tip: Use shiny cookie sheets and cake-pans for baking rather than darkened ones. Dark pans absorb more heat and can cause baked products to overbrown.

Dishes With Cheese And More Cheese

When you serve a meatless meal featuring Cheesy Vegetable Lasagna, you won't even miss the meat as three types of cheese combine for a deliciously satisfying version of this alltime favorite. If your taste calls for a main dish characteristic of our neighbors south of the border, try Chiles Rellenos Casserole. It's a savory blend of green chiles and Cheddar and Jack cheese.

Cheese dishes not only serve as an excellent source of protein for the main dish of a meal, but they are also a good accompaniment for meats. Macaroni-and-Cheese Deluxe is a great alternative to a baked potato when serving beef, owing its rich flavor to cottage cheese, American cheese, and sour cream.

FEATHER-LIGHT CHEESE CASSEROLE

15 saltine crackers, crushed
1½ cups (6 ounces) shredded Cheddar cheese
1½ cups milk
3 eggs, beaten
1 (2½-ounce) jar sliced mushrooms, drained
2 tablespoons margarine

Combine cracker crumbs, cheese, milk, eggs, and mushrooms in a medium bowl; mix well.

Melt margarine in a 1½-quart casserole; pour in cheese mixture. Bake at 350° for 45 to 50 minutes or until puffy and set. Yield: 4 servings.

Frances C. Viverette,
Rocky Mount, North Carolina.

CHEESY NOODLES AND MUSHROOMS

1 pound fresh mushrooms, sliced
¼ cup melted butter or margarine
½ cup chopped onion
¼ cup sliced scallions or green onions
1 (8-ounce) package medium egg noodles
2 cups (½ pound) shredded Cheddar cheese
½ cup half-and-half
1 teaspoon salt
⅛ teaspoon pepper
⅛ teaspoon ground nutmeg
¼ cup chopped parsley

Sauté mushrooms in butter until tender. Add onion and scallions; cook 2 minutes. Set aside.

Cook noodles according to package directions; drain and return immediately to saucepan. Add remaining ingredients except sautéed vegetables and parsley; cook over low heat until cheese melts, stirring constantly. Add sautéed vegetables, stirring gently. Sprinkle with parsley, and serve immediately. Yield: 6 servings.

Mrs. Neal Pleasant,
Houston, Texas.

CHEESY VEGETABLE LASAGNA

2 onions, chopped
4 cloves garlic, minced
7 tablespoons olive oil, divided
1 (28-ounce) can whole tomatoes, undrained
1 (6-ounce) can tomato paste
¼ cup chopped fresh parsley
2 teaspoons salt
2 teaspoons whole oregano
1 teaspoon whole basil
Freshly ground pepper to taste
1 (8-ounce) package lasagna noodles
½ pound fresh mushrooms, sliced
1 pound mozzarella cheese, shredded
1 (16-ounce) carton ricotta or cottage cheese
6 tablespoons Parmesan cheese, divided

Sauté onion and garlic until tender in 5 tablespoons olive oil. Stir in tomatoes, tomato paste, parsley, and seasonings. Bring to a boil; reduce heat, and simmer 45 minutes or until thickened.

Cook lasagna noodles according to package directions; drain.

Sauté mushrooms until tender in 2 tablespoons olive oil. Add to sauce mixture, and remove from heat.

Combine mozzarella and ricotta cheese in a medium bowl; mix well, and set aside.

Place one-third of noodles in a 13- x 9- x 2-inch baking dish. Top with one-third of sauce mixture, then one-third of cheese mixture. Sprinkle with 2 tablespoons Parmesan cheese. Repeat layers until all ingredients are used.

Bake at 375° for 30 minutes. Yield: 8 servings.

Gene Leyden,
Bluemont, Virginia.

CHILES RELLENOS CASSEROLE

6 slices bread
Butter or margarine, softened
2 cups (½ pound) shredded Cheddar cheese
2 cups (½ pound) shredded Jack cheese
1 (4-ounce) can green chiles, chopped
6 eggs
2 cups milk
2 teaspoons salt
2 teaspoons paprika
1 teaspoon whole oregano
½ teaspoon pepper
¼ teaspoon garlic powder
¼ teaspoon dry mustard

Trim crusts from bread. Spread each bread slice with butter; place, buttered side down, in an 11- x 7- x 2-inch baking dish. Top with Cheddar cheese and Jack cheese; sprinkle with chiles.

Beat eggs until frothy; add remaining ingredients, mixing well. Pour egg mixture over casserole. Cover and chill overnight or for at least 4 hours.

Uncover and bake at 325° for 50 to 55 minutes or until lightly browned. Let stand 10 minutes before serving. Yield: 6 servings.

Judy Naar,
Vienna, Virginia.

MACARONI-AND-CHEESE DELUXE

1 (8-ounce) package elbow macaroni
2 cups small-curd cottage cheese
1 (8-ounce) carton commercial sour cream
1 egg, lightly beaten
¾ teaspoon salt
Dash of pepper
2 cups (½ pound) shredded process American cheese
Paprika

Cook macaroni according to package directions; drain.

Combine cottage cheese, sour cream, egg, salt, and pepper in a large bowl; stir in shredded cheese. Add macaroni, stirring well.

Pour into a greased 9-inch baking pan, and sprinkle with paprika. Bake at 350° for 45 minutes. Yield: 6 servings.

Mrs. S. R. Griffith,
Memphis, Tennessee.

Tip: To make shredding of very soft cheese easier, put in the freezer for 15 minutes.

Making A Specialty Of Favorite Dishes

Dr. Ron Chase of Jacksonville, Florida, says that he's a sentimentalist when he cooks. "Cooking is not just a matter of eating; it's a matter of reminiscing," Ron explains. So rather than create totally new recipes, he enjoys re-creating dishes that he has enjoyed during his travels in this country and Europe.

Ron first began developing his culinary expertise when he went to college. At one point, he studied at the University of Rome and the University of Bologna. While in Rome, Ron lived above a restaurant and spent much of his time in the kitchen, where he learned the language from the cooks. While there, he also learned the secrets of some of their special recipes. In fact, Ron named his Scaloppine of Veal al Sorriso for the restaurant.

Clams Chase is another of Ron's favorite recipes, for it reminds him of a clam dish he once enjoyed in New York. With either the veal or the clam entrée, his Fenron Salad is a nice accompaniment.

Following the recipes for Ron's specialties are recipes from other men who also enjoy cooking.

SCALOPPINE OF VEAL AL SORRISO

1 cup white wine
½ cup olive oil
1 pound veal, cut into ⅜-inch-thick slices
Salt and pepper
¼ cup plus 2 tablespoons all-purpose flour
3 tablespoons vegetable oil
½ pound prosciutto or pressed turkey, sliced
6 ounces mozzarella cheese, thinly sliced
1 cup chopped fresh mushrooms
1 (4-ounce) jar pimientos, cut into strips

Combine wine and oil, mixing well; add veal. Cover and chill overnight.

Drain veal; sprinkle lightly with salt and pepper, and coat well with flour. Brown on all sides in hot oil; place in a greased 13- x 9- x 2-inch baking dish.

Place a slice of prosciutto over each veal slice; top with a slice of cheese. Sprinkle mushrooms over cheese, and arrange pimiento strips on top. Bake at 375° for 20 minutes or until cheese melts. Yield: 6 servings.

FENRON SALAD

1 large head romaine, torn
¼ to ½ rib fennel or 1½ to 2 ribs bok choy, chopped
2 hard-cooked eggs, sliced
2 tomatoes, cut into wedges
1 (3.5-ounce) can black olives, halved
¼ cup olive oil
3 tablespoons tarragon vinegar
¼ teaspoon salt
⅛ teaspoon pepper

Combine first 5 ingredients in a large mixing bowl; set aside. Combine oil, vinegar, salt, and pepper; mix well, and pour over salad. Toss gently. Yield: about 4 servings.

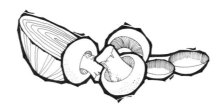

CLAMS CHASE

2 dozen cherrystone clams
2 quarts water
¼ teaspoon salt
⅛ teaspoon pepper
1 tablespoon Greek seasoning
3 tablespoons wine vinegar
1 pound jumbo shrimp
2 cups Italian-seasoned breadcrumbs
3 cloves garlic, minced
¾ cup chopped fresh mushrooms
1 cup plus 2 tablespoons olive oil, divided
Juice of 2 lemons
1 cup milk
Lemon wedges (optional)

Scrub clam shells thoroughly; rinse well. Place in salted water to cover, and chill at least 6 hours or overnight. Open shells with an oyster knife; cut clams loose from shells without removing. Set clams aside.

Combine 2 quarts water, salt, pepper, Greek seasoning, and vinegar in a large Dutch oven; bring to a boil. Add shrimp; return to a boil, and cook 3 to 5 minutes or until pink. Let cool; peel, devein, and cut into ¼-inch slices.

Combine shrimp, breadcrumbs, garlic, mushrooms, 1 cup olive oil, and lemon juice in a medium mixing bowl; mix well. Spoon about 2 rounded tablespoonfuls of mixture on top of each clam, leaving shells open.

Grease a large baking pan with 2 tablespoons olive oil; place filled clams in pan. Pour milk around clams; bake at 400° for 20 minutes. Garnish with lemon wedges, if desired. Yield: 2 dozen.

PEANUT-RAISIN PIE

1 cup finely chopped salted peanuts
1 unbaked 10-inch pastry shell
½ cup seedless raisins
3 eggs, slightly beaten
¾ cup sugar
½ cup firmly packed light brown sugar
¾ cup light corn syrup
¼ teaspoon salt
1 teaspoon vanilla extract
1 teaspoon imitation brandy extract
½ cup melted butter or margarine

Spread peanuts evenly in pastry shell; sprinkle with raisins, and set aside.

Combine eggs, sugar, corn syrup, salt, flavorings, and butter; mix well. Pour into pie shell. Bake at 375° for 1 hour or until set. Yield: one 10-inch pie.   *Robert Hammond, Asheville, North Carolina.*

FANCY BAKED CHICKEN

½ cup butter or margarine, melted
¾ cup grated Parmesan cheese
¾ to 1 teaspoon granulated garlic
½ teaspoon salt
4 whole chicken breasts, skinned and boned
1 to 1½ cups soft breadcrumbs

Combine butter, cheese, garlic, and salt; mix well. Dip each piece of chicken in mixture, reserving remainder; coat with breadcrumbs.

Place chicken in a greased 13- x 9- x 2-inch baking dish; spoon remaining butter mixture on top. Bake at 350° for 1 hour or until done. Yield: 4 servings.   *Dr. Jerry W. Price, Tarboro, North Carolina.*

ROQUEFORT DRESSING

1 (8-ounce) carton commercial sour cream
1 cup mayonnaise
1 tablespoon lemon juice
1 tablespoon anchovy paste
1 teaspoon soy sauce
¼ teaspoon Worcestershire sauce
1 teaspoon instant minced onion
3 to 4 ounces Roquefort or blue cheese, crumbled
1 tablespoon instant parsley flakes
⅓ to ¼ cup milk

Combine all ingredients; mix well, and chill until ready to serve. Yield: about 3 cups.   *P. D. Graham, Wilmington, Delaware.*

Pick A Pudding For Dessert

Pudding—whether steamed, topped with a sauce, served with ice cream, or just warm from the pan—is one dessert that you can always count on to be a hit.

Choose your favorite—dates or figs—for the delicious steamed pudding, served hot or cold.

APPLE-NUT PUDDING WITH HOT RUM SAUCE

2 cups sugar
½ cup butter or margarine, softened
2 eggs
2 teaspoons vanilla extract
½ teaspoon imitation butter flavor
2 cups all-purpose flour
2 teaspoons soda
½ teaspoon salt
2 teaspoons ground cinnamon
2 tablespoons water
4 apples, peeled and finely chopped
1 cup chopped pecans
Hot Rum Sauce

Combine sugar, butter, eggs, vanilla, and butter flavor; beat until fluffy. Add flour, soda, salt, cinnamon, and water; beat 2 minutes on medium speed of an electric mixer. Stir in apples and pecans. Spoon into a greased and floured 13- x 9- x 2-inch baking pan; bake at 350° for 1 hour or until done. Spoon into individual dishes or cut into squares; serve with Hot Rum Sauce. Yield: 15 to 18 servings.

Hot Rum Sauce:

2 tablespoons all-purpose flour
1 cup sugar
⅛ teaspoon salt
½ cup butter or margarine
1 cup water
2 teaspoons vanilla extract
2 teaspoons imitation rum extract
¼ teaspoon imitation butter flavor

Combine flour, sugar, salt, butter, and water in a medium saucepan; mix well. Cook over medium heat, stirring constantly, until mixture boils. Add vanilla extract, rum extract, and butter flavor; return to a boil. Serve hot. Yield: about 1¾ cups.
Mrs. Gene R. Grove,
Beaver, Oklahoma.

STEAMED DATE PUDDING

1⅓ cups all-purpose flour
¾ teaspoon soda
½ teaspoon salt
¾ teaspoon ground cinnamon
¾ cup coarsely chopped dates or figs
½ cup butter, softened
⅔ cup sugar
1 egg, beaten
⅓ cup milk
1 teaspoon vanilla extract
¼ cup chopped pecans or walnuts

Combine first 4 ingredients in a medium mixing bowl; stir in dates, coating well. Set aside.

Combine butter and sugar; cream until light and fluffy. Add egg, mixing well. Add flour and date mixture alternately with milk, stirring well after each addition. Stir in vanilla and pecans.

Pour batter into a well-greased 1½-quart pudding mold, and cover tightly with lid. (Or pour batter into a well-greased heatproof bowl, and cover with a double thickness of buttered aluminum foil; secure foil with string.)

Place mold on rack in a large kettle; add boiling water, filling kettle one-third full. Cover, and steam 2 to 2¼ hours. (Water should boil gently; add more water as needed.)

Remove mold from kettle; remove lid from mold to allow steam to escape. Loosen pudding from sides of mold, and invert onto serving dish. Serve hot or cold. Yield: 8 to 10 servings.
Ruth J. Jorgensen,
Rogers, Arkansas.

LEMON PUDDING

1 cup sugar
3 tablespoons all-purpose flour
Pinch of salt
Juice of 1 lemon
Grated rind of 1 lemon
1 egg yolk, beaten
1 cup milk
1 tablespoon vegetable oil
2 egg whites

Combine sugar, flour, salt, lemon juice, and rind in a large mixing bowl; mix well. Stir in egg yolk, milk, and oil. Beat egg whites until stiff but not dry; fold into lemon mixture. Pour into a greased 1½-quart casserole. Pour 1 to 1½ inches water in a baking pan, and place casserole in pan. Bake at 350° for 45 minutes or until edges are lightly browned. Yield: 6 servings.
Mrs. R. A. Dibrell,
Dallas, Texas.

BISCUIT PUDDING

8 (2-inch) biscuits
4 slices bread, trimmed
2 eggs, beaten
1 cup sugar
2½ cups milk
1 teaspoon vanilla extract
3 tablespoons melted butter or margarine
Vanilla sauce (recipe follows)

Break biscuits and bread into chunks and place in a lightly greased 9-inch square pan.

Combine remaining ingredients except vanilla sauce; pour mixture over bread. Bake at 350° for 30 to 35 minutes or until lightly browned on top. Serve hot or cold with vanilla sauce. Yield: 8 servings.

Vanilla Sauce:

½ cup sugar
2 tablespoons all-purpose flour
2 cups milk
1 teaspoon vanilla extract

Combine sugar and flour in a saucepan. Gradually stir in milk and vanilla; cook over low heat, stirring constantly, until smooth and thickened. Yield: 2 cups.
Mrs. Robert Gambill,
Nashville, Tennessee.

WOODFORD PUDDING

½ cup butter or margarine, softened
1 cup sugar
3 eggs, beaten
1 teaspoon soda
3 tablespoons buttermilk
1 cup all-purpose flour
1 teaspoon ground cinnamon
½ teaspoon ground nutmeg
1 cup blackberry jam
Vanilla ice cream

Cream butter and sugar until light and fluffy; add eggs, and beat well.

Dissolve soda in buttermilk. Combine dry ingredients. Add buttermilk mixture and dry ingredients to creamed mixture; stir well.

Stir in jam. Spoon mixture into a greased 8-inch square pan. Bake at 350° for 35 to 40 minutes or until done. Serve with ice cream. Yield: about 8 to 10 servings.
Mrs. David L. Beall,
Harrodsburg, Kentucky.

May

In the South, May brings warm weather and a need for meals that are refreshing, nourishing, and adaptable to summer living. What could be a better way to welcome this early summer season than with a cool main dish salad? We offer five that are designed to fill you up but not to leave you stuffed.

Nothing sparks the appetite like an outdoor barbecue. To help you plan yours, we offer some helpful tips and a potpourri of grilled meat recipes. After you decide on the entrée, scan our selection of cookout accompaniments to complement your menu. End your outdoor feast by serving a homemade sauce over your favorite ice cream.

To eliminate guesswork when cooking with herbs, you will find some general guidelines as well as a variety of recipes. Then take advantage of the fruit and vegetable crops that are now in season.

These Salads Are The Main Course

Southern summers call for meals that are cool and satisfying, and require little time to prepare. The answer is simplicity itself: Serve a salad as the main dish and round out the menu with bread and a refreshing beverage.

Since main dish salads need to be filling, they usually include protein-rich foods such as meats, seafood, eggs, or cheese. Crisp, fresh salad greens are almost always an ingredient.

The main dish salads included here are particularly appealing because of the colorful combinations of ingredients and interesting textures. There's a leafy-green spinach salad, a chicken-fruit combination, and a shimmering coleslaw and shrimp aspic. For extra color and flavor, garnish with radishes, cherry tomatoes, fruit, or fresh mushrooms.

SHRIMP-COLESLAW ASPIC

2½ pounds medium-size fresh shrimp
1 (3¼-ounce) package crab-boil mix
3 envelopes unflavored gelatin
3 cups cold water, divided
2¼ cups finely shredded cabbage
2¼ cups finely shredded carrots
2¼ cups mayonnaise
½ cup plus 1 tablespoon lemon juice
3 to 4 tablespoons grated onion
¾ teaspoon salt
¼ teaspoon red pepper
Bibb lettuce
Lemon slices

Combine shrimp and crab-boil mix; add boiling water to cover. Cook 3 to 5 minutes, and drain well. Rinse shrimp with cold water; peel and devein. Leave tails on 1 cup shrimp, and set aside for garnishing.

Soften gelatin in 1 cup water; place over medium heat, stirring constantly, until gelatin dissolves.

Combine gelatin mixture, 2 cups water, cabbage, carrots, mayonnaise, lemon juice, onion, salt, pepper, and 3 cups shrimp.

Spoon into an oiled 9-cup mold; chill until firm. Unmold on Bibb lettuce, and garnish with reserved shrimp and lemon slices. Yield: 10 to 12 servings.
Elizabeth Ahearn,
Stanardsville, Virginia.

CAROUSEL MANDARIN CHICKEN

2 to 3 cups cooked diced chicken
1 cup diced celery
2 tablespoons lemon juice
1 tablespoon minced onion
1 teaspoon salt
⅓ cup mayonnaise or salad dressing
1 cup seedless green grapes
1 (11-ounce) can mandarin oranges, drained
½ cup toasted slivered almonds
Leaf lettuce
Additional mandarin orange slices (optional)

Combine chicken, celery, lemon juice, onion, and salt; chill well.

Add mayonnaise, grapes, oranges, and almonds to chicken mixture; toss until well mixed. Serve on lettuce leaves. Garnish with additional orange slices, if desired. Yield: 6 servings.
Mrs. Broxie C. Stuckey,
Gordo, Alabama.

TOMATO PETAL SALAD

4 medium tomatoes, cored
1 (6½-ounce) can tuna, drained and flaked
1 (12-ounce) carton small-curd cottage cheese
4 green onions, chopped
¾ teaspoon garlic powder
½ teaspoon hot sauce
Lettuce leaves

Scoop out pulp from tomato centers, reserving pulp for other uses. Turn shell upside down to drain; chill.

Combine tuna, cottage cheese, onion, and seasonings; stir lightly until well mixed. Chill thoroughly. At serving time, quarter each tomato, cutting to within ½ inch of bottom. Carefully spread out sections of tomato to form a cup. Spoon tuna mixture into tomatoes and serve on lettuce leaves. Yield: 4 servings.
Mrs. Jack Corzine,
Greenville, South Carolina.

SEVEN-LAYER VEGETABLE SALAD

½ head lettuce, coarsely chopped or shredded
1 cup chopped celery
1 cup chopped green pepper
1 cup chopped purple onion
1 (17-ounce) can small English peas, drained
1½ cups mayonnaise
1½ teaspoons sugar
Grated Parmesan cheese
4 slices bacon, cooked and crumbled

Layer vegetables in the order listed in a 2-quart bowl; spread mayonnaise evenly over top. Sprinkle with remaining ingredients in the order listed. Cover tightly, and chill 8 hours. Yield: 4 servings.
Mrs. R. E. McGuire,
South Fulton, Tennessee.

ZESTY SPINACH SALAD

1 egg, slightly beaten
¼ cup vegetable oil
Juice of 1 lemon
1 tablespoon grated Parmesan cheese
2 tablespoons Dijon mustard
1 teaspoon sugar
1 teaspoon Worcestershire sauce
½ teaspoon salt
Dash of pepper
1¼ pounds fresh spinach
¼ pound fresh mushrooms
6 slices bacon, cooked and crumbled
2 hard-cooked eggs, chopped

Combine first 9 ingredients in a jar; tighten lid, and shake until well blended. Chill thoroughly.

Remove stems from spinach; wash leaves thoroughly, and pat dry. Tear into bite-size pieces. Quickly rinse mushrooms in cold water; pat dry, and slice thin. Combine spinach and mushrooms in a large salad bowl; cover and chill.

Toss spinach mixture with chilled dressing until well coated; garnish with bacon and hard-cooked egg. Yield: 6 servings.
Mrs. Archer Yates,
Dunwoody, Georgia.

Tip: Use the store's comparative pricing information for good buys. The unit-price data allows you to compare the cost of similar products of different sizes by weight, measure, or count.

Fire Up For Outdoor Cooking

When the air fills with the tantalizing aroma of meat sizzling over glowing coals, you know that the wonderful days of outdoor cooking are back. And everyone's favorite meats—beef, chicken, pork, and lamb—are all enhanced by the smoky flavor.

Marinating meat before cooking will improve the flavor, and also makes the meat tender and juicy. Our Barbecued Steak Kabobs call for the steak and mushrooms to be marinated in red cooking wine before being threaded on skewers with green peppers, potatoes, and cherry tomatoes. And Marinated Barbecued Chicken gets its distinctive taste from a tomato-based marinade that is flavored with orange juice, olive oil, and seasonings.

A tangy basting sauce coats Southern Barbecued Spareribs and keeps the meat from drying out. When you grill the spareribs, use a slow fire as the sauce contains sugar, making the meat more likely to burn if the fire is too hot.

To enjoy fully your over-the-coal favorites, remember these tips:

■ Before placing meat on a new or freshly scrubbed grill, rub the grill with vegetable oil so that the food won't stick to it.

■ Always use tongs, rather than a fork, to turn meat. Piercing causes loss of juices and flavor.

■ The bed of coals should be prepared well in advance of cooking; put food on the grill when the coals are ash-gray and hot with no flames.

■ Never allow the coals to flame during cooking; the flames may either burn the meat or cause it to dry out. Keep a container of water nearby, and douse flames as they appear.

BARBECUED STEAK KABOBS

3 pounds (1½-inch-thick) round or T-bone steak, cut into 1½-inch cubes
Meat tenderizer
1 pound fresh mushroom caps
1 cup red cooking wine
2 green peppers, cut into 1-inch pieces
2 (16-ounce) cans whole potatoes, drained
18 to 24 cherry tomatoes

Sprinkle meat with tenderizer; set aside 30 minutes, and again sprinkle with tenderizer. Combine meat, mushrooms, and wine in a shallow dish.

Cover and marinate 2 to 3 hours in the refrigerator, turning occasionally.

Remove meat and mushrooms from marinade. Alternate meat and vegetables on skewers. Grill 10 to 15 minutes over medium heat or until desired degree of doneness. Yield: 6 servings.

Mrs. Essie Lawson,
Trenton, Florida.

PIRATE STEAK

1 (12-ounce) can beer
½ cup chili sauce
¼ cup vegetable oil
2 tablespoons soy sauce
1 tablespoon Dijon-style mustard
½ teaspoon hot sauce
⅛ teaspoon liquid smoke
½ cup coarsely chopped onion
2 cloves garlic, crushed
1 (3-pound) sirloin steak, 1½ to 2 inches thick
1 teaspoon salt
½ teaspoon pepper

Combine first 9 ingredients in a medium saucepan; simmer 30 minutes.

Brush steak with sauce, and place on grill 4 inches from medium coals; grill 15 minutes on each side or until desired degree of doneness. Baste frequently with sauce. Remove steak from grill, and sprinkle with salt and pepper. Serve with remaining sauce. Yield: 6 to 8 servings.

Cheryl M. Howe,
Virginia Beach, Virginia.

BARBECUED FLANK STEAK

¼ cup vinegar
¼ cup vegetable oil
1 small onion, finely chopped
1 clove garlic, crushed
½ teaspoon dried basil
½ teaspoon dry mustard
⅛ teaspoon hot sauce
2 (1¼-pound) flank steaks

Combine first seven ingredients in a small bowl, stirring well. Pour over steak in a shallow baking dish; cover and refrigerate overnight.

Remove steak from marinade, and place on grill over glowing coals. Cook about 5 minutes on each side or until cooked to desired doneness. To serve, slice across the grain. Yield: about 10 servings.

Mrs. Anna Maidhof,
Lehigh Acres, Florida.

BARBECUED LAMB CHOPS

8 (2-inch-thick) rib lamb chops
Salt and pepper to taste
3 cloves garlic, halved
Pinch of rosemary
½ cup wine vinegar
¼ cup vegetable oil

Sprinkle lamb chops with salt and pepper; rub with garlic. Combine rosemary, vinegar, and oil; baste chops well with sauce.

Place chops 5 to 6 inches from medium coals. Grill 6 to 7 minutes for rare, 9 to 10 minutes for medium, 12 or more minutes for well done, or until desired degree of doneness. Baste frequently with sauce during cooking. Yield: 4 servings.

Mrs. Glen H. Orr,
Jasper, Arkansas.

SUPERBURGERS

1 pound ground beef
1 pound ground cooked ham
1 cup commercial sour cream
¼ cup finely chopped onion
¼ teaspoon Ac'cent
¾ teaspoon salt
⅛ teaspoon pepper
Commercial barbecue sauce
2 slices process American cheese, quartered
8 hamburger buns, toasted
Cherry tomatoes
Sliced sweet pickles
Lettuce
Sliced onion

Combine first 7 ingredients. Shape into 8 patties, 3¾ inches in diameter. (Mixture will be sticky.) Place on grill over hot coals; cook 4 to 8 minutes on each side or until desired degree of doneness. Baste patties frequently with barbecue sauce during cooking. Top patties with cheese during last 2 to 3 minutes of cooking.

Serve on buns. Garnish with tomatoes, pickles, lettuce, and onion. Yield: 8 servings.

Mrs. Ray Keebler,
Savannah, Georgia.

Tip: Freeze extra parsley in plastic bags; just snip off sprigs of frozen parsley as needed.

MARINATED BARBECUED PORK CHOPS

½ cup vegetable oil
¼ cup olive oil
¼ cup lemon juice
3 cloves garlic, crushed
1 tablespoon salt
1 teaspoon paprika
½ teaspoon pepper
6 bay leaves, halved
6 to 8 (1-inch-thick) loin or rib pork chops

Combine first 8 ingredients in a shallow baking dish; mix well. Add meat to marinade; cover and marinate overnight in refrigerator.

Remove chops from marinade, and place about 4 to 5 inches from coals. Grill over slow to medium coals 30 to 45 minutes or until chops are no longer pink, turning and basting occasionally. Yield: 6 to 8 servings.

Mrs. Esta Meislish,
Marietta, Georgia.

SOUTHERN BARBECUED SPARERIBS

2 cloves garlic, crushed
2 tablespoons butter or margarine, melted
2 tablespoons prepared mustard
¼ cup firmly packed brown sugar
1 cup catsup
¾ cup chili sauce
1 tablespoon celery seeds
2 tablespoons Worcestershire sauce
1 to 2 dashes hot sauce
½ teaspoon salt
1½ cups water
4 pounds spareribs or loin back ribs
Salt

Sauté garlic in butter 4 to 5 minutes in a saucepan. Add next 9 ingredients; bring to a boil.

Sprinkle spareribs with salt; place bone side down on grill over slow coals. Grill about 20 minutes; turn meaty side down and cook until browned. Turn meaty side up again, and grill ribs about 20 minutes longer. Brush meaty side with basting sauce. Continue to grill without turning 20 to 30 minutes, basting occasionally. Brush sauce on both sides of the ribs, and let cook 2 to 3 minutes on each side. Yield: about 4 to 6 servings.   *Mrs. Anne A. Shinault,*
Pulaski, Virginia.

GOLDEN GRILLED HAM

1 (1-inch-thick) slice cooked ham (about 1½ pounds)
1 cup ginger ale
1 cup orange juice
½ cup firmly packed brown sugar
3 tablespoons vegetable oil
1 tablespoon wine vinegar
2 teaspoons dry mustard
¾ teaspoon ground ginger
½ teaspoon ground cloves

Score fat edge of ham. Combine remaining ingredients; pour over ham in a shallow baking dish. Refrigerate overnight or let stand at room temperature 1 hour, spooning marinade over ham several times.

Place ham on grill over slow coals; cook about 15 minutes on each side, brushing frequently with marinade. Heat remaining marinade and serve with ham. Yield: 4 servings.

John B. Holloway, Jr.,
Tallahassee, Florida.

MARINATED BARBECUED CHICKEN

1 (8-ounce) can tomato sauce
½ cup olive oil
½ cup orange juice
¼ cup vinegar
1½ teaspoons whole oregano
1 teaspoon salt
¼ teaspoon pepper
1 clove garlic, minced
1 (2½- to 3-pound) broiler-fryer, quartered

Combine first 8 ingredients in a jar; cover and shake well.

Combine chicken and tomato marinade in a shallow dish; cover and marinate overnight in refrigerator.

Remove chicken from marinade, and place chicken bone side down on grill. Grill over medium coals 50 to 60 minutes or until tender, turning chicken and brushing with marinade about every 15 minutes. Yield: 4 servings.

Mrs. Judith Roth,
Merritt Island, Florida.

Tip: Stains or discolorations on aluminum utensils can be removed by boiling a solution of 2 to 3 tablespoons cream of tartar, lemon juice, or vinegar to each quart of water in the utensil for 5 to 10 minutes.

CHARCOAL BROILED CHICKEN

2 (2- to 3-pound) broiler-fryers, halved
½ cup soy sauce
¼ cup water
½ cup vegetable oil
2 tablespoons instant minced onion
2 tablespoons sesame seeds
1 tablespoon sugar
1 teaspoon ground ginger
¾ teaspoon salt
½ teaspoon instant minced garlic
⅛ teaspoon ground red pepper

Place chicken in a plastic bag. Combine remaining ingredients; mix well. Pour marinade into bag; close bag tightly, and place in shallow pan in refrigerator at least 12 hours, turning occasionally.

Remove chicken from marinade. Arrange, bone side down, on grill over slow coals. Grill 1 hour or until meat is tender and skin is crisp, turning and basting with marinade about every 15 minutes. Yield: 4 servings.

Martha T. Efird,
Albemarle, North Carolina.

■ These pleasantly tart barbecue sauces enhance the aroma and flavor of meats cooked on the grill. Try them with grilled pork, beef, or chicken.

PAPRIKA BARBECUE SAUCE

1 cup catsup
½ cup vinegar
½ cup butter or margarine
¼ cup paprika
Juice of 2 lemons
¼ cup firmly packed brown sugar
4 teaspoons prepared horseradish
1 tablespoon black pepper
2 teaspoons prepared mustard
1 teaspoon Worcestershire sauce
1 clove garlic, minced
¼ teaspoon hot sauce

Combine all ingredients in a large saucepan; mix well. Bring to a boil; reduce heat and simmer 10 to 15 minutes, stirring occasionally. Use on spareribs, chicken, or beef. Yield: 2 cups.

Mrs. Dean D. Piercy,
Memphis, Tennessee.

EASY BARBECUE SAUCE

1 (12-ounce) jar orange marmalade
1 (12-ounce) bottle chili sauce
¼ cup vinegar
1 tablespoon Worcestershire sauce
1½ teaspoons celery seeds

Combine all ingredients in a medium mixing bowl; mix well. Use on spareribs and other meats. Yield: about 3 cups.

Enticing Ice Cream Sauces

Go ahead and indulge yourself with one of these enticing sauces spooned over ice cream. Choose from raspberry, cherry, and a chocolate-peanut butter combination. You'll also want to try them served over pound cake and angel food cake.

CHERRY SAUCE
1 (16½-ounce) can pitted dark sweet cherries
2 tablespoons cornstarch
¼ cup sugar
¼ cup Burgundy or dry red wine

Drain cherries, reserving juice.
Combine cornstarch and sugar in a small saucepan; mix well. Gradually stir in cherry juice. Cook over medium heat, stirring constantly, until mixture boils and thickens.
Remove from heat, and stir in Burgundy and cherries. Serve warm over ice cream. Yield: about 1¼ cups.
Mrs. Reed Justus,
Memphis, Tennessee.

CHOCOLATE-PEANUT BUTTER SAUCE
1 (6-ounce) package semisweet chocolate morsels
¼ cup crunchy peanut butter
¼ cup light corn syrup
5 tablespoons whipping cream

Melt chocolate morsels in top of a double boiler. Add peanut butter, stirring until well blended. Remove from heat, and stir in corn syrup and whipping cream. Serve warm over ice cream. Yield: about 1¼ cups.
Note: Store in refrigerator. Reheat over low heat before using. If sauce becomes too thick, stir in a small amount of whipping cream.
Miss Charlotte Pierce,
Greensburg, Kentucky.

CRIMSON RASPBERRY SAUCE
1 (10-ounce) package frozen sweetened raspberries, thawed and crushed
1 tablespoon cornstarch
½ cup currant jelly

Combine raspberries and cornstarch in a saucepan, mixing well. Add jelly; cook, stirring constantly, until bubbly. Cook 1 minute. Strain. Cool and serve over ice cream. Yield: about 1¼ cups.
Mrs. Bertha Fowler,
Woodruff, South Carolina.

Munch On Some Nachos

When friends come over and settle down in front of the television, serve a substantial snack to munch on. Best-Ever Nachos may be just the snack to serve.
Tortilla chips are spread with a spicy mixture of refried beans, green chiles, and mozzarella cheese. Each nacho is then topped with more cheese, a slice of jalapeño pepper or onion, then quickly broiled. For a final topping, add a dollop of Creamy Guacamole.

BEST-EVER NACHOS
Vegetable cooking spray
2 tablespoons butter or margarine
1 clove garlic, minced
1 cup finely chopped onion
1 (4-ounce) can chopped green chiles
1 large tomato, chopped
1 tablespoon fresh cilantro or 1 teaspoon dried cilantro (optional)
2 (16-ounce) cans refried beans
4 to 6 ounces mozzarella cheese, cubed
3 (7-ounce) packages cheese-flavored tortilla chips
3 cups (¾ pound) shredded sharp Cheddar cheese
6 to 8 jalapeño peppers, sliced into rings (optional)
Pearl onion slices (optional)
Creamy Guacamole

Spray a 3-quart, deep ceramic heatproof casserole with vegetable cooking spray. Melt butter in casserole; add garlic and sauté until golden brown. Add onion and sauté until transparent. Add chiles, tomato, and cilantro, if desired; simmer until tender. Add refried beans,

stirring until mixture is smooth. Stir in mozzarella cheese; cook over low heat until cheese melts and mixture is bubbly, stirring occasionally. Cool; cover and chill well.
Select unbroken chips, and place on a cookie sheet or ovenproof platter. Top each with a generous teaspoonful of bean mixture; sprinkle with Cheddar cheese and top with a slice of jalapeño pepper or a slice of onion, if desired.
Broil 6 inches from broiler unit just until cheese melts. Top hot nachos with dollops of Creamy Guacamole. Yield: about 13 dozen.
Note: Bean mixture may be frozen for later use, if desired.

Creamy Guacamole:
2 ripe avocados, peeled and chopped
2 tablespoons picante sauce
2 tablespoons mayonnaise
1 tablespoon lemon or lime juice
½ teaspoon Worcestershire sauce
Dash of garlic powder

Combine all ingredients in container of electric blender. Blend until smooth; chill well. Serve with hot nachos. Yield: about 1½ cups.
Note: Reserve seed from 1 avocado. Place seed in guacamole to prevent mixture from darkening. May be served as a dip with plain or cheese-flavored tortilla chips.
Dave Shuppert,
Dallas, Texas.

If you've been looking for a tempting snack, spicy Best-Ever Nachos will fill the bill. A bowl of Creamy Guacamole provides the final topping.

For Eggplant Lovers

Eggplant lovers will especially like this hearty casserole that combines eggplant with tomatoes, onions, green pepper, and ground beef. The meat and vegetables, including fresh green tomatoes, are layered and topped with slices of Cheddar cheese, then baked.

FLAVORFUL EGGPLANT CASSEROLE

1 small eggplant, unpeeled and cut into ½-inch-thick slices
1 pound lean ground beef
3 medium-size green tomatoes, cut into ¼-inch-thick slices
2 medium-size green peppers, cut into ¼-inch-thick rings
2 medium onions, thinly sliced
1 (28-ounce) can whole tomatoes, drained and cut into quarters
½ teaspoon salt, divided
¼ teaspoon pepper, divided
1 pound medium-sharp Cheddar cheese, thinly sliced

Cook eggplant in boiling salted water 5 to 8 minutes or until barely tender; drain well.

Brown beef in a skillet until done, stirring to crumble; drain well.

Layer half of eggplant, green tomato, green pepper, onion, ground beef, and canned tomatoes in a lightly greased deep 2½-quart casserole; sprinkle with ¼ teaspoon salt and ⅛ teaspoon pepper. Top with half of cheese slices. Repeat layers of vegetables; reserve remaining cheese. Sprinkle casserole with ¼ teaspoon salt and ⅛ teaspoon pepper.

Cover and bake at 400° for 30 to 45 minutes or until bubbly. Top with remaining cheese slices; bake, uncovered, 5 minutes or until cheese melts. Yield: 6 to 8 servings.

Note: Reserve the juice from canned tomatoes for use in other recipes.
Mrs. T. S. Guyton,
Huntsville, Alabama.

Tip: This is a handy method for freezing casseroles: line a casserole dish with heavy-duty aluminum foil, put the food in it, seal, and freeze. When the casserole is frozen, lift out the package, and mold foil to surface of food; seal securely with freezer tape, label, and return to the freezer.

Whole Wheat—It's Naturally Good

Just one bite of freshly baked whole wheat bread is all it takes to make whole wheat a favorite at your home. For the only thing better than the aroma of freshly baked whole wheat bread is its distinctive nutlike flavor.

As the name implies, whole wheat flour is ground from the entire wheat kernel, so it provides more protein and less calories than regular white flour. And these recipes combine that whole grain goodness with honey, yogurt, fruit, and bran for muffins, cake bars, and a coffee cake layered with fresh apples.

To protect the natural flavor of whole wheat flour and ensure long shelf life during the summer, store it in a moisture-proof bag in the refrigerator or freezer.

HEARTY WHOLE WHEAT BREAD AND ROLLS

1 package dry yeast
½ cup warm water (105° to 115°)
1 tablespoon sugar
4 cups whole wheat flour
4 cups unbleached flour
½ cup sugar
1 tablespoon cocoa
2 teaspoons salt
2½ cups warm water
¼ cup vegetable oil
1 egg

Combine yeast, ½ cup warm water, and sugar in a large bowl; let stand 40 minutes.

Combine dry ingredients; add to yeast mixture with remaining ingredients. Beat until smooth.

Place dough in a greased bowl, turning to grease top. Cover and let rise in a warm place (85°), free from drafts, 1½ hours or until doubled in bulk.

Punch dough down, and let rise 1 hour and 15 minutes or until doubled in bulk.

Turn dough out on a lightly floured surface (using unbleached flour); knead about 10 minutes or until smooth and elastic. Divide dough into 3 portions.

Shape 2 portions into loaves and place in well-greased 9- x 5- x 3-inch loafpans. Cover loaves, and let rise until doubled in bulk.

Divide remaining third of dough into 8 portions. Roll each portion into a 16-inch rope. Tie a loose knot in one end of rope; then pull longer end of strip through center of knot (a French knot). Place on a greased baking sheet; cover and let rise 40 minutes or until doubled in bulk.

Place rolls on middle rack and loaves on bottom rack of a cold oven. Set oven at 400° and bake 15 to 17 minutes or until rolls are golden brown. Remove rolls; place loaves on middle rack. Reduce heat to 375°, and bake 25 minutes longer or until bread is done.

Remove loaves from pans, and cool on racks. Yield: 2 loaves and 8 rolls or 3 loaves.
Lynette L. Walther,
Palatka, Florida.

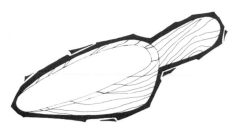

WHOLE WHEAT DESSERT WAFFLE

1½ cups whole wheat flour
½ cup unbleached flour
2 teaspoons baking powder
1 teaspoon soda
1 teaspoon ground ginger
1 teaspoon ground cloves
¼ teaspoon salt
½ cup wheat germ
½ cup safflower oil or sesame oil
½ cup honey
1 cup blackstrap molasses
3 eggs, separated
1 cup hot water
5 to 6 bananas, cut in lengthwise slices
Vanilla ice cream or whipped cream

Sift together first 7 ingredients; stir in wheat germ.

Combine oil and honey, beating well. Stir in molasses and beaten egg yolks. Add to flour mixture, mixing well. Add hot water and mix thoroughly.

Beat egg whites until soft peaks form; fold into batter. Pour ½ cup batter into a hot, lightly oiled, waffle iron. Cook about 3½ to 4 minutes or until done. Repeat process until all batter is used.

To serve, top each waffle with banana slices and a scoop of vanilla ice cream or a dollop of whipped cream. Yield: 10 (6-inch) waffles.

Note: Waffles may be prepared ahead of time and frozen. Thaw; then reheat in toaster.
Janet L. Stokes,
Virginia Beach, Virginia.

LEMON YOGURT WHEAT BARS

2 cups whole wheat flour
1 cup all-purpose flour
2 teaspoons soda
1 teaspoon baking powder
1 teaspoon salt
1 teaspoon grated lemon rind
1 (8-ounce) carton lemon yogurt
1 cup raisins
1 cup finely grated carrots
¾ cup honey
½ cup chopped nuts (optional)
2 eggs, lightly beaten
⅓ cup vegetable oil
¼ cup milk
Creamy Lemon Frosting

Combine first 6 ingredients in a large bowl, stirring well. Combine yogurt, raisins, carrots, honey, nuts, eggs, vegetable oil, and milk; add to dry ingredients, stirring until moistened.

Spread batter in a greased 13- x 9- x 2-inch baking pan. Bake at 350° for 25 to 30 minutes. Cool. Top with Creamy Lemon Frosting. Cut into bars. Yield: about 2 dozen.

Creamy Lemon Frosting:

1 (3-ounce) package cream cheese, softened
2 tablespoons butter, softened
1 teaspoon grated lemon rind
1 teaspoon lemon juice
2 cups powdered sugar

Combine cream cheese and butter, creaming until fluffy. Add lemon rind and juice; mix thoroughly. Gradually add powdered sugar, beating until light and fluffy. Yield: 1 cup.

Marion Elliott,
Washington, D.C.

CRUNCHY-TOPPED WHOLE WHEAT COFFEE CAKE

1 cup whole wheat pastry flour
½ cup all-purpose flour
¼ cup unprocessed bran
¼ cup wheat germ
1 teaspoon baking powder
1 teaspoon soda
½ teaspoon salt
½ cup butter or margarine, softened
½ cup firmly packed dark brown sugar
2 eggs
1 (8-ounce) carton plain yogurt
1 teaspoon vanilla extract
1 large apple, peeled and thinly sliced
Topping (recipe follows)
Sliced almonds (optional)

Combine first 7 ingredients in a bowl; stir well, and set aside.

Combine butter and sugar, creaming until light and fluffy; beat in eggs. Combine yogurt and vanilla; add to creamed mixture alternately with flour mixture, mixing well after each addition.

Spoon half of batter into a greased 9-inch square baking pan. Top with apple slices; sprinkle ½ cup topping over apples. Spread the remaining batter evenly on top; then sprinkle with remaining topping. Top with sliced almonds, if desired.

Bake at 350° for 35 to 40 minutes. Cool on rack for 30 minutes; cut into 12 squares. Serve warm. Yield: 12 servings.

Topping:

¼ cup firmly packed dark brown sugar
½ cup chopped pecans
½ teaspoon ground cinnamon
2 tablespoons shredded coconut (optional)

Combine all ingredients in a small bowl, stirring well. Yield: about 1⅓ cups.

Note: Thinly sliced fresh peaches or pears may be substituted for apples.

Marie Hayman,
Ocean City, Maryland.

FRUITED WHEAT MUFFINS

2 cups whole wheat flour
1½ cups unprocessed bran
1 cup peeled, chopped apple
½ cup raisins
½ cup sunflower seeds
1 tablespoon grated orange rind
1¼ teaspoons soda
½ teaspoon salt
½ teaspoon ground nutmeg
Juice of 1 orange (3 tablespoons orange juice)
About 1¾ cups buttermilk
1 egg, slightly beaten
½ cup molasses
2 tablespoons vegetable oil

Combine first 9 ingredients in a large bowl; stir well. Make a well in center.

Combine orange juice and enough buttermilk to make 2 cups. Combine buttermilk mixture, egg, molasses, and oil in a small bowl. Add to dry ingredients, stirring just until moistened.

Fill greased muffin tins two-thirds full. Bake at 350° for 25 minutes or until done. Yield: about 1½ dozen.

Linda Clark,
Charlottesville, Virginia.

Pizza, Thick Or Thin

Everybody loves a pizza; it's just that some people like a thin crust and others prefer a thick one. Mrs. John F. Woods of Memphis has solved the problem with a recipe than can go either way. Her delicious Canadian-style bacon pizza recipe will make two thick-crust or four thin-crust pizzas.

TWO-WAY PIZZA

1 package dry yeast
¾ cup warm water (105° to 115°)
2½ cups biscuit mix
Vegetable oil
1 (8-ounce) can tomato sauce
2 teaspoons Italian seasoning
Sliced olives
Chopped green pepper
Chopped onion
Sliced mushrooms
1 pound Canadian-style bacon, cut into ½-inch cubes
Shredded mozzarella and Cheddar cheese

Soften yeast in warm water; add biscuit mix, and beat until smooth. Turn dough out onto a floured surface; knead about 25 times or until dough is soft and elastic.

For thick crust: Divide dough into 2 parts; shape into balls. Roll each ball of dough into a 10-inch circle on a floured surface and place on a well-greased pizza pan, or press each ball of dough into well-greased pan. Brush with oil; bake at 425° for 5 minutes.

For thin crust: Divide dough into 4 parts and prepare as above, rolling out dough into 8-inch circles.

Combine tomato sauce and Italian seasoning; spread over dough. Sprinkle olives, green pepper, onion, and mushrooms over tomato sauce. Arrange Canadian-style bacon on top; sprinkle with cheese. Bake at 425° for 15 minutes or until bubbly. Let stand 5 to 10 minutes before cutting. Yield: two 10-inch thick-crust pizzas or four 8-inch thin-crust pizzas.

Tip: Compare costs of fresh, frozen, canned, and dried foods. To compute the best buy, divide the price by the number of servings. The lower price per serving will be the thriftiest buy.

Feast On Juicy, Ripe Strawberries

If there's a better way to enjoy fresh strawberries than just plain or with a little sugar and cream, it's when they're served in one of these delectable desserts.

Besides the custardy goodness of Old-Fashioned Strawberry Ice Cream, there's a parfait and the tartlike Strawberry Pizza. You'll also want to try Strawberries Sabayon, a Grand Marnier-flavored sauce spooned over whole berries.

Since strawberries do not ripen after being picked, buy fully ripened berries. If storage is necessary, spread the berries out on a shallow pan or tray and place in the refrigerator. Do not wash or remove the caps of strawberries until you're ready to use them.

STRAWBERRIES SABAYON

4 egg yolks
2 tablespoons sugar
¼ cup Grand Marnier
⅓ cup whipping cream, whipped
2 pints fresh strawberries, washed and hulled

Place egg yolks in top of a double boiler; beat at medium speed of electric mixer until thick and lemon colored. Gradually add sugar, beating until soft peaks form.

Place egg yolk mixture over simmering water; beat in Grand Marnier. Continue cooking and beating until mixture is fluffy. Remove from heat and beat until cool. Fold in whipped cream.

Divide strawberries equally among 6 dessert dishes. Spoon sauce over top. Yield: 6 servings.

Mrs. Bruce Fowler,
Woodruff, South Carolina.

OLD-FASHIONED STRAWBERRY ICE CREAM

1 cup sugar, divided
2 tablespoons all-purpose flour
Dash of salt
1½ cups milk
2 eggs, slightly beaten
1½ cups sieved or pureed fresh strawberries
1½ cups whipping cream
1½ teaspoons vanilla extract
1 teaspoon almond extract

Combine ¾ cup sugar, flour, and salt; set aside.

Scald milk in top of a double boiler; add a small amount of milk to sugar mixture, stirring to make a smooth paste. Stir sugar mixture into remaining milk; cook, stirring constantly, until thickened. Cover and cook 10 minutes.

Stir a small amount of hot mixture into eggs. Stir eggs into remaining hot mixture; cook, stirring constantly, 1 minute. Let cool.

Combine strawberries, remaining ¼ cup sugar, whipping cream, and flavorings; stir into custard. Pour into container of a 2-quart electric or hand-turned ice cream freezer; freeze according to manufacturer's directions. Yield: about 1¼ quarts.

Mrs. Parke LaGourgue Cory,
Neosho, Missouri.

STRAWBERRY PIZZA

1 cup self-rising flour
¼ cup powdered sugar
½ cup melted butter or margarine
1 (8-ounce) package cream cheese, softened
1 (14-ounce) can sweetened condensed milk
⅓ cup lemon juice
1 teaspoon vanilla extract
½ cup sugar
2 tablespoons cornstarch
½ cup water
2 pints strawberries, halved
Few drops of red food coloring (optional)

Combine flour and powdered sugar; add butter, mixing well. Pat dough out in a 14-inch pizza pan; bake at 350° for 10 minutes or until lightly browned.

Combine cream cheese, condensed milk, lemon juice, and vanilla; mix well and spread on cooled crust. Chill.

Combine sugar and cornstarch in a large saucepan; add water, mixing until smooth. Cook over medium heat until thickened (about 5 minutes), stirring constantly. Add strawberries; if desired, stir in food coloring. Cool completely.

Spread strawberry mixture over cream cheese layer; chill. Cut into wedges to serve. Yield: 8 to 10 servings.

Mrs. E.C. Bryant,
Greenwood, Mississippi.

CHERRY-BERRY ON A CLOUD

6 egg whites
½ teaspoon cream of tartar
¼ teaspoon salt
3 cups sugar, divided
2 (3-ounce) packages cream cheese, softened
1 teaspoon vanilla extract
1 cup whipping cream, whipped
2 cups miniature marshmallows
2 cups fresh strawberries, washed and hulled
1 (21-ounce) can cherry pie filling
1 teaspoon lemon juice

Place a 10-inch circle of brown paper on a cookie sheet.

Place egg whites in a large mixing bowl; beat at high speed of electric mixer until foamy. Add cream of tartar and salt, beating until soft peaks form. Gradually add 1¾ cups sugar, 2 tablespoons at a time, beating well after each addition.

Spread egg white mixture evenly on brown paper circle. Bake at 275° for 1 hour. Turn oven off, and let meringue layer remain in unopened oven overnight.

Combine cream cheese, 1 cup sugar, vanilla, and whipped cream; mix well. Stir in marshmallows and spread over meringue layer; refrigerate overnight.

Combine strawberries and ¼ cup sugar; stir gently, and chill 1 to 2 hours. Combine strawberries, cherry pie filling, and lemon juice; stir gently. Spread over the cream cheese layer. Yield: 16 servings.

Note: Two (10-ounce) packages frozen strawberries, thawed, may be substituted for fresh strawberries.

Aileen Leslie,
Kirksey, Kentucky.

The traditional food of Ocracoke has a flavor as special as the island itself. Shown clockwise: Stewed Shrimp with Dumplings (page 31), Shrimp and Chicken Ariosto (page 31), Corned Fish (page 32), and Oyster Fritters (page 31).

Page 98: Alternating layers of rich chocolate cake, sweetened whipped cream, and nutty chocolate filling make a luscious Double-Chocolate Torte (page 67).

Above: Satisfy warm-weather appetites with one of these cool, refreshing main dish salads: Shrimp-Coleslaw Aspic and Carousel Mandarin Chicken (page 88).

Left: Grow your own thyme, chives, basil, oregano, sage, and rosemary in containers; then try our recipes for cooking with fresh herbs that begin on page 99.

Far Left: In Sweet-and-Sour Pork (page 42), cubes of pork are battered and deep-fried, then combined with a pineapple-vegetable sauce and spooned over rice.

STRAWBERRY PARFAIT

1 pint strawberries, washed and hulled
¼ cup plus 2 tablespoons sugar
1 tablespoon cornstarch
1 tablespoon lemon juice
⅛ teaspoon ground nutmeg
Dash of salt
1 cup whipping cream, whipped and
   divided
2 tablespoons kirsch
Red food coloring (optional)
1 pint vanilla ice cream

Set aside 8 whole strawberries; puree remaining berries.

Combine sugar, cornstarch, lemon juice, nutmeg, salt, and pureed strawberries; mix well. Cook over low heat, stirring constantly, until thickened. Let cool. Fold in ½ cup whipped cream, kirsch, and food coloring, if desired; chill.

Place a whole strawberry in each of 4 parfait glasses; top with a scoop of ice cream and about 2 tablespoons strawberry mixture. Repeat layers of ice cream and strawberry mixture. Top with about 2 tablespoons whipped cream, and garnish with remaining whole strawberries. Yield: 4 servings.

Mrs. Peggy Fowler Revels,
Woodruff, South Carolina.

Fresh Ideas For Cooking With Herbs

Cooking with fresh herbs is becoming increasingly popular and with good reason, for they enhance the flavor of a multitude of dishes. Fortunately, cooking with herbs is easy to master.

Innovation is the key, and few groups have become as imaginative and creative with herb cookery as the Herb Society of Hilton Head Island, South Carolina. The original 30-member group was organized by Mrs. Esther Dickey in 1971. Since that time, the group has produced an abundance of simple recipes that emphasize the best use of herbs, and the popularity of their recipe-exchange program has spawned two additional herb groups.

Besides being dedicated experimenters, society members are gradually accumulating recipes that will one day be compiled into a cookbook. The emphasis is on fresh herbs and surprising ways to serve them. They also use herbs to replace or reduce other seasonings like salt, which is especially beneficial to people on low-sodium diets.

Tips On Harvesting And Cooking

In the course of their experimentation, the Herb Society has developed guidelines that can help the herb enthusiast. Here are some tips on harvesting and using herbs.

■ Herbs can be harvested at any stage of their growth, but the flavors are strongest when the oils are at their peak. For flowering herbs, this is usually when they are in bloom.

■ Herbs harvested for later use should be dried. Spread the herbs over a wire screen or similar device that allows the air to circulate around them, or hang them in bunches upside down; store in a warm, preferably dark, place. When the herbs are completely dry, place them in airtight containers; store away from heat and sunlight in order to preserve their flavor.

■ Revive the flavor of long-dried herbs by soaking them for 10 minutes in lemon juice.

■ Crush dried herbs gently with a mortar and pestle to enhance their flavor. Slightly bruising fresh plants will also increase their effectiveness.

■ When substituting dried herbs for fresh, use a third (or half if you like strong flavor) the amount of fresh herb called for.

■ If the dish is to cook slowly for a long time, such as soup or stew, add delicate-flavored and ground herbs late in cooking. This will keep the flavor from being steamed out. However, firm herbs, like bay leaves, require long cooking.

■ Avoid using two strong herbs like bay, rosemary, or sage together, as the flavors will fight each other. Instead, use a strong herb in combination with a milder one. The accent herbs are slightly milder than the strong herbs and include basil, tarragon, oregano, and mother-of-thyme. Medium herbs are dill, marjoram, winter savory, fennel, mint, and lemon thyme. Delicate herbs include chervil, chives, parsley, and summer savory.

Using the Popular Herbs

Try mixing and matching herbs with a variety of foods to determine which combinations you prefer. Here are some suggestions.

Basil—Tomato dishes, beef stew, lamb chops, pizza, shrimp creole, potato salad, eggplant, squash, and peas

Chives—Cottage cheese, egg dishes, meatballs, scalloped potatoes, tossed salads, tuna fish, and poultry

Dill—Cheese dips, cottage cheese, drawn butter for shellfish, sauce for chicken or fish, carrots, and peas

Bay leaf—Pot roasts, game, fish stews, poultry stuffings, tomatoes, artichokes, beets, carrots, and potato salad

Marjoram—Vegetable soups, baked fish, barbecue sauce, beef, cauliflower, green beans, spinach, and zucchini

Mint—Apple pie, applesauce, carrots, fruit salads, oatmeal, peas, tea, mint juleps, jellies, and lamb

Oregano—Chowders, Italian dishes, Mexican dishes, egg salad, broccoli, tomatoes, Swiss steak, and cheese dip

Parsley—Biscuits, cottage cheese, meatballs, potato soup, scrambled eggs, tossed salads, and creamed fish

Rosemary—Fruit cup, chicken and vegetable soups, beef stew, pizza, spaghetti sauce, cabbage, and zucchini

Sage—Chicken and vegetable soups, lamb, pot roast, poultry dressing, eggplant, chowder, and tomatoes

Tarragon—Chicken livers, chowders, consommés, veal, poultry dishes, vinegar, marinades, and asparagus

Thyme—Clam chowder, barbecue sauces, beef, chicken dishes, tomatoes, zucchini, and herb salad dressing

Some Special Recipes: While the Herb Society of Hilton Head Island has developed many recipes, here are a few that offer a different or unusual use of some common herbs.

BROILED HERB FISH FILLETS

2 fish fillets
2 to 3 teaspoons minced fresh dillweed
½ to 1 teaspoon minced fresh thyme
¾ teaspoon low-sodium seasoning
½ teaspoon grated gingerroot (optional)
¼ cup dry white wine (optional)
2 tablespoons salt-free margarine
1 teaspoon lemon juice

Place fillets, skin side down, in a lightly oiled 2-quart shallow baking dish. Sprinkle with dill, thyme, low-sodium seasoning, and gingerroot. Pour wine over and around fish, if desired; set aside.

Combine margarine and lemon juice in a small saucepan; cook over low heat until margarine melts. Pour over fillets. Broil 6 inches away from heat 7 to 10 minutes or until fish flakes easily when tested with a fork. Yield: 2 servings.

HERBED BREAST OF CHICKEN

1 medium onion
4 whole cloves
4 whole chicken breasts, skinned
2 to 3 teaspoons minced fresh lemon
    thyme or thyme
2 to 3 teaspoons minced fresh marjoram
½ to 1 teaspoon minced fresh rosemary,
    sage, or tarragon
1 teaspoon low-sodium seasoning
½ teaspoon grated gingerroot
Pepper (optional)
4 large mushrooms, sliced
⅓ cup dry white wine
Parsley

Cut 4 small slits in onion and insert a clove into each slit. Set aside.

Place chicken, meaty side up, on a large piece of foil. Sprinkle chicken with herbs, low-sodium seasoning, gingerroot, and pepper; top with mushrooms and onion. Add wine; fold foil to seal securely.

Bake at 350° for 1 hour or until done; open foil during last 10 minutes of baking time to allow browning. Cut the onion into wedges for serving. Garnish with parsley. Yield: 4 servings.

PEPPERED CHEESE BALL

1 (8-ounce) package cream cheese,
    softened
1 tablespoon commercial sour cream
1 teaspoon minced fresh marjoram
1 clove garlic, minced
Cracked peppercorns or lemon pepper

Combine cream cheese, sour cream, marjoram, and garlic in a small mixing bowl; beat until fluffy and well blended. Form mixture into a ball, and coat with pepper. Chill 2 to 3 hours; serve with crackers. Yield: one 3-inch cheese ball.

Note: Instead of forming cheese mixture into a ball, it may be placed in a small crock and topped with pepper.

HOMEMADE HERB VINEGAR

Pack a glass jar loosely with bruised leaves and tender stems of fresh herbs. Fill jar with heated cider or white or red wine. Let stand 3 weeks or longer; strain through a cloth or fine sieve before using.

Suggested herb combinations: Basil and shallots; basil, thyme, rosemary, celery seeds, and lemon balm or lemon verbena; burnet, thyme, basil, tarragon, garlic, and red pepper; basil, oregano, thyme, parsley, and dill.

For Your Cookout, Super Side Dishes

The tender, juicy meats cooked over the coals deserve only the best of vegetables to complement their wonderful flavor. This array of side dishes includes vegetables to suit every type of meat.

Cheesy Onion Casserole is particularly good with steak. Those who prefer potatoes will find the flavor of Potato-Cheese Casserole to be delightful with many grilled meats.

To make the most of the season's fresh produce, serve green beans in the Mediterranean style or combine zucchini and yellow squash with a tangy tomato sauce and green chiles for Two-Squash Casserole.

MEDITERRANEAN-STYLE GREEN BEANS

1 large onion, chopped
¼ cup olive oil or vegetable oil
½ green pepper, chopped
1 stalk celery, chopped
1 pound fresh green beans, cut into
    2-inch pieces
½ cup water
1 teaspoon salt
¼ teaspoon pepper

Sauté onion in oil over medium heat until tender. Add green pepper and celery; cover and cook over low heat 5 minutes, stirring occasionally. Add green beans, water, salt, and pepper; cover and cook 20 minutes, stirring occasionally. Yield: 5 to 6 servings.

Mrs. Jean Hansen,
Muscle Shoals, Alabama.

CHEESE-TOPPED GREEN BEANS

1 pound fresh green beans, cut into
    1-inch pieces
¼ cup dry onion soup mix
1 cup water
3 tablespoons melted butter or margarine
⅓ cup toasted slivered almonds
3 tablespoons grated Parmesan cheese
½ teaspoon paprika

Combine green beans, onion soup mix, and water; cover and cook over low heat 20 to 30 minutes or until beans are tender. Drain and spoon into a serving dish. Add butter, almonds, and cheese; toss lightly. Sprinkle with paprika. Yield: 4 to 6 servings.

Nancy A. Sturup,
Columbus, Georgia.

BARBECUED PORK AND BEANS

1 (16-ounce) can pork and beans,
    undrained
⅓ cup chopped onion
¼ cup diced green pepper
1 slice bacon, diced
1 clove garlic, minced
¼ cup catsup
2 tablespoons brown sugar or
    maple-flavored syrup
1 tablespoon Worcestershire sauce
½ teaspoon salt
¼ teaspoon dry mustard
Dash of pepper
2 tablespoons margarine

Combine all ingredients except margarine, mixing well. Spoon into a lightly greased 1-quart casserole, and dot with margarine. Bake at 425° for 35 to 40 minutes. Yield: 4 servings.

Ms. Winifred K. Crow,
Baton Rouge, Louisiana.

BAKED SWISS CAULIFLOWER

1 large head cauliflower
½ cup breadcrumbs
2¾ cups shredded Swiss cheese
1½ cups half-and-half
3 egg yolks, beaten
¼ teaspoon ground nutmeg
½ teaspoon salt
¼ teaspoon pepper
¼ cup melted butter or margarine

Wash cauliflower, and discard green leaves; break into flowerets. Cook, covered, 10 minutes in a small amount of boiling salted water; drain.

Place cauliflower in a buttered 1½-quart shallow baking dish. Combine remaining ingredients except butter, and pour over cauliflower; drizzle butter over top. Bake at 350° for 15 to 20 minutes. Yield: 6 servings.

Beth Calkins,
Nashville, Tennessee.

CHEESY ONION CASSEROLE

5 medium onions, thinly sliced
¼ cup butter or margarine
¼ cup all-purpose flour
2 cups milk
2 cups (½ pound) shredded sharp process
    American cheese
½ teaspoon salt
½ teaspoon pepper

Separate onion slices into rings; place in an ungreased 2½-quart casserole.

Melt butter in a heavy saucepan over low heat and blend in flour; cook until bubbly, stirring constantly. Gradually add milk; cook over low heat, stirring constantly, about 6 minutes or until thickened. Stir in cheese, salt, and pepper; cook just until cheese melts, stirring constantly.

Remove sauce from heat; pour over onion, mixing gently. Bake at 325° for 45 to 50 minutes or until bubbly. Yield: 6 to 8 servings.

Mrs. Margaret L. Hunter,
Princeton, Kentucky.

POTATO-CHEESE CASSEROLE

6 medium potatoes
2 (10¾-ounce) cans cream of mushroom
    soup, undiluted
2 cups milk
2 large onions, thinly sliced
2 cups (½ pound) shredded sharp
    Cheddar cheese
Salt and pepper
Paprika

Cover potatoes with salted water, and bring to a boil; reduce heat, and cook about 30 minutes or until tender. Peel and cut into ¼-inch slices; set aside. Combine soup and milk, stirring well.

Layer half of potatoes, onion, and cheese in a greased 2-quart casserole; sprinkle with salt and pepper. Pour half of soup mixture over cheese. Repeat layers; sprinkle paprika over top. Bake at 300° for 45 minutes or until bubbly. Yield: 6 to 8 servings. *Grace Owens,*
Tioga, Louisiana.

Tip: When food boils over in the oven, sprinkle the burned surface with a little salt. This will stop smoke and odor from forming and make the spot easier to clean. Also, rubbing damp salt on dishes in which food has been baked will remove brown spots.

TWO-SQUASH CASSEROLE

1 pound yellow squash, cut into ½-inch
    slices
1 pound zucchini, cut into ½-inch slices
1 medium onion, chopped
2 tablespoons bacon drippings
1 (8-ounce) can tomato sauce
1 (4-ounce) can chopped green chiles
½ teaspoon salt
1 cup (¼ pound) shredded Cheddar
    cheese
Italian breadcrumbs

Cook yellow squash and zucchini separately in a small amount of boiling salted water 5 minutes; drain well.

Sauté onion in bacon drippings until tender but not brown. Combine tomato sauce, chiles, and salt; stir well.

Place yellow squash in a 1½-quart deep casserole; add onion, spreading evenly. Pour half of sauce over onion; add zucchini, and pour remaining sauce over top. Sprinkle with cheese, and top with breadcrumbs. Bake at 350° for 30 minutes or until bubbly. Yield: about 6 servings. *Mrs. H. LeRoy Baker,*
Annandale, Virginia.

English Peas, So Good Served Fresh

Besides enjoying fresh English peas just simmered and topped with melted butter, enjoy their sweet flavor and tender texture in other dishes.

An all-time favorite combination is English peas and potatoes, and these recipes offer two variations: Harvest Soup and Creamed Peas and New Potatoes. For something different, try Vegetable Medley—a mixture of English peas, limas, and French-style green beans tossed with a mayonnaise-base sauce.

When buying English peas, select large, bright-green pods that are well filled and snap easily. Yellowish pods usually indicate overly mature, tough peas. Use the peas as soon as possible; if storage is necessary, place the unshelled peas in the refrigerator.

HARVEST SOUP

½ pound fresh English peas
4 slices bacon, cut into ½-inch pieces
2 tablespoons sliced green onion
½ cup sliced celery
½ cup thinly sliced carrot
2 cups mashed potatoes
1 (17-ounce) can cream-style corn
2 cups milk
1 teaspoon salt
1 cup (¼ pound) shredded medium-sharp
    Cheddar cheese
1 large tomato, peeled and thinly sliced
Seasoned pepper

Shell and wash peas; drain.

Fry bacon in a large saucepan until crisp, and drain on paper towels; reserve 1 tablespoon drippings.

Sauté onion, celery, and carrot in bacon drippings 2 minutes; stir in potatoes, corn, peas, milk, salt, and cheese; cook over medium heat, stirring occasionally, until cheese melts.

Top each serving with a tomato slice, bacon pieces, and a dash of seasoned pepper. Yield: 4 to 6 servings.

Note: 1½ cups frozen peas may be substituted for fresh.

Mrs. Cary Loehl,
Arcadia, California.

BRAISED RICE AND PEAS

2 pounds fresh English peas
5 cups chicken stock
¼ cup plus 2 tablespoons butter or
    margarine, divided
½ cup finely chopped onion
1½ cups uncooked regular rice
1 cup diced cooked smoked ham
½ cup grated Parmesan cheese

Shell and wash peas; drain. Simmer chicken stock in a large saucepan. (It should remain at simmer throughout preparation.)

Melt ¼ cup butter in a 3-quart saucepan; add onion and sauté just until tender. Add peas, rice, and ham to sautéed onion; cook, stirring often, 2 minutes. Stir in 2 cups stock; cook, uncovered, 5 minutes, stirring occasionally. Add 1 more cup stock; cook, stirring occasionally, until all liquid is absorbed. (Rice and peas should be tender; if not, add more stock, ½ cup at a time, cooking until tender.)

Stir in cheese and remaining 2 tablespoons of butter. Serve hot. Yield: about 8 servings.

Note: 2 cups frozen peas may be substituted for fresh peas.

T. H. Wagener,
Augusta, Georgia.

CREAMED PEAS AND NEW POTATOES

1½ pounds tiny new potatoes
1 to 1½ pounds fresh green peas
3 tablespoons sliced green onion
¼ cup butter or margarine
¼ cup all-purpose flour
1 cup milk
¼ teaspoon salt
⅛ teaspoon white pepper

Wash potatoes; peel a thin strip around center. Cook potatoes, covered, in boiling salted water 10 to 15 minutes or until tender; drain.

Shell and wash peas. Add peas and onion to a small amount of boiling salted water. Reduce heat; cover and cook 8 to 12 minutes or until tender. Drain.

Melt butter in a heavy saucepan over low heat; blend in flour. Cook 1 minute, stirring constantly. Gradually add milk; cook over medium heat, stirring constantly, until thickened and bubbly. Stir in salt and pepper.

Combine vegetables; and top with sauce. Yield: 4 to 6 servings.

Note: 1½ cups frozen peas may be substituted for fresh. Cook according to package directions.

Mrs. Hazel W. Smith,
Westfield, North Carolina.

PARTY PEAS

1½ pounds fresh English peas
3 tablespoons butter or margarine
3 tablespoons all-purpose flour
1½ cups milk
½ teaspoon salt
¼ teaspoon white pepper
2 hard-cooked eggs, chopped
¼ cup chopped fresh mushrooms
¼ cup cracker crumbs

Shell and wash peas; add peas to a small amount of boiling salted water. Reduce heat; cover and cook 8 to 12 minutes or until tender. Drain.

Melt butter in a heavy saucepan over low heat; blend in flour. Cook 1 minute, stirring constantly. Gradually add milk; cook over medium heat, stirring constantly, until thickened and bubbly. Stir in salt and pepper.

Combine peas, white sauce, eggs, and mushrooms. Spoon into a greased 1-quart casserole. Sprinkle cracker crumbs over top. Bake at 350° for 15 to 20 minutes. Yield: 4 servings.

Note: 1½ cups frozen peas may be used instead of fresh peas. Cook according to package directions.

Mrs. A. I. O. Davies,
St. Petersburg, Florida.

VEGETABLE MEDLEY

1½ cups mayonnaise
2 hard-cooked eggs, finely chopped
1 medium onion, finely chopped
1 tablespoon Worcestershire sauce
1 tablespoon prepared mustard
¼ teaspoon salt
Juice of 1 lemon
⅛ teaspoon garlic salt
Dash of hot sauce
3 pounds fresh English peas
2 (10-ounce) packages frozen baby lima beans
2 (10-ounce) packages frozen French-style green beans

Combine first 9 ingredients, stirring well. Chill several hours; when ready to use, bring to room temperature.

Shell and wash peas; add to a small amount of boiling salted water. Reduce heat; cover and cook 8 to 12 minutes or until tender. Drain.

Cook green beans and limas according to package directions; drain.

Combine vegetables; add sauce, stirring gently to coat. Serve hot. Yield: 10 to 12 servings.

Note: 3 cups frozen peas may be substituted for fresh. Cook according to package directions. *Janice Biggers,*
Corinth, Mississippi.

Serve A Winning Dessert

The racetrack is not the only place you'll find winners during Derby Week, for parties and celebrations also call for prize-winning foods. Kentucky Derby Tarts, a specialty of Mrs. Margaret Hunter of Princeton, Kentucky, combine chocolate, pecans, and a hint of bourbon in small pastry shells for a rich, luscious dessert. Topped with powdered sugar, whipped cream, and a pecan half, they'll rank first place.

KENTUCKY DERBY TARTS

2 eggs
1 cup sugar
¼ cup butter or margarine, melted
2 tablespoons bourbon
½ teaspoon vanilla extract
½ cup all-purpose flour
½ cup semisweet chocolate morsels, melted
½ cup chopped pecans
10 unbaked (3-inch) pastry shells
Powdered sugar
Whipped cream
10 pecan halves

Beat eggs just until blended. Gradually add sugar, beating until thick and light colored. Add butter, bourbon, and vanilla; mix well.

Gradually add flour, beating well. Stir in chocolate and chopped pecans. Spoon ¼ cup filling into each pastry shell. Bake at 350° for 30 minutes. Cool tarts completely.

Sift powdered sugar lightly over tarts. Top with a dollop of whipped cream, and garnish each with a pecan half. Yield: 10 (3-inch) tarts.

Mrs. Margaret L. Hunter,
Princeton, Kentucky.

Creative Cooking Is His Art

According to Bill Gaines of Richmond, "cooking is never a chore and never a bore." This enthusiastic approach to cooking applies to his work as Program Director for the Virginia Museum as well as to his many other interests, such as painting, sailing, and skiing.

"The whole point of cooking is to do what you like," Gaines says. "I prefer entertaining my friends at home rather than eating out. People who lead busy lives as I do want to be able to cook for themselves as well as for guests with recipes that are easy to prepare and tasty, too."

Gaines' creative talents are evident when he takes one basic set of ingredients—pork, rice, and fruit—and develops those ingredients into two very different dishes.

A savory marinade and pears are the secret to Sunrise Pork Tenderloin served on a bed of rice, while a curry with apples, chutney, seasonings, and tender chunks of pork is served with rice in Hurry Curry.

"I like everything curried," Gaines says."Hurry Curry is actually several recipes in one, as I use the basic sauce for chicken, shrimp, lamb, and pork."

For a surprisingly easy accompaniment to Hurry Curry, baked bananas wrapped in bacon add an interesting taste. As the bacon cooks, the bananas soak in the drippings, giving them a sweet, delicate flavor.

Bill Gaines' special recipes for Hurry Curry, Sunrise Pork Tenderloin, and Baked Bananas are followed by recipes from other men who also enjoy cooking as a hobby.

SUNRISE PORK TENDERLOIN

1 (16-ounce) can pear halves
¼ cup soy sauce
12 pork tenderloin slices (about 2 pounds)
2 tablespoons melted butter
1 teaspoon crystallized ginger
1 teaspoon ground cinnamon sugar
Pinch of ground nutmeg
Salt and pepper to taste
Hot cooked rice

Drain pears, reserving juice. Combine pear juice and soy sauce in a shallow dish. Add pork; cover, and marinate 1 hour at room temperature or overnight in refrigerator. Drain pork, reserving marinade. Sauté pork in butter until golden brown; set aside and keep warm.

Combine marinade, ginger, cinnamon sugar, nutmeg, salt, and pepper in a saucepan; simmer 5 minutes. Add pears and simmer 3 minutes, basting with marinade. Serve with pork and rice. Yield: 4 servings.

BAKED BANANAS

4 slices bacon
4 small firm bananas
Lemon juice

Cook bacon until transparent. Brush bananas with lemon juice. Wrap bacon around bananas, securing with toothpicks. Place in shallow baking dish. Bake at 375° for 25 minutes, or until desired degree of doneness, turning once. Yield: 4 servings.

HURRY CURRY

8 pork tenderloin slices (about 1½ pounds)
¼ cup melted butter, divided
1 clove garlic, crushed
½ cup chopped onion
1 cup chopped tart apple
2 teaspoons curry powder
¼ teaspoon ground cardamom
1 tablespoon all-purpose flour
1 teaspoon crystallized ginger
¼ teaspoon salt
⅛ teaspoon pepper
1 (10¾-ounce) can condensed chicken broth, undiluted
1 teaspoon lemon juice
¼ cup chutney
Hot cooked rice

Brown pork in 2 tablespoons butter in a large skillet. Remove and cut into bite-size pieces; set aside.

Add remaining butter, garlic, and onion to skillet; cook until onion is transparent. Add apple and curry powder; cook, stirring constantly, over low heat until apple is tender. Add cardamom, flour, ginger, salt, and pepper; stir until well blended. Gradually add chicken broth, stirring constantly. Stir in lemon juice, and bring to a boil. Reduce heat; simmer about 10 minutes. Stir in pork and chutney; cover and simmer 10 minutes. Serve over rice. Yield: 4 servings.

WHITE WINE OMELET

2 tablespoons chopped green onion
⅓ cup chopped onion
1⅔ cups sliced fresh mushrooms
1½ tablespoons melted butter
¼ to ⅓ cup dry white wine
1½ tablespoons butter
3 eggs, well beaten
½ cup shredded Swiss cheese

Sauté onion and mushrooms in 1½ tablespoons melted butter in a small saucepan. Add wine; simmer until liquid is absorbed. Set aside mushrooms and onions, and keep warm.

Place a 6- or 7-inch omelet pan or heavy skillet on burner, and heat until it is hot enough to sizzle a drop of water. Add remaining 1½ tablespoons butter; rotate pan as butter melts to coat bottom of pan.

Add eggs to pan. With a plastic spatula, lift cooked portions of egg at the edges so uncooked portions flow underneath. Slide pan back and forth over heat to keep mixture in motion.

When eggs are set and top is still moist and creamy, sprinkle cheese, reserving 1 tablespoon, over half of omelet. Spoon mushroom mixture over cheese. Fold unfilled side over filling; sprinkle with remaining cheese, and cover for a few seconds or until cheese melts. Slide omelet onto plate, and serve immediately. Yield: 2 servings.

Paul Fransway,
Houston, Texas.

STEAK DIANE FLAMBE

½ pound fresh mushrooms, sliced
1 medium onion, chopped
½ cup melted butter
2 tablespoons Worcestershire sauce
2 (8-ounce) rib-eye steaks
Dijon mustard
⅓ cup brandy

Sauté mushrooms and onion in butter and Worcestershire sauce in a large skillet over low heat.

Flatten steaks slightly with a meat mallet or spoon. Spread a thin layer of mustard on one side of steak. Push mushrooms and onion to side of skillet; add steaks, mustard side down. Brown steaks, stirring mushrooms and onion occasionally to keep from burning. Spread a thin layer of mustard on top side of steak; turn and brown other side of steak.

Lightly pierce steak in several places with a fork. Pour brandy over steaks and simmer, covered, about 1 minute. Uncover and ignite. When flame dies down, remove steaks to heated platter; spoon mushrooms and onion over top. Yield: 2 to 4 servings. *Don Meinke,*
Roanoke, Virginia.

Tip: New cast-iron cookware should always be seasoned before using. Rub the interior of the utensil with oil or shortening, and place in 250° or 300° oven for several hours. Wipe off oily film, and store. If scouring is necessary after using the utensil, re-season the surface immediately to prevent rusting.

If utensils are to be stored for any length of time between use, rub a light film of oil over interior. Wipe off film before using, and wash in clear water.

Radishes, A Lively Touch In Salads

Whether it's a green salad, slaw, or potato salad, radishes fit right in, adding color and a fresh, crisp texture. Their pleasantly pungent flavor perks up cabbage in Sweet and Crunchy Slaw, while their color makes Sour Cream Potato Salad attractive. Radish-Dressed Tossed Salad features a combination of salad greens along with radishes, tomatoes, and green pepper, all topped with Zesty Blue Cheese Dressing.

SOUR CREAM POTATO SALAD

4 to 4½ cups peeled and sliced potatoes
2 stalks celery, finely chopped
12 small radishes, thinly sliced
1 small onion, finely chopped
2 hard-cooked eggs, sliced
½ cup commercial sour cream
¾ cup mayonnaise
½ teaspoon dillseeds
1¼ teaspoons prepared mustard
1½ teaspoons salt
½ teaspoon seasoned salt

Cook potatoes in boiling salted water for 10 to 15 minutes or until tender. Drain; chill thoroughly.
Combine potatoes, celery, radishes, onion, and egg slices in a large mixing bowl; set aside.
Combine remaining ingredients in a small bowl; mix well, and pour over vegetables. Toss lightly. Yield: 6 servings.
Mary Eason,
Orange Park, Florida.

SWEET AND CRUNCHY SLAW

4 cups shredded cabbage
2 tomatoes, chopped
1 green pepper, chopped
2 cups chopped celery
1 cup sliced radishes
Salt and pepper to taste
1 cup sugar
¼ cup vinegar
Juice of 1 lemon

Combine vegetables in a medium bowl. Sprinkle with salt, pepper, and sugar. Toss lightly. Add vinegar and lemon juice; toss. Yield: 6 to 8 servings.
Mrs. Charles Simms,
Palestine, Illinois.

RADISH-DRESSED TOSSED SALAD

½ head iceberg lettuce, torn
¼ head Bibb lettuce, torn
1 bunch of watercress (optional)
2 tomatoes, cut into wedges
12 large radishes, thinly sliced
4 to 5 green onions, sliced
½ green pepper, thinly sliced into rings
Zesty Blue Cheese Dressing

Combine first 3 ingredients in a large bowl. Add tomatoes, radishes, onion, and green pepper. Pour Zesty Blue Cheese Dressing on top; toss well, and serve. Yield: 4 to 6 servings.

Zesty Blue Cheese Dressing:

3 ounces blue cheese, crumbled
½ cup vegetable oil
2 tablespoons vinegar
1 tablespoon lemon juice
1 teaspoon salt
1 teaspoon steak sauce
1 teaspoon anchovy paste
⅛ teaspoon pepper
1 small clove garlic, minced

Combine all ingredients in a small bowl; stir well. Yield: about 1½ cups.
Mrs. Gerald Duncan,
Jacksonville, Florida.

Round Steak—Any Way You Like It

Round steak is one of the less expensive cuts of steak and certainly one of the most versatile. Whether you like it fried, stuffed, marinated, or baked, the flavor is great and the variations endless.
In Royal Beef Rollups with Rice, the steak is rolled around a delicious filling flavored with a hint of orange. The beef rolls are baked along with vegetables, then spooned over rice for a satisfying one-dish dinner.
Give fried steak new appeal by serving it as Lemon-Flavored Cutlets. This dish owes its refreshing flavor to lemon juice and a crispy crust.
For an Oriental touch, there's a choice of two delicious stir-fried specialties: Oriental Beef and Snow Peas or Beef and Green Peppers.

BEEF AND GREEN PEPPERS

½ pound boneless round steak
Marinade (recipe follows)
6 tablespoons vegetable oil, divided
1 cup water chestnuts, sliced
2 green peppers, cut into strips
¼ teaspoon salt
¼ teaspoon Ac'cent
⅓ cup water
1 teaspoon cornstarch
2 teaspoons soy sauce
Hot cooked rice

Partially freeze meat; cut (across grain) into slices ¼ inch thick. Place meat in marinade in an airtight container; marinate 30 minutes at room temperature or 8 hours in refrigerator.
Heat 3 tablespoons oil over high heat in a wok or skillet. Add meat and marinade; stir-fry until meat is browned. Remove meat and set aside.
Heat remaining 3 tablespoons oil in wok. Add water chestnuts, green pepper, salt, and Ac'cent; stir-fry until pepper is crisp-tender. Return meat to wok.
Combine water, cornstarch, and soy sauce; stir until smooth, and pour over meat. Cook, stirring constantly, until thickened and bubbly. Serve over rice. Yield: 2 to 3 servings.

Marinade:

1 tablespoon plus 1½ teaspoons soy sauce
2 teaspoons cornstarch
1 tablespoon dry white wine
1 tablespoon sesame seed oil
Dash of pepper
1 teaspoon finely chopped ginger
1 clove garlic, crushed
¼ teaspoon Ac'cent

Combine all ingredients, stirring until cornstarch is dissolved. Yield: ¼ cup.
Diana Williams,
Greensboro, North Carolina.

BEEF BOURGUIGNON

1 cup chopped onion
3 tablespoons vegetable oil
3 pounds round steak, cut into 1-inch cubes
¼ cup all-purpose flour
1¼ teaspoons salt
⅛ teaspoon pepper
½ teaspoon whole thyme leaves
1 bay leaf
½ cup beef bouillon
1 cup dry red wine
½ pound package fresh mushrooms, sliced
2 tablespoons butter or margarine, melted
Cooked potatoes, rice, or noodles

Sauté onion in hot oil until tender. Dredge meat in flour, and brown in oil. Add salt, pepper, thyme, bay leaf, bouillon, and wine; simmer 1 hour, stirring occasionally. (Add more bouillon or wine if necessary.)

Sauté mushrooms in butter; add to meat, and simmer an additional 30 to 45 minutes or until meat is tender. Serve with potatoes or over rice or noodles. Yield: 8 servings. *Eleanor Brandt, Arlington, Texas.*

ORIENTAL BEEF AND SNOW PEAS

1 pound boneless round steak
5 tablespoons soy sauce, divided
1 tablespoon sherry
4 teaspoons cornstarch
½ cup vegetable oil, divided
1 (6-ounce) package frozen snow peas
1 clove garlic, crushed
¾ teaspoon sugar
Hot cooked rice

Partially freeze meat; cut into slices ¼ inch thick and 2 inches long.

Combine 1 tablespoon soy sauce, sherry, and cornstarch; stir vigorously until cornstarch is dissolved. Coat beef with soy sauce mixture.

Heat 6 tablespoons oil over high heat in a wok or skillet. Add meat, and stir-fry until meat is browned. Remove meat, and set aside.

Add remaining 2 tablespoons oil to wok; add snow peas, and stir-fry over high heat 2 minutes. Add meat, garlic, remaining soy sauce, and sugar to wok; cook until thickened and bubbly. Serve over hot cooked rice. Yield: 4 servings. *Mrs. R. P. Vinroot, Matthews, North Carolina.*

STUFFED SHERRIED BEEF ROLLS

About 3 pounds boneless round steak
Salt and pepper to taste
3 stalks celery, finely chopped
3 carrots, finely chopped
2 medium onions, finely chopped
¼ cup melted butter or margarine
1 (4-ounce) can mushroom stems and pieces, drained
1½ cups toasted breadcrumbs
2 teaspoons Worcestershire sauce
1 teaspoon salt
½ cup dry sherry or dry red wine
Hot cooked noodles
Cornstarch

Trim excess fat from steak. Pound steak to ¼-inch thickness; cut into 4- x 4-inch pieces, and season to taste with salt and pepper.

Sauté celery, carrots, and onion in butter until crisp-tender; stir in mushrooms, breadcrumbs, Worcestershire sauce, and 1 teaspoon salt. Place ½ cup vegetable mixture on each steak piece, spreading to within ½ inch of edge. Roll each piece jellyroll fashion; secure with a toothpick.

Place beef rolls seam side down in a lightly greased 2-quart baking dish; pour in sherry. Cover and bake at 350° for 1 to 1½ hours or until tender. Remove beef rolls from baking dish, reserving drippings. Remove toothpicks, and arrange steak rolls on noodles on a warm serving platter. Keep warm.

Measure drippings. Use 2 teaspoons cornstarch per 1 cup drippings, and gradually stir drippings into cornstarch. Cook over medium heat, stirring constantly, until thickened and bubbly. Serve sauce with steak rolls. Yield: 8 servings. *Mrs. E. A. Kraus, Louisville, Kentucky.*

LEMON-FLAVORED CUTLETS

1½ to 2 pounds boneless round steak
3 eggs, beaten
Grated rind and juice of 2 lemons
1 teaspoon salt
1 teaspoon pepper
¾ cup fine breadcrumbs
¾ cup fine cracker crumbs
Hot vegetable oil

Trim excess fat from steak; pound to ¼-inch thickness. Cut steak into serving-size pieces.

Combine eggs, lemon rind and juice, salt, and pepper; beat well. Combine breadcrumbs and cracker crumbs. Dip steak into egg mixture; then dredge in crumb mixture. Cook steak cutlets in hot oil until done, turning once. Yield: 6 servings. *Dr. Hattie C. Propst, Tahlequah, Oklahoma.*

ROYAL BEEF ROLLUPS WITH RICE

1 pound boneless round steak
1 (2-ounce) can mushroom stems and pieces, drained and finely chopped
1 medium tomato, peeled and finely chopped
¼ cup breadcrumbs
1 teaspoon grated orange rind
1 teaspoon salt
¼ teaspoon pepper
¼ cup all-purpose flour
¼ teaspoon salt
¼ teaspoon pepper
¼ cup vegetable oil
2 cups whole baby carrots
3 celery stalks, cut into 1½-inch pieces (about 2 cups)
1 cup frozen English peas
2 cups beef broth
Hot cooked rice
2 tablespoons water

Trim excess fat from steak. Pound steak to ¼-inch thickness, and cut into 3½- x 4½-inch pieces.

Combine mushrooms, tomato, breadcrumbs, orange rind, 1 teaspoon salt, and ¼ teaspoon pepper. Place 2 tablespoons vegetable mixture on each steak piece, spreading to within ½-inch of edge. Roll up each piece jellyroll fashion; secure with a toothpick or tie with string at each end. Combine flour, ¼ teaspoon salt, and ¼ teaspoon pepper.

Dredge steak rolls in flour mixture; reserve excess flour mixture. Brown steak rolls in hot oil. Place in a shallow 2-quart casserole or baking dish; add carrots, celery, peas, and broth. Cover casserole and bake at 375° for 1 hour or until tender.

Remove steak rolls from casserole, reserving drippings; remove toothpicks or string. Place steak rolls and vegetables on rice on a warm serving platter; keep warm.

Combine reserved flour mixture and 2 tablespoons water in a small saucepan, blending until smooth. Gradually stir in drippings; cook over medium heat, stirring constantly, until thickened and bubbly. Serve sauce with steak rolls. Yield: 4 servings. *Myra Schisler, Jonesboro, Arkansas.*

Tip: Be willing to alter your shopping and eating habits. Learn less-expensive nutritional alternatives and substitute whenever possible. For example, substitute reconstituted dry milk for whole milk in cooking and baking.

You'll Welcome These Pineapple Dishes

Pineapple, the traditional symbol of hospitality, appears on gateposts and doorways throughout the South. Southerners, known for expressing their hospitality through fine food, not only use this sweet fruit in desserts but also in some other delightful dishes.

SCALLOPED PINEAPPLE

3 eggs, well beaten
2 cups sugar
1 (20-ounce) can crushed pineapple, undrained
4 cups 1-inch cubes fresh bread
1 cup margarine, cut into 1-inch squares

Combine all ingredients in a medium mixing bowl and mix well. Pour into a greased 13- x 9- x 2-inch baking pan. Bake at 350° for 1 hour. Yield: 10 to 12 servings. *Mrs. Elmer Underwood, Knoxville, Tennessee.*

SWEET-AND-SOUR CHICKEN

2½ cups bite-size pieces cooked chicken
1 egg, slightly beaten
½ cup cornstarch
Vegetable oil
1 (15¼-ounce) can pineapple chunks
½ cup vinegar
½ cup sugar
1 medium-size green pepper, cut into 1-inch squares
¼ cup water
2 tablespoons cornstarch
1 teaspoon soy sauce
1 (16-ounce) can sliced carrots, drained
Hot cooked rice

Combine chicken and egg, tossing to coat chicken. Dredge chicken in ½ cup cornstarch and fry in hot oil until golden brown. Drain on paper towels, and set aside.

Drain pineapple, reserving juice. Add enough water to pineapple juice to measure 1 cup. Combine juice, vinegar, and sugar in a large skillet; stir well. Bring to a boil, stirring constantly. Add green pepper; cover and simmer mixture 2 minutes.

Combine water and 2 tablespoons cornstarch, mixing well. Add to skillet mixture; cook, stirring constantly, until thickened. Stir in pineapple, soy sauce, carrots, and chicken; cook until thoroughly heated. Serve over rice. Yield: 4 to 5 servings. *Susanne Webb, Roanoke, Virginia.*

PINEAPPLE-CHEESE BAKE

1 (20-ounce) can pineapple chunks
1 (8-ounce) can crushed pineapple
1 egg
⅓ cup sugar
3 tablespoons all-purpose flour
1½ cups (⅜ pound) shredded Cheddar cheese
½ cup miniature marshmallows

Drain pineapple, reserving juice; set aside. Combine egg and sugar in a saucepan, beating until foamy. Add flour and pineapple juice, stirring until smooth; cook over low heat until thickened, stirring constantly. Remove from heat, and stir in cheese and pineapple.

Pour into a greased 2-quart casserole; top with marshmallows. Bake at 350° for 20 minutes. Cool slightly. Yield: 6 to 8 servings. *Mrs. R. M. Neumann, Bartlesville, Oklahoma.*

PINEAPPLE-CARROT BREAD

2 cups all-purpose flour
1 teaspoon soda
1 teaspoon salt
1½ teaspoons ground cinnamon
3 eggs, beaten
2 cups sugar
1 cup vegetable oil
1 cup grated carrots
1 (8-ounce) can crushed pineapple, undrained
2 teaspoons vanilla extract
1 cup chopped pecans

Combine flour, soda, salt, and cinnamon; set aside. Combine eggs, sugar, and oil in a medium mixing bowl; mix well. Stir in carrots, pineapple, and vanilla. Add dry ingredients, mixing well. Stir in pecans.

Pour batter into 2 greased 9- x 5- x 3-inch loafpans. Bake at 325° for 1 hour and 10 minutes or until done. Yield: 2 loaves. *Mrs. Glenna Scherle, Louisville, Kentucky.*

Pimientos Add Color And Spice

Brighten up some of your favorite casseroles and salads with colorful pimiento. Our readers have added the mild spicy flavor and lively red color of pimiento to a number of dishes. For example, there is a casserole of fresh green beans brightened with fresh tomatoes as well as pimiento. And for a colorful snack, try Confetti Snack Dip.

GREEN BEAN CASSEROLE

2 cups fresh green beans, cut in 2-inch pieces
3 to 6 slices bacon
½ cup chopped onion
4 large tomatoes, peeled and chopped
2 large whole pimientos, chopped
¼ teaspoon salt
⅛ teaspoon freshly ground pepper
½ cup shredded process American cheese

Cook beans, uncovered, in boiling salted water for 2 to 3 minutes; cover and cook 20 to 30 more minutes or until tender. Drain and set aside. Fry bacon until crisp; remove from pan and drain on paper towels, reserving drippings. Crumble bacon. Sauté onion in drippings until tender.

Combine all ingredients except cheese, tossing gently. Spoon into a greased 2-quart casserole; sprinkle cheese on top. Bake at 350° for 15 to 20 minutes or until cheese is lightly browned. Yield: 6 servings.
Mrs. Earl L. Faulkenberry, Lancaster, South Carolina.

MARINATED VEGETABLE SALAD

¾ cup vinegar
½ cup vegetable oil
1 teaspoon salt
1 cup sugar
1 tablespoon water
1 teaspoon pepper
1 (16-ounce) can French-style green beans, drained
1 (17-ounce) can small peas, drained
1 (12-ounce) can shoe peg whole kernel corn, drained
1 (2-ounce) jar chopped pimiento, drained
1 cup chopped celery
1 green pepper, finely chopped
1 bunch green onions, chopped

Combine first 6 ingredients in a medium saucepan; bring to a boil, stirring to dissolve sugar. Cool.

Combine vegetables, and stir in vinegar mixture. Cover and place in refrigerator 12 hours, stirring occasionally. Yield: 8 servings. *Sally Clinton, Orlando, Florida.*

CHICKEN-CHESTNUT SOUFFLE

9 slices white bread, crusts removed
4 cups cubed cooked chicken
1 (8-ounce) can sliced mushrooms, drained
¼ cup melted margarine
1 (8-ounce) can sliced water chestnuts, drained
9 slices process sharp Cheddar cheese
½ cup mayonnaise
4 eggs, well beaten
2 cups milk
1 teaspoon salt
1 (10¾-ounce) can cream of mushroom soup, undiluted
1 (10¾-ounce) can cream of celery soup, undiluted
1 (2-ounce) jar chopped pimiento, drained
2 cups buttered coarse breadcrumbs

Line a buttered 13- x 9- x 2-inch baking dish with bread; top with chicken.

Sauté mushrooms in margarine; spoon over chicken. Top with water chestnuts and cheese. Combine mayonnaise, eggs, milk, and salt, beating well; pour over cheese.

Combine soup and pimiento, stirring well; spoon over casserole. Cover with aluminum foil and place in refrigerator about 8 hours or overnight.

Bake, uncovered, at 350° for 30 minutes. Remove from oven; top with breadcrumbs. Return to oven, and bake an additional 15 to 20 minutes, or until set. Yield: 8 servings. *Mrs. Edward K. Beckes, Franklin, Tennessee.*

POTATOES AND EGGS AU GRATIN

1 tablespoon butter or margarine
1 tablespoon all-purpose flour
¾ cup milk
½ teaspoon salt
2 teaspoons chopped pimiento
2 cups cooked, sliced potatoes
3 hard-cooked eggs, sliced
⅔ cup shredded Cheddar cheese

Melt butter in a heavy saucepan over low heat; blend in flour, and cook 1 minute. Gradually add milk; cook over medium heat, stirring constantly, until thickened and bubbly. Stir in salt and chopped pimiento.

Place half the potatoes, eggs, white sauce, and cheese in layers in a greased 1-quart casserole; repeat with remaining ingredients. Bake at 325° for 25 minutes. Yield: 4 servings. *Mrs. Roy Tucker, Columbus, Georgia.*

CONFETTI SNACK DIP

1 (1⅜-ounce) envelope onion soup mix
1 (16-ounce) carton commercial sour cream
¼ cup finely chopped green pepper
¼ cup finely chopped cucumber
¼ cup finely chopped pimiento

Combine soup mix and sour cream. Stir in remaining ingredients. Chill 1 hour to blend flavors. Serve with crackers or chips. Yield: 2¼ cups. *Mrs. Jennie Kinnard, Mabank, Texas.*

Whip Up A Treat With Avocado

The creamy texture and the nutty flavor of avocado make it a welcome ingredient in these recipes—a cool, creamy dessert, a colorful and refreshing main dish salad, and a smooth, chicken-flavored soup.

Always purchase firm avocados and allow them to ripen at room temperature. To speed ripening, place the avocado in a brown paper bag. You'll know the fruit is ripe if the skin yields when pressed. To delay ripening, store the avocado in the refrigerator. Once it's cut, prevent discoloration of the flesh by rubbing it with lime or lemon juice.

CREAMY AVOCADO SOUP

1 large ripe avocado, peeled and cubed
3 cups chicken broth
1 green onion, chopped
1 cup whipping cream
½ teaspoon salt
⅛ teaspoon pepper
Dillseeds (optional)
Shredded cheese (optional)

Combine avocado, broth, and green onion in container of electric blender; process until smooth (about 5 minutes). Add cream, salt, and pepper; stir well. Chill 1 hour. Pour into large saucepan, and heat thoroughly. Serve warm. Garnish with dillseeds or shredded cheese, if desired. Yield: 4½ cups. *William A. Smith, Punta Gorda, Florida.*

CHICKEN SALAD SUPREME

3 (5-ounce) cans boned chicken, flaked
½ cup mayonnaise
1 tablespoon lemon juice
1 tablespoon prepared mustard
1 teaspoon seasoned salt
1 cup thinly sliced celery
1 medium avocado, peeled and cubed
1 (4-ounce) jar diced pimiento
¼ cup minced parsley
Salad greens

Drain chicken, reserving broth; combine broth and next 4 ingredients, mixing well. Add chicken, celery, avocado, pimiento, and parsley; stir gently. Chill, and serve on salad greens. Yield: 4 to 6 servings. *Mrs. Jack Corzine, Greenville, South Carolina.*

AVOCADO WHIP

1 large ripe avocado
Juice of 1 large lemon
3 tablespoons sugar
1 cup vanilla ice cream, slightly softened
Melon balls (optional)
Fresh strawberries (optional)
Sliced peaches (optional)
Crème de menthe (optional)

Cut avocado in half lengthwise; remove seed. Peel, mash, and sieve avocado; stir in lemon juice and sugar. Add ice cream and beat with electric mixer until smooth. Chill in freezer for about 1 hour or until firm, but not frozen. Garnish with melon balls, strawberries, peaches, or crème de menthe, as desired; serve at once. Yield: 4 servings. *Mrs. Eva Key, Isle of Palms, South Carolina.*

Make Veal Your Specialty

Prized for its fine texture and delicate flavor, veal is undeniably a delicacy. Using rich sauces, cheese, mushrooms, olives, or rice, our readers have given veal the special treatment it deserves.

Fresh, high-quality veal should be light pink in color and velvety in appearance. Even though veal is tender, it has very little fat and is likely to be dry unless moisture is used during the cooking process. This also means that for best results, veal should be pounded, sliced thin, or cooked long and slow.

In Veal Chops Mediterranean, the loin chops are simmered in a rich sauce of beef broth, onions, olives, and pimiento and served over buttered noodles.

VEAL CHOPS MEDITERRANEAN

2 tablespoons all-purpose flour
½ teaspoon salt
⅛ teaspoon pepper
6 to 8 small veal loin chops
2 tablespoons vegetable oil
1 medium onion, thinly sliced and separated into rings
1 (10½-ounce) can beef broth, undiluted
2 tablespoons lemon juice
½ teaspoon grated lemon rind
1 (7.4-ounce) can pitted ripe olives, drained and halved
1 (2-ounce) jar diced pimiento, drained
2 tablespoons chopped fresh parsley
Hot buttered noodles

Combine flour, salt, and pepper. Coat veal chops lightly with flour mixture, reserving remainder for sauce.

Brown chops in vegetable oil; remove chops, and set aside.

Add onion to pan drippings, and sauté until tender. Sprinkle with reserved flour mixture, stirring until smooth. Add broth; bring to a boil, stirring constantly. Add lemon juice and grated rind.

Return chops to skillet; cover. Reduce heat and cook 45 to 50 minutes. Add olive halves and pimiento; cook 5 additional minutes. Sprinkle with parsley, and serve over hot buttered noodles. Yield: 6 to 8 servings.
*Mrs. Roderick W. McGrath,
Orlando, Florida.*

Tip: Chopped onions have the best flavor if they are browned in shortening before being added to casserole dishes.

VEAL STROGANOFF

½ pound fresh mushrooms, sliced
6 tablespoons butter or margarine, divided
¼ cup all-purpose flour
1½ teaspoons salt
¼ teaspoon pepper
1 to 1½ pounds cubed veal cutlets
½ cup sliced onion
½ cup red cooking wine
1 (8-ounce) carton commercial sour cream
1 tablespoon chopped fresh parsley
Hot cooked noodles

Sauté mushrooms until tender in 2 tablespoons butter; set aside.

Combine flour, salt, and pepper in a medium bowl. Cut veal into 1-inch strips, and toss in flour mixture until lightly coated.

Melt remaining butter in a 10-inch skillet; add veal and onion, and cook until browned. Stir in wine; reduce heat and simmer 10 minutes, stirring occasionally. Add sour cream, mushrooms, and parsley; cook until thoroughly heated. Serve over hot cooked noodles. Yield: 6 servings. *Carole Lake,
Houston, Texas.*

HERBED VEAL AND ONIONS

3 tablespoons butter or margarine
3 medium onions, finely chopped
⅓ cup all-purpose flour
2 teaspoons salt
¾ teaspoon pepper
2 pounds ¼-inch-thick veal
⅓ cup butter or margarine
2 cloves garlic, crushed
Pinch of rosemary leaves
1 (10½-ounce) can beef consommé, undiluted

Melt 3 tablespoons butter in a skillet; add onion, and sauté until tender. Place onion in a 2-quart shallow casserole and set aside.

Combine flour, salt, and pepper; dredge veal in flour mixture. Melt ⅓ cup butter in skillet; add veal, and brown well.

Place veal over onion in casserole. Top with garlic and rosemary. Pour consommé over top. Loosen browned particles from skillet, and add to casserole. Cover and bake at 350° for 45 minutes. Yield: 6 to 7 servings.
*Mrs. J. T. Ballard,
Wichita Falls, Texas.*

VEAL CUTLET CASSEROLE

8 (¼-inch-thick) veal cutlets
Salt and pepper
2 tablespoons prepared mustard
¼ cup all-purpose flour
1 medium onion, thinly sliced
¼ cup vegetable oil
2 tablespoons all-purpose flour
3 (8-ounce) cans tomato sauce
1 (4-ounce) can sliced mushrooms,
   undrained

Sprinkle cutlets on both sides with salt and pepper; coat with mustard, and dredge with ¼ cup flour. Set aside.

Sauté onion in oil until golden; place onion in a greased 2-quart shallow casserole. Add 2 to 3 cutlets to skillet; cook over medium heat until brown, turning once. Place in casserole; repeat procedure until all cutlets are cooked.

Stir 2 tablespoons flour into pan drippings; cook, stirring constantly, until lightly browned. Gradually add tomato sauce; cook over medium heat, stirring constantly, until thickened. Pour over cutlets; add mushrooms. Cover and bake at 350° for 1 hour. Yield: 8 servings.
Mrs. M. Griffith,
Jonesboro, Arkansas.

VEAL DELIGHT

1½ pounds veal cutlets
2 tablespoons olive oil
1 (1⅜-ounce) package onion soup mix
2 tablespoons all-purpose flour
1¼ cups water
1 cup canned tomatoes, chopped
¼ cup chopped green pepper
1 clove garlic, minced
1½ teaspoons ground oregano
1 (8-ounce) package sliced mozzarella
Hot cooked rice

Place cutlets on a sheet of waxed paper. Using a meat mallet or rolling pin, flatten to ¼-inch thickness. Brown cutlets on both sides in hot oil in a large skillet; remove from skillet, and pour off drippings.

Add soup mix and flour to skillet; gradually add water, stirring constantly until well mixed. Add tomatoes, green pepper, garlic, and oregano. Return cutlets to skillet; cover and cook over low heat for 35 to 40 minutes or until meat is tender.

Place cheese slices on top of veal mixture; cover and cook an additional 5 minutes or until cheese melts. Serve over hot cooked rice. Yield: 4 servings.
Mrs. Paul Smith,
Maitland, Florida.

VEAL SCALLOPINI A LA MARSALA

1½ pounds ⅛-inch-thick veal cutlets
Salt
Pepper
About 1½ tablespoons all-purpose flour
2 tablespoons butter or margarine
½ cup dry Marsala or Madeira wine
1 (3-ounce) can sliced mushrooms or 1
   cup sliced fresh mushrooms
2 tablespoons water

Cut veal into large pieces. Season both sides lightly with salt and pepper; sprinkle with flour.

Sauté veal in butter until well browned on both sides. Stir in wine and mushrooms; cook 1 minute over medium heat, stirring frequently.

Place veal on a serving platter. Add water to drippings, stirring and scraping bottom of skillet to loosen browned bits. Cook until bubbly; pour over veal. Yield: 4 to 5 servings.
Mrs. Charles R. Simms,
Palestine, Illinois.

Get The Most From Your Microwave Oven

A microwave oven can perform a multitude of cooking chores or it can just sit on the counter, used occasionally to reheat a cup of cold coffee. If yours is just a coffee warmer, you probably don't realize just how versatile it can be.

To help you get the most from your microwave, we at the *Southern Living* test kitchens are continually experimenting with our microwave ovens. Here we offer some basic information to help you get the best results possible. In the future we will be featuring articles on use and care of the microwave, as well as kitchen-tested recipes.

The first step in mastering microwave cookery is to understand how it differs from conventional cooking. To put it simply, microwaves agitate molecules in the food, creating heat, which is then conducted throughout the food. Therefore, the food cooks by internal heat rather than by contact with hot air or a hot pan as in conventional cooking.

The finished product will depend largely upon the techniques you use while cooking. The following tips will help you achieve top results with your microwave oven.

Containers Safe For The Microwave

Although the metal pans commonly used in conventional cooking are unsafe in the microwave, there are a variety of containers safe for use.

■ Paper products, such as paper plates and cups, can be used for defrosting; for heating snacks, sandwiches, or beverages; and for cooking bacon or other foods requiring short cooking times. When left in the oven for long cooking periods, especially with foods with a high fat content, they may catch fire. Avoid using items made from recycled paper.

■ Ceramic, porcelain, and oven glass products are safe for defrosting, heating, and cooking processes.

■ Some plastic products and dinnerware are usable, but not all are of the same quality. Look for labels indicating "Safe for Microwave."

■ A number of products are designed especially for use in the microwave. These are generally made of glass or heavy-duty plastic and are available in department stores.

■ Oven cooking bags, freezer bags, and boxes should be pierced for use in the microwave. Remove metal twist ties before placing bags in the microwave.

■ To check a dish for safety in the microwave, pour 1 cup of water into a glass measure. Place the measure in the microwave next to or in the dish being tested. Microwave at HIGH POWER for 1 minute. If the dish being tested is warm and the water cool, the dish is unsafe. Do not test dishes containing metal decor as they are not safe for use.

Covering Food In The Microwave

Covering food is a key for achieving good microwave results.

■ Paper towels and napkins absorb moisture and grease, prevent spattering, and promote even heating. They are useful when cooking bacon and heating sandwiches or bread. As with other paper products, they should be avoided for long cooking periods.

■ Waxed paper holds in heat when cooking meats, chicken, fruits, and some vegetable casseroles.

■ Heavy-duty plastic wrap holds in steam and heat when cooking vegetables and fish. It is also useful for bowls that have no cover. Place the wrap loosely over the dish, and fold back one corner to prevent excessive steam buildup.

■ The container's lid is useful when cooking types of foods that require long, slow cooking.

Techniques For Microwaving

A few special techniques make microwaving simple and assure good results.

■ Food arrangement is crucial. Since microwave energy first enters the food at the edge of the dish, arrange such foods as chicken pieces so the meatier portions are around the outside of the dish.

■ Rotate dishes periodically during the cooking period to assure more even cooking. When rotating, give the dish a quarter to half turn.

■ Be sure to prick foods with thick skins (potatoes and zucchini) or membrane coverings (chicken livers and egg yolks) to allow steam to escape; otherwise, they may burst when heat builds up inside the food.

■ Stir foods to mix the heated portions of food with unheated portions. Foods that require constant stirring when cooked conventionally, such as sauces, will require stirring only once or twice during microwaving.

■ Food continues to cook after removal from the microwave, so standing time is required on many microwaved foods. Microwave recipes usually give a range of time, 5 to 7 minutes for example.

■ Shielding with thin strips of lightweight foil to prevent overbrowning is useful when cooking unevenly shaped foods like poultry or portions of thin foods like fish.

Nibble On These For A While

Appetizers traditionally serve to whet the appetite for finer foods to come, but your guests may be content to nibble on these specialties all evening. And with these appetizers on your menu, you'd better plan to have plenty on hand in the kitchen.

Cocktail Pizzas and Hot Artichoke Spread are two easy ways to give you time to enjoy your own party since they can be prepared ahead and baked as guests arrive. And the Cheese Puffs can be tucked away in the freezer until needed. Pop them in the oven, and you'll have a delightful treat in minutes.

CHESTNUT MEATBALLS

2 cups soft breadcrumbs
½ pound pork sausage
½ pound ground beef
1 (8-ounce) can water chestnuts, drained and chopped
1 tablespoon soy sauce
¼ teaspoon onion powder
½ teaspoon garlic salt
½ cup milk
1 (16-ounce) can sweet-and-sour sauce

Combine all ingredients except sweet-and-sour sauce; mix well and shape into 1-inch balls. Place in a greased 13- x 9- x 2-inch baking dish; bake at 350° for 25 to 30 minutes. Add sauce; mix lightly to coat meatballs. Bake an additional 15 minutes. Yield: about 4 dozen.

Mrs. Carl Ramay,
Plano, Texas.

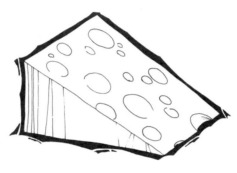

CHEESE PUFFS

1 (1-pound) loaf of unsliced sandwich bread
2 (3-ounce) packages cream cheese
1 (8-ounce) package sharp Cheddar cheese
1 cup margarine
4 egg whites, stiffly beaten

Trim crust from all sides of bread; discard crust. Cut bread into 1-inch cubes, and set aside.

Combine cheese and margarine in the top of a double boiler; cook over boiling water until cheese is melted and mixture is smooth, stirring constantly. Remove from heat.

Fold a small amount of the hot cheese mixture into egg whites; fold into remaining cheese mixture.

Use a fork to dip each bread cube into cheese mixture, coating the bread on all sides. Place bread cubes 1 inch apart on a lightly greased baking sheet; cover, and refrigerate overnight.

Remove from refrigerator, uncover, and bake at 400° for 10 to 12 minutes or

until golden brown. Serve immediately. Yield: about 8 dozen.

Note: Cheese-coated bread cubes may be frozen instead of refrigerated and may be kept up to 2 months. Freeze bread cubes on covered tray until firm; remove from tray and place in plastic freezer bags. To bake, remove from freezer, spread on baking sheets, and bake while still frozen at 400° for 12 to 15 minutes or until golden brown.

Marion Ferguson,
Birmingham, Alabama.

COCKTAIL PIZZAS

1 (1-pound) loaf of sliced sourdough bread
1 (6-ounce) can tomato paste
Whole oregano
1 (6-ounce) package pepperoni, thinly sliced
2 (6-ounce) packages sliced provolone cheese

Cut each slice of bread into 2-inch squares. Spread tomato paste on 1 side of each square; sprinkle with oregano. Place 1 slice of pepperoni on each square of bread.

Cut each slice of cheese in half; cut each half into 3 equal pieces, and place a piece of cheese on each pizza. Arrange pizzas on a large baking sheet, and broil 3 minutes or until cheese bubbles. Yield: about 5½ dozen.

Alice Pahl,
Raleigh, North Carolina.

HOT ARTICHOKE SPREAD

1 (14-ounce) can artichoke hearts, drained and chopped
1 cup mayonnaise
1 cup grated Parmesan cheese
½ teaspoon garlic powder

Combine all ingredients, mixing well. Spoon into a lightly greased 3-cup casserole. Bake at 350° for 20 minutes. Serve with assorted crackers. Yield: about 2½ cups.

Mrs. Tandy Jarvis,
Nashville, Tennessee.

Tip: Sour cream keeps best if stored in the tightly covered container in which it is purchased. If stored upside down in the refrigerator, maximum retention of texture and flavor is assured.

Save The Day With Cake

Martha Lou Derrick of Lexington, Virginia, shares her recipe for Almond Cake Squares, a simple and elegant cake that she suggests serving with morning coffee or brunch.

A delicate cake layer, rich in butter, is baked, then spread while still warm with an almond-filled topping. A few minutes under the broiler gives the cake its golden glow.

ALMOND CAKE SQUARES

3 eggs
1 cup sugar
1 cup all-purpose flour
1 cup melted butter
Almond Topping

Combine eggs and sugar; beat with electric mixer until thick and lemon colored. Stir in flour and butter; pour batter into a greased and floured 13- x 9- x 2-inch baking pan. Bake at 350° for 30 minutes. Spread Almond Topping over cake; broil cake 4 inches from heat for 3 to 5 minutes or until top is golden brown and bubbly. Cool on a wire rack; cut into 2-inch squares. Yield: about 2 dozen.

Almond Topping:
½ cup butter
½ cup sugar
½ cup sliced almonds
1 tablespoon all-purpose flour
1 tablespoon milk

Combine all ingredients in a small saucepan; cook over low heat, stirring constantly, until sugar is completely dissolved and mixture thickens. Yield: about 1½ cups.

Dip Into A Pineapple

If you're looking for an appealing appetizer for a garden-room party or a light dessert for a barbecue, Fresh Pineapple Delight is a delectable answer.

A scooped-out fresh pineapple serves as the bowl for a fluffy dip in this warm-weather refresher. Part of the scooped-out fruit flavors the dip, and the remainder is served as a dipper along with other fresh fruit.

Serve Fresh Pineapple Delight with an assortment of fresh fruit for dipping.

It's a good idea to prepare the fruit ahead to avoid any last-minute rush. To prevent cut fruit like apple wedges from discoloring on standing, squeeze lemon or lime juice over them or use ascorbic-citric mixture.

FRESH PINEAPPLE DELIGHT

1 medium pineapple
1 egg, well beaten
2 to 4 tablespoons sugar
1 teaspoon all-purpose flour
1 (8-ounce) carton whipping cream, whipped
Assorted fresh fruit

Cut a lengthwise slice from pineapple, removing about one-third of the pineapple. Scoop pulp from slice; discard rind. Scoop pulp from remaining portion of pineapple, leaving shell ½ inch thick; set shell aside.

Chop pineapple pulp into bite-size pieces, discarding core. Crush 1 cup of pineapple pieces; reserve remaining pineapple pieces for dipping.

Combine crushed pineapple (and juice that accumulates), egg, sugar, and flour in a large saucepan. Cook over low heat until thickened; cool. Fold in whipped cream, and spoon into pineapple shell.

Serve dip with reserved pineapple pieces and other fresh fruit cut into serving pieces. Yield: about 3 cups.

*Mrs. J. Rush Thompson, Jr.,
Pleasantville, New Jersey.*

Three Ways With Fresh Rhubarb

Those tall, rosy-red stalks of fresh rhubarb are available in the market now. So what better reason to try Rhubarb-Raisin Pie or Rhubarb Whip and Rosy Rhubarb Squares—three luscious desserts.

When selecting fresh rhubarb, choose large, crisp, and straight stalks of red or cherry color. Only the stalks can be used, but the condition of the leaves is an indicator of the freshness of the vegetable.

ROSY RHUBARB SQUARES

3 cups diced rhubarb
1 (3-ounce) package strawberry-flavored gelatin
1 cup all-purpose flour
2 tablespoons sugar
2 teaspoons baking powder
½ teaspoon salt
¼ cup shortening
¼ cup milk
1 egg, beaten
½ cup sugar
½ cup all-purpose flour
¼ cup butter or margarine
Whipped cream or ice cream (optional)

Combine rhubarb and gelatin; mix well, and set aside.

Combine 1 cup flour, 2 tablespoons sugar, baking powder, and salt; cut in shortening until mixture resembles coarse crumbs. Add milk and egg, mixing until smooth. Press mixture evenly into bottom and ¾ inch up sides of a greased and floured 9-inch square baking pan, using the back of a floured spoon. Spread rhubarb mixture evenly over top, and set aside.

Combine ½ cup sugar and ½ cup flour; cut in butter until mixture is crumbly. Sprinkle over rhubarb mixture; bake at 375° for 35 to 40 minutes. Cut into squares. Serve with whipped cream or ice cream, if desired. Yield: 9 servings.

*Mrs. W. P. Chambers,
Louisville, Kentucky.*

Tip: Always use standard fractional measuring cups and spoons. One of the newest items on the market is the glass measuring cup that gives the familiar measure as well as the new metric measure, which we will probably be using within the next 10 years.

RHUBARB-RAISIN PIE

1 cup sugar
2 tablespoons all-purpose flour
3 eggs, separated
⅓ cup orange juice
2 cups diced rhubarb
¼ cup raisins
1 unbaked 9-inch pastry shell
½ teaspoon vanilla extract
¼ teaspoon cream of tartar
⅓ cup sugar
Dash of ground cinnamon

Combine 1 cup sugar and flour; stir lightly. Beat egg yolks slightly; add yolks and orange juice to sugar mixture, mixing well. Stir in rhubarb and raisins. Pour into pastry shell; bake at 375° for 55 to 60 minutes, covering edges of pastry with aluminum foil after 30 minutes to prevent excess browning.

Combine egg whites, vanilla, and cream of tartar; beat until soft peaks form. Combine ⅓ cup sugar and cinnamon; gradually add to egg whites, beating until stiff peaks form. Spread meringue over warm pie, sealing edges well; bake at 350° for 12 to 15 minutes or until golden brown. Let cool. Yield: one 9-inch pie. *Mrs. R. L. Bradley, Sparta, Tennessee.*

RHUBARB WHIP

1 pound rhubarb, cut into 1-inch pieces
½ cup sugar
¼ cup water
1 (3-ounce) package strawberry-flavored gelatin
½ cup cold water
½ cup whipping cream, whipped
Fresh sliced strawberries

Combine rhubarb, sugar, and ¼ cup water in a medium saucepan; mix well and bring to a boil, stirring occasionally. Cover and cook over medium heat for 8 minutes. Add gelatin, and cook, stirring constantly, until gelatin dissolves. Remove from heat; stir in ½ cup cold water, and chill until mixture is slightly thickened. Beat on high speed of electric mixer until light and fluffy; fold in whipped cream. Spoon into serving dishes, and chill 30 to 45 minutes. Top with strawberries. Yield: 6 servings. *Mrs. Carl Ramay, Plano, Texas.*

Double-Good Cookies

When Mrs. C. C. Eckert of Orlando, Florida, makes a batch of homemade cookies, it's a double delight. Two cookies are stacked and baked with a rich, sweet filling between them. A plain cookie dough makes the top and bottom layers, and a mixture of sugar, raisins, and nuts fills them with flavor.

ICE BOX FILLED COOKIES

½ cup shortening
1 cup firmly packed brown sugar
2 eggs
½ teaspoon vanilla extract
3 to 3¼ cups all-purpose flour
½ teaspoon soda
Pinch of salt
Raisin Filling

Combine shortening, sugar, eggs, and vanilla; mix well with an electric mixer. Combine flour, soda, and salt; add to sugar mixture, mixing thoroughly. Cover; chill overnight.

Roll out dough on a lightly floured pastry cloth to ⅛-inch thickness; cut with 2-inch cookie cutter. Place half the cookies on ungreased baking sheets. Spoon 1 teaspoon Raisin Filling on each cookie; spread evenly. Place a second cookie on top of filling. Bake at 375° for 12 minutes. Yield: 2 to 3 dozen cookies.

Raisin Filling:

1 cup sugar
1 cup water
1 cup raisins
3 tablespoons all-purpose flour
1 cup nuts

Combine all ingredients except nuts in a saucepan; cook until thickened, stirring constantly. Stir in nuts. Yield: about 2 cups.

Tempt Them With Vegetable Tempura

Tempura is the name for those delectable morsels of seafood or vegetables dipped in batter and deep fried until light and crisp. After tasting vegetable tempura in a local Japanese restaurant, Mrs. Joseph Mashaw of Memphis went home and developed this version.

For an accompaniment, Mrs. Mashaw also dips banana slices in the tempura batter and fries them along with the vegetables. Then she sprinkles them with powdered sugar and serves them with the rest of the meal.

Tempura must be served immediately, as the delicate, crisp coating will soften if allowed to stand. So prepare all vegetables and fruit first; then make the batter and cook just before serving.

VEGETABLE TEMPURA

Raw vegetables
Banana slices
1 cup all-purpose flour
1 tablespoon sugar
1½ teaspoons baking powder
½ teaspoon chili powder
Salt
2 eggs, beaten
⅓ cup milk
1 tablespoon salad oil
Salad oil for frying
Powdered sugar

Prepare raw vegetables (cauliflower flowerets, green pepper strips, sliced zucchini and yellow squash, carrot sticks, whole mushrooms). Set aside vegetables and banana slices.

Combine flour, 1 tablespoon sugar, baking powder, chili powder, and ½ teaspoon salt; add eggs, milk, and 1 tablespoon salad oil. Mix just until blended (batter will be lumpy).

Sprinkle vegetables with salt to taste. Dip vegetables and banana slices into batter, shaking to remove excess. Drop a few pieces at a time into deep oil heated to 375°; cook until golden brown. Drain on paper towels. Dust banana slices with powdered sugar. Serve the tempura immediately. Yield: about 1¼ cups batter.

Relax With These Sunday Night Suppers

Sunday evening is a time for relaxing, so why not plan a light supper that can be prepared ahead. With our two menu suggestions, all you'll have to do is warm the entrée when it's suppertime.

The first menu features Beefy Vegetable Soup, full of ground beef and vegetables. There's also a vegetable salad with an herb-vinegar dressing.

Our second menu offers a vegetable salad topped with a sour cream-mayonnaise dressing and a casserole of tuna and biscuits. A tangy lemon sherbet ends the meal.

**Beefy Vegetable Soup
Variety Salad
Cracker Pie**

BEEFY VEGETABLE SOUP

2 pounds ground beef
1 cup all-purpose flour
½ cup melted margarine
2 quarts water
1 cup chopped onion
1 cup chopped carrots
1 cup chopped celery
1 (10-ounce) package frozen mixed
    vegetables
1 (28-ounce) can whole tomatoes
2 tablespoons beef-flavored instant
    bouillon
1 tablespoon Ac'cent
2 to 3 teaspoons pepper

Cook ground beef until done, stirring to crumble. Drain on paper towels; discard pan drippings.

Stir flour into margarine in a Dutch oven; cook over low heat 3 to 5 minutes, stirring contantly, until a smooth paste is formed. Gradually stir in water; cook, stirring constantly, until bubbly. Stir in cooked ground beef and remaining ingredients. Bring soup to a boil; cover and simmer 45 minutes to 1 hour. Yield: 6 to 8 servings.

*Mrs. A. P. McDonald,
Houston, Texas.*

VARIETY SALAD

2 carrots, cut into 1½- x ¼-inch strips
1 cup broccoli flowerets
1 cup cauliflower flowerets
1 small green onion, sliced
1 medium zucchini, cut into 1- x ¼-inch
    strips
1 medium onion, thinly sliced and
    separated into rings
Oregano-Vinaigrette Dressing
Lettuce leaves

Cook carrots, covered, in a small amount of boiling salted water 2 minutes. Add broccoli and cauliflower; cover and cook an additional 2 minutes. Drain and cool.

Combine all vegetables in a medium bowl; pour Oregano-Vinaigrette Dressing over vegetables, and stir lightly.

Cover and chill at least 8 hours, stirring occasionally. Serve on lettuce leaves. Yield: 4 to 6 servings.

Oregano-Vinaigrette Dressing:
½ cup vegetable oil
3 tablespoons wine vinegar
1 teaspoon dried oregano
1 small clove garlic, minced

Combine all ingredients in a jar; tighten lid securely, and shake well. Yield: about ¾ cup.

*Mrs. H. E. Olsen,
New Port Richey, Florida.*

CRACKER PIE

20 buttery round crackers, finely crushed
½ cup chopped pecans
1 teaspoon baking powder
3 egg whites
1 cup sugar
1 teaspoon vanilla extract
1 cup whipping cream, whipped
¼ cup chopped pecans

Combine cracker crumbs, ½ cup chopped pecans, and baking powder in a large bowl; set aside.

Beat egg whites until frothy. Gradually add sugar, beating until stiff and glossy. Add vanilla, and beat until blended. Fold meringue into cracker crumb mixture. Spoon mixture into a well-greased 9-inch piepan. Bake at 350° for 25 to 30 minutes.

Cool; refrigerate at least 2 hours. Top with whipped cream, and sprinkle with ¼ cup pecans. Yield: one 9-inch pie.

*Mrs. Claudia Galvan,
Dallas, Texas.*

**Company's Coming Salad
Biscuit-Topped Tuna Casserole
Lemon Cream Sherbet**

COMPANY'S COMING SALAD

1 medium head lettuce, shredded
1 cup chopped celery
1 pound fresh spinach, shredded
3 to 4 sliced green onions
½ to ¾ cup sliced radishes
½ cup drained garbanzo beans
4 hard-cooked eggs, sliced or chopped
1 (8-ounce) carton commercial sour cream
¾ cup salad dressing or mayonnaise
Commercial bacon bits or imitation bacon
    pieces
1 cup (¼ pound) shredded Cheddar
    cheese

Layer first 7 ingredients in order listed in a large salad bowl; set aside.

Combine sour cream and salad dressing, mixing well. Spread mixture evenly over entire top of salad, sealing at the edges of the bowl. Sprinkle with bacon bits and cheese. Cover tightly and refrigerate at least 8 hours. (Salad will keep 3 days if properly sealed.) Yield: 12 to 15 servings.

Note: Salad may be resealed with additional salad dressing after serving. Spread salad dressing to edge of bowl; wrap tightly, and store in refrigerator.

*Harriet B. Smith,
Alexandria, Virginia.*

BISCUIT-TOPPED TUNA CASSEROLE

1 medium onion, chopped
1 small green pepper, chopped
3 tablespoons melted butter or margarine
½ cup all-purpose flour
3 cups milk
1 teaspoon salt
⅛ teaspoon pepper
2 (7-ounce) cans solid-pack light tuna in
    oil, drained and flaked
1 cup biscuit mix
¼ cup cold water
½ cup shredded Cheddar cheese

Sauté onion and green pepper in butter until vegetables are tender. Blend in flour, and cook over low heat until bubbly. Gradually add milk; cook until smooth and thickened, stirring constantly. Stir in salt, pepper, and tuna. Spoon mixture into a lightly greased 2-quart casserole.

Combine biscuit mix and water. Mix with a fork until a soft dough forms; then beat vigorously 20 strokes.

Smooth dough into a ball on a lightly floured board; knead 5 times. Roll to ¼-inch thickness, and sprinkle with cheese. Roll dough up jellyroll fashion, and cut into 8 slices. Place on tuna mixture. Bake at 325° for 30 to 40 minutes or until lightly browned. Yield: about 6 servings.

*Mrs. Nettie Ferdig,
Noel, Missouri.*

Blueberry Buttermilk Pancakes, filled with plump, juicy blueberries, are served with Homemade Maple Syrup.

BLUEBERRY BUTTERMILK PANCAKES

1 egg
1 cup all-purpose flour
1 tablespoon sugar
1 tablespoon baking powder
½ teaspoon soda
½ teaspoon salt
1 cup buttermilk
2 tablespoons vegetable oil
½ cup blueberries, rinsed and drained
Homemade Maple Syrup

Beat egg. Stir together flour, sugar, baking powder, soda, and salt; add to egg. Add buttermilk and vegetable oil, beating until mixture is smooth. Fold in blueberries.

For each pancake, pour about ¼ cup batter onto a hot, lightly greased griddle or skillet. Turn pancakes when tops are covered with bubbles and edges look cooked. Serve with Homemade Maple Syrup. Yield: 8 (4-inch) pancakes.

Homemade Maple Syrup:

1 cup water
2 cups sugar
½ teaspoon maple flavoring

Bring water to a boil in a 1-quart saucepan; add sugar and maple flavoring, stirring to dissolve. Cook for 1 to 2 minutes, stirring constantly. Remove from heat. Yield: 1⅔ cups.

Note: Leftover syrup may be stored in the refrigerator. *Mrs. Jackie DeNisco, Indiantown, Florida.*

LEMON CREAM SHERBET

Juice and grated rind of 3 lemons
1½ cups sugar
2 cups milk
1 pint half-and-half

Combine lemon juice, lemon rind, and sugar in a large bowl; let stand at room temperature several hours. Add milk and half-and-half, mixing well. Pour into freezer trays, and freeze until almost firm (about 2 hours). Spoon mixture into a large bowl, and beat until smooth and creamy.

Spoon mixture back into freezer trays, and freeze until firm. Yield: 6 to 8 servings. *Claire Bastable, Chevy Chase, Maryland.*

Perk Up Plain Pancakes

Creative cooks have found that it's fun to dress up plain pancakes by adding special ingredients, as this selection of recipes illustrates.

Blueberry Buttermilk Pancakes and Applesauce Pancakes even sport their own homemade syrups. Light and airy Cottage Cheese Pancakes will melt in your mouth. But be cautioned: When you prepare these pancakes, be ready to serve stacks and stacks, because everyone will want seconds.

WHEAT GERM-BANANA PANCAKES

2 eggs
1½ cups milk
1 large banana, mashed
1 (8-ounce) can crushed pineapple, drained
1 cup unbleached white flour
½ cup wheat germ
1 teaspoon baking powder
½ teaspoon salt
Additional wheat germ (optional)

Beat eggs in a small mixing bowl until foamy. Add milk, banana, and pineapple; beat well.

Combine flour, wheat germ, baking powder, and salt in a bowl; stir well. Add the dry ingredients to the banana mixture, stirring just until moistened.

For each pancake, pour ⅓ cup batter onto a hot, lightly greased griddle or skillet. Sprinkle with additional wheat germ, if desired. Turn pancakes when tops are covered with bubbles and edges look cooked. Serve pancakes hot with butter and syrup. Yield: about 10 (5-inch) pancakes. *Marsha Edwards, Dallas, Texas.*

Tip: Watch the price trends on fresh fruits and vegetables. Buy when they are in season and at their lowest price.

APPLESAUCE PANCAKES

2 cups biscuit mix
1 cup milk
1 cup applesauce
2 eggs
Spiced Apple Syrup

Combine biscuit mix, milk, applesauce, and eggs in a medium mixing bowl; beat until smooth.

For each pancake, pour about ¼ cup batter onto a hot, lightly greased griddle or skillet. Turn pancakes when tops are covered with bubbles and edges look cooked. Serve hot with butter and Spiced Apple Syrup. Yield: about 2 dozen (4-inch) pancakes.

Spiced Apple Syrup:

1 cup applesauce
1 (10-ounce) jar apple jelly
½ teaspoon ground cinnamon
Dash of ground cloves
Dash of salt

Combine all ingredients in a small saucepan. Cook over low heat, stirring occasionally, until jelly melts and mixture is blended. Yield: 1½ cups.

Mrs. Helen Maurer,
Christmas, Florida.

COTTAGE CHEESE PANCAKES

4 eggs
1 cup cottage cheese
1 (8-ounce) carton commercial sour cream
¾ cup all-purpose flour
1 tablespoon sugar
¼ teaspoon salt

Beat eggs in a small mixing bowl. Add cottage cheese and sour cream, mixing well. Stir in remaining ingredients, and beat until thick.

Drop batter by tablespoonfuls onto a hot, lightly greased griddle or skillet. Turn pancakes when tops are covered with bubbles and edges look cooked. Serve hot with butter or syrup. Yield: about 3 dozen pancakes.

Mrs. John Haven,
Jonesboro, Arkansas.

POTATO PANCAKES

4 medium potatoes, peeled and grated
1 cup cooked, mashed potatoes
2 eggs, beaten
1 teaspoon salt
¼ to ½ teaspoon pepper
2 to 3 tablespoons butter or margarine

Combine first 5 ingredients in a medium-size mixing bowl; mix well.

Heat 2 tablespoons butter in a large heavy skillet. For each pancake, spoon ¼ cup batter onto skillet. Cook until brown on one side; turn and cook until crisp. Repeat until all potato mixture is used, adding an additional tablespoon butter, if needed. Yield: about 1 dozen pancakes.

Ginger Barker,
Mesquite, Texas.

Peel A Banana For Something Special

As good as fresh bananas are eaten out of hand, they are just as delicious when cooked, baked, or combined with other ingredients.

In this selection of recipes, the old Southern favorite, banana pie, is given a special new twist. The flavor of Banana Butterscotch Bread, baked with a nutty topping and filled with butterscotch morsels, will surpass most other banana breads. For an easy but elegant breakfast or dessert, try Baked Bananas with Orange Sauce.

Not only are bananas delicious, they're good for you, too. They're virtually fat free, low in sodium, and high in vitamin A and potassium. And they're one fruit that is available year-round, so you can enjoy these dishes any time.

LUSCIOUS CARAMEL BANANA PIE

1 (14-ounce) can sweetened condensed milk
2 to 3 bananas
1 (9-inch) graham cracker crust
1 cup whipping cream
¼ cup powdered sugar
1 or 2 (1⅛-ounce) English toffee-flavored candy bars, crumbled

Pour sweetened condensed milk into an 8-inch glass pieplate. Cover with foil.

Pour about ¼ inch hot water in a 2-quart shallow casserole. Place covered pieplate in casserole. Bake at 425° for 1 hour and 20 minutes or until the condensed milk is thick and caramel colored (add hot water to casserole as needed). Remove foil when done, and set aside.

Cut bananas crosswise into ⅛-inch slices, and place in the bottom of graham cracker crust. Spread caramelized milk over banana layer. Cool for at least 30 minutes.

Combine whipping cream and powdered sugar in a small mixing bowl; beat until stiff. Spread over caramel layer. Sprinkle with crumbled candy. Chill at least 3 hours or overnight before serving. Yield: one 9-inch pie.

Sherry Boger Phillips,
Knoxville, Tennessee.

BAKED BANANAS WITH ORANGE SAUCE

6 firm bananas
2 tablespoons butter or margarine, melted
⅔ cup orange juice
½ cup firmly packed brown sugar
2 tablespoons grated orange rind

Cut bananas in half lengthwise; place cut side down in a 13- x 9- x 2-inch baking dish. Brush bananas with butter. Bake at 350° for 10 minutes more.

Combine remaining ingredients; pour over bananas. Bake 15 minutes more. Yield: 6 servings.

Kathleen Stone,
Houston, Texas.

MARVELOUS BANANA CAKE

1 cup butter or margarine, softened
3 cups sugar
2 cups mashed bananas
4 eggs, beaten
4 cups sifted all-purpose flour
2 teaspoons soda
1 cup buttermilk
1 teaspoon vanilla extract
2 tablespoons bourbon
1 cup chopped pecans
Banana-Nut Frosting

Combine butter and sugar in a large bowl; cream until light. Add bananas; mix until smooth. Stir in beaten eggs.

Sift together flour and soda. Add to banana mixture alternately with buttermilk, mixing well. Stir in vanilla, bourbon, and nuts.

Pour batter into 3 greased and floured 9-inch cakepans. Bake at 350° for 35 to 40 minutes or until cake tests done. Cool for 10 minutes; remove from pans, and cool completely on wire racks. Spread Banana-Nut Frosting between layers and on top of cake. Yield: one 9-inch layer cake.

Banana-Nut Frosting:

½ cup mashed bananas
1 teaspoon lemon juice
⅓ cup butter or margarine, softened
1 (16-ounce) package plus 3 cups powdered sugar
3 tablespoons milk
1 cup flaked coconut, toasted
⅔ cup finely chopped pecans
3 drops yellow food coloring (optional)

Combine bananas and lemon juice; set aside.

Beat butter until creamy in a large bowl. Add sugar, bananas, and milk; beat until fluffy. (Additional milk may be added if needed in order to obtain proper consistency.)

Stir in coconut and chopped pecans. Add food coloring, if desired. Yield: enough frosting for one 9-inch layer cake.

Mrs. Elizabeth Kraus,
Louisville, Kentucky.

BANANA BUTTERSCOTCH BREAD

1¾ cups all-purpose flour
2 teaspoons baking powder
½ teaspoon soda
½ teaspoon salt
½ teaspoon ground cinnamon
½ teaspoon ground nutmeg
1 cup mashed bananas
¾ cup sugar
2 eggs
¼ cup melted margarine
¼ cup milk
1 (6-ounce) package butterscotch-flavored morsels
1 cup chopped nuts, divided

Combine first 6 ingredients in a large mixing bowl; set aside.

Combine banana, sugar, eggs, and margarine in a small bowl. Add banana mixture to flour mixture alternately with milk, beating well with an electric mixer. Stir in butterscotch morsels and ⅔ cup nuts.

Line bottom of a 9- x 5- x 3-inch loafpan with waxed paper; grease waxed paper and sides of pan. Spoon batter into pan; sprinkle with remaining ⅓ cup nuts. Bake at 350° for 1 hour and 20 minutes or until done. Cool 30 minutes. Serve warm. Yield: one 9- x 5- x 3-inch loaf.
Betsy Aloway,
Abbeville, Mississippi.

Savor The Light Taste Of Crab

The fresh and delicate flavor of crabmeat is always a welcome treat. You can serve crabmeat in the form of a tempting hors d'oeuvre such as Crab Mousse; in a colorful salad along with wild rice and English peas; or as an entrée like Crab Stroganoff served on a bed of spinach noodles.

If fresh crabmeat is not available, the frozen or canned varieties make a good alternative. Canned crabmeat is available in three different types: lump—solid nuggets of meat that are good to use when appearance is important; flake—smaller pieces of white meat from the crab body; and claw—brownish in color and less expensive, but good in dips, stuffings, or casseroles.

CRAB PUFF

½ pound fresh crabmeat
2 tablespoons butter or margarine
2 tablespoons all-purpose flour
1 cup hot milk
3 eggs, separated
½ cup mayonnaise
½ teaspoon salt
⅛ teaspoon pepper
1 teaspoon paprika
½ cup shredded Cheddar cheese (optional)

Remove and discard cartilage from crabmeat; set aside.

Melt butter in a heavy saucepan over low heat; blend in flour, and cook 1 minute. Gradually add milk; cook over medium heat, stirring constantly, until thickened. Let cool. Lightly beat egg yolks; stir into sauce. Fold in mayonnaise. Add crabmeat, salt, and pepper; stir lightly.

Beat egg whites until stiff peaks form. Fold into crab mixture, and spoon into a greased 1½-quart casserole. Sprinkle with paprika; top with cheese, if desired. Bake at 400° for 25 to 30 minutes. Yield: 4 to 5 servings.
Mrs. R. G. Connally,
Decatur, Georgia.

CRAB STROGANOFF

1 (3-ounce) can mushroom caps
2 tablespoons butter
1 cup finely chopped onion
½ cup finely sliced celery
2 tablespoons all-purpose flour
1 (8-ounce) carton commercial sour cream
½ teaspoon salt
Dash of pepper
1 (6½-ounce) can crabmeat
¼ cup sherry
Butter
1 (8-ounce) package spinach noodles, cooked

Drain mushrooms, reserving liquid; set aside.

Melt butter in a small saucepan. Add onion and celery; sauté over low heat 4 minutes. Add mushrooms and flour, and stir until flour is well blended.

Combine sour cream and reserved mushroom liquid, stirring well. Add sour cream mixture, salt, and pepper to vegetable mixture, stirring well. Add crabmeat and sherry; cook over low heat 5 minutes.

Butter spinach noodles generously, and arrange on a serving platter. Spoon crabmeat mixture over noodles. Yield: 4 servings.
Mrs. J. C. Taylor,
Waynesboro, Mississippi.

CRAB IMPERIAL

1 pound crabmeat
1 egg, well beaten
½ cup mayonnaise
2 tablespoons melted butter or margarine
2 tablespoons evaporated milk
2 tablespoons capers
1 teaspoon salt
¼ teaspoon pepper
½ cup grated Parmesan cheese

Combine all ingredients except cheese; stir gently until well mixed.

Spoon mixture into 6 buttered crab shells, dividing evenly, or spoon into a 1-quart buttered casserole; sprinkle with cheese. Place crab shells on cookie sheet; bake at 350° for 25 to 30 minutes. Yield: 6 servings. *Barbara A. Sullivan,*
Ocala, Florida.

CRAB AND WILD RICE SALAD

½ (4-ounce) package wild rice
2 (6-ounce) packages frozen crabmeat, thawed, drained, and flaked
1 (6-ounce) package cooked, peeled shrimp, thawed
½ cup cooked and drained English peas
½ cup chopped onion
2 tablespoons chopped pimiento
½ cup mayonnaise
1 tablespoon lemon juice
1 teaspoon curry powder
Lettuce
Cherry tomatoes or tomato wedges

Cook rice according to package directions. Combine rice, crabmeat, shrimp, peas, onion, and pimiento; stir lightly.

Combine mayonnaise, lemon juice, and curry powder; stir into crab mixture. Cover and chill. Serve on lettuce leaves; garnish with tomatoes. Yield: 5 servings. *Mrs. Warren D. Davis,*
Yulee, Florida.

BROILED CRAB AND AVOCADO

1 pound crabmeat
1 slice white bread, cut into ¼-inch cubes
1 egg, beaten
3 tablespoons prepared mustard
1 teaspoon salt
1 teaspoon pepper
2 teaspoons mayonnaise
2 large, ripe avocados
Vegetable oil

Remove any cartilage or shell from crabmeat. Combine crabmeat, bread, egg, mustard, salt, pepper, and mayonnaise; stir well.

Cut avocados in half lengthwise; remove seed. Fill center of avocados with crab mixture; brush crabmeat and avocados with oil. Broil 6 inches from broiler element for 10 minutes; baste occasionally with oil. Yield: 4 servings.

Mrs. N. V. Gall,
San Antonio, Texas.

HOT SEAFOOD SALAD

1 pound fresh crabmeat
1 cup mayonnaise
1 tablespoon Worcestershire sauce
Dash of hot sauce
½ teaspoon salt
¼ teaspoon pepper
½ cup chopped green pepper
¼ cup chopped onion
2 pounds small shrimp, cooked, peeled, and deveined
2 cups crushed potato chips, divided

Remove and discard cartilage from crabmeat; set aside.

Combine mayonnaise, Worcestershire sauce, hot sauce, salt, and pepper; mix well. Stir in green pepper, onion, shrimp, crabmeat, and 1½ cups potato chips; spoon into a greased 2½ quart casserole. Sprinkle remaining potato chips on top; bake at 400° for 25 to 30 minutes. Yield: 8 servings.

Mrs. Janis Moyer,
Farmersville, Texas.

CRAB MOUSSE

2 envelopes unflavored gelatin
½ cup cold water
1 (10¾-ounce) can tomato soup
1 (3-ounce) package cream cheese
1 medium onion, diced
¾ cup diced celery
1 medium-sized green pepper, diced
2 (6½-ounce) cans crabmeat, drained and flaked
1 (6½-ounce) can small shrimp, drained
1 cup mayonnaise
Assorted crackers or party breads

Soften gelatin in water; set aside.

Combine soup and cheese in top of a double boiler; cook, stirring constantly, until cheese melts and mixture is smooth. Remove from heat. Add softened gelatin and remaining ingredients except crackers; mix well. Spoon into a greased 5-cup mold; chill until firm. Serve with assorted crackers or party breads. Yield: 5 cups.

Mrs. Janet C. Kasper,
Fort Worth, Texas.

Show Off With Pretty Petits Fours

Those fancy little iced cakes known as petits fours look impressive, but they're not really difficult to make yourself.

One of the most practical recipes we've found is this one from Virginia Stadnick of Columbus, Georgia. One of her techniques is to glaze the top of each cake with an egg white-powdered sugar mixture before icing; this prevents cake crumbs from marring the smoothly iced surface characteristic of professionally made petits fours.

With Virginia's recipe and the step-by-step instructions illustrated in the photographs, you'll find that "impressive" doesn't mean difficult.

In addition to the usual kitchen utensils, you'll need two 8-inch square cake-pans, cake rack, candy thermometer, long bread knife, pastry brush, and decorating cone. If you want to make round petits fours, you'll also need a 2-inch round cookie cutter.

PETITS FOURS

2 cups sugar
1 cup shortening
3 cups all-purpose flour
2 teaspoons baking powder
¼ teaspoon salt
1 cup ice water
1½ teaspoons imitation butter flavor
1 teaspoon vanilla or almond extract
6 egg whites
1 egg white
1 tablespoon powdered sugar
Icing (recipe follows)
Creamy Decorator Frosting

Combine sugar and shortening in a large mixing bowl, creaming until light and fluffy.

Sift dry ingredients together; add to creamed mixture alternately with ice water, mixing well after each addition. Add flavorings, and mix well.

Beat 6 egg whites in a large mixing bowl until soft peaks form; fold into creamed mixture. Pour batter into 2 greased and floured 8-inch square pans. Bake at 325° for 40 minutes or until

cake tests done. Cool in pan 10 minutes; remove from pans and cool on wire racks.

Wrap cake tightly in foil; freeze for several hours or until firm.

Remove cake from foil and carefully trim crust from all surfaces, making sure top of cake is flat. Cut each layer of cake into 16 (2-inch) squares, or cut into circles using a 2-inch cookie cutter.

Beat 1 egg white until frothy and slightly thickened; add powdered sugar, mixing well. Brush egg white mixture lightly over top of each cake. Allow egg white glaze to dry.

Place cakes 2 inches apart on a wire rack; place rack in a large shallow pan. Quickly pour warm icing over the cakes, completely covering top and sides.

Spoon up all icing that drips through rack, and reheat to 110°; add a small amount of water, if necessary, to maintain original consistency. Continue pouring and reheating until all cakes are iced. Allow icing to dry.

Place each cake on a cutting board; using a sharp knife, trim any surplus icing from bottom edge of each.

Decorate the petits fours as desired, using a decorating cone, and Creamy Decorator Frosting. Yield: 18 round or 32 square petits fours.

Icing:
½ cup plus 3 tablespoons water
7 cups sifted powdered sugar
3 tablespoons light corn syrup
1 teaspoon vanilla or almond extract

Combine all ingredients in a medium saucepan; cook over low heat, stirring constantly, until frosting reaches 110°. Quickly pour icing over cakes as directed. Yield: enough icing for 32 petits fours.

Creamy Decorator Frosting:
1 (1-pound) package powdered sugar
¾ cup shortening
¼ cup water
½ teaspoon salt
1 teaspoon vanilla or almond extract
Few drops of food coloring

Combine sugar and shortening in a small mixing bowl; beat at low speed until smooth. Add water slowly, beating constantly. Add salt and vanilla and mix well.

Divide frosting into separate portions for each color that will be used; tint each with desired color. Frosting will keep in airtight container in refrigerator for up to 1 week. Yield: about 2½ cups frosting.

Step 1—After cake is baked and cooled, wrap in aluminum foil and freeze until firm. Carefully trim crusts from all surfaces of frozen cake, making sure top of cake is flat.

Step 2—Cut each layer of cake into 16 (2-inch) squares. For round petits fours, cut with a 2-inch cookie cutter.

Step 3—Beat 1 egg white until frothy and thickened; add 1 tablespoon powdered sugar. Brush mixture over top of cakes, and allow to dry.

Step 4—Position cakes on a wire rack placed over a large shallow pan. Quickly pour warm icing over cakes. Spoon up excess icing; reheat and continue icing.

Step 5—When petits fours are dry, use a sharp knife to trim excess icing from lower edge of each. Decorate as desired with Creamy Decorator Frosting.

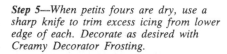

June

Gardens flourish in June, bringing an abundance of fresh produce to Southern tables. We think there is no better way to enjoy the season's bounty than with an old-fashioned vegetable dinner. To help you enjoy the summer's harvest all year long, we present recipes for jams and jellies, along with some basic preparation guidelines.

Warm weather calls for desserts that are light but full of flavor. We think you will agree that our selection of summertime pies is the ideal solution. Another way to cool off is with frozen salad. We offer five that can double as dessert, too.

For those who tend to skip breakfast, we present four non-traditional breakfast recipes that are too good to pass by. And if there are only two people at your house for breakfast, you will find more recipes selected with you in mind.

Stock Up On Jams And Jellies

Jams, jellies, and their close relatives—conserves, marmalades, and preserves—are some of the best things that can happen to summer's bounty of fresh fruit. Not only do these jellied delights preserve the luscious flavor of the season, but they're also good ways to use overripe fruit and any not suitable for canning or freezing.

BLUEBERRY JAM

1½ quarts stemmed blueberries, crushed
¼ cup lemon juice
1 (1-inch) stick cinnamon
7 cups sugar
2 (3-ounce) packages liquid fruit pectin

Combine all ingredients except fruit pectin in a Dutch oven; bring mixture to a boil, stirring occasionally, until the sugar dissolves.

Cook at a rolling boil 2 minutes, stirring frequently; remove from heat. Discard cinnamon stick. Add pectin to blueberry mixture and stir 5 minutes. Skim off foam with a metal spoon.

Quickly pour jam into hot sterilized jars, leaving ⅛-inch headspace; cover at once with metal lids, and screw metal bands tight. Process 5 minutes in boiling-water bath. Yield: 5 cups.

Eva G. Key,
Isle Of Palms, South Carolina.

PEACH CONSERVE

5 pounds underripe peaches, peeled and
    sliced
Grated rind of 1 orange
3 oranges, peeled and sectioned
7 cups sugar
¾ pound blanched almonds, cut
    lengthwise into halves or slivers

Combine all ingredients except almonds in a Dutch oven; bring to a boil, stirring occasionally until sugar dissolves. Boil gently 45 minutes, stirring frequently. Stir in almonds; cook an additional 10 minutes.

Quickly pour into hot sterilized jars, leaving ⅛-inch headspace. Cover at once with metal lids, and screw metal bands tight. Process in boiling-water bath for 10 minutes. Yield: 4½ cups.

Mrs. Beckwith Smith,
Jacksonville, Florida.

STRAWBERRY PRESERVES

About 1 quart firm, ripe strawberries
2½ cups sugar, divided

Cap and rinse strawberries; place in a large colander. Pour boiling water over berries, and let drain 1 minute.

Combine berries and 1 cup sugar in a Dutch oven. Bring to a boil; boil 7 minutes, stirring frequently. Stir in remaining 1½ cups sugar; boil an additional 7 minutes, stirring frequently.

Pour strawberry mixture into a shallow 13- x 9- x 2-inch pan; skim off foam with a metal spoon. Let stand, uncovered, in a cool place 12 hours; shake pan occasionally (do not stir) so that berries will absorb syrup and remain plump and whole.

Skim off foam with a metal spoon; pour preserves into sterilized jelly glasses, leaving ½-inch headspace. Cover with a ⅛-inch layer of paraffin. Cover with lids. Yield: about 2½ cups.

Mrs. Robert Collins,
Fairfax, Missouri.

WATERMELON PRESERVES

1 medium watermelon, quartered
1½ tablespoons salt
½-inch cube fresh gingerroot, peeled
1 (2-inch) stick cinnamon
12 whole cloves
½ teaspoon powdered alum
9 cups sugar
2 large or 3 small lemons, thinly sliced
    and seeded

Trim dark skin and pink flesh from watermelon; cut enough of rind into 1- x ¼-inch strips to make 4 pounds. Combine 2 quarts water and salt in a large, shallow glass or plastic container; add watermelon rind. Cover and chill 8 to 10 hours, stirring occasionally. Drain well.

Tie gingerroot and spices in cheesecloth; set aside.

Place watermelon rind in a Dutch oven; cover with cold water, and stir in alum. Bring to a boil, and boil 15 minutes. Drain; rinse with cold water.

Combine 2 quarts water and sugar in a Dutch oven; bring to a boil, stirring constantly. Add the watermelon rind, lemon, and spice bag; boil gently, stirring frequently, until watermelon rind is transparent and syrup is consistency of honey. Remove spice bag; ladle preserves into hot sterilized jars, leaving ⅛-inch headspace. Cover at once with metal lids, and screw bands tight. Process in boiling-water bath for 10 minutes. Yield: 8 cups.

Lucille Finley,
Richardson, Texas.

APPLE MARMALADE

1 orange
6 medium cooking apples, peeled and
    coarsely chopped
2 cups water
3 tablespoons lemon juice
5 cups sugar

Cut orange into quarters; thinly slice, removing seeds. Combine orange, apples, water, and lemon juice in a Dutch oven; bring to a boil. Lower heat, and cook gently 10 minutes or until apples are tender.

Add sugar to fruit mixture; cook, stirring constantly, over high heat until mixture reaches a full boil and sugar is completely dissolved. Continue cooking rapidly until the mixture reaches 220° on a candy thermometer.

Remove from heat, and skim off foam with a metal spoon. Quickly pour marmalade into hot sterilized jars, leaving ⅛-inch headspace; cover at once with metal lids, and screw metal bands tight. Process in boiling-water bath 10 minutes. Yield: 6 cups.

Mrs. O. V. Elkins,
Raleigh, North Carolina.

CRABAPPLE JELLY

3 pounds crabapples, stemmed and
    coarsely chopped
3 cups water
4 cups sugar

Combine crabapples and water in a large Dutch oven; cover and bring to boil. Reduce heat, and simmer 20 to 25 minutes or until crabapples are soft.

Press mixture through cheesecloth reserving juice. Pour juice into a large saucepan, and stir in sugar. Boil over high heat until mixture is the consistency of jelly.

Remove from heat; skim off foam with a metal spoon, and pour jelly into sterilized jars, leaving ½-inch headspace. Seal with a ⅛-inch layer of paraffin. Yield: 5 to 6 cups.

PEPPER JELLY

1½ cups minced green pepper
½ cup minced hot green pepper
7½ cups sugar
1½ cups (5% acid strength) white vinegar
2 (3-ounce) packages liquid fruit pectin

Combine all ingredients except fruit pectin in a Dutch oven; bring to a boil. Boil 6 minutes, stirring frequently. Stir in fruit pectin; continue boiling for 3 additional minutes, stirring frequently. Remove from heat, and skim off foam with a metal spoon.

Quickly pour jelly into sterilized jars, leaving ½-inch headspace. Cover at once with a ⅛-inch layer of paraffin. Cover with lids. Yield: 3½ cups.
Mrs. Jack Corzine,
Greenville, South Carolina.

GREEN TOMATO JAM

4½ pounds firm, medium-size green
    tomatoes, cored and cut into
    ⅛-inch-thick slices
6 cups sugar
Grated rind and juice of 1 lemon
Grated rind and juice of 1 orange

Layer tomatoes alternately with sugar in a large mixing bowl; sprinkle with citrus rind and juice. Cover and let stand at room temperature 8 hours.

Spoon tomatoes and juice into a Dutch oven; bring to a boil. Boil gently 2 to 3 hours, depending on desired degree of thickness; stir frequently. Remove from heat; skim off foam, if necessary, with a metal spoon.

Quickly pour jam into hot sterilized jars, leaving ⅛-inch headspace; cover at once with metal lids, and screw metal bands tight. Process 15 minutes in boiling-water bath. Yield: about 4½ cups.
Marge Mounsey,
El Paso, Texas.

MINT JELLY

2 cups apple juice
1½ cups sugar
1 teaspoon mint extract
Green food coloring

Combine apple juice and sugar in a large saucepan; bring to a boil, stirring often until mixture is of jelly consistency. Stir in mint extract.

Remove mixture from heat, and stir in food coloring to desired shade of green. Pour jelly into sterilized jars, leaving ½-inch headspace. Seal with a ⅛-inch layer of paraffin. Yield: 2 cups.

Tips For Jelly Making

To ensure your success with jam and jelly recipes, here are some things you need to know.

Equipment: A large flat-bottomed kettle is essential for making jellied products. An 8- to 10-quart kettle is a good size.

A jelly or candy thermometer is helpful when making jellied products without the use of commercial pectin.

A jelly bag or a fruit press extracts juice for jelly-making purposes. The bag can be made of several thicknesses of cheesecloth or of flannel with the napped side in. A special stand or colander helps hold the jelly bag while the juice is being extracted.

Containers: Jelly glasses or canning jars may be used. Be sure all jars and closures are in perfect condition. Use new lids for jars.

Have the glasses or jars ready before beginning any actual jelly or jam production. Wash the jars in warm suds, rinse in hot water, boil 10 minutes to sterilize, and keep hot until used. This prevents cracking when filled.

Wash and rinse all lids and bands. Metal lids with sealing compound may require immersion in hot water for a short time before using; follow the manufacturer's directions for this. When using porcelain-lined zinc caps, have new rings of the right size for jars. Caps may be reused, but new rings should be used. Wash the rings in hot soapy water, and rinse well.

Packing and Sealing: Prepare jars and lids ahead so they will be ready to fill.

To seal with lids, use only standard home canning jars and lids. For jars with metal lids and bands, fill the hot jars to within ⅛ inch of the top with the hot fruit mixture. Wipe the jar rim clean, and place a hot metal lid on the jar with the sealing compound next to the glass; screw the metal lid down firmly, and stand the jar upright to cool. For jars with porcelain-lined zinc caps, place a wet rubber ring on the shoulder of the empty jar. Fill the jar to within ⅛ inch of the top, screw the cap down tightly, and stand the jar upright to cool.

When using either type lid, work quickly. After the jar has been filled, use a knife to remove air bubbles by moving the blade around the jar edges.

In many instances it is wise to process jams and jellies for 10 minutes in a boiling-water bath after sealing with lids. If your recipe does not call for processing, you may prefer to seal the jars with paraffin.

The method of *sealing with paraffin* should be used only with mixtures that make fairly firm products. Use only enough paraffin to make a layer ⅛ inch thick, and prick air bubbles in the paraffin before it gets firm. Do not use paraffin that has been used before. Never melt paraffin over direct heat; use a double boiler.

For jelly, pour the hot juice mixture immediately into hot glass containers to within ½ inch of top, and cover with hot paraffin.

For jams, conserves, preserves, and marmalades, remove the fruit mixture from the heat; skim and stir about 5 minutes. This will help prevent the fruit from floating to the top. Pour the fruit mixture into hot glasses to within ½ inch of top. Remove air bubbles with a knife, and cover with a ⅛-inch layer of paraffin. Cover with lids.

Cooling and Storing: Let sealed jars stand overnight to be sure that the seal has been made. Label with name of jellied product and date; also include batch number, if you make more than one. Store in a cool, dark, dry place. Do not hold jellied products in storage longer than one year. Uncooked jams may be stored in the refrigerator for three weeks; if longer storage is needed, place them in the freezer.

Tip: Many recipes call for both the juice and rind of citrus fruits. Remember to wash and grate the fruit before juicing.

For Dinner, Make It All Vegetables

The warm, sunny days of summer bring an abundance of garden-fresh vegetables—black-eyed peas, golden squash, plump tomatoes, sweet corn, and tender pods of okra. And Southerners make the most of the season's bounty by enjoying an old-fashioned vegetable dinner.

Though traditionally thought of as side dishes, a collection of vegetable dishes makes a meal that's as nutritious as it is delicious.

To reach the table at their flavorful best with natural nutrients preserved, vegetables require some special attention during selection, storage, and preparation. The recipes featured in our menu give the proper methods of preparation. Use the following guidelines for selection and storage.

Black-eyed peas: Fresh black-eyed peas are a good source of vitamin A and a fair source of vitamin C. When dried, they are considerably lower in food value. Select pods that are well filled and snap easily. A yellowish pod usually indicates overly mature, tough peas. Also avoid pods that are mildewed, swollen, or highly specked.

Peas in the pod store better than shelled. Use them as quickly as possible to avoid loss of nutrients. The best temperature for temporary storage is 32°F.

Corn: Corn is a good source of vitamin A. Select ears with fresh, green husks; kernels should be tender, milky, and should puncture easily when slight pressure is applied. Ears should be filled to the tip, with no space between rows.

Corn should be used immediately. If necessary, ears may be stored a short time in the refrigerator.

Green beans: High in vitamin A, green beans are also a fair source of riboflavin and thiamine. Long, straight pods, crisp enough to easily snap between your fingers, are the most desirable. Once the beans start to ridge and bulge the pods, they are usually old and tough.

Green beans can be held successfully for a short time at 45° F. to 50° F. Store beans whole to prevent nutrient loss.

Okra: Okra is a good source of riboflavin and also has a fair content of vitamin C and thiamine. Good-quality pods can be either long and thin or short and chunky. They should be tender, puncturing on slight pressure.

Store okra a maximum of two weeks at 50° F. Cooking in iron, copper, or brass utensils will cause pods to become discolored. Although the reaction is harmless, it is undesirable.

Potatoes: A fair source of vitamin C, riboflavin, and thiamine, potatoes also contain an abundance of iron and phosphorus. Select firm, relatively smooth, well-shaped potatoes. They should not be badly bruised, sprouted, or wilted.

Store potatoes in a cool, dry, dark area. Do not refrigerate, as potatoes develop an undesirable sweetness when chilled below 40° F. Loss of vitamin C also increases as storage temperature is reduced. New potatoes should be stored only a few days; mature potatoes can be kept longer.

Squash: Squash is an excellent source of vitamin A and a fair source of thiamine and riboflavin. Summer squash should be young and tender. Hard rinds are desirable for winter squash, but should be avoided in summer squash as the flesh is likely to be stringy.

Summer squash is highly perishable and should be kept for only a few days. The best temperature for storage is 32° F. to 40° F.

Tomatoes: Green tomatoes contain many important minerals besides being a good source of vitamin C and a fair source of vitamin A. Ripe tomatoes offer the same nutrients and are considerably higher in vitamin A. Tomatoes should be firm, plump, fairly well formed, and free from blemishes. Avoid tomatoes that are yellow or misshapen.

Ripe tomatoes can be stored for a short time at 50° F. or lower. Green tomatoes will ripen at room temperature. Do not store unripe tomatoes at low temperatures as an unsatisfactory texture and taste can result.

FRESH GREEN BEANS

2 pounds fresh green beans
2 quarts water
½ pound diced salt pork or ham hock
Salt to taste
¼ teaspoon of sugar

Remove strings from beans; cut beans into 1½-inch pieces. Wash thoroughly. Put water in a 4-quart saucepan, and add salt pork. Cover and cook about 5 minutes. Add beans, salt, and sugar. Cover and cook over medium heat 25 to 35 minutes or until tender. Yield: 6 to 8 servings.

BLACK-EYED PEAS WITH HAM HOCKS

1 quart shelled fresh black-eyed peas
1 quart water
3 ham hocks
1 medium onion, minced
1 to 1½ teaspoons salt
¼ teaspoon pepper

Combine all ingredients in a 4-quart Dutch oven; bring to a boil. Reduce heat; cover and simmer 1 to 1½ hours or until peas are tender. (Add more water, if needed.)

Remove ham hocks from Dutch oven. Remove meat from bones, and add to peas. Yield: 6 to 8 servings.

CORN ON THE COB

8 to 10 ears fresh corn
3 to 4 quarts water
¼ cup sugar
1 tablespoon salt

Remove husks and silks from corn just before cooking. Combine water, sugar, and salt in a Dutch oven; stir to dissolve sugar and salt. Bring water to a boil and add corn. Return to a boil, and cook 8 to 10 minutes. Drain well. Yield: 8 to 10 servings.

FRIED OKRA

1 to 1¼ pounds okra
8 cups water
½ cup salt
Cornmeal
Vegetable oil

Wash okra well; drain. Cut off tip and stem ends; cut okra crosswise into ½-inch slices.

Combine water and salt; pour over okra. Soak 30 minutes; drain, rinse well, and drain again. Roll okra in cornmeal; fry in hot oil until golden brown. Drain on absorbent towels. Yield: 6 servings.

PARSLEY NEW POTATOES

3 pounds small new potatoes
5 cups water
Salt to taste
¾ cup melted butter or margarine
6 tablespoons chopped fresh parsley

Wash potatoes; peel a strip around center of each potato, if desired.

Cook potatoes in boiling salted water until tender; drain well. Combine butter and parsley; spoon over hot potatoes. Yield: 8 servings.

CHEESY SQUASH CASSEROLE

12 medium-size yellow squash
6 slices bacon
¾ cup chopped onion
3 eggs, beaten
1½ cups (about ⅓ pound) shredded
    Cheddar cheese
Salt and pepper to taste
1½ tablespoons Worcestershire sauce

Cook squash in a small amount of boiling salted water until tender; drain well, and mash. Cook bacon until crisp; drain well, reserving drippings. Crumble bacon. Sauté onion in drippings.

Combine all ingredients, stirring well; spoon into a lightly greased 1½-quart casserole. Bake at 350° for 30 minutes. Yield: 6 to 8 servings.

FRIED GREEN TOMATOES

6 large, firm green tomatoes
Salt and pepper to taste
1 cup cornmeal
Bacon drippings or shortening

Cut tomatoes into ¼-inch slices. Season with salt and pepper; dredge in cornmeal. Heat bacon drippings in a heavy skillet; add tomatoes, and fry slowly until browned, turning once. Yield: about 6 to 8 servings.

SOUTHERN CORNBREAD

2 cups cornmeal
1 teaspoon soda
1 teaspoon salt
2 eggs, beaten
2 cups buttermilk
¼ cup bacon drippings

Combine cornmeal, soda, and salt; stir in eggs and buttermilk. Heat bacon drippings in an 8-inch iron skillet until very hot; add drippings to batter, mixing well.

Pour batter into hot skillet, and bake at 450° about 25 minutes or until bread is golden brown. Yield: 8 to 10 servings.

Light, Perk-You-Up Pies

Luscious doesn't have to mean rich when it comes to dessert, not with this tempting selection of pies. And though they are light and refreshing, no flavor has been spared.

Beneath peaks of whipped cream, the filling of Grape Juice Pie is tart and delicious. Whipped cream is in the filling of Rum Bisque Pie, a fluffy combination of coconut and rum. Even chocolate pie can be light and refreshing when served as Chocolate Whipped Cream Pie.

Those who prefer the tart, fresh taste of lemon have two choices: Angel Pie and Whipped Lemon Pie.

ANGEL PIE

4 eggs, separated
½ teaspoon vanilla extract
¼ teaspoon cream of tartar
1 cup sugar
¼ to ½ cup sugar
3 tablespoons fresh lemon juice
2 tablespoons grated lemon rind
1 cup whipping cream
2 tablespoons sugar

Beat egg whites until frothy; add vanilla and cream of tartar, beating slightly. Gradually add 1 cup sugar, beating well after each addition; continue beating until stiff and glossy. Do not underbeat.

Spoon meringue into a well-greased 9-inch pieplate. Use a spoon to shape meringue into a pie shell, swirling sides high. Bake at 275° for 10 minutes; reduce heat to 250°, and bake an additional 30 to 35 minutes or until the meringue is lightly browned.

Beat egg yolks until thick and lemon colored. Gradually beat in ¼ to ½ cup sugar, lemon juice, and lemon rind. Cook in top of a double boiler, stirring constantly, until smooth and thickened. Cool slightly.

Combine whipping cream and 2 tablespoons sugar; beat until light and fluffy. Spoon half into meringue shell; spread with lemon filling, and top with remaining whipped cream. Cover and refrigerate at least 24 hours. Yield: one 9-inch pie.

Mrs. Edith Grosch,
Raleigh, North Carolina.

GRAPE JUICE PIE

¾ cup sugar
¼ cup cornstarch
1⅓ cups grape juice
1 egg, slightly beaten
2 tablespoons butter
2 tablespoons lemon juice
1 baked 9-inch pastry shell
1 cup whipping cream
1 tablespoon sugar

Combine sugar and cornstarch in a 2-quart saucepan. Stir in grape juice; cook over medium heat, stirring constantly, until thickened and bubbly. Cook 1 additional minute.

Add a small amount of hot mixture to egg, mixing well; stir egg mixture into remaining hot mixture. Add butter and lemon juice; return to heat. Bring to a boil, stirring constantly; boil gently 1 minute. Cool. Pour into pastry shell; chill thoroughly.

Combine whipping cream and sugar, beating until light and fluffy. Spread on pie; chill. Yield: 8 servings.

Carrie Bartlett,
Gallatin, Tennessee.

RUM BISQUE PIE

1 envelope unflavored gelatin
¼ cup cold water
3 eggs, separated
½ cup sugar
½ cup milk
¼ teaspoon salt
6 macaroons, finely crushed
¼ cup rum
2 tablespoons sugar
1 cup whipping cream, whipped
1 baked 9-inch pastry shell
Whipped cream (optional)
Toasted chopped almonds (optional)

Soften gelatin in cold water; set aside.

Combine egg yolks, ½ cup sugar, milk, and salt in a small saucepan; cook over low heat, stirring constantly, until thickened and smooth. Remove from heat; add gelatin and macaroons, beating well. Stir in rum.

Beat egg whites (should be at room temperature) until foamy. Gradually add 2 tablespoons sugar, beating until stiff and glossy. Fold meringue and whipped cream into cooked custard; spoon into pastry shell. Chill several hours or until set. Garnish with whipped cream and toasted almonds, if desired. Yield: one 9-inch pie.

Mrs. Thomas R. Cherry,
Birmingham, Alabama.

WHIPPED LEMON PIE

⅔ cup water
⅓ cup lemon juice
1 (3-ounce) package lemon-flavored gelatin
½ cup sugar
1 teaspoon grated lemon rind
1 cup evaporated milk
2 tablespoons lemon juice
1 (9-inch) graham cracker crust

Combine water and ⅓ cup lemon juice in a small saucepan; bring to a boil. Remove from heat; add gelatin and sugar, stirring until dissolved. Stir in lemon rind. Chill until consistency of unbeaten egg white.

Place evaporated milk in freezer about 15 to 20 minutes or until ice crystals form around edges; beat about 1 minute or until stiff. Add 2 tablespoons lemon juice, and beat about 2 minutes or until very stiff; fold into gelatin. Spoon mixture into crust. Chill several hours or until set. Yield: one 9-inch pie.
Mrs. C. Gene Crow,
Dallas, Texas.

CHOCOLATE WHIPPED CREAM PIE

2 (½-ounce) squares unsweetened chocolate
¾ cup sugar
Pinch of salt
5 tablespoons all-purpose flour
1 (13-ounce) can evaporated milk, divided
2 egg yolks, well beaten
1 cup water
2 cups miniature marshmallows
¼ cup butter
1 (9-inch) graham cracker crust
½ pint whipping cream
¼ cup sugar
Grated unsweetened chocolate

Melt chocolate squares in the top of a double boiler over boiling water. Add ¾ cup sugar, salt, flour, and ⅓ cup evaporated milk; mix well.

Add a small amount of chocolate mixture to egg yolks, and mix well; add yolk mixture to remaining hot mixture, mixing well. Stir in water and remaining evaporated milk. Cook over boiling water until smooth and thickened, stirring constantly. Remove from heat. Add marshmallows and butter, stirring until melted. Allow mixture to cool.

Pour filling into crust. Cover and chill thoroughly. Combine whipping cream and ¼ cup sugar; beat at high speed of electric mixer until stiff peaks form. Spread over filling, and sprinkle with grated chocolate. Refrigerate until serving time. Yield: one 9-inch pie.
Varniece Warren,
Hermitage, Arkansas.

Bribe Your Non-Breakfast Eaters

Morning divides the world into two groups—those who eat breakfast and those who don't. Here we offer a selection of unusual breakfast foods that will delight those who do and should prove tempting to those who don't.

Blackberry-Filled Bars and Banana Breakfast Bars are perfect for a quick breakfast on the run. Crunchy Strawberry-Yogurt Parfait provides a nutritious way to start the morning. And for an unusual hot breakfast serve Cheesy Hot Quiche Squares.

BANANA BREAKFAST BARS

¾ cup margarine, softened
½ cup firmly packed brown sugar
1 egg
4 cups quick-cooking oats
1½ cups mashed ripe banana
½ teaspoon salt
½ teaspoon ground cinnamon
½ cup chopped nuts
½ cup raisins
¼ cup chopped dried apricots

Combine margarine and sugar; cream until light and fluffy. Add egg, beating well. Stir in oats, banana, salt, and cinnamon; mix well. Add remaining ingredients, stirring well.

Spoon batter into a greased 13- x 9- x 2-inch baking pan. Bake at 350° for 45 minutes; allow to cool in pan. Cut into 2-inch bars. Yield: about 2 dozen.

Note: Bars can be frozen in airtight container for later use. Remove from freezer the night before serving.
Ruth Crowe,
Midland, Texas.

BLACKBERRY-FILLED BARS

1 cup firmly packed brown sugar
¾ cup margarine, softened
1¾ cups all-purpose flour
1 teaspoon salt
½ teaspoon soda
1½ cups quick-cooking oats
1 (10-ounce) jar seedless blackberry preserves

Combine sugar and margarine; cream until light and fluffy. Sift together flour, salt, and soda; add to creamed mixture, mixing well. Stir in oats.

Press half of mixture into a greased 13- x 9- x 2-inch baking pan. Top with preserves, spreading to within ¼ inch of edge. Press remaining crumb mixture firmly on top. Bake at 400° for 30 to 35 minutes. Cool 5 minutes. Cut into 2-inch bars. Yield: about 2 dozen.
Nancy Sparks Morrison,
Roanoke, Virginia.

CRUNCHY STRAWBERRY-YOGURT PARFAIT

2 cups fresh strawberries, sliced
Sugar (optional)
2 cups corn flakes
1 (8-ounce) carton plain yogurt

Sprinkle fresh strawberries with sugar, if desired. Place a spoonful of strawberries in each of 2 large glasses. Sprinkle each with a spoonful of corn flakes; top with a spoonful of yogurt. Repeat layers until glasses are filled. Garnish each glass with a whole berry, if desired. Yield: 2 servings.
Mrs. Mike Monroe,
Greenville, Mississippi.

CHEESY HOT QUICHE SQUARES

8 eggs
½ cup all-purpose flour
1 teaspoon baking powder
¾ teaspoon salt
4 cups (1 pound) shredded Monterey Jack cheese
1½ cups cottage cheese
¼ cup chopped jalapeño peppers

Beat eggs 3 minutes. Combine flour, baking powder, and salt; add to eggs, and mix well. Stir in cheese and chopped peppers.

Pour into a greased 13- x 9- x 2-inch baking pan; bake at 350° for 30 to 35 minutes. Let cool 10 minutes; cut into squares. Yield: about 12 servings.
Linda Ball,
Houston, Texas.

Dressing Up Pork Chops

If you think you've already prepared pork chops every way imaginable, try some of these new ideas.

Apple-Stuffed Pork Chops have an unusual stuffing: Bread cubes are combined with apples, cheese, raisins, and a touch of cinnamon. For a skillet dinner, pork chops are simmered in a tangy tomato-flavored sauce with vegetables. And if you like pork in a sweet-and-sour sauce, try Pleasing Pork Chops.

CHOPS IN SHERRY

6 loin pork chops
Salt to taste
Seasoned pepper to taste
2 tablespoons margarine, melted
1 (2½-ounce) jar sliced mushrooms, drained
½ cup sherry
1 (8-ounce) carton commercial sour cream

Sprinkle chops with salt and pepper; brown on both sides in margarine. Remove chops, and place in a shallow 2-quart casserole. Combine remaining ingredients; pour over chops. Cover and bake at 350° for 1 hour or until done. Yield: 6 servings. *Mrs. Leo Russell, Forest, Mississippi.*

PLEASING PORK CHOPS

6 (¾-inch-thick) pork chops
2 tablespoons melted shortening
½ teaspoon salt
¼ cup chopped onion
¼ cup chopped green pepper
1 clove garlic, crushed
1½ tablespoons cornstarch
1 tablespoon brown sugar
⅓ cup water
2 tablespoons vinegar
2 teaspoons soy sauce
1 (20-ounce) can pineapple chunks, undrained
3 tablespoons tomato sauce
1 teaspoon grated lemon rind
½ teaspoon salt
½ teaspoon pepper
⅓ cup pecan halves

Brown chops in shortening; remove chops, and place in a lightly greased 13-

x 9- x 2-inch baking dish. Sprinkle chops with ½ teaspoon salt.

Sauté onion, green pepper, and garlic in pan drippings. Remove from heat, and stir in cornstarch and brown sugar. Gradually add water, vinegar, and soy sauce, stirring well; add remaining ingredients except pecans. Cook over low heat, stirring constantly, 10 minutes.

Pour sauce over pork chops; cover and bake at 350° for 45 minutes. Uncover and bake an additional 15 minutes or until done. Sprinkle with pecan halves. Yield: 6 servings.
Mrs. Dollye Leathers, Houma, Louisiana.

PORK CHOP SKILLET DINNER

6 lean pork chops
½ teaspoon salt
¼ teaspoon pepper
1 tablespoon vegetable oil
½ teaspoon savory leaves, crushed
½ bay leaf
2 cups tomato juice
½ cup water
1 small cabbage, cut into wedges
6 carrots, cut in 1-inch slices
1½ cups coarsely chopped onion
3 medium potatoes, peeled and quartered
¼ teaspoon salt

Sprinkle chops with ½ teaspoon salt and pepper; brown in oil in a large skillet. Add savory, bay leaf, tomato juice, and water; cover and simmer 30 minutes.

Add remaining ingredients; cover and simmer 35 minutes or until vegetables are tender. Yield: 6 servings.
Cindy Murphy, Knoxville, Tennessee.

APPLE-STUFFED PORK CHOPS

1½ cups toasted ½-inch bread cubes
½ cup chopped apple
½ cup shredded sharp Cheddar cheese
2 tablespoons seedless golden raisins
¼ teaspoon salt
⅛ teaspoon ground cinnamon
2 tablespoons orange juice
2 tablespoons butter or margarine, melted
6 (1½-inch-thick) pork chops, cut with pockets
Salt and pepper to taste

Combine bread cubes, apple, cheese, and raisins; sprinkle with salt and cinnamon. Add orange juice and butter; stir until bread cubes are coated.

Season pocket of pork chops with salt and pepper; stuff with bread cube mixture. Sprinkle chops with salt and pepper, and place in a shallow baking dish. Bake at 350° for 1 hour and 15 minutes. Cover and bake an additional 15 minutes. Yield: 6 servings.
Mrs. Kenneth B. Waldron, Mountain Rest, South Carolina.

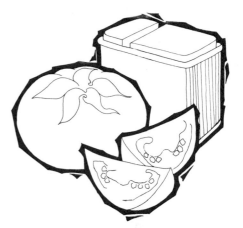

A Meal In A Loaf

For a quick and easy hot sandwich that's a meal in itself, try French Beef Slice. Made with simple ingredients, this sandwich can be prepared in just over half an hour.

French Beef Slice requires only a loaf of French bread, a pound of ground chuck, an onion, and a can each of tomato and Cheddar cheese soups. The loaf is scooped out, filled with the beef and soup mixture, then baked.

FRENCH BEEF SLICE

1 loaf French bread
1 pound ground chuck
1 medium onion, chopped
1 (10¾-ounce) can tomato soup
1 (11-ounce) can Cheddar cheese soup

Cut bread in half lengthwise; carefully scoop out inside and break into bite-size pieces. Combine ground chuck and onion in a large saucepan or Dutch oven; cook until meat is browned. Stir in soup and bread pieces.

Spoon meat mixture into bottom half of bread shell, and cover with top half of bread shell. Wrap loaf in foil; bake at 350° for 30 minutes. To serve, cut into slices. Yield: 8 to 10 servings.
Mrs. Gary L. Jones, Bay City, Texas.

Why Not Serve The Salad Frozen?

A salad often adds a cool refreshing accent to a meal, and no salad is more refreshing than a frozen fruit salad. Whether frozen in a loaf and served in slices or squares or frozen in muffin tin cups for convenient little servings, these salads can substitute as a snack or light dessert.

For a light luncheon, serve a slice of Cranberry Oriental surrounded by fresh summer fruits. Dreamy Frozen Fruit Salad is a rich, creamy mixture filled with pineapple chunks, pecans, and cherry pie filling. This salad is frozen in paper-lined muffin tins. Even the traditional Waldorf salad conforms to the season in a frozen variation that is prepared in paper baking cups for easy serving.

DREAMY FROZEN FRUIT SALAD

2 (1.5-ounce) envelopes whipped topping mix
2 (3-ounce) packages cream cheese, softened
¼ cup lemon juice
1 (14-ounce) can sweetened condensed milk
1 cup chopped pecans
1 (15¼-ounce) can pineapple chunks, drained
1 (21-ounce) can cherry pie filling

Prepare whipped topping mix according to package directions; set aside.

Combine cream cheese and lemon juice; beat until smooth. Stir in milk, pecans, and pineapple. Fold in whipped topping and pie filling. Place about 24 paper baking cups in muffin tins; spoon mixture into baking cups. Cover and freeze. Yield: about 24 servings.

Note: Frozen salads may be removed from muffin tins and stored in plastic freezer bags. *Mrs. Linda Huffaker, Tahoka, Texas.*

CRANBERRY ORIENTAL

1 (16-ounce) can whole-berry cranberry sauce
1 (8-ounce) can crushed pineapple, drained
1 teaspoon lemon juice
1 (8-ounce) carton commercial sour cream
Pinch of salt
Fresh fruit (optional)

Combine all ingredients; stir until well blended. Pour mixture into an 8½- x 4½- x 3-inch loafpan, and freeze until firm. Cut into 1-inch slices. Serve with fresh fruit, if desired. Yield: 8 servings. *Dani Beasley, Clarksville, Tennessee.*

FROZEN CHERRY SALAD

1 (8-ounce) package cream cheese, softened
1 (8-ounce) carton commercial sour cream
¼ cup sugar
¼ teaspoon salt
2 cups miniature marshmallows
½ cup chopped pecans
1 (16-ounce) can pitted dark sweet cherries, drained
1 (8¼-ounce) can crushed pineapple, drained
1 (11-ounce) can mandarin orange sections, drained

Beat cream cheese until smooth. Add sour cream, sugar, and salt; mix well. Fold in marshmallows and pecans. Add fruits, reserving a few for garnish, if desired. Spoon mixture into an 8½- x 4½- x 3-inch pan, and freeze at least 6 hours or until firm. To serve, let stand at room temperature 5 minutes, and cut into 1-inch slices. Garnish with reserved fruit. Yield: 8 servings. *Mrs. Warren D. Davis, Yulee, Florida.*

FROZEN WALDORF SALAD

1 (8¼-ounce) can crushed pineapple
2 eggs, slightly beaten
½ cup sugar
2½ cups chopped apple
⅔ cup chopped celery
⅔ cup chopped walnuts or pecans
⅔ cup miniature marshmallows
¼ cup mayonnaise
¼ cup lemon juice
1 cup whipping cream, whipped

Drain pineapple, reserving juice. Combine pineapple juice, eggs, and sugar in a medium saucepan; cook over medium heat, stirring constantly, until thickened and smooth. Cool slightly. Add pineapple and remaining ingredients except whipped cream; stir well. Fold in whipped cream.

Place about 20 paper baking cups in muffin tins; spoon salad mixture into baking cups. Cover and freeze. Yield: about 20 servings.

Note: Salads may be removed from muffin tins and stored in freezer bags. *Mrs. John M. Woleben, Jr., Williamsburg, Virginia.*

ICE CREAM SALAD

1 (3-ounce) package lemon-flavored gelatin
1 cup boiling water
1 quart vanilla ice cream, softened
1 (8-ounce) can crushed pineapple, undrained
½ cup chopped pecans

Dissolve gelatin in boiling water. Add ice cream, stirring until well blended. Stir in pineapple and pecans. Pour mixture into an 8-inch square pan, and freeze until firm. Cut into squares to serve. Yield: about 9 servings. *Laura Shipley, Fayetteville, North Carolina.*

Treat Yourself To A Quiche

Quiche—that rich custard pie filled with cheese, meat, seafood, or vegetables—is the perfect entrée for light summer meals, with simple ingredients ensuring quick and easy preparation.

Use your favorite pastry recipe to line a quiche dish or piepan; or as an alternative, you'll find that a frozen deep-dish pastry shell also works well and saves time. Then fill the pastry with one of the choices offered in these recipes.

Fresh crabmeat makes a delightful quiche filling; and when blended with eggs, half-and-half, and Swiss cheese in Almond-Topped Crab Quiche, a half pound of crabmeat is stretched into dinner for four.

Bacon and Swiss cheese is the classic combination in quiche Lorraine; these recipes also include a variation—Cheesy Ham Quiche—made with ham and Cheddar. Zucchini-Mushroom Quiche is an appealing example of using fresh vegetables as the basis for quiche.

The combinations of ingredients for quiche are limitless, so don't hesitate to experiment. In fact, quiche is a great way to make a delicious meal of leftover meats and cheeses.

CHEESY HAM QUICHE

Pastry for 9-inch pie shell
1 cup diced cooked ham
1 cup shredded Cheddar cheese
¼ teaspoon ground nutmeg
4 eggs
1 cup half-and-half
½ teaspoon salt
½ teaspoon pepper
½ teaspoon paprika
1 teaspoon parsley flakes

Line a 9-inch quiche dish or piepan with pastry; trim excess pastry around edges. Bake at 400° for 3 minutes; remove from oven, and gently prick with a fork. Bake 5 minutes longer. Let cool on a rack.

Place ham in pastry shell; top with cheese, and sprinkle with nutmeg.

Beat eggs until foamy; stir in half-and-half and seasonings. Pour over cheese in pastry shell.

Bake at 350° for 45 minutes or until firm. Yield: one 9-inch quiche.

Mrs. Martha Ann Rabon,
Stapleton, Alabama.

ALMOND-TOPPED CRAB QUICHE

Pastry for 9-inch pie shell
1 cup (¼ pound) shredded natural Swiss cheese
½ pound fresh crabmeat
2 green onions, sliced
3 eggs
1 cup half-and-half
½ teaspoon salt
½ teaspoon grated lemon rind
Dash of dry mustard
Dash of pepper
¼ cup sliced almonds

Line a 9-inch quiche dish or piepan with pastry; trim excess pastry around edges. Bake at 400° for 3 minutes; remove from oven, and gently prick with a fork. Bake 5 minutes longer. Let cool on rack.

Sprinkle cheese in pastry shell. Remove and discard cartilage from crabmeat; place crabmeat on top of cheese, and sprinkle with green onion.

Beat eggs until foamy; stir in half-and-half, salt, lemon rind, dry mustard, and pepper. Pour into pastry shell, and sprinkle with almonds.

Bake at 325° for 1 hour or until set. Let stand 10 minutes before serving. Yield: one 9-inch quiche.

Mrs. Shannon Doolittle,
Virginia Beach, Virginia.

ZUCCHINI-MUSHROOM QUICHE

Pastry for 10-inch pie shell
2 tablespoons butter or margarine
¼ pound fresh mushrooms, washed and sliced
1 small onion, chopped
1 cup milk
1 cup cooked zucchini slices, well drained
3 eggs, beaten
1 cup (¼ pound) shredded Swiss cheese, divided
½ teaspoon salt
¼ teaspoon pepper

Line a 10-inch quiche dish or piepan with pastry; trim excess pastry around edges. Bake at 400° for 3 minutes; remove from oven, and gently prick with a fork. Bake 5 minutes longer. Let cool on rack.

Melt butter in a skillet. Add mushrooms and onion; sauté until tender. Drain butter from pan.

Combine sautéed vegetables, milk, zucchini, eggs, ¾ cup cheese, salt, and pepper in a large bowl; stir well. Pour into pastry shell. Top with remaining ¼ cup cheese.

Bake at 375° for 30 minutes or until set. Yield: one 10-inch quiche.

Suzie Berg,
Charlotte, North Carolina.

PERFECT QUICHE LORRAINE

Pastry for 10-inch pie shell
1 pound bacon
1½ cups diced Swiss cheese
4 eggs, beaten
1 cup whipping cream
1 cup half-and-half
1 tablespoon all-purpose flour
¾ teaspoon salt
Dash of pepper
Dash of ground nutmeg

Line a 10-inch quiche dish or piepan with pastry; trim excess pastry around edges. Bake at 400° for 3 minutes; remove from oven, and gently prick with a fork. Bake 5 minutes longer. Let cool on rack.

Fry bacon until crisp; drain. Crumble bacon and place in pastry shell; sprinkle with cheese.

Combine remaining ingredients, stirring well; pour over cheese in pastry shell. Bake at 375° for 65 minutes or until set. Yield: one 10-inch quiche.

Shirley W. Hodge,
Delray Beach, Florida.

Hard rolls stuffed with a vegetable salad make a delicious combination for a picnic.

Take The Salad In A Roll

As the days become longer and temperatures warm, it's time to pack a picnic and head for the great outdoors. Lita Cromer of Anderson, South Carolina, shares her favorite totable. It's called Picnic Salad Rolls, a unique recipe that gives you all the makings for a salad stuffed into hard rolls and eaten like a sandwich.

PICNIC SALAD ROLLS

½ cup chopped green pepper
½ cup chopped seeded cucumber
½ cup chopped seeded tomato
½ cup chopped celery
2 tablespoons chopped onion
2 tablespoons chopped parsley
2 tablespoons chopped dill pickle
⅓ cup garlic-flavored sour cream dip
¼ cup mayonnaise or salad dressing
¼ teaspoon salt
6 hard rolls

Combine first 7 ingredients, tossing well. Combine dip, mayonnaise, and salt; mix well, and fold into vegetable mixture. Set aside.

Split rolls lengthwise; scoop out center, leaving a ½-inch shell. Spoon vegetable mixture into rolls; wrap each tightly, and chill until serving time. Yield: 6 servings.

Breakfast For Two

Plan a special breakfast or brunch with these recipes designed to serve two. If omelets are a favorite, choose Potato-Sprout Omelet filled with cottage cheese, potatoes, and alfalfa sprouts. Mexican Omelet combines olives, chiles, and Monterey Jack cheese.

Serve Sour Cream Biscuits as a breakfast accompaniment, or slice and fill with country ham for a delightful main dish. Fluffy Egg Nests perched on buttered toast also make an attractive entrée for a leisurely breakfast.

POTATO-SPROUT OMELET

1 medium potato, cut into ½-inch cubes
2 tablespoons chopped onion
2 to 4 tablespoons vegetable oil
2 eggs
⅓ cup small-curd cottage cheese
2 tablespoons milk
Salt and pepper
1 cup alfalfa sprouts
Avocado slices

Cook potato in boiling salted water until just tender; drain. Brown potatoes and onion in hot oil in a 10-inch omelet pan or heavy skillet over medium heat. Combine eggs, cottage cheese, and milk; mix until blended. Pour over potatoes. Reduce heat to low; cover, and cook about 5 to 8 minutes or until set. Season with salt and pepper to taste. Place alfalfa sprouts on half of omelet; carefully fold omelet in half. Garnish with avocado slices. Yield: 2 servings.   *Robbin Dorrier,*
Mooresville, North Carolina.

FLUFFY EGG NESTS

4 eggs
1 teaspoon seasoned salt
¼ teaspoon cream of tartar
4 slices hot buttered toast
¼ to ½ cup shredded Cheddar cheese

Separate eggs, placing each egg yolk on a saucer or in a custard cup. (Cover with plastic wrap to keep egg yolks from drying out.)

Combine egg whites, seasoned salt, and cream of tartar; beat until stiff but not dry.

Place toast on a baking sheet. Spoon equal amounts of egg whites on each slice of toast, making an indentation in center of each. Carefully slip egg yolk into each indentation; top with cheese. Bake at 350° for 15 minutes or until lightly browned and the yolks are set. Yield: 2 servings.   *Norma Patelunas,*
St. Petersburg, Florida.

MEXICAN OMELET

4 eggs, slightly beaten
2 tablespoons chopped green olives
2 tablespoons chopped green chiles
½ teaspoon salt
2 to 4 teaspoons melted butter or margarine
¼ cup shredded Monterey Jack or Cheddar cheese

Combine eggs, olives, chiles, and salt; mix until just blended. Heat butter in a 10-inch omelet pan or heavy skillet over medium heat until slightly golden at edges.

Pour in egg mixture all at once. As mixture starts to cook, gently lift edges of omelet with a fork, and tilt pan to allow the uncooked portion to run underneath. Sprinkle cheese on half of omelet. Fold omelet in half, and place on a warm platter. Yield: 2 servings.
D. Bennett Keenan,
Dallas, Texas.

SOUR CREAM BISCUITS

1 cup self-rising flour
¼ teaspoon soda
¾ cup commercial sour cream

Combine all ingredients in a bowl; stir until smooth. Turn dough out onto a lightly floured surface. Pat dough out to ½-inch thickness; cut with 2-inch biscuit cutter. Place biscuits on a lightly greased baking sheet. Bake at 450° for 10 to 12 minutes or until golden brown. Yield: 8 biscuits.   *Mrs. Bennie Cox,*
Clinton, Tennessee.

Ground Beef— A Good Buy, A Great Entrée

Small wonder that ground beef is a mainstay in the family diet, for it is one of the best meat buys available and can be the basis of a multitude of mouthwatering entrées.

From easygoing to company special, we've collected an array of recipes from our readers that are sure to find a welcome place on any dinner table.

Potato-Sprout Omelet, filled with alfalfa sprouts and garnished with avocado slices, makes a delicious breakfast for two.

Spaghetti and Beef Casserole is perfect for serving a hungry crowd, stretching 2 pounds of ground beef to serve 12.

For hamburger lovers, there are two choices: Beerburgers and Super Hamburgers. We've also included tempting variations of meatballs and meat loaf.

SUPER HAMBURGERS

1½ pounds ground beef
1 large onion, finely chopped
1 small apple, peeled and finely chopped
1 stalk celery, finely chopped
1 tomato, finely chopped
1 teaspoon chopped fresh parsley
1½ cups crisp rice cereal
1½ teaspoons pepper
1 teaspoon salt
2 tablespoons vegetable oil

Combine all ingredients except oil, mixing well. Shape into 6 patties, and brush with oil. Broil 4 to 6 minutes on each side, depending on desired degree of doneness. Yield: 6 servings.
Mrs. Hugh F. Mosher,
Huntsville, Alabama.

MEAT LOAF ROLL

1½ pounds ground chuck
1 cup soft breadcrumbs
1 egg, beaten
2 teaspoons prepared mustard
1 teaspoon prepared horseradish
1½ teaspoons salt
⅛ teaspoon pepper
¼ to ½ teaspoon rosemary leaves, crushed
½ teaspoon thyme leaves
1 teaspoon Worcestershire sauce
1 (8-ounce) can tomato sauce
1½ cups (about ⅓ pound) shredded Cheddar cheese

Combine first 10 ingredients and ½ cup tomato sauce. Shape into a 14- x 10-inch rectangle on a sheet of waxed paper. Sprinkle with cheese. Begin at short end and roll jellyroll fashion, lifting waxed paper to help roll. Press edges and ends to seal.

Place roll seam side down on baking sheet. Bake at 350° for 45 minutes. Pour remaining tomato sauce over meat loaf. Bake an additional 15 minutes. Let stand 10 minutes before serving. Yield: 6 to 8 servings. *Joy M. Custis,*
Norcross, Georgia.

SPAGHETTI AND BEEF CASSEROLE

3 tablespoons vegetable oil
2 pounds ground beef
2 medium onions, chopped
2 (4-ounce) cans mushroom stems and pieces, undrained
2 (8-ounce) cans tomato sauce
1 (6-ounce) can tomato paste
1 teaspoon ground oregano
1 teaspoon garlic powder
2 (7-ounce) packages spaghetti
1 (8-ounce) package cream cheese, softened
2 cups cottage cheese
½ cup chopped fresh or frozen chives
½ cup commercial sour cream
½ cup buttered fine, dry breadcrumbs

Heat oil in a heavy skillet. Add ground beef and onion; sauté until meat is browned, stirring to crumble. Drain off pan drippings.

Combine mushrooms, tomato sauce, tomato paste, oregano, and garlic powder; add to meat mixture, mixing well. Simmer, uncovered, 15 minutes.

Cook spaghetti according to package directions; drain. Place half of spaghetti in a buttered 13- x 9- x 2-inch baking dish.

Combine cream cheese, cottage cheese, chives, and sour cream; mix well. Spoon cream cheese mixture over spaghetti layer, spreading evenly.

Place remaining spaghetti over cream cheese mixture. Pour meat sauce over spaghetti and sprinkle with breadcrumbs. Bake at 350° for 30 minutes or until bubbly. Yield: 12 servings.
Doris Garton,
Shenandoah, Virginia.

BARBECUE CUPS

1 pound ground beef
½ cup barbecue sauce
1 tablespoon minced onion
1½ tablespoons brown sugar
1 (8-ounce) can refrigerated biscuits
¾ cup shredded Cheddar cheese

Sauté ground beef until browned, stirring to crumble; drain off pan drippings. Stir in barbecue sauce, onion, and brown sugar.

Place each biscuit in a greased muffin cup, pressing to cover bottom and sides. Spoon meat mixture into cups, and sprinkle with cheese. Bake at 400° for 10 to 12 minutes or until golden brown. Yield: 12 servings. *Mrs. Travis Massey,*
Sherwood, Arkansas.

BEERBURGERS

2 pounds ground beef
½ cup beer
⅓ cup crushed pretzels
2 tablespoons chopped onion
2 tablespoons drained pickle relish
1 teaspoon salt

Combine all ingredients, mixing well. Shape into 6 patties. Broil 4 to 6 minutes on each side, depending on desired degree of doneness. Yield: 6 servings.
Mrs. Carol Poston,
Harriman, Tennessee.

TANGY HAWAIIAN MEATBALLS

1½ pounds ground beef
1 pound ground pork
1 cup fine, dry breadcrumbs
½ cup chopped roasted blanched salted almonds
2 eggs, well beaten
2 cloves garlic, minced
Dash of hot sauce
Dash of ground nutmeg
1 to 2 tablespoons cornstarch
Vegetable oil
1 (16-ounce) can pineapple chunks
About ⅔ cup pineapple juice
2 cups vinegar
½ cup soy sauce
1½ cups sugar
¼ cup cornstarch

Combine first 8 ingredients in a large bowl; mix well. Shape meat mixture into 1- to 1¼-inch balls. Roll meatballs in 1 to 2 tablespoons cornstarch, coating lightly. Cook meatballs in hot oil until done; drain.

Drain pineapple, reserving juice; set pineapple aside. Add enough additional pineapple juice to reserved juice to make 1 cup. Combine juice, vinegar, and soy sauce in a 3-quart saucepan. Combine sugar and ¼ cup cornstarch; stir into juice mixture. Cook over medium heat, stirring constantly, until thickened and clear (about 15 minutes).

Add pineapple and meatballs to sauce; cook until thoroughly heated. Serve warm. Yield: about 5 dozen.
Note: If a milder flavored sauce is desired, substitute 1¼ cups vinegar plus ¾ cup water for the 2 cups vinegar.
Jan Uecke,
Fort Bliss, Texas.

COUNTY FAIR CASSEROLE

1 (8-ounce) package elbow macaroni
1 pound ground beef
1 cup chopped onion
1 teaspoon salt
¼ teaspoon pepper
1 (10¾-ounce) can cream of celery soup, undiluted
1 (8-ounce) carton commercial sour cream
1 (17-ounce) can English peas, drained

Cook macaroni according to package directions, and drain well.

Combine ground beef, onion, and seasonings in a heavy skillet; sauté until meat is lightly browned, stirring to crumble. Drain off pan drippings. Stir in cream of celery soup; cover and simmer 10 minutes. Stir in macaroni and remaining ingredients.

Spoon mixture into a lightly greased 2½-quart casserole. Bake at 350° for 35 minutes. Yield: 8 servings.
Margaret L. Hunter,
Princeton, Kentucky.

Soup To Sip Or Make A Meal Of

Hot or cold, rich or light, soup is a delightful addition to summer meals. Serve it as an appealing appetizer to sip before dinner, or pair it with a salad or sandwich for a light lunch.

These recipes offer both hot and cold soups in variations that range from a smooth, rich Cream of Broccoli Soup to the cool, refreshing herb-flavored Summer Tomato Soup and Cold Cucumber Soup.

COLD CUCUMBER SOUP

1½ cups commercial sour cream
1 teaspoon dillweed
1 tablespoon Worcestershire sauce
½ teaspoon celery salt
1 tablespoon lemon juice
¼ teaspoon pepper
¾ teaspoon salt
2 green onions, coarsely chopped
3 medium cucumbers, peeled, seeded, and coarsely chopped

Combine all ingredients in container of electric blender; process until smooth. Chill thoroughly. Yield: 2½ to 3 cups.   *Audrey Burnham,*
Rehoboth Beach, Delaware.

CLEAR VEGETABLE SOUP

Bones from 1 uncooked chicken
6 cups hot water
½ pound Chinese vegetable greens, cut into 1-inch strips
3 ounces smoked ham, cut into ¼-inch strips
Salt and pepper to taste

Combine chicken bones and hot water in a large saucepan. Bring to a boil; cover and cook 30 minutes. Remove bones, and strain broth.

Return broth to a boil; add vegetable greens, ham, salt, and pepper. Heat thoroughly and serve hot. Yield: about 6 cups.
Betty Kao,
Birmingham, Alabama.

CREAM OF BROCCOLI SOUP

2 cups cold water
1 tablespoon cornstarch
2 cups water
2 (10-ounce) packages frozen chopped broccoli, thawed
1 cup chopped onion
4 chicken bouillon cubes
¼ teaspoon seasoned salt
¼ teaspoon celery salt
⅛ teaspoon garlic powder
Pinch of ground nutmeg
¾ teaspoon Worcestershire sauce
⅓ cup instant nonfat dry milk
2 tablespoons evaporated milk
3 to 4 tablespoons margarine

Combine 2 cups cold water and cornstarch; stir well, and set aside.

Bring 2 cups water to a boil; stir in vegetables, bouillon cubes, and seasonings. Reduce heat, and simmer 10 minutes or until vegetables are tender. Stir cornstarch mixture and remaining ingredients into soup; heat thoroughly (do not boil). Yield: about 6 cups.
Gloria Pedersen,
Corinth, Mississippi.

SUMMER TOMATO SOUP

12 large, ripe tomatoes, peeled and quartered
6 green onions, cut into 2-inch slices
1½ cups commercial sour cream
1 tablespoon salt
1 teaspoon sugar
½ teaspoon whole marjoram leaves
½ teaspoon whole thyme leaves
1 teaspoon curry powder
2 tablespoons lime juice

Combine all ingredients in a large bowl. Pour about one-fourth of mixture into container of electric blender; process until smooth. Pour into a large bowl or pitcher; repeat with remaining mixture. Cover and chill well. Yield: 11 cups.
Mrs. Doug Hail,
Moody, Texas.

CHILLED PEANUT SOUP

¾ cup roasted peanuts
3 (10½-ounce) cans beef broth
1½ cups half-and-half
¾ teaspoon chili powder
Thinly sliced radishes (optional)

Combine peanuts and 1 can broth in container of electric blender; process until smooth. Pour into a large saucepan. Add remaining 2 cans broth, half-and-half, and chili powder.

Bring to a boil over medium heat, stirring often; reduce heat, and simmer 15 minutes. Chill. Garnish with radishes, if desired. Yield: about 6 cups.
Mrs. James Sutton,
Winston-Salem, North Carolina.

Tip: When adding vegetables to home-made soup, remember that all vegetables should not be added at the same time. Vegetables that take the longest cooking time should be added first. These include green beans, potatoes (unless diced very thin), and corn. Canned vegetables need only to be heated, so add them last.

Outdoor barbecues make for easy entertaining when you serve Charcoal Broiled Chicken (page 90), Barbecued Steak Kabobs (page 89), or Southern Barbecued Spareribs (page 90).

Page 134: Asparagus with Yogurt Dressing (page 66) makes a bright, refreshing dish for a springtime luncheon.

Left: Make the best of the season's vegetables with these cool, crisp salads: Spinach Salad with Russian Dressing (page 144), Tangy Vegetable Toss (page 144), and Marinated Vegetable Salad (page 143).

Left: For a festive summer party serve a lavish array of colorful dishes: Lamb Shish Kabobs, Green Spinach Salad, fresh fruit, Date Muffins, and Curried Rice with Pineapple. Menu and recipes begin on page 141.

Right: Enjoy the summer's harvest all year long with homemade jams and jellies. Recipes begin on page 120.

Coleslaw, The Summertime Salad

Coleslaw is a refreshing alternative to tossed salad, a just-right accompaniment for summertime foods—grilled hamburgers, fried chicken, and cold sandwiches. And these coleslaw recipes offer some appealing variations.

For Cabbage-Orange Slaw, not only are oranges used in the slaw, but it's also served in orange shells; the citrus flavor blends nicely with celery, parsley, and raisins.

Swedish Slaw owes its lively taste to the dry mustard and turmeric in the dressing. If you need a salad that can be made ahead, we suggest Marinated Coleslaw or Overnight Coleslaw.

SWEDISH SLAW

1 cup sugar
1 cup vinegar
1 teaspoon dry mustard
1 teaspoon turmeric
1 medium head cabbage, chopped
1 medium-size green pepper, chopped
1 medium onion, chopped

Combine sugar, vinegar, mustard, and turmeric in a saucepan; boil mixture 1 minute.

Combine cabbage, green pepper, and onion in a large mixing bowl. Pour hot mixture over slaw, stirring well. Chill. Yield: about 6 servings.

*Mrs. Jean Fort,
Ashland City, Tennessee.*

CORN AND CABBAGE SLAW

3 cups chopped cabbage
1 (12-ounce) can vacuum-packed golden whole kernel corn with sweet peppers
1 medium onion, chopped
½ medium-size green pepper, diced
½ cup sliced celery
½ cup mayonnaise
¼ cup cubed salad pickles
¼ teaspoon salt
⅛ teaspoon pepper

Combine all ingredients, stirring until thoroughly mixed. Chill well. Yield: 6 to 8 servings. *Mrs. Loren D. Martin, Knoxville, Tennessee.*

OVERNIGHT COLESLAW

2½ cups shredded green cabbage (about 1 medium head)
2½ cups shredded red cabbage (about 1 medium head)
1 medium-size green pepper, chopped
½ cup vegetable oil
¼ cup white wine vinegar
1 tablespoon sugar
1 teaspoon celery seeds
½ teaspoon celery salt
½ teaspoon onion salt
½ teaspoon salt
½ teaspoon pepper

Combine cabbage and green pepper in a large mixing bowl.

Combine remaining ingredients in a jar; screw lid tightly, and shake well. Pour dressing over cabbage mixture, stirring well. Chill overnight. Yield: 8 to 10 servings.

Note: ¾ cup chopped celery may be substituted for celery seeds and celery salt. *Carol G. Parker, Seattle, Washington.*

CABBAGE-ORANGE SLAW

3 large oranges
1⅔ cups shredded cabbage
2 tablespoons finely chopped celery
2 tablespoons chopped fresh parsley
2 tablespoons raisins (optional)
¼ cup mayonnaise
2 tablespoons milk or half-and-half
1 teaspoon vinegar
¼ teaspoon salt
¼ teaspoon sugar

Cut each orange in half crosswise; gently remove pulp, leaving shells intact. Remove membrane from orange pulp; drain off juice.

Combine orange sections, cabbage, celery, and parsley; add raisins, if desired. Combine remaining ingredients, mixing well. Pour dressing over cabbage mixture, stirring gently until well mixed. Fill orange shells with slaw; chill. Yield: 6 servings.

Note: Edges of orange shells may be scalloped or notched, if desired.

Marlan Mary Hornburg, Melbourne, Florida.

MARINATED COLESLAW

1 large head cabbage, shredded
2 green peppers, finely chopped
3 medium onions, finely chopped
1⅓ cups vinegar
2½ cups sugar
⅔ cup water
1½ teaspoons mustard seeds
1 teaspoon celery seeds
½ teaspoon turmeric
1½ teaspoons salt

Combine cabbage, green pepper, and onion in a large bowl; set aside.

Combine remaining ingredients in a medium saucepan, mixing well. Bring to a boil; immediately pour over vegetables. Cover and chill 12 hours, stirring occasionally. Yield: 6 to 8 servings.

Chelsa Dickerson, Hoboken, Georgia.

A New Snack Idea

A new idea for an afternoon snack comes from Mrs. Kent M. Sharp of Pulaski, Virginia. She calls her creation Little Nothings, but we think you'll agree they're something special.

Thin slices of bread are spread with fruit preserves, battered and deep fried, and then topped with powdered sugar. She suggests serving additional fruit preserves along with the crispy rolls.

LITTLE NOTHINGS

½ cup fruit preserves or marmalade
16 slices sandwich bread, crust removed
¾ cup buttermilk pancake and waffle mix
1 teaspoon sugar
¼ teaspoon ground nutmeg
1 egg
¾ cup milk
Hot vegetable oil
Powdered sugar
Additional fruit preserves or marmalade (optional)

Spread preserves over each slice of bread; roll up jellyroll fashion. Tightly wrap each bread roll in plastic wrap; chill several hours or overnight.

Combine pancake mix, sugar, and nutmeg; mix well. Add egg and milk, mixing until smooth.

Dip each bread roll into batter, and deep fry in hot oil until golden brown. Drain on paper towels; sprinkle with powdered sugar. Serve warm with additional preserves or marmalade, if desired. Yield: 1¼ dozen.

Nutmeg Makes The Difference

The warm, spicy aroma of nutmeg is surpassed only by the wonderful flavor it lends to a variety of dishes.

In these recipes, nutmeg combines with orange rind for the delightfully different Orange Spiced Doughnuts. Spicy Prune Cake and Nutmeg Sugar Cookies also owe their goodness to this spice. And should you think that nutmeg is only for desserts, be sure to try this version of Meatballs in Gravy.

ORANGE SPICED DOUGHNUTS

1 package dry yeast
¾ cup warm water (105° to 115°)
1 cup canned mashed sweet potatoes
1 cup water
¾ cup shortening
½ cup sugar
1 tablespoon salt
2 eggs
2 tablespoons grated orange rind
1 teaspoon ground nutmeg
7 cups all-purpose flour
Vegetable oil
6 cups powdered sugar
1 cup boiling water

Dissolve yeast in warm water; let stand 5 minutes.

Combine potatoes, 1 cup water, shortening, sugar, and salt in a large bowl; mix until shortening is well dispersed. Stir in yeast mixture; add eggs, orange rind, nutmeg, and flour; mix until a soft dough forms.

Turn dough out on a well-floured surface; knead 5 to 8 minutes or until smooth and elastic. Place dough in a greased bowl, turning once to grease top. Cover and let rise in a warm place (85°), free from drafts, 1½ hours or until doubled in bulk.

Punch dough down; divide in half, and shape each portion into a ball. Working with one portion at a time, place dough on a lightly floured surface; pat to ¾-inch thickness. Cut with floured doughnut cutter.

Place doughnuts several inches apart on greased baking sheets; cover and let rise in a warm place until doubled in bulk (about 1 hour and 25 minutes). At this point, doughnuts may be refrigerated overnight, if desired.

Heat 2 to 3 inches of oil to 375°; drop in 3 to 4 doughnuts at a time. Cook about 1 minute or until golden on one side; turn and cook other side about 1 minute. Drain on absorbent towels.

Combine sugar and 1 cup boiling water, stirring until sugar is dissolved. Dip warm doughnuts in glaze to coat both sides; then place on waxed paper. Yield: about 3½ dozen.

Note: After the kneading process, dough may be covered and stored in the refrigerator for up to 3 days. To prepare chilled dough, turn out on floured surface and follow above procedure for cutting, rising, and cooking.
Mrs. Milton L. Davis,
Waco, Texas.

SPICY PRUNE CAKE

2 cups all-purpose flour
1 cup diced cooked prunes
1½ cups sugar
1 teaspoon salt
1 teaspoon soda
1 teaspoon ground nutmeg
1 teaspoon ground allspice
1 teaspoon ground cinnamon
3 eggs, slightly beaten
1 cup vegetable oil
1 cup buttermilk
1 teaspoon vanilla extract
Buttermilk Sauce

Sprinkle 2 tablespoons flour over prunes, stirring until well coated. Set aside.

Sift together remaining flour, sugar, salt, soda, and spices in a large bowl. Add eggs, oil, and buttermilk; beat well (about 2 minutes). Stir in prunes and vanilla.

Spoon batter into a well-greased and floured 10-inch tube pan. Bake at 300° for 65 minutes or until done. Cool for 20 minutes in pan; remove from pan, and cool completely.

Glaze cake with half of Buttermilk Sauce. Serve remaining sauce over individual slices. Yield: one 10-inch cake.

Buttermilk Sauce:

1 cup sugar
½ cup buttermilk
½ cup butter
1 tablespoon light corn syrup
½ teaspoon soda
½ teaspoon vanilla extract

Combine all ingredients in a saucepan. Cook over medium heat, stirring occasionally, until mixture reaches a boil. Boil 2 minutes. Remove from heat, and serve warm. Yield: about 2½ cups.
Jane Carr,
Danville, Virginia.

NUTMEG SUGAR COOKIES

2 cups all-purpose flour
1 teaspoon baking powder
½ teaspoon soda
1 teaspoon ground nutmeg
½ teaspoon salt
1 cup sugar
½ cup shortening
2 eggs, beaten
2 teaspoons milk
Additional sugar

Sift together first 5 ingredients in a bowl; set aside.

Combine 1 cup sugar and shortening in a large bowl, creaming well. Add eggs and milk; beat well. Add dry ingredients, and mix well.

Drop dough by teaspoonfuls onto lightly greased cookie sheets. Slightly flatten each with a spoon; sprinkle with sugar. Bake at 375° for 10 to 12 minutes. Place on rack to cool. Yield about 5½ dozen.
Mrs. Tom Cleveland,
Lumberton, North Carolina.

MEATBALLS IN GRAVY

1 tablespoon shortening
⅓ cup chopped onion
1 pound ground beef
½ pound ground pork
1½ cup fine dry breadcrumbs
¾ cup water or milk
2 eggs, beaten
1 tablespoon salt
1 tablespoon sugar
¼ teaspoon ground nutmeg
¼ teaspoon pepper
¼ cup shortening
3 beef bouillon cubes
3 cups boiling water
2½ tablespoons all-purpose flour
5 tablespoons lemon juice
3 bay leaves

Melt 1 tablespoon shortening in a Dutch oven; add onion, and sauté until tender. Combine onion, meat, breadcrumbs, water, eggs, salt, sugar, nutmeg, and pepper; mix well, and shape into 1½-inch balls.

Melt ¼ cup shortening in Dutch oven; add meatballs. Brown lightly; drain, reserving pan drippings.

Dissolve bouillon cubes in 3 cups water; set aside.

Sprinkle flour into pan drippings, stirring until smooth. Combine bouillon and lemon juice; gradually add to flour mixture, stirring constantly. Cook over medium heat until thickened and bubbly, stirring constantly.

Add meatballs and bay leaves to sauce; reduce heat, and simmer 1 hour. Yield: 6 to 8 servings.   *Mary Mays,*
Lebanon, Kentucky.

Mango-Pineapple Preserves are a delicious way to keep the flavor of fresh mangoes around all year long.

Easy And Elegant Beef

Elegant dining doesn't always mean spending countless hours in the kitchen. Beef Fillets au Vin is a festive and delicious entrée that requires little preparation time. The fillets are simply sautéed and served with a rich mushroom and wine sauce.

BEEF FILLETS AU VIN

4 (1¼- to 1½-inch-thick) fillets of beef
3 tablespoons melted butter or margarine, divided
1 pound fresh mushrooms, cut into ¼-inch slices
1 tablespoon minced shallots or green onions
½ cup Burgundy or dry red wine
1 teaspoon butter or margarine, softened
1 teaspoon all-purpose flour
2 tablespoons Burgundy or dry red wine

Sauté fillets in 1 tablespoon butter 4 minutes on each side; remove from skillet, and keep warm. Drain and discard pan drippings.

Melt 1 tablespoon butter in skillet over low heat; sauté mushrooms and shallots 2 to 3 minutes. Stir in ½ cup Burgundy; cook over high heat until wine is reduced to half.

Combine 1 teaspoon butter and flour; stir to form a smooth paste. Add to mushroom mixture; cook, stirring constantly, 30 seconds. Add remaining tablespoon butter and 2 tablespoons Burgundy; stir until butter melts. Spoon sauce over fillets. Serve at once. Yield: 4 servings.   *Mrs. Bruce Weilbacher,*
San Antonio, Texas.

Fresh Mangoes For The Picking

South Florida is the proud producer of several tropical fruits, one of which is the mango. This marvelous fruit is good for eating at almost any stage of harvest. Green mangoes may be prepared as a filling for pie, as in Green Mango Pie. When ripe, the mango peel will change from green to an orange-yellow color. At this point, it's ready for eating directly out of hand or for making Mango-Pineapple Preserves or Mango Salad.

GREEN MANGO PIE

1¼ cups sugar
1 teaspoon ground cinnamon
½ teaspoon ground nutmeg
2 tablespoons all-purpose flour
3½ cups peeled sliced green mango
1 tablespoon lime juice
Pastry for double crust 9-inch pie

Combine first four ingredients; add mango and lime juice. Stir well, and spoon into pastry shell. Top with pastry, and crimp edges to seal. Cut several slits in the top crust to act as steam vents. Bake at 450° for 10 minutes; reduce oven temperature to 375°, and continue to bake 40 to 45 minutes or until done. Yield: one 9-inch pie.
Mrs. Claire C. Dolan,
Hialeah, Florida.

MANGO SALAD

1 (3-ounce) package orange-flavored gelatin
1 cup boiling water
¾ cup cold water
1 (3-ounce) package cream cheese, softened
1 cup chopped mango
Lettuce
Mayonnaise

Dissolve gelatin in boiling water; add cold water. Combine about ½ cup dissolved gelatin, cream cheese, and mango in container of electric blender; process until smooth. Add remaining dissolved gelatin, and pour into a 4-cup mold. Refrigerate until firm. Unmold on a bed of lettuce. Top with a dollop of mayonnaise. Yield: 5 to 6 servings.
Jeannine Allen,
McAllen, Texas.

MANGO-PINEAPPLE PRESERVES

8 cups peeled chopped mango
1 (20-ounce) can crushed pineapple
¼ cup lime juice
4 cups sugar

Combine all ingredients in a large Dutch oven. Heat slowly to boiling, stirring occasionally until sugar dissolves. Cook rapidly until fruit is clear, stirring frequently. Spoon into sterilized half-pint jars, leaving ⅛-inch headspace. Adjust caps. Process in boiling-water bath for 15 minutes. Yield: 5 half pints.
Mrs. Howard F. Lane,
Boca Raton, Florida.

Popovers— High On Flavor

Good Old Southern Popovers rise to any occasion. Hot from the oven, their golden-brown, crisp exterior and deliciously moist, chewy centers wait to be smothered in butter.

The secret to the light, delicate texture of this quick bread is that it is leavened by steam. When the thin batter (about the consistency of rich cream) is poured into hot greased muffin tins and baked at a high temperature, it quickly puffs up and over the top of the pan and bakes into an irregular shape.

Two other popover recipes are included here. For a flavorful variation, try Pimiento Popovers; onion, green pepper, and pimiento are added to the batter. Muffin Tin Popovers have a hint of sugar.

MUFFIN TIN POPOVERS

2 cups all-purpose flour
2 cups milk
4 eggs, slightly beaten
1 teaspoon sugar
¼ teaspoon salt

Combine all ingredients; beat with an electric mixer just until smooth.

Place well-greased muffin tins in oven at 450° for 3 minutes or until a drop of water sizzles when dropped in them. Remove tins from oven; fill half full with batter. Bake at 450° for 25 to 30 minutes. Serve immediately. Yield: about 20 popovers.
Stephanie E. Creim,
Bellevue, Washington.

GOOD OLD SOUTHERN POPOVERS

1½ cups all-purpose flour
1½ cups milk
3 eggs, slightly beaten
½ teaspoon salt

Combine all ingredients; beat with electric mixer just until smooth.

Place well-greased muffin tins in oven at 450° for 3 minutes or until a drop of water sizzles when dropped in them. Remove tins from oven; fill two-thirds full with batter. Bake at 450° for 30 minutes; reduce heat to 300°, and bake an additional 10 to 15 minutes. Serve immediately. Yield: 1 dozen.
Mrs. Warren A. Knight,
Sarasota, Florida.

PIMIENTO POPOVERS

1 tablespoon finely chopped onion
1 tablespoon finely chopped green pepper
2 tablespoons butter or margarine
1 tablespoon well-drained, finely chopped pimiento
2 eggs, slightly beaten
1 cup milk
1 cup all-purpose flour
½ teaspoon salt

Sauté onion and green pepper in butter about 5 minutes; remove from heat, and stir in pimiento.

Combine eggs, milk, flour, and salt; beat with electric mixer just until smooth. Stir sautéed vegetables into batter; pour batter into well-greased 6-ounce custard cups, filling half full. Bake at 400° for 40 to 45 minutes. Serve immediately. Yield: 6 servings.
Mrs. Elizabeth Kraus,
Louisville, Kentucky.

The Flavor's In The Filling

Delicate patty shells overflowing with a creamy cheese sauce full of ham, olives, and pimiento make Creamy Ham Towers a delightful dish for a luncheon or brunch. Or fill patty shells with creamed chicken or Saucy Mushrooms and Eggs.

SAUCY MUSHROOM AND EGGS

1 pound fresh mushrooms, washed and sliced
½ cup finely chopped onion
¼ cup butter or margarine
1 (10¾-ounce) can cream of mushroom soup, undiluted
¼ cup chopped fresh parsley
¼ teaspoon white pepper
6 hard-cooked eggs, chopped
2 (10-ounce) packages frozen patty shells, baked
Paprika

Sauté mushrooms and onion in butter in a large skillet about 5 minutes. Stir in soup, parsley, and pepper. Cook until bubbly, stirring constantly. Reduce heat, and stir in eggs. Cook until mixture is heated thoroughly.

Spoon filling into patty shells and sprinkle with paprika. Yield: 12 servings.
Mrs. Beverly Fink,
Indialantic, Florida.

CREAMY HAM TOWERS

1 chicken bouillon cube
½ cup hot water
1½ cups milk
¼ cup butter or margarine
¼ cup all-purpose flour
½ cup (2 ounces) shredded process American cheese
1 teaspoon prepared mustard
1 teaspoon Worcestershire sauce
2 cups cubed cooked ham
⅓ cup sliced, pitted ripe olives
2 tablespoons chopped pimiento
2 tablespoons minced fresh parsley
8 frozen patty shells, baked

Dissolve bouillon cube in hot water; stir in milk, and set aside.

Melt butter in a heavy saucepan over low heat; blend in flour. Cook 1 minute, stirring constantly. Gradually add bouillon mixture; cook over medium heat, stirring constantly, until thickened and bubbly. Add cheese, mustard, and Worcestershire, stirring until cheese melts. Stir in ham, olives, pimiento, and parsley. Heat thoroughly.

Spoon filling into patty shells. Yield: 8 servings.
Mrs. G. R. Hlavenka,
Bethlehem, Pennsylvania.

CREAMED CHICKEN IN A SHELL

½ green pepper, chopped
2 tablespoons chopped celery
1 tablespoon chopped onion
3 tablespoons butter or margarine, melted
¼ cup butter or margarine
5 tablespoons all-purpose flour
2 cups half-and-half or milk
3 cups diced cooked chicken
¾ cup sliced fresh mushrooms
2 to 3 hard-cooked eggs, thinly sliced
1 (2½-ounce) jar diced pimiento, drained
Salt and pepper to taste
2 (10-ounce) packages frozen patty shells, baked
Paprika

Sauté green pepper, celery, and onion in 3 tablespoons butter until tender. Drain and set aside.

Melt ¼ cup butter in a heavy saucepan over low heat; blend in flour. Cook 1 minute, stirring constantly. Gradually add half-and-half; cook over medium heat, stirring constantly, until thickened and bubbly. Stir in sautéed vegetables, chicken, mushrooms, eggs, and pimiento; add salt and pepper to taste.

Spoon into patty shells, and sprinkle with paprika. Yield: 12 servings.
Mrs. W. Harold Groce,
Arden, North Carolina.

July

To help you celebrate the long, lazy days of July, we bring you a special *Summer Suppers* section complete with menus, recipes, and entertaining ideas. Relax with your family and friends, and enjoy the South's favorite season.

Figs are one of summer's most versatile fruits. Their moist, sweet flavor lends itself to a variety of dishes, such as cobblers and ice cream sauces. Take advantage of other summer fruits with our assortment of cooling sherbets.

For a filling side dish or an unusual entrée, consider the collection of squash recipes in this chapter. Your family will delight over the light zucchini soufflé or yellow squash croquettes. Other seasonal selections you should not miss include some new ideas for okra and fresh plum specialties.

Pick A Fig Favorite

With all of summer's abundance of fresh fruits, figs are often overlooked. But once you've tasted their distinctive sweetness in these recipes, you'll find that the flavor is unforgettable.

Homemade fig preserves is an alltime favorite, made with whole figs simmered in syrup until plump and tender. Enjoy them as a condiment year-round and also use them in a moist, spicy fig cake. The cake included here is baked in a tube pan and drenched with Buttermilk Glaze.

Figs also add variety to the relish tray when served as pickled figs. Since the stems are left intact, they're a perfect finger food.

For dessert, bake fresh figs in a crusty cobbler, or spoon a generous serving of warm fig sauce over ice cream or pound cake.

Fresh figs are available now through early fall, ranging in color from greenish yellow to purplish brown, depending on variety. When buying, select fruit that is soft to the touch and has a bright color characteristic of the particular variety. Be sure to check the aroma of the figs for any sign of sourness. Since figs spoil quickly after picking, immediately store in the refrigerator.

FIG PRESERVE CAKE

1½ cups sugar
2 cups all-purpose flour
1 teaspoon soda
1 teaspoon salt
1 teaspoon ground nutmeg
1 teaspoon ground cinnamon
½ teaspoon ground allspice
½ teaspoon ground cloves
1 cup vegetable oil
3 eggs
1 cup buttermilk
1 tablespoon vanilla extract
1 cup fig preserves, chopped
½ cup chopped pecans or walnuts
Buttermilk Glaze

Combine dry ingredients in a large mixing bowl; add oil, beating well. Add eggs, and beat well; add buttermilk and vanilla, mixing thoroughly. Stir in preserves and pecans.

Pour batter into a greased and floured 10-inch tube pan; bake at 350° for 1 hour and 15 minutes. Let cool 10 minutes; remove from pan. Pour warm Buttermilk Glaze over warm cake. Yield: one 10-inch cake.

Buttermilk Glaze:
¼ cup buttermilk
½ cup sugar
¼ teaspoon soda
1½ teaspoons cornstarch
¼ cup margarine
1½ teaspoons vanilla extract

Combine first 5 ingredients in a saucepan; bring to a boil, and remove from heat. Cool slightly, and stir in vanilla. Yield: enough glaze for one 10-inch cake.
Mrs. Linda Barnett,
Birmingham, Alabama.

FIG PRESERVES

4 quarts fresh figs with stems
1 tablespoon soda
3 quarts boiling water
8 cups sugar
1 quart water
1 lemon, thinly sliced

Place figs in a large bowl; sprinkle with soda. Add 3 quarts boiling water, and soak 1 hour. Drain figs; rinse thoroughly in cold water.

Combine sugar and 1 quart water in a large Dutch oven; bring to a boil, and cook 10 minutes. Add figs and lemon to syrup; cook until figs are clear and tender (about 1 hour), stirring occasionally.

Spoon figs into hot sterilized jars; if necessary, continue cooking syrup until thick. Pour syrup over figs, leaving ⅛-inch headspace. Run knife around edge of jars to remove air bubbles. Top with lids, and screw metal bands tight. Process 10 minutes in boiling-water bath. Yield: 4 to 5 pints.
Note: Any remaining syrup can be poured into a hot sterilized jar, sealed, processed, and used as a topping for pancakes, toast, or ice cream.
Mrs. Elizabeth A. Lewis,
Birmingham, Alabama.

FIG COBBLER

5 to 6 cups peeled fresh figs
¾ cup sugar
3 tablespoons all-purpose flour
Butter or margarine
Pastry for 8-inch pie

Combine figs, sugar, and flour; mix well. Spoon into an 8-inch square baking pan; dot with butter.
Roll pastry to ¼-inch thickness on a lightly floured surface; cut into 9- x ½-inch strips. Arrange strips in lattice fashion over fig mixture. Trim edges as needed. Bake at 375° for 45 minutes or until golden brown. Yield: 6 servings.
Mrs. V. O. Walker,
Pennington, Texas.

PICKLED FIGS

3 quarts fresh figs with stems
½ cup soda
2 quarts boiling water
6 cups sugar
1 cup water
1 cup cider vinegar
1 (1½-ounce) package pickling spice

Place figs in a large bowl and sprinkle with soda; add 2 quarts boiling water, mixing well. Let stand 5 minutes; drain figs, and rinse 3 times.

Combine sugar, 1 cup water, and vinegar in a Dutch oven; bring to a boil. Tie pickling spice in a cheesecloth bag; add to syrup along with figs. Bring to a boil, and boil 10 minutes; remove from heat and cover. Let stand at room temperature 24 hours.

The second day, bring to a boil, and boil 10 minutes. Cover and let stand 24 hours. On third day, boil for 10 minutes; then pack into hot sterilized jars, leaving ⅛-inch headspace. Top with lids, and screw metal bands tight. Process in boiling-water bath 15 minutes. Yield: 3 to 4 pints.
Mrs. L. V. Luckett, Sr.,
Vicksburg, Mississippi.

FIG SAUCE

12 to 15 fresh ripe figs, peeled
½ cup sugar
1 cup water
1 tablespoon butter or margarine
1 tablespoon cornstarch
3 tablespoons lemon juice

Combine figs, sugar, water, and butter in a saucepan; bring to a boil, and simmer 5 to 8 minutes or just until figs are tender.

Combine cornstarch and lemon juice, mixing until smooth. Stir into fig mixture; cook over low heat, stirring constantly, until thickened and bubbly. Serve warm over ice cream or pound cake. Yield: 3½ cups.
Mrs. Thomas Lee Adams,
Kingsport, Tennessee.

summer Suppers

Summertime— Time For Food, Friends, And Easy Living

At-home barbecues, picnics in the park, and lots of good friends to share the fun are sure signs that summer in the South has arrived. Here are delicious recipes and fresh ideas to help you celebrate the long, lazy season.

When Robert and Bette Cole of Montgomery, Alabama, entertain, they enjoy combining the freshness of outdoors with the cool comfort of a glassed-in garden room. Guests can mingle in their beautiful garden or move inside to escape soaring temperatures.

With such an ideal situation, the Coles enjoy entertaining often. For their lively garden party, they invite four couples they vacation with, and the occasion doubles as a planning session for the next trip.

Guests are welcomed in the garden setting of the summerhouse and offered Freezer Lime Daiquiris to sip with Chicken Liver Turnovers and Artichoke Hearts With Caviar.

While the group enjoys appetizers, Robert grills Lamb Shish Kabobs—a savory marinated meal-on-a-skewer brightened with small onions, cherry tomatoes, and green pepper. Curried Rice with Pineapple is a perfect match for the lamb; while it bakes, Bette is free to enjoy the party.

Kabobs hot from the grill beckon the guests indoors to the tempting buffet table. Bette tosses fresh spinach with cucumber, celery, and avocado for an elegant all-green salad. The creamy blue cheese dressing is tossed along with the vegetables for ease in serving.

The bread is Bette's homemade Date Muffins baked in petite muffin cups and drenched with butter. A colorful fruit tray of melons, apples, oranges, strawberries, and pineapple completes the main course.

For dessert, it's homemade ice cream made with the juice of freshly squeezed lemons. Robert freezes the ice cream just before the party and packs it in ice to ripen so the dessert is ready when the guests are.

Take the Coles' menu and adapt it to your own party for a summer evening your guests are sure to remember.

Freezer Lime Daiquiris
Chicken Liver Turnovers
Artichoke Hearts With Caviar
Lamb Shish Kabobs
Curried Rice With Pineapple
Green Spinach Salad   Date Muffins
Fresh fruit
Lemon Ice Cream

FREEZER LIME DAIQUIRIS

2 (6-ounce) cans frozen limeade
  concentrate, thawed and undiluted
1 (6-ounce) can frozen lemonade
  concentrate, thawed and undiluted
4½ cups rum
4½ cups water
1 teaspoon sweetened reconstituted lime
  juice
Lime slices
Maraschino cherries

Combine all ingredients except lime slices and cherries in a large bowl. Cover and freeze 12 hours or overnight.

To serve, place 3 to 4 cups frozen mixture in container of electric blender; blend until smooth. Serve immediately, garnished with lime slices and cherries. Store remaining frozen mixture in the freezer; repeat blending procedure as needed. Yield: about 12 cups.

CHICKEN LIVER TURNOVERS

¼ cup chopped onion
¼ cup melted butter
½ pound chicken livers
½ teaspoon salt
¼ teaspoon garlic salt
¼ teaspoon pepper
1 tablespoon dry sherry
1 stick piecrust
Melted butter
Grated Parmesan cheese

Sauté onion until tender in ¼ cup melted butter. Add chicken livers, salt, and pepper; cook over low heat until tender, stirring occasionally. Stir in sherry. Place mixture in container of electric blender, and process until smooth. Set aside.

Prepare piecrust according to package directions. Roll out to ¼-inch thickness; cut with a 2-inch biscuit cutter.

Place about 1 teaspoon of pâté on half of each pastry circle. Fold in half to make a crescent shape; seal edges with tines of fork. Brush with melted butter, and sprinkle with Parmesan cheese. Bake at 350° for 25 to 30 minutes or until lightly browned. Yield: about 2 dozen.

Note: Turnovers may be frozen after edges are sealed. To serve, thaw and proceed as directed above.

ARTICHOKE HEARTS WITH CAVIAR

1 (8-ounce) package cream cheese, softened
2 tablespoons commercial sour cream
2 teaspoons mayonnaise
1 teaspoon lemon juice
1 (8½-ounce) can artichoke hearts, drained and chopped
2 teaspoons grated onion
Dash of garlic salt
Caviar

Combine cream cheese, sour cream, mayonnaise, and lemon juice; mix well. Add artichoke, onion, and garlic salt; mix well.

Shape mixture into a 5-inch mound; flatten slightly, and spread cavier on top. Serve with assorted crackers. Yield: about 10 servings.

LAMB SHISH KABOBS

1 (3½-pound) boned leg of lamb
1 large onion, finely chopped
½ cup vegetable oil
½ cup dry sherry
1 to 1½ tablespoons cumin seeds
1 tablespoon salt
1½ teaspoons rosemary
1 teaspoon coarsely ground black pepper
1 teaspoon garlic salt
1 (1-pint) carton cherry tomatoes
3 green peppers, cut into 1-inch squares
2 (16-ounce) jars boiling onions, drained

Remove fell (tissuelike covering) from lamb; cut lamb into 1½-inch cubes, and set aside.

Combine chopped onion, oil, sherry, and seasonings. Add lamb; cover and marinate 24 hours in refrigerator.

Remove meat from marinade. Alternate meat and vegetables on skewers. Broil 5 minutes; turn and broil an additional 5 minutes or to desired degree of doneness. Yield: 10 servings.

CURRIED RICE WITH PINEAPPLE

2½ cups uncooked regular rice
1 medium onion, chopped
½ cup butter or margarine, melted and divided
2 (10½-ounce) cans consommé
2 (10½-ounce) cans beef broth
1 teaspoon garlic salt
2 (13¼-ounce) cans pineapple chunks, drained
2 teaspoons curry powder

Brown rice in a large heavy skillet, stirring constantly; place in a 2½-quart casserole. Sauté onion until tender in 2 tablespoons melted butter. Add onion, consommé, broth, garlic salt, and 2 tablespoons melted butter to rice; bake at 350° for 1 hour.

Combine remaining butter, pineapple chunks, and curry powder; stir well. Add pineapple mixture to rice, and bake an additional 15 to 20 minutes. Yield: 10 servings.

GREEN SPINACH SALAD

1 pound fresh spinach
1 large cucumber
2 cups coarsely chopped celery
2 large ripe avocados, peeled and cubed
Blue cheese dressing (recipe follows)

Remove stems from spinach; wash leaves thoroughly, and pat dry. Tear into bite-size pieces.

Remove alternate strips of cucumber peel with vegetable peeler; slice cucumber. Add cucumber and remaining vegetables to spinach. Add dressing, tossing gently until coated. Yield: 10 servings.

Blue Cheese Dressing:

2 ounces blue cheese, crumbled
2 tablespoons half-and-half
¼ cup mayonnaise
3 tablespoons vegetable oil
2 tablespoons vinegar
½ teaspoon prepared mustard
Dash of salt
Dash of pepper
1 (0.4-ounce) package buttermilk salad dressing mix

Combine cheese and half-and-half in a small mixing bowl; beat with electric mixer until creamy. Add remaining ingredients except buttermilk salad dressing mix, and mix until smooth.

Prepare buttermilk salad dressing according to package directions. Add ½ cup buttermilk dressing to blue cheese mixture, mixing well; reserve remaining buttermilk dressing for another use. Yield: about 1¼ cups.

DATE MUFFINS

½ cup shortening
¼ cup sugar
1 egg
2 cups all-purpose flour
1 tablespoon plus 1 teaspoon baking powder
½ teaspoon salt
1 cup milk
⅔ cup chopped dates

Combine shortening and sugar, creaming until light and fluffy. Add egg, and beat until smooth. Combine dry ingredients; add to creamed mixture along with milk and dates; stir just until moistened (batter will be lumpy).

Spoon batter into greased miniature muffin tins, filling two-thirds full. Bake at 425° for 18 to 20 minutes. Yield: about 4 dozen.

LEMON ICE CREAM

1 quart whipping cream
1 quart half-and-half
1 pint milk
4 cups sugar
Juice of 8 lemons (about ¾ cup)
1 tablespoon grated lemon rind
2 teaspoons lemon extract

Combine all ingredients in a large mixing bowl; mix well. Pour mixture into container of a 1½-gallon hand-turned or electric freezer, and freeze according to manufacturer's instructions. Let ripen 30 minutes. Yield: about 1½ gallons.

Vegetable Salads: The Pick Of The Crop

You can have your pick of the vegetable crop with this sensational selection of salads. Juicy tomatoes, bright-green broccoli, cool cucumbers, and crisp squash are just the beginning of the delightful colors and textures that blend in these summer salads.

Nothing quite compares to the flavor of vine-ripe tomatoes, and you can enjoy them in a variety of salads. Tangy Vegetable Toss combines them with green pepper, onion, and cucumber and a tart dressing. In Creamy Broccoli Salad, sliced tomatoes, cauliflower, broccoli, and onion are tossed with a mayonnaise-base dressing.

If you prefer not to toss the salad, try Marinated Vegetable Salad—it's a zesty, crunchy blend of carrots, cauliflower, and zucchini.

SUMMER TOMATO TREAT

¾ cup vegetable oil
¼ cup vinegar
3 tablespoons crumbled blue cheese
1 clove garlic, minced
1 teaspoon sugar
½ teaspoon seasoned salt
¼ teaspoon pepper
6 firm ripe tomatoes, peeled and cut into wedges
1 cucumber, peeled and thinly sliced
¼ cup diced celery
1 onion, thinly sliced
1 teaspoon minced parsley

Combine first 7 ingredients in container of electric blender, and process until smooth.

Combine vegetables in a salad bowl; pour dressing over top, and sprinkle with minced parsley. Let stand at room temperature about 30 minutes before serving. Yield: 6 servings.
T. O. Davis, Waynesboro, Mississippi.

MARINATED VEGETABLE SALAD

1 (10¾-ounce) can chicken broth, undiluted
4 medium carrots, sliced
2 cups cauliflower flowerets
2 small zucchini, diagonally sliced
1 cup sliced mushrooms
¼ cup wine vinegar
1 (0.6-ounce) envelope Italian dressing mix
Lettuce leaves (optional)

Bring broth to a boil; add sliced carrots, and simmer 2 minutes. Remove from heat, and allow mixture to cool. Stir in next 5 ingredients; chill mixture 4 hours or more. Serve the salad on lettuce leaves, if desired. Yield: about 8 servings.
Mrs. Rose Naquin, Melville, Louisiana.

CREAMY BROCCOLI SALAD

1 bunch fresh broccoli
1 medium head cauliflower
3 medium tomatoes, sliced
3 small red onions, sliced and separated into rings
¼ teaspoon garlic salt
½ to ¾ cup mayonnaise
½ to ¾ cup commercial sour cream
½ teaspoon lemon juice (optional)
8 to 10 cherry tomatoes

Trim off large leaves of broccoli. Remove tough ends of lower stalks, and wash broccoli thoroughly. Cut into bite-size pieces.

Wash cauliflower, and remove green leaves. Separate cauliflower into flowerets, slicing large flowerets into bite-size pieces.

Combine broccoli, cauliflower, tomatoes, and onion in a large bowl. Combine garlic salt, mayonnaise, sour cream, and lemon juice, if desired; add to vegetables, tossing gently. Garnish with cherry tomatoes. Yield: 6 to 8 servings.
Mrs. J. D. Barnett, Etowah, Tennessee.

SUMMERTIME SALAD

2 bunches watercress, stem ends removed
½ head iceberg lettuce, torn into bite-size pieces
½ head romaine lettuce, torn into bite-size pieces
½ cup chopped green onion with tops
2 medium tomatoes, cut into wedges
2 cups diced cooked chicken
1 avocado, peeled and sliced
3 hard-cooked eggs, sliced
½ pound bacon, cooked and crumbled
2 tablespoons capers
1 (4-ounce) package blue cheese, crumbled
Additional watercress (optional)
French dressing (recipe follows)

Combine 2 bunches watercress, lettuce, and onion in a large salad bowl; toss well. Arrange tomatoes, chicken, avocado, eggs, and bacon over top. Sprinkle with capers and cheese. Garnish with additional watercress, if desired. Serve with French dressing. Yield: 10 to 12 servings.

French Dressing:

1 cup vegetable oil
¾ cup vinegar
½ cup tarragon vinegar or red wine vinegar
½ cup catsup
½ cup chili sauce
¼ cup sugar
1 tablespoon prepared mustard
1 tablespoon Worcestershire sauce
1 tablespoon prepared horseradish
1 large onion, chopped
Salt to taste

Combine all ingredients in container of an electric blender, and process well. Cover and store in refrigerator. Shake or stir dressing well before serving. Yield: 4½ cups.

TANGY VEGETABLE TOSS

6 large ripe tomatoes, quartered
1 green pepper, cut into strips
1 medium onion, sliced and separated into
   rings
1 cucumber, cut into ¼-inch slices
¾ cup white wine vinegar
¼ cup water
1½ teaspoons mustard seeds
1½ teaspoons celery salt
½ teaspoon salt
1½ tablespoons sugar
¼ teaspoon black pepper
Dash of cayenne

Combine vegetables, and set aside.
Combine vinegar, water, and seasonings in a large saucepan, mixing well.
Bring to a boil; cook, stirring constantly, 1 minute. Pour hot mixture over vegetables, tossing lightly. Chill. Yield: 6 to 8 servings. *Mrs. W. J. Scherffius, Mountain Home, Arkansas.*

SPINACH SALAD WITH RUSSIAN DRESSING

1 pound fresh spinach, torn
1 (16-ounce) can bean sprouts, well
   drained
1 small head iceberg lettuce, torn
1 cup sliced mushrooms
6 slices cooked bacon, crumbled
Russian dressing (recipe follows)

Combine vegetables and bacon in a large salad bowl. Toss with Russian dressing. Yield: 6 to 8 servings.

Russian Dressing:

¼ to ½ cup sugar
1 cup vegetable oil
½ cup catsup
¼ cup vinegar
2 tablespoons Worcestershire sauce
2 tablespoons finely chopped onion
Salt to taste

Combine all ingredients, mixing well.
Yield: about 2 cups. *Ronda Cox, Shawnee, Oklahoma.*

WATERCRESS SALAD

1 large bunch fresh watercress, torn
½ cup sliced fresh mushrooms
½ cup sliced canned hearts of palm
¼ cup toasted almonds
Salt and pepper to taste
¼ cup commercial creamy garlic salad
   dressing

Combine first 5 ingredients in a salad bowl. Add enough water to salad dressing to make ⅓ cup, mixing well. Pour over salad, and toss gently. Yield: 2 to 3 servings. *Holly Sansone, Lehigh Acres, Florida.*

Picnicking In The Park

Summertime entertaining for Atlanta's Karen and Joe League often means inviting friends to share a preconcert picnic in Piedmont Park. The Leagues, along with friends Mary Ann and John Busby, Pam Powell, and Steve Swicegood, enjoy a picnic that is anything but ordinary. Karen, Mary Ann, and Pam use their imagination for everything from the menu to the quilt-lined laundry baskets used to tote the food and serving pieces.

Once at the park, the friends choose a comfortable spot on the park's grassy slopes and spread out their picnic fare on an attractive quilt.

Scuppernong white wine accompanies this Southern summer picnic and complements the cool elegance of the fare. First course is Chilled Cucumber Soup, ladled into pottery mugs and garnished with sliced cucumber. Seafood offerings follow in the form of a beautifully garnished platter of New Orleans Pickled Shrimp and Scallops Savannah. Marinated Vegetables and Charleston Red Rice Salad accompany open-face Vidalia Sandwiches. These tempting sandwiches are slices of homemade salt-rising bread topped with Virginia ham, sliced sweet onion, and cucumber.

For dessert, which is both elegant and convenient, Peaches Champagne are

spooned into bowls and accompanied by homemade gingersnaps.

Most of this menu can be prepared a day or two ahead, leaving only the details of packing and selection of accessories to the last minute.

Here are the menu and recipes for this delightful picnic enjoyed by the Leagues and their friends.

Chilled Cucumber Soup
New Orleans Pickled Shrimp
Scallops Savannah
Vidalia Sandwiches on Salt-Rising Bread
Marinated Vegetables
Charleston Red Rice Salad
Gingersnaps   Peaches Champagne
Scuppernong White Wine

CHILLED CUCUMBER SOUP

1 large onion, chopped
4½ medium cucumbers, peeled and sliced
2 medium bay leaves
6 peppercorns
¼ cup melted butter or margarine
¼ cup all-purpose flour
5 cups chicken broth
½ cup commercial sour cream
1½ teaspoons chopped fresh dill or ½
   teaspoon dillweed
1 teaspoon salt
½ teaspoon hot sauce
1 cup whipping cream
2 tablespoons lemon juice
½ medium cucumber, peeled and sliced

Sauté onion, 4½ cucumbers, bay leaves, and peppercorns in butter in a Dutch oven until cucumber is tender and onion is transparent. Reduce heat to low; gradually stir in flour. Cook for 1 minute, stirring constantly. Add broth and cook over medium heat, stirring constantly, until mixture comes to a boil. Reduce heat; cover and simmer mixture 30 minutes.

Press cucumber mixture through a sieve into a large bowl; discard seeds and pulp. Pour half of cucumber mixture into container of electric blender; process 30 seconds on medium speed, and pour into a large bowl. Process remaining half of cucumber mixture. Stir sour cream, dill, salt, and hot sauce into cucumber mixture; cover and chill 4 to 6 hours, stirring occasionally.

Stir whipping cream and lemon juice into soup just before serving. Float cucumber slices on top of soup, reserving 6 to 8 slices. Garnish each serving with 1 slice cucumber. Yield: 6 to 8 servings.

NEW ORLEANS PICKLED SHRIMP

2 pounds uncooked shrimp
Bay leaves
6 small onions, thinly sliced
1 cup olive oil
¼ cup tarragon vinegar
2 tablespoons pickling spice
2 teaspoons salt
½ teaspoon dry mustard
Dash of cayenne pepper
Cherry tomatoes
Parsley

Place shrimp in boiling water to cover; cook 3 to 5 minutes, and drain well. Rinse shrimp with cold water; peel and devein, leaving the tails intact.

Place a layer of shrimp in a flat-bottomed container. Place 5 bay leaves on top of shrimp; cover shrimp with a layer of onion slices. Repeat layering until all shrimp are used.

Combine next 6 ingredients, mixing well. Pour marinade over shrimp. Cover; chill 24 hours, stirring mixture occasionally. Remove shrimp from marinade, and arrange in a serving dish. Garnish with cherry tomatoes and parsley. Yield: 6 servings.

Tip: Using kitchen shears for cutting many foods saves time and gives a neat-looking cut. Use shears to cut shells from shrimp, to snip parsley, and to trim piecrusts. When cutting sticky foods like marshmallows or dates, dip the shears in hot water.

SCALLOPS SAVANNAH

1 pound scallops, cut into bite-size pieces
2 tablespoons melted butter
½ cup vegetable oil
2 egg yolks, beaten
2 tablespoons instant minced onion
2 tablespoons chopped fresh parsley
1 tablespoon chopped chives
2 tablespoons lemon juice
2 tablespoons commercial sour cream
1 teaspoon dillweed
1 teaspoon lemon pepper
1 teaspoon Dijon mustard
½ teaspoon tarragon leaves
½ teaspoon salt
½ teaspoon anchovy paste
1 (2-ounce) jar diced pimiento
4 stalks celery, chopped
Parsley sprigs
Cherry tomatoes

Sauté scallops in butter 2 minutes; cool, drain, and spoon into a shallow dish. Combine remaining ingredients except parsley sprigs and tomatoes; stir well, and pour over scallops. Cover and chill overnight.

Spoon scallops onto a serving plate; garnish with parsley sprigs and tomatoes. Yield: 6 to 8 servings.

SALT-RISING BREAD

¼ cup vegetable oil
2 teaspoons salt
8 to 8¼ cups all-purpose flour
4 cups starter (recipe follows)

Stir oil, salt, and flour into starter (dough will be moderately stiff). Spoon dough into a large greased bowl; cover and let rise in a warm place (85°), free from drafts, 1 to 1½ hours or until doubled in bulk. Stir dough down.

Divide dough equally into 3 parts, and place in 3 greased 9- x 5- x 3-inch loafpans or 1-quart casseroles. Cover and let rise in warm place, free from drafts, until doubled in bulk. Bake at 375° for 50 to 60 minutes or until loaves sound hollow when tapped with fingertips. Remove from pans; cool on wire racks. Yield: 3 loaves.

Starter:

3 medium potatoes, peeled and cubed
6 cups water
½ cup all-purpose flour
2 tablespoons sugar
2 packages dry yeast
½ cup sugar
2 tablespoons sugar

Combine potatoes and water in a Dutch oven; cover and cook 10 to 15 minutes or until potatoes are tender. Drain, reserving 5 cups potato liquid. Reserve potatoes for another use.

Allow 1 cup potato liquid to cool to 120° to 130°. Combine flour, 2 tablespoons sugar, and yeast in a large bowl; stir in the 1 cup cooled potato liquid. Cover and let stand in a warm place (85°) for 4 hours. Stir in remaining 4 cups potato liquid and ½ cup sugar. Cover and let mixture stand in a warm place overnight.

Stir starter well; reserve 1 cup. Stir 2 tablespoons sugar into reserved 1 cup starter, and pour into an airtight 2-cup glass container. Store in refrigerator until ready to use for a second batch of bread.

Use remaining 4 cups starter to make Salt-Rising Bread. Yield: 5 cups.

Note: To make second batch of bread, use reserved 1 cup starter plus 3 cups plain potato water for 4 cups starter.

VIDALIA SANDWICHES ON SALT-RISING BREAD

12 slices baked Virginia ham
12 slices Vidalia or other sweet onion
12 slices unpeeled cucumber
12 slices salt-rising bread
Lettuce leaves

Place 1 slice ham, onion, and cucumber on each slice of bread in order given; serve on a lettuce-lined tray. Yield: 6 to 8 servings.

MARINATED VEGETABLES

3 cups water
¾ cup olive oil
½ cup lemon juice
6 sprigs parsley
1 teaspoon salt
12 peppercorns
¼ teaspoon ground thyme
¼ teaspoon whole oregano
⅛ teaspoon celery seeds
⅛ teaspoon mustard seeds
⅛ teaspoon ground cardamom
1 medium lemon
1 pound small yellow squash, cut in
   ¼-inch slices
1 pound small zucchini, cut lengthwise
   into strips
1 pound small okra
1 pound baby carrots, peeled
½ pound whole green beans, trimmed
3 medium-size green peppers, cut into
   ½-inch-wide strips
Lemon wedges

Combine first 11 ingredients in a Dutch oven. Cut lemon into quarters; remove pulp and reserve for other use. Cut lemon peel into strips; twist strips and drop into marinade. Bring mixture to a boil. Reduce heat; partially cover pan, and simmer 45 minutes. Pour mixture through a fine sieve; return liquid to Dutch oven.

Simmer each vegetable separately in marinade for prescribed number of minutes; remove from marinade and proceed with next vegetable: squash 7 to 10 minutes, zucchini 7 to 10 minutes, okra 6 to 8 minutes, carrots 8 minutes, green beans 8 minutes, and green pepper 4 to 6 minutes. Place each vegetable in a separate container.

Boil marinade until reduced in half; cool. Pour equal amounts of marinade over each vegetable; cover. Chill vegetables 8 hours. Remove vegetables from marinade, and arrange on a serving platter. Garnish with lemon wedges. Yield: 12 to 14 servings.

Tip: Pouring a strong solution of salt and hot water down the sink will help eliminate odors and remove grease from drains.

CHARLESTON RED RICE SALAD

2 cups water
1 (6-ounce) can tomato paste
1 cup uncooked regular rice
1 cup chopped onion
½ cup chopped green pepper
¾ teaspoon salt
French dressing (recipe follows)
Lettuce leaves

Place water in a medium saucepan; bring to a boil, and stir in tomato paste and rice. Reduce heat, and simmer 15 to 20 minutes or until rice is tender; allow to cool.

Combine rice, onion, green pepper, salt, and ½ cup French dressing. (Reserve remainder of dressing for future use.) Chill 3 to 4 hours; serve in a lettuce-lined bowl. Yield: about 6 to 8 servings.

French Dressing:

½ cup vinegar
1½ cups vegetable oil
3 to 4 cloves garlic, minced
½ teaspoon pepper
1 teaspoon dry mustard
Dash of cayenne
1 teaspoon paprika

Combine all ingredients; mix well and chill. Yield: about 2 cups.

PEACHES CHAMPAGNE

2 cups dry scuppernong white wine or
   any sweet white wine
¾ cup sugar
2 (2-inch) cinnamon sticks
12 freestone peaches
Peel of 2 oranges, cut into strips
1 (8-ounce) can almond paste
Powdered sugar

Combine wine, sugar, and cinnamon in a Dutch oven; simmer 5 minutes. Add peaches; cook over low heat 8 minutes or until fork tender. Cool peaches in liquid at least 20 minutes. Drain peaches, reserving liquid. Remove peel from peaches (peel should be easily removed with fingers); discard peel. Place peaches in a jar; add orange peel. Pour reserved liquid over peaches, and chill thoroughly.

Shape almond paste into ¾-inch balls; dust lightly with powdered sugar, and chill.

Drain peaches, reserving liquid. Cut a small slit along crease of peach; remove pit. Place an almond ball in center of each peach. Close peach and place back in jar; pour reserved liquid over peaches, and chill. Yield: 12 servings.

Note: Peaches will keep in refrigerator 4 to 5 days.

GINGERSNAPS

¾ cup shortening
1 cup sugar
1 egg
¼ cup molasses
2 cups all-purpose flour
1 tablespoon ground ginger
2 teaspoons soda
1 teaspoon ground cinnamon
½ teaspoon salt
Sugar

Cream shortening and sugar until light and fluffy. Add egg and molasses; mix well.

Combine flour, ginger, soda, cinnamon, and salt; mix well. Add about one-fourth of dry mixture at a time to creamed mixture, mixing until smooth after each addition.

Roll dough into 1-inch balls, and roll each in sugar. Place 2 inches apart on ungreased cookie sheets; bake at 350° for 12 minutes. (Tops will crack.) Yield: about 4½ dozen.

Take Along A Special Dish

Perhaps the favorite of all summer suppers down South is the covered dish picnic. Whether it be for a family, club, or church group, everyone enjoys showing off one or two special dishes, not to mention enjoying the bounty of foods on the picnic table.

The never-ending line of food always includes several versions of fried chicken. Add variety to yours with Garlic-Flavored Fried Chicken, a crisp, savory version that is first fried, then baked. Homemade bread is always welcome on the picnic table; carry along a loaf of Easy Yeast Bread or Orange Pecan Bread. Pack it into a small basket; then slice and serve it attractively in its own container.

If you want to add to the lineup of salads, try Creole Salad, a vegetable salad in gelatin that you can conveniently unmold and garnish at serving time. Cottage Cheese-Potato Salad is an interesting version of the always-welcome potato salad.

Be sure to take the necessary precautions that the foods you carry remain at safe temperatures. Salads that contain mayonnaise or salad dressing should be kept cold (below 40° F.) with ice or reusable cold packs. Foods that need to be kept hot until serving time (above 140° F.) can be carried and stored in a closed insulated container such as an ice chest.

GARLIC-FLAVORED FRIED CHICKEN

¾ cup milk
3 eggs, beaten
4 cloves garlic, minced
½ teaspoon Ac'cent
2 (2- to 3-pound) broiler-fryers
1 cup all-purpose flour
2 cups fine breadcrumbs
½ teaspoon garlic powder
½ teaspoon salt
¼ teaspoon pepper
Vegetable oil

Combine milk, eggs, garlic, and Ac'cent; set aside.

Wash chicken, and pat dry; dredge in flour. Combine breadcrumbs, garlic powder, salt, and pepper. Dip chicken in egg mixture; dredge in breadcrumb mixture, coating well.

Heat oil to 350°; cook chicken in hot oil until golden brown. Drain on paper towels, and place on a rack in shallow baking pan. Bake at 350° for 30 to 40 minutes or until done. Yield: 8 servings.
Mrs. Sue-Sue Hartstern, Louisville, Kentucky.

COTTAGE CHEESE-POTATO SALAD

3 to 4 cups cooked cubed potatoes
½ cup sliced celery
1 tablespoon chopped green pepper
1 tablespoon chopped pimiento
2 tablespoons minced onion
2 tablespoons chopped sweet pickle
1 cup mayonnaise
1 teaspoon salt
⅛ teaspoon pepper
1 teaspoon dry mustard
1 tablespoon lemon juice
1 cup small-curd cottage cheese

Combine potatoes, celery, green pepper, pimiento, onion, and pickle; toss lightly. Chill. Combine mayonnaise, seasonings, and lemon juice; add to potato mixture. Add cottage cheese; stir gently. Yield: 5 to 6 servings.
Linda Owens, Mount Vernon, Texas.

CREOLE SALAD

1 (6-ounce) package lemon-flavored gelatin
1½ cups boiling water
1½ cups tomato juice
2 tablespoons chopped onion
½ cup finely chopped green pepper
2 tablespoons finely chopped pimiento
1 cup finely chopped cucumber
½ cup finely chopped celery
Lettuce
Sliced hard-cooked eggs (optional)

Dissolve gelatin in boiling water. Add tomato juice; chill until consistency of unbeaten egg white.

Stir onion, green pepper, pimiento, cucumber, and celery into gelatin. Spoon into a 4-cup mold; chill until firm. Unmold on lettuce, and garnish with sliced hard-cooked eggs, if desired. Yield: 6 to 8 servings.
Mrs. Paul Raper, Burgaw, North Carolina.

EASY YEAST BREAD

2 packages dry yeast
½ cup warm water (105° to 115°)
½ cup butter or margarine, melted
1½ teaspoons salt
½ cup sugar
½ cup milk, scalded
3 eggs, slightly beaten
5 to 5½ cups unbleached flour
Melted shortening
1 egg yolk
2 tablespoons water

Dissolve yeast in ½ cup warm water; let stand 5 minutes.

Combine butter, salt, and sugar. Add milk, stirring until sugar dissolves; cool to 105° to 115°. Add yeast, 3 eggs, and 2 cups flour; mix well. Gradually stir in remaining flour.

Turn dough onto a floured board; knead 8 to 10 minutes. Divide dough in half; cut each half into thirds. Shape each third into an 8-inch rope. Place 3 ropes on a greased baking sheet; pinch ends together at one end to seal. (Do not stretch.) Braid ropes; pinch loose ends to seal. Repeat with remaining dough. Brush with melted shortening.

Cover and let rise in a warm place, free from drafts, 40 to 50 minutes or until doubled in bulk.

Combine egg yolk and 2 tablespoons water; brush on each loaf. Bake at 350° for 30 minutes or until bread tests done. Yield: 2 loaves.   *Mrs. Donly Ray, Birmingham, Alabama.*

ORANGE-PECAN BREAD

4 to 5 oranges
1 teaspoon soda
1¾ to 2 cups sugar
3¼ cups all-purpose flour
3 teaspoons baking powder
⅛ teaspoon salt
2 eggs
2 tablespoons melted butter or margarine
1 cup milk
1 cup chopped pecans

Peel oranges; scrape white membrane from peel. Finely chop peel. Combine 1 cup water, peel, and soda in a heavy saucepan; boil 5 minutes (watch carefully; mixture will foam). Drain well, and set aside. (Orange sections may be used in another recipe.)

Combine cooked peel, sugar, and 1 cup water in a saucepan. Boil until consistency of jelly (about 45 minutes), stirring occasionally; cool.

Combine flour, baking powder, and salt; set aside. Beat eggs and butter until frothy. Alternately add dry ingredients and milk to eggs, beginning and ending with dry ingredients. Stir just until all ingredients are moistened. Stir in orange peel mixture and pecans. Spoon batter into a well-greased 9- x 5- x 3-inch loafpan. Bake at 350° for 1 hour and 10 minutes or until bread tests done. Yield: 1 loaf. *Mrs. Jack Corzine, Greenville, South Carolina.*

PINEAPPLE POUND CAKE

½ cup shortening
1 cup butter or margarine
2¾ cups sugar
6 eggs
3 cups all-purpose flour
1 teaspoon baking powder
¼ cup milk
1 teaspoon vanilla extract
¾ cup crushed pineapple, undrained
Pineapple Glaze

Combine shortening, butter, and sugar; cream until light and fluffy. Add eggs, one at a time, beating well after each addition. Combine flour and baking powder; add to creamed mixture alternately with milk and vanilla, beating well after each addition. Stir in crushed pineapple.

Pour batter into a well-greased and floured 10-inch tube pan. Place in a cold oven; set temperature at 325°, and bake 1 hour and 15 minutes or until cake tests done. Cool 10 to 15 minutes in pan. Invert onto serving plate; drizzle Pineapple Glaze over top and sides. Yield: one 10-inch cake.

Pineapple Glaze:

¼ cup melted butter or margarine
1½ cups powdered sugar
1 cup crushed pineapple, drained

Combine butter and powdered sugar, mixing until smooth. Stir in pineapple. Yield: about 1½ cups.
Mrs. Donald C. Vanhoy, Salisbury, North Carolina.

Sip A Frosty Ice Cream Beverage

Take the heat off a sultry summer day with a frosty ice cream or sherbet beverage. These cool and colorful drinks are perfect for sipping leisurely by the pool or for serving to a houseful of guests.

Old-Fashioned Strawberry Soda, a creamy beverage garnished with whipped cream and fresh strawberries, is reminiscent of the Gay Nineties. Vanilla ice cream and ginger ale combine with refreshing fruit juices in Parsonage Punch and Cranberry-Orange Soda.

For beverages sparked with the flavor of liqueurs, try Velvet Coffee Refresher or French Vanilla Frosty. And for a taste of white wine, cool off with a tall Pineapple Sherbet Float.

FRENCH VANILLA FROSTY

1 pint French vanilla ice cream
3 tablespoons crème de cacao
3 tablespoons Drambuie
2 tablespoons chocolate-flavored syrup
1½ to 2 cups milk

Combine all ingredients in container of electric blender; process until smooth. Serve immediately. Yield: about 5 cups. *Mrs. Thomas E. Dale, Dallas, Texas.*

PARSONAGE PUNCH

1½ cups pineapple juice
1 cup orange juice
¼ cup lemon juice
2 tablespoons honey
1 tablespoon maraschino cherry juice
1 pint vanilla ice cream
2 cups ginger ale, chilled

Combine first 5 ingredients; chill at least 2 hours. Place juice mixture in a punch bowl, and scoop ice cream into juice mixture. Gradually pour in ginger ale, stirring gently. Serve immediately. Yield: about 6 cups.
Mrs. Sidney I. McGrath, Hopkinsville, Kentucky.

CRANBERRY-ORANGE SODA

2 cups cranberry juice, chilled
1 (6-ounce) can frozen orange juice concentrate, undiluted
6 scoops vanilla ice cream
1 quart ginger ale

Combine cranberry juice and orange juice concentrate in container of electric blender; process until smooth. Pour cranberry mixture evenly into 6 (12-ounce) glasses; add a scoop of ice cream to each glass. Fill glasses with ginger ale. Yield: 6 servings. *Mrs. Jack Land, Live Oak, Florida.*

PINEAPPLE SHERBET FLOAT

2½ cups pineapple sherbet
1 cup dry white wine
1 cup ginger ale

Combine all ingredients; stir gently until sherbet is partially melted. Serve in tall glasses. Yield: 4 servings.
Mrs. E. W. Hanley, Elberton, Georgia.

Enjoy a tall glass of Old-Fashioned Strawberry Soda, topped with a dollop of whipped cream and a strawberry.

Make It Dinner On The Grill

Hardly anything compares with the flavor outdoor grilling gives to food. So we've put together an entire meal that can be prepared on the grill, whether at a favorite campsite or at home in your own backyard. Besides thick, juicy hamburgers, there are several grilled vegetables, baked beans, and even a simple dessert.

It's a filling meal, enough to satisfy outdoor appetites, but it also offers other pluses to camping enthusiasts: The dishes are easy and quick to prepare and the ingredients are convenient for taking along.

Old-Fashioned Hamburgers
Cheesy Grilled Tomatoes
Grilled Squash and Onion
Smoked Baked Beans
Corn With Herb Butter Sauce
Fruit Turnovers

OLD-FASHIONED STRAWBERRY SODA

1 (10-ounce) package frozen strawberries in syrup, thawed
3 cups strawberry ice cream, divided
2 (12-ounce) cans cream soda, divided
Whipped cream
4 whole strawberries

Mash thawed strawberries with a fork until strawberries are well blended with syrup. Add 1 cup ice cream and ½ cup cream soda; stir well.

Spoon an equal amount of strawberry mixture into 4 (14-ounce) soda glasses; top with remaining ice cream, and fill glasses with remaining cream soda. Garnish each glass with a dollop of whipped cream and a strawberry. Yield: 4 servings. *Mrs. Parke LaGourgue Cory, Neosho, Missouri.*

VELVET COFFEE REFRESHER

1 quart coffee ice cream
¼ cup brandy
¼ cup crème de cacao

Combine all ingredients in container of electric blender; process until smooth. Serve immediately. Yield: about 3½ cups. *Miss Lucile Freese, Nashville, Tennessee.*

OLD-FASHIONED HAMBURGERS

1½ pounds ground beef
½ cup uncooked quick-cooking oats
¼ cup finely chopped onion
1½ teaspoons salt
¼ teaspoon pepper
⅔ cup tomato juice
6 hamburger buns
6 Cheddar cheese slices
6 onion slices
6 tomato slices

Combine first 6 ingredients. Shape into 6 patties ½ inch thick.

Place patties on grill 3 to 5 inches from coals; cook 3 to 5 minutes on each side or to desired degree of doneness.

Place patties on bottom of buns. Top each with cheese, onion, and tomato; close with bun tops. Yield: 6 servings. *Mrs. Clarence Broughton, Harrodsburg, Kentucky.*

CHEESY GRILLED TOMATOES

4 firm ripe tomatoes
Salt and pepper
¼ cup soft breadcrumbs
¼ cup shredded sharp process American
 cheese
1 tablespoon melted butter or margarine
Chopped parsley

Cut a slice from top of each tomato; sprinkle with salt and pepper.

Combine breadcrumbs, cheese, and butter; mix well. Sprinkle mixture over tomatoes, and top with parsley. Wrap tomatoes in aluminum foil; fold securely to seal.

Cook on grill over moderate heat 20 minutes or until tomatoes are thoroughly heated and the cheese is melted. Yield: 4 servings.
Mrs. Susan Wanmer,
Columbia, South Carolina.

GRILLED SQUASH AND ONION

6 medium-size yellow squash, cut into
 ½-inch slices
3 medium onions, cut into ½-inch slices
¼ teaspoon garlic salt
Salt and pepper to taste
2 tablespoons butter or margarine

Alternate squash and onion slices in rows on a large sheet of aluminum foil. Sprinkle vegetables with garlic salt, salt, and pepper; dot with butter.

Fold foil securely to seal; place on grill and cook over moderate heat for about 45 minutes or until tender. Yield: 6 servings. *Mrs. J. R. Currie,*
Huntsville, Alabama.

SMOKED BAKED BEANS

About ½ cup diced salt pork
2 (16-ounce) cans pork and beans,
 undrained
½ cup catsup
½ cup firmly packed brown sugar
2 teaspoons dry mustard

Cook salt pork until browned; drain and set aside.

Combine remaining ingredients in a heavy 2-quart casserole; top with salt pork. Place on grill over hot coals; close hood, and cook 1 hour. Yield: 4 to 6 servings. *Patsy Owsley,*
Bardwell, Kentucky.

CORN WITH HERB BUTTER SAUCE

6 ears fresh corn
Herb Butter Sauce

Husk corn right before cooking. Place each ear on a piece of aluminum foil. Brush with sauce (may serve sauce over corn after grilling, if desired); wrap foil tightly around corn. Roast on grill 10 to 20 minutes, turning frequently. Yield: 6 servings.

Herb Butter Sauce:
½ cup butter or margarine
½ teaspoon salt
¼ teaspoon paprika
¼ teaspoon whole thyme, crushed
¼ teaspoon whole marjoram, crushed

Combine all ingredients in a saucepan; place over medium coals, stirring until butter melts. Yield: ½ cup.
Charlotte Pierce,
Greensburg, Kentucky.

FRUIT TURNOVERS

2 sticks piecrust, crumbled
1 tablespoon plus 1 teaspoon nonfat dry
 milk solids
¼ cup water
1 (21-ounce) can cherry, blueberry, or
 apple pie filling

Combine piecrust sticks, dry milk solids, and ¼ cup water; stir until dough loses stickiness and leaves side of bowl.

Divide pastry into 6 portions. On a lightly floured surface, roll each portion into a 6-inch circle.

Place 2 tablespoons pie filling on each pastry circle. Moisten edges of circles; fold pastry in half, making sure edges are even.

Using a fork dipped in flour, press edges together to seal.

Place pies in a heavy skillet or in hinged basket; cook on grill over moderate heat 10 minutes on each side until lightly browned. Yield: 6 servings.
Jean Robbins,
Roanoke, Virginia.

This Fish Fry Is A Feast

Few summer outings are as much fun as the traditional Southern fish fry. When that is coupled with the great availability of salt-water fish and shellfish of Topsail Island, North Carolina, it's no wonder that Sidney Williams and Nelson Allen have chosen a fish fry for entertaining their friends.

The fun of the fish fry actually starts before daybreak for the fishermen in the group. A successful catch is almost guaranteed, for the waters off the North Carolina coast offer some of the best fishing on the East Coast.

Not only are the fishermen responsible for providing the fish for the evening meal; it is also a tradition that the morning anglers prepare the day's catch.

As guests arrive for the fish fry, the remainder of the meal comes with them. The joint efforts of the fishermen and their guests yield a bountiful menu.

Clam Dip	Crackers
Fried Fish	Marinated Shark
Down East Crab Cakes	
Boiled Shrimp With Cocktail Sauce	
Clam Fritters	Fish Chowder
Topsail Island Hush Puppies	
Coleslaw	Sliced Tomatoes

Before the first fish is slipped into vats of hot oil for cooking, guests mingle in the relaxed, informal setting and enjoy appetizers and beverages.

Sidney's specialties include boiled shrimp, clam fritters, crab cakes, fried flounder, and marinated shark. Since the guests complete the menu with favorite dishes, we've also included their recipes.

CLAM DIP

1 (6½-ounce) can minced clams
1½ cups commercial sour cream
1 teaspoon onion salt
¼ teaspoon salt
¼ teaspoon Worcestershire sauce

Drain clams, reserving 2 tablespoons liquid. Combine clams, reserved clam liquid, and remaining ingredients; stir well. Chill 3 to 4 hours. Serve with crackers. Yield: 1½ cups. *Stacy Smith, Hampstead, North Carolina.*

BOILED SHRIMP WITH COCKTAIL SAUCE

4 to 6 quarts water
3 pounds unpeeled medium shrimp
Salt
Parsley sprigs (optional)
Cocktail sauce (recipe follows)

Bring water to a boil in a Dutch oven; add shrimp, and return to a boil. Immediately remove from heat, and drain well. Heavily salt shrimp while hot and in shells; allow to cool to touch. Chill thoroughly.

Arrange shrimp on serving platter; garnish with parsley sprigs, if desired. Serve with cocktail sauce. Yield: about 12 servings.

Cocktail Sauce:
1 cup chili sauce
1 cup catsup
⅓ cup lemon juice
3 tablespoons prepared horseradish
6 drops of hot sauce

Combine all ingredients, stirring well. Yield: about 2½ cups.

FRIED FISH

12 small flounder, cleaned and dressed
Salt
2½ to 3 cups cornmeal
Vegetable oil
Lemon slices (optional)
Parsley sprigs (optional)

Dry fish thoroughly, and sprinkle lightly with salt. Dredge fish in cornmeal; fry in deep hot oil (375°) until golden brown. Do not overcook; drain on paper towels. Garnish with lemon slices and parsley sprigs, if desired. Yield: 12 servings.

MARINATED SHARK

About 8 pounds shark meat
1 quart water
1 cup dry red wine or 1 cup vinegar
¼ cup vegetable oil
3 tablespoons salt
1 tablespoon celery seeds
1 bay leaf
1 teaspoon pepper
Seafood Batter
Vegetable oil or shortening
Lemon slices (optional)

Cut shark meat into 1- x 3-inch strips; place in a large shallow baking dish.

Combine 1 quart water, wine, ¼ cup vegetable oil, and seasonings in container of electric blender; process 30 seconds at medium speed, and pour over shark meat. Marinate in refrigerator at least 4 hours; drain well.

Dip shark meat into Seafood Batter; fry in deep hot oil (375°) until golden brown. Do not overcook. Drain on paper towels. Garnish with lemon slices, if desired. Yield: 12 to 16 servings.

Seafood Batter:
1 cup all-purpose flour
2 eggs
¾ cup cold water
½ teaspoon salt
2 tablespoons vegetable oil

Combine all ingredients, and beat at medium speed of electric mixer until smooth. Yield: about 2 cups.

Note: Seafood Batter may also be used for shrimp and clams.

DOWN-EAST CRAB CAKES

1½ pounds cooked crabmeat, drained and flaked
1 cup soft breadcrumbs
2 eggs, beaten
2 tablespoons finely chopped onion
2 tablespoons finely chopped green pepper
1 teaspoon Worcestershire sauce
1 teaspoon dry mustard
¼ teaspoon ground thyme
⅛ teaspoon salt
¾ to 1 cup all-purpose flour
Hot vegetable oil or shortening
Hot sauce or seafood cocktail sauce (optional)

Combine first 9 ingredients, stirring well. Form into patties 2 inches in diameter and 1 inch thick; chill well (mixture will be slightly loose).

Dredge crab cakes in flour; fry in hot oil until golden brown, turning once. Drain on paper towels. Serve with hot sauce or seafood cocktail sauce, if desired. Yield: 6 servings.

CLAM FRITTERS

1 pint shucked clams, well drained
1 small onion, finely chopped
2 eggs, beaten
2 tablespoons all-purpose flour
½ teaspoon baking powder
½ to 1 teaspoon salt
⅛ teaspoon pepper
Hot vegetable oil or shortening

Finely chop or coarsely grind clams. Combine clams with next 6 ingredients, mixing well. Carefully drop mixture by tablespoonfuls into hot oil (370°). Fry until golden brown, turning once; drain them on paper towels. Serve hot. Yield: 6 servings.

FISH CHOWDER

1 (28-ounce) can whole tomatoes, chopped
1 (8-ounce) can tomato sauce
Dash of hot sauce
1 pound bacon
6 to 8 cups peeled, cubed potatoes
6 to 8 large onions, sliced
2 to 3 pounds fish fillets, cut into 1-inch
   pieces
Salt and pepper
1 dozen eggs (optional)

Combine tomatoes, tomato sauce, and hot sauce; stir well, and set aside.

Fry bacon in a 6-quart Dutch oven until crisp; drain on paper towels, reserving 3 tablespoons drippings. Crumble bacon, and set aside.

Return reserved bacon drippings to Dutch oven; add a 1-inch layer of potatoes, a ½-inch layer of onion, and a 1-inch layer of fish. Spoon one-third of tomato mixture over fish; sprinkle with one-third of bacon, and season with salt and pepper. Repeat layers to within 1 inch of top of Dutch oven. Cover and cook over low heat 45 minutes or until potatoes are tender.

Add unbeaten eggs, if desired, 15 minutes before serving. Cover and continue cooking 15 minutes or until eggs are cooked to desired doneness. Do not stir. Yield: 12 servings. *Edwin Butler, Jacksonville, North Carolina.*

TOPSAIL ISLAND HUSH PUPPIES

3 cups yellow cornmeal
3 cups self-rising flour
¼ cup sugar
1 teaspoon baking powder
½ teaspoon salt
1½ cups water
¾ cup evaporated milk
¼ cup vegetable oil
1 egg, beaten
Vegetable oil or shortening

Combine dry ingredients; add water, evaporated milk, ¼ cup vegetable oil, and egg. Mix well. Carefully drop batter by tablespoonfuls into deep hot oil (370°); cook only a few at a time, turning once. Fry until hush puppies are

golden brown (3 to 5 minutes). Drain well on paper towels. Yield: about 5 dozen. *L.D. Smith, Hampstead, North Carolina.*

COLESLAW

1 medium head cabbage, shredded
1 small onion, minced
½ cup sweet pickle cubes
1 cup mayonnaise
¼ cup vinegar
¼ cup sugar
1 tablespoon salt
1 teaspoon dillseeds
1 teaspoon celery seeds or celery salt
¼ teaspoon pepper
Leaf lettuce
Green pepper rings (optional)
Pimiento strips (optional)

Combine cabbage, onion, and sweet pickle in a large bowl; set aside.

Combine mayonnaise, vinegar, sugar, and seasonings; stir well. Pour dressing over vegetables, tossing well. Chill several hours. Serve in a lettuce-lined bowl; garnish with green pepper and pimiento, if desired. Yield: 12 servings. *Stacy Smith, Hampstead, North Carolina.*

Think Light For Summer Meals

Something light and cool is often the request for a summer supper, so we've planned a menu that's just that.

It's a colorful combination of the fresh fruits and vegetables of the season—flavorful and satisfying, yet reduced in calories. And since you don't want to spend your summer evenings in the kitchen, most of the dishes can be prepared in advance.

Chicken Salad Supreme
Zesty Broccoli Spears
Quick Broiled Tomatoes
Melba Toast
Luscious Fresh Fruit With Cheese
Iced Tea

CHICKEN SALAD SUPREME

6 whole chicken breasts
2 hard-cooked eggs, chopped
2 cups salad cubes or pickle relish
½ cup finely chopped onion
1 cup mayonnaise
2 tablespoons prepared mustard
1 tablespoon celery seeds
1 teaspoon whole oregano
1 teaspoon hot sauce
½ teaspoon salt
½ teaspoon paprika
¼ teaspoon pepper
Dash of cayenne
Lettuce leaves
Carrot curls (optional)
Hard-cooked eggs, cut in wedges
   (optional)

Place chicken in boiling salted water to cover, and cook until tender (about 25 minutes); drain and cool. Skin and bone chicken; coarsely chop meat.

Combine chicken, chopped eggs, salad cubes, and onion in a bowl. Combine mayonnaise and seasonings, stirring until well blended; add to chicken mixture, mixing well. Chill. Serve on lettuce leaves. Garnish with carrot curls and wedges of hard-cooked egg, if desired. Yield: about 8 servings. *Mrs. Margie D. Thomas, Richmond, Virginia.*

ZESTY BROCCOLI SPEARS

1 pound fresh broccoli
3 tablespoons olive oil
3 tablespoons lemon juice
1 medium clove garlic, thinly sliced
¼ teaspoon salt
⅛ teaspoon pepper

Trim off large outer leaves of broccoli. Remove tough ends of stalks, and wash broccoli thoroughly. Cut into serving-size spears. Cook in a small amount of boiling salted water just until tender; drain. Chill thoroughly.

Combine remaining ingredients, mixing well; pour over chilled broccoli. Yield: 6 servings.   *Mrs. Rose Naquin, Melville, Louisiana.*

QUICK BROILED TOMATOES

⅓ cup dry breadcrumbs
3 tablespoons low-calorie Italian dressing
1 tablespoon chopped parsley
3 tomatoes, halved

Combine breadcrumbs, dressing, and parsley in a small bowl; mix well.

Spoon breadcrumb mixture over cut surface of tomatoes. Broil about 4 inches from heat about 7 minutes or until topping is lightly browned. Yield: 6 servings.   *Mrs. L. W. Cross, Brewster, Massachusetts.*

LUSCIOUS FRESH FRUIT WITH CHEESE

1 (12-ounce) carton low-fat cottage cheese
4 ounces Neufchâtel cheese, softened
6 to 8 (1-inch-thick) peeled cantaloupe wedges
1 pint strawberries, capped
1 small bunch seedless grapes
6 to 8 (1-inch-thick) peeled honeydew wedges
1 pineapple, peeled, cored, and cut into bite-size chunks
3 cups watermelon cubes, seeded
Honey

Combine cottage cheese and Neufchâtel in a small bowl; mix well, and mound in center of a large platter. Arrange fruit around cheese mound. Serve with honey. Yield: about 8 servings.
Jennifer Kimmel, Nashville, Tennessee.

Munch On Cool Party Snacks

If you're planning a party or special meal on a warm Southern summer day, start by treating your guests to some cold appetizers. These appealing snacks are easy to prepare and can be assembled ahead of time and refrigerated until your guests arrive.

Try serving a combination of appetizers, such as Ham Rolls along with Quick Shrimp Dip and crackers. For an elegant touch, try Caviar Pie—a unique way to serve caviar—and smooth, flavorful Chicken Liver Pâté.

HAM ROLLS

1 (3-ounce) package cream cheese, softened
6 stuffed olives, chopped
2 tablespoons whipping cream
1 teaspoon prepared horseradish
¼ teaspoon salt
¼ teaspoon paprika
Dash of white pepper
6 slices boiled ham

Combine all ingredients except ham; mix well. Spread cream cheese mixture evenly on one side of each ham slice; roll up and secure with a wooden pick. Cover and chill. Slice rolls into 1-inch pieces; serve with toothpicks. Yield: 24 rolls.   *Patti Brown, Carrollton, Georgia.*

QUICK SHRIMP DIP

1 (4½-ounce) can shrimp, drained
¼ cup plus 2 tablespoons mayonnaise
3 tablespoons catsup
Juice of 1 lemon
1 teaspoon minced onion
1 teaspoon minced garlic
Paprika
Parsley (optional)
Crackers

Mash shrimp until fine. Combine shrimp with mayonnaise, catsup, lemon juice, onion, and garlic; mix well. Sprinkle with paprika. Garnish dip with parsley, if desired. Serve with an assortment of crisp crackers. Yield: about 1 cup.
Mrs. Sam Stone, Mantee, Mississippi.

CHICKEN LIVER PATE

1 pound chicken livers
¼ cup minced shallots
¼ cup melted butter or margarine
¼ cup cognac
¼ cup whipping cream
½ teaspoon salt
⅛ teaspoon pepper
⅛ teaspoon tarragon leaves
⅛ teaspoon whole thyme leaves
½ cup melted butter or margarine
Crackers

Sauté livers and shallots in ¼ cup butter over low heat until livers are lightly browned; remove livers and shallots from pan, and set aside.

Pour cognac into skillet; simmer until reduced to 2 tablespoons. Combine livers, shallots, cognac, cream, and seasonings; pour into container of electric blender. Process mixture for 30 seconds or until smooth. Add ½ cup butter, and process until smooth. Pour mixture into an oiled 3-cup bowl; chill several hours or overnight.Unmold pâté, and serve with crackers. Yield: about 3 cups.
Lynda Shealey, Houston, Texas.

Tip: Packaged meat should always be rewrapped before it's put in the freezer. Remove the plastic wrap and plastic or cardboard tray from meat; rewrap with heavy-duty aluminum foil or freezer wrapping paper, or put in a heavy plastic bag. Seal the package securely; label and freeze at once.

CAVIAR PIE

4 hard-cooked eggs, finely chopped
1 small onion, finely chopped
2 (3½-ounce) jars black caviar
1½ cups commercial sour cream
Chopped parsley
Crackers or party rye bread

Combine eggs and onion; press firmly into a 9-inch pie plate. Spoon the caviar evenly over egg mixture. Carefully spread sour cream over caviar; sprinkle parsley around edge of pie. Serve with crackers or party rye bread. Yield: one 9-inch pie. *Mrs. Bert E. Uebele, Jr., Boca Raton, Florida.*

Time For Fresh Fruit Cobblers

One of the best ways to enjoy the fresh fruits of summer is in an old-fashioned cobbler. Strawberries, peaches, and apples combine in these recipes for some delightful versions. There's Rosy Strawberry-Rhubarb Cobbler, a juicy Lattice-Topped Peach Cobbler, and a cake-type Apple Walnut Cobbler.

ROSY STRAWBERRY-RHUBARB COBBLER

1 cup sugar
3 tablespoons cornstarch
⅛ teaspoon salt
2 cups sliced rhubarb
1 pint fresh strawberries, washed and sliced
1 tablespoon lemon juice
1 tablespoon butter or margarine
1 (9.5-ounce) package refrigerated biscuits
1 teaspoon sugar
½ teaspoon ground cinnamon

Combine sugar, cornstarch, and salt in a 2-quart saucepan; stir in rhubarb, strawberries, lemon juice, and butter.

Cook over medium heat until bubbly and slightly thickened, stirring constantly.

Pour mixture into a 1¾-quart baking dish. Cut biscuits in half, and arrange around edge and center of dish. Combine 1 teaspoon sugar and cinnamon; sprinkle over cobbler. Bake at 400° for 15 to 20 minutes or just until biscuits are browned. Yield: about 4 to 5 servings. *Mrs. Lillian Stere, Clearwater, Florida.*

LATTICE-TOPPED PEACH COBBLER

8 cups peeled, sliced peaches
2 cups sugar
1½ cups water
½ teaspoon ground nutmeg
2½ cups biscuit mix
3 tablespoons sugar
⅔ cup milk
¼ cup melted shortening
¼ cup sugar
1 teaspoon ground cinnamon
3 tablespoons butter or margarine

Combine peaches, 2 cups sugar, water, and nutmeg in a large saucepan. Bring to a boil; boil 10 minutes or until peaches are tender. Pour into a 2-quart shallow baking dish.

Combine biscuit mix and 3 tablespoons sugar in a medium bowl. Combine milk and shortening; pour over dry ingredients. Mix with a fork until dough forms a ball.

Turn dough out on a floured surface, and knead gently 5 to 8 times. Roll dough out to ⅛-inch thickness; cut into ½-inch-wide strips with a knife or pastry wheel. Place strips on top of fruit to make a lattice.

Sprinkle top with ¼ cup sugar, and cinnamon. Dot with butter.

Bake at 400° for 12 to 15 minutes or until pastry is golden brown. Serve warm. Yield: 6 to 8 servings.

Note: Fresh nectarines may be substituted for peaches, if desired. *Mrs. Carmen Hicks, Bandera, Texas.*

APPLE WALNUT COBBLER

4 cups thinly sliced, peeled cooking apples
1½ cups sugar, divided
½ teaspoon ground cinnamon
¾ cup coarsely chopped walnuts, divided
1 cup sifted all-purpose flour
1 teaspoon baking powder
¼ teaspoon salt
1 egg, well beaten
½ cup evaporated milk
⅓ cup butter or margarine, melted
Whipped cream (optional)
Ground cinnamon (optional)

Place apples in a lightly greased 9-inch round cakepan. Combine ½ cup sugar, ½ teaspoon cinnamon, and ½ cup walnuts; sprinkle over apples.

Sift together flour, remaining sugar, baking powder, and salt. Combine egg, milk, and butter; add to dry ingredients, mixing until smooth. Pour over apple mixture. Top with remaining nuts.

Bake at 325° for 40 to 50 minutes or until top is golden brown. Spoon into serving bowls; top each with whipped cream and cinnamon, if desired. Yield: 6 to 8 servings. *Marlene Beasley, San Antonio, Texas.*

Freeze A Fruit Sherbet

There's nothing like the cool taste of sherbet to finish off a big meal or add refreshment to a hot July afternoon. Crushed or pureed fruits and fruit juices provide an assortment of flavors and a rainbow of colors.

How about churning that ice-cold watermelon into a smooth creamy Watermelon Sherbet? Or try a luscious Orange Sherbet that gets its sparkle from an orange carbonated beverage.

If you like avocados, you're sure to enjoy Mexican Sherbet. The bright-green color comes from a blend of mashed avocado, fresh lemon juice, and grated lemon rind.

WATERMELON SHERBET

1 cup sugar
3 tablespoons lemon juice
4 cups diced seeded watermelon
⅛ teaspoon salt
1 envelope unflavored gelatin
¼ cup cold water
1 cup whipping cream

Combine sugar, lemon juice, watermelon, and salt; refrigerate 30 minutes. Spoon mixture into container of an electric blender; process until smooth.

Soften gelatin in cold water; place over low heat, and stir until gelatin is dissolved. Add to watermelon mixture, stirring well. Add whipping cream, and beat until fluffy. Pour into freezer can of a 1-gallon hand-turned or electric freezer. Freeze according to manufacturer's instructions. Yield: 1 quart.

Dorothy N. Duty,
Pasadena, Texas.

MEXICAN SHERBET

1½ cups sugar
1½ cups water
¾ cup lemon juice
2 tablespoons grated lemon rind
1½ cups mashed avocado

Combine sugar and water in a saucepan; bring to a boil, and boil 5 minutes. Cool. Add lemon juice, rind, and avocado; stir well. Freeze mixture until slushy; remove from freezer, and beat well. Return to freezer, and freeze until firm. Yield: 8 to 10 servings.

Eva G. Key,
Isle of Palms, South Carolina.

FROZEN FRUIT SHERBET

5 large bananas, mashed
3 cups sugar
1 (30-ounce) can apricot halves, drained and chopped
1 (15¼-ounce) can crushed pineapple
Juice of 3 lemons
1 (12-ounce) can frozen orange juice concentrate, thawed and undiluted
3 cups water

Combine all ingredients. Pour into freezer can of a 1-gallon hand-turned or electric freezer. Freeze according to manufacturer's instructions. Yield: about 1 gallon.

Note: May be served in tall glasses with ginger ale. *Jean Keasler,*
Newton, North Carolina.

ORANGE SHERBET

1 (8-ounce) can crushed pineapple
2 (14-ounce) cans sweetened condensed milk
6 (12-ounce) cans orange carbonated beverage

Combine pineapple and milk in freezer can of a 1-gallon hand-turned or electric freezer; mix well. Add orange carbonated beverage, stirring well. Freeze according to manufacturer's instructions. Yield: 1 gallon. *Beth Hall,*
Columbus, Georgia.

CREAMY PINEAPPLE SHERBET

½ cup sugar
½ cup boiling water
Juice of 1 lemon
½ cup crushed pineapple
1 cup milk
1 cup whipping cream, whipped

Combine sugar and boiling water, stirring until sugar is dissolved. Add lemon juice, pineapple, and milk. Freeze until slushy; remove from freezer, and fold in whipped cream. Return to freezer, and freeze until firm. Yield: about 6 servings.

Mrs. R. A. Dibrell,
Dallas, Texas.

Tip: To store leftover egg yolks, put them in a small jar, cover with cold water, and refrigerate. Drain and use within a couple of days.

Sauces Made To Microwave

If you're not making sauces in your microwave oven, you're missing one of the best uses of the oven. Microwave sauces are easy, save time, and don't entail the problems of lumping, scorching, and constant stirring.

From our test kitchens come easy main dish and dessert sauces. Our basic white sauce has three variations for topping meats, vegetables, and fish.

For dessert lovers, we offer two toppings that can be ready on a moment's notice: Chocolate-Peanut Butter Sauce for a quick ice cream topping and Elegant Cherry Sauce, for ice cream or ice cream-filled crêpes. It's also good over roast duck.

Since wattage of microwave ovens varies, the cooking times will vary. We give a time range in our recipes to allow for the difference. To prevent overcooking, always check for doneness at the lower end of the range.

A glass measure or casserole dish is perfect for cooking sauces in the microwave. Use a utensil large enough to prevent the sauce from boiling over. A sauce yielding 1 to 1½ cups should be cooked in a 1-quart or larger container.

Just about any sauce will convert to microwaving. Since sauces don't evaporate as they do when cooked conventionally, you may need to increase thickening agent or decrease liquid.

Use high power for microwaving most sauces; however, use a lower setting for sauces with eggs or very sweet sauces to assure a smooth consistency.

Microwaved sauces need to be stirred occasionally to mix the cooked portion near the outside of the dish with the uncooked portion in the center. Thorough stirring at 1 minute intervals is sufficient for most sauces.

The microwave oven is excellent for heating prepared ice cream toppings. Sauces coming in glass containers can be heated in their original container; however, if the container is full, spoon just the amount you need into another container. This makes stirring easier and cuts heating time.

Canned sauces must be poured into a microwave-safe dish for heating. Stir the sauce at 30-second to 1-minute intervals, and check frequently for doneness until you become familiar with the amount of time it will take for heating. Remember, the larger the quantity being microwaved, the more time it will take to heat.

BASIC WHITE SAUCE

2 tablespoons butter or margarine
2 tablespoons all-purpose flour
¼ teaspoon salt
1 cup milk

Place butter in a 4-cup glass measure. Microwave at HIGH for 30 seconds or until butter melts. Blend in flour and salt; stir well. Gradually add milk, stirring well. Microwave at HIGH for 2 minutes; stir well. Microwave at HIGH for 1 to 2½ minutes, stirring at 1-minute intervals until thickened and bubbly. Yield: 1 cup.

Cheese Sauce Variation: To 1 cup hot white sauce, add ¾ cup shredded sharp Cheddar cheese and ⅛ teaspoon dry mustard; stir until cheese melts. Serve over vegetables or hamburgers. Yield: about 1¼ cups.

Creamy Dill Sauce Variation: To 1 cup hot white sauce, stir in ¼ cup commercial sour cream and 1 teaspoon dried dillweed. Serve over vegetables, fish, or schnitzel. Yield: about 1¼ cups.

Curry Sauce Variation: To 1 cup hot white sauce, stir in 2 teaspoons curry powder. Serve over meats. Yield: about 1 cup.

CHOCOLATE-PEANUT BUTTER SAUCE

1 (6-ounce) package milk chocolate morsels
1 (5⅓-ounce) can evaporated milk
¼ cup creamy peanut butter

Combine chocolate morsels and milk in a 4-cup glass measure. Microwave at HIGH for 2 to 2½ minutes or until chocolate melts, stirring twice.

Stir in peanut butter until melted. Serve over ice cream, and top with chopped peanuts, if desired. Yield: about 1½ cups.

Note: Cover any leftover sauce, and store in refrigerator. To reheat, place in glass measure and microwave at HIGH, stirring occasionally. (Time will vary with amount of sauce reheated.)

ELEGANT CHERRY SAUCE

1 tablespoon cornstarch
⅛ teaspoon ground cinnamon
1 (16-ounce) can pitted dark sweet cherries
2 tablespoons brandy
½ teaspoon lemon juice

Combine cornstarch and cinnamon in a 4-cup glass measure. Drain cherries, reserving liquid. Add enough cherry liquid to dissolve cornstarch; stir well. Add remaining liquid and cherries. Microwave at HIGH for 3 to 4 minutes or until thickened, stirring twice.

Stir in brandy and lemon juice. Serve over ice cream or roast duck. Yield: 2 cups.

Yellow Squash And Zucchini— Summer Favorites

Some of the best ways to enjoy yellow straight or crookneck squash and zucchini are given right here: stuffed and baked, in casseroles, as croquettes, a soufflé—even crêpes stuffed with a delicious tomato-cheese-zucchini filling.

Small to medium-size squash are more likely to have tender, edible skin. Since squash bruise easily, handle them with care. Like most vegetables with a high water content, squash keep best in a cool, dry place. It's wise to use fresh squash as soon as possible.

PARMESAN-STUFFED SQUASH BOATS

6 medium-size yellow squash
6 slices bacon
1 large onion, chopped
1 teaspoon grated green pepper
1 chicken bouillon cube
½ cup boiling water
1 cup dry breadcrumbs
1 teaspoon salt
½ teaspoon pepper
½ teaspoon celery salt
¼ cup butter or margarine, melted
Parmesan cheese
Fresh parsley

Wash squash thoroughly. Place squash in boiling salted water to cover; simmer 10 to 15 minutes or until tender but still firm. Drain and cool slightly. Trim off stems. Cut squash in half lengthwise; remove and reserve pulp, leaving a firm shell. Set aside.

Fry bacon until crisp; remove from pan, and drain on paper towels. Crumble bacon. Drain off bacon drippings, reserving 2 tablespoons in pan. Sauté onion and green pepper in drippings until golden brown.

Add bouillon cube to ½ cup boiling water; stir until dissolved. Combine bouillon mixture, bacon, onion and green pepper, breadcrumbs, 1 teaspoon salt, pepper, celery salt, butter, and

Yellow squash and zucchini lend themselves to a variety of dishes.

squash pulp; mix well. Place squash shell in a 13- x 9- x 2-inch baking dish. Spoon pulp mixture into shells; sprinkle with cheese. Broil about 3 minutes or until lightly browned. Serve on bed of fresh parsley. Yield: 6 servings.

Kay Alloway,
North Myrtle Beach, South Carolina.

HAM AND CHEESE STUFFED ZUCCHINI

3 medium zucchini
¼ cup finely chopped onion
1 tablespoon butter or margarine
1 cup finely chopped ham
¾ cup small-curd cottage cheese
⅔ cup cooked rice
1 egg, slightly beaten
1 tablespoon chopped parsley
¼ teaspoon salt
⅛ teaspoon basil
3 (1-ounce) slices sharp process American cheese

Wash squash thoroughly. Place in a small amount of boiling salted water; cover and simmer 10 to 15 minutes or until tender but still firm. Drain and cool slightly. Cut squash in half lengthwise; remove pulp, leaving a firm shell. Set aside.

Sauté onion in butter until tender. Combine onion, ham, cottage cheese, rice, egg, parsley, salt, basil, and zucchini pulp; mix well. Place zucchini shells in a 9-inch baking dish; spoon filling into shells. Bake, covered, at 350° for 25 minutes. Cut each slice of cheese into 8 strips; place 4 strips cheese on each zucchini half. Bake, uncovered, 5 more minutes. Yield: 6 servings.

Joyce DeLong,
Annandale, Virginia.

ZUCCHINI SOUFFLE

¼ cup butter or margarine
¼ cup all-purpose flour
1⅓ cups milk
1 teaspoon salt
Dash of pepper
1 tablespoon minced onion
1¼ cups grated zucchini
5 eggs, separated
1 teaspoon cream of tartar
½ cup shredded sharp Cheddar cheese

Melt butter in a heavy saucepan over low heat; blend in flour and cook 1 minute, stirring constantly. Gradually add milk; cook, stirring constantly, until smooth and thickened. Stir in salt, pepper, and onion; remove from heat, and let cool. Squeeze grated zucchini to remove as much liquid as possible; stir into sauce.

Beat egg yolks until thick and lemon colored; add to squash mixture; mix well.

Beat egg whites and cream of tartar until stiff, but not dry; fold into squash mixture. Pour into a greased 2-quart casserole or soufflé dish; sprinkle with cheese. Place dish in a baking pan filled with 1 inch of water. Bake at 350° for 1 hour and 15 minutes or until a knife inserted in center comes out clean. Yield: 6 to 8 servings.

Phyllis Patterson,
San Antonio, Texas.

ZUCCHINI CREPES

1 cup all-purpose flour
¼ teaspoon salt
2 eggs
½ cup milk
½ cup water
2 tablespoons butter or margarine, melted
Vegetable oil
Zucchini filling (recipe follows)

Combine flour, salt, and eggs; mix well. Add milk, water, and butter; beat until smooth. Cover mixture; refrigerate at least 2 hours. (This allows flour particles to swell and soften so crêpes are light in texture.)

Brush the bottom of a 6- or 7-inch crêpe pan or heavy skillet with vegetable oil; place pan over medium heat until oil is hot, but not smoking.

Pour 2 to 3 tablespoons batter into pan; quickly tilt pan in all directions so batter covers the pan in a thin film. Cook about 1 minute.

Lift edge of crêpe to test for doneness. Crêpe is ready for flipping when it can be shaken loose from pan. Flip the crêpe, and cook about 30 seconds on the other side. (This side is rarely more than a spotty brown and is the side on which the filling is placed.) Place the crêpe on a towel to cool; stack crêpes between layers of waxed paper to prevent sticking. Set aside 8 crêpes; freeze remaining crêpes for later use.

Spoon about ¼ cup zucchini filling in center of each crêpe. Fold sides of crêpe over filling; turn and tuck ends under. Place crêpes, seam side down, in a lightly greased 12- x 8- x 2-inch baking dish. Bake at 300° for 10 to 15 minutes. Yield: 8 servings.

Zucchini Filling:

2 cups thinly sliced zucchini
½ cup chopped onion
½ cup chopped green onion
½ cup finely chopped green pepper
3 cloves garlic, minced
1 (16-ounce) can tomato sauce
½ cup cottage cheese
½ cup Parmesan cheese

Sauté zucchini, onion, green pepper, and garlic in butter until tender; add tomato sauce, and simmer 10 minutes. Stir in cheese. Yield: about 4 cups.

Patti Buckley,
Kenner, Louisiana.

ZUCCHINI CASSEROLE

2 slices bacon
½ cup chopped mushrooms
¼ cup minced onion
Dash of instant minced garlic
½ cup melted butter or margarine
2 medium zucchini, grated
1¼ cups cracker crumbs, divided
1 egg, beaten
½ teaspoon salt
¼ teaspoon pepper
½ cup shredded Swiss cheese

Fry bacon until crisp; drain on paper towels. Crumble bacon.

Sauté mushrooms, onion, and garlic in butter just until tender. Combine bacon, mushroom mixture, zucchini, 1 cup cracker crumbs, egg, salt, and pepper; stir well. Pour zucchini mixture into a greased 1½-quart casserole.

Combine Swiss cheese and remaining ¼ cup cracker crumbs; sprinkle over zucchini mixture. Bake at 350° for 40 minutes. Yield: 6 servings.

Jacqueline Skeen,
Houston, Texas.

SQUASH CROQUETTES

2 cups finely chopped yellow squash
1 cup finely chopped onion
1 egg, beaten
1 teaspoon salt
1 teaspoon pepper
½ cup plus 1 tablespoon all-purpose flour
Hot vegetable oil

Combine first 5 ingredients; mix well. Stir in flour. Drop by tablespoonfuls into ½ inch of hot oil. Cook until browned, turning once; drain. Yield: 6 servings.

Mrs. Marie Elrod,
Warner Robins, Georgia.

SQUASH PATTIES

1 cup all-purpose flour
1 teaspoon sugar
½ teaspoon salt
¾ cup milk
1 egg
¼ cup vegetable oil
3 cups grated yellow squash
1 medium onion, chopped
2 to 3 teaspoons crushed red pepper

Combine first 6 ingredients; beat with an electric mixer until smooth. Add remaining ingredients; stir well.

Drop mixture by tablespoonfuls onto a hot, greased skillet. Cook until golden brown, turning once. Drain on paper towels. Yield: about 2 dozen.

Mrs. Dwight Curtis,
Grannis, Arkansas.

COUNTRY CLUB SQUASH

8 medium-size yellow squash
½ cup chopped onion
1 (8-ounce) carton commercial sour cream
½ to ¾ teaspoon salt
¼ teaspoon pepper
¼ teaspoon basil
1 cup soft breadcrumbs
½ cup grated medium Cheddar cheese
⅓ cup butter or margarine, melted
½ teaspoon paprika
8 slices bacon, cooked and crumbled

Wash squash; trim off ends. Cook squash and onion in boiling salted water until tender; drain and mash. Combine squash, sour cream, salt, pepper, and basil; pour into a greased 2-quart casserole. Combine breadcrumbs, cheese, butter, and paprika; sprinkle over squash mixture. Top with bacon. Bake at 300° for 30 minutes. Yield: 6 to 8 servings.   *Mrs. Sherry Means,*
Atlanta, Georgia.

ITALIAN SQUASH

6 medium zucchini
3 cups soft breadcrumbs
½ cup grated Parmesan cheese
1 small onion, minced
3 tablespoons minced fresh parsley
1 teaspoon salt
⅛ teaspoon pepper
2 eggs, beaten
2 tablespoons butter or margarine
Grated Parmesan cheese

Wash squash thoroughly. Place in a small amount of boiling salted water.

Cover and simmer 5 minutes. Drain and cool slightly. Trim off stems. Cut squash in half lengthwise; remove and reserve pulp, leaving a firm shell. Set shells aside.

Combine zucchini pulp, breadcrumbs, ½ cup cheese, onion, parsley, salt, pepper, and eggs; mix well. Spoon mixture into zucchini shells. Dot with butter; sprinkle with cheese. Bake at 350° for 30 minutes. Yield: 6 servings.

Note: Any leftover stuffing can be spooned into a casserole dish and baked with the squash.   *Mrs. Sandra Horn,*
Houston, Texas.

The Specialty Is Seafood

After a busy day, Dr. Fred Berley enjoys retiring to the kitchen for an evening of creative cooking. A retired Navy rear admiral, Dr. Berley has been in private medical practice in Jacksonville, Florida, for 19 years.

With cooking, Dr. Berley often combines another hobby: fishing. His Florida Bouillabaisse is an outstanding example, for much of the seafood used in this stew is his catch from a successful fishing trip.

Besides Florida Bouillabaisse, Dr. Berley has shared his recipe for a light, crusty French bread. These are followed by specialties from several other men who also enjoy cooking as a hobby.

FLORIDA BOUILLABAISSE

1 cup olive oil
1 bay leaf, crushed
¼ teaspoon whole thyme leaves
1 clove garlic, minced
½ cup diced onion
½ cup diced green pepper
¼ cup diced celery
¼ cup sliced carrot
1 leek, sliced (optional)
1 (48-ounce) can tomato juice
6 fresh crab bodies and claws
1 cup bite-size pieces fresh lobster
2 to 3 cups bite-size pieces sea bass or other firm fish
1½ cups peeled and deveined shrimp
1 cup bite-size pieces conch (optional)
1 cup shucked clams
1 cup sweet white wine
½ cup lemon juice

Heat oil in a Dutch oven over low heat; add bay leaf, thyme, and garlic. Sauté 1 to 2 minutes. Stir vegetables into oil, and sauté until onion is tender. Add tomato juice; increase heat to medium, and add crab. Bring mixture to a boil; cover and simmer 1½ to 2 hours.

Pour tomato juice-crab mixture through a cone-shaped ricer, reserving liquid. Use a pestle to grind crab bodies and claws in the ricer, catching liquid in a shallow bowl. Stir crab liquid into reserved tomato juice mixture; discard crab and vegetables.

Return tomato juice mixture to Dutch oven; add remaining seafood. Cook over medium heat 10 minutes. Stir in wine and lemon juice; cook an additional 5 minutes. Yield: 10 to 12 servings.

FRENCH BREAD

3 cups warm water (105° to 115°)
1⅛ teaspoons dry yeast
Pinch of sugar
About 10 cups unbleached all-purpose flour
2 tablespoons sugar
4½ teaspoons salt

Combine water, yeast, and a pinch of sugar in a medium bowl; set aside.

Combine 10 cups flour, 2 tablespoons sugar, and salt in a large mixing bowl; stir well.

Spoon about one-third of flour mixture into bowl of food processor. Pour one-third of yeast mixture through chute; process with steel blade until dough forms a ball. Turn dough out onto a floured surface. Repeat process with remaining flour mixture and yeast mixture, using one-third of each at a time.

Press the 3 balls of dough together; knead until smooth and elastic (dough will be very stiff). Place in a well-greased bowl, turning once to grease top. Cover and let rise in a warm place (85°), free from drafts, until doubled in bulk. Punch down; cover and let rise until doubled in bulk.

Turn dough out on a floured surface, and divide into 3 equal portions; shape each portion into a 14- to 16-inch loaf. Place 2 loaves on 1 greased baking sheet and remaining loaf on another. Cover and let rise until doubled in bulk. Cut ¼-inch-deep slashes in top of each loaf, using a sharp knife or razor blade.

Place a loafpan of boiling water on lower shelf of oven. Place 1 baking sheet of bread on lower shelf of oven, and bake at 400° for 30 minutes; move bread to upper shelf, and bake an additional 5 minutes. Repeat baking process with remaining baking sheet of bread. Allow to cool on wire racks. Yield: 3 loaves.

Note: Conventional mixing procedures may be used to make bread. Place yeast mixture in a large bowl, and gradually stir in flour mixture; then proceed with remaining directions.

COUNTRY PRIDE PORK CHOPS

½ cup soy sauce
¼ cup firmly packed brown sugar
¼ cup dry sherry
1 teaspoon ground cinnamon
½ teaspoon garlic salt
½ teaspoon monosodium glutamate
Dash of ground ginger
4 (1-inch-thick) center cut pork chops

Combine first 7 ingredients; stir well. Arrange pork chops in a single layer in a dish. Pour marinade over chops; cover and refrigerate overnight.

Grill chops 6 to 8 inches from heat over gray-white coals 1 hour or until done, basting with marinade and turning occasionally. Yield: 4 servings.
Jim Hudson,
Cary, North Carolina.

BEEF ROAST BARBECUE

2 tablespoons shortening
1 (4-pound) rump roast
⅓ cup cider vinegar
½ cup water
½ cup catsup
1 teaspoon salt
1 teaspoon liquid smoke
½ teaspoon garlic salt
Piquant Barbecue Sauce

Melt shortening in an ovenproof Dutch oven. Brown roast slowly on all sides; remove from heat. Combine remaining ingredients except barbecue sauce; pour over roast. Cover and bake at 350° for 2 hours or until tender; baste occasionally.

Remove roast to platter; reserve pan drippings. Let roast stand at room temperature 10 to 15 minutes; slice roast to desired thickness.

Stir Piquant Barbecue Sauce into pan drippings. Place beef slices in sauce mixture; simmer 5 to 10 minutes or until heated. Yield: 12 to 14 servings.

Piquant Barbecue Sauce:

1 cup catsup
¼ cup water
¼ cup red wine vinegar
½ cup chopped onion
½ cup chopped celery
2 tablespoons brown sugar
2 tablespoons Worcestershire sauce
½ teaspoon liquid smoke

Combine all ingredients in a small saucepan; cook over low heat until vegetables are tender, stirring occasionally. Yield: about 1½ cups.
Dr. Wilbur Wilson,
Cynthiana, Kentucky.

MOLDED GAZPACHO SALAD

1½ tablespoons unflavored gelatin
¼ cup cold water
1½ cups tomato juice
1 cucumber, peeled and finely chopped
4 large tomatoes, peeled and finely chopped
1 large green pepper, finely chopped
¼ cup sliced radishes
2 tablespoons finely chopped green onion
½ cup finely chopped celery
Dash of hot sauce
¼ cup olive oil
1½ tablespoons wine vinegar
1 tablespoon fresh lemon juice
1 teaspoon salt
Creamy Dressing

Soften gelatin in ¼ cup cold water, and set aside.

Heat tomato juice in a large saucepan; add gelatin, stirring until dissolved. Add vegetables and seasonings; mix well, and chill until slightly thickened. Stir well, and pour into an oiled 6-cup mold; chill until firm. Unmold the salad, and serve with Creamy Dressing. Yield: 8 to 10 servings.

Creamy Dressing:

½ cup mayonnaise
¾ cup commercial sour cream
¾ cup minced fresh parsley

Combine all ingredients, mixing well. Yield: 1¼ cups.
Rex Lyons,
Midway, Kentucky.

Tips For Freezing Fruits And Vegetables

Freezing is one of the simplest and least time-consuming ways to preserve foods at home. The following hints will help you preserve the natural color, fresh flavor, and nutritive value of most fruits and vegetables.

Getting Ready To Freeze

—Some varieties of fruits and vegetables freeze better than others. If you question how well a product will freeze, you should test it first. To test, freeze three or four packages and then sample.

—Green onions, lettuce, other salad greens, and radishes do not freeze well. Tomatoes freeze better as a juice or cooked product.

—Select containers for freezing that will hold only enough of a fruit or vegetable for one meal. Containers with flat sides and uniform shapes will stack well and save freezer space.

—Rigid plastic containers can be reused indefinitely. Cardboard cartons may be reused if lined with plastic.

Preparing Fruits and Vegetables

—All fruits need to be washed in cold water before freezing, but avoid overhandling as it may bruise delicate fruits.

—Some fruits darken during freezing if not treated with a suitable antidarkening agent. If you use an ascorbic or citric acid mixture to prevent darkening, follow the manufacturer's directions for proper use.

—Use young, barely mature vegetables fresh from the garden for freezing. Wash vegetables in cold water and sort according to size or cut into uniform pieces.

—Practically every vegetable, except green pepper, maintains better frozen quality if blanched before packing. Most vegetables require blanching for only a few minutes. Check a blanching timetable, available in most cookbooks, to determine proper blanching time.

—After blanching, vegetables should be cooled quickly and thoroughly by plunging them into cold water.

—Drain cooled vegetables thoroughly. Dry pack is recommended for almost all vegetables because preparation for freezing and serving is easier.

Packing and Storage

—Allow ample headspace when freezing products. Headspace is necessary because food expands as it freezes. A guide to the amount of headspace to allow is available in most cookbooks.

—Label containers to identify their contents by using gummed labels, freezer tape, or crayon-type pencils.

—For the quickest freezing, leave a little space between containers so air can circulate freely. Place containers closer together after they are frozen.

—Most fruits and vegetables maintain high quality when frozen for 8 to 12 months; citrus products, for 4 to 6 months. It's a good idea to post a list of frozen foods near the freezer and keep a record of when they were frozen.

—If power to the freezer is interrupted, do not open the door unnecessarily. Food in a loaded freezer will stay frozen 2 days and in a half-filled freezer about one day. If power is not resumed within this time, use dry ice to prevent spoilage. If you can't get dry ice, locate a locker plant and move your food there in insulated boxes.

—You may safely refreeze foods that have thawed if they still contain ice crystals or if they have been held no longer than one or two days at refrigerator temperature after thawing.

Okra The Way You Like It

Fried, cooked in a casserole, or made into fritters, okra is a true Southern favorite. We've selected five mouth-watering recipes from our readers that we know you'll enjoy.

Fresh corn and tomatoes are sautéed with sliced okra for a colorful side dish called Okra Surprise. Fried okra lovers will enjoy Okra and Green Tomatoes fried in a seasoned batter, or Okra Fritters flavored with onion and tomato. For a hearty vegetable dish, try Okra and Corn in Cream or cheesy-topped Okra Casserole.

OKRA SURPRISE

3 cups sliced okra
2 cups fresh corn cut from cob, cooked
4 or 5 large ripe tomatoes, peeled and chopped
3 tablespoons melted margarine
Salt and pepper to taste

Thoroughly rinse sliced okra under running water; drain well. Combine okra and remaining ingredients in a large skillet; cover and simmer 15 minutes. Yield: 8 servings.

Mrs. William S. Bell,
Chattanooga, Tennessee.

OKRA AND GREEN TOMATOES

½ pound okra
2 medium-size very green tomatoes, unpeeled
1 egg
2 tablespoons milk
½ cup all-purpose flour
¼ cup cornmeal
1 teaspoon salt
Salt and pepper to taste
Hot vegetable oil

Wash okra well; drain. Cut off tip and stem ends; cut okra into 1-inch slices. Cut tomatoes into 1-inch cubes; set aside.

Combine egg and milk, beating well. Combine flour, cornmeal, and 1 teaspoon salt.

Sprinkle okra and tomatoes with salt and pepper to taste; dip into egg mixture, and dredge in flour mixture. Cook in ¼ inch hot oil until golden brown. Drain on paper towels. Yield: 4 servings.

Eunice B. Sherrill,
Birmingham, Alabama.

OKRA CASSEROLE

½ cup chopped onion
½ cup chopped green pepper
⅓ cup melted margarine
2 tablespoons all-purpose flour
1 teaspoon salt
½ teaspoon pepper
2 cups chopped tomato
1¼ cups sliced okra
½ teaspoon dried basil leaves
4 slices process American cheese, cut in half to form triangles

Sauté onion and green pepper in margarine. Stir in flour, salt, and pepper; blend well. Stir in tomato, okra, and basil. Spoon mixture into a lightly greased 1½-quart casserole; top with cheese. Bake at 350° for 20 to 25 minutes or until bubbly. Yield: 6 servings.

Mrs. Leon Johnson,
Fordyce, Arkansas.

OKRA AND CORN IN CREAM

1½ cups fresh corn cut from cob
¼ cup melted butter or margarine
2 cups sliced okra (½ inch thick)
1 teaspoon salt
Dash of pepper
½ cup half-and-half

Cook corn in butter over low heat about 7 minutes, stirring occasionally. Add okra; cover and cook 10 minutes, stirring occasionally. Stir in salt, pepper, and half-and-half; heat thoroughly. Yield: 4 servings. *Mrs. R. S. Duff,*
Hurricane, West Virginia.

OKRA FRITTERS

1 cup thinly sliced okra
½ cup chopped onion
½ cup chopped tomato
¼ cup all-purpose flour
¼ cup cornmeal
½ teaspoon salt
½ teaspoon curry powder
¼ teaspoon pepper
1 egg, beaten
Hot peanut oil

Combine first 9 ingredients, stirring well. Drop mixture by tablespoonfuls into hot oil; cook until golden brown, turning once. Yield: 6 servings.

Mrs. Horace Estes,
Gurdon, Arkansas.

Breads Fresh From The Garden

Your bread assortment will never be dull when you rely on summer's fresh fruits and vegetables for flavor. From this fresh produce comes a variety of quick breads, from muffins to loaves.

Grated zucchini and crushed pineapple give a delicate, moist texture to Spiced Zucchini Bread, while juicy-ripe peaches make Georgia Peach Bread distinctive.

Fresh Lemon Muffins, flavored with fresh lemon juice and grated lemon rind are great for morning meals or served with a fruit plate for a luncheon. Their light texture comes from folding beaten egg whites into the batter.

And why not try asparagus in bread? Asparagus Squares are pleasingly moist and spicy, with a blend of cinnamon, nutmeg, and ginger.

FRESH LEMON MUFFINS

1 cup all-purpose flour
1 teaspoon baking powder
¼ teaspoon salt
½ cup butter or margarine, softened
½ cup sugar
2 egg yolks, well beaten
3 tablespoons lemon juice
2 egg whites, at room temperature
1 tablespoon grated lemon rind
2 tablespoons sugar
¼ teaspoon ground cinnamon

Combine flour, baking powder, and salt; set aside.

Beat butter until creamy; gradually add ½ cup sugar, and beat until light and fluffy. Beat in egg yolks. Add dry ingredients to creamed mixture alternately with lemon juice, mixing just until combined (do not overmix).

Beat egg whites until stiff; gently stir in lemon rind. Fold into muffin mixture. Spoon batter into greased muffin tins, filling three-fourths full. Combine 2 tablespoons sugar and cinnamon; top each muffin with ½ teaspoon sugar mixture.

Bake at 375° for 20 to 25 minutes or until done. Yield: about 1 dozen.
Mrs. Nan Fountain,
Greenville, Mississippi.

GEORGIA PEACH BREAD

3 cups sliced fresh peaches
6 tablespoons sugar
2 cups all-purpose flour
1 teaspoon baking powder
1 teaspoon soda
¼ teaspoon salt
1 teaspoon ground cinnamon
1½ cups sugar
½ cup shortening
2 eggs
1 cup finely chopped pecans
1 teaspoon vanilla extract

Place peaches and 6 tablespoons sugar in container of electric blender; process until pureed. (Mixture should yield about 2¼ cups.)

Combine flour, baking powder, soda, salt, and cinnamon; set aside.

Combine 1½ cups sugar and shortening; cream well. Add eggs, and mix well. Add peach puree and dry ingredients, mixing until ingredients are moistened. Stir in nuts and vanilla.

Spoon batter into 2 well-greased and floured 9- x 5- x 3-inch loafpans. Bake at 325° for 55 to 60 minutes or until done. Cool 10 minutes in pan; turn out on rack, and let cool completely. Yield: 2 loaves.
Anne Ringer,
Warner Robins, Georgia.

SPICED ZUCCHINI BREAD

3 cups all-purpose flour
2 teaspoons soda
1 teaspoon salt
½ teaspoon baking powder
1½ teaspoons ground cinnamon
¾ cup finely chopped walnuts
3 eggs
2 cups sugar
1 cup vegetable oil
2 teaspoons vanilla extract
2 cups coarsely shredded zucchini
1 (8-ounce) can crushed pineapple, well drained

Combine flour, soda, salt, baking powder, cinnamon, and nuts; set aside.

Beat eggs lightly in a large mixing bowl; add sugar, oil, and vanilla; beat until creamy. Stir in zucchini and pineapple. Add dry ingredients, stirring only until dry ingredients are moistened.

Spoon batter into 2 well-greased and floured 9- x 5- x 3-inch loafpans. Bake at 350° for 1 hour or until done. Cool 10 minutes before removing from pans; turn out on rack, and cool completely. Yield: 2 loaves.
Mrs. Bettina Hambrick,
Muskogee, Oklahoma.

ASPARAGUS SQUARES

2 cups all-purpose flour
1½ cups sugar
2½ teaspoons baking powder
1 teaspoon soda
1 teaspoon salt
1½ teaspoons ground cinnamon
1 teaspoon ground nutmeg
½ teaspoon ground ginger
1 cup buttermilk
¾ cup vegetable oil
3 eggs, lightly beaten
1½ cups cooked asparagus stems and pieces, chopped
1 cup chopped walnuts

Sift together dry ingredients; add buttermilk and oil, beating until smooth. Add remaining ingredients; mix just until blended.

Spoon batter into a greased and floured 13- x 9- x 2-inch baking pan. Bake at 325° for 45 to 50 minutes or until bread tests done. Cut into squares. Yield: about 15 servings.
Sandra Moore,
Bowling Green, Kentucky.

Plum Good Ideas To Try

During the summer months, juicy plums fill the produce section.

A ripe plum will be full colored and have a slightly soft tip end. Plums will ripen rapidly at room temperature. Refrigerate the ripened fruit immediately in a moisture-proof container; it will keep well for three to five days.

The characteristic flavor of the plum comes from the contrast between the tart skin and the sweet flesh. So for most recipes, as for eating out of hand, you will want to leave the skin on.

PLUM KUCHEN

8 fresh plums (about 1 pound)
2 tablespoons all-purpose flour
Pastry (recipe follows)
1 teaspoon ground cinnamon
⅔ to 1 cup sugar
2 eggs, beaten

Cut each plum into 8 wedges, discarding pits. Sprinkle 2 tablespoons of flour evenly in bottom of pastry shell. Arrange plum wedges, side by side, overlapping slightly. Combine cinnamon and sugar; sprinkle over plums. Pour eggs over top, covering surface evenly.

Bake at 400° for 30 minutes or until top is lightly browned. Yield: 6 to 8 servings.

Pastry:

½ cup butter, melted
1 tablespoon white vinegar
2 tablespoons sugar
1¼ cups all-purpose flour

Combine butter and vinegar; add sugar and flour, mixing well. Roll dough out to fit a 10-inch piepan; press evenly into bottom and halfway up sides. Prick bottom with a fork. Bake at 400° for 10 minutes. Yield: one 10-inch pie shell.
Karen S. Bain,
Charlottesville, Virginia.

PLUM PIE WITH ITALIAN SWEET CRUST

6 cups pitted and sliced fresh plums
1¼ cups sugar
¼ cup all-purpose flour
2 tablespoons butter
½ teaspoon salt
Juice of 1 lemon
Grated rind of 1 lemon
Italian Sweet Crust
Whipped topping or ice cream (optional)

Combine first 7 ingredients; pour into a 1½-quart shallow baking dish. Cover with Italian Sweet Crust, pinching edges of crust to sides of baking dish. Bake at 400° for 45 minutes. Serve hot with whipped topping or a scoop of ice cream, if desired. Yield: 6 to 8 servings.

Italian Sweet Crust:
2 egg yolks
⅓ cup sugar
⅓ cup butter, softened
1 teaspoon grated lemon rind
1 tablespoon rum
1 cup plus 2 tablespoons all-purpose flour
¼ teaspoon salt

Combine egg yolks, sugar, butter, rind, and rum; beat well. Combine flour and salt; gradually add to beaten mixture, stirring well. Shape dough into a ball; chill. Roll out dough between layers of waxed paper; cut dough to cover top of 1½-quart baking dish. Yield: pastry for one 9-inch pie.
Mrs. Florence L. Costello,
Chattanooga, Tennessee.

CHILLED PURPLE PLUM SOUP

2 pounds fresh purple plums, pitted and
quartered
3 cups water
¼ cup honey
1 tablespoon lemon juice
2 tablespoons sugar
½ teaspoon salt
1 stick cinnamon, broken in pieces
1 teaspoon whole cloves
2 teaspoons cornstarch
2 tablespoons water
½ teaspoon almond extract
2 cups whipping cream

Place plums in a large saucepan; add 3 cups water, honey, lemon juice, sugar, and salt. Tie cinnamon and cloves in a cheesecloth bag; place in saucepan with plum mixture. Bring mixture to a boil; reduce heat and simmer 10 minutes, or until plums are tender.
Combine cornstarch and 2 tablespoons water; gradually pour into plum mixture, stirring constantly. Bring mixture to a boil; cook 2 to 3 minutes until slightly thickened. Remove from heat, and discard spice bag. Stir in almond extract. Chill. Add cream, mixing well. Stir before serving. Yield: about 6 to 8 servings. *Mrs. Amelia Shearouse, Orlando, Florida.*

FRESH FRUIT COMPOTE

1 cup sugar
4 cups water
2 apples, peeled, cored, and quartered
2 peaches, peeled, pitted, and quartered
2 pears, peeled, cored, and quartered
3 fresh plums, pitted and quartered
¼ pound cherries, seeded
1 cup fresh strawberries, hulled
2 tablespoons lemon juice
2 to 3 sticks cinnamon
Whipped cream (optional)

Combine sugar and water in a large saucepan; bring to a boil. Add fruits, lemon juice, and cinnamon; cook over medium heat 10 minutes, stirring occasionally. Chill. Serve with whipped cream, if desired. Yield: 6 to 8 servings. *Martha Underwood, Jackson, Mississippi.*

Serve These Biscuits Anytime

Biscuits are the perfect way to round out any meal. Warm, fragrant, and butter-flavored, Parker House-Style biscuits are so light in texture they will melt in your mouth.

Raised from a yeast dough, the biscuits are cut and folded over in the traditional Parker House fashion. Each biscuit is then dipped in butter and baked until golden.

PARKER HOUSE-STYLE BISCUITS

2 packages dry yeast
2 tablespoons warm water (105° to 115°)
5 cups self-rising flour
¼ cup sugar
1 cup shortening
2 cups buttermilk
½ to ¾ cup melted butter or margarine

Dissolve yeast in water (mixture will be thick).
Sift together flour and sugar in a large bowl; cut in shortening until mixture resembles coarse meal. Add buttermilk and yeast mixture, stirring well.
Turn dough out onto a well-floured surface. Roll out to ¼-inch thickness. Cut with a 2¼-inch cutter. With dull edge of knife, make a crease just off center on each round. Brush biscuits with some of the melted butter. Fold over so top overlaps slightly; press edges together. Dip biscuits in remaining butter. Place on an ungreased baking sheet. Bake at 400° for 15 minutes or until golden brown. Yield: 3 dozen biscuits.
Note: Dough can be stored in an airtight container in refrigerator 1 week.
Mary Ann Pittard,
Burlington, North Carolina.

Beefed-Up Main Dishes

There's a lot to be said for the versatility of beef. One of the best things is that it can be prepared in main dishes that are suitable for any occasion, from casual to elegant.

For a one-dish supper, serve Cornbread Tamale Bake, a savory mixture of ground beef and cheese with a crusty cornbread topping. If meat loaf is a favorite, Beef-Vegetable Loaf offers an interesting variation. Several vegetables are baked in the loaf for extra flavor and moistness.

Company meals call for extra-special entrées, and these recipes offer some delightful choices.

COMPANY POT ROAST

½ cup chopped onion
¼ cup melted butter or margarine
1 (4-pound) chuck roast
1 bay leaf, crumbled
2 tablespoons grated orange rind
1 teaspoon salt
¼ teaspoon ground allspice
⅛ teaspoon pepper
1 (10½-ounce) can consommé, undiluted

Sauté onion in butter in a large Dutch oven until tender; add meat and brown on both sides.

Combine seasonings and consommé; pour over meat. Cover and simmer 3½ hours or until tender. Yield: 6 to 8 servings.
Mrs. Robert Deleot, Atlanta, Georgia.

BEEF EN DAUBE

2½ pounds round or sirloin steak, cut into ½-inch cubes
2 tablespoons melted butter
1 tablespoon brandy
12 small fresh mushrooms
24 small pitted Spanish olives
3 tablespoons all-purpose flour
1 tablespoon tomato paste
2 cups beef broth
½ cup claret
1 tablespoon currant jelly
1 bay leaf
Hot cooked rice

Quickly brown meat in butter in a Dutch oven. Add brandy, stirring well. Remove meat with a slotted spoon, and set aside. Add mushrooms to Dutch oven; cook, stirring occasionally, until tender. Add olives, flour, and tomato paste; stir until flour is dissolved.

Gradually add broth, stirring constantly; cook over medium heat until mixture reaches a boil. Stir in claret, currant jelly, and bay leaf.

Return meat to Dutch oven; cook over low heat 45 to 50 minutes or until meat is tender. Remove bay leaf. Serve over rice. Yield: 6 to 8 servings.
Mrs. H. S. Wright, Leesville, South Carolina.

BEEF STROGANOFF

¼ cup all-purpose flour
Dash of pepper
1½ pounds round steak, cut into ½-inch strips
¼ cup butter or margarine
1 (4-ounce) can sliced mushrooms, drained
½ cup chopped onion
1 small clove garlic, minced
1 (10½-ounce) can beef broth, undiluted
1 (8-ounce) carton commercial sour cream
⅓ cup dry sherry
Hot cooked noodles

Combine flour and pepper; sprinkle over beef, coating thoroughly.

Melt butter in a large skillet over medium heat; add beef, and sauté until lightly browned. Add mushrooms, onion, and garlic; cook until onion is

tender. Add broth; cover and cook over low heat, stirring occasionally, until meat is tender (about 1 hour). Stir in sour cream and sherry; heat well. Serve over hot noodles.
Mrs. R. I. Bradford, Jr., Madison, Tennessee.

SAVORY BEEF AND VEGETABLES

1 (8-ounce) can tomato sauce
2 tablespoons brown sugar
1 teaspoon salt
¼ teaspoon pepper
1 teaspoon caraway seeds
3 tablespoons Worcestershire sauce
2 tablespoons cider vinegar
2 beef bouillon cubes
¼ cup dry white wine
2 pounds round steak, cut into 1-inch cubes
1 (8-ounce) can button mushrooms, drained
1 (16-ounce) jar boiling onions, drained
½ cup green pepper strips
2 tablespoons cornstarch
Hot buttered noodles

Combine first 9 ingredients, mixing well. Add steak, mushrooms, onions, and green pepper; stir lightly. Marinate 24 hours in refrigerator.

Remove steak and vegetables from marinade. Add cornstarch to marinade, stirring well; pour into a skillet. Add steak and vegetables to skillet; simmer 20 minutes, stirring occasionally. Serve over hot buttered noodles. Yield: 4 to 6 servings.
Mrs. James A. Tuthill, Virginia Beach, Virginia.

CORNBREAD TAMALE BAKE

2 pounds ground beef
1 clove garlic, minced
½ cup chopped onion
½ cup chopped green pepper
1½ tablespoons chili powder
1½ teaspoons salt
1 teaspoon ground oregano
1 teaspoon whole basil
3 cups peeled, chopped tomato
½ cup water, divided
2 tablespoons all-purpose flour
1 cup (¼ pound) shredded Cheddar cheese
1 cup (¼ pound) shredded mozzarella cheese
½ cup sliced ripe olives
1 (6-ounce) package cornbread mix

Combine ground beef and garlic in a skillet; sauté over medium heat until meat is browned, stirring to crumble. Add onion and green pepper; cook until tender. Stir in seasonings, tomato, and ¼ cup water. Cover and simmer 10 to 15 minutes.

Stir remaining ¼ cup water into flour, and add to meat mixture; cook over medium heat, stirring constantly, until thickened and bubbly. Remove from heat; add cheese and olives, stirring until cheese melts. Spoon into a greased 9-inch square baking dish.

Prepare cornbread mix according to package directions; spread over meat mixture. Bake at 425° for 15 to 20 minutes. Yield: 5 to 6 servings.
Mrs. S. Bruce Jones, Nashville, Tennessee.

SPICY MEATBALLS AND SAUSAGE

½ pound Italian sausage, sliced
1½ pounds lean ground beef
1 cup chopped onion
½ cup chopped green pepper
1 clove garlic, crushed
5 slices bacon, cooked and crumbled
2 jalapeño peppers, seeded and chopped
1 tablespoon chili powder
½ teaspoon salt
¼ teaspoon dried oregano leaves
2½ cups water
1 (12-ounce) can tomato paste
1 (16-ounce) can kidney beans, drained
Hot cooked rice

Brown sausage in a Dutch oven; remove and set aside, reserving 2 tablespoons drippings.

Shape ground beef into 60 (¾-inch) meatballs. Sauté meatballs, onion, green pepper, and garlic in reserved drippings until meatballs are browned, stirring gently. Add sausage, bacon, jalapeño peppers, and seasonings. Add water and tomato paste, stirring gently. Bring to a boil; cover and simmer for 1½ hours, stirring occasionally.

Stir kidney beans into meat mixture; cover and simmer 15 minutes. Serve over hot cooked rice. Yield: about 8 servings.
Mrs. Debbie Formosa, Nashville, Tennessee.

BEEF-VEGETABLE LOAF

2 pounds ground beef
2 cups soft breadcrumbs
½ cup shredded carrot
¼ cup sliced celery
¼ cup chopped onion
¼ cup chopped green pepper
2 eggs
1 teaspoon dry mustard
1 teaspoon parsley flakes
1½ teaspoons salt
½ teaspoon pepper
1 (16-ounce) can whole tomatoes, drained
    and chopped
¼ cup catsup
½ cup water

Combine first 12 ingredients mixing well. Place mixture in a 13- x 9- x 2-inch baking pan, and shape into a 10- x 6-inch loaf. Pour catsup over meat loaf; add water to pan. Bake at 350° for 1 hour and 15 minutes, basting occasionally with drippings. Yield: 8 servings.
Dorothy Davenport,
North Wilkesboro, North Carolina.

Summer Is Sandwich Time

Sandwiches are fun to serve, especially during the summer when meals tend to be more relaxed. But if you serve them often, you may find it a challenge to create new ways to prepare them. If you need inspiration, here are recipes you'll want to try. We offer a variety of fillings that include meat, cheese, vegetables, and fruit.

EGGSCLUSIVE SANDWICHES

4 hard-cooked eggs, chopped
½ cup finely chopped celery
1 tablespoon chopped parsley
1½ teaspoons chopped pimiento
¼ teaspoon salt
⅛ teaspoon pepper
⅓ cup mayonnaise or salad dressing
12 slices buttered toast
2 tomatoes, sliced
8 slices bacon, cooked
4 lettuce leaves

Combine eggs, celery, parsley, pimiento, salt, and pepper; add mayonnaise, and mix well. Spread 4 slices of toast with egg mixture; top each with

another slice of toast. Arrange tomato slices, bacon, and lettuce on top of toast. Top with remaining toast. Cut each sandwich into quarters to serve, using wooden picks to hold layers together. Yield: 4 sandwiches.
Mrs. James L. Twilley,
Macon, Georgia.

BAKED CHICKEN SANDWICHES

1 (10¾-ounce) can cream of chicken soup,
    undiluted
1½ cups diced cooked chicken
1 (4-ounce) jar chopped pimiento
¾ cup milk
3 tablespoons all-purpose flour
2 tablespoons minced onion
18 slices sandwich bread
Butter or margarine, softened
3 eggs, well beaten
3 cups finely crushed potato chips

Combine soup, chicken, pimiento, milk, flour, and onion in a medium saucepan. Cook over low heat until thickened and bubbly. Cool thoroughly.

Trim crust from bread. (Reserve crust for use in another recipe.) Spread butter on both sides of bread. Spread about ¼ cup chicken mixture on each of 9 slices of bread; top with remaining 9 slices. Wrap each sandwich tightly with foil and freeze until ready to use.

Remove sandwiches from freezer; unwrap and slice in half diagonally. Dip each half in egg, and dredge in potato chips. Arrange on a large baking sheet; bake at 325° for 30 minutes. Yield: 9 servings.
Mrs. James S. Tiffany,
Dallas, Texas.

ASPARAGUS GRILL SANDWICHES

8 slices sandwich bread
Butter or margarine
8 slices cooked ham or 16 slices cooked
    bacon
4 slices onion
4 slices tomato
16 asparagus spears, cooked
4 slices process American cheese
Cheese sauce (recipe follows)

Spread one side of each slice of bread with butter. Place 4 slices of bread, buttered side down, on a hot griddle. On each slice place 2 slices of ham or 4 slices of bacon, 1 slice of onion and tomato, 4 asparagus spears, and 1 slice of cheese. Place remaining 4 slices of

bread, buttered side up, on top of cheese. Cook until sandwiches are golden brown on bottom; turn sandwiches to brown top slices of bread. Pour cheese sauce over sandwiches before serving. Yield: 4 sandwiches.

Cheese Sauce:

2 tablespoons butter or margarine
2 tablespoons all-purpose flour
1 cup milk
1 cup (¼ pound) shredded sharp Cheddar
    cheese

Melt butter in a heavy saucepan over low heat. Add flour, and cook 1 minute, stirring constantly. Gradually add milk; cook over medium heat, stirring constantly, until thickened and bubbly. Add cheese, and stir until melted. Yield: about 1 cup.
Mrs. Ginger McVay,
Miami, Florida.

APPLE SANDWICHES

2 apples, finely chopped
¼ cup raisins
6 to 8 ounces cooked ham, finely diced
¼ cup (1 ounce) shredded mild Cheddar
    cheese
½ cup mayonnaise
2 teaspoons lemon juice
12 slices hot buttered toast
6 lettuce leaves

Combine apple, raisins, ham, cheese, mayonnaise, and lemon juice; mix well. Spread about ½ cup of apple mixture on each of 6 slices of toast. Top with lettuce leaves and remaining toast. Cut sandwiches in half, and serve immediately. Yield: 6 servings.
Mrs. Harvey Kidd,
Hernando, Mississippi.

Crab Crêpes, Baked Until Crisp

Mrs. Jack Boozer of Ormond Beach, Florida, prepares a scrumptious crêpe that will remind you of egg rolls. The crêpes are rolled around a filling of crabmeat, bean sprouts, celery, and green onion, then brushed with an egg wash that makes them crisp when baked. Their crowning touch is a rich Parmesan Cheese Sauce.

CRAB CREPES

1 cup all-purpose flour
1 teaspoon salt
3 eggs, beaten
1 cup water
1 egg, beaten
1 teaspoon water
Salad oil
Crabmeat Filling
Parmesan Cheese Sauce

Combine flour, salt, and 3 eggs; mix well. Add 1 cup water, stirring well. Refrigerate at least 2 hours. (This allows flour particles to swell and soften so crepes are light in texture.)

Combine 1 egg and 1 teaspoon water; beat well, and set aside.

Brush the bottom of a 6- or 7-inch crêpe pan or heavy skillet with salad oil; place over medium heat until just hot, not smoking.

Pour 2 tablespoons batter into pan; quickly tilt pan in all directions so batter covers the pan in a thin film. Cook about 1 minute. (If necessary, add 1 tablespoon water to batter to maintain thin consistency.)

Lift edge of crêpe to test for doneness. The crêpe is ready for flipping when it can be shaken loose from pan. Flip the crêpe, and cook for about 30 seconds on the other side. (This side is rarely more than spotty brown and is the side on which the filling is placed.) Place hot crêpe on a towel to cool; stack crêpes between layers of waxed paper to prevent sticking. Prepare filling while crêpes are cooling.

Spoon ¼ cup of filling in center of each crêpe; do not spread filling. Roll up crêpe, leaving ends open. Secure seam with a toothpick; brush each crêpe on all sides with egg mixture. Heat 1 inch salad oil to 360°; cook crêpes 2 to 3 at a time in hot oil until golden brown. Drain on paper towels.

Place crêpes on ungreased jellyroll pan. (There will be additional draining as crêpes bake.) Bake at 400° for 20 minutes. Prepare cheese sauce while crêpes are baking.

Spoon 1 tablespoon Parmesan Cheese Sauce over each crêpe; serve immediately. Yield: 16 crepes.

Crabmeat Filling:

1 pound crabmeat
1 cup drained bean sprouts
1 cup minced celery
1 tablespoon minced green onion
1 teaspoon monosodium glutamate
1 teaspoon salt

Combine all ingredients; stir well. Yield: about 4 cups.

Parmesan Cheese Sauce:

2 tablespoons butter or margarine
2 tablespoons all-purpose flour or instant-blending flour
1 cup warm milk
¼ cup grated Parmesan cheese
Salt and pepper to taste

Melt butter in a heavy saucepan over low heat, and blend in flour. Cook 3 or 4 minutes, stirring constantly.

Gradually add milk to flour mixture; cook over low heat, stirring constantly, 6 to 8 minutes or until thickened. Add cheese, salt, and pepper; stir until cheese melts. Yield: 1 cup.

Pick A Cherry Cake Or Salad

From our readers come two recipes making delicious use of fresh, juicy cherries. Paige Smith of Chattanooga, Tennessee, contributes an elegant fruit salad drizzled with a sherry dressing; an enticing cake recipe comes from Eleanor Brandt of Arlington, Texas.

The taste test is the best indicator of good-quality cherries. They should be of good flavor and juicy. When selecting on the basis of appearance, look for fresh, firm, well-matured, and well-colored fruit.

CHERRY CAKE

1 teaspoon soda
½ cup buttermilk
¾ cup butter or margarine, softened
1½ cups sugar
3 eggs
2 cups all-purpose flour
½ teaspoon ground allspice
½ teaspoon ground cloves
1 cup pitted fresh Bing cherries, halved

Stir soda into buttermilk; set aside.

Cream butter and sugar until light and fluffy. Add eggs, one at a time, beating well after each addition. Add buttermilk mixture; beat well.

Combine dry ingredients; stir into creamed mixture, blending well. Stir in cherries. Spoon batter into a greased 13- x 9- x 2-inch baking pan. Bake at 350° for 35 to 40 minutes or until cake tests done. Yield: 12 to 15 servings.

Fresh cherries are at their peak in July. Enjoy this juicy, inviting fruit right from the basket or in a delicious salad or cake.

CHERRY SALAD WITH SHERRY DRESSING

1 cup chopped fresh Bing cherries
½ cup chopped celery
½ cup chopped walnuts
1 cup fresh pineapple chunks, chilled, or 1 (8-ounce) can pineapple chunks, drained and chilled
Lettuce leaves
Sherry Salad Dressing
Mint sprigs (optional)

Combine cherries, celery, and walnuts; stir well and chill. Stir in pineapple just before serving (cherry juice will discolor pineapple). Serve fruit on lettuce leaves. Top with Sherry Salad Dressing; garnish with mint sprigs, if desired. Yield: 4 to 6 servings.

Sherry Salad Dressing:

3 tablespoons vegetable oil
2 tablespoons commercial sour cream
1 tablespoon lemon juice
1 tablespoon cream sherry
¼ teaspoon sugar
Pinch of salt
Dash of white pepper

Combine all ingredients; beat well. Yield: about ½ cup.

Tip: Most fruits are best stored in the refrigerator. Allow melons, avocados, and pears to ripen at room temperature; then refrigerate. Berries should be sorted to remove imperfect fruit before refrigerating; wash and hull just before serving.

Ice Cream Bursting With Coconut

Here's an ice cream that is an irresistible blend of freshly grated coconut and coconut milk in a rich, creamy custard. Fresh Coconut Ice Cream is so delicious, it's well worth the time it takes to prepare the fresh coconut.

To make the task easier, use this procedure: Puncture the eyes of the coconut with a nail or ice pick, and drain off the milk. Tap the shell with a hammer or meat cleaver about a third of the way down from the eyes, turning the shell as you tap. When the shell is cracked, pry it open and remove the meat in pieces, using a table knife. Peel the meat, and wipe it with a cloth; then grate.

Once all ingredients are combined, the custard for Fresh Coconut Ice Cream gets more than the overnight chilling recommended for ice cream custards. It's chilled for three days prior to freezing to ensure extra smoothness. Should there be leftovers, Fresh Coconut Ice Cream will keep well for about a month when it is stored in an airtight container.

FRESH COCONUT ICE CREAM

3 cups whipping cream
2 cups half-and-half
1 coconut
1 (5.33-ounce) can evaporated milk
1½ cups sugar

Scald whipping cream and half-and-half; let cool completely.

Puncture coconut; drain, reserving milk. Crack coconut, and remove meat; peel, and finely grate. Combine grated coconut, reserved coconut milk, and whipping cream mixture with remaining ingredients; mix well. Cover and place in refrigerator for 3 days, stirring occasionally.

Pour mixture into container of a 1-gallon hand-turned or electric freezer. Freeze according to manufacturer's instructions. Yield: about 3½ quarts.

Marjorie F. Jeffrey,
Gainesville, Florida.

A New Twist For Pork

A delicious recipe for pork blade steaks comes from Mrs. Jack B. Long of Picayune, Mississippi. The steaks are smothered in sauce featuring basil and peach nectar and served on a bed of hot cooked rice.

PEACHY PORK STEAKS

4 to 6 (½-inch-thick) pork blade steaks
1 tablespoon vegetable oil
Salt and pepper
¾ teaspoon dried basil leaves
1 cup peach nectar
½ cup water
1 tablespoon vinegar
2 beef bouillon cubes or 2 teaspoons
   instant beef bouillon
Hot cooked rice
1 tablespoon cornstarch
1 tablespoon cold water
2 teaspoons fresh chopped parsley

Cook steaks in hot oil over medium heat in a large skillet until lightly browned on both sides. Drain off pan drippings. Sprinkle steaks with salt, pepper, and basil.

Combine peach nectar, ½ cup water, vinegar, and bouillon cubes; pour over steaks. Simmer 30 minutes or until steaks are tender. Place steaks over rice on a serving platter, and keep warm.

Combine cornstarch and water; add to nectar mixture and cook, stirring constantly, until thickened. Stir in parsley. Spoon half of gravy over steaks. Serve remaining gravy with steaks. Yield: 4 to 6 servings.

Candy In The Ice Cream

If there's any way to make homemade ice cream any better, ice cream fanciers will find it. Such is the case with Marilyn Poage of San Antonio, who has created a delectable variation that has bits of chocolate-peanut candy bars stirred into a rich vanilla custard. She calls her specialty Candy Crunch Ice Cream, and it has become a favorite of family and friends at summer parties.

Candy Crunch Ice Cream: a rich vanilla custard studded with bits of chocolate-peanut candy bars.

Rather than adding the candy before freezing, Marilyn suggests stirring it into the frozen custard after the dasher is removed. For best flavor and texture, allow the ice cream to ripen an hour before serving.

CANDY CRUNCH ICE CREAM

2 quarts milk
2 (14-ounce) cans sweetened condensed
   milk
1 pint whipping cream
2 to 3 teaspoons vanilla extract
1 (16-ounce) package SNICKERS Peanut
   Bars, cut into ¼-inch cubes

Combine all ingredients except candy, stirring well. Pour mixture into a 1-gallon hand-turned or electric freezer. Freeze according to the manufacturer's directions. Remove dasher, and stir in candy. Let ripen about 1 hour before serving. Yield: 1 gallon.

Capture the moist, sweet flavor of figs in Fig Preserves, Fig Cobbler, Fig Preserve Cake, or Fig Sauce to spoon over ice cream (page 140).

Above: Planned around an entrée of Catfish Parmesan, an appealing meal can be prepared in less than an hour. Menu and recipes appear on page 184.

Right: Tantalize summer appetites with an ice-cold glass of Gazpacho (page 172).

August

With the temperature still soaring, August is time to give meals a lift with cold soups. You will find them enjoyable as a first course, with a sandwich, or even as a frosty fruit dessert. In addition to their refreshing flavor, you will find them convenient as they can be prepared well ahead of serving time.

In this chapter you will also meet some gourmet cooks who share their culinary expertise. You should try your skill with the recipe for home-made green noodles—these can be made by hand or with a special pasta machine.

Since so many fresh vegetables are still in season, you will want to try them in a variety of dishes. Choices range from a corn-zucchini casserole to deep-fried carrot balls. Then whatever your plans may be, we offer six entrée selections to fit the occasion and satisfy the appetite.

Cooking With Gourmets

With more and more Southerners experimenting with different cuisines, it's not surprising that gourmet cooking groups are being formed throughout the region.

Such is the case in Chapel Hill, North Carolina, where five years ago several aspiring gourmet cooks enrolled in a nearby cooking school. Not only were their culinary skills enhanced, but friendships evolved because of their mutual interest in good food.

Alice Welsh and Bill Neal decided that the good times and good fellowship of gourmet cooking shouldn't be limited to a series of classes. So Alice and Bill along with Jenny Fitch, Carroll Kyser, Mary Hill, and Helen Gottschalk decided to meet twice a month in one of their homes to prepare, sample, and critique individual creations. According to Jenny, "All the group members are well traveled and enjoy experimenting and trying the foods of the world in greater depth."

At the group's occasional organizational meetings, they decide on specific foods they wish to concentrate on or perfect. It may be Italian food one month, while another meeting might be spent working with phyllo pastry or preparing hors d'oeuvres or Chicken Kiev for the freezer.

The menu for monthly luncheons is decided on by the hostess, but each member is responsible for bringing the ingredients and preparing a dish. Fortunately, all members have large kitchens that allow each cook a work area.

The meeting starts early in the day to allow people time for preparation and to learn each other's techniques. Although the dishes are prepared relatively fast, most require at least an hour of intricate work.

Lunch is a fitting reward for the morning's work. As you might expect, conversation centers around the food—pointers, praise, and a critique of the recipes and methods of preparation.

Some menus get added flavor from the fresh vegetables and herbs grown by several members in their home gardens. In fact, the group spends several meetings canning and freezing summer produce rather than preparing a complete menu.

When the gourmet group met at Jenny Fitch's, they prepared and enjoyed this gourmet luncheon.

Enjoy This Gourmet Luncheon

Iced Tomato Soup is the beginning of this delightful luncheon. For the main dish, homemade spinach pasta is tossed with a delicate shrimp-mushroom sauce.

Dessert is Savarin, a handsome cake laced with rum syrup.

Iced Tomato Soup
Green Pasta With Shrimp-
Mushroom Italienne
Salad Composée
Figure-8 Bread
Savarin
White Wine

ICED TOMATO SOUP

1 small onion, quartered
1 to 2 cloves garlic, pressed
3 to 4 large ripe tomatoes, peeled and seeded
1 to 2 tablespoons olive oil
1 teaspoon sugar
1 tablespoon paprika
Salt to taste
2 cups tomato juice
1 ripe avocado, diced
Fresh basil
Parmesan Rounds

Combine first 8 ingredients in container of electric blender; process until tomatoes are pureed. Remove from blender container, and chill overnight. Just before serving, return to blender container; process 30 seconds. Stir in avocado; garnish with basil. Serve with Parmesan Rounds. Yield: 4 cups.

Parmesan Rounds:

6 to 8 slices white bread
Melted butter or margarine
Grated Parmesan cheese

Cut each bread slice into four 1½-inch rounds. Place on cookie sheet, and bake at 250° for 10 minutes or until lightly browned. Remove from oven; brush with butter, and sprinkle with Parmesan cheese. Broil 2 inches from heat until golden brown (watch carefully). Yield: 2 to 2½ dozen.

Tip: Don't throw away cheese that has dried out or any small leftover pieces. Grate the cheese; cover and refrigerate for use in casseroles or other dishes.

GREEN PASTA WITH SHRIMP-MUSHROOM ITALIENNE

1 (10-ounce) package frozen chopped spinach
3 cups instant-blending flour
2 teaspoons salt
2 eggs
4 egg yolks
1 teaspoon butter or margarine
4 quarts boiling water
1½ teaspoons salt
1 tablespoon vegetable oil
Shrimp-Mushroom Italienne
Grated Parmesan cheese

Cook spinach according to package directions; drain. Place spinach on paper towels; squeeze until barely moist.

Combine flour and salt on a smooth surface, forming a mound. Make a well in center of flour mixture. Break 1 whole egg in well; draw part of flour into egg, using fingertips of one hand. Add remaining whole egg, and draw in additional flour. Add egg yolks, one at a time, and work in remaining flour to form a dough. Add spinach and butter; knead dough 10 minutes.

Shape dough into a ball, and place in a plastic bag; fasten bag securely. Let rest in refrigerator 1 hour.

Cut dough into 8 pieces, and return 7 pieces to bag. Pat remaining portion into a 4-inch square.

To shape pasta by machine: Pass each portion of dough through smooth rollers of pasta machine on widest setting. Fold dough into thirds. Repeat rolling and folding about 10 times or until dough becomes smooth and pliable.

Move rollers to the next to the widest setting; pass dough through rollers. Continue moving width gauge to narrower settings; pass dough through once at each setting, dusting with flour if needed.

Roll dough to thinness desired, about 1/16 inch. Pass each dough sheet through the cutting rollers of machine. Spread ribbons on dry towel; let stand 30 minutes or until dry.

To shape pasta by hand: Roll each portion of dough to 1/16-inch thickness on a lightly floured surface. Turn dough over occasionally.

Cut dough with sharp knife into ⅛- to ¼-inch strips. Place strips on a dry towel. Let stand, uncovered, 30 minutes or until pasta is dry.

Cooking: Combine boiling water, 1½ teaspoons salt, and vegetable oil in large Dutch oven; bring to a boil. Add pasta, and cook ½ to 1 minute. Drain;

toss lightly with Shrimp-Mushroom Italienne. Spoon into serving dish; sprinkle liberally with Parmesan cheese. Serve immediately. Yield: 6 to 8 servings.

Shrimp-Mushroom Italienne:

18 anchovy fillets
Olive oil
1½ pounds fresh mushrooms, sliced
Juice of 2 lemons
6 cloves garlic, pressed
2 to 3 tablespoons chopped fresh parsley
1¾ pounds medium shrimp, cooked, peeled, and deveined

Mash anchovies with a fork, and set aside.

Heat ⅜ inch olive oil in a large skillet, and add mushrooms; cook 1½ minutes, tossing mushrooms lightly and shaking pan often. Stir in anchovies and lemon juice; bring to a boil, and cook 1 minute. Stir in garlic; cook an additional minute. Add parsley and shrimp, tossing lightly. Yield: 6 to 8 servings.

SALAD COMPOSEE

2 medium carrots, cut into 2- x ¼-inch strips
⅓ head cauliflower, cut into flowerets
½ bunch broccoli, cut into bite-size pieces
6 ounces fresh whole green beans
1 large head Romaine or leaf lettuce
24 to 30 cherry tomatoes
6 small beets, diced
Vinaigrette Dressing

Cook first 4 vegetables separately in boiling salted water. Cook carrots, cauliflower, and broccoli 2 minutes; green beans 5 minutes or until crisp-tender.

Immerse vegetables in ice water to cool; drain. Chill vegetables.

Arrange lettuce on individual serving plates; arrange cauliflower, broccoli, green beans, and tomatoes separately on lettuce; garnish with carrots and beets. Pour dressing over vegetables. Yield: 6 servings.

Vinaigrette Dressing:

1 cup olive oil
¼ cup wine vinegar
2 teaspoons dry mustard
1 teaspoon salt
2 shallots or scallions, minced

Combine olive oil and vinegar; add remaining ingredients, mixing thoroughly. Yield: about 1½ cups.

FIGURE-8 BREAD

1½ cups warm water (105° to 115°)
1 teaspoon sugar
1 tablespoon plus 1¼ teaspoons dry yeast
4 to 4½ cups unbleached flour
1 tablespoon salt
1 egg
1 tablespoon cold water
Coarse sea salt or kosher salt

Combine warm water, sugar, and yeast in a large mixing bowl; stir slightly, and let stand 15 minutes.

Stir in 1½ cups flour into yeast mixture; cover and let rise in a warm place (85°) 1 hour or until doubled in bulk. Mixture will be bubbly. Add salt and enough of remaining flour to form a soft dough; mix well.

Turn dough out on a lightly floured surface, and knead about 5 minutes or until smooth and elastic. Let dough rest 10 minutes.

Divide dough in half; shape each half into a 20-inch cylinder. Gently transfer each cylinder to a greased 15½- x 12-inch baking sheet, shaping cylinders into 2 circles and joining the ends in the center of the pan to form an 8-shape. Pinch ends together to seal. Place an oiled ovenproof bowl in center of each circle to maintain shape.

Cover and let rise in a warm place 1 hour or until doubled in bulk.

Combine egg and 1 tablespoon water in a small bowl; beat well. Gently brush dough with egg mixture; sprinkle with sea salt.

Bake on upper shelf at 500° for 1 minute; reduce heat to 400°, and bake 20 minutes or until loaf sounds hollow when tapped. Cool on wire rack. Yield: 1 loaf.

SAVARIN

1 package dry yeast
¼ cup warm milk (105° to 115°)
2 cups all-purpose flour
¼ cup plus 2 tablespoons sugar
1 teaspoon salt
4 eggs
½ cup butter, softened
Rum syrup (recipe follows)
Light rum
About ½ cup apricot jam, melted
Whole fresh cherries, pitted and stems removed
Sliced fresh peaches
Fresh blueberries
Fresh raspberries
Fresh strawberries
Sweetened whipped cream
Mint sprigs

Combine yeast and milk in a small bowl; let stand 5 minutes.

Place flour in a large bowl; add yeast mixture, stirring gently but well. Add sugar, salt, and eggs; beat at low speed of electric mixer until smooth. Add butter, 1 tablespoon at a time, beating well after each addition.

Spoon dough into a greased 10-inch tube pan. Cover and let rise in a warm place (85°), free from drafts, 2½ to 3 hours or until doubled in bulk. Place pan in a 500° oven; immediately reduce heat to 350°, and bake 15 to 20 minutes.

Invert cake on a cooling rack, and place in a large, shallow pan. Spoon rum syrup over hot cake, also using syrup that drips through rack. Sprinkle lightly with rum. Place cake on serving plate before proceeding.

Brush apricot jam over cake; arrange fruit in an attractive design on top. Brush apricot jam over fruit to prevent darkening. Pipe or spoon sweetened whipped cream around base of cake. Garnish with mint sprigs. Yield: one 10-inch cake.

Rum Syrup:

1½ cups water
1 cup sugar
¼ cup light rum

Combine water and sugar in a small saucepan; bring to a boil, and cook until sugar dissolves. Cool and stir in rum. Yield: about 2 cups.

Tip: When making coffee for a crowd, allow 1 pound of coffee plus 2 gallons water for 40 servings.

Cold Soups Put The Chill On Summer

In appealing combinations of vegetables or fruits skillfully seasoned with herbs and spices, chilled soups have a lot to offer summer meals.

Served as an appetizer, cold soups spark taste buds with their light, delicate flavor. Teamed with a sandwich or salad, they make a satisfying meal. And when dessert is a frosty fruit soup, it's a fitting end to a delicious meal.

Cold soups are versatile, delicious, and refreshing without question, but they're also practical for a very good reason: quick and easy preparation, something that can be done in advance since they store so well.

To make cold soups even more appealing, serve them in stemmed glasses or crystal bowls nestled in crushed ice. And don't forget the garnishes—a sprinkling of chopped parsley, a dollop of sour cream, or slices of summer fresh fruit and vegetables.

GAZPACHO

1 (10¾-ounce) can tomato soup
1½ cups tomato juice
1¼ cups water
½ to 1 cup chopped cucumber
½ to 1 cup chopped tomato
½ cup chopped green pepper
½ cup chopped Spanish onion
2 tablespoons olive oil
2 tablespoons wine vinegar
1 tablespoon commercial Italian dressing
1 tablespoon lemon or lime juice
1 clove garlic, minced
¼ teaspoon salt
¼ teaspoon pepper
¼ teaspoon hot sauce
⅛ teaspoon garlic salt
Dash of Worcestershire sauce
Cucumber slices (optional)

Combine all ingredients, except cucumber slices, in a large bowl; chill at least 6 hours. Garnish each serving with cucumber slices, if desired. Yield: about 6 servings. *Mrs. H. Davis Collier, Jr., Jacksonville, Florida.*

SHRIMP-CUCUMBER BISQUE

1 medium leek or 8 large green onions
3 tablespoons butter or margarine
2 medium cucumbers, peeled and sliced
2 bay leaves
1½ tablespoons all-purpose flour
3 cups chicken broth
1 teaspoon salt
1 cucumber, peeled, seeded, and grated
1 cup whipping cream
1½ tablespoons lemon juice
1 tablespoon finely chopped parsley
⅔ cup finely chopped cooked shrimp
Commercial sour cream

Slice white portion of leek; reserve green top for another use.

Melt butter in a Dutch oven; add leek, 2 sliced cucumbers, and bay leaves. Cover and cook over low heat about 20 minutes or until vegetables are tender; remove bay leaves.

Stir flour into cucumber mixture; cook 1 minute, stirring constantly. Gradually add broth; cook over medium heat, stirring constantly, until thickened. Stir in salt.

Pour soup mixture into container of electric blender; process for 30 seconds. Chill soup at least 4 hours. Just before serving, stir in grated cucumber, whipping cream, lemon juice, parsley, and shrimp. Top each serving with a dollop of sour cream. Yield: 6 servings.
Lucile Freese, Nashville, Tennessee.

REFRESHING TOMATO CREAM SOUP

5 cups tomato juice
1 cup commercial sour cream
¾ cup diced cooked ham
¼ cup grated onion
2 tablespoons lemon juice
1 teaspoon grated lemon rind
½ teaspoon salt
Dash of pepper
1 cantaloupe, halved and seeded
1 cucumber
1 tablespoon dried basil leaves

Combine tomato juice and sour cream in a large bowl, stirring with a whisk. Add ham, onion, lemon juice, lemon rind, salt, and pepper; stir well. Cover and chill at least 4 hours.

Scoop out cantaloupe balls, or peel melon and cut into cubes. Peel cucumber, and scoop into balls. Combine melon, cucumber, and basil in a bowl. Cover and chill 3 hours.

To serve, spoon soup into individual bowls; garnish with chilled melon and cucumber balls. Yield: 6 to 8 servings.
Eleanor Brandt, Arlington, Texas.

FRUIT SOUP DESSERT

2 cups firmly packed mixed dried fruit
½ cup raisins
1 (3-inch) cinnamon stick
1 quart water
1 orange, cut into ¼-inch slices
1 (20-ounce) can unsweetened pineapple juice
½ cup currant jelly
¼ cup sugar
2 tablespoons quick-cooking tapioca
¼ teaspoon salt

Combine dried fruit, raisins, cinnamon, and water in a Dutch oven; bring to a boil. Reduce heat, and simmer until dried fruit is tender (about 15 minutes). Add remaining ingredients. Return to a boil; cover and reduce heat. Simmer 15 minutes, stirring occasionally. Chill thoroughly. Yield: 8 to 10 servings.
Maybelle Pinkston, Corryton, Tennessee.

■ Orange juice and champagne combine to make Carrot Orange Soup so light you'll want to sip it as a beverage.

CARROT-ORANGE SOUP

1 orange, cut into ¼-inch slices
6 cups orange juice, divided
1½ tablespoons chopped crystallized ginger
½ whole nutmeg, grated
2 cups finely grated carrots
¾ cup champagne
1 tablespoon grated orange rind

Combine orange slices, ½ cup orange juice, ginger, and nutmeg; simmer 3 to 5 minutes. Strain; discard orange slices. Cool orange juice mixture.

Combine orange juice mixture, remaining orange juice, and carrots; chill. Stir in champagne and orange rind; serve at once. Yield: 10 to 12 servings.
Norman Johnson, Birmingham, Alabama.

Crisp-tender cauliflower and carrots combine with crunchy, raw vegetables in Garden Salad with Tomato-Cream Cheese Dressing.

Salads Add A Lively Touch

If your meals could use a lift, we suggest rounding out the menu with one of these cool, refreshing salads. Choices range from crisp vegetable salads to plump fruits molded in gelatin.

Feta cheese and ripe olives add a lively touch to garden-fresh vegetables in Grecian Tossed Salad, while a light dressing nicely blends the flavors.

Garden Salad With Tomato-Cream Cheese Dressing owes its appeal to interesting textures—crisp-tender cauliflower and carrots combined with several crunchy, raw vegetables.

If the menu calls for fruit salad, consider these molded delights. Layered Berry Salad features a creamy filling between layers of raspberry and blueberry gelatin. In Double Grape-Cantaloupe Salad, white grape juice adds flavor, yet leaves the salad clear to show off the bright-orange cantaloupe and green grapes.

Tip: Many gelatin molds do not have their size stamped on them. You can determine the capacity of a mold by measuring the number of cups of water it will hold.

GARDEN SALAD WITH TOMATO-CREAM CHEESE DRESSING

1 small head cauliflower
1 cup diced cooked carrots, chilled
½ cup sliced radishes
3 slices Spanish or Bermuda onion, separated into rings
2 tomatoes, cut in wedges
1 small cucumber, sliced
1 cup diced celery
Lettuce leaves
Hard-cooked egg slices
1 small green pepper, sliced into rings
Tomato-Cream Cheese Dressing

Wash cauliflower, and break into flowerets. Cook, covered, in a small amount of boiling salted water about 5 to 8 minutes or until crisp-tender. Drain well, and chill.

Combine cauliflower and the next 6 ingredients. Spoon cauliflower mixture onto lettuce leaves; top with hard-cooked egg slices and green pepper rings. Serve with Tomato-Cream Cheese Dressing. Yield: 8 servings.

Tomato-Cream Cheese Dressing:

1 (3-ounce) package cream cheese, softened
½ cup condensed tomato soup, undiluted
2 teaspoons lemon juice
½ teaspoon salt
¾ cup mayonnaise

Combine all ingredients in container of an electric blender; process until smooth. Store in refrigerator until ready to use. Yield: 2 cups.

Mrs. Helen Mize,
Lakeland, Florida.

LAYERED BERRY SALAD

1 (3-ounce) package red raspberry-flavored gelatin
2 cups boiling water
2 envelopes unflavored gelatin
½ cup cold water
1 cup sugar
1 cup half-and-half
1 (8-ounce) package cream cheese, softened
1 teaspoon vanilla extract
½ cup chopped pecans
1 (3-ounce) package black raspberry-flavored gelatin
1 cup boiling water
1 (15-ounce) can blueberries, undrained

Dissolve red raspberry gelatin in 2 cups boiling water. Pour into a 9-inch square pan. Chill until firm.

Soften unflavored gelatin in cold water. Combine sugar and half-and-half in a saucepan. Heat but do not boil. Add softened gelatin, stirring until dissolved. Remove from heat; add cream cheese and vanilla, beating until smooth. Stir in pecans. Pour over red raspberry layer. Chill until firm.

Dissolve black raspberry gelatin in 1 cup boiling water; stir in blueberries. Allow to cool. Pour over cream cheese layer, and chill until firm. Cut into squares to serve. Yield: 9 servings.

Linda R. Bell,
Signal Mountain, Tennessee.

DOUBLE GRAPE-CANTALOUPE MOLD

3 envelopes unflavored gelatin
4½ cups white grape juice, divided
4 small cantaloupe wedges, peeled and halved crosswise
¾ cup diced cantaloupe
1 cup seedless green grapes
Lettuce leaves (optional)

Soften gelatin in 1 cup grape juice; let stand 5 minutes. Place over low heat, stirring until gelatin dissolves; stir in remaining grape juice. Chill until consistency of unbeaten egg white.

Pour a ⅛-inch layer of thickened gelatin into a lightly oiled 6-cup mold. Arrange cantaloupe wedges around edge. Chill until gelatin is firm and cantaloupe wedges set.

Fold diced cantaloupe and grapes into remaining gelatin; spoon into mold, and chill until firm. Unmold on lettuce leaves, if desired. Yield: 6 to 8 servings.

Mrs. Cindy Murphy,
Knoxville, Tennessee.

GRECIAN TOSSED SALAD

½ head iceberg lettuce, torn
4 to 5 endive leaves, torn
½ cucumber, thinly sliced
1 tomato, cut into wedges
¼ cup chopped green pepper
3 green onions, chopped
4 radishes, sliced
½ cup crumbled feta cheese
6 ripe olives, sliced
¼ cup olive oil
2 tablespoons vinegar
1 teaspoon whole oregano

Combine first 9 ingredients in a salad bowl. Combine remaining ingredients in a jar; screw lid tightly, and shake well. Toss with salad just before serving. Yield: 8 servings. *Mrs. Mary Pappas, Richmond, Virginia.*

Beverages For A Summer Day

Fresh fruits and juices, ginger ale, and rum combine in these recipes and add up to lots of new ideas for summer coolers. All are as appealing to the eye as to the taste.

If you want to fill the punch bowl for a crowd, try Bubbling Jade Punch or refreshing Pineapple Punch. For a thicker, icier punch filled with bananas, cherries, and crushed pineapple, try Tropical Ice.

If you enjoy the taste of rum, serve Easy Rum Slush; its light tart taste will make it an all-summer favorite.

FOUR-FRUIT REFRESHER

3 cups cranberry juice, chilled
1½ cups apple juice, chilled
¾ cup orange juice, chilled
¼ cup plus 2 tablespoons lemon juice, chilled
1½ (33.8-ounce) bottles ginger ale, chilled
Orange slices (optional)

Combine juice and ginger ale; stir gently. Serve over ice cubes, and garnish with orange slices, if desired. Yield: 12 cups. *Susanne L. Webb, Roanoke, Virginia.*

BUBBLING JADE PUNCH

1 (3-ounce) package lime-flavored gelatin
1 cup boiling water
2 cups cold water
1 (6-ounce) can frozen lemonade concentrate, thawed and undiluted
1 cup pineapple juice, chilled
1 (33.8-ounce) bottle ginger ale, chilled
Whole fresh strawberries (optional)

Dissolve gelatin in boiling water; stir in cold water, lemonade concentrate, and pineapple juice; chill well.
Pour mixture into punch bowl; add ginger ale. Garnish with strawberries, if desired. Yield: about 10 cups.
Mrs. Kathryn M. Elmore, Demopolis, Alabama.

EASY RUM SLUSH

1 (6-ounce) can frozen orange juice concentrate, undiluted
1 (6-ounce) can frozen lemonade concentrate, undiluted
1 to 1¼ cups light rum
Ice cubes

Combine orange juice concentrate, lemonade concentrate, and rum in container of electric blender. Add ice to within 1 inch of container top; blend well. Yield: about 5½ cups.
Mrs. Paul E. Kline, Palm Beach Gardens, Florida.

PINK COCONUT FROST

1 (6-ounce) can frozen pink lemonade concentrate, undiluted
¾ to 1½ cups gin
3 tablespoons cream of coconut
1 to 2 tablespoons maraschino cherry juice
16 to 20 ice cubes
Maraschino cherries

Combine all ingredients except cherries in container of electric blender; process until frothy. Serve garnished with a maraschino cherry. Yield: about 4 cups. *Mrs. William Evans, Birmingham, Alabama.*

Tip: Place fresh cranberries in the refrigerator unwashed; they can be kept in the refrigerator for one to four weeks. Wash before using.

SPICED GRAPE TEA

2½ tablespoons tea leaves
1 teaspoon whole allspice
10 cups boiling water
2 cups sugar
2 cups grape juice
Juice of 4 lemons
Juice of 2 oranges

Stir tea leaves and allspice into boiling water; steep 5 minutes. Strain tea; stir in sugar and fruit juices. Cool; serve over ice cubes. Yield: 12 cups.
Note: Tea may be served hot.
Mrs. W. Snellgrove, LaGrange, Georgia.

PINEAPPLE PUNCH

1 (46-ounce) can pineapple juice, chilled
3 cups cranberry juice cocktail, chilled
1 (33.8-ounce) bottle ginger ale, chilled
1 cup light rum (optional)
1 lemon, thinly sliced

Combine pineapple juice, cranberry juice cocktail, and ginger ale in a punch bowl. Stir in rum, if desired. Add lemon slices. Yield: about 12 cups.
Mrs. Leisa Kilgore, Gardendale, Alabama.

TROPICAL ICE

2 cups mashed bananas
1 (20-ounce) can crushed pineapple, undrained
1 (4-ounce) jar maraschino cherries, drained and chopped
2 cups orange juice
1 tablespoon lemon juice
1 cup sugar
1 (33.8-ounce) bottle ginger ale, chilled

Combine first 6 ingredients; stir well, and freeze until firm.
To serve, partially thaw fruit mixture. Place in punch bowl, and break into chunks with a fork. Add ginger ale; stir until slushy. Yield: 12 cups.
Becky Barnett, West Point, Mississippi.

Stuff Lettuce With Flavor

If you're looking for a lettuce salad that's packed with flavor, try Cheesy Stuffed Lettuce, a recipe shared by Mrs. M. L. Shannon of Fairfield, Alabama.

A head of iceberg lettuce is hollowed out, then stuffed with a pimiento cheese and ham filling lightly seasoned with curry. After thorough chilling, it's sliced into wedges and served with your favorite French dressing.

Besides being an appealing salad course, Cheesy Stuffed Lettuce is also appropriate as a light main dish when sliced into larger portions.

CHEESY STUFFED LETTUCE

1 medium head iceberg lettuce
1 cup (¼ pound) shredded Cheddar
   cheese
½ cup mayonnaise
¼ teaspoon curry powder
½ cup chopped cooked ham
2 tablespoons chopped celery
2 tablespoons chopped pimiento
¼ cup minced fresh parsley
Commercial French dressing

Wash lettuce, and remove core. Hollow out center of lettuce, leaving a ½- to ¾-inch shell; set aside.

Combine cheese, mayonnaise, and curry powder in a mixing bowl; mix well. Stir in ham, celery, pimiento, and parsley; spoon into lettuce shell, and chill several hours. To serve, slice into wedges; top with French dressing. Yield: 6 servings.

Two Nectarine Favorites

Although nectarines can be used in recipes calling for peaches, they are not "fuzzless peaches." Here nectarines add their natural goodness to a spicy butter and a lively version of chicken salad.

Nectarine selections developed in recent years produce larger, firmer, more desirable fruit. Since most of the new selections have full, red color before they mature, color is not a good indication of maturity. Select nectarines that are well rounded and bright looking. Avoid any hard, dull, or slightly shriveled fruit—signs they were picked before maturity.

NECTARINE CHICKEN SALAD

3 cups cubed cooked chicken
2 cups peeled, cubed nectarines
¼ cup chopped green pepper
1 (8-ounce) can water chestnuts, drained
   and sliced
1 tablespoon lemon juice
1 tablespoon sugar
¾ teaspoon salt
¼ teaspoon pepper
¼ teaspoon rosemary
½ cup mayonnaise
Lettuce leaves (optional)
Fresh nectarine slices (optional)

Combine first 10 ingredients, tossing well. Chill thoroughly. Serve on a bed of lettuce and garnish with nectarine slices, if desired. Yield: 6 servings.
Ella M. Crockett,
Murfreesboro, Tennessee.

NECTARINE BUTTER

4 pounds nectarines, quartered
2 cups sugar
2 teaspoons grated lemon rind
¼ cup lemon juice
½ teaspoon ground cloves
2 teaspoons ground cinnamon

Place nectarines in a large Dutch oven; cover with water, and bring to a boil. Reduce heat, and simmer 30 to 40 minutes or until tender. Drain. Place nectarines in container of electric blender, and process until pureed; then press mixture through a sieve or food mill. Stir in sugar, lemon rind, lemon juice, and spices; mix well.

Pour nectarine mixture into a 13- x 9- x 2-inch baking pan; bake at 300° for 1 hour and 45 minutes or until thickened, stirring about every 20 minutes. Spoon quickly into hot sterilized jelly glasses, leaving ⅛-inch headspace; top with lids, and screw metal bands tight. Process in boiling-water bath 10 minutes. Yield: about 4 half pints.
Mrs. E. T. Williams,
Baton Rouge, Louisiana.

Special Desserts Make Smooth Endings

The just-right dessert can turn a meal into something special. This array of desserts, all varied in flavors and ingredients, is absolutely irresistible.

If your menu calls for a light, informal dessert, select simple Date Nut Cake. For an extra-rich treat, try Crunchy Peanut Butter Parfaits or Tropical Sour Cream Pie.

DAFFODIL SPONGE CAKE

1 cup sifted cake flour
½ cup sugar, divided
4 egg yolks
½ teaspoon lemon extract
10 egg whites, at room temperature
1 teaspoon cream of tartar
½ teaspoon salt
¾ cup sugar
½ teaspoon vanilla extract

Sift flour and ½ cup sugar together 3 times; set aside.

Beat egg yolks at high speed of electric mixer 4 minutes or until thick and lemon colored. Add lemon extract; beat at medium speed 5 more minutes or until thick. Set aside.

Beat egg whites until foamy. Add cream of tartar and salt; beat until soft peaks form. Add ¾ cup sugar, 2 tablespoons at a time; continue beating 5 minutes or until stiff peaks form.

Sprinkle one-fourth of flour mixture over egg whites; gently fold in with a rubber spatula. Repeat procedure with remaining flour, adding one-fourth of the mixture at a time. Divide egg white mixture in half.

Fold vanilla extract into half of the egg white mixture. Gently fold the beaten egg yolks into remaining egg white mixture.

Pour half of the yellow mixture into an ungreased 10-inch tube pan, then gently add half of the white mixture; repeat procedure.

Bake at 350° for 55 to 60 minutes or until cake springs back when touched lightly with fingers. Invert cake; cool (about 40 minutes). Loosen cake from sides of pan, using a small metal spatula. Remove cake from pan; place on a serving platter. Yield: one 10-inch cake.
Mrs. Mabel B. Couch,
Chelsea, Oklahoma.

PEPPERMINT WAFER DESSERT

1½ teaspoons unflavored gelatin
2 tablespoons cold water
1 (8-ounce) package soft-type peppermint
 sticks
½ cup whipping cream
1½ cups whipping cream, whipped
1 (8½-ounce) package chocolate wafers

Soften gelatin in water; set aside.
Combine candy and ½ cup whipping cream in top of a double boiler; cook, stirring often, until candy melts. Add gelatin, stirring until dissolved. Chill mixture until slightly thickened; fold in whipped cream.

Line bottom of a 9-inch square pan with wafers; break additional wafers in half and stand around the sides of pan. Spoon half the peppermint mixture into pan; cover with a layer of wafers. Spoon remaining peppermint mixture over top. Chill dessert at least 8 hours. Yield: 9 servings.

Mrs. Mildred Sherrer,
Bay City, Texas.

CRUNCHY PEANUT BUTTER PARFAITS

¾ cup quick-cooking oats, uncooked
⅓ cup firmly packed brown sugar
¼ cup chopped peanuts
3 tablespoons butter or margarine, melted
½ cup firmly packed brown sugar
¼ cup all-purpose flour
2 cups milk
2 egg yolks, beaten
⅔ cup peanut butter
½ teaspoon vanilla extract

Combine oats, ⅓ cup brown sugar, peanuts, and butter, stirring well. Spread oat mixture in an ungreased 13- x 9- x 2-inch baking pan; bake at 350° for 15 minutes, stirring occasionally. Cool; crumble.

Combine ½ cup brown sugar, flour, milk, and egg yolks in a saucepan; cook, stirring constantly, over low heat until thickened and bubbly. Cook 1 additional minute, stirring constantly. Stir in peanut butter and vanilla. Cover surface with waxed paper; chill.

Spoon alternate layers of peanut butter pudding and oat mixture into 4 parfait glasses. Yield: 4 servings.

Mrs. William T. Hunter,
Princeton, Kentucky.

DATE NUT CAKE

1 cup sugar
½ cup vegetable oil
4 eggs
1 cup all-purpose flour
1 teaspoon salt
1 (1-pound) package pitted dates
4 cups pecan halves

Combine sugar, oil, and eggs, mixing well. Stir in flour and salt; add dates and nuts. Spoon mixture into a greased and floured 9- x 5- x 3-inch loafpan. Place in a cold oven; set oven at 300°, and bake 2 hours. Remove cake from pan immediately, and cool on a wire rack. Yield: one 9-inch loaf.

Mrs. Pete Beckham,
Philadelphia, Mississippi.

TROPICAL SOUR CREAM PIE

1 (8-ounce) can crushed pineapple,
 undrained
1 tablespoon sugar
1 cup milk
1 (4¾-ounce) package vanilla-flavored
 pudding and pie filling mix
1 (8-ounce) carton commercial sour cream
1½ cups flaked coconut, divided
1 medium banana, sliced
1 baked 9-inch pastry shell
1 (4½-ounce) carton frozen whipped
 topping, thawed

Combine pineapple, sugar, milk, and pudding mix in a medium saucepan; cook over medium heat, stirring constantly, until mixture comes to a boil. Remove from heat. Add a small amount of hot mixture to sour cream, mixing well; add sour cream mixture to remaining hot mixture, mixing well. Stir in 1 cup coconut; cool.

Place banana slices in pastry shell. Spoon custard over bananas; spread with whipped topping, and sprinkle with remaining ½ cup coconut. Chill at least 3 hours before serving. Yield: one 9-inch pie.

Gailya Godfrey,
Charlotte, North Carolina.

Tip: To help a pastry shell keep its shape while baking, line it with fitted waxed paper and fill with dried peas or rice. Bake about 5 minutes or until shell sets; remove the paper and dried peas or rice.

Melons Make It Light And Cool

Along with the bounty of cantaloupe, watermelon, and honeydew melon comes an enticing array of recipes for enjoying them.

To begin a meal, serve Melon Balls in Watermelon Sauce. Watermelon juice is mixed with rum and sugar and poured over bite-size pieces of cantaloupe and honeydew melon.

Melons can also end a meal as deliciously as they begin it, with rich desserts like Cantaloupe Cream Pie and Cantaloupe Ice Cream.

Of course, summer fruit salads wouldn't be complete without melons. We suggest Melon-Citrus Mingle and, for a nice change of pace, Cantaloupe Cooler Salad. In this salad, juicy chunks of cantaloupe are piled on lettuce leaves and topped with thin slices of onion and crumbled bacon. As different as the flavors are, they're nicely mingled with Blender Poppy Seed Dressing.

CANTALOUPE COOLER SALAD

1 large or 2 small cantaloupes
Lettuce leaves
1 large onion, thinly sliced and separated
 into rings
½ pound (about 12 slices) bacon, cooked
 and crumbled
Blender Poppy Seed Dressing

Peel cantaloupe, and cut into bite-size pieces; arrange on lettuce leaves. Top cantaloupe with onion and crumbled bacon. Drizzle dressing over salad. Yield: 8 servings.

Blender Poppy Seed Dressing:

¾ cup vegetable oil
⅓ cup honey
¼ cup red wine vinegar
2 tablespoons poppy seeds
1 tablespoon minced onion
1 tablespoon Dijon mustard
1 teaspoon salt

Combine all ingredients in container of electric blender; process on low speed 30 seconds. Chill thoroughly; stir well before serving. Yield: 1¼ cups.

Beverly Goodwin,
Dillon, South Carolina.

MELON-CITRUS MINGLE

1 honeydew melon, halved
1 large cantaloupe, halved
10 pink grapefruit, peeled and sectioned
10 oranges, peeled and sectioned
Juice of 4 to 6 oranges
1 pineapple, peeled and cubed, or 1 (20-ounce) can pineapple chunks in own juice
6 to 8 medium bananas, cut into ¼-inch slices
½ pound Bing cherries, pitted, or 1 (2-ounce) jar maraschino cherries, drained

Scoop out melon balls, or peel melons and cut into cubes.

Combine all ingredients in a large plastic container; stir gently to coat bananas with fruit juices and prevent darkening. Cover tightly; chill well. Yield: about 20 servings.

Note: May be stored in refrigerator 1 week. *Mrs. Robert W. Dilks, Knoxville, Arkansas.*

CANTALOUPE CREAM PIE

1 cup sugar
2 tablespoons all-purpose flour
3 eggs, beaten
1 cup pureed cantaloupe
1 teaspoon vanilla extract
2 tablespoons butter or margarine
1 baked 8-inch pastry shell
1 cup whipping cream, whipped

Combine sugar and flour in a saucepan; add eggs, mixing well. Stir in cantaloupe puree. Cook over medium heat 8 to 10 minutes, stirring constantly, until mixture boils and thickens. Remove from heat, and stir in vanilla and butter. Cool.

Pour filling into pastry shell; spread evenly with whipped cream. Chill. Yield: one 8-inch pie.

Kathleen D. Stone, Houston, Texas.

CANTALOUPE ICE CREAM

6 egg yolks, beaten
1 cup milk
1¼ cups sugar
2 large ripe cantaloupes, peeled and pureed
¼ cup lemon juice
2 cups whipping cream

Combine egg yolks, milk, and sugar in a large mixing bowl; beat until sugar

is dissolved. Add remaining ingredients, mixing well. Pour into freezer trays. Cover and freeze about 1 hour or until firm around edges.

Spoon mixture into a mixing bowl, and beat on medium speed of an electric mixer 2 to 3 minutes or until smooth. Return mixture to freezer trays; cover and freeze until firm. Yield: 12 to 15 servings. *Marian Zeigler, Orangeburg, South Carolina.*

MELON BALLS IN WATERMELON SAUCE

¼ small watermelon
½ cup sugar
2 tablespoons light rum
2 cups cantaloupe balls
4 cups honeydew melon balls

Cut watermelon into cubes; press cubes through a strainer or food mill to make 2 cups juice.

Combine watermelon juice, sugar, and rum in a large bowl; stir until sugar dissolves. Add melon balls, tossing well. Cover and chill 2 hours or overnight. Yield: 8 servings.

Mrs. James W. Bachus, Austin, Texas.

A Fresh Peach Of A Cake

Summer brings a bountiful crop of fresh fruit to Southern tables, and peaches are one of the alltime favorites. To help you enjoy their juicy goodness, we've selected an array of recipes ranging from salad to desserts.

Peachy Picnic Cake features a sweet coconut glaze atop fresh peach slices, while Macaroon-Stuffed Peaches are peach halves stuffed with a luscious macaroon-peach filling.

For a special summertime entrée, there are chicken breasts stuffed with peaches and cashews and topped with Creamy Fresh Peach Sauce. Our salad selection tops peach halves with a creamy pineapple-coconut mixture.

PEACH-STUFFED CHICKEN BREASTS

6 whole chicken breasts, boned and skinned
1½ teaspoons salt, divided
⅛ teaspoon pepper
3 fresh peaches, peeled and diced
½ cup chopped onion
½ cup coarsely chopped cashews
⅛ teaspoon ground ginger
½ cup butter or margarine
Creamy Fresh Peach Sauce

Place each chicken breast on a sheet of waxed paper. Flatten to ¼-inch thickness, using a meat mallet or rolling pin; sprinkle 1 teaspoon salt and pepper over inside of breasts. Set chicken aside.

Combine peaches, onion, cashews, and ginger, stirring well. Place ¼ cup filling in center of each breast; fold side of chicken over filling and secure with a toothpick.

Melt butter in a 13- x 9- x 2-inch baking pan; place breasts top side down in butter. Bake at 375° for 25 minutes; turn chicken and bake 20 additional minutes. Serve with Creamy Fresh Peach Sauce. Yield: 6 servings.

Creamy Fresh Peach Sauce:

2 fresh peaches, peeled and sliced
1 (8-ounce) carton commercial sour cream
½ cup firmly packed brown sugar
2 teaspoons Dijon mustard
1 tablespoon brandy
¼ teaspoon salt

Combine all ingredients in a saucepan; place over low heat for 8 minutes or until heated thoroughly. Yield: 2 cups. *Mrs. James S. Tiffany, Dallas, Texas.*

EASY PEACH SALAD SUPREME

½ cup crushed pineapple, drained
½ cup shredded coconut
½ cup cottage cheese
½ cup commercial sour cream
4 fresh peaches, peeled, seeded, and halved

Combine pineapple, coconut, cottage cheese, and sour cream in a medium bowl, stirring well. Chill.

Fill peach halves with mixture and serve immediately. Yield: 8 servings.

Miss Kathy Strode, Tompkinsville, Kentucky.

MACAROON-STUFFED PEACHES

6 firm, ripe, fresh peaches
1 cup coconut macaroon crumbs
2 tablespoons sugar
¼ cup melted unsalted butter
2 egg yolks, beaten

Dip peaches, 2 at a time, into deep boiling water; boil 20 seconds. Using a slotted spoon, lift peaches from boiling water, and dip into cold water. Carefully peel skin from peaches. Cut peaches in half lengthwise; discard seeds. Remove and reserve enough pulp to leave a ¼-inch shell. Set the peach shells aside.

Chop pulp; combine pulp and remaining ingredients, stirring well. Spoon macaroon mixture into peach shells; place in a buttered 12- x 8- x 2-inch baking dish. Bake at 375° for 25 minutes or until barely tender; baste occasionally with pan drippings. May be served hot or cold. Yield: 6 servings.

T. H. Wagener,
Augusta, Georgia.

PEACHY PICNIC CAKE

¼ cup butter or margarine
1 cup sugar
2 eggs
¾ teaspoon almond extract
1¾ cups all-purpose flour
2 teaspoons baking powder
½ teaspoon salt
¾ cup milk
1½ cups thinly sliced fresh peaches
About 2 tablespoons lemon juice
½ cup butter or margarine
¾ cup firmly packed brown sugar
½ cup flaked coconut
2 tablespoons half-and-half
1 teaspoon almond extract

Combine ¼ cup butter and sugar; beat well. Add eggs, one at a time, beating well after each addition. Add ¾ teaspoon almond extract; mix well.

Combine flour, baking powder, and salt; mix well. Add to creamed mixture alternately with milk, beginning and ending with flour mixture. Spoon into a well-greased 9-inch square baking pan. Bake at 350° for 30 minutes or until cake tests done. Cool cake slightly on a wire rack.

Combine peaches and lemon juice; gently stir peaches to coat all surfaces with juice. Drain peaches; arrange on top of cake.

Melt butter in a small saucepan. Add brown sugar, coconut, half-and-half, and 1 teaspoon almond extract; mix well. Pour butter mixture over peaches, spreading evenly to sides of pan. Broil 2 minutes or until topping is bubbly and lightly browned. Cool slightly, and cut into squares. Yield: 9 to 12 servings.

Kay Martin,
Clanton, Alabama.

Fresh Vegetables For Every Taste

Whether you like them fried, baked in a casserole, or stir-fried, nothing tops the flavor of fresh vegetables.

In Corn-Zucchini Bake, two summer favorites are combined with Swiss cheese and onion in a colorful casserole. Our Yellow Squash Casserole tops a layer of the squash with green pepper, onion, pimiento, and mayonnaise.

If you like eggplant, try deep frying small breaded fingers of the vegetable, or enjoy Eggplant with Almonds, this time sliced, breaded, and baked.

CORN-ZUCCHINI BAKE

1 pound zucchini, cut into ½-inch slices
¼ cup chopped onion
1 tablespoon butter or margarine
2 cups cooked fresh corn
2 eggs, beaten
1 cup (¼ pound) shredded Swiss cheese
¼ to ½ teaspoon salt
¼ cup breadcrumbs
2 tablespoons grated Parmesan cheese
1 tablespoon melted butter or margarine
Cherry tomatoes
Parsley

Cook zucchini in a small amount of water until tender; drain and mash.

Sauté onion in 1 tablespoon butter until tender. Combine zucchini, onion, corn, eggs, Swiss cheese, and salt; mix well. Pour mixture into a greased 1-quart casserole.

Combine breadcrumbs, Parmesan cheese, and melted butter; sprinkle over zucchini mixture. Bake at 350° for 40 minutes. Garnish with cherry tomatoes and parsley. Yield: 6 servings.

Mrs. E. L. Hackman,
Hagerstown, Maryland.

CARROT BALLS

1 pound carrots, cooked and mashed
2 eggs, well beaten
2 tablespoons all-purpose flour
1 tablespoon butter or margarine, melted
½ teaspoon salt
Hot vegetable oil

Combine all ingredients except vegetable oil; mix well. Shape into 1-inch balls, and fry in deep oil until golden brown; drain. Yield: about 6 servings.

Mrs. Irma Eisner,
St. Petersburg, Florida.

CELERY AND CHEESE CASSEROLE

6 cups ½-inch slices celery
¼ cup water
3 tablespoons butter or margarine, divided
½ teaspoon dried tarragon leaves, crushed
2 tablespoons all-purpose flour
½ cup milk
1 (10¾-ounce) can cream of chicken soup, undiluted
½ cup shredded Cheddar cheese
¼ teaspoon paprika

Combine celery, water, 1 tablespoon butter, and tarragon in a medium saucepan. Bring to a boil; cover and simmer 10 minutes. Pour mixture into a greased 2-quart shallow casserole; set aside.

Melt remaining 2 tablespoons butter in a heavy saucepan over low heat; add flour, stirring until smooth. Cook 1 minute, stirring constantly. Gradually add milk; cook over medium heat, stirring constantly, until thickened and bubbly.

Add soup and cheese to white sauce, stirring until smooth. Spoon sauce evenly over celery mixture, and sprinkle with paprika. Bake, uncovered, at 350° for 15 minutes or until bubbly. Yield: about 6 to 8 servings.

Mrs. Sarah S. Ramsey,
Greensboro, North Carolina.

FRIED EGGPLANT

1 medium eggplant
⅔ cup fine, dry breadcrumbs
⅓ cup grated Parmesan cheese
1½ to 2 teaspoons salt
½ teaspoon celery salt
¼ teaspoon pepper
2 eggs
2 tablespoons milk

Peel eggplant, and cut into finger-size strips. Set aside.

Combine breadcrumbs, cheese, salt, celery salt, and pepper; stir well. Combine eggs and milk; mix well. Roll eggplant strips in breadcrumb mixture; dip in egg mixture, and roll again in breadcrumb mixture. Fry in hot oil (375°) until golden brown. Drain on paper towels. Yield: about 6 servings.

Mrs. Mae McClaugherty,
Marble Falls, Texas.

EGGPLANT WITH ALMONDS

1 medium eggplant
Salt and pepper
1 egg, beaten
1 cup Italian-style breadcrumbs
2 cups (½ pound) shredded mozzarella
   cheese
¾ cup sliced almonds

Peel eggplant, and cut into ½-inch-thick slices. Salt and pepper eggplant lightly. Dip each slice in egg; coat with breadcrumbs. Place slices in a buttered 15- x 10-x 1-inch baking pan. Bake at 375° for 15 minutes. Sprinkle cheese and almonds over eggplant slices. Bake 5 more minutes. Yield: 4 to 6 servings.

Gayla Scott,
Durham, North Carolina.

YELLOW SQUASH CASSEROLE

¼ cup melted butter or margarine
1 pound yellow squash, thinly sliced
½ teaspoon salt
¼ teaspoon pepper
1 egg, beaten
½ cup mayonnaise
¼ cup chopped green pepper
⅓ cup chopped onion
1 tablespoon chopped pimiento
1 teaspoon sugar
½ cup shredded mild cheese

Pour melted butter into a 1½-quart casserole; add squash, and sprinkle with salt and pepper.

Combine egg, mayonnaise, green pepper, onion, pimiento, and sugar; mix well, and pour over squash. Sprinkle evenly with cheese; bake at 350° for 35 to 40 minutes. Yield: 4 to 5 servings.

Dale W. Barr,
Birmingham, Alabama.

CHINESE SPINACH

1½ to 2 pounds fresh spinach
2 tablespoons vegetable oil
1 tablespoon soy sauce
1 small onion, thinly sliced
½ pound fresh mushrooms, sliced
1 cup canned bean sprouts, drained

Wash and drain spinach; tear into bite-size pieces.

Combine oil and soy sauce in a skillet or wok. Add onion and mushrooms; cook, stirring occasionally, until tender. Add spinach and bean sprouts; cook about 2 to 3 minutes until spinach is crisp-tender, stirring occasionally. Yield: 4 servings.

Mrs. Sue Dunlap,
Savannah, Georgia.

Searching For An Entrée

Whether it be dinner for guests or a family meal, planning a menu usually means deciding first on the entrée.

If your plans call for entertaining, impress your guests with Cornish hens served on a bed of rice and topped with a savory cranberry-flavored sauce, or offer pork chops and mushrooms baked in wine.

For a delicious one-dish dinner, try Moussaka Casserole or the Veal and Wild Rice Casserole.

MOUSSAKA CASSEROLE

2 medium eggplants, peeled
Salt
½ pound ground beef
½ pound ground lamb
2 medium onions, chopped
1 (6-ounce) can tomato paste
½ cup chopped fresh parsley
½ cup dry red wine
½ cup water
2 eggs
¼ cup plus 2 tablespoons Parmesan
   cheese, divided
½ cup plus 2 tablespoons soft
   breadcrumbs, divided
1 teaspoon salt
½ teaspoon ground cinnamon
¼ teaspoon pepper
Dash of ground nutmeg
Vegetable oil
Sauce (recipe follows)
2 tablespoons melted butter or margarine

Cut eggplant into ½-inch-thick slices; sprinkle both sides with salt. Place in a bowl, and set aside.

Brown meat in a large skillet; add onion and cook until tender. Stir in tomato paste, parsley, wine, and water; simmer 3 to 5 minutes, uncovered. Remove from heat, and let cool slightly.

Combine eggs and ¼ cup Parmesan cheese; beat well. Add to meat mixture. Stir in ¼ cup breadcrumbs, 1 teaspoon salt, cinnamon, pepper, and nutmeg.

Drain eggplant slices; pat dry with absorbent paper. Fry in vegetable oil until lightly browned on both sides; drain on absorbent paper.

Sprinkle 2 tablespoons breadcrumbs in a greased 13- x 9- x 2-inch baking pan. Top with eggplant; cover with meat mixture. Top with sauce. Cover with foil, and bake at 350° for 45 minutes.

Combine butter, 2 tablespoons Parmesan cheese, and remaining ¼ cup breadcrumbs; sprinkle over casserole. Bake 20 additional minutes, uncovered, until golden brown. Yield: 6 to 8 servings.

Sauce:

¼ cup butter or margarine
¼ cup all-purpose flour
¼ teaspoon salt
Dash of pepper
¼ teaspoon ground nutmeg
2 cups milk
2 egg yolks, beaten
2 tablespoons lemon juice

Melt butter in a heavy saucepan. Combine flour, salt, pepper, and nutmeg; add to butter, stirring until smooth. Gradually add milk, and cook over medium heat, stirring constantly, until thickened and bubbly. Reduce heat to low. Stir some of hot mixture into yolks; add to remaining sauce mixture, stirring constantly, and cook 2 minutes. Remove from heat; stir in lemon juice. Cover until needed. Yield: about 2 cups.

Florence Greenberg,
Jacksonville, Florida.

Tip: To keep such foods as pork chops, strawberries, or diced green pepper from sticking together while freezing, place in a single layer on a cookie sheet and freeze until solid. Then remove from cookie sheet, and store in freezer bags or containers.

CREAMY CHIPPED BEEF AND TOAST

12 to 16 slices bread
6 slices bacon
2 tablespoons butter or margarine
2 (3-ounce) packages dried beef, coarsely chopped
2 tablespoons all-purpose flour
1½ cups milk
4 hard-cooked eggs, coarsely chopped
2 tomatoes, chopped

Trim crusts from bread; fit bread into lightly greased muffin cups, using 1 slice per cup. Bake at 400° for 12 to 15 minutes. Set aside.

Fry bacon until done, and drain well on paper towels; discard drippings. Crumble bacon, and set aside.

Melt butter in skillet; add beef and sauté 3 to 5 minutes. Stir in flour. Add milk and cook, stirring constantly, until thickened and bubbly. Stir in eggs and tomatoes; remove from heat. Spoon into toast cups (allow 2 toast cups per serving); garnish with crumbled bacon. Yield: 6 to 8 servings. *Lucy Littleton, Auburn, Alabama.*

VEAL AND WILD RICE CASSEROLE

3 pounds boneless veal, cut into cubes
¼ cup melted margarine
1 cup chopped onion
½ cup chopped celery
3 tablespoons melted margarine
1 (4-ounce) package wild rice, cooked
1 (10¾-ounce) can cream of mushroom soup, undiluted
1 (8-ounce) carton commercial sour cream
1 (2½-ounce) can sliced mushrooms, undrained
1 teaspoon Worcestershire sauce
½ cup sherry
1 tablespoon salt
¼ cup grated Romano cheese

Sauté veal in ¼ cup margarine until lightly browned; drain and set aside.

Sauté 1 cup chopped onion and ½ cup chopped celery in 3 tablespoons margarine until tender.

Combine all ingredients except cheese; mix well. Spoon into a greased 2-quart casserole, and sprinkle with cheese. Bake at 350° for 1 hour. Yield: 8 to 10 servings.

Mrs. Shannon Doolittle, Virginia Beach, Virginia.

CORNISH HENS WITH CRANBERRY SAUCE

2 (1½-pound) Cornish hens, split lengthwise
Salt and pepper
2 slices bacon, cut in half
1 tablespoon lemon juice
1 chicken bouillon cube
1 cup hot water
2 tablespoons all-purpose flour
1 cup water
3 tablespoons whole-berry cranberry sauce
1 (4-ounce) can sliced mushrooms, drained
Hot cooked rice

Sprinkle hens with salt and pepper; place cut side down in a large, shallow roasting pan. Place half a slice of bacon on top of each hen, and sprinkle with lemon juice.

Dissolve bouillon cube in 1 cup hot water, and pour in pan. Bake at 375° for 1 hour and 15 minutes or until juice runs clear when thigh is pierced with a fork; baste often with pan drippings.

Remove hens to serving platter. Pour pan drippings into a medium saucepan. Add flour to pan drippings, blending well. Cook over low heat until browned, stirring constantly. Gradually add remaining 1 cup water; cook, stirring constantly, until smooth and thickened. Stir in cranberry sauce and mushrooms; add salt and pepper to taste. Simmer 10 minutes. Serve sauce over rice. Yield: 4 servings.

Mrs. N. E. Wilson, Danville, Illinois.

HAM LOAF

1 cup milk
2 eggs, beaten
1 cup cracker crumbs
1 pound cooked smoked ham, ground
1 pound ground lean pork
¾ cup firmly packed brown sugar
¼ cup vinegar
¼ cup water
1½ tablespoons dry mustard

Combine milk, eggs, and cracker crumbs; add meat; mixing well. Shape into a loaf, and place on a shallow baking pan.

Combine remaining ingredients; bring to a boil. Pour over ham loaf. Bake at 350° for 1 hour and 15 minutes. Yield: 6 to 8 servings. *Mrs. G. T. Peters, Jonesboro, Arkansas.*

GOURMET PORK CHOPS

4 (1-inch-thick) loin pork chops
Salt and pepper
¼ cup all-purpose flour
3 tablespoons peanut oil
½ cup finely chopped onion
1 clove garlic, minced
½ cup dry white wine
1 cup chicken stock
½ pound fresh mushrooms, sliced
2 tablespoons butter or margarine
¼ teaspoon dried thyme
1 bay leaf

Sprinkle pork chops with salt and pepper; dredge in flour. Brown chops in hot oil over medium heat; drain well on paper towels. Place chops in casserole dish, and set aside.

Stir onion and garlic into pan drippings in skillet; cook until onion is tender. Add wine and stock; simmer 3 to 5 minutes.

Sauté mushrooms in butter until tender; add mushrooms, thyme, and bay leaf to skillet.

Pour wine sauce over chops. Cover; bake at 350° for 45 minutes or until tender. Remove bay leaf. Yield: about 4 servings. *Mrs. C. Robert Bauer, Charlottesville, Virginia.*

Bake The Bread With Cheese

With the addition of Parmesan cheese, basic hot roll mix becomes Parmesan Rolls that taste like you made them from scratch.

Sharp Cheddar gives Onion-Cheese Bread its distinctive flavor. Although made from scratch, this bread contains simple ingredients and can be prepared in a jiffy.

ONION-CHEESE BREAD

1½ cups milk
1 tablespoon instant minced onion
3 cups all-purpose flour
1 tablespoon baking powder
1 teaspoon salt
¼ teaspoon pepper
1 egg, beaten
¾ cup shredded sharp Cheddar cheese
3 tablespoons melted butter or margarine

Combine milk and onion in a small mixing bowl; mix well, and let stand 10 minutes.

Combine flour, baking powder, salt, and pepper in a large mixing bowl. Add egg, cheese, butter, and milk mixture; stir only to moisten.

Spread batter evenly in a greased and floured 13- x 9- x 2-inch baking pan. Bake at 375° for 45 minutes or until lightly browned. Yield: 15 servings.

Susan Settlemyre,
Chapel Hill, North Carolina.

PARMESAN ROLLS

½ cup grated Parmesan and Romano
   cheese
1 (13¾-ounce) package hot roll mix
Melted butter or margarine
1 egg, beaten (optional)

Combine cheese and flour mixture from hot roll mix. Prepare dough; let rise according to package directions.

Divide dough into 16 equal portions; shape as desired, and place on a lightly greased baking sheet. Brush rolls with butter. Cover and let rise in a warm place until doubled in bulk (about 30 to 45 minutes). Brush with egg, if desired. Bake at 375° for 12 to 15 minutes or until golden brown. Yield: 16 rolls.

Shirley Hodge,
Delray Beach, Florida.

A Catch Of Seafood Specialties

With the South's vast expanse of shoreline and therefore great availability of seafood, fish and shellfish add a wide variety of flavors to Southern meals. From clam chowder to baked fish, here are some seafood favorites.

Two delicious recipes for fish fillets are included: halibut fillets baked and served in an apple cider sauce, and mackerel fillets baked with lots of lemon juice and butter.

Shrimp Creole is always a favorite; this version features a highly seasoned tomato sauce with green chiles and crushed red pepper.

If you don't live along the coast and often have to settle for the sea's bounty in its canned or frozen form, you'll enjoy recipes like Creamy Lobster and Crab Supreme, both cooked in rich cream sauces.

SPICY SHRIMP CREOLE

⅓ cup vegetable oil
¼ cup all-purpose flour
1 pound shrimp, peeled and deveined
1 clove garlic, minced
½ cup chopped onion
2 tablespoons minced parsley
½ cup chopped green pepper
1 cup water
1 (8-ounce) can tomato sauce
1 (10-ounce) can tomatoes and green
   chiles
2 bay leaves
2 teaspoons salt
½ teaspoon crushed red pepper (optional)
Hot cooked rice

Heat oil in a heavy skillet over high heat; add flour and cook, stirring constantly, until golden brown. Reduce heat; stir in shrimp and cook, stirring constantly, 3 minutes. Stir in garlic, onion, parsley, and green pepper; cook 2 minutes. Gradually add water, stirring constantly; cook over medium heat until thickened. Stir in tomato sauce, tomatoes and green chiles, bay leaves, salt, and red pepper, if desired; bring to a boil. Cover and simmer 20 minutes, stirring occasionally. Serve over hot cooked rice. Yield: 4 to 5 servings.

Nancy K. Noland,
Lake Charles, Louisiana.

CREAMY LOBSTER

¼ cup butter or margarine
2 (7-ounce) cans lobster, drained
2 tablespoons chopped green onion
3 tablespoons all-purpose flour
½ to 1 teaspoon salt
Dash of cayenne pepper
⅛ teaspoon ground nutmeg
1½ cups milk or half-and-half
Buttered toast
Chopped parsley

Melt butter in a Dutch oven. Add lobster and onion; sauté 5 minutes or until onion is tender. Combine flour, salt, cayenne, and nutmeg; stir into lobster. Gradually add milk and cook over medium heat, stirring constantly, until thickened and bubbly.

Spoon lobster over toast. Sprinkle with parsley. Yield: 4 to 6 servings.

Cynthia D. Harper,
Snow Hill, North Carolina.

CRAB SUPREME

⅓ cup butter or margarine
⅓ cup all-purpose flour
1 (16-ounce) carton commercial sour
   cream
2 (6-ounce) packages frozen crab, thawed
   and drained
2 (4-ounce) cans button mushrooms,
   drained
1 tablespoon minced onion
1 tablespoon chopped parsley
¼ teaspoon ground nutmeg
Hot cooked rice
1 whole pimiento, cut into strips

Melt butter in a heavy saucepan over low heat; blend in flour, and cook 1 minute, stirring constantly. Gradually stir in sour cream. Add crab, mushrooms, onion, parsley, and nutmeg; mix well. Cover; cook over low heat 20 to 25 minutes, stirring often. Serve over rice. Garnish with pimiento. Yield: 6 to 8 servings.

Mrs. Joe W. Yarbrough, Jr.,
Marion, Kentucky.

Tip: Fish and onion odors can be removed from the hands by rubbing them with a little vinegar, followed by washing in soapy water.

OYSTERS BIENVILLE

1 pound shrimp, cooked, peeled, and
  deveined
¼ cup butter or margarine
¼ cup all-purpose flour
2 cups half-and-half
¼ to ⅓ cup grated Parmesan cheese
1 teaspoon salt
½ teaspoon pepper
2 pints oysters
Ground red pepper (optional)
12 patty shells

Place one-third of shrimp in container of electric blender; process 30 seconds or until shredded. Repeat blending process with remaining two-thirds shrimp, processing one-third each time. Set shrimp aside.

Melt butter in a large, heavy saucepan over low heat; blend in flour and cook 1 minute, stirring constantly. Gradually add half-and-half; cook over medium heat, stirring constantly, until thickened and bubbly. Stir in shrimp, cheese, salt, and pepper; remove sauce from heat, and set aside.

Place oysters and oyster liquid in a saucepan; season with red pepper, if desired. Simmer about 1 minute or until oyster edges curl. Remove oysters from liquid with a slotted spoon; stir oysters into sauce. Add oyster liquid to desired consistency (sauce should be quite thick). Cook over medium heat 5 to 10 minutes or until thoroughly heated. Spoon mixture into patty shells. Yield: 12 servings.   Nancy K. Noland,
              Lake Charles, Louisiana.

CLAM CHOWDER

1 small onion, chopped
4 slices bacon, coarsely chopped
2 (8-ounce) cans minced clams, undrained
4 medium potatoes, finely diced
1½ teaspoons salt
¼ teaspoon pepper
2 tablespoons cornstarch
4 cups milk, divided
2 tablespoons butter or margarine

Cook onion and bacon in a Dutch oven until bacon is lightly browned. Stir in clams, potatoes, salt, and pepper; cover and simmer until potatoes are tender.

Dissolve cornstarch in a small amount of milk, and add to clam mixture. Add butter and remaining milk. Cook over medium heat, stirring constantly, until thickened (do not boil). Yield: 8 to 10 servings.   Mrs. T. V. Padgett III,
              Augusta, Georgia.

LEMON-BAKED MACKEREL

4 to 6 mackerel fillets
Seasoned salt
Pepper
Butter or margarine
1 cup butter or margarine
Juice of 6 lemons
3 to 4 tablespoons Worcestershire sauce

Sprinkle fillets with seasoned salt and pepper; dot with butter. Arrange in a greased 13- x 9- x 2-inch baking pan. Bake at 350° for 10 minutes. Place under broiler to lightly brown fillets.

Combine 1 cup butter, lemon juice, and Worcestershire sauce in a small saucepan. Place over low heat until butter melts. Pour sauce over fillets, and continue baking at 350° for 20 to 30 minutes or until fish flakes easily when tested with a fork. Yield: 4 to 6 servings.
              Marilyn R. Coomer,
              Louisville, Kentucky.

HALIBUT WITH CIDER

1½ to 2 pounds halibut fillets
1 cup apple cider
½ cup water
2 tablespoons butter or margarine
1½ tablespoons all-purpose flour
2 tablespoons half-and-half
1 tablespoon chopped parsley
½ teaspoon lemon juice
½ teaspoon salt
¼ teaspoon pepper

Place fillets in greased 13- x 9- x 2-inch baking dish. Combine cider and water; pour over fish. Cover with foil; bake at 350° for 10 to 12 minutes or until fish flakes easily when tested with a fork. Place fish on serving dish and keep warm. Pour liquid through a sieve; set aside.

Melt butter in a heavy saucepan over low heat; blend in flour and cook 1 minute, stirring constantly. Gradually add reserved liquid; cook over medium heat, stirring constantly, until slightly thickened. Stir in remaining ingredients. Spoon sauce over fish. Yield: 4 to 6 servings.   Ruth E. Cunliffe,
              Lake Placid, Florida.

Tip: Burned food can be removed from an enamel saucepan by using the following procedure: Fill the pan with cold water containing 2 to 3 tablespoons salt, and let stand overnight. The next day, cover and bring water to a boil.

Serve A Blackberry Flan

In the South, summer is the season for fresh blackberries, and Blackberry Flan is an elegant way to serve them. Mounds of whipped cream crown this variation of the traditional dessert. If fresh blackberries are not available, using frozen ones will achieve the same delicious results.

BLACKBERRY FLAN

⅓ cup butter or margarine, softened
⅔ cup sugar
3 egg yolks
⅓ cup milk
1 cup all-purpose flour
¼ teaspoon salt
½ teaspoon soda
1 teaspoon cream of tartar
½ teaspoon almond extract
Blackberry Filling
Whipped cream

Combine butter and sugar; cream until light and fluffy. Add egg yolks and milk, beating well. Add dry ingredients; mix well, and stir in almond extract.

Pour batter into a greased 10-inch flan pan. Bake at 350° for 20 to 25 minutes. Remove from pan; cool. Spoon filling into center of flan. Serve with whipped cream. Yield: about 8 servings.

Blackberry Filling:
¼ cup all-purpose flour
1 cup sugar
¼ teaspoon salt
½ teaspoon allspice
3 cups fresh or frozen blackberries
1 tablespoon butter or margarine

Combine flour, sugar, salt, and allspice in a saucepan; gently stir in berries. Add butter; cook over low heat, stirring occasionally, until thickened. Cool. Yield: about 3¼ cups.
              Bobbie Stewart,
              Comfort, Texas.

September

School bells ring and schedules become more hectic when September rolls around. For a fast meal that is flavorful, too, consider our complete quick and easy menu. It features baked Catfish Parmesan, an easy rice accompaniment, and peaches simmered in wine. You will also want to look over our ideas for packing a school lunch.

Since September marks the beginning of football season, we thought you would like a menu suited for a tailgate party. Ours features Mexican specialties such as chicken chalupas, beef-filled tacos, and Sangría.

Preserve the fall pear harvest with a relish or savory mincemeat. Your effort now will be appreciated all year long. And for that family who is always on the go, try one of our one-dish meals. From a tasty shrimp dish to a sausage casserole, there is a recipe to please every appetite.

Make It Quick And Easy

Something quick. Something easy. That's often the request from readers whose busy life-styles send them in every direction except the kitchen.

Whether it's preparing a spur-of-the-moment dinner for unexpected guests or a family supper at the end of a busy day, you want to save time and trouble without compromising flavor and quality.

Dishes that use mixes, canned or frozen fruits and vegetables, or other convenience foods will save you that valuable time. This menu is an appealing collection of such dishes, prepared from start to finish in less than an hour.

Catfish Parmesan   Tartar Sauce
Turkish Pilaf
Sweet-and-Sour Green Beans
Dill Pickle Sticks
Bermuda Onion Slices
Commercial Hard Rolls
Peaches in Wine Sauce
Iced Tea

For the entrée, fresh or frozen catfish are baked in an herb-flavored cheese and breadcrumb coating—ready in just 25 minutes. The tartar sauce is a matter of combining a few simple ingredients.

Instant rice is the basis for the savory Turkish Pilaf, so it can be prepared in a jiffy while the fish bakes. You'll even have plenty of time to perk up canned green beans with bacon, onion, and a sweet-and-sour dressing.

Dessert is also ready to serve in only minutes. It's peach halves glazed with brown sugar and simmered in a rich, wine-flavored sauce.

CATFISH PARMESAN

6 skinned, pan-dressed catfish, fresh or frozen
1 cup dry breadcrumbs
¾ cup grated Parmesan cheese
¼ cup chopped parsley
1 teaspoon paprika
½ teaspoon whole oregano
¼ teaspoon whole basil
2 teaspoons salt
½ teaspoon pepper
½ cup melted butter or margarine
Lemon wedges
Parsley

Pat fish dry. Combine breadcrumbs, Parmesan cheese, and seasonings; stir well. Dip catfish in butter, and roll each in crumb mixture.

Arrange fish in a well-greased 13- x 9- x 2-inch baking dish. Bake at 375° about 25 minutes or until fish flakes easily when tested with a fork. Garnish with lemon wedges and parsley. Yield: 6 servings.

TARTAR SAUCE

1 cup mayonnaise
1 tablespoon chopped onion
¼ cup sweet pickle relish
1 tablespoon lemon juice

Combine all ingredients, mixing well. Yield: 1¼ cups.

TURKISH PILAF

2 cups instant rice, uncooked
¼ cup butter or margarine
1 (16-ounce) can tomatoes, cut into eighths
2 beef bouillon cubes
1 cup boiling water
1 medium onion, sliced
1 clove garlic, minced
1 teaspoon salt
1 teaspoon sugar
¼ teaspoon pepper
1 bay leaf

Brown rice in butter in a medium saucepan; stir in remaining ingredients. Bring to a boil; then reduce heat. Cover and simmer 15 to 17 minutes, stirring occasionally. Remove bay leaf before serving. Yield: 6 servings.

SWEET-AND-SOUR GREEN BEANS

4 slices bacon
1 cup finely diced onion
2 (15½-ounce) cans cut green beans, undrained
2 tablespoons sugar
Dash of pepper
¼ cup vinegar

Cut bacon in ½-inch pieces. Partially cook bacon; add onion, and sauté until onion is lightly browned.

Drain beans, and add liquid to bacon and onion; cook until liquid is reduced to ½ cup. Add beans and remaining ingredients. Heat thoroughly. Yield: about 6 servings.

PEACHES IN WINE SAUCE

1 (29-ounce) can peach halves
3 tablespoons butter or margarine
2 tablespoons lemon juice
⅓ cup firmly packed brown sugar
⅓ cup rosé
½ cup whipping cream
1 tablespoon cornstarch

Drain peaches, reserving 2 tablespoons liquid; set aside.

Melt butter in an 8-inch skillet over medium heat; add lemon juice and peaches, turning peaches to coat with butter. Sprinkle with brown sugar; add wine. Cover and simmer about 5 minutes until peaches are lightly glazed. Stir in whipping cream, and simmer several minutes.

Combine reserved peach liquid and cornstarch, stirring until smooth. Add to peach mixture; cook over low heat until thickened, stirring constantly. Serve warm. Yield: 4 to 6 servings.

Box Lunches Score Before The Game

What better way to kick off an afternoon of football than with a tailgate box lunch on the stadium parking lot? One look at the menu tells you that the game is in Texas.

Tailgate Tacos al Carbon
Pico de Gallo   Hot Sauce
Chicken Chalupas
Guacamole   Refried Beans
Texas-Size Pralines
Sangría

David and Kathryn Waldrep invited four of David's former SMU fraternity brothers and their wives to bring their lawn chairs and join them at the Cotton Bowl before the game to enjoy some of Kathryn's spectacular Mexican food. This same group has formed a supper club that meets regularly, and from these dinners Kathryn has gained the reputation of being the perfect hostess.

Lunches were packed in bright-red boxes tied with red and blue ribbons, which also held a napkin and plasticware. Inside the box, each guest found a taco, chalupa, and praline wrapped individually in plastic wrap. (Kathryn had some extras packed away for heartier eaters.) A colorful assortment of garnishes and sauces was spread on the tailgate of their station wagon.

TAILGATE TACOS AL CARBON

½ cup vegetable oil
3 tablespoons lemon juice
1 tablespoon wine vinegar
½ teaspoon garlic salt
½ teaspoon whole thyme
½ teaspoon chili powder
1 teaspoon whole oregano
1 large onion, minced
2 pounds tenderloin or sirloin
10 (8-inch) flour tortillas

Combine first 8 ingredients; spoon over tenderloin and marinate in refrigerator 8 hours. Drain well. Grill tenderloin over hot coals 7 to 8 minutes or until medium rare to medium. Slice meat into thin strips.

Wrap a stack of tortillas in a damp kitchen towel or foil, and heat in a 325° oven 15 minutes. Place several strips of meat on a tortilla and roll up tortilla. Repeat with remaining tortillas and meat. Serve with Pico de Gallo or other hot sauce. Yield: 4 to 5 servings.

Note: To heat tortillas in a microwave oven, place a tortilla on a paper plate; cover with waxed paper. Microwave on high power 15 to 20 seconds or until warm and softened.

PICO DE GALLO

8 long green chiles, seeded and chopped
2 small banana peppers, seeded and chopped
5 green onions with tops, chopped
5 medium tomatoes, peeled and chopped
¼ cup chopped fresh or dried cilantro leaves
2 tablespoons vegetable oil
1 teaspoon vinegar
Salt to taste

Combine all ingredients; stir well. Chill until needed. May be stored in refrigerator up to 2 weeks. Yield: about 3 cups.

HOT SAUCE

1 cup chili sauce
½ cup chopped onion
3 tablespoons lemon juice
2 tablespoons vegetable oil
1 teaspoon brown sugar
2 teaspoons vinegar
1 clove garlic, crushed
½ teaspoon hot sauce
¼ teaspoon dry mustard
¼ teaspoon salt

Combine all ingredients in a saucepan; bring to a boil. Reduce heat and simmer 5 minutes, stirring occasionally. Yield: about 1¼ cups.

CHICKEN CHALUPAS

12 corn tortillas
Vegetable oil
Chicken Filling
Shredded lettuce
Chopped tomatoes
Chopped ripe olives
Chopped onions
Shredded Longhorn Cheddar cheese
Commercial sour cream
Guacamole
Refried Beans

Fry tortillas in hot oil until brown and crisp; drain on absorbent paper. Top each tortilla with Chicken Filling and the remaining toppings as desired. Yield: 12 servings.

Chicken Filling:

4 chicken breasts
2 medium onions, chopped
2 medium tomatoes, chopped
Dash of whole oregano
1 clove garlic, minced
Salt and pepper to taste

Place chicken in a large saucepan; add 5 cups water. Bring to a boil; cover, and simmer until tender. Remove chicken from broth; cool and shred or slice. Set aside.

Combine 4 cups broth, onions, tomatoes, oregano, garlic, salt, and pepper. Cook until about half of liquid remains. Add the chicken; simmer until all liquid is absorbed. Yield: enough for 12 chalupas.

GUACAMOLE

6 ripe avocados, peeled and mashed
1 tomato, peeled and finely chopped
¼ cup finely chopped onion
2 tablespoons lemon juice or vinegar
Hot sauce to taste
Garlic salt to taste

Combine first 5 ingredients; blend well. Season to taste with garlic salt. Yield: about 5½ cups.

Note: Reserve 2 or 3 seeds from avocados. Place in guacamole to prevent mixture from darkening.

REFRIED BEANS

1 pound dried pinto beans
1 (1½- to 2-pound) pork roast
1 tablespoon chili powder
2 teaspoons hot sauce
2 teaspoons cumin
3 cloves garlic, minced
1 tablespoon sugar
1½ to 2 teaspoons garlic salt
½ teaspoon salt

Wash beans thoroughly; cover with water, and soak overnight.

Drain beans, and place in a heavy, large Dutch oven; add enough water to cover beans. Add pork roast and next 5 ingredients; bring to a boil. Reduce heat; cover and simmer 6 to 8 hours, adding more water during cooking, if necessary.

Remove roast; trim fat and remove pork from bone. Shred pork with a fork and set aside. Mash beans; add pork to beans, and mix well. Season to taste with garlic salt and salt. Yield: 12 to 15 servings.

Note: To reheat, combine 2 cups bean mixture and 2 tablespoons melted butter in a skillet. Heat the mixture over low heat until warm, stirring occasionally.

Tip: Fall is the time to check your spices to see if they have lost their aroma. The spice should smell strong and clear as soon as you open the container. If it doesn't, now is the time to replace it. This is the peak time of year for using spices, and you'll want to get the most in flavor and aroma.

TEXAS-SIZE PRALINES

3 cups sugar
1 cup buttermilk
1 teaspoon soda
1 teaspoon vanilla extract
1 tablespoon butter or margarine
2 to 2½ cups pecan halves

Combine sugar, buttermilk, soda, and vanilla in a heavy Dutch oven; cook over medium heat to 234° (soft ball stage), stirring constantly.

Remove from heat; stir in butter. Beat 2 to 3 minutes, just until mixture begins to thicken. Stir in pecans. Working rapidly, drop mixture by tablespoonfuls onto lightly buttered waxed paper; let cool. Yield: about 2 dozen (3-inch) pralines.

SANGRIA

½ cup plus 2 tablespoons Sangría Base
1 (25.4-ounce) bottle Burgundy
1 (10-ounce) bottle lemon-lime carbonated beverage
½ cup club soda
1 large orange, thinly sliced and seeded
1 lemon, thinly sliced and seeded

Combine first 4 ingredients; stir well. Serve over ice; garnish with orange slices and lemon slices. Yield: about 5 cups.

Sangría Base:

3 pounds sugar (about 6½ cups)
1½ quarts water
4 large oranges, sliced and seeded
5 lemons, sliced and seeded
2 limes, sliced and seeded

Combine sugar and water in a large saucepan; simmer, uncovered, until volume is reduced to half. Add fruit to syrup; mash fruit well. Cool fruit mixture; remove rinds. Chill.
Note: Sangría Base can be stored in the refrigerator for later use.

Make Meat Loaf The Main Attraction

If you think of serving meat loaf only for casual family meals, you're in for a surprise. For these recipes add touches of elegance to meat loaf, creating uncommonly good, affordable entrées for special occasions.

What could be more handsome than a Wellington, more pennywise than

ground beef? And when you consider how easy the pastry is with piecrust mix, you have three good reasons for serving Meat Loaf Wellington.

Triple Meat Loaf gets its name from a trio of meats—ground beef, pork, and veal. It's a deftly seasoned combination that's extra moist and flavorful. Shaped into individual servings, Saucy Meat Loaves are baked in tangy tomato sauce and served on a bed of fluffy rice.

Another selection is a meat roll stuffed with mushroom filling. There's also an Italian-style loaf layered with cheese and hard-cooked eggs, then topped with a wine-tomato sauce.

MEAT LOAF WELLINGTON

3 pounds ground beef
1 (10¾-ounce) can cream of mushroom soup, undiluted
1 envelope beefy onion soup mix
1 cup seasoned dry breadcrumbs
3 eggs
¼ teaspoon pepper
1 (4¾-ounce) can liverwurst spread
1 (6-ounce) can chopped mushrooms, drained
1 (11-ounce) package piecrust mix
1 egg, beaten
1 teaspoon cold water
Parsley sprigs (optional)
Spiced crabapples (optional)

Combine first 6 ingredients in a large bowl; mix well, and pack into a lightly greased 9- x 5- x 3-inch loafpan. Bake at 350° for 1 hour and 45 minutes. Invert over a rack, and allow to drain. Let cool, and remove meat loaf from pan.

Combine liverwurst spread and mushrooms; set aside.

Prepare piecrust mix according to package directions for a double crust pie. Shape dough into a ball, and place on a lightly floured surface; roll dough into an 18- x 15-inch rectangle.

Spread about one-fourth of liverwurst mixture on top of meat loaf. Place loaf lengthwise in middle of pastry, top side down. Spread remaining liverwurst on bottom and sides of loaf. Bring long sides of pastry over underside of loaf; overlap slightly to form a seam, trimming off excess pastry. Combine 1 egg and water; brush on seam to seal. Trim ends of pastry to make even; fold over ends of loaf, and brush with egg mixture to seal.

Place meat loaf, seam side down, on a lightly greased baking sheet. Brush with egg mixture.

Roll out pastry trimmings; cut into decorative shapes, and arrange on top of loaf.

Brush with remaining egg mixture. Bake at 425° for 15 to 20 minutes or until golden brown. Let stand 10 minutes before slicing. Garnish meat loaf with parsley and spiced crabapples, if desired. Yield: 10 to 12 servings.
Miss Marlan Hornburg,
Melbourne, Florida.

TRIPLE MEAT LOAF

1 pound lean ground beef or sirloin
1 pound ground pork
1 pound ground veal
3 slices bread, torn into small pieces
1 teaspoon ground sage
1 (1⅜-ounce) package dry onion soup mix
1 (single-serving) envelope cream of mushroom soup mix
1 small green pepper, chopped
1 large stalk celery, thinly sliced
1 tablespoon steak sauce
1 tablespoon mayonnaise
1 tablespoon commercial sour cream
1 (8-ounce) can tomato sauce
¼ teaspoon garlic powder
1 teaspoon salt
½ teaspoon pepper
1 egg, beaten

Combine all ingredients, mixing well. Place mixture in a 13- x 9- x 2-inch baking pan, and shape into a 12- x 6-inch loaf. Bake at 350° for 1½ hours or until done. Yield: 8 to 10 servings.
Mrs. H. Mark Webber,
New Port Richey, Florida.

SAUCY MEAT LOAVES

1½ pounds ground beef
1 cup soft breadcrumbs
1 medium onion, finely chopped
1 egg, beaten
1¼ teaspoons salt
¼ teaspoon pepper
1 cup tomato sauce, divided
2 tablespoons brown sugar
2 tablespoons vinegar
2 tablespoons prepared mustard
½ cup water
Hot cooked rice

Combine first 6 ingredients and ½ cup tomato sauce in a large mixing bowl; mix well, and shape into 6 individual meat loaves. Place in a greased 9-inch square baking pan.

Combine ½ cup tomato sauce, brown sugar, vinegar, mustard, and water; mix well, and pour over meat loaves. Bake at 350° for 35 to 40 minutes, basting occasionally. Serve on rice. Yield: 6 servings. *Mrs. Louise Holmes, Winchester, Tennessee.*

STUFFED MEAT LOAF

1 pound ground beef
1 pound ground pork
1 cup dry breadcrumbs
½ cup shredded carrot
½ cup milk
¼ cup chopped onion
2 eggs, beaten
2 teaspoons salt
1 teaspoon Worcestershire sauce
⅛ teaspoon pepper
1 (4-ounce) can mushrooms, drained and chopped
1 tablespoon onion
2 tablespoons melted butter or margarine
2 cups soft breadcrumbs
1 tablespoon chopped fresh parsley
½ teaspoon poultry seasoning
¼ teaspoon salt

Combine first 10 ingredients in a large mixing bowl, mixing well. Shape mixture into a 14- x 8-inch rectangle on well-greased aluminum foil.

Sauté mushrooms and 1 tablespoon onion in butter until tender; add remaining ingredients, mixing well. Spread evenly over meat mixture, leaving a ½-inch border; roll up jellyroll fashion, beginning with long side. Bring up sides and ends of foil, and fold over roll to seal securely; place in a 15- x 10- x 1-inch jellyroll pan. Bake at 375° for 1 hour; open foil, and continue baking for 15 minutes. Yield: about 8 servings.
Mrs. Pete Beckham, Philadelphia, Mississippi.

ITALIAN MEAT LOAF

2 pounds meat loaf mixture (ground beef, pork, and veal)
1 cup commercial meat loaf sauce
½ cup Italian-seasoned breadcrumbs
⅓ cup chopped onion
¼ cup grated Parmesan cheese
2 hard-cooked eggs, sliced
1 or 2 slices Swiss cheese
2 tablespoons olive oil
1 (8-ounce) can tomato herb sauce
¼ cup dry red wine
½ cup shredded Cheddar cheese
Green pepper rings (optional)

Combine meat, meat loaf sauce, breadcrumbs, and onion in a large mixing bowl; mix well. Place half of mixture in a 13- x 9- x 2-inch baking pan, and shape into a 9- x 5-inch loaf. Sprinkle Parmesan over meat; top with egg slices, then Swiss cheese.

Shape remaining meat mixture over filling. Pinch edges of meat together to seal. Brush loaf with olive oil, and bake at 350° for 1 hour.

Combine tomato herb sauce and wine; mix well. Spoon half over meat loaf. Bake 15 minutes longer.

Add Cheddar cheese to remaining sauce mixture, stirring well; spoon over meat loaf, and bake 10 minutes longer. Garnish with green pepper rings, if desired. Yield: 6 to 8 servings.
Mrs. Linda Sherer, Hampton, Virginia.

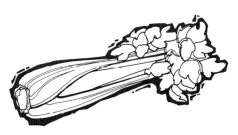

GLAZED HAM LOAF

1 pound ground cooked ham
1 pound ground fresh pork
½ cup crushed corn flakes
1 egg, beaten
2 tablespoons chili sauce
2 tablespoons half-and-half
½ teaspoon prepared mustard
2 tablespoons chopped green pepper
¼ cup chopped celery
¼ cup chopped onion
2 tablespoons vegetable oil
½ cup firmly packed brown sugar
2 tablespoons prepared mustard
¼ teaspoon ground cloves
Pineapple slices (optional)
Maraschino cherries (optional)

Combine meat, corn flakes, egg, chili sauce, half-and-half, and ½ teaspoon mustard; mix well. Sauté pepper, celery, and onion in oil until tender; stir into meat mixture.

Combine brown sugar, 2 tablespoons mustard, and cloves; mix well. Spread mixture in a 9- x 5- x 3-inch loafpan; top with pineapple slices and cherries, if desired. Pack meat mixture into loafpan. Bake at 350° for 1 hour and 30 minutes. Remove from pan before slicing. Yield: 6 servings.
Mrs. W. P. Chambers, Louisville, Kentucky.

Sharing The Best Of Eggplant

There's no denying the versatility of eggplant when you consider that it's equally delicious either stuffed with a savory filling, baked in a casserole, or battered and fried. Our recipes emphasize that versatility with dishes like Cheesy Stuffed Eggplant, Eggplant Supreme, and Parmesan Fried Eggplant.

For best flavor, be sure to select good-quality eggplant. Those that are very shiny are a good choice; if dull, the eggplant is overripe. Also avoid any with dark spots, as this indicates decay.

Eggplant flesh darkens rapidly when cut, so don't peel until just before cooking. To prevent darkening, rub cut surfaces with lemon or lime juice.

SEAFOOD STUFFED EGGPLANT

1 large eggplant
1 medium onion, chopped
¼ cup chopped fresh parsley
¼ green pepper, chopped
2 cloves garlic, finely chopped
3 tablespoons bacon drippings
4 slices bread
1 cup cooked, peeled, deveined shrimp
1 (3.66-ounce) can smoked oysters
½ teaspoon salt
⅛ teaspoon pepper
1 (6½-ounce) can crabmeat, drained and flaked (optional)
2 tablespoons dry breadcrumbs
2 tablespoons grated Parmesan cheese

Cut eggplant in half lengthwise. Carefully scoop out pulp, leaving shells intact; chop pulp. Cook pulp in a small amount of boiling salted water until tender; drain well.

Sauté onion, parsley, green pepper, and garlic in bacon drippings until tender. Remove from heat; add eggplant, mixing well.

Soak bread in water; squeeze out any excess. Add bread to eggplant mixture, along with shrimp, oysters, salt, and pepper; stir in crabmeat, if desired.

Spoon stuffing evenly into eggplant shells. Combine breadcrumbs and cheese; sprinkle over top. Place eggplant in a shallow pan; pour ¼ inch hot water into pan. Bake at 350° for 30 minutes or until shells are tender. Yield: 2 servings. *Pat Andrus, Scott, Louisiana.*

CHEESY STUFFED EGGPLANT

2 small eggplant
½ pound ground beef
1 large onion, finely chopped
1 medium tomato, chopped
3 cloves garlic, pressed
3 tablespoons vegetable oil
¼ cup chopped parsley
1 teaspoon salt
½ teaspoon pepper
½ teaspoon whole oregano
1 cup water
¼ pound Cheddar cheese, cut into 8
   strips
Chopped parsley (optional)

Wash eggplant and cut in half length-wise. Remove pulp, leaving a ¼-inch shell; set shells aside. Cut pulp into ½-inch cubes.

Sauté eggplant pulp, ground beef, chopped onion, tomato, and garlic in oil until beef is browned and onion is tender. Stir in ¼ cup parsley, salt, pepper, and oregano.

Stuff shells with eggplant mixture, and place in a 13- x 9- x 2-inch baking dish; pour water into dish. Cover tightly with aluminum foil, and bake at 350° for 30 minutes. Top each eggplant half with 2 strips of cheese. Bake, uncovered, an additional 5 minutes or until cheese melts. Garnish eggplant with chopped parsley, if desired. Yield: 4 servings.
Rhonda Given,
Harvest, Alabama.

EGGPLANT TOPHATS

1 medium eggplant
¾ cup cracker crumbs
¼ cup evaporated milk
Vegetable oil
6 thin slices onion
6 thick slices tomato
6 thin slices Cheddar cheese
Salt and pepper

Cheddar cheese tops the ground beef and tomato filling of Cheesy Stuffed Eggplant.

Peel eggplant, and cut into 6 slices ½ inch thick. Dredge each slice in cracker crumbs; dip in milk, and coat with remaining cracker crumbs. Fry in hot vegetable oil until golden brown. Drain on paper towels. Place eggplant slices on a lightly greased baking sheet.

Top each eggplant slice with 1 slice onion, tomato, and cheese. Sprinkle with salt and pepper. Bake at 350° for 25 minutes. Yield: 6 servings.
Patricia Chapman,
Huntsville, Alabama.

EGGPLANT-SHRIMP MEDLEY

2 medium eggplant
1 cup finely chopped shallots
1 cup finely chopped celery
1 cup finely chopped green pepper
½ cup butter or margarine, melted
2 pounds uncooked shrimp, peeled and
   deveined
⅓ cup finely chopped fresh parsley
2 teaspoons salt
½ teaspoon hot sauce

Trim stem from eggplant. Cook eggplant whole in boiling water 15 minutes. Remove from water, and let cool. Peel the eggplant, and then cut into ¾-inch cubes.

Sauté shallots, celery, and green pepper in butter 10 minutes. Add eggplant, and sauté 10 minutes. Add remaining ingredients; simmer 10 minutes or until shrimp is done. Yield: 6 servings.
Patti Buckley,
Kenner, Louisiana.

EGGPLANT SUPREME

1 medium eggplant, peeled and cubed
¾ cup sliced fresh mushrooms
2 tablespoons chopped onion
2 tablespoons chopped green pepper
2 tablespoons butter or margarine
2 tablespoons all-purpose flour
1 teaspoon salt
⅛ teaspoon pepper
½ cup half-and-half
3 tablespoons chopped pimiento
2 slices bacon, cooked and crumbled
2 tablespoons buttered breadcrumbs
1 tablespoon grated Parmesan cheese

Cook eggplant 10 minutes in a small amount of boiling water; drain well.

Sauté mushrooms, onion, and green pepper in butter in a large skillet until tender. Stir in flour, salt, and pepper.

Add eggplant, half-and-half, pimiento, and bacon; stir well.

Spoon mixture into a lightly greased 1½-quart casserole. Top with breadcrumbs and Parmesan cheese. Bake at 350° for 30 minutes. Yield: 6 servings.
Mrs. C. F. Coates,
Oklahoma City, Oklahoma.

PARMESAN FRIED EGGPLANT

1 medium eggplant, peeled and cut into
   ½-inch slices
1½ teaspoons salt, divided
⅔ cup breadcrumbs
⅓ cup grated Parmesan cheese
¼ teaspoon pepper
1 egg
2 tablespoons milk
⅓ cup all-purpose flour
Hot vegetable oil

Sprinkle eggplant slices with ¾ teaspoon salt. Let stand 30 minutes; pat dry with paper towels.

Combine breadcrumbs, Parmesan cheese, remaining ¾ teaspoon salt, and pepper; mix well, and set aside. Combine egg and milk; beat well, and set mixture aside.

Dredge eggplant slices in flour; dip in egg mixture, and coat with breadcrumb mixture. Fry in hot vegetable oil until golden brown; drain on paper towels. Yield: 4 servings. *Mrs. Dorothy Apgar,*
Flagler Beach, Florida.

Limas Fresh From The Pod

Enjoying a seemingly endless bounty of fresh vegetables is one of the pluses of the South's long growing season, and lima beans are always a favorite. Here, freshly shelled limas are combined with cheese, bacon, sour cream, and other vegetables to create some fine casseroles.

When buying fresh lima beans, select pods that are well filled, firm, crisp, and unblemished. Remember that a pound of unshelled beans is equivalent to about a cup of shelled beans.

Frozen limas may be substituted in the following recipes when fresh ones are not available.

SPICY LIMA BEAN CASSEROLE

3½ cups fresh lima beans
1 cup chopped onion
1 cup chopped green pepper
1 clove garlic, minced
3 tablespoons hot vegetable oil
1 teaspoon salt
1 tablespoon cornstarch
1 tablespoon chili powder
1 cup whole ripe olives, sliced
1 cup shredded Cheddar cheese, divided

Cook beans in boiling salted water until tender; drain, reserving liquid. Add enough water to liquid to measure 1¼ cups. Set aside.

Sauté onion, green pepper, and garlic in hot oil; set aside.

Combine salt, cornstarch, and chili powder; mix well. Stir in ¼ cup bean liquid, and mix well. Add remaining bean liquid, sautéed onion mixture, sliced olives, beans, and ½ cup of cheese; mix well. Spoon into a well-greased 1½-quart deep-dish casserole; sprinkle with remaining ½ cup of cheese. Bake at 375° for 30 minutes. Yield: 6 to 8 servings.
Mrs. Don Young,
Berwyn, Pennsylvania.

LIMA BEAN CASSEROLE

2 cups cooked and drained lima beans
1 (16-ounce) can tomatoes, chopped
1 cup cooked, diced luncheon meat or
   ham
½ teaspoon salt
1 teaspoon sugar
Dash of pepper
½ cup soft breadcrumbs
2 tablespoons melted butter or margarine

Combine beans, tomatoes, luncheon meat, and seasonings; mix well, and spoon into a buttered 1½-quart casserole. Spread breadcrumbs over top; drizzle with butter. Bake at 350° for 30 minutes. Yield: 5 to 6 servings.
Mrs. E. S. Grogan,
Martinsville, Virginia.

SUPER LIMA BEANS

4 slices bacon
1 large onion, chopped
4 cups cooked and drained lima beans
1 (10¾-ounce) can tomato soup, undiluted
2 tablespoons melted butter or margarine
½ cup soft breadcrumbs

Cook bacon until crisp; remove from skillet, crumble, and set aside. Sauté onion in bacon drippings until tender; add beans, soup, and bacon, mixing well. Spoon into a greased 1½-quart casserole. Combine butter and breadcrumbs; sprinkle over top. Bake at 375° for 30 minutes. Yield: 5 to 6 servings.
Opal M. Rogers,
Tempe, Arizona.

LIMA BEANS IN SOUR CREAM

¼ cup plus 2 tablespoons chopped onion
   or shallots
2 tablespoons chopped pimiento
2 tablespoons melted butter or margarine
2 cups cooked and drained lima beans
½ cup commercial sour cream
¼ teaspoon salt
⅛ teaspoon pepper

Sauté onion and pimiento in butter until tender; stir in beans, sour cream, salt, and pepper. Cook just until heated. Yield: 5 to 6 servings.
Mrs. J. W. Riley, Jr.,
Kingsport, Tennessee.

Pack A Lunch For School

Finding the time and ideas for packing a nutritious and satisfying lunch for your schoolchildren day after day can be quite a challenge. A fresh and flavorful selection of foods packed attractively and carefully will bring smiles to their faces every time they open their lunch.

To make the job easier for you, there's Quick Vegetable Soup. Start with a can of alphabet soup, add a few fresh vegetables and seasonings, and you've got a convenience soup that tastes homemade. Slices of individually wrapped cheeses pack well and with a few crackers make a nice accompaniment to hot soup.

Sour Cream-Banana Bread, sliced and spread with peanut butter and honey, will be a welcome change from the usual peanut butter and jelly sandwich. And instead of cookies or candy, try packing nutritious Granola for dessert. It's easy to prepare, and one batch makes about 10½ cups.

SOUR CREAM-BANANA BREAD

3 tablespoons butter or margarine,
    softened
1 cup sugar
1 egg, beaten
½ cup commercial sour cream
2 cups all-purpose flour
2 teaspoons baking powder
1 teaspoon soda
½ teaspoon salt
¾ cup mashed banana
1 tablespoon lemon juice

Combine butter and sugar, creaming until light and fluffy. Add egg and sour cream; mix well.

Combine dry ingredients; alternately add to creamed mixture with banana, mixing well after each addition. Add lemon juice, stirring until blended. Spoon into a well-greased and floured 8½- x 4½- x 3-inch loafpan. Bake at 375° for 50 minutes or until bread tests done. Yield: 1 loaf. *Diane E. France, Bel Air, Maryland.*

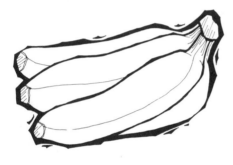

GRANOLA

6 cups regular oats, uncooked
1 cup flaked coconut
1 cup wheat germ
½ cup shelled sunflower seeds
½ cup sesame seeds
½ cup chopped almonds
⅓ cup chopped cashew nuts
¾ cup honey
½ cup vegetable oil
⅓ cup water
¼ cup firmly packed brown sugar
1½ teaspoons vanilla extract
1 teaspoon salt
1 cup raisins (optional)

Combine first 7 ingredients in a large bowl; mix well and set aside.

Combine remaining ingredients except raisins; pour over oats mixture; mix well. Spread mixture evenly into 2 lightly greased 15- x 10- x 1-inch jelly-roll pans. Bake at 350° for 30 minutes

or until golden brown, stirring every 5 minutes. Cool. Add raisins, if desired, and mix well. Store in an airtight container. Yield: about 10½ cups.
*Jennifer Kimmel,
Nashville, Tennessee.*

QUICK VEGETABLE SOUP

1 (46-ounce) can tomato juice
2 (10½-ounce) cans alphabet vegetable
    soup, undiluted
3 medium potatoes, diced
3 carrots, sliced
2 stalks celery, diced
1 medium onion, finely chopped
Salt and pepper to taste

Combine all ingredients in a large Dutch oven; mix well. Bring to a boil; reduce heat and simmer 30 minutes or until vegetables are tender. Yield: 8 to 10 servings. *Mrs. Florence Keel, Memphis, Tennessee.*

Make The Dressing Special

The finishing touch to any salad is the dressing selected for it. Mrs. Michael Champagne of Covington, Louisiana, suggests this zesty combination of ingredients for Special Italian Dressing. Not only is it great for salad greens; it is also good served over avocado or with antipasto.

SPECIAL ITALIAN DRESSING

1⅓ cups vegetable oil
½ cup tarragon vinegar
2 tablespoons minced garlic
1 teaspoon salt
2 teaspoons freshly ground pepper
3 tablespoons chopped fresh parsley
1 teaspoon whole basil leaves
1 teaspoon whole oregano
1 tablespoon plus 1 teaspoon anchovy
    paste
⅓ cup pimiento-stuffed olives
1 tablespoon capers
¼ cup grated Parmesan cheese
1 tablespoon plus 1 teaspoon lemon juice
2 teaspoons sugar
4 green onions with tops, coarsely
    chopped

Combine all ingredients in container of electric blender; blend well. Refrigerate at least 1 hour before serving. Yield: about 2 cups.

Marinated Salads With A Plus

Advance preparation is just one of the pluses of marinated vegetable salads. They are also easy to assemble, and most begin with ingredients you already have on hand.

For Senator's Salad, canned green beans and English peas are the basic ingredients, with green pepper, celery, and onion added for extra flavor and texture, pimiento for color. The marinade is a simple combination of oil and vinegar. Green Vegetable and Egg Salad is similar, using frozen vegetables and a mayonnaise-base dressing.

VEGETABLE-SHRIMP SALAD

1 (10-ounce) package frozen cauliflower
1 (10-ounce) package frozen brussels
    sprouts
1 (10-ounce) package frozen broccoli
    spears
1 (10-ounce) package frozen lima beans
1 pound cooked, peeled, and deveined
    shrimp
1 cup whole pitted ripe olives
¼ cup chopped pimiento
1 cup lemon juice
½ cup vegetable oil
2 tablespoons chopped parsley
2 teaspoons salt
1 teaspoon monosodium glutamate
1 teaspoon whole basil
Lettuce leaves (optional)

Cook each vegetable separately; follow package directions, but cook only 3 minutes or until vegetables are crisp-tender. Drain and cool.

Cut cauliflower into small flowerets. Cut brussels sprouts in half lengthwise; cut broccoli in half crosswise.

Combine vegetables, shrimp, olives, and pimiento in a large bowl; toss lightly, and set aside.

Combine next 6 ingredients, mixing well. Pour dressing over vegetables; toss lightly to coat. Cover and chill thoroughly. Toss again before serving. Serve on lettuce leaves, if desired. Yield: 6 to 8 servings. *Alta Cronin, Charlottesville, Virginia.*

Crisp-tender vegetables, ripe olives, and shrimp are the flavorful combination in Vegetable-Shrimp Salad. The marinade is an herb-seasoned blend of lemon juice and oil.

SENATOR'S SALAD

1 (16-ounce) can cut green beans, drained
1 (17-ounce) can small English peas, drained
½ cup chopped green pepper
2 stalks celery, chopped
1 small onion, sliced
1 (2-ounce) jar diced pimiento, drained
1 cup vegetable oil
¾ cup vinegar
½ cup sugar
Salt and pepper

Combine vegetables, tossing lightly. Combine oil, vinegar, and sugar; mix well. Pour over vegetables, and toss lightly. Stir in salt and pepper to taste. Cover and chill overnight. Yield: 8 to 10 servings. *Mrs. Charles Wilson, Louisville, Kentucky.*

How About A One-Dish Meal?

Whatever your family's main dish preferences may be, they're sure to enjoy some of these convenient one-dish meals. They range from easily prepared Country Sausage Casserole to make-ahead Spinach and Beef Casserole.

For a hearty main dish, serve cornbread-topped Ham and Lima Casserole or Red Flannel Hash flavored with onion and sour cream. Chow mein noodles add a crunchy texture to Oriental Beef Supper, and Spanish Rice Casserole is a combination of sausage, rice, and tomatoes.

RED FLANNEL HASH

¼ cup chopped onion
3 tablespoons butter or margarine
3 cups cubed cooked potatoes
2 cups chopped cooked corned beef
1½ cups chopped cooked beets
¼ cup commercial sour cream
1 teaspoon salt
¼ teaspoon pepper

Sauté onion in butter until tender. Add potatoes, corned beef, beets, sour cream, salt, and pepper to skillet; cook over medium heat 10 to 15 minutes or until hash is well browned on bottom. Serve from skillet. Yield: 4 to 6 servings. *Anna May Simmons, Gainesville, Florida.*

MARINATED VEGETABLE-BACON BOWL

1 (8½-ounce) can English peas, drained
1 pound fresh mushrooms, sliced
1 medium-size sweet onion, sliced
1 small head cauliflower, broken into flowerets
⅔ cup vegetable oil
¼ cup lemon juice
1¼ teaspoons salt
½ teaspoon dry mustard
Dash of cayenne pepper
¼ cup cooked, crumbled bacon or imitation bacon bits

Combine vegetables, tossing lightly. Combine remaining ingredients except bacon, mixing well. Pour dressing over vegetables, and toss lightly. Cover and chill at least 3 hours, stirring occasionally. Sprinkle bacon over salad just before serving. Yield: 6 to 8 servings. *Mrs. Murray B. Reed, Hagerstown, Maryland.*

GREEN VEGETABLE AND EGG SALAD

1 (10-ounce) package frozen baby lima beans
1 (10-ounce) package frozen English peas
1 (10-ounce) package frozen French-style green beans
1 small onion, finely chopped
1 cup mayonnaise
¾ teaspoon prepared mustard
¾ teaspoon Worcestershire sauce
¾ teaspoon hot sauce
3 hard-cooked eggs, mashed

Cook each frozen vegetable separately, following package directions; drain well. Combine all vegetables, and toss them lightly.

Combine remaining ingredients, mixing well. Spoon egg mixture over vegetables; stir gently. Cover and chill overnight. Yield: 8 servings. *Pam H. Carswell, Macon, Georgia.*

SPINACH AND BEEF CASSEROLE

6 slices bacon
1 pound lean ground beef
½ cup finely chopped onion
1 teaspoon garlic salt
½ teaspoon salt
½ teaspoon pepper
¼ pound fresh mushrooms, sliced
1 (8-ounce) can tomato sauce
1 (8-ounce) carton commercial sour cream
1 cup cottage cheese
½ cup grated Parmesan cheese
2 cups (½ pound) shredded mild Cheddar
    cheese, divided
4 eggs, beaten
½ teaspoon basil leaves
2 (10-ounce) packages frozen chopped
    spinach, thawed

Fry bacon in a skillet until crisp; drain bacon on paper towels and discard drippings. Crumble bacon.

Cook ground beef and onion over medium heat until browned, stirring to crumble. Add garlic salt, salt, pepper, and mushrooms; cook 3 minutes, stirring occasionally. Drain off drippings.

Combine tomato sauce, sour cream, cottage cheese, Parmesan cheese, 1 cup Cheddar cheese, eggs, and basil; mix well. Stir in crumbled bacon.

Squeeze liquid from spinach; add spinach and beef mixture to tomato sauce mixture, stirring well. Spoon mixture into a 13- x 9- x 2-inch baking dish; sprinkle with remaining Cheddar cheese. Chill at least 3 hours. Bake at 350° for 30 minutes. Yield: 6 to 8 servings.
Mrs. Warren D. Davis,
Yulee, Florida.

ORIENTAL BEEF SUPPER

1 pound ground beef
1 (10¾-ounce) can cream of mushroom
    soup, undiluted
1 (16-ounce) can bean sprouts, drained
1 (8-ounce) can water chestnuts, drained
    and sliced
1 (4-ounce) can mushrooms, undrained
1 cup diced celery
½ cup uncooked instant rice
¼ cup soy sauce
2 tablespoons instant minced onion
½ teaspoon salt
¼ teaspoon pepper
1 (3-ounce) can chow mein noodles

Cook ground beef until browned, stirring to crumble; drain off pan drippings. Add remaining ingredients except noodles; simmer 20 minutes. Spoon mixture into a serving dish, and sprinkle with noodles. Yield: 6 to 8 servings.
Donna L. Ellett,
Simpsonville, South Carolina.

HAM AND LIMA CASSEROLE

1½ cups cubed cooked ham
1 cup cooked lima beans
1 (8.5-ounce) can cream-style corn
1 cup (¼ pound) shredded sharp Cheddar
    cheese
2 tablespoons minced onion
1 teaspoon Worcestershire sauce
⅔ cup biscuit mix
⅓ cup cornmeal
1 egg
¼ cup milk

Combine ham, lima beans, corn, cheese, onion, and Worcestershire sauce; mix well. Spoon into a greased 1½-quart casserole. Cover and bake at 400° for 15 minutes.

Combine remaining ingredients; spoon over hot mixture, spreading evenly. Bake, uncovered, 20 minutes. Yield: 4 servings.
Carolyn Brantley,
Greenville, Mississippi.

SPANISH RICE CASSEROLE

1 pound mild bulk sausage
1½ cups uncooked regular rice
1 medium onion, chopped
3 onion bouillon cubes or 3 teaspoons
    instant onion bouillon
2 cups boiling water
1 (10-ounce) can tomatoes with green
    chiles
2 to 3 teaspoons chili powder
½ teaspoon garlic powder
½ teaspoon pepper
5 slices bacon, cut in half crosswise

Cook sausage over medium heat until brown, stirring to crumble; drain on paper towels, reserving drippings in skillet. Combine rice and onion; brown lightly in reserved drippings.

Dissolve bouillon in water. Combine sausage, rice mixture, bouillon, tomatoes, chili powder, garlic powder, and pepper; stir well. Spoon into a greased 2-quart casserole. Bake at 350° for 20 minutes. Place bacon strips over rice; bake an additional 35 minutes or until bacon is lightly browned. Yield: 4 servings.
Mrs. Patsy M. Smith,
Lampasas, Texas.

COUNTRY SAUSAGE CASSEROLE

1 pound mild bulk sausage
½ small onion, chopped
2 tablespoons all-purpose flour
2 cups canned whole tomatoes, chopped
2 cups drained, canned whole kernel corn
1 tablespoon sugar
½ cup buttered breadcrumbs

Cook sausage until browned, stirring to crumble; drain off pan drippings, reserving 2 tablespoons in skillet. Sauté onion and flour in reserved drippings until browned. Add sausage, tomatoes, corn, and sugar; mix well. Pour sausage mixture into a 2-quart casserole; sprinkle with breadcrumbs. Bake at 425° for 20 to 25 minutes. Yield: about 6 servings.
Mabel Parker,
Union Mills, North Carolina.

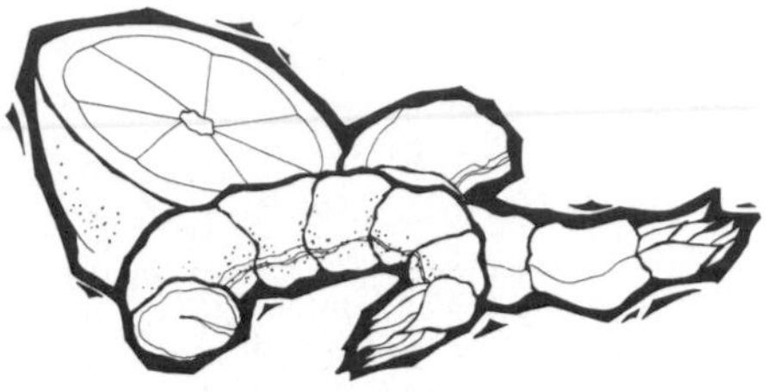

SHRIMP DELIGHT

2 cups uncooked regular rice
¼ cup sliced green onion
¼ cup vegetable oil
1 quart chicken broth
2 tablespoons soy sauce, divided
1 clove garlic
1 bay leaf
2 teaspoons salt
½ teaspoon pepper
1 tablespoon lemon juice
2 tablespoons melted butter or margarine
1 pound shrimp, cooked, peeled, and
    deveined
1 (8-ounce) carton commercial sour cream
1 cup shredded sharp Cheddar cheese

Sauté rice and onion in oil until rice is browned; stir in broth, 1 tablespoon soy sauce, garlic, bay leaf, salt, pepper, and lemon juice. Cover and cook 25 minutes or until all liquid is absorbed. Remove garlic and bay leaf.

Combine butter, shrimp, and remaining soy sauce in a saucepan; cook just until heated through.

Combine shrimp mixture and rice mixture; mix well. Spoon half of shrimp-rice mixture into a greased 2½-quart casserole; gently spread sour cream over rice. Spoon remaining rice over sour cream; sprinkle with cheese. Bake at 450° for 10 to 15 minutes or until bubbly. Yield: 6 to 8 servings.
Mrs. R. M. Lancaster,
Brentwood, Tennessee.

Shortcut Your Bread Baking

No one can resist the aroma of freshly baked bread warm from the oven. To make the end results as easy as they are good, we've gathered an assortment of recipes using convenience products.

Caramel Breakfast Rolls are easily assembled with frozen bread dough the night before serving and refrigerated until time to bake. For these sweet rolls, choose between a raisin-nut or pineapple-cherry topping.

Serve Petite Ham and Cheese Biscuits for a nutritious snack or as an accompaniment to tossed salad. They're made quick and easy with refrigerated biscuits. Biscuit mix is the shortcut to both Marmalade Biscuit Squares and beef-filled Cheeseburger Biscuits.

PETITE HAM AND CHEESE BISCUITS

1 (11-ounce) package refrigerated
   buttermilk biscuits
1 (4½-ounce) can deviled ham
¼ cup melted butter or margarine
½ cup grated Parmesan cheese
Lemon pepper marinade

Cut each biscuit into quarters; arrange evenly in two greased 8-inch round cake pans.

Combine deviled ham and butter, mixing well; spread on biscuit pieces. Spoon cheese on top; sprinkle lightly with lemon pepper marinade. Bake at 400° for 12 to 15 minutes. Yield: 40 appetizers.   *Mrs. J. Edwin Parrish,*
Maitland, Florida.

MARMALADE BISCUIT SQUARES

2 tablespoons butter or margarine,
   softened
½ cup orange marmalade
2 cups biscuit mix
½ cup cold water

Combine butter and marmalade, mixing well; spread mixture evenly in a greased 8-inch square baking pan.

Combine biscuit mix and water in a medium bowl; stir vigorously until a soft dough is formed. Turn out on a floured surface; knead lightly about 5 times. Roll dough into an 8-inch square about ½ inch thick. Place on top of marmalade mixture; cut into 36 squares. Bake at 425° for 15 to 20 minutes; immediately invert onto a serving dish. Yield: 3 dozen.   *Mrs. Mary Pappas,*
Richmond, Virginia.

CARAMEL BREAKFAST ROLLS

2 (1-pound) loaves frozen bread dough,
   thawed
1 cup firmly packed brown sugar
1 (5½-ounce) package regular vanilla
   pudding and pie filling mix
½ cup butter or margarine, melted
¼ cup milk or half-and-half
½ cup chopped nuts, divided
½ cup raisins, divided

Cut 1 loaf of dough into small pieces; place dough pieces in a greased 13- x 9- x 2-inch baking dish.

Combine brown sugar, pudding mix, butter, and milk; mix well. Drizzle half of the brown sugar mixture over dough pieces; sprinkle with ¼ cup nuts and ¼ cup raisins.

Cut remaining loaf of dough into small pieces; place dough pieces over first layer. Drizzle remaining brown sugar mixture over dough pieces; sprinkle with remaining nuts and raisins. Cover and refrigerate several hours or overnight. Bake at 325° for 50 to 60 minutes. Yield: 10 to 12 servings.

Note: Chopped maraschino cherries and crushed pineapple may be substituted for nuts and raisins.

Marcie Johnston,
Lubbock, Texas.

Caramel Breakfast Rolls are easy to prepare with frozen bread dough and are refrigerated overnight before baking.

CHEESEBURGER BISCUITS

¾ pound ground beef
½ cup finely chopped onion
¼ cup finely chopped celery
2 tablespoons vegetable oil
¼ cup tomato paste
½ cup water
½ teaspoon salt
¼ teaspoon chili powder
½ teaspoon Worcestershire sauce
¼ cup chopped pitted ripe olives
3 cups biscuit mix
1 cup milk
2 (1-ounce) slices process American
   cheese, halved

Sauté beef, onion, and celery in oil until vegetables are tender. Add tomato paste, water, salt, chili powder, Worcestershire sauce, and olives, mixing well; simmer 10 minutes, stirring occasionally. Set aside.

Combine biscuit mix and milk, stirring until a soft dough is formed. (More biscuit mix may be added, if it is needed.)

Beat vigorously 30 seconds, and turn out on a lightly floured surface; knead 10 times. Roll the dough to ½-inch thickness.

Cut into eight 4-inch circles; place 4 dough circles on a greased baking sheet. Spoon one-fourth of the meat mixture onto each, leaving a ¼-inch border; top each with a cheese slice.

Place remaining dough circles on top, pressing edges to seal. Bake at 375° for 25 minutes or until biscuits are golden brown. Yield: 4 servings. *Kathy Jones, Ozark, Alabama.*

Pasta For The Main Dish

Everyone seems to enjoy pasta in one form or another, and our readers are constantly sending us evidence of their creative ways with pasta. This group of recipes includes a sausage-onion-tomato-green pepper combination served over spaghetti; a layered beef and macaroni casserole that serves 12; and an elaborate version of lasagna. Vermicelli with Mushrooms features sautéed onions, mushrooms, and peas over vermicelli.

VINTAGE LASAGNA

1 medium zucchini, thinly sliced
1 medium onion, thinly sliced
2 tablespoons olive oil or melted
   margarine
1 teaspoon garlic powder
1 pound ground beef
1 medium onion, chopped
1 (15½-ounce) jar spaghetti sauce
2 (8-ounce) cans tomato sauce
1 teaspoon whole basil
1 tablespoon whole oregano
Salt and pepper to taste
1 tablespoon hot sauce
1 (4-ounce) can sliced mushrooms,
   undrained
1 (1-pound) package lasagna noodles
3 hard-cooked eggs, sliced
½ cup sliced green olives
1 (12-ounce) carton cream-style cottage
   cheese
1 cup shredded mozzarella cheese

Sauté zucchini and sliced onion in olive oil in a medium skillet until crisp-tender. Remove from skillet, and sprinkle with garlic powder; set aside.

Cook beef and chopped onion in skillet, stirring to crumble meat; drain well. To meat mixture add spaghetti sauce, tomato sauce, basil, oregano, salt, pepper, hot sauce, and mushrooms; simmer over low heat 30 minutes.

Cook lasagna noodles according to package directions; drain.

Reserve 1 cup meat sauce; set aside. In a 13- x 9- x 2-inch baking dish, alternate layers of meat sauce, noodles, egg slices, olives, cottage cheese, mozzarella cheese, and zucchini mixture; repeat layers three times. Spread reserved meat sauce on top.

Bake at 375° for 35 minutes; let stand 5 minutes before serving. Yield: 10 to 12 servings. *Carole McAllister, Bixby, Oklahoma.*

BEEF-MACARONI COMBO

3 pounds ground beef
¾ cup chopped onion
1 (28-ounce) can whole tomatoes,
   undrained
1 (16-ounce) can whole tomatoes,
   undrained
2 (6-ounce) cans tomato paste
1 (8-ounce) package elbow macaroni
1 cup milk
½ teaspoon garlic salt
1 (8-ounce) package cream cheese,
   softened
1 cup (¼ pound) shredded Cheddar
   cheese
1 cup (¼ pound) grated Parmesan cheese,
   divided

Cook ground beef and onion in a large skillet until beef is browned; drain off drippings. Add tomatoes and tomato paste; simmer 20 minutes or until thick.

Cook macaroni according to package directions; drain and set aside.

Combine milk, garlic salt, cream cheese, Cheddar cheese, and ½ cup Parmesan cheese in top of double boiler; cook, stirring occasionally, until cheese melts. Stir in macaroni.

For 6 servings, alternately layer half of meat and macaroni mixtures, beginning and ending with meat mixture, into a lightly greased 1½-quart casserole. Sprinkle with ¼ cup Parmesan cheese. Bake at 350° for 20 minutes or until bubbly.

Layer remaining meat and macaroni mixture in a 1½-quart casserole lined with aluminum foil; sprinkle with remaining Parmesan cheese; freeze for later use. Yield: 12 servings.

*Jo Miller,
Stephenville, Texas.*

SAUSAGE SPAGHETTI DINNER

2 pounds smoked link sausage, cut into
   2-inch pieces
2 large onions, chopped
1 (28-ounce) can whole tomatoes,
   undrained and chopped
2 (8-ounce) cans tomato sauce
2 teaspoons salt
½ teaspoon pepper
1 bay leaf
2 tablespoons Worcestershire sauce
1 large green pepper, chopped
1 (7-ounce) package thin spaghetti
Grated Parmesan cheese (optional)

Cook sausage in a Dutch oven over medium heat until browned, stirring occasionally. Add onion and cook until lightly browned. Stir in tomatoes, tomato sauce, salt, pepper, bay leaf, and Worcestershire sauce; cover and simmer about 35 minutes. Add green pepper; simmer an additional 10 minutes.

Prepare spaghetti according to package directions; drain. Serve sauce over spaghetti. Sprinkle with Parmesan cheese. Yield: 6 servings.
*Mrs. S. A. Ingersoll,
Mobile, Alabama.*

Tip: When you need just a few drops of onion juice for flavor, sprinkle a little salt on a slice of onion; scrape the salted surface with a knife or spoon to obtain the juice.

VERMICELLI WITH MUSHROOMS

¾ cup chopped onion
1 clove garlic, minced
½ cup melted margarine, divided
1 pound fresh mushrooms, cleaned and
    sliced
1 (10-ounce) package frozen peas, thawed
1½ tablespoons lemon juice
1 teaspoon salt
¼ teaspoon pepper
¼ teaspoon whole oregano (optional)
1 (12-ounce) package vermicelli
Grated Parmesan cheese

Sauté onion and garlic in ¼ cup margarine for 3 minutes, stirring occasionally. Add mushrooms; cook 5 minutes, stirring occasionally. Stir in peas, lemon juice, salt, pepper, and oregano; cook over low heat 5 minutes.

Cook vermicelli according to package directions; drain. Add remaining ¼ cup margarine, and stir well. Spoon mushroom mixture over vermicelli. Serve with Parmesan cheese. Yield: about 4 servings.
Roxanne Gaudin,
Evansville, Indiana.

Put A Tomato In The Pie

When the tomato-growing season comes to an end, Ray M. Jackson of Birmingham collects the green tomatoes to make this special pie. While this idea is new and different, the flavor is surprisingly similar to that of old-fashioned apple pie.

Green tomatoes and grapes fill Green Tomato Pie. The flavor is much like old-fashioned apple pie.

GREEN TOMATO PIE

Pastry for double-crust 10-inch pie
1¾ cups sugar
½ cup all-purpose flour
¼ teaspoon salt
1 teaspoon ground allspice
4 cups peeled small green tomato wedges
2 cups seedless green grapes, halved
1 teaspoon grated lemon rind
2 tablespoons daiquiri cocktail mix
¼ cup light rum
4 large mint leaves, minced
3 tablespoons melted butter or margarine

Roll half of pastry to ⅛-inch thickness; fit into a 10-inch piepan.

Combine sugar, flour, salt, and allspice, stirring well. Add tomatoes and grapes; stir gently to coat with flour mixture. Add remaining ingredients; spoon into pastry shell.

Roll out remaining pastry to ⅛-inch thickness; carefully place over pie, leaving 1-inch rim beyond edge of pan. Seal and flute edges; cut slits in top for steam to escape. Decorate with scraps of pastry cut into decorative shapes.

Cover pastry edges with aluminum foil to prevent excessive browning. Bake at 450° for 15 minutes. Reduce heat to 350° and bake an additional 30 minutes. Remove foil and continue to bake for 15 minutes. Yield: one 10-inch pie.

Try These Pear Pleasers

While enjoying the season's bounty of fresh pears, give a thought to preserving some to enjoy during the rest of the year. You'll enjoy Pear Marmalade spread on your morning toast or Pear Relish and Mustard Pear Pickles, two delicious ways to complement your meals. Mary Hogue of Jackson, Mississippi, shares with us her recipe for Pear Mincemeat and a note on how to turn it into a savory mincemeat pie.

Choose firm pears for preserving.

PEAR MINCEMEAT

12 to 15 large pears, peeled and ground
10 to 12 apples, peeled and chopped
2¼ cups firmly packed brown sugar
1 cup sugar
1 tablespoon salt
½ cup vinegar
1 unpeeled orange, ground
2¾ cups raisins, ground
1 teaspoon ground nutmeg
2 teaspoons ground cinnamon
½ teaspoon ground ginger
1 teaspoon ground cloves

Combine all ingredients in a large saucepan or Dutch oven; bring to a boil, stirring constantly. Spoon mixture into hot sterilized jars, leaving ⅛-inch headspace. Adjust lids; process 20 minutes in a boiling-water bath. Yield: 3½ quarts.

Note: To make Pear Mincemeat Pie, add ¼ cup sugar to approximately 4½ cups of pear mincemeat. Heat mincemeat to boiling. Pour mixture into a 9-inch unbaked pastry shell; dot with butter. Cover with top crust; slit crust in several places to allow steam to escape. Seal and flute edges. Cover edge of pastry with strip of aluminum foil to prevent excessive browning. Bake at 375° for 30 to 40 minutes; remove foil for last 15 minutes of baking. Yield: one 9-inch pie.
Mary A. Hogue,
Jackson, Mississippi.

MUSTARD PEAR PICKLES

1 cup all-purpose flour
4 cups water
1 quart white vinegar
1¾ cups sugar
2 tablespoons salt
1 tablespoon turmeric
1 tablespoon celery seeds
1 tablespoon mustard seeds
2 quarts pears, peeled and chopped
2 cups chopped onion
7 green peppers, cut into small strips

Stir together flour and water. Combine flour mixture with next 6 ingredients in a saucepan. Bring to a boil, and simmer 4 minutes, stirring constantly.

Combine pears, onion, and green peppers in a large saucepan or Dutch oven. Stir in vinegar mixture; bring to a boil. Cook 4 additional minutes, stirring constantly.

Spoon mixture into hot sterilized jars, leaving ⅛-inch headspace. Adjust lids

and process 10 minutes in a boiling-water bath. Yield: about 4 quarts.
Mrs. Winfield Towles,
Indianapolis, Indiana.

PEAR RELISH

4 quarts pears, peeled and ground
6 large onions, finely chopped
½ cup hot peppers, ground
½ cup sweet red peppers, ground
1 quart cider vinegar
3 cups sugar
1 teaspoon turmeric
1 teaspoon ground cinnamon
1 teaspoon ground cloves
¼ cup salt

Combine all ingredients; let stand 1 hour. Drain well, discarding liquid. Heat mixture to a boil; reduce heat, and simmer 15 minutes.

Spoon mixture into hot sterilized jars, leaving ⅛-inch headspace. Adjust lids; process 10 minutes in boiling-water bath. Yield: 2 quarts. *Mary J. DeFoor,*
Rusk, Texas.

PEAR MARMALADE

4 cups peeled and chopped pears
4 cups sugar
1 (8-ounce) can crushed pineapple, undrained
1 (1¾-ounce) package powdered fruit pectin

Combine pears and sugar in a large saucepan. Cook over medium heat, stirring constantly, until pears are tender, about 15 to 20 minutes. Mash pears and stir in pineapple; bring to a boil. Stir in pectin, and bring to a boil again.

Spoon mixture into hot sterilized jars, leaving ⅛-inch headspace. Adjust lids; process in boiling-water bath 5 minutes. Yield: 3½ pints. *Aliese Trigg,*
Douglasville, Georgia.

Try A Little Bit

When you need a bite-size sweet for a coffee or tea or to serve as dessert for a cocktail buffet, Little Bits are a delectable choice. They have the look and taste of miniature cheesecakes.

LITTLE BITS

Butter
Graham cracker crumbs
3 eggs, separated
¾ cup sugar
2 (8-ounce) packages cream cheese, softened
Sour Cream Filling

Butter 1½-inch muffin tins, and coat generously with graham cracker crumbs; set aside.

Cream egg yolks, sugar, and cream cheese until fluffy. Beat egg whites until stiff; fold into creamed mixture.

Spoon cream cheese mixture into muffin tins, filling three-fourths full. Bake at 350° for 20 minutes. Cool 10 to 15 minutes (centers will fall, forming an indentation). Carefully remove from muffin tins; spoon 1 teaspoon Sour Cream Filling into each indentation. Store in refrigerator. Yield: 4 dozen.

Sour Cream Filling:

1 (8-ounce) carton commercial sour cream
¾ cup sugar
½ teaspoon vanilla extract

Combine all ingredients in a 9-inch pieplate; stir well. Bake at 400° for 5 minutes. Stir well, and bake an additional 3 minutes. Yield: 1 cup.
Mrs. Harry B. Dawson,
Jacksonville, Florida.

The center of Little Bits sinks slightly on cooling, forming an indentation that holds Sour Cream Filling.

October

Fall brings a bountiful harvest in the South with tastes and aromas as exhilarating as the brisk days of October. From mulled apple cider to a moist persimmon cake, you will find recipes that use the season's produce to its fullest. And we have included guidelines for selection and storage, too.

To take the chill off a crisp fall day, try a steaming pot of homemade soup or stew. Whether you choose filling Meatball Stew or Spicy Vegetable Soup, the result is the same—a satisfying meal-in-a-bowl.

With October comes that special holiday for children—Halloween. And we offer treats sure to please even the toughest goblin. Another way to please children of all ages on any day is to bake a big batch of homemade cookies.

Soups And Stews Take The Chill Off

Piping hot soups and stews, thick and rich with seasonings, add warmth to a crisp fall day. Flavored with beef, chicken, seafood, or vegetables, they are a satisfying main dish for even the heartiest of appetites.

Meatball Stew, chock-full of onions, potatoes, and carrots, is thick enough to eat with a fork. Although convenience foods are used to shorten preparation time, this robust stew has a distinctive homemade flavor.

For a steaming pot of Spicy Vegetable Soup, use leftover vegetables you have on hand. This nutritious blend of ingredients is even better the day after it's made when the flavors have had time to blend.

Cheese is an essential ingredient in two of our chowder recipes: Cream cheese flavors Shrimp and Corn Chowder, and Ham 'n Cheese Chowder is thick with shredded Cheddar.

And what Southerner can think of soups and stews without thinking of gumbo? We recommend spicy Seafood Gumbo and Chicken Gumbo.

MEATBALL STEW

1½ pounds ground beef
1 egg, slightly beaten
¾ cup soft breadcrumbs
¼ cup finely chopped onion
1 teaspoon salt
1 tablespoon vegetable oil
1 (10½-ounce) can beef broth
1 (10¾-ounce) can tomato soup
¼ teaspoon dried thyme
1 (16-ounce) can sliced carrots, drained
1 (16-ounce) can whole white potatoes, drained
1 (16-ounce) jar small boiled onions, drained

Combine beef, egg, breadcrumbs, onion, and salt; mix well, and shape into 1-inch balls. Brown well in hot oil; drain off excess drippings.

Combine beef broth and tomato soup, mixing well; pour over meatballs. Add thyme, carrots, potatoes, and onions; simmer, stirring occasionally, 15 to 20 minutes or until soup is thoroughly heated. Yield: 6 to 8 servings.
Martha T. Efird,
Albemarle, North Carolina.

CHICKEN, HAM, AND OYSTER SOUP

4 (16-ounce) cans stewed tomatoes
4 chicken bouillon cubes
1 teaspoon salt
1 teaspoon whole basil leaves, crushed
½ teaspoon rubbed sage
8 drops hot sauce
1 cup diced onion
1 cup diced green pepper
1 cup sliced mushrooms
¼ cup melted butter or margarine
2 (10½-ounce) cans tomato soup, undiluted
1½ cups water
1½ cups diced cooked chicken
1½ cups diced cooked ham
2 (12-ounce) cans fresh oysters, drained
¼ cup dry white wine
½ cup sliced pimiento-stuffed olives

Combine tomatoes, bouillon cubes, salt, basil, sage, and hot sauce in a Dutch oven; stir well. Bring to a boil; lower heat, and simmer 30 minutes.

Sauté onion, green pepper, and mushrooms in butter 5 minutes. Stir vegetables, soup, water, chicken, and ham into tomato mixture; simmer 5 minutes. Add oysters and wine to soup; simmer 5 to 8 minutes or until edges of oysters curl. Stir olives into soup before serving. Yield: 10 to 12 servings.
Mrs. Eunice Palmer,
Morris Chapel, Tennessee.

SPICY VEGETABLE SOUP

1½ pounds meaty soup bones
6 cups water
1 teaspoon whole oregano
1 tablespoon garlic salt
2 teaspoons salt
½ to 1 teaspoon pepper
2 small bay leaves
1 tablespoon minced parsley
2 medium potatoes, cut into ½-inch pieces
¾ cup diced carrots
¾ cup frozen whole kernel corn
1 (28-ounce) can tomatoes, undrained
½ cup frozen English peas
2 onions, quartered
½ to ¾ cup uncooked barley

Combine first 8 ingredients in a large Dutch oven; bring to a boil, and cook over low heat about 30 minutes. Add remaining ingredients, and simmer 1½ hours. Remove soup bones; cut meat from bones, and return meat to soup. Yield: 6 to 8 servings.
Mrs. John J. O'Neill,
Welaka, Florida.

HOMEMADE SOUP

1 pound pork chops
7 cups water
2 teaspoons salt
½ teaspoon pepper
5 tablespoons dried onion flakes
1 (16-ounce) can tomatoes
½ cup diced carrots
1 cup fresh or frozen black-eyed peas
1 cup snapped fresh green beans
1 cup whole kernel white corn
1½ cups diced potatoes
1 cup shredded cabbage

Combine first 5 ingredients in a large Dutch oven; cook about 45 minutes or until meat is tender. Discard bones, and cut meat into bite-size pieces. Skim fat off top of broth. Add remaining ingredients except potatoes and cabbage. Cook 30 minutes; add potatoes and cabbage, and cook soup an additional 30 minutes. Yield: 6 to 8 servings.
Mrs. John Uecke,
Fort Belvoir, Virginia.

SEAFOOD GUMBO

2 (32-ounce) bottles tomato juice
1 (8-ounce) bottle clam juice
1 (16-ounce) can stewed tomatoes
1 (3-ounce) package crab boil
1 cup chopped green onion
1 cup chopped red onion
1 cup chopped celery
½ cup chopped green pepper
2 tablespoons vegetable oil
½ teaspoon garlic salt
1 (12-ounce) can fresh oysters
1 (18-ounce) package frozen cut okra
2 pounds medium shrimp, cooked, peeled, and deveined
1 pound fresh crabmeat
Hot cooked rice (optional)

Combine tomato juice, clam juice, tomatoes, and crab boil in a large Dutch oven; bring to a boil. Reduce heat; cover and place over low heat.

Sauté onion, celery, and green pepper in oil until tender. Add vegetable mixture to tomato juice mixture. Cover and simmer over low heat 1 to 1½ hours or until seasoned to taste. (The longer the bag of crab boil simmers, the spicier the mixture will be.) Remove crab boil. Add garlic salt; cover and simmer an additional 2 hours.

Drain oysters, reserving liquid. Add oyster liquid and okra to gumbo 30 minutes before end of cooking time. Add shrimp, crabmeat, and oysters 10 minutes before end of cooking time; simmer until edges of oysters begin to curl. Serve over hot cooked rice, if desired. Yield: 12 to 15 servings.

Linda Barnett,
Birmingham, Alabama.

CHICKEN GUMBO

2 tablespoons all-purpose flour
½ cup vegetable oil
1 slice bacon, diced
1 onion, chopped
½ green pepper, chopped
1 clove garlic, minced
1 teaspoon soy sauce
1 tablespoon Worcestershire sauce
1 teaspoon salt
Dash of pepper
Dash of hot sauce
1 (16-ounce) can tomatoes
4 whole chicken breasts
2 to 3 cups water
1 cup frozen cut okra
1½ teaspoons filé powder
Hot cooked rice

Combine flour and vegetable oil in a large Dutch oven; stir over medium heat until flour is lightly browned. Stir in bacon, and cook 1 minute. Add onion, green pepper, and garlic; cook until onion is transparent. Add the next 8 ingredients. Simmer 45 minutes or until chicken is tender.

Remove chicken; discard bones and skin. Chop chicken, and return to Dutch oven. Add okra, and cook 10 minutes. Stir in filé just before serving. Serve gumbo over hot cooked rice. Yield: 6 to 8 servings.

Mrs. Fred Horner, Jr.,
Uvalde, Texas.

HAM 'N CHEESE CHOWDER

½ cup water
Dash of salt
2 cups peeled and cubed potatoes
3 tablespoons butter or margarine
1 cup chopped onion
3 tablespoons all-purpose flour
Dash of pepper
3 cups milk
1½ cups diced cooked ham
1½ cups (6 ounces) shredded Cheddar
  cheese
Croutons (optional)

Place ½ cup water and salt in a small saucepan; bring to a boil. Add potatoes, and reduce heat; cook 15 minutes or until potatoes are tender. Drain potatoes, reserving liquid. Set potatoes aside. Add enough water to potato liquid to make 1 cup; set aside.

Melt butter in a 3-quart Dutch oven; add onion, and sauté until tender. Blend in flour and pepper. Stir in milk and potato liquid; cook over medium heat until mixture is bubbly and slightly thickened. Add cooked potatoes and ham; heat gently. Remove from heat, and stir in cheese. Top with croutons, if desired. Yield: 6 to 8 servings.

Mrs. Leon Johnson,
Fordyce, Arkansas.

SHRIMP AND CORN CHOWDER

1 tablespoon butter or margarine
¼ cup chopped green onion
1 clove garlic, minced
⅛ teaspoon pepper
2 (10¾-ounce) cans cream of potato soup,
  undiluted
2 cups milk
1 (3-ounce) package cream cheese,
  softened
1 (8¾-ounce) can whole kernel corn,
  undrained
1½ pounds fresh shrimp, peeled and
  deveined

Melt butter in a large Dutch oven; add onion, garlic, and pepper. Sauté until tender. Stir in soup, milk, cream cheese, and corn; bring to a boil, stirring occasionally.

Add shrimp; then cover, reduce heat, and cook 5 to 7 minutes. Serve hot. Yield: about 8 servings.

Mrs. Cathy Darling,
Maidsville, West Virginia.

Now Comes Autumn's Delectable Harvest

Golden pumpkins, juicy apples, plump sweet potatoes, crunchy pecans, and sweet persimmons paint the Southern countryside with the rich, warm hues of the autumn season.

It's time for fall harvest, and the excitement returns each year as orchard owners nail up signs encouraging passers-by to stop and gather some of the bounty themselves—and roadside stands pop up along the highways offering an alternative for the less adventuresome.

Faced with such an abundance, it's often difficult to know which are the best choices. So here are some tips to help you choose and properly store your selections.

And since you'll want to capture the season's robust flavors in breads, pies, cakes, and dishes like Stuffed Baked Sweet Potatoes and Pumpkin Drop Cookies, we offer a whole temptation of recipes.

Apples: "Most people want to purchase an apple that's big, juicy, and red, but they aren't always the best for cooking or eating," explains Rachel Graves, who helps her husband, Jim, manage their apple farm near Syria, Virginia.

"The flavor and texture varies among apples of the same type, as well as among different types," Jim adds. "Some big, red apples have no flavor at all, but that's impossible to tell without tasting them."

The apple you select should depend on personal preference. "Some people cultivate a taste for cooking apples and prefer them over eating apples," comments Rachel, "just as some people prefer to eat rare roast beef while others like it well done."

The sweetest apples are the Delicious type, with Red Delicious being sweeter than Golden. The Graves think the Golden Delicious is the best all-purpose apple because it is sweet enough to classify as an eating apple and also holds its consistency when cooked.

Red and Golden Delicious apples are grown all across the South; so are Winesap and York, popular for cooking and eating, and Stayman, widely used for cooking.

While McIntosh and Rome Beauty apples are not commonly grown in the South, they are popular because of their common availability in grocery stores.

McIntosh is excellent for applesauce and eating out of hand, while Rome Beauty is a popular cooking apple.

Apples are a wise choice for between-meal snacks because they contain moderate amounts of several important nutrients, including calcium, phosphorus, and iron. Store apples in the refrigerator or other cool place where the temperature can be maintained at 38° to 40°.

Pecans: A longtime Southern favorite, pecans are considered by many to be a luxury, but that shouldn't be the case according to Michael Wetherbee, a Georgia pecan grower. "Both walnuts and almonds, two competitive nuts, are sometimes priced just as much as pecans," he explains.

Wetherbee suggests buying shelled pecans rather than unshelled because the valuable time required for shelling makes them worth the higher price. If you choose to shell your own, you can usually expect about 4¼ cups or 1 pound of shelled pecans from 2 pounds of unshelled. If you plan to chop pecans for cooking, remember that pecan pieces are usually less expensive than halves.

Nutritionally, most people think of pecans as being high in calories, as well as fats; however, keep in mind that they also contain protein, iron, vitamin A, thiamine, riboflavin, and niacin.

While pecans are harvested during the fall months, they are easily stored for year-round enjoyment. Pecans maintain freshness longer when unshelled, storing up to one year in the refrigerator; shelled, up to nine months. Pecans may be frozen as long as two years, either shelled or unshelled. At room temperature, unshelled pecans will stay fresh for four months; shelled, two months. Store all pecans in tightly covered containers.

Persimmons: If you've ever bitten into a persimmon to discover a highly astringent taste, you know that only ripe persimmons have a pleasing sweet flavor. John McAvoy, an Alabama farmer, says you can tell a persimmon is ripe when it starts to shrivel. Although McAvoy usually waits until frost to pick his persimmons, he says they're ready when they start falling off the tree.

There are two types of persimmons grown in the South, although very few of either are grown commercially, according to McAvoy. "The American persimmon (native type), which is the smaller of the two, will not ripen after being picked so it must be left on the tree until fully ripe," he continued, "but

most Oriental persimmons will ripen after they are picked."

Because persimmons are a delicate fruit, they should be refrigerated as soon as ripe and used within a few days. Oriental persimmons are high in vitamin A, while the American type is a good source of vitamin C.

Pumpkins: It's unfortunate that most people reach for a can of pumpkin rather than selecting a fresh one straight from the field. Besides missing the fun of selecting your own pumpkin, you'll also be missing the more distinctive flavor of fresh pumpkin.

Mrs. Elmo Tant, wife of a North Carolina pumpkin grower, says, "When selecting pumpkins for cooking purposes, it's good to remember that this is one time that the biggest is not the best." Mrs. Tant suggests selecting smaller pumpkins since they have more tender flesh and contain less water, resulting in less waste. You'll find that a 5-pound pumpkin will yield about 4½ cups of mashed cooked pulp.

Although pumpkins are most popular during autumn, they can be stored to prolong your enjoyment. Pumpkins maintained at about 68° will keep about one month; stored in the refrigerator, most whole pumpkins will keep for two or three months.

Sweet potatoes: While a sweet potato is not really a yam, that's how most Southerners know them. And there is a good reason for this, according to L. J. Duplechain, executive director of the Louisiana Sweet Potato Commission.

"Southerners call their moist-meated sweet potatoes 'yams' to distinguish them from the dry-meated types grown in the more northern areas," Duplechain explained.

"The two types are altogether different," he said. "The moist type, which is the best for baking, is orange-copper colored with a much sweeter taste and smoother texture than the whitish-tan dry type.

"Most people think they should store sweet potatoes in the refrigerator, but that is absolutely incorrect—they should never be refrigerated," he said. "The best temperature for storing is 65°, but never below 55°. If refrigerated, the potatoes will turn black, lose flavor, and rot."

Sweet potatoes make a nutritious addition to meals, containing large amounts of vitamins A and C.

Feasting On A Harvest Of Flavors

Southerners celebrate fall harvest with old-fashioned sweet potato pie, spicy cider and apple butter, cakes and cookies moist with pumpkin or persimmons—and almost everything crunchy with pecans.

It's a veritable feast of flavors, and this collection of recipes offers a wealth of delightful ways to enjoy the harvest to the fullest. Besides old favorites, there are some new variations: apple pie tangy with cranberries, persimmons tossed in a salad, pumpkin baked in muffins.

APPLE BUTTER

1 gallon sweet apple cider
7 pounds (about 3 dozen medium) tart cooking apples, cored, peeled, and quartered
1 tablespoon ground cinnamon
2 teaspoons ground nutmeg
¾ teaspoon ground cloves
Sugar to taste

Bring cider to a boil in a large saucepan or Dutch oven; boil until reduced by half. Add apples; allow mixture to return to a boil. Reduce heat; simmer, stirring frequently, 4 to 5 hours or until mixture is dark brown and consistency of marmalade. Stir in remaining ingredients.

Pour hot mixture into sterilized jars, leaving ¼-inch headspace; cover at once with metal lids, and screw metal bands tight. Process in boiling-water bath for 10 minutes. Yield: 4 pints.
Pam Brown,
Atlanta, Georgia.

With the brisk days of fall comes an abundance of produce—pumpkins, apples, sweet potatoes, pecans.

Page 204: Chocolate-Covered Pecan Fritters and Miniature Pecan Pies (page 205) are delectable ways to savor the crunchiness of pecans.

Above: Warm up those brisk fall days with Hot Mulled Cider and a slice of Apple Bread or Autumn Apple Pie (page 205).

Right: Sweet Potatoes are the basis of some of the South's favorite dishes: Sweet Potato Pie, Stuffed Baked Sweet Potatoes, and Sweet Potato Cake (page 207).

Far Right: A sprinkling of powdered sugar adds the final touch to this moist Persimmon Cake (page 205).

AUTUMN APPLE PIE

2 cups sugar
¼ cup cornstarch
½ teaspoon ground cinnamon
5 cups peeled, sliced apples
2 cups fresh cranberries
½ teaspoon grated lemon rind
Pastry for deep-dish double crust
   9-inch pie
Milk
1 tablespoon sugar
Ice cream (optional)

Combine 2 cups sugar, cornstarch, and cinnamon; set aside. Combine apples, cranberries, and lemon rind; sprinkle with sugar mixture. Spoon into a pastry-lined deep-dish 9-inch pieplate.

Roll out remaining pastry, and place over fruit; press edges together to seal. Make several slits in top to allow steam to escape. Brush top with milk, and sprinkle with 1 tablespoon sugar. Bake at 350° for 1 hour or until golden brown. Serve warm; top with ice cream, if desired. Yield: 8 servings.
Linda Schooler,
Amarillo, Texas.

APPLE BREAD

½ cup margarine, softened
1 cup sugar
2 eggs
2 cups all-purpose flour
½ teaspoon salt
1 teaspoon soda
2 tablespoons buttermilk
1 teaspoon vanilla extract
2 cups peeled, diced apples
Topping (recipe follows)

Combine margarine and sugar in a large mixing bowl, creaming until light and fluffy. Add eggs, and mix well. Stir in flour and salt.

Dissolve soda in buttermilk; add to batter, mixing well. Stir in vanilla and apples. Spoon into a greased and floured 9- x 5- x 3-inch loafpan. Sprinkle with topping; bake at 325° for 1 hour and 10 minutes or until bread tests done. Yield: 1 loaf.

Topping:
2 tablespoons margarine, softened
2 tablespoons sugar
2 tablespoons all-purpose flour
1 teaspoon ground cinnamon

Combine all ingredients in a medium mixing bowl; mix with pastry blender until consistency of coarse crumbs. Yield: about ¼ cup. *Penny Owen,*
Raleigh, North Carolina.

HOT MULLED CIDER

1 medium orange, cut into 5 slices
2 quarts apple cider
½ cup firmly packed light brown sugar
1 teaspoon whole allspice
16 whole cloves
10 cinnamon sticks

Cut 2 orange slices into quarters, and set aside.

Combine remaining orange slices, cider, sugar, allspice, cloves, and 2 cinnamon sticks in a 3-quart saucepan; bring to a boil. Reduce heat, and simmer 15 minutes. Stir well, and pour into serving mugs; garnish each with a quarter of an orange slice and a cinnamon stick. Yield: 8 servings.
Mrs. Opal D. Cooper,
Bentonville, Arkansas.

PECAN SQUARES

2 tablespoons butter or margarine
2 eggs
¾ teaspoon vanilla extract
¾ teaspoon lemon extract
1 cup firmly packed brown sugar
¼ cup plus 1 tablespoon all-purpose flour
⅛ teaspoon soda
⅛ teaspoon salt
1 cup coarsely chopped pecans
Powdered sugar (optional)

Melt butter in an 8-inch square pan. Set aside.

Combine eggs and flavorings; beat until thickened. Add sugar, beating well.

Combine flour, soda, and salt; stir in pecans. Add to egg mixture, beating until well blended.

Pour mixture over butter in pan; bake at 325° for 40 to 45 minutes or until done. Cool. Sprinkle lightly with powdered sugar, if desired. Cut into 2-inch squares. Yield: 16 squares.
Grace Samples,
Staunton, Virginia.

MINIATURE PECAN PIES

½ cup sugar
1 cup dark corn syrup
2 tablespoons butter or margarine
¼ teaspoon salt
3 eggs
1 cup coarsely chopped pecans
½ teaspoon vanilla extract
16 (2-inch) unbaked tart shells

Combine sugar, corn syrup, butter, and salt in a saucepan; bring to a boil,

stirring constantly. Remove from heat.

Break eggs into a medium bowl; remove 1 tablespoon egg white, and set aside. Beat remaining eggs with a fork until well combined. Gradually add hot mixture to beaten eggs, stirring constantly. Stir in pecans and vanilla.

Beat reserved egg white until foamy; lightly brush on inside of each tart shell. Spoon filling into tart shells, filling three-fourths full. Bake at 450° for 5 minutes; reduce heat to 325°, and bake 12 minutes or until filling is set. Yield: 16 (2-inch) pies. *Mrs. M. W. Sears,*
Sumter, South Carolina.

CHOCOLATE-COVERED PECAN FRITTERS

2 (6¼-ounce) packages vanilla caramels
2 tablespoons evaporated milk
2 cups pecan halves
1 (8-ounce) bar milk chocolate, broken
   into squares
⅓ bar paraffin, broken into pieces

Combine caramels and milk in top of double boiler; heat until caramels melt, stirring occasionally. Beat with wooden spoon until creamy; stir in pecans. Drop by teaspoonfuls onto buttered waxed paper; let stand 15 minutes.

Combine chocolate and paraffin in top of double boiler; heat until melted and smooth, stirring occasionally. Using a toothpick, dip each fritter into chocolate mixture. Place on waxed paper to cool. Yield: 4 dozen.
Mrs. George E. Robison,
Mobile, Alabama.

PERSIMMON CAKE

3 cups all-purpose flour
2 cups sugar
1 teaspoon ground cinnamon
½ teaspoon salt
1 teaspoon soda
1 cup vegetable oil
3 eggs, slightly beaten
1½ cups persimmon pulp
1 cup chopped walnuts
Powdered sugar

Combine first 9 ingredients, mixing well. Pour into a greased and floured 10-inch Bundt pan. Bake at 325° for 1 hour or until done. Remove from pan while warm. Dust with powdered sugar. Yield: one 10-inch cake.
Mrs. Larry Bailey,
Denton, Texas.

PERSIMMON PIE

1 cup all-purpose flour
¾ cup sugar
½ teaspoon baking powder
¼ teaspoon salt
¼ teaspoon ground cinnamon
Dash of ground nutmeg
1 cup persimmon pulp
⅓ cup milk
1 egg, beaten
1 teaspoon vanilla extract
1 unbaked 9-inch pastry shell

Combine dry ingredients, mixing well; stir in persimmon pulp, milk, egg, and vanilla. Pour into pastry shell, and bake at 350° for 30 to 35 minutes or until a knife inserted in center comes out clean. Cool. Yield: one 9-inch pie.
Pat Andrus,
Scott, Louisiana.

PERSIMMON PUDDING

2 cups self-rising flour
2 cups sugar
1 teaspoon ground cinnamon
2 eggs, beaten
2 cups milk
2 cups persimmon pulp
1 cup shredded raw sweet potato
2 tablespoons melted butter or margarine

Combine flour, sugar, and cinnamon; mix well. Stir in eggs and milk. Add remaining ingredients, mixing well. Pour into a greased 13- x 9- x 2-inch baking pan. Bake at 350° for 45 minutes or until set. Yield: 15 servings.
M. L. Hayes,
Charlotte, North Carolina.

PERSIMMON FRUIT SALAD

1 (11-ounce) can mandarin oranges, drained
2 cups diced apple
2 bananas, sliced
½ cup peeled, sliced persimmons
¼ cup chopped black walnuts
½ cup salad dressing or mayonnaise
¼ cup whipped cream
1 teaspoon sugar

Combine fruits and nuts, stirring gently. Combine remaining ingredients; mix well, and pour over fruit mixture. Toss lightly. Chill 1 to 2 hours. Yield: 4 to 6 servings. *Captain Hugh Poole,*
Conyers, Georgia.

■ To prepare fresh pumpkin for these and other recipes, follow this procedure: Use one small pumpkin; wash well, and cut in half crosswise. Place halves, cut side down, in a 15- x 10- x 1-inch jellyroll pan. Bake at 325° for 45 minutes or until fork tender; cool 10 minutes. Peel pumpkin, and discard seeds. Puree pulp in food processor, or mash thoroughly. Cover and place in refrigerator. Cooked pumpkin will keep well for four or five days.

PUMPKIN DROP COOKIES

1 cup cooked, mashed pumpkin
½ cup butter or margarine, softened
1 cup firmly packed brown sugar
¾ cup sugar
1 egg
1 teaspoon ground cinnamon
½ teaspoon ground nutmeg
1¼ cups all-purpose flour
1½ teaspoons salt
1 teaspoon baking powder
¼ teaspoon soda
¾ cup quick-cooking oats, uncooked
1 cup chopped pecans or black walnuts
1 cup raisins
1 (6-ounce) package semisweet chocolate morsels

See above for the proper procedure for cooking fresh pumpkin.
Combine butter and sugar, creaming thoroughly. Add pumpkin, egg, cinnamon, and nutmeg; beat mixture until light and fluffy. Add flour, salt, baking powder, and soda, mixing well. Stir in remaining ingredients.
Drop by teaspoonfuls onto lightly greased cookie sheets. Bake at 375° for 12 to 15 minutes. Cool cookies on wire rack. Yield: about 6 dozen.
Rena C. Nixon,
Mount Airy, North Carolina.

PUMPKIN MUFFINS

1 cup cooked, mashed pumpkin
1 cup white seedless raisins
½ cup water
2 eggs
1¼ cups sugar
¾ teaspoon ground cinnamon
¾ teaspoon ground cloves
½ teaspoon salt
⅓ cup vegetable oil
1¾ cups all-purpose flour
1½ teaspoons baking powder
½ teaspoon soda

See above for the proper procedure for cooking fresh pumpkin.
Soak raisins in ½ cup water; set aside (do not drain).
Combine eggs, pumpkin, sugar, spices, salt, and oil; beat well. Stir in raisins and water; set aside.
Combine remaining ingredients in a large mixing bowl; make a well in center. Pour in pumpkin mixture, stirring just until moistened (batter will be slightly lumpy).
Spoon batter into greased muffin pans, filling two-thirds full. Bake at 400° for 25 minutes. Yield: about 2 dozen muffins.
Mrs. Mary Dishon,
Stanford, Kentucky.

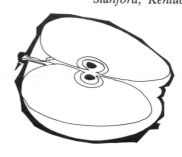

PUMPKIN ROLL

⅔ cup cooked, mashed pumpkin
3 eggs
1 cup sugar
1 teaspoon lemon juice
¾ cup all-purpose flour
1 teaspoon baking powder
½ teaspoon salt
2 tablespoons ground cinnamon
1 teaspoon ground ginger
½ teaspoon ground nutmeg
1 cup finely chopped walnuts
Powdered sugar
Filling (recipe follows)

See above for the proper procedure for cooking fresh pumpkin.
Beat eggs at high speed of electric mixer 5 minutes or until pale yellow; gradually beat in sugar. Stir in pumpkin and lemon juice.
Combine flour, baking powder, salt, cinnamon, ginger, and nutmeg; fold into pumpkin mixture. Pour batter into a greased and floured 15- x 10- x 1-inch jellyroll pan, spreading evenly; sprinkle with nuts. Bake at 375° for 15 minutes or until top of cake springs back when lightly touched.
Sprinkle powdered sugar on a towel. Loosen edges of cake, and immediately invert onto towel. Roll up cake in towel, beginning with narrow edge. Cool cake completely. Unroll cake; spread with filling to ½ inch of edges. Re-roll cake; chill. Store in refrigerator. Yield: 10 to 12 servings.

Filling:

1 cup powdered sugar
2 (3-ounce) packages cream cheese, softened
¼ cup butter, softened
½ teaspoon vanilla extract

Combine all ingredients in a small bowl; beat at medium speed of electric mixer until smooth and creamy. Yield: about 1¼ cups.　*Irene Pohlman, Baltimore, Maryland.*

SWEET POTATO CAKE

3 cups all-purpose flour
2 cups sugar
2 teaspoons baking powder
1 teaspoon soda
¼ teaspoon salt
2 teaspoons ground cinnamon
1 cup vegetable oil
1 (15¼-ounce) can crushed pineapple, undrained
2 teaspoons vanilla extract
3 eggs
2 cups grated raw sweet potatoes
1 cup chopped pecans

Combine dry ingredients; add oil, pineapple, and vanilla. Mix until well blended. Add eggs, one at a time, beating well after each addition. Stir in sweet potatoes and pecans. Pour into a greased and floured 10-inch tube pan. Bake at 350° for 1 hour and 15 minutes. Yield: one 10-inch cake.
Mrs. T. Meade, Dayton, Ohio.

SWEET POTATO PIE

2 cups cooked, mashed sweet potatoes
1 egg, slightly beaten
¼ cup sugar
¼ cup milk
2 tablespoons margarine, melted
1 teaspoon ground cinnamon
1 unbaked 9-inch pastry shell

Combine first 6 ingredients, and beat at medium speed of electric mixer until well blended. Spoon into pastry shell. Bake at 425° for 35 minutes or until knife inserted halfway between center and edge of pie comes out clean; cool before serving. Yield: one 9-inch pie.
Mrs. Elizabeth A. Lewis, Birmingham, Alabama.

STUFFED BAKED SWEET POTATOES

6 medium-size sweet potatoes
½ cup orange juice
3 tablespoons butter or margarine
1 teaspoon salt
1 (8-ounce) can crushed pineapple, drained
½ cup chopped pecans

Bake sweet potatoes at 375° for 1 hour or until tender. Cut a 1-inch lengthwise strip from top of each potato; carefully scoop pulp from shell.

Combine potato pulp, orange juice, butter, and salt; beat at medium speed of electric mixer until fluffy. Stir in pineapple. Stuff shells with potato mixture, and sprinkle with pecans. Bake at 375° for 12 minutes. Yield: 6 servings.
Mrs. Glenna Scherle, Louisville, Kentucky.

Add The Warm Taste Of Ginger

No one will deny the old-fashioned goodness of gingersnaps, and an Arkansas reader submits one of the best versions we've tasted. You'll want to save three of these spicy cookies to prepare Cocktail Meatballs.

For Tasty Nut Muffins, ginger teams up with cinnamon and nutmeg for a muffin that is as good as the name implies. You'll also want to try our mouthwatering chicken and vegetable selections, both of them sparked with the flavor of ginger.

CHICKEN WITH CASHEWS

2 large whole chicken breasts, skinned, boned, and halved
¼ cup water
¼ cup dry sherry
¼ cup soy sauce
1 tablespoon plus 1 teaspoon cornstarch
2 tablespoons dark corn syrup
1 tablespoon vinegar
¼ cup peanut oil
½ cup coarsely chopped green pepper
½ cup cashews
2 tablespoons sliced green onion
2 cloves garlic, minced
¼ teaspoon ground ginger
Hot cooked rice

Cut chicken into 1-inch pieces; set aside. Combine water, sherry, soy sauce, cornstarch, syrup, and vinegar; mix well and set aside.

Heat wok to 375° or high heat for 2 minutes. Pour oil around top of wok to coat sides; heat 1½ to 2 minutes. Add chicken; stir-fry 2 to 3 minutes, or until chicken turns white, and push up sides of wok. Add green pepper and cashews; stir-fry 30 seconds, and push up sides. Add onion, garlic, and ginger; stir-fry 1 minute, and push up sides. Add cornstarch mixture; bring to a boil, stirring constantly. Cook 1 additional minute, stirring all ingredients with sauce. Serve over hot cooked rice. Yield: 4 servings.　*Mrs. Archer Yates, Dunwoody, Georgia.*

COCKTAIL MEATBALLS

1½ pounds ground chuck
¼ cup seasoned breadcrumbs
1 medium onion, chopped
2 teaspoons prepared horseradish
2 cloves garlic, crushed
¾ cup tomato juice
2 teaspoons salt
¼ teaspoon pepper
2 tablespoons margarine
1 medium onion, chopped
2 tablespoons all-purpose flour
1½ cups beef broth
½ cup dry red wine
2 tablespoons brown sugar
2 tablespoons catsup
1 tablespoon lemon juice
3 gingersnaps, crumbled

Combine first 8 ingredients, mixing well. Shape into 1-inch balls; place in a 13- x 9- x 2-inch baking dish. Bake at 450° for 20 minutes. Remove from oven, and drain off excess fat.

Heat margarine in a large skillet; sauté onion until tender. Blend in flour; gradually add beef broth, stirring constantly. Add remaining ingredients. Cook over low heat 15 minutes; add meatballs, and simmer 5 minutes. Yield: about 4 dozen.　*Kathy Jones, Ozark, Alabama.*

FRESH VEGETABLE POTPOURRI

2 tablespoons vegetable oil
½ cup chopped onion
3 cloves garlic, finely minced
1 (½-inch) slice fresh gingerroot, peeled
    and finely chopped
½ head fresh broccoli, broken into
    flowerets and 1-inch pieces
2 carrots, thinly sliced
2 stalks celery, sliced into 1-inch pieces
1 green pepper, sliced into 1-inch pieces
1 large onion, cut into 8 wedges
½ cup sliced almonds
½ cup soy sauce
1 tablespoon honey or sugar
2 to 3 tablespoons all-purpose flour
1 cup water
Hot cooked rice (optional)

Heat oil in a 10-inch skillet; add chopped onion, garlic, and gingerroot. Cook on low heat until onion is tender. Add remaining vegetables, almonds, soy sauce, and honey; heat to boiling. Reduce to low heat and cover. Cook 8 to 10 minutes or until vegetables are crisp-tender.

Combine flour and water; stir into vegetable mixture. Cook 5 to 7 minutes or until vegetables are tender and sauce is thickened, stirring occasionally. Serve over hot cooked rice, if desired. Yield: 6 servings.   *Mrs. Sandy Wallace,*
Pompano Beach, Florida.

TASTY NUT MUFFINS

2 eggs, beaten
½ cup honey
1 cup vegetable oil
1 cup chopped nuts
1 teaspoon vinegar
1¼ cups milk
2 cups whole wheat flour
1 cup all-purpose flour
1 teaspoon baking powder
1 teaspoon salt
1 teaspoon soda
¾ teaspoon ground allspice
¾ teaspoon ground ginger
¾ teaspoon ground cinnamon

Combine eggs, honey, and oil; mix well. Stir in nuts, and set aside.

Stir vinegar into milk; combine dry ingredients and add to egg mixture alternately with milk mixture, stirring only to blend. Spoon batter into greased and floured muffin pans, filling two-thirds full. Bake at 375° for 20 minutes or until done. Yield: about 1½ dozen.
Robbin Dorrier,
Mooresville, North Carolina.

BEST-EVER GINGERSNAPS

1 cup sugar
2 cups all-purpose flour
½ teaspoon salt
1 teaspoon soda
1 teaspoon ground cinnamon
1 teaspoon ground ginger
½ teaspoon ground cloves
¾ cup shortening
¼ cup molasses
1 egg, slightly beaten
Sugar

Combine 1 cup sugar, flour, salt, soda, and spices; stir lightly. Cut in shortening to resemble coarse crumbs. Stir in molasses and egg.

Shape dough into 1-inch balls, and roll them in sugar. Place on ungreased baking sheets; bake at 350° for 10 minutes. Remove from baking sheets immediately. (Cookies will firm quickly as they cool.) Yield: about 4½ dozen.
Mrs. Steve Toney,
Helena, Arkansas.

Sour Cream Makes The Difference

Coffee cake gets extra moistness and pancakes are fluffier when sour cream is an ingredient. In this collection of recipes, it also lends its smooth, custard-like texture and pleasantly tart taste to a dip for fresh fruit and Creamy Avocado and Zucchini Salad.

In most cooked dishes, like Easy Hamburger Stroganoff, be sure to add the sour cream last and keep the temperature low. If heated at too high a temperature or held over low heat for an extended period, sour cream will curdle. If overstirred, sour cream will become thin; you can avoid this problem by folding it very carefully into the other ingredients.

ORANGE SOUR CREAM DIP

1 (6-ounce) can frozen orange juice
    concentrate, thawed and undiluted
1¼ cups milk
1 (3¾-ounce) package vanilla-flavored
    instant pudding and pie filling mix
¼ cup commercial sour cream
1 medium-size fresh pineapple
Assorted fresh fruits

Combine orange juice concentrate, milk, and pudding mix; beat with electric mixer until smooth (about 2 minutes). Stir in sour cream; chill 2 hours.

Cut pineapple in half lengthwise. Scoop out pulp, leaving shells intact; set aside shells. Cut pineapple pulp into chunks. Combine pineapple chunks and other assorted fruits; spoon into 1 pineapple shell. Spoon dip into remaining shell. Yield: 10 to 12 servings.
Martha Ann Edminster,
East Freetown, Massachusetts.

EASY HAMBURGER STROGANOFF

1 pound ground beef
1 medium onion, chopped
2 tablespoons all-purpose flour
½ teaspoon salt
½ teaspoon garlic salt
¼ teaspoon pepper
1 (8-ounce) can mushroom stems and
    pieces, drained
1 (10¾-ounce) can cream of chicken soup
1 (8-ounce) carton commercial sour cream
1 (8-ounce) package egg noodles, cooked
    and drained

Cook ground beef and onion until beef is browned and onion is tender. Stir in flour, salt, garlic salt, pepper, and mushrooms; cook over medium heat 5 minutes, stirring mixture constantly.

Stir soup into meat mixture; simmer 10 minutes, stirring occasionally. Stir in sour cream, and cook only until thoroughly heated. Serve over hot cooked noodles. Yield: 4 servings.
Susan Erickson,
State University, Arkansas.

CREAMY AVOCADO AND ZUCCHINI SALAD

½ cup commercial sour cream
¼ cup mayonnaise
2 tablespoons milk
1 teaspoon salt
½ teaspoon Italian seasoning
⅛ teaspoon garlic salt
3 medium avocados, peeled and cubed
3 medium zucchini, thinly sliced
Salad greens

Combine first 6 ingredients, stirring well. Add avocado and zucchini; toss gently. Serve on salad greens. Yield: 6 to 8 servings.   *Gloria Patrick,*
Tibbie, Alabama.

Sour Cream-Walnut Coffee Cake owes its delicate texture and moistness to sour cream.

floured 10-inch tube pan or Bundt pan; sprinkle with one-third of nut mixture. Repeat layers twice; bake at 350° for 1 hour or until done. Let stand 5 minutes before removing from pan. Place on serving dish, and drizzle with glaze. Yield: one 10-inch coffee cake.

Powdered Sugar Glaze:

1½ cups powdered sugar
2 tablespoons water
½ teaspoon vanilla extract

Combine all ingredients, mixing well. Yield: about 1 cup.   *Anne Ringer, Warner Robins, Georgia.*

Don't Forget These Special Squash

You know acorn squash by the green rind and acorn shape, butternut by its cream color and bulbous base. But once you taste these winter squash, you remember them for their delicious flavor.

Acorn squash is easy to prepare—simply slice, top with brown sugar, and bake. Or try layering the slices with ham and apples for a main-dish casserole called Harvest Ham Bake.

Like acorn squash, butternut combines well with apples for such tasty side dishes as Squash and Apple Casserole. You'll also want to enjoy the moist, spicy Squash Bread, prepared with either type squash.

FLUFFY SOUR CREAM PANCAKES

3 eggs, separated
1½ cups commercial sour cream
1 teaspoon soda
1¼ cups all-purpose flour
2 teaspoons sugar
1 teaspoon baking powder
½ teaspoon salt
3 tablespoons butter or margarine, softened

Beat egg yolks well. Combine sour cream and soda; stir into egg yolks. Combine flour, sugar, baking powder, and salt; stir into sour cream mixture. Add butter, and beat on medium speed of electric mixer 30 seconds. Beat egg whites until stiff peaks form; fold into batter.

For each pancake, pour about ¼ cup batter onto a hot, lightly greased griddle. Turn pancakes when tops are covered with bubbles and edges look cooked. Yield: 4 to 5 servings.

Mrs. Michael Champagne, Covington, Louisiana.

SOUR CREAM-WALNUT COFFEE CAKE

¾ cup butter or margarine, softened
1½ cups sugar
3 eggs
2 teaspoons vanilla extract
3 cups all-purpose flour
1½ teaspoons baking powder
1½ teaspoons soda
½ teaspoon salt
1 pint commercial sour cream
¾ cup firmly packed light brown sugar
2 teaspoons ground cinnamon
1 cup coarsely chopped walnuts
Powdered Sugar Glaze

Combine butter and sugar, creaming until light and fluffy. Add eggs, one at a time, beating well after each addition. Stir in vanilla.

Combine flour, baking powder, soda, and salt; add to creamed mixture alternately with sour cream, mixing well after each addition.

Combine brown sugar, cinnamon, and walnuts, mixing well. Spoon about one-third of batter into a greased and

SQUASH AND APPLE CASSEROLE

3 cups cubed, cooked butternut squash
1½ cups stewed apples
Salt
¾ cup firmly packed brown sugar
6 tablespoons butter or margarine
Ground cinnamon

Place 1 cup squash in a buttered casserole; top with ½ cup apples. Sprinkle lightly with salt and ¼ cup sugar; dot with 2 tablespoons butter. Repeat layers twice; sprinkle top with cinnamon. Bake at 350° for 45 minutes or until lightly browned. Yield: 6 to 8 servings.

Jane Teschner, Narragansett, Rhode Island.

HARVEST HAM BAKE

2 medium acorn squash
1½ pounds ham, sliced ½-inch thick
⅓ cup firmly packed brown sugar
2 tablespoons dry mustard
2 teaspoons water
3 medium cooking apples, cut into ½-inch slices
¼ teaspoon ground nutmeg
2 tablespoons butter or margarine
2 cups apple cider

Wash squash; cut into ¼-inch slices, and remove seeds. Place slices in a 2½-quart casserole and arrange ham slices on top.

Combine sugar, mustard, and water; spread over ham.

Arrange apples over ham; sprinkle with nutmeg, and dot with butter. Pour cider over casserole. Bake, uncovered, at 350° for 1½ hours, basting often. Yield: 6 to 8 servings.

Mrs. E. A. Kraus,
Louisville, Kentucky.

SQUASH AND APPLE BAKE

2 pounds butternut squash (about 2 small)
2 cooking apples, cut into ½-inch slices
½ cup firmly packed brown sugar
¼ cup butter or margarine, melted
1 tablespoon all-purpose flour
1 teaspoon salt
½ teaspoon ground mace

Cut each squash in half lengthwise; remove seeds. Peel squash, and cut into ½-inch slices. Arrange in a lightly greased 12- x 8- x 2-inch baking dish; top with apple slices.

Combine remaining ingredients, mixing well; spoon over apple slices. Cover tightly with foil. Bake at 350° for 1 hour and 15 minutes or until squash is tender. Yield: 6 to 8 servings.

Mrs. Gary Ferguson,
Dallas, Texas.

BUTTERNUT SQUASH CASSEROLE

2 cups cooked, mashed butternut squash
3 eggs, beaten
1 cup sugar
½ cup milk
⅓ cup butter or margarine, melted
2 tablespoons flaked coconut
½ teaspoon ground ginger
½ teaspoon coconut flavoring

Combine all ingredients, mixing well; pour into a lightly greased 1-quart casserole. Bake at 350° for 1 hour or until set. Yield: 5 to 6 servings.

Mrs. Mary Dishon,
Stanford, Kentucky.

SQUASH BREAD

1½ cups all-purpose flour
1 cup sugar
1 teaspoon soda
¼ teaspoon baking powder
½ teaspoon salt
½ teaspoon ground cinnamon
½ teaspoon ground nutmeg
1 cup cooked, mashed butternut or acorn squash
2 eggs, beaten
¼ cup melted margarine

Combine first 7 ingredients; stir lightly, and set aside.

Combine squash, eggs, and margarine; mix well. Add to flour mixture, stirring only until blended. Pour into a greased and floured 9- x 5- x 3-inch loafpan. Bake at 350° for 50 to 60 minutes or until bread tests done. Yield: 1 loaf.

Mary Borne,
Houma, Louisiana.

Perk Up Potatoes With Stuffing

Everyone enjoys a baked potato smothered with butter and sour cream, but for a change try flavoring the potato with herbs, Roquefort cheese, or a combination of bacon and Parmesan cheese.

For Creamy Stuffed Potatoes, the potato pulp is scooped out, then blended with sour cream, crumbled bacon, green onion, and Parmesan cheese.

Chunks of ham add interest to a creamy potato filling in Ham Stuffed Potatoes, while Roquefort cheese delicately flavors Potatoes Roquefort.

Eight can be served from only four potatoes with Tuna Stuffed Potatoes. The potatoes are halved and the pulp blended with flaked tuna, Cheddar cheese, green pepper, pimiento, and green onion. Beaten egg white, mayonnaise, and shredded Cheddar cheese are combined and spread over this hearty stuffing for a light, puffy topping.

HAM STUFFED POTATOES

4 large baking potatoes
Vegetable oil
1 egg, separated
½ cup finely chopped cooked ham
¼ cup milk
½ teaspoon salt
¼ teaspoon pepper

Scrub potatoes thoroughly and rub skins with oil; bake at 400° for 1 to 1¼ hours or until done.

Allow to cool to touch. Slice skin away from top of each potato. Carefully scoop out pulp, leaving shells intact; mash pulp.

Beat egg yolk; add ham, milk, salt, and pepper. Stir into potato pulp, mixing well. Beat egg white until stiff peaks form; fold into potato mixture. Stuff shells with mixture; bake at 450° for 10 minutes or until lightly browned. Yield: 4 servings. *Mrs. Wayne Snellgrove,*
La Grange, Georgia.

TUNA STUFFED POTATOES

4 large baking potatoes
Vegetable oil
1 cup mayonnaise
½ cup shredded Cheddar cheese
¼ cup chopped green pepper
¼ cup chopped pimiento
¼ cup chopped green onion or scallions
2 (7-ounce) cans tuna, drained and flaked
2 tablespoons shredded Cheddar cheese
¼ cup mayonnaise
1 egg white, stiffly beaten

Scrub potatoes thoroughly, and rub skins with oil; bake at 400° for 1 to 1¼ hours or until done.

Allow to cool to touch. Cut potatoes in half lengthwise; scoop out pulp, leaving shells intact. Combine pulp, 1 cup mayonnaise, ½ cup cheese, green pepper, pimiento, onion, and tuna; stir lightly. Stuff shells with potato mixture; bake at 400° for 10 minutes.

Fold 2 tablespoons cheese and ¼ cup mayonnaise into egg white; spread evenly over potatoes. Bake an additional 10 minutes or until lightly browned. Yield: 8 servings.

Mrs. R. M. Lancaster,
Brentwood, Tennessee.

POTATOES ROQUEFORT

6 medium baking potatoes
Vegetable oil
½ cup firmly packed Roquefort cheese
¼ cup whipping cream
1 teaspoon salt
¼ teaspoon pepper
⅓ cup toasted breadcrumbs
¼ clove garlic, pressed
3 tablespoons melted butter or margarine

Scrub potatoes thoroughly, and rub skins with oil; bake at 400° for 1 to 1¼ hours or until potatoes are done.

Allow to cool to touch. Slice skin away from top of each potato. Scoop out pulp, leaving shells intact; mash pulp. Add cheese; beat with an electric mixer until blended. Gradually add whipping cream; stir in salt and pepper. Stuff shells with potato mixture.

Combine breadcrumbs, garlic, and butter, mixing well; sprinkle over potatoes. Bake at 350° for 20 to 25 minutes or until lightly browned. Yield: 6 servings. *Mrs. Marie H. Webb, Roanoke, Virginia.*

HERB STUFFED POTATOES

6 medium baking potatoes
Vegetable oil
½ cup butter or margarine
1 tablespoon finely chopped onion
1 tablespoon chopped fresh parsley
½ cup evaporated milk
¼ teaspoon crushed basil leaves
¼ teaspoon crushed tarragon leaves
1 teaspoon salt
¼ teaspoon pepper
Butter or margarine

Scrub potatoes thoroughly, and rub skins with oil; bake at 400° for 1 hour or until done.

Allow to cool to touch. Slice skin away from top of each potato. Carefully scoop out pulp, leaving shells intact; mash pulp. Add ½ cup butter, onion, parsley, milk, and seasonings to potato pulp, mixing well; stuff shells with potato mixture, and dot with butter. Bake at 350° for about 30 minutes. Yield: 6 servings. *Mrs. A. C. Frese, Birmingham, Alabama.*

Tip: Bake potatoes in half the usual time: Let them stand in boiling water for 15 minutes before baking in a very hot oven.

CREAMY STUFFED POTATOES

4 large baking potatoes
Vegetable oil
8 slices bacon
½ cup chopped green onion
¼ cup grated Parmesan cheese
1 cup commercial sour cream
1 teaspoon salt
½ teaspoon pepper
½ teaspoon paprika, divided

Scrub potatoes thoroughly and rub skins with oil; bake at 400° for 1 to 1¼ hours or until done.

Allow to cool to touch. Slice skin away from top of each potato. Carefully scoop out pulp, leaving shells intact; mash pulp.

Cook bacon until crisp; drain and crumble, reserving 3 tablespoons drippings in skillet. Sauté onion in bacon drippings until tender. Combine potato pulp, bacon, onion, cheese, sour cream, salt, and pepper, mixing well. Stuff shells with potato mixture; sprinkle each with ⅛ teaspoon paprika. Bake at 350° for 15 to 20 minutes or until heated thoroughly. Yield: 4 servings. *Marian Lokey, Marietta, Georgia.*

His Recipes Offer Elegance With Ease

When Bill Cliett of Gainesville, Florida, entertains, he likes to prepare dishes that take advantage of the fresh citrus so plentiful in the state. His Frozen Orange Soufflé and Sopa de Lima (lime soup) are two examples.

The soufflé is a refreshing blend of ladyfingers layered with rich custard and delicately flavored with orange and Cognac. The soup is a surprising combination: chopped chicken, chicken broth, and tomato lightly seasoned with lime.

As assistant principal of one of the city's middle schools, Bill can often combine his love of cooking with his career. Besides giving food demonstrations in his school's home economics classes, he recently taught an adult education course on preparing international menus.

Following the recipes for Bill's citrus specialties, we've included favorite recipes from other men cooks.

FROZEN ORANGE SOUFFLE

4 tablespoons Cognac, divided
10 ladyfingers, split lengthwise
½ cup plus 1 tablespoon sugar
2½ tablespoons water
Grated rind of 1 orange
4 egg yolks
1 pint whipping cream, whipped
Fresh orange slices

Cut a piece of waxed paper or aluminum foil long enough to fit around a 7-cup soufflé dish, allowing a 1-inch overlap. Fold paper lengthwise into thirds. (Foil should be greased.) Wrap around dish, allowing paper to extend 2 inches above rim to form a collar. Secure with freezer tape or string.

Sprinkle 2 tablespoons Cognac over split ladyfingers; set aside.

Combine sugar, water, and orange rind in a small saucepan; bring to a boil, and boil 3 minutes. While mixture is boiling, beat egg yolks until thick and lemon colored; add remaining 2 tablespoons Cognac, beating well. Very slowly and in a steady stream, add hot syrup to egg mixture; beat constantly. Fold in whipped cream.

Pour a third of mixture into prepared soufflé dish; top with half of ladyfingers. Repeat procedure, and chill until slightly set. Add remaining mixture, and freeze until firm. Garnish with fresh orange slices. Yield: 8 servings.

SOPA DE LIMA

1½ quarts chicken stock
2 cups cooked, cubed chicken
½ green pepper, chopped
1 tomato, peeled and chopped
½ onion, chopped
Juice of 2 limes
¼ teaspoon salt
Dash of pepper
9 slices lime
Corn tortilla chips, crushed

Combine first 8 ingredients in a Dutch oven, and bring to a boil. Reduce heat, and simmer 20 minutes. Place a slice of lime in each serving bowl; ladle soup on top. Sprinkle with tortilla chips. Yield: 9 cups.

Tip: Cooking vegetables with the least amount of water possible will preserve vitamins and maintain flavor. Save the cooking liquid, and add to soup stock or gravy for additional food value and flavor.

STUFFED MUSHROOMS

1½ to 2 pounds large fresh mushrooms
1 (8-ounce) package cream cheese,
   softened
1 (4½-ounce) can deviled ham
1 tablespoon Worcestershire sauce
Dash of hot sauce
¼ teaspoon garlic powder
½ teaspoon celery salt
1 tablespoon grated Parmesan cheese
Sliced pimiento-stuffed olives

Rinse mushrooms and pat dry; remove stems. (Mushroom stems may be frozen for use in other recipes.) Place caps on a greased baking sheet.

Combine remaining ingredients except olives; mix until well blended. Spoon mixture into mushroom caps; top each with an olive slice. Bake at 325° for 20 minutes. Yield: about 4 dozen.
Ted Kleisner,
Savannah, Georgia.

SMOTHERED STEAK

1 (2½-pound) boneless round steak, cut
   into serving pieces
Seasoned salt to taste
Pepper to taste
All-purpose flour
¼ cup vegetable oil
1 teaspoon garlic salt
1 tablespoon Worcestershire sauce
Dash of hot sauce
2 tablespoons red wine vinegar
2 cups plus 2 tablespoons water
4 green pepper rings

Sprinkle steak with seasoned salt and pepper; dredge in flour. Heat oil in a large skillet; brown meat on both sides.

Combine 3 tablespoons flour, garlic salt, Worcestershire sauce, hot sauce, wine vinegar, and 2 tablespoons water; stir until smooth. Add remaining water; stir until well blended. Pour mixture over steak, and top with green pepper rings. Cover and cook over low heat 50 to 60 minutes or until tender. Yield: 6 to 8 servings. *Donald K. Cullen,*
Hallsville, Texas.

CRUNCHY MEAT LOAF ORIENTAL

2 pounds ground beef
1 medium onion, chopped
¾ cup fine breadcrumbs
1 medium-size green pepper, chopped
3 tablespoons soy sauce
⅓ cup catsup
2 eggs
¼ cup milk
1½ teaspoons salt
¼ teaspoon pepper
½ cup finely chopped water chestnuts

Combine all ingredients, mixing well. Shape into 12- x 6-inch loaf, and place on a rack in a shallow baking pan. Bake at 375° for 1 hour or until done. Yield: about 6 servings. *Randall De Trinis,*
Brevard, North Carolina.

TOMATO JUICE COCKTAIL

2 quarts ripe tomatoes
2 medium onions, quartered
2 large bay leaves
7 whole cloves
½ teaspoon cayenne pepper or ground red
   pepper
1 cup water
2 tablespoons sugar
2 tablespoons vinegar
1 tablespoon salt
2 tablespoons lemon juice

Wash tomatoes thoroughly. Remove blemishes and stem ends; cut into quarters. Combine tomatoes, onion, bay leaves, cloves, cayenne pepper, and water in large saucepan or Dutch oven. Cook over low heat about 1 hour.

Remove from heat, and put vegetables through a food mill or sieve. Add remaining ingredients to tomato juice, and bring to a boil. Pour mixture into hot sterilized jars, leaving ½-inch headspace. Adjust lids, and process in boiling-water bath 10 minutes. Chill juice before serving. Yield: 2 quarts.
John C. Kittrell, Jr.,
Alexandria, Virginia.

MACAROON-SHERBET FROZEN DESSERT

18 (1-inch) coconut macaroons, finely
   crushed
1 teaspoon vanilla extract
½ to 1 cup chopped walnuts
1 pint whipping cream, whipped
1 pint lemon sherbet, softened
1 pint lime sherbet, softened
1 pint raspberry sherbet, softened

Fold crushed macaroons, vanilla, and walnuts into whipped cream; spread half of mixture into a 13- x 9- x 2-inch pan.

Alternately place scoops of lemon, lime, and raspberry sherbet over mixture; level with a spatula. Top with remaining whipped cream mixture. Freeze until firm. To serve, cut into squares. Yield: 12 to 15 servings.
James O. Michelinie,
Louisville, Kentucky.

Try Brussels Sprouts

Brussels sprouts smothered in a creamy blue cheese sauce or topped with crunchy buttered almonds make an exceptional side dish for any meal. We offer these and other new ways to enjoy the full flavor of this versatile vegetable.

CREAMY BRUSSELS SPROUTS

1 (4-ounce) package crumbled blue cheese
½ cup mayonnaise
1 tablespoon lemon juice
2 teaspoons garlic salt
1 (16-ounce) carton commercial sour
   cream
3 (10-ounce) packages frozen brussels
   sprouts

Combine cheese and mayonnaise, stirring until smooth. Add lemon juice and garlic salt. Stir in sour cream, mixing well. Cover; chill overnight.

To serve, cook brussels sprouts according to package directions; drain. Warm sour cream mixture in top of a double boiler; add cooked brussels sprouts. Serve immediately. Yield: 8 to 10 servings. *Fannie Goodner,*
Ooltewah, Tennessee.

BRUSSELS SPROUTS MEDLEY

3 cups water
2 chicken bouillon cubes
3 (10-ounce) packages frozen brussels
   sprouts
1½ cups sliced carrots
1½ cups sliced celery
⅓ cup butter or margarine
¾ cup dry-roasted cashew halves
¼ teaspoon salt
¼ teaspoon whole thyme leaves, crushed
⅛ teaspoon pepper

Place water and bouillon cubes in a medium saucepan; bring to a boil. Add brussels sprouts, carrots, and celery; return to a boil. Reduce heat and cover; simmer 15 minutes or until vegetables are tender. Drain; place in a serving bowl.

Melt butter in a small skillet; add nuts and seasonings. Cook on low heat for 3 to 4 minutes. Remove from heat, and pour over vegetables. Yield: 8 to 10 servings. *Mrs. William B. Moore, Selma, Alabama.*

Recipes For Busy Days

Busy days call for meals you can prepare in a hurry. Here is an assortment of time-saving recipes that will help you fill out those busy-day menus.

Apple Ham Casserole is an easy entrée and a good way to use leftover baked ham. For an interesting quick bread, try Easy Beer Bread—self-rising flour gives it its speedy rise.

BRUSSELS SPROUTS AMANDINE

2 (10-ounce) packages frozen brussels sprouts
1 cup water
2 teaspoons instant chicken bouillon granules
½ teaspoon salt
1 (10¾-ounce) can cream of chicken soup, undiluted
1 (2-ounce) jar diced pimiento, undrained
⅛ teaspoon whole thyme leaves
⅛ teaspoon pepper
2 teaspoons butter or margarine
½ cup sliced almonds

Place brussels sprouts, water, bouillon, and salt in a medium saucepan. Cook over medium-high heat until mixture comes to a boil; reduce heat and cover. Simmer 8 to 10 minutes or until tender. Drain.

Combine soup, pimiento, and seasonings; stir in brussels sprouts. Spoon into a greased 1½-quart casserole.

Melt butter in a small skillet; add almonds, and cook 3 minutes. Remove butter mixture from heat, and spoon over top of casserole.

Bake at 350° for 20 minutes or until hot and bubbly. Yield: 6 servings. *Mrs. Harvey T. Kidd, Hernando, Mississippi.*

Tip: For a quick way to peel tomatoes, hold tomato over flame or heat for 1 minute. You may prefer to dip tomato in boiling water for 1 minute, and then plunge it into cold water. The skin should slip off easily by either method.

APPLE HAM CASSEROLE

3 cups diced, cooked ham
2 tablespoons prepared mustard
2 apples, cored and sliced
2 tablespoons lemon juice
½ cup firmly packed light brown sugar
1 teaspoon grated orange rind
2 tablespoons all-purpose flour

Place ham in a greased 1½-quart casserole; spread mustard over ham. Arrange apple slices evenly over top, and sprinkle with lemon juice.

Combine sugar, orange rind, and flour; mix well, and sprinkle evenly over apples. Bake at 350° for 35 minutes. Yield: 4 servings. *Eleanor Brandt, Arlington, Texas.*

CREAMY CORN

1 (3-ounce) package cream cheese, softened
¼ cup milk
1 tablespoon butter or margarine
½ teaspoon onion salt
1 (16-ounce) can whole kernel corn, drained

Combine cream cheese, milk, butter, and onion salt in a small saucepan; cook over low heat, stirring often, until cheese melts. Stir in corn; cook, stirring constantly, until thoroughly heated. Yield: 4 servings. *Opal M. Rogers, Tempe, Arizona.*

SOUR CREAM PANCAKES

1 cup buttermilk biscuit mix
1 teaspoon baking powder
1 egg, lightly beaten
1 (8-ounce) carton commercial sour cream
3 to 5 tablespoons milk

Combine first 4 ingredients, mixing well. Add milk gradually, using enough to obtain desired consistency.

For each pancake, pour about ¼ cup batter onto a hot, lightly greased griddle. Turn pancakes when tops are covered with bubbles and edges look cooked. Yield: about 8 pancakes. *Mary Anne Pusey, Mount Airy, Maryland.*

BANANA FRITTERS

1¾ cups biscuit mix
½ cup milk
2 eggs
4 bananas, peeled and sliced
Hot vegetable oil
Powdered sugar

Combine biscuit mix, milk, and eggs; mix well with electric mixer. Add bananas; stir gently to coat. Drop each coated slice into deep oil heated to 375°. Fry until golden, turning once. Drain on paper towels; sprinkle with powdered sugar. Serve hot. Yield: about 5 dozen. *Mary Lou Entwisle, Metairie, Louisiana.*

EASY BEER BREAD

2 cups self-rising flour
3 tablespoons sugar
1 (12-ounce) can beer
1 tablespoon melted butter or margarine

Combine flour, sugar, and beer; stir just until all ingredients are moistened. Pour into a greased 9- x 5- x 3-inch loafpan. Bake at 375° for 30 to 35 minutes or until bread tests done. Brush with melted butter. Remove bread from pan, and cool on wire rack. Yield: 1 loaf. *Mrs. Sue Weeks, Kinston, Alabama.*

Hot Sandwiches For A Quick Supper

Hearty sandwiches, served open-faced with a sauce, stuffed with a filling, or layered with meat and cheese, make the perfect hot supper for a busy day.

Take an English muffin, top it with a slice of turkey, ham, tomato, a broccoli spear, and hollandaise sauce, and you've got a hot sandwich that's a meal in itself.

Our Corned Beef and Cheese Sandwich and Hot Ham Sandwiches can be prepared in advance, wrapped in foil, and then heated before serving time.

HOT HAM SANDWICHES

¼ cup butter or margarine, softened
2 tablespoons finely chopped onion
2 tablespoons mustard with horseradish
2 teaspoons poppy seeds or sesame seeds
6 hamburger buns
6 slices cooked ham
6 slices Swiss cheese

Combine butter, onion, mustard, and poppy seeds; mix well. Spread on both sides of hamburger buns. Place 1 ham slice and 1 cheese slice on bottom of each bun; cover with top bun. Wrap each sandwich in foil. Bake at 350° for 25 minutes. Yield: 6 servings.
Mrs. Pam H. Carswell,
Macon, Georgia.

CORNED BEEF AND CHEESE SANDWICH

1 (12-ounce) can corned beef
2 cups (½ pound) shredded Cheddar cheese
¼ cup chopped onion
¼ cup catsup or barbecue sauce
2 hard-cooked eggs, chopped
12 pimiento-stuffed olives, chopped
3 tablespoons mayonnaise
12 hot dog or hamburger buns

Combine first 7 ingredients; mix well. Spoon corned beef mixture into buns; wrap each bun separately in aluminum foil, sealing well.

Place foil-wrapped buns on a cookie sheet; bake at 400° for 15 minutes. Yield: 12 servings.
Note: Sandwiches may be made ahead of time; wrap in foil, and refrigerate. Bake as directed.
Mrs. Loren Martin,
Knoxville, Tennessee.

OPEN-FACED SANDWICHES

8 slices cooked turkey breast
8 slices cooked ham
8 slices tomato
8 spears broccoli, cooked
4 English muffins, split
1 (1¼-ounce) package hollandaise sauce mix

Layer 1 slice turkey, 1 slice ham, 1 slice tomato, and 1 spear broccoli on each English muffin half.

Prepare hollandaise sauce according to package directions; spoon over each sandwich. Broil 2 minutes or until sandwiches are heated. Yield: 4 servings.
Mrs. Omega W. Brown,
Orlando, Florida.

Two Servings And No Leftovers

Preparing tempting, nutritious meals for just two is easy with this collection of recipes designed to eliminate the leftovers.

For the main dish, there are three choices: chicken and mushrooms baked in sherry, flounder fried in an oniony coating, and zucchini stuffed with a savory filling.

Vegetable Stir-Fry is a quick and attractive side dish, an appealing accompaniment with either the chicken or fish. For an extra-special end to any meal, serve Quick Peach Cobbler topped with vanilla ice cream.

SHERRIED CHICKEN

1 small broiler-fryer, halved
Seasoned salt
2 tablespoons tarragon vinegar
2 tablespoons vegetable oil
1 clove garlic, minced
2 tablespoons chopped fresh parsley
2 tablespoons melted butter or margarine
½ cup plus 2 tablespoons sherry, divided
1 cup sliced fresh mushrooms

Sprinkle chicken with seasoned salt.
Combine vinegar, vegetable oil, garlic, and parsley. Sauté 1 portion of chicken in half the vinegar mixture until lightly browned, turning once. Repeat procedure with remaining chicken and vinegar mixture.

Place both chicken halves in a greased 13- x 9- x 2-inch baking pan;

add butter and ½ cup sherry. Bake at 350° for 1 hour or until done. Add 2 tablespoons sherry and mushrooms; bake 5 to 10 minutes or until thoroughly heated. Yield: 2 servings.
Mrs. Andrew L. Cooley,
Fayetteville, North Carolina.

SEASONED FRIED FLOUNDER

1 cup all-purpose flour
1½ teaspoons instant minced onion
1 teaspoon salt
½ teaspoon pepper
1 (16-ounce) package frozen flounder fillets, thawed
1 tablespoon onion juice
Hot vegetable oil

Combine flour, minced onion, salt, and pepper; mix well. Sprinkle fish with onion juice, and coat well with flour mixture. Fry in about ¼ inch of hot oil until golden brown, turning once. Yield: 2 servings.
Phyllis E. Winfrey,
Athens, Georgia.

VEGETABLE STIR-FRY

2½ tablespoons vegetable oil
10 to 12 large mushrooms, sliced
1 medium onion, sliced and separated into rings
1 medium zucchini, thinly sliced
1 tablespoon soy sauce
½ teaspoon salt
¼ teaspoon pepper
¼ teaspoon sugar

Heat oil in a large skillet. Add remaining ingredients; stir-fry over high heat about 5 minutes or until zucchini is crisp-tender. Yield: 2 servings.
Martha Brunton,
Winfield, Kansas.

STUFFED ZUCCHINI MAIN DISH

2 (6- to 8-inch) zucchini
1 small onion, finely chopped
2 tablespoons butter or margarine
1 (15-ounce) can red kidney beans,
    slightly mashed
1 cup (¼ pound) shredded sharp Cheddar
    cheese
¾ cup spaghetti sauce, divided
¼ teaspoon whole oregano
¼ teaspoon whole basil
¼ teaspoon salt
⅛ teaspoon pepper
¼ cup grated Parmesan cheese, divided

Slice zucchini in half lengthwise; scoop out and discard seeds. Cook shells in boiling salted water for 3 minutes; drain and set aside.

Sauté onion in butter until tender. Combine onion, kidney beans, Cheddar cheese, ½ cup spaghetti sauce, oregano, basil, salt, and pepper; mix well.

Arrange zucchini shells in a lightly buttered 12- x 8- x 2-inch baking dish. Spoon bean mixture into zucchini. Top each with 1 tablespoon of remaining spaghetti sauce and 1 tablespoon Parmesan cheese.

Cover zucchini and bake at 325° for 20 to 25 minutes or until thoroughly heated. Yield: 2 servings.
Mrs. Patricia Mose,
Hagerstown, Maryland.

QUICK PEACH COBBLER

1½ teaspoons cornstarch
1 tablespoon water
1 (8¾-ounce) can sliced peaches,
    undrained
½ cup buttermilk baking mix
2 teaspoons sugar
2 tablespoons milk
1 tablespoon vegetable oil
Vanilla ice cream

Dissolve cornstarch in cold water; add to peaches, and cook over medium heat about 5 minutes or until mixture is thickened and bubbly. Pour into a 1-quart baking dish.

Combine baking mix and sugar; add milk and vegetable oil, stirring to form a soft dough. Drop dough by spoonfuls on top of peaches. Bake at 400° for 20 minutes or until golden brown. Serve hot with ice cream. Yield: 2 servings.

Note: Canned apricots, cherries, or apples may be substituted for peaches.
Mrs. Allen Churchwell,
Waycross, Georgia.

Special Breads Perk Up The Morning

Whether it's a delicate sweet loaf of Strawberry Jam Bread or a coffee ring flavored with cinnamon and coconut, a special breakfast bread is sure to perk up your morning. These loaf breads are filled with fruits and nuts, are easy to make, and range in flavors from Orange-Pecan to Spiced Apple.

And if you want to serve French toast, our Overnight French Toast Deluxe makes it easy. The bread is sliced the night before and placed in an egg and milk mixture. It takes only minutes the next morning to sauté the bread and serve it topped with powdered sugar.

SPICED APPLE LOAF

1 (15-ounce) jar spiced apple rings
¼ cup firmly packed brown sugar
¼ teaspoon ground ginger
¼ teaspoon ground cinnamon
¼ teaspoon ground nutmeg
¼ cup butter or margarine, softened
1 cup sugar
2 eggs
1 teaspoon vanilla extract
2½ cups all-purpose flour
1 tablespoon baking powder
1 teaspoon salt
1 teaspoon ground cinnamon
¾ cup milk
½ cup chopped walnuts

Remove peel from apple rings; thoroughly mash rings with a fork. Combine apple, brown sugar, ginger, ¼ teaspoon cinnamon, and nutmeg; stir well. Set aside.

Combine butter and sugar; cream well. Add eggs, one at a time, beating well after each addition. Stir in vanilla.

Combine flour, baking powder, salt, and 1 teaspoon cinnamon. Stir one-third flour mixture into creamed mixture until blended. Add half of milk to creamed mixture; stir until blended. Repeat procedure, ending with dry ingredients. Stir in nuts.

Pour a third of batter into a greased and floured 9- x 5- x 3-inch loafpan; spread one-third apple mixture over batter. Repeat procedure twice, ending with apple mixture. Bake at 350° for 60 minutes. Cool in pan 10 minutes; turn out on wire rack. Yield: 1 loaf.
Diane E. France,
Bel Air, Maryland.

ORANGE-PECAN LOAVES

1½ cups orange juice
2 cups sugar
1 cup finely chopped dates
1 cup coarsely chopped pecans
2 eggs, slightly beaten
¼ cup grated orange rind
¼ cup melted butter
3½ cups all-purpose flour
2 teaspoons baking powder
1 teaspoon soda
1 teaspoon salt
⅓ cup sugar
3 tablespoons frozen orange juice
    concentrate, thawed and undiluted
⅓ cup chopped orange sections

Combine orange juice, 2 cups sugar, dates, pecans, eggs, orange rind, and butter; mix well. Combine next 4 ingredients; mix well. Pour pecan mixture into dry ingredients, and stir well.

Pour batter evenly into two greased and floured 9- x 5- x 3-inch loafpans. Bake at 350° for 1 hour. Cool in pan 5 minutes; turn out on wire rack.

Combine ⅓ cup sugar and orange juice concentrate in a small saucepan; cook, stirring frequently, over low heat 5 minutes. Stir in orange sections. Brush loaves with glaze. Yield: 2 loaves.
Jane Beverly,
Fayetteville, Tennessee.

PINEAPPLE-NUT BREAD

2 cups all-purpose flour, divided
¾ cup sugar
1 teaspoon baking powder
½ teaspoon salt
1 egg
2 tablespoons melted butter or margarine
1 teaspoon vanilla extract
1 teaspoon soda
1 (8¼-ounce) can crushed pineapple,
    undrained
1 cup seedless golden raisins
½ to 1 cup coarsely chopped pecans

Combine 1½ cups flour, sugar, baking powder, and salt; set aside.

Beat egg; add butter and vanilla. Dissolve soda in pineapple, and add to egg mixture. Add dry ingredients, and stir just enough to moisten. Combine raisins and pecans; sprinkle with remaining ½ cup flour; stir into batter.

Spoon batter into a greased and floured 8½- x 4½- x 3-inch loafpan. Bake at 350° for 50 to 60 minutes or until bread tests done. Yield: 1 loaf.
Mrs. Gary Mattke,
Edmond, Oklahoma.

STRAWBERRY JAM BREAD

3 cups all-purpose flour
1 teaspoon salt
¾ teaspoon cream of tartar
½ teaspoon soda
1½ cups sugar
1 cup butter or margarine, softened
1 teaspoon vanilla extract
¼ teaspoon lemon juice
4 eggs
1 cup strawberry jam
½ cup buttermilk
1 cup chopped nuts

Combine flour, salt, cream of tartar, and soda; set aside.

Combine sugar, butter, vanilla, and lemon juice in a large mixing bowl; cream until light and fluffy. Add eggs, one at a time, beating well after each addition. Stir together jam and buttermilk; add to creamed mixture alternately with dry ingredients, mixing just until blended. Stir in nuts.

Spoon batter into 2 greased 9- x 5- x 3-inch loafpans. Bake at 350° for 55 minutes or until bread tests done. Cool 15 minutes; remove from pans onto cooling racks. Yield: 2 loaves.

Mrs. Jo Ellen Greenhaw,
Athens, Alabama.

BUTTERFLAKE COFFEE RING

¾ cup sugar
¾ teaspoon ground cinnamon
¾ cup milk, divided
2 (8-ounce) packages refrigerated butterflake dinner rolls
¼ cup shredded coconut
Glaze (recipe follows)

Combine sugar and cinnamon in a small bowl. Place ½ cup milk in a separate small bowl. Dip each roll in milk; roll in sugar mixture. Place 12 rolls in a well-greased 6-cup ring mold; slightly overlap rolls. Sprinkle with coconut; pour ¼ cup milk over top. Overlap remaining rolls over first layer.

Bake at 375° for 25 minutes or until lightly browned. Invert on serving platter. Drizzle with glaze while still warm. Yield: 6 to 8 servings.

Glaze:
½ cup powdered sugar
1 tablespoon milk
¼ teaspoon vanilla extract
2 tablespoons chopped pecans

Combine first 3 ingredients; stir well. Add pecans. Yield: about ¼ cup.

Mrs. Marshall Marvelli,
Winston-Salem, North Carolina.

SURPRISE DATE MUFFINS

1½ cups graham cracker crumbs
2 teaspoons baking powder
2 teaspoons sugar
Pinch of salt
1 egg, well beaten
2 tablespoons melted margarine
½ cup chopped dates
½ cup chopped nuts
½ cup warm milk

Combine first 4 ingredients; stir in egg and margarine, mixing well. Stir in dates and nuts. Add milk and stir just until moistened.

Spoon batter into greased muffin pans, filling two-thirds full. Bake at 400° for 15 minutes or until done. Yield: about 10 muffins.

Mrs. R. E. Londeree,
St. Petersburg, Florida.

OVERNIGHT FRENCH TOAST DELUXE

8 (¾-inch thick) slices French bread
4 eggs
1 cup milk
1 tablespoon sugar
⅛ teaspoon salt
2 tablespoons orange juice
½ teaspoon vanilla extract
¼ cup butter or margarine, divided
Powdered sugar

Place bread in a 13- x 9- x 2-inch baking dish. Combine eggs, milk, sugar, salt, orange juice, and vanilla; beat well. Pour mixture over bread slices; turn slices over to coat evenly. Cover and refrigerate overnight.

Melt 2 tablespoons butter in a large skillet; remove 4 slices bread from dish, and sauté in butter 4 minutes on each side or until browned. Repeat procedure with remaining butter and bread slices. Sprinkle toast with powdered sugar; serve immediately. Yield: 4 servings.

Carmen A. Jones,
Aurora, North Carolina.

Keep The Cookie Jar Filled

Now is the time to keep the cookie jar filled with homemade goodies for after-school snacks and bag lunches. Drop cookies, filled with chocolate morsels, nuts, fruits, or cereals, offer a choice of flavors and textures to suit every taste.

Included are two variations of the favorite chocolate chip cookies, Pineapple Cookies with bits of crushed pineapple and Banana Oatmeal Cookies—a change from the traditional oatmeal.

DELUXE CHOCOLATE CHIP COOKIES

2 cups firmly packed brown sugar
1 cup butter or margarine, softened
2 eggs
1 teaspoon vanilla extract
2 cups all-purpose flour
½ teaspoon baking powder
2 cups crisp rice cereal
1 (6-ounce) package semisweet chocolate morsels
1 cup shredded coconut
1 cup chopped nuts

Combine sugar and butter in a large mixing bowl, creaming until light and fluffy. Add eggs and vanilla; beat well.

Combine flour and baking powder; stir into batter. Stir remaining ingredients into batter.

Drop batter by heaping teaspoonfuls onto lightly greased baking sheets. Bake at 350° for 10 to 12 minutes or until lightly browned. Cool on wire racks. Yield: about 7½ dozen.

Mrs. Sherrye Perkins,
Dothan, Alabama.

PINEAPPLE COOKIES

1¾ cups all-purpose flour
½ teaspoon soda
¼ teaspoon baking powder
¼ teaspoon salt
½ cup firmly packed brown sugar
½ cup sugar
½ cup shortening
1 egg
1 teaspoon vanilla extract
½ cup drained crushed pineapple
½ cup chopped nuts (optional)

Combine flour, soda, baking powder, and salt; set aside.

Combine sugar and shortening in a large mixing bowl; cream until light and fluffy. Add egg and vanilla; beat well. Add dry ingredients, mixing well. Stir in pineapple; add nuts, if desired.

Drop batter by heaping teaspoonfuls onto lightly greased baking sheets. Bake at 350° for 10 minutes or until lightly browned. Cool on wire racks. Yield: about 5 dozen.

Note: Batter may be covered and stored in refrigerator 1 week; bake cookies as desired.

Mrs. Genelle Lawrence,
Scottsville, Kentucky.

DOUBLE CHOCOLATE CHIP COOKIES

1 (6-ounce) package semisweet chocolate morsels, divided
1½ cups all-purpose flour
1 teaspoon baking powder
½ teaspoon salt
1 cup sugar
½ cup shortening
1 egg
1 teaspoon vanilla extract
2 tablespoons milk
¾ cup coarsely chopped walnuts

Melt ½ cup chocolate morsels in the top of a double boiler; set aside to cool.

Combine flour, baking powder, and salt; set aside.

Combine sugar and shortening in a large mixing bowl, creaming well. Add cooled chocolate, egg, and vanilla; beat well. Stir in milk. Add dry ingredients, and mix well. Stir in remaining ½ cup chocolate morsels and walnuts.

Drop batter by heaping teaspoonfuls onto lightly greased baking sheets. Bake at 350° for 10 minutes or until done. Carefully transfer cookies to racks to cool (cookies will be soft). Yield: about 5½ dozen.
Patsy Parker,
Morganton, North Carolina.

BANANA OATMEAL COOKIES

¾ cup shortening
1 cup sugar
1 egg
1 cup mashed bananas
1 cup quick-cooking oats, uncooked
1½ cups all-purpose flour
½ teaspoon soda
½ teaspoon baking powder
¼ teaspoon salt
¾ teaspoon ground cinnamon
¼ teaspoon ground nutmeg

Combine shortening and sugar in a large mixing bowl; cream until light and fluffy. Beat in egg; then stir in bananas and oats.

Combine remaining ingredients, and stir into creamed mixture. Drop batter by teaspoonfuls onto greased cookie sheets. Bake at 400° for 13 minutes. Cool cookies on wire racks. Yield: about 6 dozen.
Janis S. Koenig,
Yonges Island, South Carolina.

A Peach Of A Coffee Cake

Here's a coffee cake that looks and tastes special. Made from a sweet yeast dough, Peach Flip is curved into a horseshoe shape, then topped with peach preserves and a powdered sugar glaze. It comes to us from Gloria Duncan of Jackson, Tennessee.

PEACH FLIP

2 packages dry yeast
½ cup warm water (105° to 115°)
½ cup butter
½ cup sugar
2 teaspoons salt
½ cup scalded milk
3 eggs
5 to 5½ cups all-purpose flour
⅔ cup sugar
2 teaspoons ground cinnamon
1 cup chopped walnuts
¼ cup melted butter, divided
1 cup peach or apricot preserves, divided
Glaze (recipe follows)

Dissolve yeast in warm water; set aside. Combine ½ cup butter, ½ cup sugar, salt, and milk; cool to lukewarm. Add eggs and yeast; stir well. Stir in enough flour to form a stiff dough.

Turn dough out onto a lightly floured board; knead 3 to 5 minutes or until smooth. Place in a greased bowl, turning to grease top. Cover; let rise in a warm place (85°), free from drafts, until doubled (about 1½ hours).

Combine ⅔ cup sugar, cinnamon, and walnuts; stir well. Set aside.

Punch dough down, and divide in half. Roll each half into a 20- x 10-inch rectangle. Brush with 2 tablespoons melted butter, and spread with ¼ cup peach preserves to within ½ inch of edge. Sprinkle with half the cinnamon mixture. Roll up jellyroll fashion, beginning with long edge; pinch edges together to seal. Place roll, seam side down, on greased baking sheet; curve roll to form a horseshoe shape.

With kitchen shears, clip about halfway through roll, beginning and ending about 2 inches from ends.

Cover and let rise in a warm place about 30 minutes. Spoon ¼ cup peach preserves over top of each coffee cake. Bake at 350° for 20 to 25 minutes or until golden brown. Drizzle with glaze while warm. Yield: 18 to 20 servings.

Glaze:

1 cup powdered sugar
1 teaspoon vanilla extract
2 to 3 tablespoons milk

Combine all ingredients in a small bowl; mix well. Yield: about 1 cup.

Stir-Fry The Cabbage

Chinese cabbage is a cabbage, yet it looks a lot like romaine lettuce because of the oval-shaped head, fringed leaves, and white stalks.

In her recipe for Stir-Fried Vegetables, Caroline Degen of St. Petersburg, Florida, combines Chinese cabbage with green pepper, bean sprouts, bamboo shoots, water chestnuts, and spinach for a delicious, crisp-tender side dish.

STIR-FRIED VEGETABLES

¼ cup vegetable oil
2 cups coarsely shredded Chinese cabbage
1 cup sliced green pepper
1 (16-ounce) can bean sprouts, drained
1 (8-ounce) can bamboo shoots, drained
1 (8-ounce) can water chestnuts, drained and sliced
3 cups coarsely chopped spinach
2 tablespoons soy sauce
½ teaspoon salt

Heat wok or skillet at 375° for 2 to 3 minutes; add oil, and heat 1 minute. Add cabbage, green pepper, bean sprouts, bamboo shoots, and water chestnuts; stir-fry 5 minutes. Cover and cook over low heat for 3 to 5 minutes. Stir in spinach, soy sauce, and salt; stir-fry about 2 minutes or until spinach wilts. Yield: 6 servings.

Put Chicken On The Table

Economical doesn't mean dull when it comes to chicken. To prove that point, we offer some exceptional entrées that put the emphasis on the versatility of chicken. Recipes range from the zesty, Italian-style Chicken Breasts Romano to a delicately flavored chicken à la king.

In Sweet Lemon Chicken, a sweet-and-sour variation, chicken is simmered in a lemonade-base sauce and served with rice. You'll also want to try chicken breasts baked with a topping of spinach, Parmesan cheese, and bread-crumbs in an unexpected delight called Chicken Rockefeller.

Green grapes are stirred into the stuffing for Wild Rice-Stuffed Chicken. When almost done, the chicken is basted with soy sauce and wine.

CHICKEN BREASTS ROMANO

⅓ cup all-purpose flour
½ teaspoon salt
¼ teaspoon pepper
3 whole chicken breasts, split and skinned
2 tablespoons melted shortening or vegetable oil
¼ cup minced onion
2 cups tomato juice
2 tablespoons grated Romano or Parmesan cheese
1 tablespoon sugar
½ teaspoon salt
½ teaspoon garlic salt
½ teaspoon whole oregano
¼ teaspoon basil leaves
1 teaspoon vinegar
1 (4-ounce) can sliced mushrooms, drained
1 tablespoon minced parsley
½ cup grated Romano or Parmesan cheese
Hot cooked spaghetti (optional)
Parsley sprigs (optional)

Combine flour, ½ teaspoon salt, and pepper. Dredge chicken in flour mixture, and brown in hot shortening. Drain chicken on paper towels. Pour off all but 1 tablespoon of pan drippings.

Sauté onion in reserved drippings until tender. Add next 10 ingredients, stirring well. Return chicken to skillet; cover and simmer 45 minutes or until tender. At serving time, sprinkle chicken with ½ cup Romano cheese. Serve over spaghetti and garnish with parsley sprigs, if desired. Yield: 6 servings.
Margaret Beasley,
Timpson, Texas.

CHICKEN A LA KING

¼ cup chopped green pepper
1 (2-ounce) can sliced mushrooms, drained
¼ cup melted butter or margarine
¼ cup all-purpose flour
1 teaspoon salt
⅛ teaspoon pepper
1 cup chicken broth
1 cup half-and-half
1 cup diced cooked chicken
¼ cup chopped pimiento
1 (10-ounce) package frozen patty shells, baked

Sauté green pepper and mushrooms in butter in a 10-inch skillet until green pepper is tender. Combine flour, salt, and pepper; add to vegetables, stirring until smooth. Cook 1 minute, stirring constantly. Gradually add chicken broth and half-and-half; cook over medium heat, stirring constantly, until thickened and bubbly.

Stir in chicken and pimiento; cook until thoroughly heated. Divide filling among patty shells. Yield: 6 servings.
Mrs. R. H. McCoin,
Greenville, Missouri.

Tip: Cut raw turnips into strips and serve as a snack or hors d'oeuvre. They're good served with a dip.

SWEET LEMON CHICKEN

¼ cup all-purpose flour
1 teaspoon salt
1 (3-pound) broiler-fryer, cut up
2 tablespoons vegetable oil
1 (6-ounce) can frozen lemonade concentrate, thawed and undiluted
½ cup water
3 tablespoons brown sugar
3 tablespoons catsup
1 tablespoon vinegar
1 tablespoon cornstarch
1 tablespoon cold water
2 cups hot cooked rice

Combine flour and salt. Dredge chicken in flour mixture, and brown in hot oil in a large skillet. Drain chicken on paper towels, and return to skillet.

Combine lemonade concentrate, water, sugar, catsup, and vinegar; stir well, and pour over chicken. Bring to a boil, and reduce heat; cover and simmer 45 to 50 minutes or until tender.

Remove chicken to serving platter, and keep warm. Measure pan drippings, and add enough water to make 1¼ cups liquid. Combine cornstarch and 1 tablespoon cold water, stirring until smooth. Add cornstarch mixture to pan drippings, and return to skillet; cook, stirring constantly, until smooth and thick. Serve the sauce with hot rice. Yield: 4 to 6 servings.
Lilly S. Bradley,
Salem, Virginia.

WILD RICE-STUFFED CHICKEN

1 (6-ounce) package long grain and wild
    rice mix
¼ cup melted butter or margarine
½ teaspoon onion salt
½ teaspoon whole thyme, crushed
1½ cups seedless green grapes, halved
1 (3- to 3½-pound) broiler-fryer
Salt to taste
2 tablespoons soy sauce
2 tablespoons white wine
Seedless green grapes (optional)

Cook rice mix according to package directions. Add butter, onion salt, thyme, and 1½ cups grapes; stir well.

Season cavity of chicken with salt; place breast side up on a rack in a shallow roasting pan. Stuff lightly with half of rice mixture. Truss chicken, and bake at 375° for 1½ hours. Combine soy sauce and wine; use to baste chicken during last 30 minutes of baking time.

Spoon remaining rice mixture into a lightly greased 1-quart casserole; bake at 375° for 15 to 20 minutes. Remove chicken to serving platter, and spoon the rice around it. Garnish with seedless green grapes, if desired. Yield: about 6 servings. *Carolyn Epting,*
Leesville, South Carolina.

CHICKEN ROCKEFELLER

1 (10-ounce) package frozen chopped
    spinach
1 egg, beaten
¼ cup grated Parmesan cheese, divided
1 cup Italian-style breadcrumbs
6 whole chicken breasts, split, boned, and
    skinned
Salt and pepper to taste
3 tablespoons melted butter or margarine

Cook spinach according to package directions; drain well, and allow to cool. Combine spinach, egg, and 1 tablespoon Parmesan; set aside. Combine breadcrumbs and remaining Parmesan in a shallow pan; set aside.

Sprinkle chicken breasts with salt and pepper; roll each in breadcrumb mixture. Place in a greased 13- x 9- x 2-inch baking dish.

Place 1 heaping tablespoon of spinach mixture on each chicken breast, spreading to form a small mound. Sprinkle with remaining breadcrumb mixture, and drizzle with butter. Bake at 350° for 40 minutes. Yield: 6 servings.
Elise Golde Davies,
Tuscaloosa, Alabama.

CHICKEN IN ORANGE-ALMOND SAUCE

1 (2-pound) broiler-fryer, cut up
Salt
¼ cup melted butter or margarine
2 tablespoons all-purpose flour
Dash of ground ginger
⅛ teaspoon ground cinnamon
1½ cups orange juice
½ cup slivered almonds
½ cup seedless raisins
1 cup orange sections
Hot cooked rice

Sprinkle chicken with ¼ teaspoon salt. Brown in butter in a large skillet over low heat. Drain chicken on paper towels. Pour off all but 2 tablespoons of pan drippings.

Blend flour, spices, and ¼ teaspoon salt into reserved pan drippings; cook over low heat, stirring constantly, until bubbly. Gradually add orange juice; cook until smooth and thickened, stirring constantly. Stir in slivered almonds and raisins.

Add chicken to sauce; cover and cook over low heat 30 minutes or until chicken is tender. Just before serving, add orange sections. Serve with rice. Yield: 6 servings. *Jay Amonette,*
Tulsa, Oklahoma.

CURRIED CHICKEN SALAD

3 cups diced cooked chicken
1 (20-ounce) can pineapple chunks,
    drained
3 tablespoons instant minced onion
3 tablespoons water
2 tablespoons melted butter or margarine
1¼ teaspoons curry powder
⅓ cup mayonnaise
1 tablespoon lemon juice
½ teaspoon salt
Dash of red pepper
½ cup coarsely chopped pecans
⅓ cup golden seedless raisins
1 apple, diced
Lettuce (optional)
Flaked coconut (optional)

Combine chicken and pineapple; chill thoroughly.

Soak onion in water for 10 minutes. Combine onion, butter, and curry powder; cook 3 to 5 minutes over low heat, stirring occasionally. Cool. Combine onion mixture, mayonnaise, lemon juice, salt, and red pepper in a large bowl; mix well. Stir in chicken mixture, pecans, raisins, and apple; chill.

At serving time, spoon salad onto lettuce and garnish with coconut, if desired. Yield: 6 servings.
Karen Dotterman,
San Antonio, Texas.

Treats Without Tricks

When the goblins come calling on Halloween, you can easily avoid their pranks and tricks with these enchanting treats. Offer them Caramel Popcorn—it's honey flavored and filled with almonds, pecan halves, and cashews.

For a cheese-flavored surprise, have a big batch of Sesame-Cheese Popcorn on hand. Caramel Apples are always a Halloween favorite, and our recipe should please even the most devilish of spooks.

CARAMEL POPCORN

3 quarts freshly popped popcorn
1 cup blanched slivered almonds
1 cup pecan halves
1 cup cashew nuts
½ cup butter or margarine
1 cup firmly packed brown sugar
¼ cup honey
1 teaspoon vanilla extract

Combine popcorn and nuts in a lightly greased 14- x 11- x 2-inch roasting pan; mix well and set aside.

Melt butter over low heat in a medium saucepan. Add brown sugar and honey; bring to a boil, and boil 5 minutes without stirring. Add vanilla, stirring well. Pour syrup over popcorn mixture, stirring until popcorn is evenly coated. Bake at 250° for 1 hour, stirring every 15 minutes. Cool completely, and break into pieces. Store in airtight containers. Yield: about 4 quarts.
Adrienne Parker,
Nashville, Tennessee.

SESAME-CHEESE POPCORN

½ cup melted butter or margarine
2 tablespoons sesame seeds
1 (1¼-ounce) envelope cheese sauce mix
½ teaspoon salt
4 quarts freshly popped popcorn

Combine butter and sesame seeds in a small saucepan. Stir over low heat until sesame seeds are lightly browned; set mixture aside.

Sprinkle cheese sauce mix and salt over popcorn. Drizzle butter mixture over popcorn, tossing well to evenly coat popcorn. Yield: 4 quarts.

James L. Strieber,
Odenton, Maryland.

CARAMEL APPLES

12 small apples
2 cups firmly packed light brown sugar
½ cup milk
½ cup shortening
½ teaspoon salt
1 teaspoon vanilla extract

Wash and dry apples; remove stems. Insert wooden skewers into stem end of each apple. Set aside.

Combine next 4 ingredients in a heavy saucepan; mix well. Bring to a boil and boil 2 minutes, stirring constantly. Remove from heat and add vanilla. Beat with a wire whisk about 10 minutes or until mixture thickens and loses its gloss.

Dip apples in syrup, covering entire surface; allow excess to drip off. Place apples on lightly buttered waxed paper to cool. Store in cool place. Yield: 12 servings.

Jeanette Burgess,
Scranton, South Carolina.

Macaroni Makes The Salad

For a change from the traditional tossed salad, serve macaroni instead. The versatility of macaroni, coupled with its chewy texture and mild flavor, makes it perfect for combining with meat, seafood, fruit, and vegetables for some delightful salads.

Minestrone Salad, served on a bed of romaine and surrounded by tomatoes, makes a colorful addition to the table. And be sure to try Pineapple Macaroni Salad, full of pineapple and bananas.

MINESTRONE SALAD

1 (8-ounce) package elbow macaroni
1 (16-ounce) can navy beans, drained
3 medium carrots, peeled and shredded
1½ cups chopped celery
¼ cup chopped parsley
¾ cup mayonnaise or salad dressing
½ cup vegetable oil
2 tablespoons cider vinegar
1½ teaspoons seasoned salt
¼ teaspoon seasoned pepper
Romaine
Tomato slices

Cook macaroni according to package directions; drain. Rinse with cold water, and drain.

Combine macaroni, navy beans, carrots, celery, and parsley; mix well. Combine next 5 ingredients; mix well. Pour mayonnaise mixture over macaroni mixture, stirring well. Chill at least 1 hour.

Line a salad bowl with romaine. Spoon macaroni salad into bowl; arrange tomato slices around edge of salad. Yield: 8 servings.

Mrs. Clara Ackman,
Williamstown, Kentucky.

HAM AND MACARONI SALAD

3 cups elbow macaroni
2½ cups chopped cooked ham
6 hard-cooked eggs, chopped
4 to 5 green onions, thinly sliced
¼ cup chopped green pepper
3 to 4 tablespoons chopped sweet pickles
¾ to 1 cup mayonnaise
¼ teaspoon paprika
Salt and pepper to taste

Cook macaroni according to package directions; drain. Rinse with cold water, and drain.

Combine all ingredients, stirring lightly; cover and chill several hours before serving. Yield: 10 servings.

Mrs. Sarah S. Ramsey,
Greensboro, North Carolina.

PINEAPPLE MACARONI SALAD

1 cup elbow macaroni
2 eggs
1 (20-ounce) can pineapple chunks
½ cup sugar
¼ cup lemon juice
¼ teaspoon salt
2 bananas, sliced
1 cup whipping cream, whipped

Cook macaroni according to package directions; drain. Rinse with cold water; drain and set aside.

Beat eggs in a medium saucepan. Drain pineapple, reserving juice. Combine pineapple juice, sugar, lemon juice, and salt; stir well. Slowly add pineapple juice mixture to eggs, stirring constantly. Cook egg mixture over medium heat, stirring constantly, until thickened and bubbly.

Stir together macaroni, egg mixture, and pineapple (mixture will be thin). Chill 24 hours.

Just before serving, add bananas and whipped cream; mix well. Yield: 6 to 8 servings.

Mrs. Gloria Pedersen,
Corinth, Mississippi.

SHRIMP MACARONI SALAD

2½ cups shell macaroni
1½ pounds small cooked shrimp
⅔ cup chopped celery
1 medium onion, chopped
1 cup salad dressing or mayonnaise
¾ cup catsup
½ cup sweet pepper relish
Juice of 1 lemon
2 dashes hot sauce
½ teaspoon salt
¼ teaspoon pepper

Cook macaroni according to package directions; drain. Rinse with cold water; drain.

Combine macaroni, shrimp, celery, and onion, mixing well. Stir together remaining ingredients. Pour salad dressing mixture over macaroni mixture; stir well. Chill. Yield: 8 to 10 servings.

Mrs. Fay Brown,
Oak Ridge, Tennessee.

Call For Cauliflower

Cauliflower makes a versatile accompaniment to meals when French fried, baked with English peas for a two-vegetable side dish, or tossed in a salad.

Mrs. R. E. Bunker of Bartlett, Texas, also suggests serving cauliflower as a main dish. In her Main-Dish Cauliflower, the flowerets are topped with chunks of ham and baked in a cheese sauce.

When selecting cauliflower, look for a head that is firm, compact, and creamy white. Size of the head is not an indication of quality. Cauliflower is past its prime if the head has brown bruises, a speckled appearance, or has started breaking apart; withered or yellow leaves also indicate poor quality.

MAIN-DISH CAULIFLOWER

1 large head cauliflower
1 cup chopped cooked ham
¼ cup butter or margarine
¼ cup all-purpose flour
1½ cups milk
½ pound sharp Cheddar cheese, diced
1 cup soft breadcrumbs
2 tablespoons melted butter or margarine

Remove large outer leaves, and break cauliflower into flowerets; wash thoroughly. Place in a small amount of boiling salted water; cover and cook about 20 minutes or until tender. Drain well. Place cauliflower in a lightly greased 2-quart casserole; sprinkle with ham.

Melt ¼ cup butter in a heavy saucepan; blend in flour, and cook until bubbly. Gradually add milk; cook over medium heat, stirring constantly, until thickened and bubbly. Add cheese, stirring until melted. Spoon sauce over cauliflower and ham.

Combine breadcrumbs and remaining butter; spoon over sauce. Bake at 350° for 30 minutes. Yield: 6 servings.

Mrs. R. E. Bunker,
Bartlett, Texas.

CAULIFLOWER AND PEAS WITH CURRIED ALMONDS

1 large head cauliflower or 2 (10-ounce) packages frozen cauliflower
1 (10-ounce) package frozen English peas
2 tablespoons butter or margarine, divided
2 tablespoons all-purpose flour
1½ cups commercial sour cream
1 teaspoon onion salt
1 teaspoon curry powder
½ cup slivered almonds

Wash cauliflower, and break into flowerets. Cook, covered, in a small amount of boiling salted water 10 minutes; drain well. Cook peas according to package directions; drain.

Melt 1 tablespoon butter in a heavy saucepan over low heat; add flour, stirring until smooth. Cook 1 minute, stirring constantly. Add sour cream; cook over low heat, stirring constantly, just until well heated.

Combine cauliflower, peas, sour cream mixture, and onion salt; mix well. Spoon into a lightly greased 1½-quart casserole.

Melt remaining butter in saucepan; stir in curry powder and almonds. Cook over medium heat, stirring frequently, until almonds are golden (3 to 5 minutes). Spoon almonds over cauliflower. Bake at 325° for 25 minutes. Yield: 6 servings.

Mrs. Ledlie Wilson,
Georgetown, Kentucky.

HERBED CAULIFLOWER CASSEROLE

1 medium head cauliflower
3 tablespoons margarine
¼ cup all-purpose flour
2 cups milk
¾ teaspoon salt
Dash of pepper
1 cup herb-seasoned stuffing mix
¼ cup water
2 tablespoons melted margarine

Remove large outer leaves, and break cauliflower into flowerets; wash thoroughly. Cook, covered, in a small amount of boiling salted water 10 minutes; drain. Place in a lightly greased 2-quart casserole.

Melt 3 tablespoons margarine in a heavy saucepan; add flour, stirring until smooth. Cook 1 minute, stirring constantly. Gradually add milk; cook over medium heat, stirring constantly, until thickened and bubbly. Stir in salt and pepper. Spoon sauce over cauliflower.

Combine stuffing mix, water, and remaining margarine; stir well, and sprinkle over sauce. Bake at 350° for 30 minutes or until golden brown. Yield: 6 servings.

Mrs. Virginia Mathews,
Jacksonville, Florida.

CAULIFLOWER SALAD

1 large head cauliflower
½ pound bacon, cooked and crumbled
2 medium tomatoes, diced
1 bunch green onions, chopped
1 cup diced Cheddar cheese
½ cup pimiento-stuffed olives, sliced
½ cup mayonnaise

Remove outer green leaves, and break cauliflower into flowerets; wash thoroughly. Toss cauliflower with remaining ingredients. Yield: 10 to 12 servings.

Margaret Connelly,
Fort Worth, Texas.

FRENCH-FRIED CAULIFLOWER AU GRATIN

1 small head cauliflower
1 egg
1 tablespoon water
Fine cracker crumbs
Salad oil
Cheese sauce (recipe follows)

Wash cauliflower, and break into flowerets. Cook, covered, in a small amount of boiling salted water about 10 minutes or until crisp-tender; drain.

Combine egg and water; beat well. Dredge flowerets in cracker crumbs; then dip in egg. Dredge again in cracker crumbs. Deep fry in hot salad oil (375°) until golden brown. Serve with cheese sauce. Yield: 6 servings.

Cheese Sauce:

2 tablespoons butter or margarine
2 tablespoons all-purpose flour
1 cup milk
¼ teaspoon salt
Dash of pepper
1 cup (¼ pound) shredded Cheddar cheese

Melt butter in a heavy saucepan over low heat; add flour, stirring until smooth. Cook 1 minute, stirring constantly. Gradually add milk; cook over medium heat, stirring constantly, until thickened and bubbly. Add salt, pepper, and cheese, stirring until cheese melts. Serve with fried cauliflower. Yield: about 1 cup.

Mrs. William O. Warren,
Hermitage, Arkansas.

Explore Clay Cookery

Have you ever made stew in a clay cooker? Or stuffed pork chops? While clay cookers are widely acclaimed for baking poultry, they give that same natural moistness to a wide selection of other dishes.

Explore these entrée ideas, and don't be afraid to experiment with some of your favorite recipes. Because manufacturers' directions vary for soaking cookers, check your instructions before using.

CORNISH HENS WITH WILD RICE STUFFING

1 (6-ounce) package long grain and wild rice mix
1 medium onion, minced
3 tablespoons melted butter or margarine, divided
1 large Delicious apple, peeled, cored, and coarsely shredded
1 egg, beaten
1 tablespoon minced fresh parsley
⅛ teaspoon ground thyme
2 (1 pound 6-ounce) Cornish hens
Salt and pepper

Soak clay cooker in water according to manufacturer's directions. Prepare rice according to package directions.

Sauté onion in 2 tablespoons butter until onion is tender, but not brown.

Combine rice, onion, apple, egg, parsley, and thyme; stir lightly.

Sprinkle inside of hens with salt and pepper. Stuff hens lightly with some of the rice mixture; set remaining rice aside. Close cavity, and secure with toothpicks; truss. Brush hens with 1 tablespoon butter, and place breast side up in cooker. Sprinkle hens with salt and pepper. Cover cooker, and place in a cold oven. Bake at 400° for 2 hours. Remove cooker from oven, and place on a heat-resistant pad. (Do not uncover so hens will remain hot.)

Reduce oven temperature to 350°. Spoon extra rice into a lightly greased 1-quart casserole. Bake at 350° for 30 minutes. Serve with Cornish hens. Yield: 2 to 4 servings.
Kathleen A. Wilson,
Port Arthur, Texas.

OVEN BEEF STEW

1½ pounds lean boneless beef, cut into 1-inch cubes
3 tablespoons vegetable oil
1 (16-ounce) can whole tomatoes
2 large onions, quartered
1 medium rutabaga, peeled and cut into 8 wedges
1 teaspoon salt
1 teaspoon pepper
1 teaspoon sugar
½ teaspoon thyme leaves
1 (9-ounce) package frozen cut green beans
¼ cup all-purpose flour
¼ cup water

Soak clay cooker in water.

Sauté meat in oil in a skillet until brown; transfer to cooker. Add tomatoes, onion, and rutabaga; sprinkle with seasonings.

Cover cooker, and place in a cold oven. Bake at 400° for 1 hour and 30 minutes. Add beans; cover and bake an additional 30 minutes. Remove meat and vegetables from cooker using a slotted spoon; place in a serving dish.

Transfer meat drippings to a saucepan. Combine flour and water in a jar; tighten lid, and shake well. Stir flour mixture into meat drippings; cook over medium heat, stirring constantly, until thickened and bubbly. Serve gravy over meat and vegetables. Yield: 6 servings.
Mrs. Mildred Sherrer,
Bay City, Texas.

STUFFED BAKED PORK CHOPS

2 cups soft breadcrumbs
1 small onion, minced
¼ cup melted butter or margarine
½ teaspoon Worcestershire sauce
¼ teaspoon salt
Dash of pepper
6 (1¼-inch-thick) pork chops, cut with pockets
1½ cups water
3 tablespoons catsup

Soak clay cooker in water.

Combine breadcrumbs, onion, butter, Worcestershire sauce, salt, and pepper.

Stuff pockets of pork chops with breadcrumb mixture, and secure with toothpicks. Place chops in cooker. Combine water and catsup, stirring well; pour over pork chops.

Cover cooker, and place in a cold oven. Bake at 400° for 45 minutes to 1 hour. Yield: 6 servings.
Mrs. J. W. Hopkins,
Abilene, Texas.

Dessert With A Dixie Flavor

Traditional French crêpes take a Southern twist in this recipe for Dixie Dessert Crêpes from James Strieber of Crofton, Maryland. The crêpes are filled with ice cream, then topped with a creamy chocolate-peanut sauce.

DIXIE DESSERT CREPES

⅔ cup instant-blending flour
1 tablespoon sugar
⅛ teaspoon salt
2 eggs
¾ cup milk
1 tablespoon vegetable oil
¼ teaspoon vanilla extract
Butter
3 to 3½ cups vanilla ice cream
Chocolate-Peanut Topping
¼ cup chopped peanuts

Combine flour, sugar, and salt; set aside. Combine eggs, milk, oil, and vanilla; beat well. Add dry ingredients, mixing until smooth.

Brush the bottom of a 6-inch crêpe pan with butter; place over medium heat until hot.

Pour 1½ to 2 tablespoons batter into pan; quickly tilt pan in all directions so batter covers the pan in a thin film. Cook about 1 minute.

Lift edge of crêpe to test for doneness. Crêpe is ready for flipping when it can be shaken loose from pan. Flip crêpe, and cook about 30 seconds on other side. (This side is rarely more than spotty brown.) Place on a towel to cool. Stack crêpes between layers of waxed paper to prevent sticking.

Fill each crêpe with ¼ cup ice cream. Spoon Chocolate-Peanut Topping over each, and sprinkle with chopped peanuts. Yield: 12 to 14 crêpes.

Note: All-purpose flour may be substituted for instant-blending flour. If you do this, refrigerate batter 1 to 2 hours to allow flour particles to swell and soften so the crêpes are light in texture.

Chocolate-Peanut Topping:

½ cup semisweet chocolate morsels
½ cup chunky peanut butter
½ cup marshmallow cream
½ cup hot water

Combine all ingredients in a small saucepan. Cook over medium heat, stirring frequently, until thoroughly heated and smooth. Yield: 1⅓ cups.

November

November marks the beginning of the merry holiday season in the South. Celebrations range from quiet family dinners to gala get-togethers for special friends. To help you celebrate, we present a special *Holiday Dinners* section featuring complete menus and entertaining ideas, as well as tempting recipes.

In this chapter you will also find some creative recipes for preparing wild duck. They range from a well-seasoned gumbo to an elegant duck liver pâté. And since cool weather calls for warming meals, we offer some spicy chili variations.

Because Southerners love seafood just about any way it is prepared, we present some delightful ways to enjoy your favorite shellfish. And for a casual dinner gathering, look over our complete menu designed to make the preparation easy on you.

Wild About Duck In Pine Bluff

If you think the only way to cook duck is baking it in an orange sauce, then you're in for some surprises. Because Arkansas is a hunter's wonderland and the No. 1 sport in Pine Bluff is duck hunting, the people there have created a variety of duck specialties. They have graciously shared their specialties, with recipes and a complete menu centered around duck.

When the duck season begins in November, the men of Pine Bluff head for the rice fields. The sport of hunting not only generates close friendships among the hunters, but their wives frequently gather while the men are away. One such gathering is a luncheon at Pat Lile's home. She serves a well-known Pine Bluff specialty, Duck and Wild Rice Casserole, a family recipe shared by her friend, Susan Stobaugh.

After the hunting season, the hunters and their wives often gather to enjoy the rewards of the hunt together. And that's the case when Sue and Henry Trotter entertain the group with an elegant dinner. Sue's specialty is Sherried Baked Duck, a dish she can prepare the day before the party and just reheat at serving time.

The people of Pine Bluff not only take pride in their wild duck, but also in the rice grown in this area of Arkansas. Sue Trotter serves the rice shaped in a ring mold and filled with pickled beets.

Duck gumbo is a favorite of the Teryl Brooks family. Helen Brooks learned the art of making gumbo from her husband's mother, a great Louisiana cook. Helen says the secret to good gumbo is starting with a dark roux made in a heavy iron pot. Her Pine Bluff version reflects that Louisiana influence, as she combines the duck with spicy smoked sausage and oysters.

"This gumbo is always better when made a day before serving to allow the flavors to blend," says Helen. "We always serve it over hot cooked rice; then add filé to thicken."

"It's hard to convince people they're eating duck," says Jane Starling about the tender bits of Charcoaled Marinated Duck Breasts she serves with crackers as an hors d'oeuvre.

For this specialty, Jane soaks the duck breasts in salt water and places them in a savory marinade for several hours. Then the duck breasts are wrapped in bacon before her husband grills them over slow coals.

The soaking in salt water and marinating takes the wild game taste out of the duck, and the flavor of the bacon permeates the duck during the grilling to give it an unbeatable taste. According to Jane, "It's the easiest way to prepare ducks—once you've fixed them like this, you won't want them any other way."

There are also three other duck appetizers you'll want to try. Two are skillfully seasoned pâtés—one made with duck livers, the other with the meat. And there's Chafing Dish Orange Duck, bite-size pieces of roast duck chilled in a well-seasoned orange sauce, then served piping hot with melba toast rounds.

smooth. Add mushrooms; cook 1 minute, stirring constantly. Gradually stir in mushroom liquid-broth mixture; cook over medium heat, stirring constantly, until thickened and bubbly. Stir in duck, rice, half-and-half, and parsley; spoon into a greased 2-quart shallow casserole. Sprinkle almonds over top.

Cover and bake at 350° for 15 to 20 minutes; uncover and bake 5 to 10 additional minutes or until thoroughly heated. Yield: 6 to 8 servings.

Note: If desired, 3 cups cubed cooked chicken may be substituted for the duck.

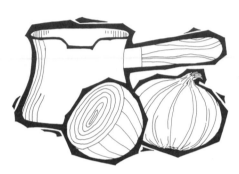

Cooking Duck With Pine Bluff

■ At a luncheon for the hunter's wives, **Pat Lile** centers her menu around a well-known Pine Bluff favorite: Duck and Wild Rice Casserole.

DUCK AND WILD RICE CASSEROLE

2 large wild ducks, cleaned
3 stalks celery, cut into 2-inch pieces
1 onion, halved
1½ teaspoons salt
¼ teaspoon pepper
1 (6-ounce) package long-grain and wild-rice mix
1 (4-ounce) can sliced mushrooms
½ cup chopped onion
½ cup melted margarine
¼ cup all-purpose flour
1½ cups half-and-half
1 tablespoon chopped fresh parsley
½ cup slivered almonds

Combine first 5 ingredients in a large Dutch oven; cover with water, and bring to a boil. Reduce heat; cover and simmer 1 hour or until ducks are tender. Remove ducks from stock; strain stock, and reserve. When ducks cool, remove meat from bones; cut into bite-size pieces, and set aside.

Cook rice according to directions on the package.

Drain mushrooms, reserving liquid. Add enough duck broth to mushroom liquid to make 1½ cups.

Sauté chopped onion in margarine until tender; add flour, stirring until

■ **Henry and Sue Trotter** entertain friends with an elegant dinner that features ducks baked in a sherry sauce.

Sherried Baked Duck
Rice Ring with Beets
Scalloped Oysters
Plantation Squash
Hot Curried Fruit
Rolls   Butter
Tiny Pecan Pies
Chablis   Coffee

SHERRIED BAKED DUCK

1 quart dry sherry
½ cup vegetable oil
2 cups water
¼ cup butter
1 teaspoon red pepper
2 teaspoons white pepper
2 tablespoons parsley flakes
4 (2-ounce) bottles onion juice
8 wild ducks, cleaned
Salt
8 bay leaves
2 large onions, quartered
Orange slices (optional)
Parsley sprigs (optional)

Combine first 8 ingredients in a large saucepan; heat well.

Sprinkle ducks with salt. Place 1 bay leaf and an onion quarter in cavity of each duck; place ducks, breast down, in a large roaster.

Pour half of hot sherry mixture over ducks; cover and bake at 350° for 3 hours or until tender, basting occasionally with pan drippings.

Reheat the remaining sherry mixture, and pour over ducks; cover and let stand in refrigerator for 1 to 2 hours or until ready to reheat and serve.

Before reheating, cut ducks in half and return to roaster. Cover and bake at 350° for 30 minutes or until hot. Place on serving platter; garnish with orange slices and parsley sprigs, if desired. Yield: 8 servings.

Note: This dish is best when prepared a day in advance. Store in refrigerator, and heat before serving.

RICE RING WITH BEETS

2 (6-ounce) packages long-grain and wild-rice mix
¼ cup butter or margarine, melted
2 tablespoons chopped parsley
1 (4-ounce) can sliced mushrooms, drained
½ green pepper, chopped
1 small onion, chopped
4 cups chicken or duck broth
1 clove garlic, minced
½ teaspoon salt
¼ teaspoon pepper
About 1 cup sweet sliced pickled beets
Small whole beets (optional)
Parsley (optional)

Place rice and butter in a large skillet; cook over medium heat, stirring constantly, until rice is golden brown (about 5 minutes). Add next 8 ingredients and seasoning envelopes from packages of rice; mix well. Pour into an ungreased 2-quart casserole. Bake at 325° for 1 hour.

Remove rice from oven, and firmly pack hot rice into a greased 6-cup ring mold. Place serving plate on top of mold; invert and let stand 10 minutes before removing mold.

Fill center of rice ring with sliced pickled beets; garnish with whole beets and parsley, if desired. Yield: about 10 to 12 servings.

SCALLOPED OYSTERS

2 cups cracker crumbs
1 pint oysters, drained
1 teaspoon salt
½ teaspoon pepper
½ cup butter or margarine, cut into ¼-inch slices
2 cups milk

Sprinkle one-third of cracker crumbs in a greased 2-quart casserole. Spoon half of oysters evenly over crumbs; sprinkle with ½ teaspoon salt and ¼ teaspoon pepper. Place half of butter slices over oysters. Repeat layers. Top with the remaining cracker crumbs.

Pour milk over oyster mixture. Bake at 350° for 45 minutes. Yield: about 8 servings.

PLANTATION SQUASH

12 medium-size yellow squash
2 (10-ounce) packages frozen chopped spinach
1 (3-ounce) package cream cheese, softened
3 eggs, well beaten
6 tablespoons melted butter or margarine
1½ tablespoons sugar
½ teaspoon seasoned salt
½ teaspoon onion salt
2 teaspoons coarsely ground black pepper
1 cup round buttery cracker crumbs
Paprika
1 pound bacon, cooked and crumbled

Wash squash thoroughly. Drop in boiling water; cover and simmer 8 to 10 minutes or until tender but still firm. Drain and cool slightly; trim off stems. Cut squash in half lengthwise. Scoop out pulp, leaving firm shells; mash pulp.

Cook spinach according to package directions; drain well, and add to squash pulp. Add cream cheese, mixing until well blended. Stir in next 6 ingredients; spoon into squash shells.

Sprinkle squash with cracker crumbs, paprika, and bacon. Place on lightly greased baking sheets; cover with foil, and bake at 325° for 30 minutes. Yield: 12 servings.

Note: To prepare ahead, spoon filling into shells and chill. When ready to bake, sprinkle with cracker crumbs, paprika, and bacon. Bake at 325° about 30 to 40 minutes or until well heated.

HOT CURRIED FRUIT

1 (16-ounce) can peach halves
1 (16-ounce) can pear halves
1 (15¼-ounce) can pineapple chunks
1 tablespoon cornstarch
2 tablespoons brown sugar
1 teaspoon curry powder
1 (16-ounce) jar spiced apple rings, drained

Drain peaches, pears, and pineapple, reserving juice; pour juice into a medium saucepan. Combine cornstarch, sugar, and curry powder; stir into fruit juice. Cook juice over medium heat, stirring occasionally, until mixture begins to thicken.

Stir all fruit into hot mixture; cook until thoroughly heated. Serve hot. Yield: 8 to 12 servings.

TINY PECAN PIES

¾ cup firmly packed brown sugar
1 tablespoon butter or margarine, softened
1 egg
Dash of salt
1 teaspoon vanilla extract
⅔ cup coarsely chopped pecans
Pastry shells (recipe follows)

Combine first 5 ingredients in a small bowl; beat at medium speed of electric mixer just until smooth.

Layer ½ teaspoon pecans, 1 teaspoon filling, and ½ teaspoon pecans in each pastry shell. Bake pies at 325° for 25 minutes or until filling is set. Yield: 2 dozen.

Pastry Shells:

1 (3-ounce) package cream cheese, softened
½ cup butter or margarine, softened
1 cup all-purpose flour

Combine cream cheese and butter in a small bowl; stir until smooth. Add flour, mixing well. Chill dough 1 hour; shape into 24 (1-inch) balls. Place in ungreased 1¾-inch muffin tins, shaping each into a shell. Yield: 2 dozen.

Tip: Wine should be stored at an even temperature of 50 to 60 degrees. It is important that bottles of corked table wines be kept on their side so that the corks are kept moist and airtight. If the bottle has a screw cap, it may remain upright.

■ **Mrs. Thomas E. Gillespie** uses a mold with a duck design for her pâté. Then she outlines the imprint of the duck with peppercorns and embellishes the design with grated carrots, chopped parsley, sour cream, and nutmeg.

DUCK PATE

3 large wild ducks, cleaned
3 stalks celery, cut into 2-inch pieces
1 onion, sliced
1½ teaspoons salt
¼ teaspoon pepper
4 stalks celery, cut into 1-inch pieces
4 green onions, cut into 1-inch pieces
1 green pepper, coarsely chopped
2 tablespoons lemon juice
1 tablespoon Worcestershire sauce
¼ teaspoon hot sauce
¾ teaspoon salt
½ cup mayonnaise

Combine first 5 ingredients in a large Dutch oven; cover with water, and bring to a boil. Reduce heat; cover and simmer about 1 hour or until ducks are tender. Remove ducks from stock; cool and remove meat from bones.

Grind meat, 1-inch celery pieces, green onion, and green pepper in a meat grinder or food processor; stir in remaining ingredients. Spoon into a 1-quart mold; chill 3 to 4 hours or overnight. Unmold and garnish as desired; serve with whole wheat wafers. Yield: about 3½ cups.

■ A favorite of **Jane and Jeff Starling**, Charcoaled Marinated Duck Breasts are sliced thin and served as an hors d' oeuvre with crackers and a favorite barbecue sauce.

CHARCOALED MARINATED DUCK BREASTS

8 whole duck breasts, split, boned, and
    skinned
1½ cups commercial Italian salad dressing
3 tablespoons Worcestershire sauce
¾ teaspoon garlic powder
¾ teaspoon ground cloves
Juice of 3 lemons
16 slices bacon

Soak duck breasts in salt water about 3 hours. Wipe with paper towels, and place in a shallow pan.

Combine next 5 ingredients; pour mixture over duck breasts. Place in refrigerator, and marinate at least 3 hours or overnight.

Remove duck breasts from marinade, and wrap each in a bacon slice; secure with toothpick.

Grill over slow coals 7 minutes on each side or until bacon is done. Slice duck breasts thin, and serve as an hors d'oeuvre with crackers and your favorite barbecue sauce. Yield: 12 to 16 servings.

Note: Duck breasts may be served unsliced as an entrée.

■ **Helen Brooks** adds oysters and spicy smoked sausage to her version of duck gumbo.

DUCK, OYSTER, AND SAUSAGE GUMBO

2 large wild ducks, cleaned
2 stalks celery with leaves, cut into 2-inch
    pieces
1 medium onion, sliced
1 tablespoon salt
Chicken broth
1 pound hot smoked sausage, cut into
    1-inch pieces
½ cup vegetable oil
½ cup all-purpose flour
¾ cup finely chopped celery
1 large onion, finely chopped
1 green pepper, finely chopped
Salt and pepper to taste
6 green onions with tops, finely chopped
2 tablespoons chopped fresh parsley
1 pint oysters, undrained
Hot cooked rice
Gumbo filé

Combine first 4 ingredients in a large Dutch oven; cover with water, and bring to a boil. Reduce heat; cover and simmer about 1 hour or until ducks are tender. Remove ducks from stock; reserve stock. When ducks cool, remove meat from bones; cut meat into bite-size pieces, and set aside.

Return skin and bones to stock; cover and simmer an additional hour. Strain stock; add enough chicken broth to make 2½ quarts liquid. Set aside.

Cook sausage over medium heat about 5 minutes, stirring occasionally. Drain on paper towels, and set aside.

Heat oil in a 5-quart heavy iron pot or Dutch oven; stir in flour. Cook over medium heat at least 30 minutes, or until a dark roux is formed, stirring constantly. Add chopped celery, chopped onion, and green pepper; cook over medium heat 10 minutes, stirring constantly. Remove from heat, and

gradually stir in reserved hot stock. Bring mixture to a boil; then reduce heat, and simmer 20 minutes.

Add duck, sausage, salt, and pepper to stock mixture; simmer 20 minutes. Stir in green onion and parsley; simmer 20 minutes. Add oysters; simmer an additional 10 minutes. Serve gumbo over hot cooked rice. Thicken each serving with gumbo filé. Yield: 8 to 10 servings.

Note: Gumbo is best when made a day ahead, refrigerated, and reheated.

■ Tender chunks of roast duck flavored with orange juice and selected seasonings are served from a chafing dish for this appetizer. The recipe is a favorite of **Mrs. Louis L. Ramsay, Jr.**

CHAFING DISH ORANGE DUCK

6 wild ducks, cleaned
Salt and pepper
1½ cups finely chopped carrot
1½ cups finely chopped apple
¾ cup finely chopped onion
¾ cup finely chopped celery
½ cup butter or margarine
2 cups orange juice
Juice of 2 lemons
Grated rind of 1 lemon
Grated rind of 1 orange
½ cup firmly packed brown sugar
3 tablespoons red wine vinegar
1½ tablespoons Worcestershire sauce
¼ teaspoon hot sauce
2 tablespoons catsup
¼ cup cornstarch
Chopped fresh parsley (optional)

Sprinkle ducks with salt and pepper; place about ¼ cup carrot, ¼ cup apple, 2 tablespoons onion, and 2 tablespoons celery in cavity of each duck.

Place ducks in a large roaster, and add water to cover. Cover and bake at 350° for 3 to 3½ hours or until ducks are very tender; remove ducks, and let cool to touch. Reserve broth. Remove meat from bones, and cut into bite-size pieces. Chill broth; skim fat from top, and reserve 2 cups broth.

Melt butter in a medium saucepan; stir in orange and lemon juice, rind, sugar, and vinegar. Cook over medium heat, stirring constantly, until sugar is dissolved. Stir in Worcestershire sauce, hot sauce, catsup, 1 teaspoon salt, and ¼ teaspoon pepper.

Combine cornstarch and reserved duck broth, mixing well; stir into hot mixture. Cook over medium heat, stirring constantly, until smooth and slightly thickened. Stir in duck meat, and chill overnight.

When ready to serve, heat in a chafing dish; garnish with chopped parsley, if desired. Serve with melba toast rounds. Yield: about 2 quarts.

Note: This dish may be prepared ahead and frozen.

■ Only the duck livers are used in this pâté from **Mrs. Edward E. Brown.**

DUCK LIVER PATE

2 tablespoons finely minced green onion
1 pound duck livers (about 2 cups)
2 tablespoons melted butter or margarine
⅓ cup brandy
¼ cup whipping cream
½ teaspoon salt
⅛ teaspoon ground allspice
⅛ teaspoon pepper
Pinch of ground thyme
½ cup melted butter or margarine
1 hard-cooked egg, sliced (optional)
Chopped fresh parsley (optional)

Sauté green onion and livers in 2 tablespoons butter until livers are done; spoon into container of electric blender or food processor.

Place brandy in a small saucepan; boil until amount is reduced to 3 tablespoons. Add brandy, whipping cream, and seasonings to liver mixture; blend 1 minute or until smooth. Add ½ cup butter; blend well.

Spoon pâté into a 2½- to 3-cup mold; chill 3 to 4 hours or overnight. Serve in mold, or unmold; garnish with hard-cooked egg and parsley, if desired. Serve with crackers. Yield: about 2½ cups.

Note: Chicken livers may be substituted for duck livers.

It's A Great Time For Shellfish

From our Eastern shores to the Florida Keys and the Gulf Coast, the South is blessed with an abundant year-round supply of fresh seafood. Of all the delicacies these waters yield, there is none more prized than shellfish—shrimp, crab, oysters, scallops, and clams.

Without question, **shrimp** is the South's favorite, not only because of its flavor but also for its ease of preparation. And even if fresh shrimp is not available, today's processing methods produce a frozen product that is nearly as good.

The most important thing to remember when preparing shrimp is to avoid overcooking. Besides enjoying shrimp simply with a cocktail sauce, savor its delicate flavor in dishes like West Indian Curried Shrimp spooned over fluffy rice.

Crabmeat is one of the sweetest and most versatile shellfish, equally appealing as appetizer, salad, or main dish. In our Crab Casserole, it's combined with a lightly seasoned white sauce and baked with a breadcrumb topping.

If fresh crabmeat isn't available, the canned or frozen type is a good alternative. Whatever type you use, be sure to check crabmeat for pieces of shell and cartilage. Even though crabmeat is expensive, there is no waste and 1 pound generally serves four.

Oysters were one of the first foods enjoyed by the Indians and early settlers along our Southern coast. It's not surprising that they are still a favorite, whether eaten raw on the half shell with hot sauce, baked in a casserole, or simmered in a stew.

Scallops are often a forgotten delicacy. And if you haven't tried what is probably the sweetest of the shellfish, there is a treat in store. Let us tempt you with Scallop Casserole, a pleasing blend of fresh scallops and a well-seasoned cheese sauce.

When buying fresh scallops, remember that a creamy-white or light-pink color and a mild, faintly sweet aroma are indications of freshness. One pound of scallops yields about 2 cups cooked.

Clams, prized for their distinctive flavor, are part of a tradition in shellfish cookery: a clambake. While thought of as a New England event, one can be just as easily staged in the South.

Like oysters, clams on the half shell are a delicious appetizer. You'll also want to enjoy them in Seafood Linguine.

SEAFOOD LINGUINE

1 medium onion, chopped
1 clove garlic, minced
½ green pepper, chopped
⅓ cup chopped fresh parsley
¼ cup olive oil
1 (15-ounce) can tomato sauce
1 (28-ounce) can tomatoes, chopped
½ cup water
1 teaspoon lemon juice
1 teaspoon whole basil leaves
1 teaspoon whole oregano
¼ teaspoon garlic powder
Salt and pepper to taste
1 dozen fresh clams in shells
1 pound medium shrimp, peeled and deveined
1 (6-ounce) package frozen crabmeat, thawed and drained
6 to 8 frozen crab claws
1 (12-ounce) package linguine or spaghetti
Grated Parmesan cheese

Sauté onion, garlic, green pepper, and parsley in hot oil in a Dutch oven. Add next 8 ingredients; simmer about 20 minutes or until thickened.

Scrub clams with a brush under running water. Add all shellfish to sauce; cover and simmer about 20 minutes or until clams open and shrimp turn pink.

Cook linguine according to package directions; drain. Place on warm platter, and top with sauce. Sprinkle with Parmesan cheese. Yield: 8 servings.
Mrs. Charles W. Kelly,
Smyrna, Georgia.

WEST INDIAN CURRIED SHRIMP

1 medium onion, chopped
1 clove garlic, crushed
¼ cup melted butter
2 teaspoons curry powder
1 green mango, peeled and cubed
2 tablespoons lime juice
1 cup coconut milk
½ teaspoon salt
¼ teaspoon white pepper
2 pounds peeled and deveined shrimp, uncooked
Hot cooked rice

Sauté onion and garlic in butter in a large skillet. Add curry powder and mango, stirring well; cook about 5 minutes over low heat. Add next 4 ingredients, and cook about 10 minutes.

Add shrimp to sauce; cook about 10 to 15 minutes or until shrimp is done, stirring occasionally. Serve over rice. Yield: 4 to 6 servings.
Mrs. Archer Yates,
Dunwoody, Georgia.

CRAB CASSEROLE

2 cups crabmeat
2 tablespoons butter or margarine
1 tablespoon all-purpose flour
1 cup milk
2 egg yolks
¼ teaspoon salt
⅛ teaspoon pepper
1 teaspoon lemon juice
1 teaspoon minced green pepper
½ teaspoon minced onion
⅓ cup buttered breadcrumbs

Remove any cartilage or shell from crabmeat. Set aside.

Melt butter in a heavy saucepan over low heat; add flour, stirring until smooth. Cook 1 minute, stirring constantly. Gradually add milk; cook over medium heat, stirring constantly, until thickened and bubbly.

Beat egg yolks until thick and lemon colored. Stir some of hot mixture into yolks; add to remaining hot mixture, stirring constantly. Stir in salt, pepper, lemon juice, green pepper, and onion. Add crabmeat, stirring well.

Pour crabmeat mixture into a greased 1½-quart casserole. Sprinkle with breadcrumbs; bake at 350° for 20 to 25 minutes. Yield: 4 servings.
Claire A. Bastable,
Chevy Chase, Maryland.

OYSTER SOUP

2 tablespoons chopped onion
2 tablespoons butter or margarine
3 tablespoons all-purpose flour
3 cups milk
1 teaspoon salt
1 pint oysters, undrained
½ teaspoon chopped parsley

Sauté onion in butter until tender; add flour, stirring until smooth. Cook 1 minute, stirring constantly. Gradually add milk; cook over medium heat, stirring constantly, until thickened and bubbly. Stir in salt.

Cook oysters over medium-low heat until edges start to curl up (about 5 minutes); stir into sauce. Sprinkle parsley over soup, and serve hot. Yield: 4 servings.
Therese Borel,
St. Martinville, Louisiana.

Tip: Make 1 cup sour milk by combining 1 tablespoon lemon juice or vinegar and enough regular milk to make 1 cup.

OYSTER CASSEROLE

2 cups toasted breadcrumbs
½ cup melted butter or margarine
2 pints oysters
¼ cup whipping cream
2 teaspoons dry sherry
1 teaspoon pepper
1 teaspoon Worcestershire sauce
½ teaspoon salt
Dash of cayenne pepper

Combine breadcrumbs and butter, stirring until well coated. Sprinkle one-third of breadcrumbs in a greased 9-inch square baking dish.

Drain oysters, reserving ¼ cup liquid. Spoon half of oysters evenly over breadcrumbs. Repeat layers.

Combine whipping cream, reserved oyster liquid, sherry, and seasonings; stir well. Pour over oysters, and sprinkle with remaining breadcrumbs. Bake at 425° for 30 minutes. Yield: 6 servings.
Mrs. Ralph Kenley,
Charlotte, North Carolina.

SCALLOP CASSEROLE

5 tablespoons margarine
5 tablespoons all-purpose flour
2½ cups milk
1 teaspoon salt
½ teaspoon white pepper
1½ cups (⅜ pound) shredded Cheddar cheese
½ teaspoon dry mustard
1 pound fresh scallops
½ cup finely chopped celery
¼ cup diced pimiento
½ teaspoon paprika
¾ cup fine dry breadcrumbs
3 tablespoons melted margarine
Lemon slices

Melt 5 tablespoons margarine in a heavy saucepan over low heat; add flour, stirring until smooth. Cook 1 minute, stirring constantly. Gradually add milk; cook over medium heat, stirring constantly, until thickened and bubbly. Stir in salt and pepper. Add cheese and mustard, stirring until cheese melts.

Add scallops, celery, pimiento, and paprika to sauce; stir well. Spoon mixture into a lightly greased 1½-quart shallow casserole. Combine breadcrumbs and 3 tablespoons melted margarine; spoon over casserole. Bake at 350° for 30 minutes. Serve with lemon slices. Yield: 4 servings.
Charles E. Cook,
Norfolk, Virginia.

SHRIMP AND RICE CASSEROLE

1 pound cooked, peeled, deveined shrimp
1 (16-ounce) can whole tomatoes, chopped
3 cups cooked rice
1 green pepper, cut into 1-inch strips
2 teaspoons salt
¼ teaspoon garlic powder
¼ teaspoon savory

Combine all ingredients, mixing well. Spoon mixture into a greased 1¾-quart casserole. Bake at 350° for 35 minutes. Yield: 4 servings.
Mrs. Leo Scherle,
Louisville, Kentucky.

QUICK BROILED SHELLFISH

2 (6-ounce) packages frozen crab and shrimp, thawed and drained
¼ cup mayonnaise
¼ cup plain yogurt
2 tablespoons minced fresh parsley
2 teaspoons instant minced onion
½ teaspoon salt
¼ teaspoon curry powder
¼ teaspoon white pepper

Combine all ingredients, mixing well. Spoon mixture into 4 (6-ounce) oven proof dishes. Broil 4 to 5 minutes. Yield: 4 servings.
Jane Beresford,
Short Hills, New Jersey.

SHRIMP DE JONGHE

½ cup butter or margarine, melted
½ cup dry white wine
⅓ cup chopped parsley
½ teaspoon paprika
Dash of cayenne
2 cloves garlic, minced
2 cups soft breadcrumbs
4 cups cooked, peeled, deveined shrimp
Parsley (optional)

Combine first 6 ingredients; stir in breadcrumbs. Place shrimp in a greased 11- x 7- x 2-inch baking pan; spoon breadcrumb mixture evenly over shrimp. Bake at 350° for 25 minutes. Garnish dish with parsley, if desired. Yield: 6 to 8 servings.
Mrs. Debra Lancaster,
Hawkinsville, Georgia.

Here Come The Holidays

Southern traditions are never more apparent than during the holidays as families and friends gather to celebrate the season. For some, it's a family dinner complete with turkey and all the trimmings; for others, it's hosting an elegant dinner party or inviting friends in for dessert and coffee. But regardless of the occasion, the warm hospitality is always there and so is a lavish array of favorite foods.

The Ron Lash family of Oklahoma City shares a traditional holiday meal that begins with Tomato Potage, a hot tomato soup. Oyster Dressing trims the turkey, while Candied Sweet Potatoes and cranberries molded into a salad take their places as customary side dishes *(page 249)*.

Moving on to Tennessee, we encountered a couple in Lookout Mountain who graciously open their home each year to friends for an evening of elegant dining. For this party, all the food was prepared by the host. Paul and Caroline Anderson's menu is one to be remembered, from the entrée of Cornish Hens With Orange Glaze to Italian-Style Ice Cream for dessert *(page 243)*.

To begin this special holiday section, we offer a collection of classic desserts—all as special as the season. Filled with candied fruits, nuts, and the flavors of wines and liqueurs, these desserts have that special holiday touch.

For instance, beneath the coconut-sprinkled Divinity Frosting of Ambrosia Cake are three moist layers spread with an orange-flavored filling.

For some families, an old-fashioned steamed pudding is traditional. Our Christmas Pudding is a close cousin and is best served warm, drenched with its own Brandy-Butter Sauce.

Curls of sweet chocolate add a festive touch to Frozen Vanilla Soufflé, which seems to magically rise above the rim of its container. Though rich and creamy, this soufflé is light enough to end an elaborate dinner.

Equally light is Elegant Pineapple Mousse, a rum-laced filling molded in a ladyfinger-lined springform pan. The delicate mousse is sprinkled with macadamia nuts, while a garnish of red cherries adds sparkle.

Also included in this collection of recipes is Coffee Ice Cream Pie, Tropical Bananas Foster, and other desserts—all perfect for the holiday season.

These golden cream puffs, brimming with Tutti-Frutti Filling, are topped with vanilla glaze and garnished with candied cherries.

AMBROSIA CAKE

1 cup butter, softened
2 cups sugar
4 eggs
1 teaspoon butter flavor
1 teaspoon vanilla extract
3 cups sifted cake flour
2½ teaspoons baking powder
½ teaspoon salt
1 cup milk
Orange Filling
Divinity Frosting
½ cup flaked coconut

Cream butter and sugar until fluffy; add eggs, one at a time, beating well after each. Add flavorings; beat 2 minutes on high speed of electric mixer.

Sift together flour, baking powder, and salt; add to creamed mixture alternately with milk, beating on low speed just until blended. Beat on high speed for 1 minute.

Pour batter into 3 greased and floured 9-inch round cakepans. Bake at 350° for 20 to 25 minutes or until cake tests done. Cool in pans 10 minutes; remove from pans, and cool completely.

Spread Orange Filling between layers; spread top and sides of cake with Divinity Frosting. Sprinkle with coconut. Yield: one 9-inch layer cake.

Orange Filling:

1 cup sugar
3 tablespoons cornstarch
¼ teaspoon salt
¾ cup orange juice
¼ cup lemon juice
½ cup water
3 egg yolks, beaten
1 tablespoon grated orange rind

Combine sugar, cornstarch, and salt in a small saucepan; gradually stir in fruit juices and water. Cook over medium heat, stirring constantly, until mixture thickens and boils.

Slowly stir a small amount of hot mixture into egg yolks; add to remaining hot mixture, stirring constantly. Boil 1 minute longer, stirring constantly. Remove from heat, and stir in orange rind. Let cool. Yield: about 2 cups.

Divinity Frosting:

1½ cups sugar
½ teaspoon cream of tartar
½ cup water
3 egg whites
½ teaspoon vanilla extract

Combine sugar, cream of tartar, and water in a heavy saucepan. Cook over medium heat, stirring constantly, until mixture is clear. Cook without stirring until candy thermometer reaches 240°.

Beat egg whites until soft peaks form; continue to beat egg whites while slowly adding syrup mixture. Add vanilla; continue beating until stiff peaks form and frosting is thick enough to spread. Yield: enough frosting for one 9-inch cake. *Jeanne Owens Glasscock, Celeste, Texas.*

SPICY RAISIN LAYER CAKE

2 cups sugar
½ cup shortening
4½ cups all-purpose flour
½ teaspoon salt
1 teaspoon ground nutmeg
1 tablespoon ground allspice
1 tablespoon ground cinnamon
2 teaspoons soda
2 cups buttermilk
1 teaspoon vanilla extract
1 cup blackberry jam
1 cup peach preserves
1 cup raisins
Raisin Filling

Combine sugar and shortening in a large mixing bowl, creaming well.

Combine flour, salt, and spices; stir lightly. Stir soda into buttermilk; add to creamed mixture alternately with flour mixture, stirring only until blended after each addition. Stir in vanilla, jam, preserves, and raisins.

Spoon batter into 3 wax paper-lined 9-inch round cakepans. Bake at 350° for 30 to 35 minutes or until cake tests done. Cool in pans 10 minutes; remove to wire racks, and cool completely.

Spread Raisin Filling between layers and on top of cake. Yield: one 9-inch cake.

Raisin Filling:

1 cup raisins
½ cup peach preserves
¼ cup butter
½ cup boiling water
1 tablespoon all-purpose flour

Combine all ingredients in a heavy saucepan; cook over medium heat, stirring constantly, until thickened. Let cool. Yield: 2 cups.   *Kathi E. Parker, St. Bethlehem, Tennessee.*

WINE CAKE PUDDING

3 eggs, separated
1¼ cups milk, scalded
¼ cup all-purpose flour
1 cup sugar
⅛ teaspoon salt
2 tablespoons melted margarine
¼ cup lemon juice
Grated rind of 1 lemon
¼ cup white wine

Lightly beat egg yolks; add milk, mixing well. Combine flour, sugar, and salt in a large mixing bowl; stir lightly. Add egg yolk mixture to dry ingredients along with margarine, lemon juice, lemon rind, and wine; mix well.

Beat egg whites until stiff peaks form; fold into egg yolk mixture. Spoon into 6 greased custard cups, and place cups in a 13- x 9- x 2-inch baking pan; pour 1 inch of hot water into pan. Bake at 325° for 45 minutes. Yield: 6 servings.
Mrs. Farmer L. Burns, New Orleans, Louisiana.

CHRISTMAS PUDDING

1½ cups all-purpose flour
1½ teaspoons baking powder
¾ teaspoon soda
½ teaspoon salt
1 teaspoon ground cinnamon
½ teaspoon ground allspice
½ cup finely chopped candied pineapple
1½ cups finely chopped candied mixed fruit
¼ cup shortening
¼ cup sugar
¾ cup molasses
2 eggs, slightly beaten
¾ cup milk
½ cup chopped nuts
Brandy-Butter Sauce
Candied red and green cherries (optional)

Combine first 6 ingredients; add candied pineapple and candied mixed fruit, stirring until well coated. Set aside.

Combine shortening and sugar, creaming well; stir in molasses. Add eggs, mixing well. Add flour mixture alternately with milk, stirring well after each addition. Stir in nuts.

Spoon mixture into a greased and floured 2-quart ovenproof mold. Cover with a tight lid or aluminum foil; bake at 350° for 1 hour or until pudding springs back when touched. Immediately unmold onto serving plate. Drizzle with ¾ cup Brandy-Butter Sauce, garnish with candied cherries, if desired. Spoon remaining sauce over each serving. Yield: 8 to 10 servings.

Brandy-Butter Sauce:

2 cups powdered sugar
¼ cup cornstarch
¼ cup water
½ cup butter
¼ teaspoon salt
2 tablespoons brandy flavor

Combine sugar and cornstarch in a small mixing bowl; stir in water.

Melt butter in a small saucepan; stir in cornstarch mixture and salt. Bring to a boil, stirring constantly. Reduce heat; simmer 3 minutes, stirring constantly. Stir in brandy flavor. Yield: about 2 cups.
Cindy Murphy, Knoxville, Tennessee.

ELEGANT PINEAPPLE MOUSSE

1 (20-ounce) can crushed pineapple
2 envelopes unflavored gelatin
5 eggs, separated
1¼ cups sugar, divided
¼ teaspoon salt
1 cup milk, scalded
⅓ cup lime juice
⅓ cup light rum
1 cup whipping cream, whipped
14 to 16 ladyfingers
¼ cup chopped macadamia nuts or pecans
Maraschino cherries (optional)

Drain pineapple, reserving ¼ cup juice; set aside.

Soften gelatin in reserved pineapple juice. Combine egg yolks, ¾ cup sugar, and salt in top of double boiler; gradually stir in milk. Cook over boiling water, stirring constantly, until thickened; stir in softened gelatin, lime juice, rum, and pineapple. Chill mixture until slightly thickened.

Beat egg whites until soft peaks form; gradually add ½ cup sugar, beating until stiff. Fold in pineapple custard and whipped cream.

Split ladyfingers in half lengthwise, and use to line sides and bottom of a 9½-inch springform pan. Spoon in filling, and chill several hours or overnight. Sprinkle with nuts. Garnish with cherries, if desired. Yield: 12 servings.
Elizabeth Kraus, Louisville, Kentucky.

FROZEN VANILLA SOUFFLE

4 egg yolks, beaten
1 cup sugar
⅛ teaspoon salt
1 cup milk
1 cup half-and-half
1½ teaspoons vanilla extract
1 pint whipping cream, whipped
Sweet chocolate curls

Cut a piece of aluminum foil long enough to fit around a 1-quart soufflé dish, allowing a 1-inch overlap. Fold paper lengthwise into thirds. Wrap around dish, allowing paper to extend 3 inches above rim to form a collar. Secure with cellophane tape.

Combine egg yolks, sugar, salt, and ¼ cup milk in top of double boiler; mix well. Combine remaining ¾ cup milk, half-and-half, and vanilla in a small saucepan; heat well, and gradually stir into egg mixture. Cook over boiling water, stirring constantly, until thickened; let cool.

Fold whipped cream into custard, and spoon into prepared soufflé dish. Freeze until firm; garnish with chocolate curls. Yield: 6 to 8 servings.

Mrs. Harland Stone,
Ocala, Florida.

MARASCHINO RUSSIAN CREAM

¾ cup milk
3 tablespoons sugar
⅛ teaspoon salt
2 eggs, beaten
1 teaspoon vanilla extract
1 (3-ounce) package lemon-flavored gelatin
1 cup warm water
¼ cup maraschino cherry juice
½ teaspoon almond extract
Whipped cream
Maraschino cherries

Scald milk in top of double boiler. Combine sugar, salt, and eggs in a small bowl, mixing well. Stir a small amount of hot milk into egg mixture; add to remaining hot milk. Cook, stirring constantly, until thickened. Remove from heat, and stir in vanilla. Chill.

Dissolve gelatin in warm water in a medium mixing bowl; stir in cherry juice and almond extract. Place bowl in ice water, and stir until gelatin is slightly thickened. With bowl in ice water, beat gelatin mixture on high speed of electric mixer until stiff peaks form.

Add chilled custard to gelatin mixture; beat on high speed of electric mixer an additional 30 seconds. Spoon into individual molds, and chill until firm. Unmold and garnish with whipped cream and maraschino cherries. Yield: 6 to 8 servings. *Mrs. Dora Farrar,*
Gadsden, Alabama.

COFFEE ICE CREAM PIE

½ cup melted butter
1 (7-ounce) can flaked coconut
2 tablespoons all-purpose flour
½ cup chopped pecans
½ gallon coffee ice cream, softened
1 cup whipping cream
¼ cup powdered sugar
Sweet chocolate curls
½ to ⅔ cup Kahlúa or other coffee-flavored liqueur

Combine butter, coconut, flour, and pecans; mix well, and press on bottom and sides of a 10-inch piepan. Bake at 375° for 10 to 12 minutes or until lightly browned; cool. Spoon ice cream into pie shell, and freeze until firm.

Beat whipping cream until foamy; gradually add powdered sugar, beating until soft peaks form. Spread over pie; top with chocolate curls. Pour 1 tablespoon Kahlúa over each serving. Yield: one 10-inch pie. *Mrs. Zack Jennings,*
Batesville, Arkansas.

TUTTI-FRUTTI CREAM PUFFS

1 cup water
½ cup butter or margarine
½ teaspoon salt
1 cup all-purpose flour
4 eggs
Tutti-Frutti Filling
Vanilla Glaze
Candied red and green cherries (optional)

Bring water to a boil in a medium saucepan; add butter, and continue boiling until butter melts. Quickly add salt and flour all at once; beat with a wooden spoon until mixture forms a ball that leaves sides of pan. Remove from heat, and cool slightly.

Add eggs to flour mixture, one at a time, beating well after each addition. (Mixture will separate as each egg is added; continue beating until smooth and shiny.)

Spoon batter by rounded tablespoonfuls onto greased baking sheets. Bake at 400° for 50 minutes or until puffed and golden. (Do not open oven during baking.) Cool thoroughly on a wire rack.

With a sharp knife, cut shells in half horizontally. Fill bottom halves with Tutti-Frutti Filling, and cover with top halves. Spoon Vanilla Glaze over each;

garnish with candied cherries, if desired. Serve immediately or refrigerate. Yield: 1 dozen.

Tutti-Frutti Filling:

1 (3¾-ounce) package vanilla pudding and pie filling mix
1½ cups milk
1 (11-ounce) can mandarin orange sections, drained and halved
½ cup currants
¼ cup finely chopped candied pineapple
¼ cup finely chopped green candied cherries
1½ teaspoons rum flavor
1 cup whipping cream, whipped

Combine pudding mix and milk; cook according to package directions, and let cool. Fold in fruit, rum flavor, and whipped cream. Yield: about 4½ cups.

Vanilla Glaze:

1 cup powdered sugar
1½ tablespoons milk
½ teaspoon vanilla extract

Combine all ingredients, beating until smooth. Yield: about ½ cup.

Mrs. Elizabeth Moore,
Huntsville, Alabama.

TROPICAL BANANAS FOSTER

½ cup butter
½ cup firmly packed brown sugar
3 large firm bananas
1 (8¼-ounce) can sliced pineapple, drained
¼ teaspoon ground cinnamon
2 tablespoons banana-flavored liqueur
¼ cup light rum
Vanilla ice cream

Melt butter in skillet over medium heat, and add sugar; cook until bubbly, stirring constantly.

Peel bananas, and slice in half crosswise; then quarter each piece lengthwise. Quarter each pineapple slice. Stir bananas, pineapple, and cinnamon into brown sugar sauce; cook over medium heat until bananas are slightly soft, basting constantly with sauce. Add liqueur, stirring gently.

Place rum in a small, long-handled pan; heat just until warm. Ignite and pour over fruit. Serve immediately over ice cream. Yield: 6 to 8 servings.

Mrs. Larry D. Elder,
Spartanburg, South Carolina.

Beverages To Toast The Season

Special beverages are a must for toasting the season. If eggnog is a tradition at your house, you should enjoy two new variations—Sparkling Eggnog with ice cream and ginger ale, or brandy-laced Holiday Eggnog Deluxe.

If your entertaining plans call for serving a large group, fill the punch bowl with Anytime Wine Punch or Double Sherbet Punch. You'll also find two coffee-based beverages to help end the evening on a festive note.

CREAMY IRISH COFFEE

½ cup plus 1 tablespoon firmly packed brown sugar
2 quarts hot strong coffee
¾ cup Irish whiskey
1 pint vanilla ice cream

Combine brown sugar and coffee, stirring to dissolve sugar. Stir in whiskey. Place ice cream in a large pitcher; add coffee mixture. Stir until ice cream is slightly melted. Serve at once. Yield: about 12 cups.

Note: Recipe may be doubled and served in a punch bowl.
Sonja Blackwood,
San Angelo, Texas.

HOLIDAY EGGNOG DELUXE

6 eggs, separated
¾ cup plus 2 tablespoons sugar
½ teaspoon vanilla extract
¼ teaspoon ground nutmeg
¼ cup plus 2 tablespoons rum
¾ cup brandy
3 cups whipping cream
2 cups milk
3 tablespoons sugar
Ground nutmeg

Beat egg yolks until thick and lemon colored; gradually add ¾ cup plus 2 tablespoons sugar, vanilla, and ¼ teaspoon nutmeg, beating well. Slowly stir in rum and brandy; cover the container, and refrigerate overnight.

Place chilled mixture in a punch bowl; gradually stir in cream and milk.

Beat egg whites in a large mixing bowl until soft peaks form. Gradually add 3 tablespoons sugar, and beat until stiff. Fold whites into chilled mixture. Sprinkle with nutmeg as desired. Yield: 2½ quarts.
Mrs. Barbara A. Sullivan,
Ocala, Florida.

SPARKLING EGGNOG

6 eggs
¼ cup sugar
¼ teaspoon ground cinnamon
¼ teaspoon ground ginger
¼ teaspoon ground cloves
2 quarts orange juice, chilled
½ cup lemon juice, chilled
1 quart vanilla ice cream
1 quart ginger ale, chilled
Ground nutmeg

Place eggs in a large mixing bowl; beat until thickened. Add sugar, cinnamon, ginger, and cloves; beat well. Stir in orange juice and lemon juice; set aside.

Scoop vanilla ice cream into a punch bowl; gradually stir in ginger ale. Add egg mixture, and stir until well blended. Sprinkle with nutmeg as desired. Yield: about 4½ quarts.
Mrs. Mary Dishon,
Stanford, Kentucky.

QUICK VIENNESE MOCHA

6 cups milk
1 (1-ounce) package instant cocoa mix
2 tablespoons instant coffee powder
¼ to ½ cup whipping cream
1 tablespoon sugar
6 (4-inch) sticks cinnamon or ground cinnamon (optional)

Heat milk in a 2-quart saucepan. Combine cocoa mix and coffee; stir into milk. Heat, stirring constantly until dry ingredients are dissolved.

Combine cream and sugar; beat until stiff, and set aside.

Pour hot mixture into individual mugs; top each with a dollop of whipped cream. Serve with cinnamon sticks or sprinkle with ground cinnamon, if desired. Yield: 6 to 8 servings.
Mrs. Margaret L. Hunter,
Princeton, Kentucky.

HOLIDAY FRUIT PUNCH

3 cups sugar
1 gallon water
1 (64-ounce) bottle cranberry juice
1 (32-ounce) bottle apple juice
2 cups orange juice
1½ cups lemon juice
2 cups strong tea
Ice cubes

Combine sugar and water in a large Dutch oven; heat to boiling. Remove from heat; cool. Combine fruit juices and tea; add to cooled sugar syrup. Chill thoroughly.

Just before serving, pour juice mixture into a punch bowl over ice cubes. Yield: about 2 gallons.

Note: Colored ice cubes may be used, if desired. Blend food coloring with water before freezing. *Ramona Hook,*
Hazelwood, Missouri.

DOUBLE SHERBET PUNCH

1 (12-ounce) can frozen orange juice concentrate
1 (6-ounce) can frozen lemonade concentrate
3 cups pineapple juice
1 quart pineapple sherbet
1 quart lime sherbet
1½ quarts ginger ale, chilled

Mix orange juice concentrate and lemonade concentrate as directed on container label.

Combine orange juice, lemonade, and pineapple juice. Refrigerate 2 hours or until serving time.

When ready to serve, pour juice mixture into punch bowl; add sherbet to punch in small scoops. Add ginger ale, and stir slightly. Serve immediately. Yield: about 6 quarts. *Mary Jo Ealey,*
Smithfield, Virginia.

ANYTIME WINE PUNCH

1 gallon Burgundy or rosé
1 (6-ounce) can frozen lemonade, thawed and undiluted
1 (6-ounce) can frozen limeade, thawed and undiluted
1 (12-ounce) can apricot nectar
2 (32-ounce) bottles lemon-lime carbonated beverage, chilled
1 (16-ounce) package frozen whole strawberries

Combine first 4 ingredients; chill. When ready to serve, pour chilled mixture into an ice-filled punch bowl. Pour in carbonated beverage, and stir gently. Float strawberries on top. Yield: about 2 gallons.

Note: A blend of 2 quarts Burgundy and 2 quarts rosé may be substituted for 1 gallon of wine, if desired.

*Carole Lake,
Houston, Texas.*

GOLDEN GIN PUNCH

1 cup gin
1 cup Galliano or banana-flavored liqueur
⅓ cup thawed lemonade concentrate, undiluted
⅓ cup thawed lemon concentrate, undiluted
1 (32-ounce) bottle club soda, chilled
1 (32-ounce) bottle ginger ale, chilled
Ice ring
Orange slices (optional)
Maraschino cherries (optional)

Combine first 4 ingredients; chill. When ready to serve, combine chilled mixture, club soda, and ginger ale in a punch bowl with an ice ring. Garnish with orange slices and maraschino cherries, if desired. Yield: 3 quarts.

*Rita D. Hutson,
Lithonia, Georgia.*

PLANTATION SYLLABUB

5 cups sugar, divided
3 quarts apple cider
¼ cup light corn syrup
1 cup lemon juice
2 teaspoons aromatic bitters
8 egg whites
2 quarts milk
1 quart half-and-half

Combine 4 cups sugar, apple cider, corn syrup, lemon juice, and bitters; stir to dissolve sugar. Chill several hours.

Beat egg whites, gradually adding 1 cup sugar; beat until stiff peaks form. Spoon meringue by teaspoonfuls onto cookie sheet; freeze.

To serve, combine milk, half-and-half, and cider mixture; beat with whisk until frothy. Pour into punch bowl, and float meringues on top. Yield: 50 cups.

*Charlotte Watkins,
Lakeland, Florida.*

Tasty Beginnings For That Special Occasion

Whether your entertaining plans call for a cocktail dinner or the traditional holiday feast, tasty hors d'oeuvres are the beginning of a memorable occasion.

Something light is in order when an elaborate dinner is to follow. Offer your guests tangy Smoked Oyster Dip to enjoy with crunchy vegetables. Or serve cheese in a Ham-and-Cheese Roll to spread on crisp crackers.

Cocktail dinners require an assortment of appetizers, both hot and cold, light and filling. We offer such delightful choices as Sweet-and-Sour Party Meatballs; cool, creamy Crab Pâté; and delicate Gouda-Shrimp Puffs.

SMOKED OYSTER DIP

1 (8-ounce) package cream cheese, softened
1½ cups mayonnaise
4 dashes of hot sauce
1 tablespoon lemon juice
1 (4¼-ounce) can chopped black olives
1 (3.66-ounce) can smoked oysters, drained and chopped

Combine first 4 ingredients, mixing well. Stir in olives and oysters. Serve with raw vegetables or crackers. Yield: about 2 cups.
*Eloise Haynes,
Greenville, Mississippi.*

CRAB PATE

1 (10¾-ounce) can cream of mushroom soup, undiluted
1 envelope unflavored gelatin
3 tablespoons cold water
¾ cup mayonnaise
1 (8-ounce) package cream cheese, softened
1 (6½-ounce) can crabmeat, drained and flaked
1 small onion, grated
1 cup finely chopped celery
Parsley sprigs

Heat soup in a medium saucepan over low heat; remove from heat. Dissolve gelatin in cold water; add to soup, stirring well. Add next 5 ingredients, and mix well. Spoon into an oiled 4-cup mold. Chill until firm. Unmold and garnish with parsley. Serve with assorted crackers. Yield: about 4 cups.
*Mrs. N. Callicott,
Sedona, Arizona.*

SWEET-AND-SOUR PARTY MEATBALLS

1 pound ground round steak
1 pound ground pork
2 cups soft breadcrumbs
2 tablespoons finely chopped onion
2 eggs, beaten
1 teaspoon salt
¼ teaspoon pepper
1 tablespoon butter or margarine
3 tablespoons cornstarch
1 cup vinegar
¾ cup sugar
3 drops hot sauce
1 tablespoon Worcestershire sauce
1 green pepper, diced
1 (20-ounce) can pineapple chunks, drained
1 (8-ounce) can tomato sauce

Combine first 7 ingredients, mixing well; shape into 1-inch meatballs. Brown in butter over medium heat; drain. Place meatballs in a 13- x 9- x 2-inch baking dish.

Combine cornstarch, vinegar, and sugar in a medium saucepan; cook over low heat, stirring constantly until clear and thickened. Stir in remaining ingredients; pour over meatballs. Bake at 300° for 40 minutes. Yield: about 6 dozen.
*Robyn Phillips,
Thomasville, Alabama.*

GOUDA-SHRIMP PUFFS

½ cup vegetable oil
¼ cup butter or margarine
½ cup water
¾ cup plus 2 tablespoons all-purpose
    flour
3 eggs
Dash of hot sauce
¼ teaspoon salt
Dash of pepper
1 cup (¼ pound) shredded Gouda cheese
1 tablespoon chopped chives
1 (4½-ounce) can shrimp, drained and
    chopped

Heat vegetable oil to 350° in an electric skillet.

Melt butter in a medium saucepan; add water, and bring to a boil. Add flour, stirring until mixture leaves sides of pan; remove from heat. Add eggs, one at a time, beating well at medium speed of electric mixture after each addition. Stir in remaining ingredients.

Drop mixture by teaspoonfuls into hot skillet; fry about 5 minutes or until golden brown, turning once. Drain on paper towels. May be kept warm in a 200° oven about 1 hour before serving. Yield: about 3 dozen.
Mrs. H. S. Wright,
Leesville, South Carolina.

HAM-AND-CHEESE ROLL

1 (8-ounce) package cream cheese,
    softened
2 cups (½ pound) shredded Cheddar
    cheese
1 teaspoon grated onion
1 teaspoon dry mustard
½ teaspoon paprika
1 (2¼-ounce) can deviled ham
1 tablespoon parsley flakes
½ cup chopped pecans
Parsley sprigs

Combine first 7 ingredients, mixing well; chill thoroughly. Shape into an 8-inch roll, and coat with pecans. Chill. Garnish with parsley, and serve with crackers. Yield: one 8-inch cheese roll.
Mrs. Charles DeHaven,
Owensboro, Kentucky.

Holiday Breads To Give Or Keep

Nothing can compare to the aroma that fills the kitchen during the holiday bread-baking season. Full of fruits, nuts, and spices, these breads are especially good fresh from the oven. Bake several for guests, or tie some with ribbons to carry to friends.

Our quick breads include Apricot-Cranberry Loaf and Kahlúa Fruit-Nut Bread—a date-nut loaf flavored with coffee liqueur. Sugarplum Coffee Ring is a delicately textured yeast bread well worth the preparation time.

MARASCHINO CHERRY NUT BREAD

¼ cup shortening
1 cup sugar
1 teaspoon salt
2 eggs
1½ cups all-purpose flour
1½ teaspoons baking powder
1 (8-ounce) bottle maraschino cherries
½ cup chopped pecans

Combine shortening, sugar, salt, and eggs in a medium mixing bowl; beat well, and set aside.

Combine flour and baking powder; mix well. Drain cherries, reserving liquid. Add flour mixture to creamed mixture alternately with reserved cherry liquid, mixing well after each addition. Stir in cherries and pecans. Spoon into a greased and floured 9- x 5- x 3-inch loafpan. Bake at 350° for 1 hour. Let cool in pan 10 minutes. Remove to wire rack, and cool completely. Yield: 1 loaf.
Mrs. John B. Thompson,
Anniston, Alabama.

ORANGE TEA BREAD

2 cups all-purpose flour
½ cup sugar
1 teaspoon salt
1 teaspoon soda
1 egg, beaten
¼ cup butter or margarine, melted
1 teaspoon grated orange rind
1 teapoon grated lemon rind
1 cup orange juice
1 cup chopped pecans

Combine flour, sugar, salt, and soda; add remaining ingredients, mixing well. Pour into a greased 9- x 5- x 3-inch loafpan. Bake at 350° for 50 minutes. Yield: 1 loaf.
Mrs. George Sellers,
Newport News, Virginia.

NORWEGIAN CHRISTMAS BREAD

1 cup milk, scalded
½ cup butter, softened
½ cup sugar
1 teaspoon salt
2 packages dry yeast
½ cup warm water (105° to 115°)
1 tablespoon all-purpose flour
1 cup diced mixed candied fruit
½ cup chopped pecans
4½ to 5 cups all-purpose flour
1 cup regular or quick-cooking oats,
    uncooked
1 egg, beaten
Melted butter
1 tablespoon sugar
⅛ teaspoon ground cinnamon

Combine milk, ½ cup butter, ½ cup sugar, and salt in a large bowl; stir until butter melts. Cool to lukewarm.

Combine yeast and water in a small mixing bowl; let stand 5 minutes.

Combine 1 tablespoon flour, fruit, and pecans; stir well, and set aside.

Stir 2 cups flour into milk mixture, beating until smooth. Add yeast mixture, fruit mixture, oats, and egg; stir well. Add 2½ to 3 cups flour, beating until a soft dough is formed.

Turn dough out onto a floured surface, and knead until elastic (5 to 8 minutes). Form dough into a ball; place in a well-greased bowl, turning to grease top. Cover and let rise in a warm place (85°), free of drafts, 1½ to 2 hours or until doubled in bulk.

Divide dough in half, and shape each half into a smooth ball. Place each on a buttered baking sheet, and press lightly to flatten bottom. Cover; let rise in a warm place (85°), free of drafts, until doubled in bulk.

Bake at 350° for 30 minutes or until loaves sound hollow when tapped on top with finger.

Brush hot loaves with melted butter. Combine 1 tablespoon sugar and cinnamon; sprinkle over loaves. Cool on wire racks. Yield: 2 loaves. *Gabriel Beaugh,*
Lake Charles, Louisiana.

KAHLUA FRUIT-NUT BREAD

1 cup pitted dates, chopped
½ cup Kahlúa or other coffee-flavored liqueur
½ cup warm water
1 teaspoon grated orange rind
⅔ cup firmly packed brown sugar
2 tablespoons shortening
1 egg, beaten
2 cups all-purpose flour
1 teaspoon salt
1 teaspoon soda
⅔ cup chopped pecans

Combine dates, Kahlúa, water, and orange rind; set aside.

Cream sugar and shortening until light and fluffy; add egg, mixing well.

Stir together flour, salt, and soda; add to creamed mixture alternately with date mixture. Stir in pecans. Pour into a greased and floured 9- x 5- x 3-inch loafpan. Bake at 350° for 1 hour or until loaf tests done. Place on rack to cool. Yield: 1 loaf.
*F. E. Holmes,
De Bary, Florida.*

HAWAIIAN BANANA NUT BREAD

3 cups all-purpose flour
2 cups sugar
1 teaspoon soda
1 teaspoon salt
1 teaspoon ground cinnamon
1 cup chopped nuts
3 eggs, beaten
1½ cups vegetable oil
2 cups mashed ripe bananas
1 (8-ounce) can crushed pineapple, drained
2 teaspoons vanilla extract

Combine dry ingredients; stir in nuts and set aside.

Combine remaining ingredients; add to dry ingredients, stirring just until moistened.

Spoon batter into 2 greased and floured 9- x 5- x 3-inch loafpans. Bake at 350° for 1 hour and 5 minutes or until done. Cool 10 minutes before removing from pans. Remove to wire racks; cool completely. Yield: 2 loaves.
*Mrs. Marge Killmon,
Annandale, Virginia.*

APRICOT-CRANBERRY LOAF

2 cups all-purpose flour
¾ cup sugar
1 tablespoon baking powder
½ teaspoon salt
1 cup diced dried apricots
1 cup chopped cranberries
½ cup coarsely chopped nuts
2 eggs
¼ cup milk
¼ cup melted butter or margarine
1 teaspoon grated lemon rind

Combine flour, sugar, baking powder, and salt in a large bowl. Stir in apricots, cranberries, and nuts, coating well. Make a well in the center of mixture.

Beat eggs slightly in a small bowl; stir in milk, butter, and lemon rind. Pour into center of flour mixture; stir until dry ingredients are moistened.

Pour batter into a greased 9- x 5- x 3-inch loafpan. Bake at 350° for 1 hour or until loaf tests done. Let cool in pan 10 minutes. Remove to wire rack, and cool completely. Yield: 1 loaf.
*Mrs. Grace L. Grogaard,
Baltimore, Maryland.*

GOLDEN BLUEBERRY MUFFINS

2 cups all-purpose flour
½ teaspoon salt
1 cup firmly packed brown sugar
½ cup shortening
2 eggs
½ cup buttermilk
1 teaspoon soda
2 cups frozen blueberries, thawed and drained
½ cup all-purpose flour

Combine 2 cups flour and salt; set aside.

Cream sugar and shortening; add eggs, one at a time, beating well after each addition.

Combine buttermilk and soda, stirring well; add to sugar mixture alternately with flour mixture, stirring just to combine. Combine berries and ½ cup flour; gently fold into batter.

Spoon batter into greased muffin tins, filling two-thirds full. Bake at 350° for 20 to 25 minutes or until golden brown. Yield: about 2 dozen muffins.
Note: Two cups fresh blueberries may be substituted for frozen.
*Mrs. LaGourge Cory,
Neosho, Missouri.*

SUGARPLUM COFFEE RING

½ cup milk
⅓ cup shortening
⅓ cup sugar
1 teaspoon salt
1 package dry yeast
¼ cup warm water (105° to 115°)
2 eggs
3¼ to 3¾ cups all-purpose flour
1 cup sugar
1¼ teaspoons ground cinnamon
¼ cup plus 2 tablespoons melted butter or margarine
½ cup quartered red candied cherries
½ cup toasted slivered almonds
⅓ cup dark corn syrup

Scald milk; stir in shortening, ⅓ cup sugar, and salt. Stir until shortening is melted. Cool to lukewarm.

Combine yeast and water; let stand 5 minutes. Add to milk mixture; stir in eggs and 1 cup flour, beating well. Add enough flour to make a soft dough.

Place dough in a lightly greased bowl, turning to grease top. Cover and let rise in a warm place (85°), free from drafts, 2 hours or until doubled in bulk. Punch dough down; cover and let dough rest 10 minutes.

Divide dough into 36 pieces; shape into balls. Combine 1 cup sugar and cinnamon; mix well. Dip balls of dough in butter; roll in sugar mixture. Place 12 balls in a staggered row in a well-greased, one-piece 10-inch tube pan. Sprinkle one-third of the cherries and one-third of the almonds over balls. Repeat layers twice.

Combine remaining butter and corn syrup, mixing well; drizzle mixture over top of dough. Cover and let rise in a warm place (85°), free from drafts, 1 hour or until doubled in bulk. Bake at 350° for 35 minutes; cool 5 minutes in pan. Serve warm. Yield: one 10-inch coffee ring.
*Mrs. Elizabeth Moore,
Huntsville, Alabama.*

ORANGE MUFFINS

1 cup margarine, softened
1 cup sugar
2 eggs
1 teaspoon soda
¾ cup buttermilk
3 cups all-purpose flour
Grated rind of 1 orange
¼ cup orange juice
1 teaspoon lemon extract
1 cup currants
Orange Sauce

Cream margarine and sugar until light and fluffy. Add eggs, one at a time, beating well after each addition.

Combine soda and buttermilk, stirring well; add to creamed mixture alternately with flour. Stir in orange rind, orange juice, lemon extract, and currants; mix well. Fill greased miniature muffin pans three-fourths full. Bake at 400° for 10 to 12 minutes or until lightly browned. Remove from muffin tins; dip top and sides of warm muffins in Orange Sauce. Place on wire rack to drain. Yield: about 7½ dozen.

Orange Sauce:

¾ cup orange juice
1½ cups sugar

Combine orange juice and sugar in a small saucepan; bring to a boil, stirring until sugar dissolves. Chill. Yield: about 1 cup.
Pat Barker,
Tallahassee, Florida.

Soup And Sandwiches Keep It Casual

Give yourself and your friends a break from the hustle and bustle of the holidays by planning an evening of relaxed entertaining. With dishes that can be prepared ahead or require little time, our menu sets the pace.

Holiday Potato Soup
Confetti Sandwiches
Cream Cheese-Onion Dip
Fresh Vegetables
French Silk Tarts
Coffee

HOLIDAY POTATO SOUP

4 medium potatoes, diced
3 medium onions, sliced
1 (10¾-ounce) can cream of chicken soup, undiluted
1 tablespoon butter or margarine
3¼ cups milk
½ cup half-and-half
1 teaspoon salt
¼ teaspoon pepper
Chopped parsley

Place potatoes and onion in a small amount of water in a medium saucepan. Cover and cook about 20 minutes or until done. Drain well and mash.

Combine mashed vegetables with remaining ingredients except parsley; mix well. Heat thoroughly in top of double boiler, stirring occasionally. Garnish with parsley. Yield: 6 to 8 servings.
Jo Gwyn Baldwin,
Abilene, Texas.

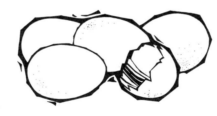

CONFETTI SANDWICHES

9 hard-cooked eggs, chopped
½ cup commercial sour cream
⅓ cup chopped fresh spinach
¼ cup grated carrot
¼ cup chopped pimiento-stuffed olives
¼ cup chopped ripe olives
6 English muffins, split, toasted, and buttered
1 cup (¼ pound) shredded Cheddar cheese
6 slices bacon, cooked and crumbled
12 slices dill pickle
12 slices ripe olives
12 slices pimiento-stuffed olives

Combine eggs, sour cream, spinach, carrot, and chopped olives; mix well, and spread evenly on each muffin half. Then sprinkle with shredded cheese and crumbled bacon.

Broil sandwiches about 6 inches from heat for 3 minutes or until cheese melts; top with pickle and olive slices. Yield: 6 servings.
Mrs. Beverly Fink,
Indialantic, Florida.

CREAM CHEESE-ONION DIP

2 chicken bouillon cubes
2 tablespoons water
2 (3-ounce) packages cream cheese, softened
2 tablespoons minced onion
⅛ teaspoon garlic powder
2 tablespoons mayonnaise
Dash of pepper
Dash of hot sauce

Dissolve bouillon cubes in water; add remaining ingredients, mixing well. Serve with fresh vegetables. Yield: about 1 cup.
Mrs. Bonnie J. Sellers,
Ruston, Louisiana.

FRENCH SILK TARTS

½ cup plus 2 tablespoons butter or margarine, softened
1 cup sugar
2 (1-ounce) squares unsweetened chocolate, melted and cooled
1½ teaspoons vanilla extract
2 drops almond extract
3 eggs
12 baked 3-inch pastry shells
Whipped cream
Chopped pecans (optional)

Combine butter and sugar, creaming until light and fluffy; stir in chocolate and flavorings. Add eggs, one at a time; after each addition, beat 5 minutes at medium speed of electric mixer.

Chill mixture 1 to 2 hours. Spoon into pastry shells. Top with whipped cream; sprinkle with chopped pecans, if desired. Yield: 12 tarts.
Mrs. W. Harold Groce,
Arden, North Carolina.

Chicken, Ham, and Oyster Soup (page 198) is a satisfying meal in-a-bowl.

Page 240: Festive holiday desserts include the following: (clockwise) Ambrosia Cake, Frozen Vanilla Soufflé, Christmas Pudding with Brandy-Butter Sauce, and Elegant Pineapple Mousse. Recipes begin on page 229.

Above: Welcome holiday guests with a tempting assortment of appetizers: Sweet-and-Sour Party Meatballs (page 233), Ham-and-Cheese Roll (page 234), and Smoked Oyster Dip (page 233).

Right: Toast the season with this colorful array of holiday beverages: Creamy Irish Coffee, Golden Gin Punch, Anytime Wine Punch, Holiday Eggnog Deluxe, and Quick Viennese Mocha. Recipes begin on page 232.

Left: Sherried Baked Duck is an ideal entrée for an elegant buffet dinner. Accompaniments include Plantation Squash and Rice Ring with Beets. Menu and recipes begin on page 224.

Salads Fit For The Feast

Let the salad put the sparkle in your holiday dinner. For what could be more seasonal than ambrosia shimmering in orange-pineapple gelatin and tart cranberry relish molded in a layered delight, more colorful than tomato aspic studded with shrimp.

But that's not all this array of salads has to offer. Fruits and nuts give coleslaw a festive touch in a variation called Apple-Pineapple Slaw, while Snowcap Cheese Molds owes its flair to maraschino cherries, flaked coconut, and a honey dressing.

APPLE-PINEAPPLE SLAW

3 cups shredded cabbage
1 (8¼-ounce) can pineapple chunks, drained
1 cup unpeeled diced apple
1 cup miniature marshmallows
1 cup chopped celery
½ cup mayonnaise
½ cup chopped pecans

Combine all ingredients, mixing well. Yield: 6 to 8 servings.
Mrs. Robert A. Bailey,
Knoxville, Tennessee.

TOMATO ASPIC WITH SHRIMP

1 tablespoon unflavored gelatin
⅓ cup water
1 (24-ounce) can tomato juice
¼ teaspoon salt
⅛ teaspoon pepper
Juice of 1 lemon
½ cup chopped celery
½ cup sliced pimiento-stuffed olives
1 pound shrimp, cooked, peeled, and deveined
Lettuce
Cottage cheese
Sliced pimiento-stuffed olives (optional)

Dissolve gelatin in water; set aside. Pour tomato juice into a small saucepan; add salt and pepper. Bring to a boil; remove from heat, and stir in gelatin. Cool.

Stir next 4 ingredients into gelatin mixture, and pour into a lightly oiled 6-cup ring mold; chill salad until set.

Unmold on lettuce-lined serving plate, and fill center with cottage cheese. Garnish with sliced olives, if desired. Yield: 6 to 8 servings.
Mrs. H. K. Anderson,
Hattiesburg, Mississippi.

CRANBERRY-CHEESE RIBBON SALAD

1 envelope unflavored gelatin
1 cup cold water
1 (3-ounce) package strawberry-flavored gelatin
¾ cup boiling water
1 (14-ounce) jar cranberry-orange relish
¼ cup lemon juice, divided
1 tablespoon grated orange rind
1 (8-ounce) package cream cheese, softened
1 (4½-ounce) container frozen whipped topping, thawed

Stir unflavored gelatin into cold water in a small saucepan; bring to a boil, stirring until gelatin is dissolved. Remove from heat, and set aside.

Dissolve strawberry gelatin in boiling water; stir in relish, 2 tablespoons lemon juice, and orange rind. Pour into a lightly oiled 6-cup mold. Chill until slightly thickened.

Combine cream cheese and 2 tablespoons lemon juice, beating until fluffy. Stir in whipped topping and unflavored gelatin mixture. Spread evenly over strawberry layer. Chill until set. Yield: 8 to 10 servings. *Shirley Hodge,*
Delray Beach, Florida.

AMBROSIA MOLD

1 (3-ounce) package orange-pineapple-flavored gelatin
1 tablespoon sugar
1 cup boiling water
¾ cup cold water
2 oranges, peeled and sectioned
1¼ cups seedless grapes, halved
⅔ cup flaked coconut
1 cup whipping cream, whipped

Dissolve gelatin and sugar in boiling water; stir in cold water. Chill until partially set. Stir in oranges, grapes, and coconut; fold in whipped cream. Pour into a lightly oiled 6-cup mold; chill until set. Yield: 6 to 8 servings.
Mrs. Richard Eppink,
Keswick, Virginia.

CHRISTMAS WREATH FROZEN SALAD

2 (3-ounce) packages cream cheese, softened
1 cup mayonnaise
½ cup red maraschino cherries, halved
½ cup green maraschino cherries, halved
1 (20-ounce) can crushed pineapple, drained
½ cup chopped pecans
2½ cups miniature marshmallows
1 cup whipping cream, whipped

Combine cream cheese and mayonnaise, mixing well. Stir in cherries, pineapple, pecans, and marshmallows; fold in whipped cream. Pour into an 8-cup ring mold; freeze. Yield: 8 to 10 servings. *Mrs. Barbara Chambers,*
Slidell, Louisiana.

CHEESY LEMON MOLD

1 (3-ounce) package lemon-flavored gelatin
1 cup boiling water
1 (6-ounce) can frozen orange juice concentrate, undiluted
1 (8-ounce) package cream cheese, softened
1 cup flaked coconut
1 cup grated carrots
1 (8-ounce) can crushed pineapple, undrained

Dissolve gelatin in boiling water; stir in orange juice. Beat cream cheese until smooth; gradually add gelatin mixture, beating until smooth. Stir in remaining ingredients. Pour into a lightly oiled 6-cup mold; chill until set. Yield: 10 to 12 servings. *Mrs. Archer Yates,*
Dunwoody, Georgia.

SNOWCAP CHEESE MOLDS

1 teaspoon unflavored gelatin
¼ cup cold water
¼ teaspoon salt
1 (12-ounce) carton cream-style cottage
  cheese
2 (3-ounce) packages cream cheese,
  softened
1 cup seedless green grapes
½ cup chopped pecans
2 tablespoons chopped chives
1 cup whipping cream, whipped
Lettuce
1 (15¼-ounce) can pineapple slices,
  drained
Flaked coconut
Maraschino cherries (optional)
Honey Dressing

Stir gelatin into cold water in a small
saucepan; bring to a boil, and stir in
salt. Combine cottage cheese and cream
cheese, mixing until well blended; add
gelatin mixture, mixing well. Stir in
grapes, pecans, and chives; fold in
whipped cream. Spoon into 8 individual
molds, and chill until set.

Arrange lettuce on each serving plate,
and top with a pineapple slice. Unmold
salad on pineapple slice, and sprinkle
with flaked coconut; garnish with maraschino cherries, if desired. Serve with
Honey Dressing. Yield: 8 servings.

Honey Dressing:
¼ cup sugar
1 teaspoon dry mustard
1 teaspoon paprika
1 teaspoon celery seeds
¼ teaspoon salt
⅓ cup honey
½ cup vinegar
1 tablespoon lemon juice
1 teaspoon grated onion
1 cup vegetable oil

Combine first 5 ingredients; mix well.
Add honey, vinegar, lemon juice, and
onion. Gradually add vegetable oil,
beating constantly with electric mixer.
Yield: 2 cups.   *Vivian Carter,*
                        Pisgah, Alabama.

*Tip: Once pimientos have been opened,
keep them in the refrigerator. Pour a little vinegar or water over them and
cover tightly; they will stay fresh for
days.*

Cook The Saucy Cranberry

It's hard to imagine any holiday
spread without an accompanying dish of
cranberry sauce or relish. But this saucy
little berry also finds its way into
breads, desserts, and salads that are
equally welcome on the holiday table.
It's also the crowning touch for Supreme Ham Loaf; this savory loaf is
topped with cranberry sauce.

SUPREME HAM LOAF

1 pound ground cooked ham
½ teaspoon onion powder
1 pound ground fresh pork
2 eggs, slightly beaten
¼ teaspoon salt
¼ teaspoon seasoned pepper
1 cup cracker crumbs
¾ cup firmly packed brown sugar
1½ teaspoons dry mustard
¼ cup vinegar
1 (16-ounce) can whole-berry cranberry
  sauce

Combine first 7 ingredients; mix well.
Shape mixture into a 9- x 5-inch loaf;
place in a greased 10- x 6- x 2-inch
baking dish.

Combine sugar, mustard, and vinegar; mix well and spoon half over ham
loaf. Bake at 350° for 1 hour and 20
minutes, basting twice with remaining
sugar mixture. Top with cranberry
sauce, and bake an additional 10 minutes. Yield: 6 to 8 servings.
                        Mabel B. Couch,
                        Chelsea, Oklahoma.

BERRY GRAPEFRUIT CUP

2 cups fresh cranberries
1 cup sugar
1 cup water
3 grapefruit, peeled, seeded, and sectioned

Sort and wash cranberries. Combine
sugar, water, and cranberries; boil 5 to
10 minutes, or until skins pop. Cool.
Combine with grapefruit; chill. Yield: 8
servings.   *Mrs. Bettie Hamilton,*
                   Kinston, North Carolina.

CRANBERRY SURPRISE DESSERT

2½ cups fresh cranberries
1½ cups sugar, divided
¼ cup chopped nuts
2 eggs
1 cup all-purpose flour
½ cup butter, melted
¼ cup margarine, melted
Whipped cream (optional)
Vanilla ice cream (optional)

Wash cranberries; place in a greased
10-inch piepan; sprinkle with ½ cup
sugar. Top with nuts, and set aside.

Beat eggs until lemon colored; gradually add remaining sugar, beating well.
Add flour, butter, and margarine; mix
well. Pour batter evenly over cranberries. Bake at 325° for 1 hour or until
golden brown. Cool; spoon into individual serving dishes, and top with
whipped cream or ice cream, if desired.
Yield: 8 to 10 servings.
                        Mrs. Russell T. Shay,
                   Murrells Inlet, South Carolina.

CRANBERRY BREAD

1 cup sugar
3 tablespoons butter or margarine
½ cup orange juice
Grated rind of 1 orange
2 cups all-purpose flour
1 tablespoon baking powder
½ teaspoon soda
½ teaspoon salt
1 cup fresh cranberries, coarsely chopped
¾ cup pecans, coarsely chopped
Melted butter or margarine

Combine sugar, butter, orange juice,
and rind in a medium saucepan; bring
to a boil. Pour into a liquid measure;
add water, if necessary, to make ¾ cup
of liquid.

Combine dry ingredients; stir in cranberries and pecans, tossing to coat. Add
hot juice mixture, and stir well. Spoon
into 2 greased and floured 7½- x 3- x
2-inch loafpans. Bake at 350° for 40 to
45 minutes or until bread tests done.
Brush with melted butter immediately.
Cool 10 minutes before removing from
pan. Yield: 2 loaves.
                        Mrs. Blake V. Watson,
                        Lenoir, North Carolina.

CRANBERRY CONSERVE

2 pounds fresh cranberries
2 (20-ounce) cans crushed pineapple
1 (12-ounce) can frozen orange juice
  concentrate, undiluted
3 cups sugar
3 (2-inch) sticks cinnamon
1 tablespoon whole cloves
2 cups seedless raisins
2 cups whole almonds
2 cups broken pecans

Wash cranberries thoroughly; drain. Drain pineapple, reserving juice. Combine pineapple juice, orange juice concentrate, and enough water to make 1 quart liquid; pour mixture into a large Dutch oven. Add sugar, stirring until dissolved.

Place spices in a cheesecloth bag; tie tightly. Add bag to fruit juices, and bring to a boil; boil 10 minutes. Stir in cranberries; allow mixture to return to a boil. Continue boiling about 5 minutes, stirring frequently, or until berries begin to pop. Add pineapple and raisins; return to a boil. Boil 5 minutes, stirring frequently. Cool slightly; add almonds and pecans.

Pack into hot sterilized jars, leaving ⅛-inch headspace. Seal. Process 10 minutes in boiling-water bath. Yield: 8 pints.
Mrs. C. C. Stalder,
Orlando, Florida.

CRANBERRY CHRISTMAS SALAD

2 oranges
1 pound fresh cranberries, ground
4 tart apples, seeded and ground
¾ cup sugar
1 cup chopped pecans
⅓ cup crushed pineapple
⅓ cup halved, seeded red grapes
1 (6-ounce) package raspberry-flavored
  gelatin
½ pint whipping cream, whipped

Grate rind of one orange. Peel remaining orange; remove seeds from both. Grind oranges; pour into a large mixing bowl. Stir in rind and next 6 ingredients; let stand 1 hour.

Prepare gelatin according to package directions; chill until partially set. Fold in whipped cream. Combine gelatin mixture with fruit, mixing well. Chill. Serve in a chilled bowl. Yield: 18 to 20 servings.
Mrs. Michael R. Woods,
Independence, Kansas.

LEMONY CRANBERRY RELISH

2 (16-ounce) cans whole-berry cranberry
  sauce
1 cup orange marmalade
Juice and grated rind of 1 lemon
½ cup chopped walnuts

Combine all ingredients. Chill until ready to serve. Yield: 4 cups.
Janelle Banks,
Garwood, Texas.

Dinner Party Matches Elegance With Ease

In celebration of the holiday season, Caroline and Paul Anderson of Lookout Mountain, Tennessee, host an elegant dinner party for their friends.

One of the unusual features of the party is that Paul prepares all the food, something he enjoys doing when they entertain. Since both Paul and Caroline have busy work schedules, they carefully compile a menu of dishes that can be prepared the day of the party.

The menu is lavish, yet preparation is easy because many of Paul's recipes begin with convenience products. For example, the basis for his Creamy Mushroom Soup is commercial cream of mushroom soup to which he adds sour cream, shredded cheese, fresh mushrooms, and wine to give it a distinctively rich flavor.

For the entrée, Cornish hens are skillfully seasoned with herbs and baked with a glaze of orange marmalade. The Seasoned Rice takes only minutes to prepare using instant rice, chicken broth, and a blend of herbs. Paul says the magic in his Magic Muffins is simply adding eggs, milk, sugar, and margarine to a prepared biscuit mix.

To complete the meal with a colorful holiday touch, there's Italian-Style Ice Cream for dessert: vanilla ice cream laced with Cherry Heering and studded with almonds and red and green maraschino cherries.

Here's a look at the complete menu for the Andersons' holiday celebration and Paul's recipes.

Creamy Mushroom Soup
Spinach Salad Supreme
Cornish Hens with Orange Glaze
Sweet Potato Pudding   Seasoned Rice
Broccoli with Hollandaise Sauce
Magic Muffins
Italian-Style Ice Cream
Chablis   Coffee

CREAMY MUSHROOM SOUP

4 (10¾-ounce) cans cream of mushroom
  soup, undiluted
2 cups half-and-half
2 cups milk
1 (8-ounce) carton commercial sour cream
1 (8-ounce) package process cheese
  spread, shredded
⅛ teaspoon cayenne pepper
1 pound fresh mushrooms, sliced
¼ cup dry white wine

Combine first 6 ingredients in a large Dutch oven; stir well. Cook over low to medium heat until cheese is melted, stirring frequently.

Stir mushrooms into soup; cook over low heat 20 to 30 minutes, stirring frequently. Stir wine into soup just before serving. Yield: 14 to 16 servings.

SPINACH SALAD SUPREME

4 pounds fresh spinach, torn into bite-size
  pieces
8 small green onions, thinly sliced
½ pound small fresh mushrooms, sliced
8 hard-cooked eggs, coarsely chopped
16 slices bacon, cooked and crumbled
1 (0.9-ounce) package mild Italian
  dressing mix
1 tablespoon bacon drippings

Place spinach in a large salad bowl; top with onion, mushrooms, eggs, and crumbled bacon.

Prepare dressing mix according to package directions, substituting 1 tablespoon bacon drippings for 1 tablespoon of oil. Pour over salad and toss lightly. Yield: 14 to 16 servings.

For the entrée, Paul seasons Cornish hens with herbs and bakes them with a glaze of orange marmalade.

SEASONED RICE

3 (10¾-ounce) cans chicken broth
3 tablespoons soy sauce
3 tablespoons butter or margarine
3 chicken bouillon cubes
¾ teaspoon celery seeds
¾ teaspoon parsley flakes
⅛ teaspoon whole basil leaves
⅛ teaspoon tarragon leaves
⅛ teaspoon ground savory or thyme
⅛ teaspoon pepper
4½ cups instant rice

Combine chicken broth and soy sauce; measure and add enough water to make 4½ cups liquid. Combine broth mixture and remaining ingredients except rice in a Dutch oven. Bring to a boil and stir in rice; cover. Remove from heat, and let stand 5 minutes. Yield: 14 to 16 servings.

CORNISH HENS WITH ORANGE GLAZE

2 teaspoons salt
2 teaspoons whole basil leaves
2 teaspoons tarragon leaves
2 teaspoons whole thyme leaves
2 teaspoons ground savory
½ teaspoon pepper
16 (1- to 1¼-pound) Cornish hens
1 cup melted butter or margarine
1 cup orange marmalade
Watercress
Peeled orange slices

Combine seasonings, stirring well. Sprinkle cavity of hens with seasonings; brush skins of each with butter, and sprinkle with seasonings.

Truss hens, and place breast side up on a rack in a shallow roasting pan. Pour enough water into pan to cover bottom (about ⅛ inch deep). Place in upper half of oven, and bake at 325° for 45 minutes.

Brush hens with butter, and spoon 1 tablespoon marmalade on breast of each hen. Bake an additional 30 to 45 minutes or until juice runs clear when thigh is pierced with a fork. Place on serving platter; garnish with watercress and orange slices. Yield: 16 servings.

Note: Recipe may be reduced to individual servings; use ⅛ teaspoon salt, ⅛ teaspoon of each herb, and a dash of pepper per hen.

SWEET POTATO PUDDING

1 (16-ounce) can whole sweet potatoes, drained
1 (32-ounce) can whole sweet potatoes, undrained
Grated rind of 3 oranges
Juice of 3 oranges
1½ teaspoons ground cinnamon
¾ teaspoon ground allspice
¾ teaspoon ground cloves
1½ cups butter or margarine
9 egg yolks, beaten
1½ cups milk
9 egg whites, stiffly beaten

Combine potatoes, orange rind, orange juice, spices, and butter in a large saucepan. Cook over medium heat, stirring occasionally, until liquid is reduced to half.

Purée potato mixture in food processor or electric blender. Cool thoroughly.

Stir egg yolks and milk into potatoes; fold in egg whites. Pour potato mixture into a 3-quart soufflé dish. Bake at 350° on top rack of oven for 1½ hours or until top is browned (pudding will not be set). Serve immediately. Yield: 14 to 16 servings.

Tip: Separate raw eggs while still cold from the refrigerator, but let whites come to room temperature if they need to be stiffly beaten.

BROCCOLI WITH HOLLANDAISE SAUCE

4 (10-ounce) packages frozen broccoli spears
12 egg yolks
Juice of 2 lemons
2 teaspoons salt
⅛ teaspoon cayenne pepper
⅛ teaspoon hot sauce
2 cups melted butter or margarine

Cook broccoli according to package directions; drain well, and place in serving dish.

Combine remaining ingredients except butter in container of electric blender; turn on and off rapidly. Set blender on high speed, and gradually add butter. Pour over broccoli. Yield: 14 to 16 servings.

MAGIC MUFFINS

4 cups biscuit mix
½ cup sugar
¼ cup melted margarine
2 eggs, beaten
1½ cups milk

Combine all ingredients in a medium mixing bowl, stirring just until moistened. Spoon batter into greased muffin pans, filling two-thirds full. Bake at 400° for 15 to 20 minutes. Yield: 20 muffins.

ITALIAN-STYLE ICE CREAM

1 tablespoon butter or margarine
1 to 2 (2¾-ounce) packages slivered
  almonds
⅛ to ¼ teaspoon salt
½ gallon vanilla ice cream
1 (10-ounce) jar red maraschino cherries,
  drained and chopped
1 (5-ounce) jar green maraschino cherries,
  drained and chopped
1 cup Cherry Heering or other
  cherry-flavored liqueur

Melt butter in a shallow baking pan; add almonds, stirring to coat with butter. Lightly sprinkle almonds with salt. Bake at 400° for 3 to 5 minutes or until golden; cool.

Combine all ingredients in a large mixing bowl; stir well. Spoon into a 9-inch square pan. Cover and freeze until firm. Yield: 14 to 16 servings.

Homemade Mincemeat is the basis for treats like Mincemeat Chiffon Pie.

Start With Homemade Mincemeat

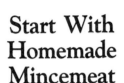

The holiday season wouldn't be complete without a mincemeat dessert. And we've come up with some new ideas with this old favorite.

At the heart of it all is a good homemade mincemeat. Mrs. L. R. Carroll of Easton, Maryland, has the perfect starter for all of these holiday treats.

HOMEMADE MINCEMEAT

2 pounds lean beef, cut into 2-inch cubes
2 pounds suet, cut into 2-inch cubes
6 oranges
6 lemons
2 (10-ounce) packages currants
2 (15-ounce) packages raisins
2 pounds apples, unpeeled and chopped
6 (10¾-ounce) jars sweet pickled
  watermelon rind, drained and chopped
3 (1-pound) packages brown sugar
1 cup grape juice
1 tablespoon ground cinnamon
1 teaspoon ground ginger
1 tablespoon ground cloves
1 tablespoon ground allspice
2 teaspoons ground nutmeg

Cover meat and suet with boiling water. Cook until beef is tender; drain.

Juice oranges and lemons, reserving juice and rind. Put rinds, beef, suet, currants, and raisins through a food grinder; place in a large kettle. Add apples, watermelon rind, sugar, reserved orange and lemon juice, grape juice, and spices; blend thoroughly. Cook until thoroughly heated.

Pack into hot sterilized jars, leaving 1-inch headspace. Adjust lids; process pints or quarts in pressure canner at 10 pounds pressure (240°) for 20 minutes. Yield: 15 pints or 7½ quarts.

MINCEMEAT CHIFFON PIE

1 envelope unflavored gelatin
½ cup cold water
¼ cup rum
1½ cups prepared mincemeat
3 egg whites
⅛ teaspoon salt
⅓ cup sugar
1 cup whipping cream, whipped
1 baked 9-inch pastry shell
Maraschino cherries

Soften gelatin in cold water; stir over low heat until gelatin is dissolved. Remove from heat, and stir in rum and mincemeat. Chill, stirring occasionally, until mixture mounds when dropped from a spoon.

Beat egg whites until stiff but not dry. Add salt and sugar, and beat well. Fold gelatin mixture into egg whites; fold in whipped cream. Spoon into pastry shell. Garnish as desired with cherries. Chill until firm. Yield: one 9-inch pie.

Mrs. Charles R. Simms,
Palestine, Illinois.

Tip: Keep staples—such as sugar, flour, rice, and spices—in tightly covered containers at room temperature. Staples that are frequently replenished should be rotated so that the oldest is always used first.

Store spices away from any direct source of heat as the heat will destroy their flavor.

MINCEMEAT DROP COOKIES

½ cup shortening
½ cup sugar
1 egg
1 cup prepared mincemeat
2 cups all-purpose flour
½ teaspoon soda
½ teaspoon salt

Cream shortening and sugar until light and fluffy; add egg and beat well. Add mincemeat, mixing well.

Combine flour, soda, and salt; mix well, and stir into creamed mixture. Drop by teaspoonfuls onto greased cookie sheets. Bake at 350° for 18 to 20 minutes. Yield: about 5 dozen.
Mrs. H. E. Griffith,
Thomaston, Alabama.

MINCEMEAT SPICE CAKE

2 eggs
½ cup shortening
1 cup firmly packed brown sugar
½ teaspoon salt
½ cup prepared mincemeat
1¾ cups all-purpose flour
½ teaspoon soda
1 teaspoon ground cinnamon
½ teaspoon ground cloves
½ cup buttermilk
¼ cup chopped nuts
Fluffy Frosting

Separate 1 egg; set aside egg white for frosting.

Combine shortening, sugar, egg yolk, remaining egg, and salt in a large mixing bowl; mix well. Add half the mincemeat and mix well.

Combine flour, soda, cinnamon, and cloves; mix well. Add to creamed mixture alternately with buttermilk. Stir in nuts and remaining mincemeat. Spoon into a greased and floured 8-inch square pan. Bake at 350° for 50 to 55 minutes or until cake tests done. Let cake cool completely. Spread Fluffy Frosting over top of cake. Yield: one 8-inch cake.

Fluffy Frosting:
½ cup sugar
2 teaspoons water
2 teaspoons light corn syrup
Pinch of salt
1 egg white
½ teaspoon vanilla extract

Combine sugar, water, corn syrup, and salt in a small saucepan; mix well. Cover and cook over low heat until sugar dissolves, about 2 or 3 minutes. Uncover pan; bring mixture to a boil, and boil without stirring until syrup spins a 6- to 8-inch thread or until candy thermometer registers 236°.

While syrup cooks, beat egg white at high speed of electric mixer until stiff but not dry. Pour hot syrup in a thin stream over egg white, beating constantly at high speed. Continue beating until mixture will hold a stiff peak. Add vanilla, and mix well. Yield: enough for one 8-inch cake. *Mrs. Dora Farrar,*
Gadsden, Alabama.

Side Dishes You've Been Looking For

Looking for a side dish to round out that special menu? Bright-green broccoli sautéed with corn and mushrooms, English peas nestled in a colorful rice ring, onions baked in a puffy soufflé show how familiar vegetables can be transformed into spectacular side dishes to complement that holiday ham or turkey. And should your entrée call for the fresh flavor of a fruit accompaniment, you'll be delighted with Baked Oranges and Orange-Glazed Pears.

SAUTEED BROCCOLI

½ cup butter or margarine
1 (10-ounce) package frozen broccoli spears, thawed and coarsely chopped
1 (10-ounce) package frozen whole kernel corn, thawed and drained
1 (4-ounce) can sliced mushrooms, drained
3 tablespoons sliced almonds (optional)
Salt and pepper to taste

Melt butter in a large skillet, and add remaining ingredients. Sauté 10 minutes, stirring often. Yield: 4 to 5 servings. *Mrs. Lee Ferguson,*
Clinton, Mississippi.

BRUSSELS SPROUTS WITH CHEESE SAUCE

1 pound fresh or 2 (10-ounce) packages frozen brussels sprouts
1 (10¾-ounce) can cream of mushroom soup, undiluted
⅓ cup milk
¼ cup shredded mild Cheddar cheese
2 tablespoons dry sherry
Dash of hot sauce

Drop brussels sprouts into a small amount of boiling water; return to a boil. Cover and cook 5 to 10 minutes or until tender; drain.

Combine remaining ingredients in a small saucepan; place over low heat, stirring until the cheese melts. Pour over brussels sprouts. Serve immediately. Yield: 6 to 8 servings.
Jeanne Owen,
Lewisville, Texas.

RICE-CARROT RING

3 cups cooked regular rice
2 cups grated carrots
¼ cup grated onion
2 tablespoons all-purpose flour
1 (11-ounce) can Cheddar cheese soup, undiluted
1 egg, slightly beaten
1 teaspoon salt
¼ teaspoon pepper
1 teaspoon Worcestershire sauce
Dash of hot sauce
1 (10-ounce) package frozen English peas or broccoli spears
Carrot curls (optional)
Radish roses (optional)

Combine rice, carrots, onion, and flour in a large bowl. Add next 6 ingredients, mixing well. Pack mixture into a greased 8-inch ring mold. Bake at 350° for 30 minutes. Allow to cool 10 minutes.

Cook peas according to package directions; drain.

Invert rice ring onto platter, and fill center with peas. Garnish with carrot curls and radish roses, if desired. Yield: 6 servings. *Susan Erickson,*
State University, Arkansas.

CREAMED CELERY

4 cups ½-inch celery pieces
2 tablespoons butter or margarine
3 tablespoons all-purpose flour
2 cups milk
1 teaspoon salt
½ teaspoon paprika
½ cup pecan halves or pieces
¾ cup buttered breadcrumbs

Cook celery in a small amount of boiling salted water just until tender (about 6 to 8 minutes); drain.

Melt butter in a heavy saucepan over low heat; add flour, stirring until smooth. Cook 1 minute, stirring constantly. Gradually add milk; cook over medium heat, stirring constantly, until thickened and bubbly.

Add salt, paprika, and celery to white sauce; spoon into a greased 1½-quart casserole. Top with pecans and breadcrumbs. Bake at 400° for 15 minutes. Yield: 6 servings.   *Mrs. Russell Spear, Hilliard, Florida.*

CORN CASSEROLE

2 eggs
¼ cup milk
½ cup cracker crumbs
1 (17-ounce) can cream-style corn
¼ cup melted butter or margarine
¼ cup grated carrot
¼ cup chopped green pepper
1 tablespoon chopped celery
1 tablespoon chopped onion
⅛ teaspoon hot sauce
½ teaspoon sugar
½ teaspoon salt
½ cup shredded Cheddar cheese

Combine eggs and milk; beat until well blended. Add cracker crumbs; set aside until all liquid is absorbed.

Add remaining ingredients except cheese to cracker crumb mixture, stirring well. Spoon mixture into a greased 1-quart casserole. Bake at 350° for 45 minutes; sprinkle with cheese while hot. Yield: 4 to 5 servings.

Mrs. Leon Johnson, Fordyce, Arkansas.

ONION SOUFFLE

3 large onions, sliced
2 tablespoons butter or margarine
1 cup water
1 tablespoon all-purpose flour
3 tablespoons sugar
1 tablespoon melted butter or margarine
2 tablespoons half-and-half
¼ teaspoon salt
3 eggs, separated
½ to 1 teaspoon sugar
¼ cup finely chopped pecans

Combine onion, 2 tablespoons butter, and water in a medium saucepan; cover tightly, and cook over medium heat 15 to 20 minutes or until water is absorbed. Mash onions; stir in flour, 3 tablespoons sugar, 1 tablespoon butter, half-and-half, and salt. Add egg yolks, mixing well.

Beat egg whites until stiff but not dry; fold into onion mixture. Spoon into a buttered 1-quart casserole; sprinkle with ½ teaspoon sugar and pecans. Bake at 350° for 30 minutes or until firm. Yield: 4 to 6 servings.   *Mrs. James S. Tiffany, Dallas, Texas.*

BAKED ORANGES

4 oranges
2 cups sugar
Butter or margarine

Cover oranges with boiling water, and boil until fork tender (about 30 minutes). Drain oranges, reserving 1 cup liquid. Cut oranges in half; remove seeds, and arrange in baking dish.

Combine sugar and reserved liquid; boil 5 minutes. Pour syrup over orange halves, and dot each with butter. Cover and bake at 400° for 30 minutes. Yield: 8 servings.   *Mrs. Warren A. Knight, Sarasota, Florida.*

ORANGE-GLAZED PEARS

1 cup orange juice
2 tablespoons apricot preserves
2 (16-ounce) cans pear halves, drained

Combine orange juice and preserves in a heavy skillet; place over medium heat, and bring to a boil. Reduce heat.

Place pears, cut side down, in skillet; simmer 15 minutes, basting often. Arrange pears in a shallow serving dish; top with sauce. Chill at least 1 hour. Yield: 6 to 8 servings.

Mrs. Sue-Sue Hartstern, Louisville, Kentucky.

Make-Aheads Save You Time

With last-minute shopping, drop-in guests, and spur-of-the-moment parties, it's a relief when menus include foods that can be prepared partially or completely in advance.

The dough for Party Refrigerator Rolls can be kept in the refrigerator up to one week; bake part of the dough and save the rest for later. Beefy Vegetable Casserole is prepared a day ahead of time and refrigerated overnight. For snacks or appetizers, freeze Tasty Little Pizza Snacks; they can be thawed quickly and reheated whenever unexpected company appears.

RED BEAN SLAW

5 slices bacon
¾ cup chopped onion
1 cup mayonnaise
¼ cup vinegar
1 tablespoon sugar
2 tablespoons parsley flakes
1 teaspoon salt
1 teaspoon whole oregano
½ teaspoon pepper
3 cups shredded cabbage
2 (16-ounce) cans kidney beans, drained
1 cup diced celery

Cook bacon; drain, reserving ¼ cup drippings. Set bacon aside.

Sauté onion in bacon drippings until tender; remove from heat. Stir in mayonnaise, vinegar, sugar, parsley, salt, oregano, and pepper; mix well.

Crumble bacon into a large bowl. Add cabbage, beans, and celery. Stir in mayonnaise mixture; chill. Yield: 6 to 8 servings.   *Mrs. Carl Ramay, Plano, Texas.*

CHICKEN AND WILD RICE

1 (3-pound) broiler-fryer
1 large onion, thinly sliced and separated into rings
½ teaspoon salt
1 teaspoon curry powder
⅛ teaspoon pepper
1 cup cooking sherry
1 (6-ounce) package long-grain and wild-rice mix
2 tablespoons butter or margarine
½ pound fresh mushrooms, sliced
1 (10½-ounce) can cream of mushroom soup, undiluted
1 cup commercial sour cream

Place chicken, onion, salt, curry powder, pepper, and sherry in a large Dutch oven; add enough water to cover chicken. Heat to boiling; cover and reduce heat. Simmer 1 hour.

Remove chicken; let cool. Bone chicken, and dice meat. Reserve 2½ cups chicken broth.

Cook rice according to package directions, using reserved chicken broth for liquid; set aside.

Melt butter in a small skillet; add mushrooms and cook until tender. Place mushrooms and chicken in a large bowl. Stir in rice, soup, and sour cream, mixing well. Spoon mixture into a foil-lined 13- x 9- x 2-inch baking pan; cover with foil and freeze. Remove foil package from baking pan, and return to freezer.

To serve, place foil package in 13- x 9- x 2-inch baking pan; thaw and bake at 350° for 50 minutes. Remove foil cover; bake 10 additional minutes. Serve hot. Yield: 6 to 8 servings.
Shelia J. Heatwole,
Virginia Beach, Virginia.

PARTY REFRIGERATOR ROLLS

½ cup sugar
1 cup buttermilk
¾ cup shortening
1 teaspoon salt
1 cup cooked, mashed potatoes
2 packages dry yeast
¼ cup warm water (105° to 115°)
2 eggs, beaten
6 cups all-purpose flour
Melted butter or margarine

Combine sugar, buttermilk, shortening, and salt in a medium saucepan; heat until shortening is melted. Remove from heat; stir in mashed potatoes. Cool to lukewarm.

Dissolve yeast in warm water. Combine sugar mixture, eggs, and half of the flour in a large mixing bowl; add yeast mixture, beating until smooth. Stir in enough remaining flour to make a soft dough.

Turn dough out on a lightly floured board; knead about 8 minutes or until smooth and elastic. Place in a greased bowl, turning to grease top. Cover tightly with aluminum foil; store in refrigerator until doubled in bulk. (Dough may be kept in refrigerator for a week.)

Punch dough down; place on a lightly floured board. Divide dough into thirds. Roll out one-third of dough into a circle about 10 inches in diameter and ⅛ inch thick; brush with melted butter. Cut into 12 wedges; roll each wedge tightly, beginning at wide end. Seal points. Repeat with remaining dough, or cover and store in the refrigerator.

Place rolls on a greased baking sheet. Cover and let rise in a warm place (85°), free from drafts, until doubled in bulk (about 50 minutes). Bake at 425° for 6 minutes or until golden brown. Yield: 3 dozen.
Carolyn Webb,
Jackson, Mississippi.

BEEFY VEGETABLE CASSEROLE

1 (5-ounce) package fine egg noodles
3 tablespoons butter or margarine
¼ cup chopped onion
¼ cup chopped green pepper
½ cup sliced fresh mushrooms
½ cup diced celery
1⅓ pounds ground beef
1 (17-ounce) can cream-style corn
1 (16-ounce) can whole tomatoes
1 (10¾-ounce) can tomato soup, undiluted
¾ teaspoon salt
½ teaspoon pepper
1½ teaspoons Worcestershire sauce
1½ tablespoons butter or margarine
1 cup shredded Cheddar cheese (optional)

Cook noodles according to package directions; drain and set aside.

Melt 3 tablespoons butter in a large Dutch oven; add onion, green pepper, mushrooms, and celery. Cook on medium heat until vegetables are tender. Add beef; cook until browned. Stir in corn, tomatoes, soup, salt, pepper, and Worcestershire sauce. Add noodles; cook over low heat 10 minutes. Remove from heat; pour mixture into a 3-quart casserole; cool. Cover and refrigerate overnight.

Dot top of casserole with 1½ tablespoons butter; sprinkle with cheese, if desired. Bake at 325° for 50 to 60 minutes or until hot and bubbly. Yield: 6 to 8 servings.
Beverly Stanley,
Jenks, Oklahoma.

TASTY LITTLE PIZZA SNACKS

1 pound Italian sausage
1 pound hot bulk sausage
1 cup chopped onion
½ green pepper, chopped
1 tablespoon whole oregano
1 tablespoon fennel seeds
1 teaspoon garlic salt
1 pound process American cheese, cut into small cubes
1 pound mozzarella cheese, cut into small cubes
3 (8-ounce) loaves party rye bread

Remove casings from Italian sausage; crumble into a large skillet. Add hot sausage, onion, and green pepper; cook until meat is browned. Drain well on absorbent paper.

Return meat mixture to skillet, and add seasonings; heat gently over low heat. Stir in cheese until melted, and remove from heat.

Spread a scant tablespoon of meat mixture on each bread slice. Place slices in a single layer on large baking sheets; freeze. When slices are frozen, place in plastic bags and store in freezer until needed.

To serve, thaw and place on lightly greased baking sheets. Bake at 425° for 8 to 10 minutes. Yield: about 11 dozen.
Mrs. Bill Anthony,
North Little Rock, Arkansas.

AMBROSIA CREAM CHEESE MOLD

1 envelope unflavored gelatin
½ cup cold water
1 (15½-ounce) can unsweetened pineapple chunks, undrained
⅓ cup sugar
Juice of one lemon
2 (3-ounce) packages cream cheese, softened
1 orange, peeled, sectioned, and diced
½ cup chopped pecans
½ cup flaked coconut
Lettuce (optional)
Lemon slices (optional)

Soften gelatin in water; let mixture stand 5 minutes.

Drain pineapple, and reserve juice; add enough water to juice to make 1 cup. Place juice in a 2-quart saucepan; heat to boiling; add gelatin mixture, and stir until dissolved. Remove from heat; stir in sugar, lemon juice, and cream cheese, using a wire whisk to blend. Chill until gelatin is partially set; fold in pineapple chunks, orange, pecans, and coconut.

Spoon mixture into a lightly greased 1-quart mold; chill until firm. Unmold on lettuce leaves, and garnish with lemon slices, if desired. Yield: 6 servings.
Mrs. Dene Elmore,
Demopolis, Alabama.

CHOCOLATE-CHIP COFFEE CAKE

2 cups all-purpose flour
1½ cups sugar
½ cup butter or margarine, softened
2 teaspoons baking powder
2 eggs
¾ cup milk
1 teaspoon vanilla extract or almond extract
1 (6-ounce) package mini-semisweet chocolate morsels
Powdered sugar

Combine first 4 ingredients in a small mixing bowl; mix on low speed of electric mixer until mixture resembles fine crumbs. Remove 1 cup crumb mixture, and set aside.

Add eggs, milk, and vanilla to remaining crumb mixture; mix until well blended. Stir in chocolate morsels. Pour batter into a greased 11- x 7- x 1½-inch baking pan; sprinkle with reserved 1 cup crumb mixture.

Bake at 350° for 35 to 40 minutes or until cake tests done. Cool slightly; dust top with powdered sugar. Yield: 1 coffee cake.

Note: Bake coffee cake ahead, and let cool completely; remove from pan, wrap in foil, and freeze. To serve, thaw and place foil package in 300° oven; heat 20 minutes or until warmed. Dust top with powdered sugar. *Jan Wisland, Whitefish Bay, Wisconsin.*

BEETS WITH PINEAPPLE

1 (16-ounce) can sliced beets
1 (15½-ounce) can pineapple chunks, undrained
2 tablespoons vinegar
2 tablespoons sugar
2 tablespoons cornstarch

Drain beets, reserving ½ cup liquid. Combine beets, reserved beet liquid, pineapple, and vinegar in a 2-quart saucepan. Stir together sugar and cornstarch; add to beet mixture. Cook over medium heat until clear and thickened. Serve hot, or chill and serve cold. Yield: 6 to 8 servings.
Barbara A. Sullivan,
Ocala, Florida.

FROSTY CRANBERRY PIE

1¼ cups crushed corn flakes
¼ cup butter or margarine, melted
1 (8-ounce) package cream cheese, softened
1 cup whipped topping
1 (16-ounce) can whole-berry cranberry sauce
Additional whipped topping (optional)

Combine crushed corn flakes and butter in a medium bowl; press mixture firmly and evenly into a lightly greased 9-inch piepan. Bake at 350° for 8 minutes. Cool completely.

Beat cream cheese until fluffy; fold in whipped topping. Mash cranberry sauce with a fork; fold into cream cheese mixture. Spoon filling into cooled crust;

freeze until firm. Remove from freezer 15 to 20 minutes before serving. Garnish with additional whipped topping, if desired. Yield: one 9-inch pie.
Mrs. R. E. Londere,
St. Petersburg, Florida.

DATE NUT ROLL

2 cups vanilla wafer crumbs
2 cups finely chopped pecans
1 (8-ounce) package chopped dates
½ cup sweetened condensed milk
1 tablespoon water

Combine all ingredients in a large mixing bowl; mix well. Divide mixture in half; shape each half into an 8- x 1-inch roll. Wrap rolls in waxed paper; chill overnight. To serve, slice as desired. Yield: 2 (8- x 1-inch) rolls.
Mrs. Ruth P. Gunter,
Winnsboro, South Carolina.

Holiday Cooking Is A Family Affair

Preparing the holiday dinner at the Ron Lash home in Oklahoma City is a family affair. The kitchen buzzes with activity as family members assemble their specialties for the annual feast.

Jan and Ron both contribute favorites passed on to them by their mothers, and some new dishes have been added along the way for their traditional family-style dinner. Everyone except 21-year-old Terry has a favorite to prepare. And even Terry gets assigned an occasional job when he happens to peek into the kitchen.

Ron's department is roasting the turkey and supervising preparation of the Oyster Dressing. The two youngest family members, Leanne and Bill, tear the bread and add the ingredients as Ron gives instructions for "a little more" of this and "not so much" of that.

Eighteen-year-old Sandy likes to bake yeast bread, and her Dinner Rolls prove she knows what she's doing. The dough can be shaped into a variety of shapes—Parker House and cloverleaf are her favorites.

A favorite side dish of the entire family is Nutty Bananas. Handed down by Jan's mother, the recipe layers bananas with a sweetened mayonnaise mixture and ground peanuts. The other accompaniments include a molded cranberry salad, Escalloped Corn, Pineapple Bake, and the traditional Candied Sweet Potatoes.

Tomato Potage
Roast Turkey   Oyster Dressing
Cranberry Mold   Escalloped Corn
Candied Sweet Potatoes
Nutty Bananas   Pineapple Bake
Dinner Rolls   Butter
Pumpkin Date Cake   Pecan Pie

For their old-fashioned holiday feast, the Ron Lash family enjoys a collection of individual specialties: (clockwise) Nutty Bananas, Pineapple Bake, Oyster Dressing, Roast Turkey, Candied Sweet Potatoes, Cranberry Mold, Dinner Rolls, and Escalloped Corn.

OYSTER DRESSING

2 (1½-pound) loaves day-old sandwich
  bread
5 eggs, beaten
1½ cups milk
⅓ cup finely chopped onion
⅓ cup finely chopped celery
1 teaspoon salt
½ teaspoon pepper
¼ teaspoon rubbed sage
Dash of garlic powder
Dash of monosodium glutamate (optional)
2¾ to 3¼ cups turkey broth
1 quart oysters, drained

Tear bread into large pieces, and place in a lightly greased 17- x 13- x 2-inch baking pan. Combine eggs and milk, mixing well.

Add egg mixture, onion, celery, and seasonings to bread; mix well to evenly coat bread. Add enough turkey broth to moisten bread thoroughly. Add oysters, and mix well.

Cover and bake at 350° for 45 minutes. Remove cover, and bake an additional 35 to 45 minutes or until set. Yield: 18 to 20 servings.

CRANBERRY MOLD

1 orange
2 cups fresh cranberries
2 unpeeled apples, cored
1 cup sugar
1 (6-ounce) package lemon-flavored gelatin
1½ cups hot water
Lettuce

Quarter orange; remove seeds and rind, reserving one-fourth rind. Put orange, reserved orange rind, cranberries, and apples through a food mill. Add sugar to fruit mixture, mixing well. Cover and let stand 1 hour.

Dissolve gelatin in hot water; add to fruit mixture. Pour into an oiled 6-cup mold, and chill until firm. Unmold on lettuce-lined serving dish. Yield: 8 to 10 servings.

TOMATO POTAGE

¼ cup plus 2 tablespoons melted butter
  or margarine
2 tablespoons olive oil
2 large onions, thinly sliced
1 teaspoon dried thyme leaves
1 teaspoon dried basil leaves
¼ teaspoon salt
¼ teaspoon pepper
1 (28-ounce) can Italian-style tomatoes
3 tablespoons tomato paste
½ cup all-purpose flour
2 (10¾-ounce) cans chicken broth
2½ cups water
1 teaspoon sugar
Chopped fresh parsley

Heat butter and oil in a 4-quart Dutch oven; add onion, thyme, basil, salt, and pepper. Sauté over low heat until onion is tender. Stir in tomatoes and tomato paste.

Combine flour and 1 can broth in a small bowl, stirring until well blended; add to tomato mixture, stirring well. Add water, sugar, and remaining broth. Bring to a boil; then reduce heat, and simmer 30 minutes, stirring often. Let cool.

Pour soup mixture, one-fourth at a time, into container of electric blender; process until smooth. Return mixture to Dutch oven, and heat thoroughly. Garnish with chopped parsley, if desired. Yield: 6 to 8 servings.

ROAST TURKEY

Select a 12- to 14-pound turkey. Remove giblets, and rinse turkey thoroughly with cold water; pat dry. Sprinkle cavity with salt. Tie ends of legs to tail with cord or string, or tuck them under flap of skin around tail. Lift wingtips up and over back so they are tucked under bird.

Brush entire bird with melted butter or margarine; place on a roasting rack, breast side up. Insert meat thermometer in breast or meaty part of thigh, making sure it does not touch bone. Bake at 325° until meat thermometer reaches 185° (about 4½ to 5 hours). If turkey starts to get too brown, cover lightly with aluminum foil.

When turkey is two-thirds done, cut the cord or band of skin holding the drumstick ends to the tail; this will ensure that the inside of the thighs is cooked. Turkey is done when drumsticks are easy to move up and down. Garnish with grapes, if desired. Yield: 20 to 24 servings.

ESCALLOPED CORN

3 cups drained whole kernel corn
⅔ cup cracker crumbs
⅔ cup milk
¼ cup chopped green onion tops
¼ cup melted butter or margarine
1 egg, slightly beaten
½ teaspoon salt
¼ teaspoon sugar
¼ teaspoon paprika
Parsley sprigs

Combine all ingredients except parsley, mixing well. Spoon into a lightly greased 1½-quart casserole. Bake at 350° for 25 minutes. Garnish with parsley. Yield: 6 servings.

CANDIED SWEET POTATOES

10 medium-size sweet potatoes, cooked
1 teaspoon salt
1½ cups light corn syrup
½ cup melted butter or margarine
½ cup chopped pecans
20 large marshmallows

Peel potatoes; slice into thirds, and arrange in a lightly greased 13- x 9- x 2-inch baking dish. Sprinkle with salt; pour corn syrup and butter evenly over potatoes, and sprinkle with pecans.
Bake at 350° for 35 minutes. Arrange marshmallows over potatoes; bake an additional 10 to 12 minutes or until marshmallows are lightly browned. Yield: 10 servings.

NUTTY BANANAS

1 cup mayonnaise or salad dressing
¼ cup milk
2 to 3 tablespoons sugar
6 bananas
2 cups salted blanched peanuts, finely ground
Maraschino cherries (optional)

Combine mayonnaise, milk, and sugar; mix well. Slice 2 bananas, and place in a 2-quart serving dish.
Spread one-third of mayonnaise mixture over bananas; sprinkle with one-third of ground peanuts. Repeat layers twice. Garnish with maraschino cherries, if desired. This dish may be assembled 1 hour before serving and refrigerated. Yield: 6 to 8 servings.

PINEAPPLE BAKE

1¼ cups cracker crumbs
1½ cups sugar
1½ cups milk
2 eggs, beaten
1 (20-ounce) can pineapple chunks, drained
3 to 4 tablespoons melted butter or margarine
1 (8-ounce) can pineapple slices, drained (optional)
Maraschino cherries (optional)

Combine first 5 ingredients in a medium mixing bowl, mixing well. Pour into a lightly greased 13- x 9- x 2-inch baking dish. Pour butter evenly over casserole.
Garnish with pineapple slices, and place a maraschino cherry in the center of each slice, if desired. Bake casserole at 350° for 25 minutes. Yield: about 6 to 8 servings.

DINNER ROLLS

⅔ cup milk
½ cup sugar
2 teaspoons salt
6 tablespoons butter or margarine
⅔ cup warm water (105° to 115°)
2 tablespoons sugar
2 packages dry yeast
4 eggs, beaten
6 cups all-purpose flour

Scald milk in a small saucepan; stir in ½ cup sugar, salt, and butter. Cool to lukewarm.
Combine water and 2 tablespoons sugar in a large mixing bowl; add yeast, stirring to dissolve. Stir in cooled milk mixture and eggs; mix well. Add 3 cups flour, mixing well. Add remaining 3 cups flour, and mix well.
Turn dough out on a floured surface, and knead until smooth and elastic (about 8 to 10 minutes). Place in a well-greased bowl, turning to grease top. Cover and let rise in a warm place (85°), free from drafts, until doubled in bulk (about 1½ hours).

Punch dough down. Shape into ¾-inch balls; place 3 in each cup of well-greased muffin pans. Cover and let rise in a warm place until doubled in bulk. Bake at 375° for 10 minutes. Yield: about 2½ dozen.

PUMPKIN DATE CAKE

½ cup chopped dates
½ cup chopped walnuts
2 tablespoons all-purpose flour
¼ cup butter
1 cup firmly packed brown sugar
⅔ cup cooked, mashed pumpkin
1 teaspoon vanilla extract
2 eggs
½ cup all-purpose flour
½ teaspoon baking powder
¼ teaspoon soda
½ teaspoon ground cinnamon
½ teaspoon ground nutmeg
¼ teaspoon ground ginger
Whipped cream
Date halves (optional)

Combine chopped dates, walnuts, and 2 tablespoons flour; mix well. Set aside.
Melt butter over low heat; stir in brown sugar. Remove from heat; stir in pumpkin and vanilla. Add eggs, one at a time, beating well after each addition.
Combine remaining dry ingredients; add to pumpkin mixture, mixing well. Stir in floured date mixture. Pour into a greased 8-inch square pan. Bake at 350° about 30 minutes. Serve warm. Top each serving with whipped cream; garnish with a date half, if desired. Yield: about 6 to 8 servings.

PECAN PIE

3 eggs, beaten
⅔ cup sugar
⅓ teaspoon salt
⅓ cup melted butter
1 cup dark corn syrup
1 unbaked 9-inch pastry shell
1 cup pecan halves

Combine eggs, sugar, salt, butter, and corn syrup in a medium mixing bowl, mixing well. Pour into pastry shell; arrange pecan halves on top. Bake at 375° for 45 minutes. Yield: one 9-inch pie.

Leftover Ham And Turkey Put You Ahead

After the family feast is over, you come out ahead if you have any turkey or ham left over, for these are the bases for an appealing array of entrées.

Breakfast Ham and Egg Casserole is made ahead, then conveniently baked at serving time. The Turkey Salad Bake is crunchy with walnuts and celery, and topped with cheesy potato chips. An unusual and attractive way to use leftover ham is to grind it and bake it into Hawaiian Ham Cakes, served with a curry-flavored pineapple sauce. And the flavorful cornmeal pastry atop Golden Turkey Pie will make this dish a favorite at your house any time of year.

LAYERED HAM AND TURKEY BAKE

1½ cups egg noodles, uncooked
2 quarts boiling water
¼ cup butter or margarine
½ cup chopped onion
½ cup chopped celery
¼ cup all-purpose flour
1¾ cups turkey or chicken broth
1 (10¾-ounce) can cream of celery soup, undiluted
2 cups diced cooked ham
2 cups diced cooked turkey or chicken
2 tablespoons chopped pimiento
1 teaspoon poultry seasoning

Cook noodles in 2 quarts boiling water 10 minutes or until tender. Drain; set aside.

Melt butter in a 2-quart saucepan over medium heat; add onion and celery. Cook until vegetables are tender. Add flour, stirring until smooth. Cook 1 minute, stirring constantly. Stir in broth and soup; cook over medium heat, stirring constantly, until thickened and bubbly. Reduce heat; simmer 5 minutes, stirring occasionally. Remove from heat; stir in ham, turkey, pimiento, and poultry seasoning.

Place half of noodles in a lightly greased 13- x 9- x 2-inch baking dish; top with half of meat mixture. Repeat layers. Bake at 350° for 30 to 35 minutes or until hot and bubbly. Yield: 6 to 8 servings. *Mrs. Harvey Kidd, Hernando, Mississippi.*

HAWAIIAN HAM CAKES

1 (8-ounce) can pineapple slices, undrained
2 cups ground cooked ham
½ cup dry breadcrumbs
1 egg, beaten
¼ cup finely chopped onion
2 tablespoons margarine
4 frozen commercial patty shells, thawed
Pineapple-Curry Sauce

Drain pineapple, reserving ½ cup juice for sauce; set pineapple slices and juice aside.

Combine ham, breadcrumbs, egg, and onion; mix well. Shape ham mixture into 4 patties. Melt margarine in a large skillet; add ham patties and cook until browned on both sides. Drain on absorbent paper; let cool to touch.

Place a patty shell on waxed paper; roll out to a 7-inch square. Place ham cake in center of square; top with a pineapple slice. Bring corners of pastry over top of ham cake; pinch ends together to seal. Repeat procedure with remaining patty shells, ham cakes, and pineapple slices.

Place ham cakes on a lightly greased baking sheet. Bake at 425° for 20 minutes or until pastry is golden brown. Serve hot with Pineapple-Curry Sauce. Yield: 4 servings.

Pineapple-Curry Sauce:

1 (10¾-ounce) can cream of mushroom soup, undiluted
½ cup reserved pineapple juice
1 teaspoon curry powder
¼ teaspoon ground ginger
1 (8¼-ounce) can pineapple chunks, drained

Combine first 4 ingredients in a 1-quart saucepan; heat to boiling, stirring occasionally. Stir in pineapple chunks; remove from heat. Yield: 2 cups.
Mrs. Marie Webb, Roanoke, Virginia.

HEARTY TURKEY STEW

2 cups diced cooked turkey
2½ cups frozen lima beans
1 (17-ounce) can whole kernel corn, undrained
1 medium onion, chopped
2 cups turkey or chicken broth
1 cup canned tomatoes
½ teaspoon salt
¼ teaspoon ground ginger
¼ teaspoon pepper

Combine all ingredients in a 3-quart Dutch oven; heat to boiling. Reduce heat; simmer 1 hour or until thick, stirring occasionally. Serve hot. Yield: 6 servings. *Evelyn M. Wilson, Burnsville, North Carolina.*

SWEET-AND-SOUR TURKEY

1 (15¼-ounce) can pineapple chunks, undrained
2 tablespoons vegetable oil
½ cup chopped onion
2 cups thinly sliced (1½-inch-long) carrot sticks
1¼ cups water
3 chicken bouillon cubes
¼ cup firmly packed brown sugar
2 tablespoons cornstarch
¼ teaspoon ground ginger
¼ cup catsup
2 tablespoons vinegar
1 tablespoon soy sauce
2 cups diced cooked turkey or chicken
1 cup thinly sliced green pepper strips
Egg Fried Rice

Drain pineapple, reserving juice for rice. Set pineapple aside.

Heat oil in a 10-inch skillet; add onion and cook over medium heat until tender. Add carrots, 1¼ cups water, and bouillon cubes; heat mixture to boiling. Cover; reduce heat and simmer 5 minutes.

Combine sugar, cornstarch, and ginger; stir in catsup, vinegar, and soy sauce, mixing well. Slowly stir cornstarch mixture into vegetables in skillet. Cook over medium heat, stirring constantly, until thickened and bubbly. Stir in turkey, green pepper, and pineapple; cover and simmer 5 minutes. Serve hot over Egg Fried Rice. Yield: 6 servings.

Egg Fried Rice:

Reserved pineapple juice
1 tablespoon butter or margarine
¾ teaspoon salt
2¼ cups instant rice, uncooked
4 eggs, beaten
4 green onions, chopped

Add enough water to reserved juice to make 2¼ cups. Combine juice mixture, butter, and salt in a 10-inch skillet; heat to boiling. Stir in rice; cover and remove from heat. Let stand 5 minutes or until water is absorbed.

Return skillet to medium heat; push rice to one side of skillet. Pour eggs into other side of skillet; top with green onion. Cook eggs until partially set; stir eggs and rice together and cook until done. Yield: about 3 cups.
Mrs. James S. Tiffany, Dallas, Texas.

TURKEY SALAD BAKE

1 (4-ounce) package potato chips
½ cup (2 ounces) shredded sharp Cheddar cheese
1 tablespoon margarine
½ cup chopped walnuts
2 cups diced cooked turkey
2 cups thinly sliced celery
2 teaspoons grated onion
¼ teaspoon salt
½ cup mayonnaise or salad dressing
1½ to 2 tablespoons lemon juice

Crush potato chips to make 2 cups; combine potato chips and cheese. Place half of potato chip mixture into a lightly greased 8-inch square baking dish. Set remaining potato chip mixture aside.

Melt margarine in a small skillet over low heat; add walnuts and sauté until lightly toasted (about 15 minutes), stirring occasionally. Drain nuts on absorbent paper.

Combine nuts, turkey, celery, onion, salt, mayonnaise, and lemon juice; spoon over potato chip mixture in baking dish. Sprinkle with remaining potato chip mixture. Bake at 450° for 12 to 15 minutes or until hot and bubbly. Yield: 4 to 5 servings.
Mrs. Margaret L. Hunter,
Princeton, Kentucky.

GOLDEN TURKEY PIE

½ cup all-purpose flour
1¼ teaspoons salt
¼ teaspoon rubbed sage
⅛ teaspoon ground mace
⅛ teaspoon pepper
½ cup butter or margarine
1½ cups turkey or chicken broth
1 cup milk
1 teaspoon lemon juice
3 cups diced cooked turkey
Seasoned Pastry

Combine flour and seasonings, stirring well; set aside.

Melt butter in a heavy 2-quart saucepan over low heat; add flour mixture, stirring until smooth. Cook 1 minute, stirring constantly. Gradually stir in broth, milk, and lemon juice; cook over medium heat, stirring constantly, until thickened and bubbly. Stir in turkey; heat thoroughly.

Pour filling into a lightly greased 1½-quart casserole; top with Seasoned Pastry. Trim edges and flute pastry as desired. Make slits along top of pastry. Bake at 425° for 25 minutes or until golden brown. Yield: 4 to 6 servings.

Seasoned Pastry:

½ cup all-purpose flour
½ cup cornmeal
½ teaspoon salt
½ teaspoon rubbed sage
⅓ cup butter or margarine, softened
3 tablespoons water

Combine first 4 ingredients; cut in butter until mixture resembles coarse crumbs. Add water; mix well with a fork. Shape dough into a ball; turn dough out onto a lightly floured surface. Roll dough out to ¼-inch thickness to fit the top of a 1½-quart casserole. Yield: crust for 1 casserole.
Mrs. W. P. Chambers,
Louisville, Kentucky.

BREAKFAST HAM AND EGG CASSEROLE

Softened butter or margarine
14 to 15 slices bread
3 cups diced cooked ham
2 cups (½ pound) shredded Cheddar cheese
1 teaspoon salt
½ teaspoon pepper
6 eggs
3 cups milk

Spread butter on both sides of bread slices; cut bread into small cubes. Combine bread cubes, ham, cheese, salt, and pepper; stir well.

Beat eggs until foamy; stir in milk. Add egg mixture to ham mixture, stirring well. Pour into a lightly greased 13- x 9- x 2-inch baking pan; cover and refrigerate overnight.

Bake, uncovered, at 350° for 1 hour or until golden brown. Serve immediately. Yield: 10 to 12 servings.
Mrs. Norma Dickson,
Enterprise, Alabama.

PINEAPPLE UPSIDE-DOWN HAM LOAF

¼ cup firmly packed brown sugar
3 tablespoons vinegar
1 teaspoon dry mustard
3 slices canned pineapple
3 maraschino cherries
2 cups ground cooked ham
1 cup (½ pound) ground pork
2 eggs, slightly beaten
1 cup cracker crumbs
1 cup milk
1 tablespoon minced onion
¼ teaspoon salt
⅛ teaspoon pepper

Combine brown sugar, vinegar, and dry mustard; stir well. Pour into a well-greased 9- x 5- x 3-inch loafpan. Place pineapple slices in a row in loafpan; put a cherry in the center of each ring.

Combine remaining ingredients, mixing well. Spoon mixture into loafpan, and shape into a loaf.

Bake at 350° for 1½ hours. Remove from oven; let stand 5 to 10 minutes. Invert loafpan on a wire rack to drain off pan drippings. Remove loaf from pan; place on a serving platter. Yield: 8 servings. *Mrs. Earl L. Faulkenberry,*
Lancaster, South Carolina.

Try A Turnip Or Rutabaga Combination

Rutabagas and turnips, so plentiful now, take on special flavor when combined with other ingredients. Rutabaga au Gratin is a cheesy casserole, Turnip Supreme is enhanced with bacon and onion, and Creamy Rutabaga is flavored with brown sugar and nutmeg.

Rutabagas and turnips taste somewhat alike, but differ in appearance. Turnips have whitish skin with a purple collar, while rutabagas have yellow-orange flesh. Since rutabagas are so large and firm, you might find it easier to cut them into quarters before you remove their waxy peel.

PARSLEYED TURNIPS AND CARROTS

3 cups peeled and diced turnips
3 cups peeled and diced carrots
¼ cup melted butter or margarine
2 tablespoons minced fresh parsley
½ teaspoon salt
Dash of pepper

Cook turnips and carrots, covered, in small amount of boiling salted water for 20 minutes or until tender; drain. Add remaining ingredients; toss well. Yield: 6 to 8 servings. *Betty Ruth Holtum,*
Vienna, Virginia.

TURNIPS AND POTATOES

1 pound turnips, peeled and sliced
2 cups peeled and sliced potatoes
½ cup sliced onion
½ teaspoon salt
½ teaspoon pepper
2 cups water
1 tablespoon butter or margarine

Combine all ingredients except butter in a saucepan. Bring to a boil; cover and simmer 20 minutes or until vegetables are tender. Drain liquid; add butter to vegetables, and mash to desired consistency. Yield: 6 servings.

Nita J. Jones,
Corpus Christi, Texas.

SCALLOPED TURNIPS

3 medium turnips, peeled and sliced
2 tablespoons butter or margarine
2 tablespoons all-purpose flour
1½ cups milk
1 teaspoon salt
⅛ teaspoon pepper
½ cup shredded mild Cheddar cheese

Cook turnips, uncovered, in boiling salted water for 15 minutes or until tender. Drain; transfer to a lightly greased 2-quart casserole.

Melt butter in a heavy saucepan over low heat; blend in flour, and cook 1 minute, stirring constantly. Gradually stir in milk; cook over medium heat, stirring constantly, until thickened and bubbly. Stir in salt and pepper.

Pour sauce over turnips; sprinkle with cheese. Bake at 450° for 10 minutes. Yield: 6 servings.

Mrs. Parke LaGourgue Cory,
Neosho, Missouri.

HASH BROWN TURNIPS

2 tablespoons butter or margarine
3 cups cubed cooked turnips
½ cup chopped onion
½ teaspoon salt
¼ teaspoon pepper
Pinch of poultry seasoning

Melt butter in a medium skillet; add remaining ingredients. Cook over medium heat, stirring occasionally, until golden. Yield: 4 servings.

Mrs. Sandy Wallace,
Pompano Beach, Florida.

TURNIP SUPREME

6 to 8 medium turnips
1 large onion
4 slices bacon
½ teaspoon sugar
½ teaspoon cayenne
1 teaspoon paprika

Peel and quarter turnips and onion; cook in boiling salted water until tender. Drain and set aside.

Fry bacon until crisp; drain and reserve drippings. Crumble bacon. Add bacon, bacon drippings, sugar, and seasonings to vegetables; toss well. Spoon into a greased 2-quart casserole. Bake at 350° for 15 minutes or until heated thoroughly. Yield: 6 servings.

Kay McElhone,
McAllen, Texas.

RUTABAGA AU GRATIN

6 tablespoons melted butter or margarine, divided
¼ cup all-purpose flour
2 cups milk
1 cup (¼ pound) shredded Cheddar cheese
1 teaspoon salt
⅛ teaspoon pepper
4 cups diced cooked rutabagas
½ cup breadcrumbs

Combine ¼ cup butter and flour in a heavy saucepan over low heat. Cook 1 minute, stirring constantly. Gradually stir in milk; cook over medium heat, stirring constantly, until smooth and thickened. Add cheese and seasonings, stirring until the cheese is melted.

Place rutabaga in a lightly greased 1½-quart casserole; top with sauce. Combine breadcrumbs with remaining 2 tablespoons butter; sprinkle over casserole. Bake at 400° for 15 minutes. Yield: 6 servings.

Mrs. John P. Trimble,
Conroe, Texas.

CREAMY RUTABAGA

1 small rutabaga, peeled and diced
1 tablespoon sugar
¼ cup evaporated milk
¼ cup firmly packed light brown sugar
2 tablespoons butter or margarine
Salt to taste
Ground nutmeg

Cook rutabaga in 1 inch of boiling salted water 10 minutes. Stir in sugar, and cook until very tender; drain well.

Combine all ingredients except nutmeg; beat on high speed of electric mixer until creamy. Sprinkle with nutmeg. Yield: 4 to 6 servings.

Mrs. Ben A. Say,
Atlanta, Georgia.

TURNIP SOUFFLE

6 medium turnips, peeled and sliced
2 tablespoons butter or margarine
½ cup milk
¼ cup shredded Cheddar cheese
½ teaspoon salt
¼ teaspoon pepper
⅛ teaspoon cayenne
2 eggs, separated

Cook turnips in boiling salted water 20 to 30 minutes or until tender; drain and mash. Cool slightly. Add remaining ingredients except egg whites; stir well.

Beat egg whites until stiff but not dry; fold into turnip mixture. Spoon mixture into a lightly greased 1½-quart casserole or soufflé dish. Bake at 375° for 1 hour or until lightly browned. Yield: 6 servings.

Mrs. Charles Gleason,
Marrero, Louisiana.

Created Especially For Two

If you prepare meals for just two, then these recipes are designed with you in mind. For a special breakfast or brunch, serve Eggs Benedict; the hollandaise is scaled down to just the right amount for two. Add some sliced tomatoes, grapefruit, and a glass of wine to complete the menu.

Entrée dishes for two are always welcome, and here are two featuring pork and chicken.

EGGS BENEDICT

2 English muffins, halved and buttered
4 poached eggs
Hollandaise sauce (recipe follows)

Broil muffins until lightly browned. Top each muffin half with a poached egg, and cover with hollandaise sauce. Yield: 2 servings.

Hollandaise Sauce:

3 egg yolks
2 tablespoons lemon juice
½ cup butter
¼ teaspoon salt
Dash of cayenne pepper

Beat egg yolks in top of double boiler; gradually add lemon juice to egg yolks, stirring constantly. Add about one-third of butter to egg mixture; cook over hot (not boiling) water, stirring constantly, until butter melts.

Add another third of butter, stirring constantly; as sauce thickens, stir in remaining butter. Stir in salt and cayenne; cook until thickened. Yield: about ½ cup. *Jennifer Kimmel,*
Nashville, Tennessee.

CASHEW CHICKEN

2 tablespoons soy sauce
1 tablespoon cornstarch
1 whole chicken breast, skinned, boned, and cut into ⅛-inch strips
¼ cup vegetable oil, divided
⅓ cup roasted cashew nuts
1 small onion
¼ pound green beans, cut diagonally in ½-inch pieces
2 medium carrots, peeled and cut diagonally in ⅛-inch slices
1 stalk celery, sliced
1 clove garlic, minced
½ cup chicken broth
1 teaspoon cornstarch

Combine soy sauce and 1 tablespoon cornstarch; mix well. Add chicken, and stir until coated; set aside.

Heat 1 tablespoon oil in wok until hot; add nuts, stirring constantly, until browned (about 30 seconds). Remove nuts, and set aside. Add another tablespoon oil to pan; add chicken, and stir-fry 1 to 2 minutes. Remove chicken, and set aside.

Cut onion into ¼-inch slices; cut slices in half crosswise. Add remaining oil to wok, and heat to smoking. Add vegetables and garlic; cover and cook 1 minute, shaking wok to prevent vegetables from sticking. Remove cover; cook, stirring constantly, an additional 2 to 4 minutes.

Combine broth and 1 teaspoon cornstarch. Add chicken and broth mixture to vegetables; stir until thickened. Stir in cashews. Yield: 2 servings.
Mrs. Michael Champagne,
Covington, Louisiana.

EASY SKILLET PORK CHOPS

2 or 3 (½- to ¾-inch-thick) loin pork chops
1½ tablespoons butter or margarine
¾ cup chopped onion
½ teaspoon salt
⅛ teaspoon pepper
1 teaspoon cornstarch
2 teaspoons prepared mustard
1 cup water
1 beef bouillon cube
1 teaspoon Worcestershire sauce

Sauté pork chops in butter until brown; set aside, reserving drippings. Sauté onion in drippings until tender. Add salt, pepper, cornstarch, and mustard; stir well. Add water, bouillon, and Worcestershire; stir until bouillon is dissolved. Place pork chops in skillet; simmer 20 to 30 minutes. Yield: 2 servings. *Carole Lake,*
Houston, Texas.

Offer An Eggnog Dessert

Eggnog, that favorite holiday beverage, is the delicious base for these three desserts. Eggnog Christmas Cookies are decorated with candied fruit and decorator candies. On the elegant side, choose between Eggnog Bavarian Parfait and Creamy Eggnog Tarts—both can be prepared ahead.

EGGNOG CHRISTMAS COOKIES

1 cup butter, softened
2 cups sugar
1 cup commercial eggnog
½ teaspoon ground nutmeg
1 teaspoon soda
About 5½ cups sifted all-purpose flour
2 egg whites, slightly beaten
Decorator candies
Candied fruit

Combine butter and sugar, creaming until light and fluffy; add eggnog, nutmeg, and soda, mixing well. Add enough flour to make a stiff dough; then roll dough into a ball and chill.

Divide dough in half; roll out each half on a lightly floured surface to ⅛-inch thickness.

Cut dough with shaped cookie cutters. Place on lightly greased cookie sheets. Brush each with egg white, and

decorate with decorator candies and candied fruit as desired. Bake at 375° for 6 to 8 minutes or until lightly browned. Yield: about 9 dozen.
Mrs. Daniel Krieg,
Lubbock, Texas.

EGGNOG BAVARIAN PARFAIT

1 quart commercial eggnog
1 (13½-ounce) container frozen whipped topping, thawed
1 (4-ounce) jar red maraschino cherries, drained and chopped
1 (4-ounce) jar green maraschino cherries, drained and chopped

Pour eggnog into a large bowl; fold in whipped topping. Pour into parfait glasses; spoon cherries into each and freeze. Let stand at room temperature 20 minutes before serving. Yield: 10 to 12 servings. *Mrs. Homer L. Thomas,*
Brownwood, Texas.

CREAMY EGGNOG TARTS

1 (3⅛-ounce) package vanilla-flavor pudding and pie filling mix
1 envelope unflavored gelatin
Dash of ground nutmeg
3 cups commercial eggnog
¼ cup light rum
½ cup whipping cream, whipped
1 dozen individual tart shells, baked
Ground nutmeg

Combine pudding mix, gelatin, and nutmeg in a saucepan; add eggnog. Cook over medium heat until mixture comes to a boil; remove from heat, and stir in rum. Pour into a large mixing bowl, and chill 3 hours or until just set.

Beat mixture with electric mixer until light and fluffy; fold in whipped cream. Chill 30 minutes. Spoon into individual tart shells; chill until serving time. Top each with a sprinkle of nutmeg. Yield: 12 tarts. *Mrs. Jack Corzine,*
St. Louis, Missouri.

Something Sweet To Snack On

These sweet treats are perfect to have on hand for snacks: They're quickly mixed, baked, and sliced into small bars or squares for serving.

No-Bake Date Bars are not even baked, and they're thick and chewy with oats and dates. For bars rich in chocolate, coconut, and pecans, try Chocolate Dream Bars; they're baked in two rich layers.

CARROT SQUARES

¾ cup shortening
½ cup firmly packed brown sugar
2 eggs, separated
Juice of 1 lemon
1 tablespoon grated lemon rind
1 cup all-purpose flour
1 teaspoon baking powder
¼ cup warm water
1½ cups grated carrots

Combine shortening and sugar; cream until light and fluffy. Add egg yolks, lemon juice, and lemon rind, mixing well. Stir in flour, baking powder, and water; mix well.

Beat egg whites until soft peaks form; fold egg whites and carrots into batter. Spoon mixture into a greased 9-inch square dish. Bake at 350° for 1 hour. Cut into 3-inch squares, and serve immediately. Yield: 9 servings.

Mrs. Maurice Shofer,
Baltimore, Maryland.

CHOCOLATE DREAM BARS

⅓ cup butter or margarine, softened
⅓ cup firmly packed brown sugar
1 cup all-purpose flour
2 eggs
1 cup firmly packed brown sugar
¼ cup all-purpose flour
½ teaspoon baking powder
1 teaspoon vanilla extract
1 (3½-ounce) can shredded coconut
1 cup chopped pecans
½ cup semisweet chocolate morsels

Combine butter and ⅓ cup sugar; beat until light and fluffy. Add 1 cup flour, and mix well. Press into the bottom of a lightly greased 13- x 9- x 2-inch baking pan. Bake at 350° for 12 minutes or until lightly browned.

Combine eggs, 1 cup sugar, ¼ cup flour, baking powder, vanilla, and coconut; mix well. Stir in pecans and chocolate morsels. Spoon mixture over hot crust; bake 20 to 25 minutes longer or until lightly browned. Cool completely; cut into small bars. Yield: about 2 dozen.
Mrs. Donald C. Vanhoy,
Salisbury, North Carolina.

NO-BAKE DATE BARS

2 (8-ounce) packages pitted dates
1½ cups shredded coconut
½ cup butter or margarine
½ cup water
¼ cup honey
⅛ teaspoon salt
2½ cups regular oats, uncooked
⅔ cup chopped nuts
1 teaspoon vanilla extract

Combine first 6 ingredients in a large, heavy saucepan; cook over medium heat until mixture reaches a boil, stirring frequently. Reduce heat; cook 3 to 4 minutes, mashing dates until mixture is thick and blended. Remove from heat.

Stir in oats, nuts, and vanilla. Spoon mixture into a 9-inch square pan that has been lined with waxed paper. Place in refrigerator, and chill 1½ to 2 hours. Cut into 18 bars; lift waxed paper from pan, and separate bars. Store bars in refrigerator in an airtight container. Yield: 1½ dozen.
Linda Clark,
Elizabethton, Tennessee.

PEANUT BUTTER FINGERS

½ cup butter
½ cup sugar
½ cup firmly packed brown sugar
1 egg
⅓ cup creamy peanut butter
½ teaspoon soda
¼ teaspoon salt
½ teaspoon vanilla extract
1 cup all-purpose flour
1 cup quick-cooking oats, uncooked
1 (6-ounce) package semisweet chocolate morsels
½ cup powdered sugar
¼ cup crunchy peanut butter
2 to 4 tablespoons milk

Combine butter and sugar; cream until light and fluffy. Add egg, creamy peanut butter, soda, salt, and vanilla; beat well. Stir in flour and oats.

Spoon batter into a greased 9-inch square pan. Bake at 350° for 25 minutes; remove from oven and sprinkle immediately with chocolate morsels. Let stand 5 minutes; then spread chocolate as a frosting.

Combine powdered sugar, crunchy peanut butter, and milk; stir until smooth. Drizzle over chocolate frosting. Cut into bars when cool. Yield: 15 to 18 bars.
Mrs. Byron Schisler,
Jonesboro, Arkansas.

FROSTED COFFEE BARS

½ cup hot coffee
½ cup raisins
¼ cup shortening
1 cup firmly packed brown sugar
1 egg, beaten
1½ cups all-purpose flour
½ teaspoon baking powder
½ teaspoon soda
½ teaspoon salt
½ teaspoon ground cinnamon
¼ cup chopped nuts
1 tablespoon hot coffee
½ cup powdered sugar

Combine ½ cup coffee and raisins; stir in shortening, brown sugar, and beaten egg.

Combine flour, baking powder, soda, salt, and cinnamon; stir into coffee mixture. Stir in nuts. Pour into a greased 9-inch square baking pan. Bake at 350° for 20 to 25 minutes.

Combine 1 tablespoon coffee and powdered sugar; drizzle over top while still hot. Cool; cut into 1½-inch squares. Yield: 3 dozen.
Mrs. Robert Collins,
Fairfax, Missouri.

Meals at Pleasant Hill, a restored Shaker Village, include ample servings of freshly baked breads. Recipes begin on page 275.

Above: Red Bean Slaw (247) and Party Re-frigerator Rolls (page 248) can both be made ahead and refrigerated.

Left: Cottage cheese fills the center of this colorful salad, Tomato Aspic with Shrimp (page 241).

Right: Ambrosia Cream Cheese Mold (page 249), a creamy congealed salad, is sweet enough to be served for dessert.

A freshly baked loaf of quick bread will make a welcome gift. Share colorful Apricot-Cranberry Loaf (page 235) or Maraschino Cherry Nut Bread (page 234).

Brunch Makes The Morning

A good way to warm up a winter morning is to have friends over for a leisurely brunch. You can plan the menu around any one of these sumptuous egg dishes. Whether you prefer a classic quiche, eggs scrambled with a rich seafood sauce, or a puffy baked omelet, the recipes here are sure to please.

For something really different, try Scotch Eggs. They're hard-cooked eggs wrapped in sausage and breadcrumbs and fried to a crisp golden brown.

SOUR CREAM-HAM OMELET

5 eggs, separated
1½ cups chopped cooked ham
1 cup commercial sour cream, divided
¼ teaspoon salt
2 tablespoons butter or margarine

Beat egg whites until stiff but not dry; set aside. Beat egg yolks until thick and lemon colored; stir in ham, ½ cup sour cream, and salt. Fold egg whites into egg yolk mixture.

Heat butter in an ovenproof 10-inch omelet pan or heavy skillet until hot enough to sizzle a drop of water. Pour in egg mixture all at once, and gently smooth surface. Reduce heat and cook omelet about 5 minutes or until puffy and light brown on bottom, gently lifting omelet at edge to judge color.

Bake at 325° for 12 to 15 minutes or until a knife inserted in center comes out clean. Tip skillet and loosen omelet with a spatula; slide omelet onto serving plate. To serve, slice in wedges and garnish with remaining sour cream. Yield: 4 servings. *Nancy Sloan, Lake Village, Arkansas.*

EASY SAUSAGE QUICHE

Pastry for 9-inch pie shell
1 pound bulk pork sausage
3 eggs
⅔ cup milk
1 teaspoon salt
Dash of pepper
Dash of cayenne pepper
1½ cups (6 ounces) shredded Cheddar cheese, divided

Line a 9-inch quiche dish or piepan with pastry; trim excess pastry around edges. Bake at 400° for 3 minutes; remove from oven, and gently prick with a fork. Bake 5 minutes longer. Let cool on a rack.

Cook sausage until browned; drain.

Combine eggs, milk, and seasonings in a medium mixing bowl; beat lightly. Stir in sausage.

Sprinkle ¾ cup cheese over pastry shell; top with sausage mixture. Sprinkle with remaining ¾ cup cheese. Bake at 375° for 50 minutes or until set. Yield: one 9-inch quiche.
Robbin Dorrier, Mooresville, North Carolina.

CHEESE SOUFFLE

½ cup butter or margarine
½ cup all-purpose flour
2 cups milk
1½ teaspoons salt
½ teaspoon paprika
Dash of hot sauce
2 cups (½ pound) shredded sharp Cheddar cheese
8 eggs, separated

Lightly butter a 3-quart soufflé dish. Cut a piece of aluminum foil long enough to circle the dish, allowing a 1-inch overlap. Fold foil lengthwise into thirds, and lightly butter one side. Wrap foil, buttered side against the dish, so it extends 3 inches above the rim. Securely attach foil with string.

Melt butter in top of double boiler. Blend in flour; cook 1 minute, stirring constantly. Gradually stir in milk; cook over medium heat, stirring constantly, until thickened and bubbly. Stir in salt, paprika, hot sauce, and cheese.

Beat egg yolks until thick and lemon colored. Stir some of hot mixture into yolks; add to remaining hot mixture, stirring constantly.

Beat egg whites (at room temperature) until stiff but not dry; gently fold into cheese sauce. Spoon into prepared soufflé dish. Bake at 475° for 10 minutes. Reduce oven temperature to 400°, and bake an additional 25 minutes or until puffy and golden brown. Remove collar before serving. Yield: 8 servings. *Mrs. Marshall Marvelli, Winston-Salem, North Carolina.*

SCOTCH EGGS

2 eggs, beaten
¼ cup water
6 hard-cooked eggs, peeled
1½ cups dry breadcrumbs
1 pound bulk sausage

Combine beaten eggs and water; mix well. Roll hard-cooked eggs in breadcrumbs; dip eggs in beaten egg mixture; roll eggs in breadcrumbs until completely coated. Set aside for 15 minutes.

Divide sausage into 6 equal portions. Shape each portion into a patty and wrap completely around egg, pressing edges together to seal well. Dip sausage-covered egg in beaten egg mixture; roll egg in breadcrumbs. Set aside for 15 minutes.

Drop eggs into deep oil heated to 375°; cook 7 to 9 minutes. Drain on paper towels. Slice or quarter to serve. Yield: 6 servings. *Lura Peace, Emerson, Arkansas.*

SHRIMP AND CRAB SCRAMBLED EGGS

1 (6-ounce) package frozen shrimp, thawed and drained
1 (6½-ounce) can crabmeat, drained and flaked
1 tablespoon chopped chives
3 tablespoons dry sherry
¼ cup plus 2 tablespoons butter or margarine
2 tablespoons all-purpose flour
¾ cup milk
12 eggs
1 teaspoon salt
1 teaspoon seasoned salt
⅛ teaspoon pepper
3 drops of hot sauce

Combine shrimp, crabmeat, chives, and sherry. Melt 2 tablespoons butter in a heavy saucepan over low heat; blend in flour, stirring until smooth. Cook 1 minute, stirring constantly. Gradually stir in milk; cook over medium heat, stirring constantly, until thickened and bubbly. Stir in shrimp mixture. Set aside.

Combine eggs, salt, seasoned salt, pepper, and hot sauce; beat well. Combine shrimp mixture and eggs. Melt remaining butter in a skillet over medium heat; add egg mixture.

As eggs begin to set, lift cooked portion so that uncooked portion can flow to bottom. Cook until eggs are set but still moist (3 to 5 minutes). Yield: 8 to 10 servings. *Mrs. Helena Miehe, Birmingham, Alabama.*

Start The Day With An Omelet

For a special way to start the morning, try a cheesy ham-filled omelet. Pat Mestayer of Raceland, Louisiana, beats her egg whites separately to give her Ham and Cheese Omelet a light and airy texture. Complete the breakfast menu with fresh fruit for a breakfast that looks as good as it tastes.

HAM AND CHEESE OMELET

4 eggs, separated
½ teaspoon all-purpose flour
2 tablespoons milk
½ medium onion, chopped
1 tablespoon chopped fresh parsley
½ teaspoon salt
Dash of pepper
3 tablespoons butter or margarine, divided
3 slices cooked ham, cut into pieces
3 slices process American cheese

Beat egg whites until stiff but not dry. Beat egg yolks until thick and lemon colored. Combine yolks, flour, milk, onion, parsley, salt, and pepper; mix well. Fold into egg whites.

For each omelet, melt 1 tablespoon of butter in an 8-inch skillet until just hot enough to sizzle a drop of water; pour in one-third egg mixture. As mixture starts to cook, gently lift edges of omelet and tilt pan to allow the uncooked portion to flow underneath. When mixture is set and no longer flows freely, sprinkle one-third of ham on half of omelet; cover ham with one slice of cheese. Fold omelet in half, and place on a warm platter. Repeat procedure with remaining ingredients. Yield: 3 servings.

Making Candy In A Microwave

Old-fashioned candy is only minutes away when made in a microwave oven. Because microwaves cook from all sides, candies not only cook quickly but require minimum attention. In fact, candies that require constant stirring if prepared conventionally will have their same creamy texture with only occasional stirring when microwaved.

Double-Good Fudge, Southern Pralines, and Nutty Toffee can be made in a matter of minutes in a microwave oven.

To acquaint you with the ease of microwave candymaking, we offer some favorite candy recipes and instructions for microwave preparation. Since wattage of microwave ovens varies, the cooking times will vary. A time range is given in our recipes to allow for the difference. To prevent overcooking, always check for doneness at the lower end of the range.

Follow these guidelines to achieve the best results.

—The cold-water technique is recommended for testing doneness since a candy thermometer cannot be used while microwaving. Some of our candy recipes specify cooking to the soft ball stage; others specify hard crack stage. The mixture is at the soft ball stage when a small amount dropped into cold water can be picked up but flattens. For the hard crack stage, mixture should separate into hard, brittle threads when given the cold-water test.

If a candy thermometer is used, allow 1 to 2 minutes for the temperature to rise and stabilize before taking a reading. Remove thermometer before returning mixture to microwave oven.

—Use a microwave-safe dish that is large enough to allow the candy mixture to expand while cooking. A deep dish works better than a shallow one because the height is needed to prevent boil-overs in the oven.

In our recipes, we recommend a specific size dish to use. If you do not have the proper size, always substitute a larger dish. If you still have a problem with boilovers, securely cover the mixture with the container's lid.

—Most candy that is to be beaten after cooking, such as fudge, should be cooled to lukewarm (110° to 120°) before beating.

MILLIONAIRES

1 (14-ounce) package caramels
1½ tablespoons milk
2 cups coarsely chopped pecans
1 (12-ounce) package semisweet chocolate morsels
1 tablespoon vegetable shortening

Remove any chocolate caramels in package, and reserve for another use. Unwrap remaining caramels, and place in a 2-quart casserole. Microwave at HIGH for 1 to 1¼ minutes; stir well.

Add milk to caramels, and microwave at HIGH for 1½ to 2 minutes, stirring every 30 seconds. Stir until mixture is smooth; add pecans, mixing well. Drop by teaspoonfuls onto buttered waxed paper. Cool; cover and chill.

Combine chocolate morsels and shortening in a 4-cup glass measure. Microwave at MEDIUM for 3 to 4 minutes or until morsels are softened; stir well. Dip caramel centers into chocolate, and return to waxed paper. Chill. Store candy in refrigerator. Yield: about 2½ dozen.

PEANUT BRITTLE

1 cup sugar
½ cup light corn syrup
1½ cups raw peanuts
¼ teaspoon salt
1 tablespoon butter or margarine
1 teaspoon vanilla extract
1 teaspoon soda

Combine sugar, corn syrup, peanuts, and salt in a deep 3-quart casserole; mix well. Microwave at HIGH for 7½ to 9½ minutes or until light brown.

Add butter and vanilla, mixing well. Microwave at HIGH for 1 minute or until mixture reaches hard crack stage (300°). Stir in soda; pour onto a buttered cookie sheet, spreading thinly. Let cool. Break into pieces. Yield: about 1 pound.

SOUTHERN PRALINES

1½ cups firmly packed light brown sugar
⅔ cup half-and-half
⅛ teaspoon salt
2 tablespoons butter or margarine
1½ cups pecan halves

Combine sugar, half-and-half, and salt in a deep 3-quart casserole; mix well. Stir in butter; microwave at HIGH for 7 to 9½ minutes or until mixture reaches soft ball stage (235°), stirring once.

Stir in pecans; cool about 1 minute. Beat by hand until mixture is creamy and begins to thicken (about 3 minutes). Drop by tablespoonfuls onto waxed paper; let stand until firm. Yield: about 2 dozen.

Tip: Tinted coconut makes a child's cake more festive. Fill a pint jar a third to half full of coconut. Add a few drops of cake coloring to 1 to 2 tablespoons water, and add to coconut; cover jar, and shake well to distribute color.

DOUBLE-GOOD FUDGE

2 cups sugar
⅔ cup half-and-half
¼ cup light corn syrup
1 (1-ounce) square unsweetened chocolate
¼ cup butter or margarine
2 teaspoons vanilla extract
Peanut Butter Layer

Combine sugar, half-and-half, corn syrup, and chocolate in a deep 4- to 5-quart casserole; mix well. Cover with waxed paper, and microwave at HIGH for 3½ to 5 minutes or until bubbly. Stir well.

Cover and microwave at MEDIUM HIGH for 6½ to 9½ minutes or until mixture reaches soft ball stage (235°). Add butter and vanilla; do not stir. Let mixture cool to lukewarm; then beat until thick and creamy.

Pour candy into a buttered 9-inch square pan, spreading with a spatula to form an even layer. Top with Peanut Butter Layer. Chill and cut into squares. Store candy in refrigerator. Yield: about 2¾ pounds.

Peanut Butter Layer:

1 cup sugar
1 cup firmly packed light brown sugar
½ cup half-and-half
2 tablespoons light corn syrup
¼ cup butter or margarine
½ cup crunchy peanut butter
½ cup marshmallow cream
2 teaspoons vanilla extract

Combine sugar, half-and-half, and corn syrup in a deep 4- to 5-quart casserole; mix well. Add butter; cover with waxed paper. Microwave at HIGH for 5 to 8 minutes or until mixture reaches soft ball stage (235°), stirring twice. Add peanut butter, marshmallow cream, and vanilla; stir until smooth. Pour over chocolate layer.

NUTTY TOFFEE

2 cups sugar
⅔ cup butter or margarine
2 tablespoons water
1 tablespoon light corn syrup
1 teaspoon vanilla extract
1 (6-ounce) package semisweet chocolate morsels
1 cup finely chopped pecans

Combine sugar, butter, water, and corn syrup in a deep 3-quart casserole. Microwave at HIGH for 11 to 13½ minutes or until mixture reaches hard crack stage (300°), stirring once. Stir in

vanilla. Pour into an ungreased 15- x 10- x 1-inch jellyroll pan, spreading to edges of pan.

Sprinkle chocolate morsels over toffee; let stand 1 minute or until chocolate begins to melt. Spread chocolate over entire candy layer; sprinkle with pecans. Let stand until set. Break into pieces. Yield: about 1½ pounds.

Chicken In A Biscuit

Here's a new idea for leftover chicken. Mrs. Sarah Phelps of Baltimore uses convenient, refrigerated crescent dinner rolls to make her golden-brown Chicken in a Biscuit.

She combines chopped chicken with cream cheese, pimientos, and onion, wraps it in the dough, tops it with breadcrumbs, and bakes it. The result is a pastry so plump that two or three will make a filling meal.

CHICKEN IN A BISCUIT

1 (3-ounce) package cream cheese, softened
2 tablespoons milk
2 cups finely chopped cooked chicken
2 tablespoons drained, chopped pimiento
2 tablespoons minced onion or chives
Salt and pepper to taste
1 (8-ounce) can refrigerated crescent dinner rolls
¼ cup melted butter or margarine
¼ cup Italian-style breadcrumbs

Combine cream cheese and milk; beat until smooth. Add chicken, pimiento, onion, salt, and pepper; stir well.

Separate dinner roll dough into 2 rectangles, firmly pressing perforations to seal; cut each rectangle into four 4- x 5-inch rectangles. Place a heaping tablespoonful of chicken mixture onto each rectangle. Fold sides and ends of dough toward center; moisten edges with water, and pinch to seal. Shape into biscuits. Place seam side down on cookie sheet; brush with butter, and sprinkle with breadcrumbs. Bake at 350° for 25 minutes or until golden brown. Yield: 8 biscuits.

His Cooking Is Virginia Style

Clifton Potter of Lynchburg, Virginia, traces his interest in cooking all the way back to childhood camping experiences as a Boy Scout. His cooking expertise has advanced from grilling hamburgers over the campfire to winning first place in *The Roanoke Times* and *World News* Favorite Reader Recipes Contest.

"Cooking is relaxing for me and so unlike my profession," said Clif, who is a professor of history at Lynchburg College and a writer of fiction and nonfiction. Clif and his wife, Dorothy Bundy, also study international foods and are members of the Lynchburg College Gourmet Group.

Many of Clif's specialties are based on foods traditional in the Old Dominion. For example, Virginia Crêpes are filled with Smithfield ham and oysters from the Chesapeake Bay.

VIRGINIA CREPES

1 pint oysters, undrained
About ¾ cup milk
¼ cup butter or margarine
½ cup all-purpose flour
1 egg yolk, beaten
⅛ teaspoon salt
¼ teaspoon white pepper
2 tablespoons sherry
1 cup finely diced country ham
1 (8-ounce) can sliced mushrooms, drained
Entrée Crêpes
Paprika

Place undrained oysters in a saucepan; bring to a boil, and cook about 2 minutes or until edges begin to curl. Drain, reserving liquid. Add enough milk to oyster liquid to make 2¼ cups; set oysters and liquid aside.

Melt butter in a heavy saucepan over low heat. Stir in flour, and cook 1 minute, stirring constantly. Gradually add reserved liquid mixture; spoon a small amount of sauce into egg yolk, and mix well. Gradually stir egg mixture into sauce; cook over medium heat, stirring constantly, until sauce is thickened and bubbly. Stir in salt, pepper, and sherry.

Combine oysters, ham, and mushrooms; stir in 1 cup cream sauce. Spoon about 2 tablespoons filling onto the center of each crêpe. Roll up and place seam side down in a greased 13- x 9- x 2-inch baking dish. Pour the remaining sauce over the crêpes; sprinkle with paprika. Bake at 350° for 15 to 20 minutes or until lightly browned. Yield: about 1 dozen.

Entrée Crêpes:
1 cup all-purpose flour
¾ cup water
¾ cup milk
3 eggs
2 tablespoons melted butter or margarine
¼ teaspoon salt

Combine all ingredients in container of an electric blender; process 1 minute. Scrape down sides of blender container with rubber spatula; process an additional 15 seconds. Refrigerate batter 1 hour. (This allows flour particles to swell and soften so the crêpes are light in texture.)

Brush the bottom of an 8-inch crêpe pan with melted butter; place pan over medium heat until butter is just hot, not smoking.

Pour 3 to 4 tablespoons batter into pan; quickly tilt pan in all directions so batter covers the pan in a thin film. Cook about 1 minute.

Lift edge of crêpe to test for doneness. Crêpe is ready for flipping when it can be shaken loose from pan. Flip crêpe, and cook about 30 seconds on other side. (This side is rarely more than spotty brown.)

Stack crêpes between layers of waxed paper to prevent sticking. Yield: about 1 dozen.

CRANBERRY-APPLE PIE

Pastry (recipe follows)
1 cup sugar
2 tablespoons all-purpose flour
½ teaspoon ground cinnamon
3 cups pared apple slices
2 cups cranberries, sliced in half
¼ cup currants
2 tablespoons butter or margarine

Line a 9-inch piepan with half of pastry; set aside. Combine sugar, flour, and cinnamon; mix well and set aside.

Place half of apple slices in pastry shell; top with half of cranberries, and half of currants. Sprinkle half the sugar mixture over fruit. Repeat layers; dot with butter. Cover with top crust; make slits in several places to allow steam to escape. Seal and flute edges. Bake at 400° for 10 minutes. Reduce heat to 350° and continue baking an additional 55 minutes or until crust is golden brown. Cool before serving. Yield: one 9-inch pie.

Pastry:
1½ cups all-purpose flour
¼ teaspoon salt
¼ cup shortening
¼ cup margarine
3 tablespoons cold water

Combine flour and salt in a bowl; cut in shortening and margarine with pastry blender until mixture resembles coarse meal. Sprinkle cold water over surface; stir with a fork until dry ingredients are moistened. Shape into a ball. Yield: pastry for 1 double-crust 9-inch pie.

CREAMY SWEET CHEESE SPREAD

1 (8-ounce) package cream cheese, softened
¼ cup butter or margarine, softened
1 tablespoon Kahlúa or other coffee-flavored liqueur
1 teaspoon sesame seeds, toasted
Whole wheat wafers

Combine cream cheese and butter, mixing well. Stir in Kahlúa and sesame seeds. Serve with whole wheat wafers. Yield: about 1¼ cups. *Frank Holmes, DeBary, Florida.*

BEEF CUBES IN WINE SAUCE

¼ cup vegetable oil
3 pounds boneless chuck roast, cut into 1-inch cubes
3 tablespoons all-purpose flour
1½ cups water
1 (1⅜-ounce) envelope onion soup mix
½ bay leaf
⅛ teaspoon garlic powder
⅛ teaspoon ground thyme
5 carrots, cut into 1-inch slices, cooked and drained
½ (16-ounce) jar boiled onions, drained
1 (4-ounce) can button mushrooms, drained, or 12 small fresh mushrooms sautéed in butter
2½ cups red cooking wine
Hot cooked noodles or rice (optional)

Heat oil in a heavy, medium skillet; brown beef slowly on all sides. Place beef in a 4-quart casserole; reserve pan drippings.

Stir flour into pan drippings; cook over low heat 1 minute, stirring constantly. Gradually stir in water; add onion soup mix. Cook over medium heat, stirring constantly, until thickened and bubbly. Pour over meat, and stir in bay leaf, garlic powder, and thyme.

Bake at 300° for 2 hours or until meat is very tender. Add carrots, onions, mushrooms, and cooking wine; bake an additional 15 minutes or until vegetables are thoroughly heated. Serve over noodles or rice, if desired. Yield: 6 to 8 servings.   *Lee Roy Perdue,*
Wrens, Georgia.

SPINACH CASSEROLE

2 (10-ounce) packages frozen chopped
    spinach
4 cups cottage cheese
¼ cup melted butter or margarine
1 cup (¼ pound) shredded Cheddar
    cheese
3 eggs, beaten
¼ teaspoon salt
3 tablespoons all-purpose flour

Cook spinach according to package directions; drain. Place spinach on paper towels; squeeze until barely moist. Combine with remaining ingredients, mixing well. Pour into a buttered 2½-quart casserole. Bake, uncovered, at 350° for 1 hour, or until center is set. Yield: 6 to 8 servings.
Dr. Kenneth E. Gawrenski,
Petersburg, Virginia.

BROWNIE PUDDING

1 cup all-purpose flour
¼ cup sugar
2 tablespoons cocoa
2 teaspoons baking powder
½ teaspoon salt
½ cup milk
2 tablespoons melted shortening
1 teaspoon vanilla extract
¾ cup chopped walnuts
¾ cup firmly packed brown sugar
¼ cup cocoa
1½ cups hot water
Vanilla ice cream

Combine flour, ¼ cup sugar, 2 tablespoons cocoa, baking powder, and salt. Add milk, shortening, and vanilla; mix well. Stir in nuts. Pour batter into a greased 8-inch square baking pan.

Combine brown sugar and remaining ¼ cup cocoa; sprinkle over batter. Pour water over top. Bake at 350° for 40 minutes. Serve warm over vanilla ice cream. Yield: 6 to 8 servings.
Emmett Ramey,
Austin, Texas.

CORNBREAD WAFFLES

1½ cups cornmeal
½ cup all-purpose flour
2½ teaspoons baking powder
¾ teaspoon salt
1 tablespoon sugar
1 egg, well beaten
2 tablespoons melted butter or margarine
1¼ cups milk
¼ cup water

Combine cornmeal, flour, baking powder, salt, and sugar; mix well. Combine remaining ingredients, mixing well; add to dry ingredients, stirring just until moistened. Bake in preheated waffle iron. Yield: 3 waffles.   *Mack Herring,*
Mount Olive, North Carolina.

Complement The Flavor Of Pork

Cheddar cheese, rice, and green pepper complement the natural flavor of pork chops in this special recipe submitted by Mrs. Marlene Miller of Trenton, Florida. Fiesta Pork Bake calls for six rib pork chops baked in a casserole. The casserole is easy to assemble and bakes in just an hour.

FIESTA PORK BAKE

2 tablespoons butter or margarine, melted
6 rib pork chops
Salt and pepper to taste
1 (1⅜-ounce) package dry onion soup mix
1 large green pepper, chopped
1 cup uncooked regular rice
½ cup catsup
1 teaspoon Worcestershire sauce
2 cups boiling water
1 cup (¼ pound) shredded Cheddar
    cheese

Coat a shallow 2-quart casserole with melted butter. Sprinkle chops with salt and pepper, and arrange in casserole; top with soup mix, green pepper, and rice. Combine catsup and Worcestershire sauce; spread over rice. Pour in boiling water; cover, and bake at 350° for 55 to 60 minutes or until done. (Additional ½ cup water may be added if casserole becomes too dry.) Remove from oven, and top with cheese. Cover and allow to stand 10 minutes. Yield: 6 servings.

Layer Gingerbread With Fruit

Imagine moist layers of gingerbread filled with a sweet combination of dried fruits and nuts. Serve this favorite of Mrs. Lewis Carroll of Easton, Maryland, with coffee for a special dessert.

OLD ENGLISH GINGERBREAD

1 cup sugar
1 cup shortening
1 cup molasses
2 eggs
3½ cups all-purpose flour
1 teaspoon soda
1 tablespoon ground ginger
1½ teaspoons ground nutmeg
1 teaspoon ground cinnamon
1 cup buttermilk
Fruit filling (recipe follows)
Powdered sugar

Combine sugar and shortening; cream until light and fluffy. Add molasses; beat well. Add eggs, one at a time, beating well after each addition.

Combine dry ingredients; stir well. Add dry ingredients to batter alternately with buttermilk, beating just until combined. Grease and flour three 9-inch cakepans; line with waxed paper. Pour batter evenly into cakepans; bake at 350° for 30 minutes. Cool layers in pans 10 minutes; remove from pans, and cool completely on wire racks. Spread fruit filling between layers of cake. Sprinkle top with powdered sugar. Yield: one 9-inch layer cake.

Fruit filling:

1 cup raisins
1½ cups water
½ cup sugar
1 tablespoon cornstarch
½ cup chopped dried figs
½ cup chopped dates
¼ cup chopped dried apricots
1 tablespoon lemon juice
1¾ teaspoons grated lemon rind
½ cup chopped nuts

Soak raisins in water about 5 minutes.
Combine sugar and cornstarch; mix well. Combine all ingredients except nuts in a saucepan; cook, stirring constantly, over medium heat until thickened. Stir in nuts. Cool slightly. Yield: enough filling for three 9-inch layers.

Make A Perfect Chiffon Cake

The light, rich chiffon cake is in a class all by itself, even though it has some characteristics of both sponge and butter cakes.

Sponge cakes use stiffly beaten egg whites as leavening; so do chiffon cakes, but baking powder is also included. Butter cakes are made with solid shortening; chiffon cakes use oil. Similar because some type of shortening is used in the batter, chiffon cakes are quicker and easier to prepare than butter cakes, as the process of creaming butter and sugar is eliminated.

Despite some similarities, chiffon cakes are not mixed by the same procedure as either sponge or butter cakes. The proper method is illustrated in the step-by-step photographs, using the recipe for Vanilla Chiffon Cake included here. To ensure your success, also refer to the following tips.

—Proper beating of the egg whites is the beginning of a light, tender-textured chiffon cake. For egg whites to beat to greatest volume, they must be at room temperature. Make sure the bowl and utensils used for beating egg whites are clean. Do not use a plastic bowl, as it may retain a greasy film that will inhibit foaming.

The function of cream of tartar in chiffon cakes is to stabilize the foam. Sugar is also added at the soft-peak stage to increase stability. However, sugar can retard foaming if not added slowly; add only 1 to 2 tablespoons at a time, continuing to beat until stiff peaks form.

—When combining the stiffly beaten egg whites with the egg yolk mixture, follow this procedure: Using a rubber spatula, fold gently with a down, up, and over motion; rotate the bowl after each stroke. Continue folding until there are no streaks remaining in the batter. Never stir, as it will force air out of the egg whites.

—Bake a chiffon cake in an ungreased tube pan on the bottom rack of the oven. The cake is done when it springs back and leaves no imprint when it is lightly pressed with your fingertips.

—To keep the cake from falling or shrinking, turn upside down in the pan to cool. Before removing from pan, loosen from sides by sliding a metal spatula around pan.

Despite its delicate texture, Vanilla Chiffon Cake is sturdy enough to hold a frosting, yet rich enough to serve plain.

VANILLA CHIFFON CAKE

1 cup sifted all-purpose flour
1 cup sugar, divided
1½ teaspoons baking powder
¼ teaspoon salt
¼ cup vegetable oil
4 egg yolks
¼ cup water
1 teaspoon vanilla extract
4 egg whites, at room temperature
½ teaspoon cream of tartar

Sift together flour, ½ cup sugar, baking powder, and salt in a small mixing bowl. Make a well in center; add oil, egg yolks, water, and vanilla. Beat at high speed of electric mixer about 5 minutes or until satin smooth.

Combine egg whites and cream of tartar in a large mixing bowl; beat at medium speed until soft peaks form. Add remaining ½ cup sugar, 2 tablespoons at a time, and beat about 4 minutes at medium speed or until stiff peaks form. (Peaks should stand up straight when beaters are lifted from bowl.)

Pour egg yolk mixture in a thin, steady stream over entire surface of egg whites; then gently fold yolk mixture into whites.

Pour batter into an ungreased 10-inch tube pan, spreading evenly with a spatula. Bake at 325° for 1 hour or until cake springs back when touched lightly. Remove from oven; invert pan, and cool completely before removing from pan. Yield: one 10-inch cake.

Mrs. John A. Shoemaker,
Louisville, Kentucky.

Step 1—*Sift dry ingredients into a small mixing bowl. Make a well in center; add oil, egg yolks, water, and vanilla. Beat at high speed of electric mixer about 5 minutes or until satin smooth.*

Step 2—*Combine egg whites and cream of tartar in a large mixing bowl; beat at medium speed until soft peaks form. Add ½ cup sugar, 2 tablespoons at a time, beating until stiff peaks form.*

Step 3—*Pour egg yolk mixture in a thin, steady stream over entire surface of egg whites.*

Step 4—*Using a rubber spatula, gently fold yolk mixture into whites. Pour batter into an ungreased 10-inch tube pan, spreading evenly. Bake at 325° for 1 hour or until cake springs back when lightly touched.*

Step 5—*Invert pan, and allow cake to cool completely before removing from pan.*

Garlic Can Be Subtle Or Pungent

Pungent or subtle, garlic adds the right accent to these entrées and side dishes. Garlic tastes sharpest when finely minced or crushed, and uncooked. Garlic Dressing is a pungent example.

Garlic becomes milder and more subtle in Mixed Vegetable Stir-Fry. Here, cooking large pieces of garlic tames its potency and imparts a sweet, nutlike flavor.

When buying garlic, select firm, plump bulbs that have dry, unbroken skins. Store in a cool, dry place that is well ventilated. The flavor will remain sharp for up to four months.

CHICKEN TETRAZZINI

1 (6-pound) hen
2 teaspoons salt
½ teaspoon pepper
½ cup butter or margarine
2 medium-size green peppers, chopped
¼ cup plus 1 tablespoon all-purpose flour
2 cups milk
2 (10¾-ounce) cans cream of mushroom soup, undiluted
2 (2-ounce) jars chopped pimiento
1 clove garlic, crushed
¼ teaspoon garlic salt
1 teaspoon Worcestershire sauce
½ cup cooking sherry
2 (4-ounce) cans sliced mushrooms, drained
6 cups (1½ pounds) shredded process American cheese, divided
¾ cup grated Parmesan cheese
1 (1-pound) package spaghetti noodles
1 cup sliced almonds
1 (4-ounce) can whole mushrooms, drained

Place hen in a large Dutch oven, and cover with water. Add salt and pepper. Bring to a boil. Cover and reduce heat; simmer until tender. Remove hen from broth, reserving broth. Cool hen; remove meat from bones. Dice meat.

Melt butter in a small Dutch oven over low heat. Add green pepper; sauté until tender. Add flour and stir until smooth; cook 1 minute, stirring constantly. Gradually stir in milk. Add soup, pimiento, garlic, garlic salt, Worcestershire sauce, sherry, sliced mushrooms, chicken, 4 cups American cheese, and Parmesan cheese; stir well. Cook over medium heat 10 minutes, stirring occasionally.

Add enough water to reserved broth to measure 5 quarts. Bring broth to a boil in a large Dutch oven. Cook noodles in boiling broth until tender; drain and rinse.

Lightly grease two 13- x 9- x 2-inch baking dishes. Spread half of noodles evenly into 2 baking dishes; spread half of chicken mixture evenly over noodles. Repeat layers once, using remaining noodles and chicken mixture. Sprinkle remaining cheese evenly over both casseroles; top with almonds and remaining mushrooms. Bake at 350° for 10 to 15 minutes or until thoroughly heated. Yield: 16 to 20 servings.

Note: Casseroles can be frozen for later use. Cover with aluminum foil; seal securely, label, and freeze. To serve, thaw in refrigerator. Bake at 350° for 35 minutes or until bubbly. Remove foil during last 10 minutes of baking.
Mrs. Ann Davis,
Waco, Texas.

GARLIC SHRIMP

2 tablespoons vegetable oil
2 tablespoons butter or margarine
8 cloves garlic, chopped
1 pound shrimp, peeled and deveined
Salt and pepper to taste
Lemon or lime wedges

Heat oil and butter in a large skillet. Add garlic and shrimp; sprinkle with salt and pepper. Sauté 2 to 3 minutes or until shrimp turn pink. Turn shrimp with spatula; cook 2 minutes longer on other side. Remove shrimp to serving platter; garnish with lemon wedges. Yield: 2 to 3 servings.
Mrs. James W. Bachus,
Austin, Texas.

MIXED VEGETABLE STIR-FRY

2 tablespoons vegetable oil
1 medium clove garlic, cut in half
2 carrots, diagonally sliced ¼-inch thick
2 stalks celery, diagonally sliced ¼-inch thick
3 to 4 green onions, cut into 1-inch pieces
2 medium-size yellow squash, diagonally sliced ¼-inch thick
1 green or red pepper, cut into ½-inch strips
1 tablespoon soy sauce
Salt and pepper to taste
1 tablespoon sliced almonds (optional)

Heat vegetable oil in a wok or a heavy skillet. Add the garlic, and sauté over medium heat until garlic is golden brown. Discard garlic.

Add carrots and celery; stir-fry 3 to 4 minutes or until partially cooked. Add onion, squash, and green pepper; stir-fry 2 to 4 minutes or until vegetables are crisp-tender. Add soy sauce, salt, and pepper; mix lightly. Sprinkle with almonds, if desired. Yield: 4 servings.
Mrs. Nancy Reel,
Kirbyville, Texas.

COMPANY HASH BROWNS

4 large baking potatoes, peeled and cut into 1-inch cubes
½ pound fresh mushrooms, thinly sliced
4 tablespoons melted butter or margarine, divided
¼ cup olive or vegetable oil
¾ teaspoon salt
⅛ teaspoon pepper
¾ cup cooked English peas
2 tablespoons chopped parsley
2 cloves garlic, minced

Cook potatoes in boiling salted water, uncovered, for 4 minutes; drain.

Sauté mushrooms in 2 tablespoons butter in small skillet until tender; set aside.

Heat oil in large skillet; add potato cubes. Cook until tender and golden brown, turning as necessary. Sprinkle with salt and pepper. Add mushrooms and butter mixture, peas, and remaining butter; cook over low heat until hot. Add parsley and garlic; stir gently, mixing well. Yield: about 6 servings.
Lilly S. Bradley,
Salem, Virginia.

SAVORY BROCCOLI

1 pound fresh broccoli, cut into spears
¼ cup olive oil
2 cloves garlic
2 red or green peppers, cut into strips
2 tablespoons vinegar
¼ cup beef broth
Salt and white pepper to taste

Cook broccoli in boiling salted water 10 minutes or until tender; drain.

Heat oil in large skillet; add garlic and sauté until golden brown. Remove garlic and set aside. Add red pepper to skillet; sauté 2 to 3 minutes. Crush garlic; add garlic, vinegar, broth, salt, and pepper to red pepper; stir well. Simmer 10 minutes. Add broccoli, and cook until heated. Arrange broccoli and red pepper on serving platter; pour pan juices over vegetables. Yield: 4 to 6 servings. *Mrs. Maruja Hatheway, Austin, Texas.*

GARLIC DRESSING

1 cup vegetable oil
½ cup sugar
¼ cup red wine vinegar
⅔ cup catsup
½ cup chili sauce
1 large onion, finely chopped
4 cloves garlic, crushed
1 teaspoon salt
1 teaspoon paprika
Juice of 1 lemon

Combine oil, sugar, and vinegar; beat with wire whisk until blended. Add remaining ingredients, mixing well. Yield: 3½ cups.

Note: Three-fourths cup of mayonnaise may be added to make Thousand Island Dressing. *Judy Eveloff, Springfield, Illinois.*

GARLIC SPOONBREAD

¾ cup cornmeal
1½ cups water
2 cups (½ pound) shredded sharp
  Cheddar cheese
¼ cup butter or margarine, softened
2 cloves garlic, crushed
½ teaspoon salt
1 cup milk
5 egg yolks, beaten
½ pound bacon, cooked and crumbled
4 egg whites

Combine cornmeal and water in a large saucepan; cook over medium heat until thickened. Remove from heat. Add cheese, butter, garlic, and salt; stir until cheese melts. Gradually stir in milk; add egg yolks, stirring well. Add bacon, reserving a small amount for garnish; mix well.

Beat egg whites until stiff but not dry. Gently fold egg whites into cornmeal mixture. Pour into a lightly greased 2½-quart soufflé dish. Bake at 325° for 65 minutes. Sprinkle reserved bacon on top, and serve immediately. Yield: 6 to 8 servings. *Mrs. John Rucker, Louisville, Kentucky.*

Spice Up Meals With Chili

A steaming bowl of chili is perfect for serving on a cool autumn day, and it makes an ideal dish for casual entertaining—especially before or after a football game.

Everyone likes chili with a different degree of spiciness, different kinds of beans, and sometimes different combinations of meat, as these recipes prove. Our Double-Meat Chili starts with dried pinto beans and features a combination of ground beef or venison and lean ground pork.

ROUNDUP CHILI

1 to 1½ pounds ground beef
1 (28-ounce) can tomatoes, undrained
3½ cups water
2 (16-ounce) cans kidney beans, undrained
1 (6-ounce) can tomato paste
2 to 3 stalks celery, chopped
1 green pepper, chopped
1 large onion, chopped
1 tablespoon chili powder
Salt and pepper to taste

Cook ground beef in a Dutch oven until browned, stirring frequently to crumble. Drain off pan drippings. Stir in remaining ingredients; simmer 2 to 2½ hours, stirring occasionally. Yield: 5 to 6 servings. *Mrs. Barbara Bodensick, Newport News, Virginia.*

OLD-FASHIONED SPICY CHILI

2 pounds ground beef
1 medium onion, chopped
4 cloves garlic, minced
2 tablespoons ground cumin
2 teaspoons salt
4 to 6 tablespoons chili powder
2 tablespoons all-purpose flour
1½ tablespoons sugar
2 (16-ounce) cans kidney beans, undrained
1 (16-ounce) can whole tomatoes, undrained and chopped
1 (6-ounce) can tomato paste

Combine first 5 ingredients in a large Dutch oven; cook over medium heat, stirring to crumble meat, until meat is browned and onion is tender. Drain off pan drippings. Stir in chili powder, flour, and sugar. Add remaining ingredients; stir well (mixture will be very thick). Cover and simmer 30 minutes over low heat. Yield: 8 servings. *Cathy Huddleston, Charlotte, North Carolina.*

SIMPLE CHILI

1 clove garlic, crushed
2 large onions, chopped
2 tablespoons vegetable oil
2 pounds lean ground beef
2 (16-ounce) cans whole tomatoes, undrained and chopped
1 (6-ounce) can tomato paste
2 tablespoons chili powder
½ teaspoon vinegar
⅛ teaspoon ground red pepper
1 teaspoon salt
2 (16-ounce) cans kidney beans, undrained and mashed
2 whole cloves
1 small bay leaf

Sauté garlic and onion in oil. Add ground beef; cook over low heat until browned, stirring to crumble. Add remaining ingredients; simmer, uncovered, 1 hour. Yield: 10 servings. *Mrs. S. D. Thomas, Dothan, Alabama.*

DOUBLE-MEAT CHILI

½ pound dried pinto beans
2 (28-ounce) cans whole tomatoes, undrained and chopped
1½ pounds (about 5 large) onions, chopped
1 pound (about 4 large) green peppers, chopped
2 cloves garlic, crushed
½ cup chopped parsley
2½ pounds ground beef or venison
1 pound lean ground pork
½ cup melted butter or margarine
1½ tablespoons vegetable oil
½ cup chili powder
2 tablespoons salt
1½ teaspoons pepper
1½ teaspoons cumin seeds
1½ teaspoons monosodium glutamate

Sort and wash pinto beans. Place in a 6-quart Dutch oven, and cover with water 2 inches above beans. Let beans soak overnight.

Cook beans in water over medium heat about 1 hour or until tender. Reduce heat; add tomatoes and simmer 5 minutes. Add onion and green pepper; cook about 10 minutes or until tender, stirring often. Stir in garlic and parsley.

Cook meat in butter and oil until browned, stirring to crumble; add to bean mixture. Stir in remaining ingredients; cover and simmer 1 hour. Uncover and simmer an additional 30 minutes. Yield: 12 to 15 servings. *DeLea Lonadier, Montgomery, Louisiana.*

RANCH CHILI AND BEANS

3 pounds ground beef
6 cups water
2 bay leaves
8 cloves garlic, crushed
4 to 6 tablespoons chili powder
2 teaspoons salt
1 teaspoon ground cumin
1 teaspoon oregano leaves
¼ teaspoon pepper
¼ to ½ teaspoon cayenne pepper
2 to 3 tablespoons paprika
1 tablespoon sugar
2 (15-ounce) cans ranch-style beans

Cook ground beef in a large Dutch oven until browned, stirring to crumble; drain off pan drippings. Add water and bay leaves; cover and simmer over low heat 1½ hours. Add next 9 ingredients; simmer 30 minutes. Stir in beans; simmer an additional 15 to 20 minutes. Yield: 6 to 8 servings.
Mrs. Diana McConnell,
Denton, Texas.

Serve Versatile Rice

As long as there's rice on the pantry shelf, you have the beginnings of an array of tempting side dishes.

Rice Medley is a fine example. It's quickly prepared using instant rice and gets extra color and flavor from pecans, raisins, and an assortment of vegetables. Then there's Golden Rice and a puffy soufflé, both rich with Cheddar cheese.

RICE-SHRIMP SALAD

3 cups cooked regular rice, cooled
2 tablespoons commercial French salad
   dressing
1 cup cooked, diced shrimp
1 cup chopped celery
½ cucumber, peeled and sliced
¼ cup minced onion
1 tablespoon vegetable oil
1 tablespoon lemon juice
1 teaspoon salt
⅛ teaspoon hot sauce
Lettuce (optional)
Tomato wedges (optional)

Combine all ingredients except lettuce and tomatoes, tossing lightly; chill. Serve on lettuce leaves and garnish with tomato wedges, if desired. Yield: about 4 servings.
Cindy Murphy,
Knoxville, Tennessee.

RICE MEDLEY

2 cups uncooked instant rice
3 medium carrots, cut into 2-inch strips
1 cup chopped onion
1 bunch scallions or green onions, cut
   into 1-inch lengths
½ cup seedless raisins
¼ cup butter or margarine
2 cups water
1 (10-ounce) package frozen English peas
2 teaspoons salt
1 cup pecan halves
1 tablespoon butter or margarine

Combine rice, carrots, onion, scallions, and raisins; sauté in ¼ cup butter about 5 minutes or until rice is lightly browned, stirring frequently. Add water, peas, and salt; bring to a boil, separating frozen peas. Reduce heat; cover and simmer 5 minutes.

Sauté pecans lightly in 1 tablespoon butter; stir into rice mixture. Yield: 8 servings.
Mrs. Loren Martin,
Knoxville, Tennessee.

GOLDEN RICE

2 cups cooked regular rice
2 cups (½ pound) shredded Cheddar
   cheese
3 cups grated carrots
2 eggs, beaten
⅔ cup milk
1 tablespoon minced onion
1 teaspoon salt
¼ teaspoon pepper

Combine all ingredients, stirring well. Spoon into a greased 1½-quart casserole. Bake at 350° for 1 hour or until set. Yield: 6 servings.
Patty Soule,
Austin, Texas.

RICE-CHEESE SOUFFLE

2 tablespoons butter or margarine
2 tablespoons all-purpose flour
1 cup milk
¼ teaspoon salt
1 cup (¼ pound) shredded Cheddar
   cheese
3 eggs, separated
1 cup cooked regular rice
¼ teaspoon cream of tartar

Melt butter in a heavy saucepan over low heat; add flour, and cook 1 minute, stirring constantly. Gradually add milk; cook over medium heat, stirring constantly, until thickened. Add salt and

cheese; stir until cheese melts. Remove from heat; cool slightly.

Beat egg yolks slightly; stir into cheese sauce along with rice.

Combine egg whites and cream of tartar, beating until stiff but not dry; fold into rice mixture. Pour into a lightly greased 1-quart casserole or soufflé dish. Bake at 325° for 40 minutes or until soufflé is golden brown. Yield: 4 to 6 servings.
Mrs. Robert Collins,
Fairfax, Missouri.

Try A Special Fruit Salad

When Banana-Mixed Fruit Salad is on the menu, any meal is special. This medley of four kinds of fruit and walnuts is a favorite of Mrs. B. Blackmon of Evergreen, Alabama. The whipped cream dressing she serves with it is so delicious you'll want to serve it on all your fruit salads.

BANANA-MIXED FRUIT SALAD

1 (8¼-ounce) can pineapple chunks
3 medium oranges, peeled and sectioned
⅓ cup coarsely chopped walnuts
1 to 2 medium apples
3 bananas
Whipped Cream Fruit Dressing
Lettuce (optional)

Drain pineapple, reserving 2 tablespoons juice for dressing. Combine pineapple, oranges, and nuts in a large bowl.

Just before serving, cube apples and slice bananas; add to fruit mixture. Stir in enough dressing to moisten. Serve promptly; place on lettuce leaves, if desired. Yield: 6 to 8 servings.

Whipped Cream Fruit Dressing:

1 egg, beaten
2 tablespoons sugar
2 tablespoons pineapple juice
2 tablespoons lemon juice
½ cup whipping cream

Combine egg, sugar, and juices in top of a double boiler. Cook until thickened, stirring constantly. Let mixture cool.

Beat whipping cream until soft peaks form; fold into cooled mixture. Serve with any fruit salad. Yield: about 1½ cups.

December

Southern hospitality shines during the festive month of December as friends and families gather to celebrate the season with good food and fellowship. You can add the flavor of a country inn to your festivities with the home-style recipes from four of the South's best inns. The specialties range from a peanut-stuffed turkey to a groaning board of holiday breads or desserts.

Because Christmas just would not be Christmas without tins filled with homemade candies, we offer thirteen special recipes plus candy-making tips. And to start the round of seasonal parties, we present a feast of foods designed for a gala open house.

Before you plan your holiday salads, consider our festive suggestions. From a cabbage-fruit combination to a tart cranberry selection, you will find just the one you want.

Share The Holidays With Candy

These homemade candies set the holiday mood as brightly as a gaily decorated tree. From fudge and pralines to peanut brittle and mints, candies are a special part of Christmas in the South.

For generations, Southerners have made a fine art of candymaking. Recipes are handed down from mother to daughter, with each generation adding special touches of its own.

Our readers have shared candy recipes that are their traditional favorites. With such delights as Date Logs, Apricot Balls, and Peanut Butter Creams, you'll want to make several flavors—for family and guests or to give as gifts.

For Never-Fail Candy

To ensure your success with these holiday confections, here are some tips on candymaking.

—Use the size saucepan recommended in the candy recipe. (Candy mixtures usually triple in volume when boiling.) A heavy, straight-sided saucepan generally works best.

—A good candy thermometer is almost a necessity. Always test a thermometer (even a new one) by letting it stand in boiling water for 10 minutes. If the thermometer doesn't register 212°, allow for the inaccuracy when cooking each batch. Refer to the chart for temperatures of the different stages used in candymaking.

—When using a candy thermometer, make sure the thermometer bulb is in the boiling mixture but is not touching the bottom of the pan.

—If you do not have a candy thermometer, the cold-water test may be used to check all candy stages except thread stage. Drop a small amount of syrup into a cup of ice-cold water; then test with your fingers to determine consistency (see chart). For thread stage, syrup should spin a 2-inch thread when dropped from a spoon.

—To prevent sugaring, follow directions in recipe for stirring and covering. Use moderate heat so candy does not come to the boiling point too quickly. When the recipe calls for beating, cool the candy to 110° first.

—Avoid doubling a candy recipe. It is better to make a second batch.

—During humid or rainy weather, cook candy until candy thermometer registers 1 to 2 degrees higher than the recipe directions specify.

TESTS FOR CANDY STAGES

Stage	Temperature	Cold-Water Test
Thread	230° to 234°	*
Soft ball	234° to 240°	Syrup forms a soft ball that flattens when removed from water
Firm ball	242° to 248°	Syrup forms a firm ball that does not flatten when removed from water
Hard ball	250° to 268°	Syrup forms a hard, yet pliable, ball when removed from water
Soft crack	270° to 290°	When dropped into water, syrup separates into threads that are hard but not brittle
Hard crack	300° to 310°	When dropped into water, syrup separates into threads that are hard and brittle

*Syrup spins 2-inch thread when dropped from a spoon

PRALINES

1 cup buttermilk
1 teaspoon soda
3 cups sugar
1 cup butter or margarine, melted
2 tablespoons light corn syrup
Pinch of salt
1 teaspoon vanilla extract
3 cups broken pecans

Combine buttermilk and soda in a 5-quart saucepan, stirring until soda is dissolved; add sugar, butter, corn syrup, and salt. Bring mixture to a boil; cook, stirring constantly, until mixture reaches soft ball stage (236°). Remove from heat, and let stand until lukewarm (110°).

Add vanilla and pecans to candy, beating until mixture begins to thicken and loses its gloss. Drop by tablespoonfuls onto a lightly buttered baking sheet or waxed paper; let stand until firm. Store in an airtight container. Yield: about 18 pralines.

Mrs. Ned T. McElmuray,
Bowie, Texas.

COCONUT CANDY

2 cups firmly packed brown sugar
2 cups sugar
¼ cup light corn syrup
1⅓ cups half-and-half
¼ cup melted butter or margarine
¼ teaspoon salt
1 teaspoon vanilla extract
1½ cups flaked coconut

Combine sugar, corn syrup, and half-and-half in a large Dutch oven. Cook over medium heat to soft ball stage (238°), stirring constantly. Remove from heat; add butter and salt without stirring. Cool to lukewarm (110°).

Add vanilla to candy, and beat with a wooden spoon until mixture is creamy and loses its gloss. Fold in coconut; pour into a greased 9-inch square pan. Cut into 1-inch squares. Yield: about 6 dozen squares. *Mrs. W. P. Chambers,*
Louisville, Kentucky.

PENUCHE

6 cups sugar, divided
2 cups evaporated milk
2 tablespoons corn syrup
¼ teaspoon soda
½ cup butter
1 teaspoon vanilla extract
2 cups chopped pecans

Place 2 cups sugar in a heavy skillet; cook over low heat until melted and golden brown, stirring constantly.

Combine remaining sugar, evaporated milk, and corn syrup in a large saucepan; bring to a boil while sugar is caramelizing.

Slowly pour caramelized sugar into boiling sugar mixture, stirring constantly. Cook, stirring occasionally, to soft ball stage (236°). Remove from heat, and immediately add soda; stir vigorously as it foams. Add butter, stirring only until melted. Cool about 20 minutes or until lukewarm.

Add vanilla, and beat until thick and creamy. Stir in pecans. Pour into a buttered 13- x 9- x 2-inch pan. Cool and cut into 1-inch squares. Yield: about 8 dozen squares. *Mrs. Louis E. Howell,*
Orange, Texas.

ENGLISH TOFFEE

1 pound butter or margarine
2 tablespoons water
2 cups sugar
½ teaspoon salt
2 cups finely chopped walnuts
1 (8-ounce) bar milk chocolate

Combine butter and water in a 4-quart Dutch oven; cook over medium heat until butter melts. Add sugar and salt, mixing well. Bring to a boil, stirring constantly. Boil gently until mixture begins to lighten in color. Add 1 cup walnuts; continue cooking, stirring constantly, until candy thermometer registers 298°.

Pour syrup mixture into a buttered 15- x 10-inch jellyroll pan, spreading to edges of pan. Cool slightly; mark into 1-inch squares with sharp edge of a knife. Cool thoroughly.

Melt chocolate in top of a double boiler over boiling water. Spread chocolate over toffee; sprinkle remaining walnuts over chocolate. Let stand until chocolate is firm. Break toffee into squares. Yield: about 3 pounds.
Mrs. Herbert F. Schneider,
Northbrook, Illinois.

FUDGE SCOTCH RING

1 cup walnut halves
1 (6-ounce) package semisweet chocolate morsels
1 (6-ounce) package butterscotch morsels
1 (14-ounce) can sweetened condensed milk
1 cup coarsely chopped walnuts
½ teaspoon vanilla extract
Red and green candied cherries

Line bottom of a 9-inch piepan with a 12-inch square of aluminum foil. Place a custard cup in center of pan. Place walnut halves around custard cup, forming a 2-inch wide ring; set aside.

Combine chocolate and butterscotch morsels and condensed milk in top of a double boiler; place over hot (not boiling) water. Stir until morsels have melted and mixture begins to thicken. Remove from heat; stir in chopped walnuts and vanilla. Chill about 1 hour.

Spoon chocolate-butterscotch mixture in mounds over walnut halves; remove custard cup. Decorate with candied cherries. Yield: one 8-inch ring.
Mrs. Gay Bridges,
Oneida, Tennessee.

PEANUT BUTTER CREAMS

¼ cup powdered sugar
½ cup sweetened condensed milk
1 cup creamy peanut butter
1 (6-ounce) package semisweet chocolate morsels
7 tablespoons chocolate-flavored decorator candies

Combine sugar, condensed milk, and peanut butter in a medium mixing bowl; stir until well blended. Stir in chocolate morsels, and chill until firm. Shape into ¾-inch balls, and roll each in decorator candies. Refrigerate until firm. Yield: 6 to 7 dozen.
Mrs. Gene Crow,
Dallas, Texas.

POTATO CANDY

¼ cup hot mashed potatoes
1 teaspoon melted butter
1¾ cups powdered sugar
1½ cups flaked coconut
Dash of salt
¼ teaspoon grated lemon or orange rind
½ teaspoon vanilla extract

Combine potatoes and butter in a medium bowl. Gradually add sugar, beating until thoroughly blended. Add remaining ingredients, mixing well. Drop by teaspoonfuls onto waxed paper. Let stand until firm. Yield: about 2 dozen.
Adele Cohill,
Nokomis, Florida.

NEVER-FAIL PEANUT BRITTLE

3 cups sugar
1 cup light corn syrup
½ cup water
1 pound raw peanuts
1 tablespoon butter or margarine
2 teaspoons soda
1 teaspoon salt

Combine sugar, corn syrup, and water in a Dutch oven; cook over low heat until mixture spins a thread (230° to 234°). Add peanuts; cook to soft crack stage (about 290°), stirring constantly. Remove from heat. Add butter, soda, and salt; mix well.

Spread mixture thinly onto 2 warm, buttered 15- x 10- x 1-inch jellyroll pans. Cool and break into pieces. Yield: about 2 pounds.
Debbie Ashley,
Grand Prairie, Texas.

PARTY MINTS

1 (1-pound) package powdered sugar
½ cup margarine, softened
2 tablespoons evaporated milk
4 to 5 drops of peppermint flavoring
Few drops of desired food coloring

Combine all ingredients in a large mixing bowl. Beat at high speed of electric mixer until well blended. Knead until smooth.

Shape mints in rubber candy molds, and place on baking sheets. Cover with a paper towel, and let stand overnight to harden. Yield: 8½ to 9 dozen mints.
Florence L. Costello,
Chattanooga, Tennessee.

KENTUCKY COLONELS

½ cup butter, softened
3 tablespoons sweetened condensed milk
⅓ cup plus 2 teaspoons bourbon
7½ cups powdered sugar
½ cup finely chopped pecans
1 (6-ounce) package semisweet chocolate morsels
1 tablespoon melted paraffin
Pecan halves

Combine butter, condensed milk, and bourbon in a large mixing bowl; add sugar, and knead until mixture is well blended and does not stick to hands. Knead in chopped pecans. Shape into 1-inch balls.

Combine chocolate morsels and paraffin in top of a double boiler; place over hot water, stirring until chocolate is melted. Using a toothpick, dip each ball of candy into chocolate mixture. Place on waxed paper. Remove toothpick, and gently press a pecan half on each. Yield: about 6 dozen.

Note: If desired, 1 tablespoon melted shortening may be substituted for paraffin in chocolate mixture. Chocolate will be soft to the touch and slightly sticky.
Joyce Johnson,
Reeds Spring, Missouri.

FAST FUDGE

2 cups sugar
⅔ cup evaporated skim milk
12 large marshmallows
½ cup butter
Few grains of salt
1 (6-ounce) package semisweet chocolate
   morsels
1 cup chopped nuts
1 teaspoon vanilla extract

Combine first 5 ingredients in a large saucepan. Cook over medium heat until mixture comes to a boil, stirring constantly; boil 5 minutes, stirring constantly. Remove from heat.

Add chocolate morsels to marshmallow mixture, stirring until melted. Add nuts and vanilla, stirring well. Spread evenly in a buttered 8-inch square pan. Cut into 1-inch squares when cool. Yield: about 5 dozen square.

Mrs. Charlene Keebler,
Savannah, Georgia.

DATE LOGS

½ cup margarine
1 (8-ounce) package chopped dates
1 cup sugar
1 egg
1 teaspoon vanilla extract
2 cups crisp rice cereal
2 cups chopped pecans
1 cup flaked coconut

Combine first 5 ingredients in a large saucepan; cook over low heat for 10 minutes, stirring constantly. Remove from heat; add cereal and pecans, mixing well.

Shape into two 11-inch logs, and roll each in coconut. Cool and slice thin. Yield: two 11-inch logs. *Marie Bilbo,*
Meadville, Mississippi.

APRICOT BALLS

3 (6-ounce) packages dried apricots, cut
   into small pieces
1 (14-ounce) package flaked coconut
1 cup chopped nuts
1 (14-ounce) can sweetened condensed
   milk
½ cup powdered sugar

Combine apricots, coconut, and nuts in a large mixing bowl; add condensed milk, mixing well. Shape into 1-inch balls, and roll each in powdered sugar. Yield: about 9 dozen.

Mrs. Charles DeHaven,
Owensboro, Kentucky.

Taste The Holidays At Southern Country Inns

From a historic setting in the Shenandoah Valley to a contemporary retreat in the Ozark Mountains of Arkansas, country inns take on a festive spirit during the Christmas season. Though the inns are often in out-of-the-way rural surroundings, their bountiful tables and restful accommodations make the journey worthwhile.

The meals at the inns are characterized by an abundance of good food, and during the holidays each inn offers specialties fit for a feast. On these pages we sample a turkey dinner with all the trimmings from Middletown, Virginia's, Wayside Inn; feast on holiday side dishes from the Colonial Inn in Hillsborough, North Carolina; add traditional Shaker breads from Kentucky's Inn at Pleasant Hill; and complete the celebration with homemade desserts from Arkansas' Red Apple Inn.

The Wayside Inn, tucked away in Virginia's Shenandoah Valley, has welcomed visitors with distinctive food and warm Southern charm since 1797. Located about 75 miles west of Washington, D.C., this restored country inn has maintained a traditional menu offering some of the same foods that were favorites of early travelers.

On Christmas Day, guests feast on roast turkey and Wayside's delicious Peanut Dressing, which is skillfully seasoned and filled with salted Virginia-grown peanuts. Vegetables served family style complement the dinner.

Homemade bread and real whipped butter are served with every meal. Ambrosia Pie, a coconut custard topped with whipped cream, mandarin oranges, and coconut, is the featured dessert on Christmas Day.

For over 200 years, the Colonial Inn has upheld a reputation for friendliness, comfort, and exceptional Old-South cooking. Located only 11 miles from Durham and Chapel Hill, it still holds historical significance as a hospitality center.

When traveling the area in Revolutionary War days, Cornwallis chose the inn for his headquarters. One of the inn's specialties, Cornwallis Yams, reflects that bit of history. The yams are especially suited to the holiday season, as they're flavored with sugar and spices before baking, then sprinkled with flaked coconut.

The Colonial Inn is known for serving a great variety of vegetables and other side dishes. "We built our reputation on Southern hospitality and Old-South cooking, and vegetables are part of it," explains Pete Thompson, innkeeper.

Some stop at Pleasant Hill, Kentucky, about a 25-mile drive from Lexington, to tour the restored village where Shakers lived from 1805 to 1910. Others stop to stay overnight in the original, but modernized, buildings. But serious visitors come to sample the food, served three times a day, surrounded by the simplicity of Shaker tradition.

The kitchen staff follows many recipes adapted from old Shaker journals, and waitresses in Shaker dress serve heaping bowls of vegetables. Pleasant Hill still maintains its own herb and vegetable gardens, and in the summer much of the produce served is grown in the village. Ovens produce a variety of hot breads.

For the Shakers, Christmas Day was like any other day, with the exception of exchanging spiritual gifts of friendship and forgiveness and gathering gifts for the poor. The daily practices of abstinence and hard work continued, and the beliefs in simplicity, humility, and charity were upheld.

Home-style baking and secluded accommodations beckon travelers through the Ozark Mountains to the Red Apple Inn. In addition to overnight guests, many visitors make the 65-mile drive from Little Rock to Heber Springs just to enjoy a leisurely dinner or Sunday lunch.

During the Christmas season, the inn's menu reflects the holiday spirit with specialty desserts. Plum Pudding, Orange-Pecan Pie, and a chocolate Yule Log covered with Mocha Butter Cream Frosting and topped with pistachio nuts are added to the array of regularly featured desserts.

Homemade Bread Is The Specialty At Pleasant Hill

Like the surroundings in this restored Shaker village, the food at Pleasant Hill is plain and simple. Included in the fare is an unbelievably delicious assortment of homemade breads.

Prepared daily, thick slices of White Bread, Whole Wheat Rolls, and crisp

Corn Sticks are served at each meal. A country breakfast and relaxing afternoon tea add more breads to the selection. Pumpkin Muffins, Lemon Bread, and Cranberry Fruit-Nut Bread are just a few that you can choose from.

WHITE BREAD

1 package dry yeast
¼ cup warm water (105° to 115°)
2 cups milk
½ cup shortening
¼ cup sugar
1 tablespoon plus 1 teaspoon salt
2 cups water
12 cups instant blending flour

Soften yeast in ¼ cup warm water; set aside.

Scald milk; add shortening, sugar, and salt, stirring until shortening melts. Stir in 2 cups water and yeast mixture. Gradually add flour, stirring after each addition; dough should be stiff.

Turn dough out on a floured surface, and knead until smooth and elastic. Shape into a ball, and place in a greased bowl. Cover and let stand in a warm place (85°), free from drafts, for 1 hour or until doubled in bulk.

Divide dough into 4 equal portions, and shape into balls. Cover and let stand 10 to 15 minutes. Place each portion in a greased and floured 9- x 5- x 3-inch loafpan; cover and let rise 1 to 1¼ hours or until dough rises to top of pan. Bake at 375° for 30 minutes or until done. Yield: 4 loaves.

WHOLE WHEAT ROLLS

2 packages dry yeast
2 cups warm milk (105° to 115°)
1 egg
½ cup sugar
1 teaspoon salt
3½ cups whole wheat flour
1 cup plus 1 tablespoon shortening, melted
3 to 3½ cups all-purpose flour
3 tablespoons melted butter or margarine

Dissolve yeast in milk in a large bowl. Stir in egg, sugar, and salt. Add whole wheat flour and shortening, mixing well. Gradually add enough all-purpose flour to form a moderately stiff dough, beating well after each addition.

Place dough in a lightly greased bowl, turning to grease top. Cover and let rise in a warm place (85°), free from drafts, for 1½ hours or until doubled in bulk. Punch down; cover and let rise 30 minutes or until doubled in bulk.

Lightly grease muffin pans. Shape dough into 1-inch balls; place 3 balls in each muffin cup. Brush tops with melted butter. Cover and let rise 45 minutes or until doubled in bulk. Bake at 400° for 12 to 15 minutes or until golden brown. Yield: about 4 dozen rolls.

CORN STICKS

1 cup plus 2 tablespoons cornmeal
1 cup buttermilk
½ cup all-purpose flour
1 egg
2 tablespoons vegetable oil
½ teaspoon baking powder
1 tablespoon sugar
½ teaspoon soda
½ teaspoon salt

Combine all ingredients, beating well. Place a well-greased cast-iron corn-stick pan in 450° oven for 3 minutes or until a drop of water sizzles when dropped on pan. Remove pan from oven; spoon batter into pan, filling half full. Bake at 450° for 10 to 13 minutes or until golden brown. Yield: about 20 corn sticks.

LEMON BREAD

½ cup shortening
1 cup sugar
2 eggs
1½ cups all-purpose flour
1½ teaspoons baking powder
¼ teaspoon salt
½ cup milk
Grated rind of 1 lemon
½ cup chopped nuts (optional)
Glaze (recipe follows)

Combine shortening and sugar, creaming until light and fluffy. Add eggs, one at a time, beating after each addition.

Combine flour, baking powder, and salt; add to creamed mixture alternately with milk, mixing well after each addition. Stir in lemon rind; add nuts, if desired.

Pour batter into a well-greased 9- x 5- x 3-inch loafpan. Bake at 350° for 60 minutes. Pour glaze over bread. Cool 10 to 15 minutes before removing from pan. Yield: 1 loaf.

Glaze:

⅓ cup sugar
2 tablespoons lemon juice

Combine sugar and lemon juice, mixing well. Yield: about ⅓ cup.

CRANBERRY FRUIT-NUT BREAD

2 cups all-purpose flour
1 cup sugar
1½ teaspoons baking powder
1 teaspoon salt
½ teaspoon soda
¼ cup shortening
¾ cup orange juice
1 egg, beaten
1 teaspoon grated orange rind
1 cup cranberries, coarsely chopped
½ cup chopped nuts

Combine first 5 ingredients in a medium bowl; cut in shortening until mixture resembles coarse meal. Combine orange juice, egg, and orange rind; stir just enough to moisten dry ingredients. Stir in cranberries and nuts.

Pour batter into a greased and floured 9- x 5- x 3-inch loafpan. Bake at 350° for 1 hour and 5 minutes or until bread tests done. Cool 10 minutes before removing from pan. Yield: 1 loaf.

PUMPKIN MUFFINS

¾ cup firmly packed brown sugar
½ cup butter or margarine, softened
¼ cup molasses
1 egg, beaten
1 cup cooked or canned, mashed pumpkin
1¾ cups all-purpose flour
1 teaspoon soda
¼ teaspoon salt
¼ cup pecans

Combine sugar, butter, and molasses; beat well. Add egg and pumpkin, beating until smooth. Stir together remaining ingredients; add to pumpkin mixture, stirring just until moistened (batter will be lumpy).

Fill lightly greased muffin pans half full. Bake at 375° for 20 minutes. Yield: about 15 muffins.

Sample Vegetables From The Colonial Inn

Colonial Inn is well known for its warm Southern hospitality and its good cooking.

Each day about a dozen vegetables are included on the menu. The selection might range from Cornwallis Yams and Corn Pudding to Broccoli with Hollandaise. Colorful Congealed Vegetable Salad, Baked Apples, and Pickled Beets are especially nice additions to Christmas dining tables.

CONGEALED VEGETABLE SALAD

6 tablespoons sugar
1 teaspoon salt
1 (6-ounce) package lime-flavored gelatin
3¼ cups boiling water
¼ cup vinegar
2 cups shredded cabbage
1 cup shredded carrot
Lettuce
Cottage cheese
Spiced apple rings (optional)
Parsley sprigs (optional)

Combine sugar, salt, and gelatin; add boiling water, stirring until gelatin dissolves. Stir in vinegar. Chill until partially set. Fold in cabbage and carrot. Spoon into an 8-cup ring mold, and chill until firm.

Unmold salad on lettuce leaves; fill center with cottage cheese. Garnish with apple rings and parsley sprigs, if desired. Yield: 10 to 12 servings.

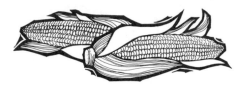

BROCCOLI WITH HOLLANDAISE SAUCE

1 (2-pound) bunch fresh broccoli
Hollandaise sauce (recipe follows)

Trim off large leaves of broccoli. Remove tough ends of lower stalks, and wash broccoli thoroughly. If stalks are more than 1 inch in diameter, make lengthwise slits in stalks.

Cook broccoli in a small amount of boiling salted water 15 to 20 minutes or until tender. Drain well; serve with hollandaise sauce. Yield: 4 to 5 servings.

Hollandaise Sauce:

¼ cup butter
2 egg yolks, slightly beaten
¼ cup melted butter
1 tablespoon lemon juice
Pinch of salt
Dash of cayenne

Combine ¼ cup butter and egg yolks in top of a double boiler. Place over hot water (do not let water boil). Beat constantly with a whisk until butter melts. Gradually add ¼ cup melted butter, beating well. Add lemon juice and salt, beating well. Cook, beating constantly, until mixture thickens. Remove from heat, and stir in cayenne. Serve immediately. Yield: about ⅔ cup.

CORNWALLIS YAMS

6 medium-size sweet potatoes
1 cup sugar
½ teaspoon salt
½ teaspoon ground cinnamon
½ teaspoon ground nutmeg
½ cup butter
3 eggs, beaten
½ cup crushed pineapple
1½ cups milk
½ cup flaked coconut

Wash sweet potatoes, and place in a large saucepan; cover with water, and bring to a boil. Cover and simmer about 30 minutes or until tender.

Peel potatoes and mash. Add next 8 ingredients, mixing well. Pour into a greased 13- x 9- x 2-inch baking dish. Bake at 350° for 45 minutes. Sprinkle with coconut. Yield: 12 to 14 servings.

CORN PUDDING

½ cup sugar
3 tablespoons all-purpose flour
3 eggs
1 (17-ounce) can whole kernel corn, drained
2 cups milk
½ teaspoon salt
¼ cup butter or margarine

Combine sugar and flour in a medium mixing bowl; add eggs, beating well. Stir in corn, milk, and salt.

Melt butter in a lightly greased 1¾-quart casserole; pour in corn mixture. Bake at 400° for 1 hour or until firm. Serve hot. Yield: 6 servings.

GREEN BEANS AMANDINE

2 pounds fresh green beans
1 small ham hock
1 cup water
⅓ cup minced onion
⅔ cup slivered almonds
3 tablespoons melted butter or margarine
1 teaspoon salt

Remove strings from beans; cut beans into 1½-inch pieces, and wash thoroughly. Place in a 5-quart Dutch oven; add ham hock and water. Bring to a boil; then reduce heat. Cover and simmer for 1 hour. Drain off any excess liquid.

Sauté onion and almonds in butter until onion is tender. Add to beans, along with salt; toss lightly. Yield: 8 servings.

BAKED APPLES

6 large baking apples, peeled and cored
6 tablespoons sugar
1½ teaspoons ground cinnamon
1½ teaspoons ground nutmeg
2 tablespoons butter or margarine
½ to ¾ cup apple juice
Red food coloring (optional)

Place apples in a shallow 2-quart casserole; pour 1 tablespoon sugar into cavity of each apple. Sprinkle each with ¼ teaspoon cinnamon and ¼ teaspoon nutmeg; top with 1 teaspoon butter.

Heat apple juice to boiling; add red food coloring, if desired. Pour juice into casserole. Bake apples, uncovered, at 400° for 50 to 60 minutes or until tender, basting occasionally with juice. Yield: 6 servings.

PICKLED BEETS

2 tablespoons sugar
¾ teaspoon salt
½ teaspoon dry mustard
¼ teaspoon ground cloves
⅓ cup cider vinegar
⅓ cup water
2 (16-ounce) cans small whole beets, drained
1 medium onion, thinly sliced
Orange slices (optional)

Combine first 6 ingredients, stirring well. Add beets and onion; toss well to coat. Cover and chill several hours. Garnish with orange slices, if desired. Yield: 10 to 12 servings.

An old-fashioned Christmas feast includes the following: Roast Turkey with Peanut Dressing; Giblet Gravy; Wayside Scalloped Potatoes; Virginia Corn Relish; Fresh Cranberry Sauce; Southern-Style Green Beans; Shenandoah Apple Juice Shrub; Ambrosia Pie. Menu and recipes begin on page 282.

Pages 278-279: Delight every taste with this array of old-fashioned Christmas candy pictured clockwise beginning at far left: Penuche, Fudge Scotch Ring, English Toffee, Peanut Butter Creams, Potato Candy, Never-Fail Peanut Brittle, Party Mints, Kentucky Colonels, Date Logs, Fast Fudge, Apricot Balls, Pralines. Recipes begin on page 272.

Page 280: The Red Apple Inn's moist Plum Pudding (page 281) is filled with fruit and topped with a rum-laced hard sauce.

Sample Desserts From The Red Apple Inn

The Red Apple Inn, located near Heber Springs, Arkansas, has quite a reputation for offering outstanding desserts.

You can bring the flavor of this country inn to your holiday table with whipped cream-topped Apricot Tarts or with Red Apple Pie. For an elegant, light dessert, offer Grand Marnier Soufflé served with Crème Fraîche Sauce.

GRAND MARNIER SOUFFLE

¼ cup plus 2 tablespoons sugar
¼ cup plus 2 tablespoons cornstarch
Grated rind of 2 oranges
1¼ cups milk
3 tablespoons Grand Marnier or other
    orange-flavored liqueur
1½ tablespoons butter, melted
6 egg yolks, beaten
8 egg whites, at room temperature
½ cup sugar
Crème Fraîche Sauce

Combine first 3 ingredients in a medium saucepan; stir in milk, liqueur, and butter with a wire whisk. Cook over medium heat until thickened, stirring constantly. Remove from heat. Add some of hot mixture to egg yolks, stirring constantly. Add yolk mixture to hot mixture, stirring constantly. Cook over medium heat 1 minute, stirring constantly; remove from heat, and allow to cool.

Beat egg whites until soft peaks form; gradually add ½ cup sugar, beating until stiff. Fold into cooled custard.

Pour mixture into 8 (10-ounce) custard cups. Set cups in a pan; pour 1 to 1½ inches of hot water into pan. Bake at 350° for 1 hour and 20 minutes. Serve immediately with Crème Fraîche Sauce. Yield: 8 servings.

Crème Fraîche Sauce:

⅓ cup commercial sour cream
1 cup whipping cream
1 tablespoon plus 2 teaspoons cream
    cheese (1 ounce), softened
⅓ cup powdered sugar
1 teaspoon amaretto

Combine all ingredients in container of electric blender; blend until thickened. Chill. Yield: about 1¾ cups.

BAVARIAN CREAM PIE

1 teaspoon unflavored gelatin
¼ cup cold water
3 eggs, separated
½ cup sugar
½ cup milk
1 teaspoon vanilla extract
¼ cup sugar
1 baked 9-inch pastry shell
1 cup whipping cream, whipped
Grated milk chocolate

Soften gelatin in water in top of a double boiler; place over boiling water, stirring until gelatin is dissolved. Combine egg yolks, ½ cup sugar, and milk; beat slightly, and stir into gelatin. Cook over boiling water, stirring constantly, about 10 minutes or until mixture coats a spoon. Stir in vanilla. Remove from heat, and cool slightly.

Beat egg whites until foamy; gradually add ¼ cup sugar; continue beating until stiff peaks form. Fold into custard. Spoon into pastry shell; top with whipped cream. Garnish with grated chocolate. Chill. Yield: one 9-inch pie.

YULE LOG

5 eggs, separated
1 cup powdered sugar
3 tablespoons cocoa
2 to 3 tablespoons powdered sugar
1 cup whipping cream
¼ cup powdered sugar
Mocha Butter Cream Frosting
Chopped pistachio nuts

Grease a 13- x 9- x 2-inch baking pan; line with waxed paper. Grease and flour paper; set aside.

Beat egg yolks until thick and lemon colored; gradually add 1 cup powdered sugar, beating constantly until sugar is dissolved. Stir in cocoa.

Beat egg whites until stiff, and fold into yolk mixture. Spread mixture evenly in prepared pan. Bake at 350° for 20 minutes.

Sift 2 to 3 tablespoons powdered sugar on a linen towel. Loosen sides of warm cake from pan, and turn out onto sugared surface. Remove waxed paper from cake. Starting with long side, roll cake and towel together, jellyroll fashion; cool thoroughly on wire rack, seam side down.

Combine whipping cream and ¼ cup powdered sugar in a small mixing bowl; beat until stiff.

Unroll cake, and spread with whipped cream. Re-roll cake, and place, seam side down, on serving platter. Frost with Mocha Butter Cream Frosting, and sprinkle with pistachio nuts. Chill 1 to 2 hours. Yield: 12 to 14 servings.

Mocha Butter Cream Frosting:

1 cup unsalted butter, softened
1 cup powdered sugar
1 tablespoon cocoa
2 teaspoons Kahlúa or other
    coffee-flavored liqueur

Combine butter and sugar in a small mixing bowl; cream until light and fluffy. Add cocoa and Kahlúa, beating well. Yield: about 2 cups.

Note: If desired, 2 teaspoons strong coffee may be substituted for Kahlúa.

PLUM PUDDING

3 cups all-purpose flour
1 teaspoon soda
½ teaspoon salt
2 teaspoons ground cinnamon
½ teaspoon ground allspice
½ teaspoon ground cloves
2 cups seedless raisins
1 cup peeled, chopped cooking apple
1 cup currants
1 cup light molasses
1 cup cold water
2 cups finely chopped suet
Hard sauce (recipe follows)

Combine flour, soda, salt, and spices in a large mixing bowl; mix well. Stir in raisins, apple, and currants.

Combine molasses, water, and suet; add to dry ingredients, mixing well. Spoon mixture into a well-buttered 10-cup mold; cover tightly.

Place mold on shallow rack in a large, deep kettle with enough boiling water to come halfway up mold. Cover kettle; steam pudding 3 hours in continuously boiling water (replace water as needed). Unmold and serve with hard sauce. Yield: 8 to 10 servings.

Hard Sauce:

½ cup butter or margarine, softened
1 cup powdered sugar
2 to 4 tablespoons rum, sherry, or
    brandy

Combine butter and powdered sugar, beating until smooth. Add rum; beat until fluffy. Chill. Yield: ¾ cup.

SOUR CREAM CHOCOLATE CAKE

4 (1-ounce) squares unsweetened chocolate
1 cup hot water
2 eggs, beaten
2 cups sugar
1 cup commercial sour cream
2 teaspoons vanilla extract
2 cups all-purpose flour
1 teaspoon soda
½ teaspoon salt
Frosting (recipe follows)

Combine chocolate and hot water in a small saucepan; place over low heat, stirring until chocolate is melted. Remove from heat, and set aside.

Combine eggs and sugar in a medium mixing bowl, mixing well; add sour cream, chocolate mixture, and vanilla. Mix well.

Combine flour, soda, and salt; gradually add to chocolate mixture, mixing well. Pour into 2 greased and floured 8-inch cakepans. Place in a cold oven, and set at 300°; bake about 55 minutes. Let cake cool before removing from pans. Spread frosting between layers and on top and sides of cake. Yield: one 8-inch layer cake.

Frosting:

2 cups sugar
¼ cup cocoa
½ cup margarine
1 tablespoon light corn syrup
½ cup milk
1 cup chopped pecans
1 teaspoon vanilla extract

Combine sugar and cocoa in a small saucepan, mixing well. Add margarine, corn syrup, and milk; bring to a boil, and boil 2 minutes. Remove from heat, and cool 5 minutes. Beat until thick enough to spread. Stir in pecans and vanilla. Yield: enough frosting for one 8-inch layer cake.

ORANGE-PECAN PIE

1 cup light corn syrup
¼ cup melted butter
¼ cup sugar
1 cup chopped pecans
1 tablespoon orange juice
1 tablespoon grated orange rind
3 eggs, beaten
½ teaspoon salt
1 unbaked 9-inch pastry shell

Combine first 8 ingredients in a medium mixing bowl; mix well. Pour into pastry shell. Bake at 350° for 45 minutes. Yield: one 9-inch pie.

BASIC PASTRY

2 cups all-purpose flour
1 teaspoon salt
⅔ cup plus 2 tablespoons shortening
4 to 6 tablespoons cold water

Combine flour and salt; cut in shortening with pastry blender until mixture resembles coarse cornmeal. Sprinkle cold water evenly over surface; stir with a fork until all dry ingredients are moistened. Shape dough into a ball; chill. Yield: enough pastry for one 9-inch double crust pie or 6 tart shells.

Note: This pastry is used for Apricot Tarts and Red Apple Pie.

APRICOT TARTS

Basic Pastry
About 2 tablespoons whipping cream
1 (22-ounce) can apricot pie filling
1 cup apricot jam
Whipped cream

Roll half of pastry to ⅛-inch thickness; cut out 3 (7-inch) circles. Fit circles into tart pans 4½ inches across and 2½ inches deep; trim excess pastry from edges. Prick shell thoroughly. Repeat procedure with remaining half of pastry.

Bake the tart shells at 475° for 8 to 10 minutes. Remove shells from pans, and cool completely.

Brush inside of each shell with a thin layer of whipping cream; fill each shell with ⅓ cup pie filling, and set aside.

Cook jam over medium heat, stirring constantly, just until melted; strain, discarding residue. Cool jam 5 minutes. Spoon 2 tablespoons jam over pie filling in each shell. Chill tarts thoroughly. To serve, top each with a dollop of whipped cream. Yield: 6 servings.

RED APPLE PIE

Basic Pastry
1½ cups sugar
¼ cup butter or margarine
2 tablespoons orange juice
2 tablespoons lemon juice
1 tablespoon plus 2 teaspoons grated orange rind
½ teaspoon ground cinnamon
7 cups peeled, thinly sliced cooking apples
Whipping cream

Roll half of pastry to ⅛-inch thickness; fit into a deep 9-inch piepan.

Combine next 6 ingredients in a medium saucepan; cook, stirring constantly, over medium-high heat just until mixture reaches a boil.

Place a thin layer of apple slices in piepan; drizzle apples with sugar mixture. Repeat layers until all ingredients are used, ending with sugar mixture.

Roll out remaining pastry to ⅛-inch thickness, and cut into ¾-inch strips. Arrange the strips in lattice design over apples. Brush pastry lightly with whipping cream. Bake at 400° for 60 minutes. Yield: one 9-inch pie.

Feasting At The Wayside Inn

Dining areas with a gracious 18th-century atmosphere welcome guests to Wayside Inn. On Christmas Day, waitresses dressed in colonial attire serve a traditional feast of roast turkey with all the trimmings—a sumptuous holiday meal like those that generations of guests at Wayside Inn have enjoyed.

Shenandoah Apple Juice Shrub
Roast Turkey With Peanut Dressing
Giblet Gravy
Wayside Scalloped Potatoes
Southern-Style Green Beans
Fresh Cranberry Sauce
Virginia Corn Relish
Old-Fashioned Yeast Bread
Ambrosia Pie

SHENANDOAH APPLE JUICE SHRUB

1 quart apple juice, chilled
Lime sherbet
Fresh mint (optional)

Pour apple juice into 4 large mugs or glasses. Top each with a generous scoop of sherbet. Garnish with a sprig of fresh mint, if desired. Yield: 4 servings.

Note: Cranberry juice or any other fruit juice or sherbet can be substituted for a refreshing drink.

ROAST TURKEY WITH PEANUT DRESSING

1 (12- to 14-pound) turkey
Salt
Peanut Dressing
Melted butter, margarine, or vegetable oil

Remove giblets from large cavity and remove neck from neck cavity; reserve for giblet gravy. Rinse turkey thoroughly with cold water, and pat dry. Rub both cavities lightly with salt.

Fill neck cavity with a small amount of Peanut Dressing, and fasten skin to back with a skewer; lightly stuff large cavity. Fold wingtips across the back; tuck drumsticks under band of skin at tail, or tie them to the tail.

Brush entire bird with melted butter; place on roasting rack, breast side up. Insert meat thermometer in thickest part of thigh, making sure it does not touch bone. Bake at 325° until meat thermometer reaches 185° (about 4½ to 5 hours).

If turkey starts to brown too much, cover loosely with a tent of aluminum foil. When turkey is two-thirds done, cut band of skin or string holding drumsticks. Turkey is done when drumsticks are easy to move up and down.

Let turkey stand 15 to 20 minutes before carving. Garnish as desired. Yield: 14 to 16 servings.

Peanut Dressing:

¾ cup finely chopped onion
1½ cups finely chopped celery
½ cup chopped fresh parsley
1 cup melted margarine
12 cups soft breadcrumbs
2 cups salted peanuts, chopped
1 tablespoon salt
1 teaspoon pepper
1 tablespoon rubbed sage
4½ cups water

Sauté onion, celery, and parsley in margarine in a large Dutch oven until tender. Add remaining ingredients; mix well, and spoon into turkey cavities. Spoon remaining dressing into a greased baking dish; bake at 350° for 45 minutes to 1 hour or until lightly browned around edges. Yield: about 12 servings.

Tip: Avoid purchasing green-tinted potatoes. The term used for this condition is "light burn," which causes a bitter flavor. To keep potatoes from turning green once you have bought them, store in a dark, cool, dry place.

GIBLET GRAVY

3 cups water
1 teaspoon salt
Giblets from 1 turkey
Turkey neck
1 medium onion, chopped (optional)
1 cup chopped celery (optional)
½ teaspoon poultry seasoning (optional)
6 tablespoons all-purpose flour
Salt and pepper

Combine 3 cups water and 1 teaspoon salt in a medium saucepan; bring to a boil. Add giblets and turkey neck; reduce heat. Cover and simmer 15 minutes. Remove liver, and continue simmering about 1½ hours or until tender. Remove meat from broth, discarding neck; chop giblets, and return to broth.

If desired, add onion, celery, and poultry seasoning to broth mixture. Cook until vegetables are tender.

Blend flour with a small amount of water, mixing to form a smooth paste; stir into broth. Cook, stirring constantly, until thickened and bubbly. Season to taste with salt and pepper. Yield: 3 cups.

WAYSIDE SCALLOPED POTATOES

8 large potatoes, peeled and sliced
1 large onion, sliced
¼ cup butter or margarine
½ cup all-purpose flour
½ teaspoon dry mustard
2 cups milk
1 teaspoon Worcestershire sauce
4 cups (1 pound) shredded sharp Cheddar cheese
¼ cup breadcrumbs
Paprika

Cook potatoes and onion in a small amount of boiling salted water about 10 to 12 minutes or until tender; drain well.

Melt butter in a large, heavy saucepan over low heat; add flour and mustard, stirring until smooth. Cook 1 minute, stirring constantly. Gradually add milk; cook over medium heat, stirring constantly, until thickened and bubbly. Add Worcestershire sauce and cheese, stirring until cheese melts.

Alternate layers of potato-onion mixture and cheese sauce in a lightly greased 2-quart shallow casserole. Top with breadcrumbs, and sprinkle with paprika. Bake at 350° for 30 minutes or until bubbly. Yield: 10 servings.

SOUTHERN-STYLE GREEN BEANS

3 pounds fresh green beans
5 cups water
1 (½-pound) ham hock
2 teaspoons salt
¼ teaspoon pepper

Remove strings from beans, and cut beans into 2-inch pieces. Wash the beans thoroughly.

Pour water into a Dutch oven; add ham hock, and bring to a boil. Reduce heat, and simmer 1 hour. Add beans, salt, and pepper; cook 30 minutes or until tender. Yield: 10 to 12 servings.

FRESH CRANBERRY SAUCE

1 pound fresh cranberries
2 cups sugar
2 cups water
2 tablespoons grated orange rind

Carefully sort and wash cranberries. Combine cranberries, sugar, and water in a saucepan; cook 10 minutes or until all berries burst. Add orange rind, and mash berries slightly. Yield: about 3 cups.

VIRGINIA CORN RELISH

½ cup vinegar
½ cup sugar
½ teaspoon salt
½ teaspoon celery seeds
¼ teaspoon mustard seeds
¼ teaspoon hot sauce
1 (12-ounce) can whole kernel corn, undrained
2 tablespoons chopped green pepper
1 tablespoon instant minced onion
1 tablespoon chopped pimiento

Combine vinegar, sugar, salt, celery seeds, mustard seeds, and hot sauce in a medium saucepan; mix well. Bring to a boil; continue boiling 2 minutes or until sugar dissolves. Remove from heat, and stir in remaining ingredients; let cool.

Refrigerate relish in airtight container for 2 days to allow flavors to blend. Yield: 10 to 12 servings.

OLD-FASHIONED YEAST BREAD

2 packages dry yeast
½ cup warm water (105° to 115°)
1 egg, well beaten
1 cup milk
¼ cup sugar
2 tablespoons butter or margarine
1 tablespoon salt
5 to 6 cups sifted all-purpose flour
Melted butter or margarine

Dissolve yeast in warm water in a large mixing bowl; add egg, stirring well. Let stand 10 minutes.

Combine milk, sugar, 2 tablespoons butter, and salt in a small saucepan. Scald milk mixture, and cool to lukewarm; add to yeast mixture. Gradually stir in enough flour to make a soft dough that leaves sides of bowl.

Turn dough out on a lightly floured surface, and knead 5 minutes or until smooth and elastic. Shape into a ball; place in a greased bowl, turning to grease top. Cover and let rise in a warm place (85°), free from drafts, 1½ hours or until doubled in bulk.

Punch dough down, and knead 1 minute. Shape into a ball, and place in greased bowl; cover and let rise 1 hour or until doubled in bulk.

Punch dough down again, and divide into 3 equal portions. Shape each portion into a 6- x 3-inch loaf. Place loaves in 3 greased 7- x 3½- x 2-inch loafpans. Cover and let rise 1 hour or until doubled in bulk. Bake at 325° for 20 minutes or until loaves sound hollow when tapped.

Remove loaves from pans; brush with melted butter, and cool on wire racks. Yield: 3 loaves.

AMBROSIA PIE

⅔ cup sugar
¼ cup cornstarch
½ teaspoon salt
3 cups milk
4 egg yolks, well beaten
2 tablespoons butter or margarine, softened
1 tablespoon plus 1 teaspoon vanilla extract
1 cup flaked coconut
1 baked 9-inch pastry shell
½ pint whipping cream
¼ cup powdered sugar
¼ cup flaked coconut, toasted
Mandarin orange sections

Combine sugar, cornstarch, and salt in a large saucepan; mix well. Combine milk and egg yolks, mixing well; stir into sugar mixture. Cook over medium heat, stirring constantly, until mixture thickens and boils; boil 1 minute, stirring constantly. Remove from heat; add butter, vanilla, and 1 cup coconut. Let cool, and spoon into pastry shell.

Whip cream until slightly thickened; add powdered sugar, beating until light and fluffy. Spread over pie filling; sprinkle with toasted coconut, and garnish with mandarin orange sections. Yield: one 9-inch pie.

Make The Party An Open House

Christmas is meant for sharing, and what could be more in keeping with that spirit than opening your home to friends and relatives during the holiday season.

An array of delectable party food is essential to the festivities. We suggest Irresistible Salmon Mousse, Holiday Cheese Ball, tangy meatballs served hot from a chafing dish, and a dip to enjoy with fresh vegetables. For a sweet touch, there's a lemon-glazed pound cake and Pecan Rolls.

The beverage is up to you, but we offer two possibilities: Merry Christmas Punch and Golden Spiked Punch.

SPICED MEATBALLS

1 pound ground beef
¾ cup seasoned breadcrumbs
2 tablespoons finely chopped onion
1 tablespoon catsup
4 drops of hot sauce
½ teaspoon prepared horseradish
2 eggs, well beaten
½ teaspoon salt
¼ teaspoon pepper
½ teaspoon Ac'cent
1 tablespoon grated Parmesan cheese
2 to 3 tablespoons butter or margarine
½ cup catsup
½ cup chili sauce
¼ cup cider vinegar
½ cup firmly packed brown sugar
2 tablespoons finely chopped onion
1 tablespoon Worcestershire sauce
1 teaspoon Ac'cent
4 drops of hot sauce
½ teaspoon dry mustard
3 drops of Angostura bitters
1 teaspoon salt
¼ teaspoon pepper
Chopped green onion (optional)

Combine first 11 ingredients in a large mixing bowl; mix well, and shape into 1-inch balls. Sauté in butter until browned; drain well, and set aside.

Combine remaining ingredients except green onion in a large saucepan; bring to a boil. Reduce heat, and simmer 5 minutes. Add meatballs, and simmer an additional 10 minutes. Transfer to chafing dish, and keep warm. Garnish with chopped green onion, if desired. Yield: about 3½ dozen.

*Mrs. Howard A. Thompson,
Kingsport, Tennessee.*

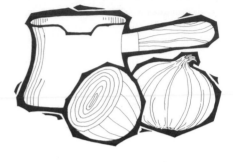

IRRESISTIBLE SALMON MOUSSE

2 envelopes unflavored gelatin
½ cup water
1 (15½-ounce) can red salmon
1 cup mayonnaise
2 tablespoons vinegar
2 tablespoons catsup
Dash of cayenne pepper
Dash of pepper
15 pimiento-stuffed olives, sliced
2 hard-cooked eggs, chopped
2 tablespoons sweet pickle relish or chopped sweet pickle
1 cup whipping cream, whipped
Lettuce
Lemons (optional)
Paprika (optional)
Parsley sprigs (optional)

Combine gelatin and water in a small saucepan; place over medium heat until gelatin is dissolved, stirring constantly. Remove from heat, and set aside.

Drain salmon, and remove skin and bones. Flake salmon with a fork; add mayonnaise, vinegar, catsup, cayenne, and pepper. Mix well; then stir in olives, eggs, relish, and the dissolved gelatin.

Fold in whipped cream. Spoon mixture into a well-greased 5½- to 6-cup mold. Chill overnight. Unmold on lettuce. If desired, garnish with lemon halves dipped in paprika and topped with sprigs of parsley. Yield: one (5½-cup) mousse.
*Karen L. Brown,
Lubbock, Texas.*

HOLIDAY CHEESE BALL

4 cups (1 pound) shredded Cheddar
    cheese
4 (3-ounce) packages cream cheese,
    softened
½ cup chopped pimiento-stuffed olives
3 tablespoons mayonnaise
⅛ teaspoon celery salt
½ teaspoon Worcestershire sauce
2 tablespoons minced onion
Dash of garlic salt
Chopped fresh parsley
Sliced pimiento-stuffed olives
Chopped pecans

Combine first 8 ingredients in a large
mixing bowl; mix well with hands, and
shape into a ball. Garnish with parsley,
olives, and pecans. Yield: 1 cheese
ball.   *Penny Owen,*
                Raleigh, North Carolina.

PECAN ROLLS

1 (7-ounce) jar marshmallow cream
1 (1-pound) package powdered sugar
1 teaspoon vanilla extract
1 (14-ounce) package assorted vanilla and
    chocolate caramels
3 tablespoons water
1 to 1½ cups chopped pecans

Combine first 3 ingredients, mixing
well with hands. Shape mixture into 5
(4- x 1-inch) rolls. (Mixture will be very
dry.) Chill 2 to 3 hours.
Combine caramels and water in top
of a double boiler; cook until melted.
Dip rolls in melted caramel, and roll
each in pecans; chill 1 hour. Cut into
slices to serve. Yield: 5 rolls.
                Mrs. Arthur L. Barton,
                    Marion, Alabama.

FESTIVE EGG DIP

1 (8-ounce) package cream cheese,
    softened
3 tablespoons milk
3 hard-cooked eggs, finely chopped
2 tablespoons mayonnaise
2 teaspoons chopped chives
1 teaspoon prepared mustard
¼ teaspoon salt
⅛ teaspoon pepper

Combine cream cheese and milk in a
small mixing bowl; beat until creamy.
Add remaining ingredients, mixing until
light and fluffy. Serve with fresh vegetables. Yield: 1⅔ cups. *Mrs. E. J. Bell,*
            Birmingham, Alabama.

BUTTERMILK POUND CAKE

1 cup shortening
2 cups sugar
4 eggs
¼ teaspoon soda
1 cup buttermilk
3 cups all-purpose flour
¼ teaspoon salt
2 tablespoons vanilla extract
2 tablespoons lemon extract
1 teaspoon almond extract
Lemon Glaze

Combine shortening and sugar,
creaming until light and fluffy. Add
eggs, one at a time, beating well after
each addition. Dissolve soda in buttermilk. Combine flour and salt; add to
creamed mixture alternately with buttermilk, mixing well after each addition.
Stir in flavorings.
Pour batter into a greased and
floured 10-inch tube pan. Bake at 350°
for 1 hour and 15 minutes or until cake
tests done. Cool 10 minutes; remove
from pan, and spoon on Lemon Glaze.
Yield: one 10-inch cake.

Lemon Glaze:

1 cup powdered sugar
¼ cup melted butter or margarine
¼ cup lemon juice

Combine all ingredients in a small
bowl, mixing well. Yield: enough glaze
for one 10-inch cake.

                    Mrs. Doris Gray,
                    Lubbock, Texas.

GOLDEN SPIKED PUNCH

1 (4/5-quart) fifth bourbon
1 (6-ounce) can frozen orange juice
    concentrate, thawed and undiluted
1 (6-ounce) can frozen lemonade
    concentrate, thawed and undiluted
¾ cup lemon juice
3 quarts lemon-lime carbonated beverage,
    chilled
Lemon slices
Orange slices

Combine first 4 ingredients; stir well.
Chill several hours. Add carbonated
beverage and sliced fruit. Serve over
ice. Yield: about 1 gallon.
Note: An additional quart of carbonated beverage may be added, if desired.
                Mrs. Pamela McWhirt,
                Fredericksburg, Virginia.

MERRY CHRISTMAS PUNCH

Grated rind of 1 orange
Grated rind of 1 lemon
2 cups water
2 cups sugar
2 teaspoons almond extract
3 cups fresh orange juice, strained
1½ cups fresh lemon juice, strained
3 pints cranberry juice cocktail
1 quart ginger ale

Combine orange and lemon rind,
water, and sugar in a medium saucepan;
bring to a boil, and cook 5 minutes. Let
cool; stir in almond extract and fruit
juice. Pour over ice; stir in ginger ale.
Yield: about 1¼ gallons.
                Mrs. J. E. Sypher,
            Charlotte, North Carolina.

Salads With A Holiday Flair

Here are salads that are as festive and
colorful as the season. Tart Cranberry
Salad, made with fresh cranberries, is a
flavorful accompaniment for the classic
turkey dinner. For a sweeter taste, try
Frosted Lime-Cheese Salad. A green
gelatin layer spread with a cream cheese
frosting can be garnished with maraschino cherries, watercress, and walnut
halves for that special holiday look.
In addition to these congealed salads,
try our Cabbage and Fruit Salad. Apple
wedges, miniature marshmallows, and
pineapple chunks are tossed with shredded cabbage in a savory dressing, then
topped with pecan halves.

COTTAGE CHEESE-POTATO SALAD

3 cups diced cooked potatoes
½ cup diced celery
1 tablespoon chopped green pepper
1 tablespoon chopped pimiento
2 tablespoons minced onion
2 tablespoons chopped sweet pickle
1 teaspoon salt
1 tablespoon lemon juice
1 cup mayonnaise
1 cup cream-style cottage cheese

Combine first 6 ingredients. Combine
remaining ingredients, mixing well; add
to potato mixture, stirring gently. Chill.
Yield: 5 to 6 servings. *Phyllis England,*
                Deer Lodge, Tennessee.

HEAVENLY FROSTED SALAD

1 (15¼-ounce) can crushed pineapple
1 (3-ounce) package lemon-flavored gelatin
1 (3-ounce) package lime-flavored gelatin
2 cups boiling water
1½ cups cold water
2 bananas, peeled and chopped
1 cup chopped pecans
2 tablespoons all-purpose flour
¾ cup sugar
1 egg, well beaten
1 (1.5-ounce) envelope whipped topping mix
1 (8-ounce) package cream cheese, softened

Drain pineapple, reserving ½ cup juice; set aside.

Combine gelatin in a large mixing bowl; add 2 cups boiling water, stirring until dissolved. Stir in 1½ cups cold water. Add bananas, pineapple, and pecans; pour into a 13- x 9- x 2-inch baking pan. Chill until firm.

Combine flour and sugar in a medium saucepan, mixing well; stir in egg and reserved pineapple juice. Cook over medium heat, stirring constantly, until smooth and thickened; cool.

Prepare whipped topping mix according to package directions; add cream cheese, and beat until smooth. Fold in cooked mixture; spread over gelatin mixture. Chill. Yield: 15 servings.

Linda Thompson,
High Point, North Carolina.

TART CRANBERRY SALAD

1 pound fresh cranberries, ground
1 (20-ounce) can crushed pineapple
1 (6-ounce) package cherry-flavored gelatin
¾ cup sugar
2 cups boiling water
½ cup cold water
2 tablespoons lemon juice
1 small orange, seeded and ground
1 cup finely chopped celery
1 cup chopped pecans

Carefully sort and wash cranberries; grind and set aside.

Drain pineapple, reserving juice; set aside.

Combine gelatin and sugar in a large mixing bowl; add boiling water, and stir until dissolved. Stir in cold water, lemon juice, and pineapple juice. Chill until partially set; stir in pineapple, cranberries, orange, celery, and pecans. Pour into a 9-cup mold; chill until firm. Yield: 15 to 20 servings.

Mrs. S. Bruce Jones,
Nashville, Tennessee.

CABBAGE AND FRUIT SALAD

1 tablespoon all-purpose flour
½ cup sugar
1 tablespoon cornstarch
¼ teaspoon salt
⅛ teaspoon pepper
⅛ teaspoon dry mustard
1 (8¼-ounce) can pineapple chunks
½ to ¾ cup vinegar
2 eggs, beaten
6 cups shredded cabbage
1 cup miniature marshmallows
1 red apple, cored and cut into wedges
Pecan halves

Combine first 6 ingredients in a medium saucepan; mix well and set aside.

Drain pineapple, reserving juice; set pineapple aside. Add enough water to juice to make 1½ cups liquid; stir liquid and vinegar into dry ingredients. Add eggs, mixing well; cook over medium heat, stirring constantly, until smooth and thickened. Cool.

Combine cabbage, marshmallows, apple, and pineapple in a large mixing bowl; pour sauce over top, and mix well. Garnish with pecans; serve immediately. Yield: 8 servings.

Mrs. Earl L. Faulkenberry,
Lancaster, South Carolina.

FROSTED LIME-CHEESE SALAD

1 (3-ounce) package lime-flavored gelatin
1 cup boiling water
½ cup finely chopped celery
1 tablespoon chopped pimiento
1 (8-ounce) can crushed pineapple, undrained
1 cup small-curd cottage cheese
½ cup chopped walnuts
1 (3-ounce) package cream cheese, softened
1 tablespoon mayonnaise
1 teaspoon lemon juice
Walnut halves (optional)
Watercress (optional)
Maraschino cherries (optional)

Dissolve lime gelatin in boiling water; chill until slightly thickened. Fold in celery, pimiento, pineapple, cottage cheese, and chopped walnuts; pour into an 8-inch square pan. Chill until firm.

Combine cream cheese, mayonnaise, and lemon juice, mixing well; spread mixture over gelatin. Cut into squares; garnish with walnut halves, watercress, and maraschino cherries, if desired. Yield: 9 servings.

Mrs. Margaret L. Hunter,
Princeton, Kentucky.

GREEN-AND-WHITE VEGETABLE SALAD

1 bunch fresh broccoli
1 medium head cauliflower, broken into flowerets
1½ cups finely chopped celery
6 green onions, finely chopped
¾ cup salad dressing or mayonnaise
¼ cup whipping cream
2 tablespoons sugar
1 teaspoon salt
¼ teaspoon pepper

Remove large leaves of broccoli, and cut off tough ends of lower stalks; discard. Wash broccoli thoroughly, and cut into 1-inch pieces. Combine vegetables in a large bowl.

Combine remaining ingredients, mixing well. Pour over vegetables; toss lightly to coat. Cover and chill thoroughly. Yield: 8 to 10 servings.

Sharlande Sledge,
Springfield, Missouri.

Speed Up Dinner With Frozen Foods

Rather than spending hours in the kitchen after a busy day, let frozen foods help you prepare gourmet dishes that are as easy as opening a package. These recipes use a wide range of frozen foods—juices, vegetables, fish, and fruits—in everything from entrée to dessert.

SEAFOOD GUMBO

3 tablespoons vegetable oil
3 tablespoons all-purpose flour
2 tablespoons butter or margarine
1 medium onion, chopped
1 clove garlic, minced
1 quart plus 2 cups water
2 tablespoons Worcestershire sauce
4 to 5 dashes hot sauce
3 to 4 bay leaves
1½ teaspoons salt
½ teaspoon pepper
1 (10-ounce) package frozen cut okra
1 (6-ounce) package frozen crabmeat, thawed and undrained
2 (6-ounce) packages frozen cooked shrimp
1 pint fresh oysters, drained
Cooked rice

Heat oil in a 3-quart Dutch oven; add flour, stirring constantly. Cook on medium heat, stirring constantly, 10 to 15 minutes or until roux is the color of a copper penny.

Melt butter in a small skillet; add onion and garlic and cook until tender. Stir into roux mixture. Gradually add water, Worcestershire sauce, hot sauce, bay leaves, salt, and pepper; simmer 1 hour.

Add okra; cook 15 minutes, stirring occasionally to separate okra. Stir in seafood; cook over medium heat 5 minutes or until oysters curl at edges. Serve hot over cooked rice. Yield: 4 to 6 servings. *Winifred K. Crow, Baton Rouge, Louisiana.*

HERBED FISH AND POTATO BAKE

1 (10-ounce) package frozen chopped spinach
1 (3-ounce) package instant mashed potatoes
½ cup commercial sour cream
Dash of pepper
1 (16-ounce) package frozen perch fillets, thawed
¼ cup milk
½ cup herb-flavored stuffing mix, crushed
2 tablespoons butter or margarine, melted
Lemon wedges

Prepare spinach according to package directions; drain well.

Prepare instant potatoes according to package directions, reducing water by ¼ cup. Stir in drained spinach, sour cream, and pepper. Spoon mixture into a lightly greased 10- x 6- x 2-inch baking dish.

Remove skin from fish fillets. Dip one side of each fillet in milk, then in stuffing mix. Fold fillets in half, coating side out; place fish on potato mixture. Drizzle butter over fish.

Bake at 350° for 30 to 35 minutes or until fish flakes when tested with a fork. Serve warm with lemon wedges. Yield: 4 to 5 servings. *Barbara L. Williams, Lawrenceville, Georgia.*

CAULIFLOWER AND ASPARAGUS SUPREME

1 (10-ounce) package frozen cut asparagus
1 (10-ounce) package frozen cauliflower
1 (10¾-ounce) can cream of celery soup, undiluted
½ cup milk
1 cup (¼ pound) shredded process American cheese
1 teaspoon prepared mustard
1 teaspoon Worcestershire sauce
⅓ cup wheat germ
2 tablespoons melted butter or margarine

Prepare vegetables according to package directions; drain.

Combine soup, milk, cheese, mustard, and Worcestershire sauce in a 2-quart saucepan; cook over medium heat, stirring frequently, until cheese is melted. Remove from heat; stir in cooked vegetables.

Place vegetable mixture in a lightly greased 1½-quart shallow casserole. Combine wheat germ and butter; sprinkle over casserole. Bake at 375° for 20 to 25 minutes. Yield: 6 servings. *Susie Beckes, Franklin, Tennessee.*

GREEN VEGETABLE MEDLEY

1 (10-ounce) package frozen English peas
1 (10-ounce) package frozen lima beans
1 (9-ounce) package frozen French-style green beans
1 cup water
Salt
¼ cup finely chopped onion
2 tablespoons butter or margarine, melted
1 tablespoon all-purpose flour
½ cup commercial sour cream
½ cup mayonnaise
½ teaspoon whole basil leaves, crushed
¼ teaspoon salt
⅛ teaspoon pepper
¾ cup shredded sharp Cheddar cheese

Place peas in a colander; pour hot water over peas to remove frost. Set peas aside.

Combine lima beans, green beans, and 1 cup salted water in a saucepan. Bring to a boil; reduce heat and simmer 3 minutes. Drain; set aside.

Sauté onion in butter in a large skillet until tender. Stir in flour; remove from heat. Add vegetables, sour cream, mayonnaise, and seasonings; spoon mixture into a lightly greased 1½-quart casserole.

Bake at 325° for 15 minutes; sprinkle cheese on top, and bake 5 minutes longer. Yield: 6 to 8 servings. *Mrs. Don Heun, Louisville, Kentucky.*

EASY RUM ROLLS

1 (1-pound) loaf frozen bread dough, thawed
2 tablespoons melted butter or margarine
1 cup sugar
½ cup water
⅓ cup rum or 2 teaspoons rum extract
Powdered sugar
Maraschino cherries (optional)

Cut dough into 12 pieces; place each dough piece in a greased muffin cup. Brush tops of dough with melted butter. Cover; let rise in a warm place (85°), free from drafts, until dough rises ½ inch above muffin cups (about 2 to 2½ hours). Bake at 375° for 12 to 15 minutes or until golden brown.

Combine sugar, water, and rum in a small saucepan; bring to a rapid boil over medium heat. Reduce heat and simmer 2 minutes.

Remove rolls from pan onto a wire rack; prick tops of rolls with a fork. Spoon rum syrup over hot rolls to coat. Sift powdered sugar on each roll and top with a cherry, if desired. Let rolls cool.

Wrap rolls tightly in foil to store. To serve, place foil package in 350° oven; heat about 15 minutes. Serve hot. Yield: 1 dozen. *Mrs. W. P. Chambers, Louisville, Kentucky.*

FROZEN RASPBERRY SALAD

1½ cups miniature marshmallows
⅓ cup orange juice
1 (3-ounce) package cream cheese, softened
¼ cup mayonnaise
1 (10-ounce) package frozen raspberries, thawed
½ cup whipping cream, whipped
¾ cup chopped pecans
Lettuce (optional)

Combine marshmallows and orange juice in top of a double boiler; cook over boiling water, stirring frequently, until marshmallows are melted. Let cool.

Add cream cheese and mayonnaise to cooled juice mixture; beat until smooth. Stir in next 3 ingredients. Pour mixture into a lightly oiled 7½- x 3- x 2-inch loafpan; freeze overnight.

Remove loafpan from freezer 10 to 15 minutes before serving; invert salad onto a lettuce-lined serving platter, if desired. Yield: 8 servings. *Mrs. H. J. Sherrer, Bay City, Texas.*

Strawberry Crunch Cake is filled with strawberries and a pecan-sugar mixture. It's topped with a strawberry glaze and a dollop of whipped cream.

STRAWBERRY CRUNCH CAKE

2 (10-ounce) packages frozen sliced strawberries, thawed
2 cups all-purpose flour
1 teaspoon baking powder
½ teaspoon soda
½ teaspoon salt
1¼ cups sugar
1 cup butter or margarine, softened
2 eggs
1 cup commercial sour cream
⅓ cup firmly packed light brown sugar
½ cup chopped pecans
1 teaspoon ground cinnamon
Strawberry Glaze
Whipped cream

Drain strawberries, reserving juice for glaze. Combine flour, baking powder, soda, and salt; set aside.

Combine 1¼ cups sugar and butter in a large mixing bowl, creaming well. Add eggs; beat until smooth. Slowly mix in sour cream. Add flour mixture, and stir well.

Combine brown sugar, pecans, and cinnamon; set aside for topping.

Pour half of batter into a lightly greased 13- x 9- x 2-inch baking pan. Spoon strawberries over batter; sprinkle with half of topping mixture. Top with remaining batter, and sprinkle with remaining topping.

Bake at 350° for 30 to 35 minutes or until cake tests done. Let cool; cut into 15 squares. Top each square with Strawberry Glaze and whipped cream. Yield: 15 servings.

Strawberry Glaze:
Reserved strawberry juice
1 tablespoon plus 1 teaspoon cornstarch
2 teaspoons lemon juice

Combine strawberry juice and cornstarch in a small saucepan; cook over medium heat, stirring constantly, until thickened. Remove from heat; stir in lemon juice. Serve warm over cake. Yield: 1¼ cups.

Mrs. Donald C. Vanhoy,
Salisbury, North Carolina.

ORANGE-LEMON MIST

1 (6-ounce) can frozen orange juice concentrate, thawed
1½ to 1¾ cups water
¼ cup lemon juice
2 tablespoons Triple Sec or other orange-flavored liqueur
1 pint orange sherbet
Fresh mint leaves (optional)

Combine orange juice concentrate, water, and lemon juice in container of electric blender; cover and blend until frothy. Add Triple Sec and sherbet; blend until combined. Serve immediately; garnish with fresh mint leaves, if desired. Yield: 4 to 5 servings.

Mrs. J. John Stearman,
Louisville, Kentucky.

Make The Dressing With Rice

Mrs. J. A. Satterfield of Fort Worth offers a delicious idea for a casual supper party with her Chicken and Rice Dressing. Flavored with sausage, green onion, and celery, the rice dressing bakes along with the chicken for ease in preparation.

CHICKEN AND RICE DRESSING

2 tablespoons melted margarine
1 tablespoon lemon juice
1 (3- to 4-pound) broiler-fryer, cut up
Salt and pepper to taste
1½ cups uncooked instant rice
1 (14½-ounce) can chicken broth
½ cup water
¼ pound bulk pork sausage
¾ cup chopped green onion
1 cup chopped celery

Combine margarine and lemon juice; brush chicken with mixture, and sprinkle with salt and pepper. Place in a 13- x 9- x 2-inch baking dish; bake at 400° for 30 minutes.

Combine rice, chicken broth, and water in a medium saucepan; bring to a boil. Reduce heat; cover and simmer about 5 minutes or until all broth is absorbed. Set aside.

Cook sausage, onion, and celery in a skillet until sausage is done, stirring occasionally to crumble sausage. Combine rice and sausage mixture. Season with salt and pepper to taste; stir well. Spoon mixture around chicken, and bake for an additional 30 minutes. Yield: 6 servings.

Perk Up Plain Vegetables

This collection of vegetable recipes boasts a variety of simple additions that make a good vegetable even better. Most include ingredients you have on hand and can be mixed up in minutes.

A luscious pimiento-and-cheese sauce highlights the flavor in Lima Beans Deluxe. For something sweet, try the Sweet Potato Casserole with a crunchy, nutty topping.

BRUSSELS SPROUTS AND RICE

1 (10¾-ounce) can cream of celery soup, undiluted
1 cup milk
1 cup water
1 tablespoon butter or margarine
1 teaspoon salt
⅔ cup uncooked regular rice
2 (10-ounce) packages frozen brussels sprouts

Combine soup, milk, water, butter, and salt in a medium saucepan; bring to a boil. Stir in rice and cover; reduce heat and simmer 15 minutes, stirring occasionally.

Stir in brussels sprouts; cover and cook 15 minutes or until brussels sprouts are tender. Yield: 6 to 8 servings.
Mrs. Kenneth George,
Dickson, Tennessee.

LIMA BEANS DELUXE

2 tablespoons butter or margarine
2 tablespoons all-purpose flour
1 cup milk
1 teaspoon salt
⅛ teaspoon pepper
2 cups cooked and drained lima beans
½ cup chopped pimiento
1 cup (¼ pound) shredded Cheddar
  cheese
2 tablespoons catsup
2 tablespoons melted butter or margarine
½ cup soft breadcrumbs

Melt 2 tablespoons butter in a heavy saucepan over low heat; blend in flour and cook 1 minute, stirring constantly. Gradually add milk; cook over medium heat, stirring constantly, until thickened and bubbly. Stir in salt and pepper.

Add beans, pimiento, cheese, and catsup to sauce; mix well and pour into a greased 1½-quart casserole. Combine melted butter and breadcrumbs; mix well and sprinkle over top. Bake at 375° for 30 minutes. Yield: 6 servings.
Mrs. Mae McClaugherty,
Marble Falls, Texas.

TURNIP AU GRATIN

2 cups peeled and cubed turnips
1 tablespoon butter or margarine
1 tablespoon all-purpose flour
1 cup milk
¾ cup shredded Cheddar cheese
½ teaspoon salt
¼ teaspoon pepper
3 tablespoons melted butter or margarine
½ cup breadcrumbs
Paprika

Cook turnips in boiling salted water to cover just until tender. Drain, and spoon into a greased 1-quart casserole.

Combine 1 tablespoon butter and flour in a small saucepan; cook over low heat until bubbly. Gradually add milk; cook, stirring constantly, until smooth and thickened.

Add cheese, salt, and pepper, stirring until cheese melts. Spoon sauce over turnips. Combine 3 tablespoons melted butter with breadcrumbs, tossing well; sprinkle over casserole. Sprinkle with paprika. Bake, uncovered, at 350° for 15 minutes. Yield: 4 servings.
Mrs. Robert W. Daray,
Natchitoches, Louisiana.

Tip: For a successful cake, measure ingredients accurately, follow recipe without making substitutions, and use size pans recommended.

ITALIAN-STYLE EGGPLANT AND ZUCCHINI

⅔ cup all-purpose flour
1½ teaspoons salt, divided
1 medium eggplant, peeled and cut into
  ¼-inch slices
⅓ cup milk
Hot vegetable oil
2 medium zucchini, thinly sliced
1 medium onion, chopped
⅛ teaspoon red pepper
2 cups cottage cheese
2 eggs
½ cup dry breadcrumbs
1 (8-ounce) package mozzarella cheese,
  diced
1 (15½-ounce) jar spaghetti sauce with
  mushrooms

Combine flour and 1 teaspoon salt, mixing well. Dip eggplant slices in milk; dredge in flour mixture, and fry in hot oil until golden brown. Drain on paper towels, and set aside. Reserve drippings in skillet.

Add zucchini and onion to skillet, and sauté until barely tender; stir in red pepper.

Combine cottage cheese, eggs, and remaining ½ teaspoon salt in a small bowl; mix well, and set aside.

Arrange half of eggplant slices in a lightly greased 13- x 9- x 2-inch baking dish. Spoon half of zucchini mixture over eggplant. Top with half of breadcrumbs, half of cottage cheese mixture, half of mozzarella cheese, and half of spaghetti sauce. Repeat layers. Bake at 350° for 1 hour or until bubbly. Yield: 6 to 8 servings.
Mrs. James Tuthill,
Virginia Beach, Virginia.

SWEET POTATO CASSEROLE

3 cups cooked, mashed sweet potatoes
1 cup sugar
2 eggs
1 teaspoon vanilla extract
⅓ cup milk
½ cup butter or margarine
1 cup firmly packed brown sugar
⅓ cup all-purpose flour
⅓ cup butter or margarine
1 cup finely chopped pecans

Combine sweet potatoes, sugar, eggs, vanilla, milk, and ½ cup butter; beat with electric mixer until smooth. Spoon into a greased 2-quart shallow casserole. Combine brown sugar, flour, ⅓ cup butter, and pecans; sprinkle over top of casserole. Bake at 350° for 30 minutes. Yield: 8 to 10 servings. *Nancy Sturup,*
Columbus, Georgia.

Bake A Holiday Tradition

Start a holiday tradition at your house with this outstanding fruitcake. It's chock full of candied fruits, raisins, and pecans, which give it a chewy texture and wonderful flavor.

OLD-SOUTH FRUIT CAKE

1 cup butter, softened
1 cup sugar
5 eggs
1½ teaspoons vanilla extract
1 teaspoon almond extract
3 cups all-purpose flour, divided
2 teaspoons baking powder
¼ cup orange juice
1 tablespoon lemon juice
7½ cups chopped pecans
¼ pound chopped candied orange peel
1 pound candied pineapple, chopped
¼ pound chopped candied lemon peel
¼ pound chopped candied citron
1 pound candied cherries, chopped
1 (15-ounce) package golden raisins
Candied cherries (optional)

Combine butter and sugar, creaming until light and fluffy. Add eggs, one at a time, beating well after each addition; stir in extract. Combine 2 cups flour and baking powder; add to creamed mixture alternately with orange and lemon juice.

Dredge pecans, chopped fruits, and raisins in remaining flour; stir to coat well. Stir mixture into batter.

Spoon into a greased and waxed paper-lined 10-inch tubepan; bake at 250° for 3 hours or until cake tests done. Remove from oven. Cool cake about 10 minutes before removing from pan. Garnish with candied cherries, if desired. Chill before slicing. Yield: one 10-inch cake. *Mrs. Winfield C. Towles,*
Indianapolis, Indiana.

Christmas Cookies By The Batch

The mouth-watering aromas of brown sugar and spices, nuts and candied fruit chopped and ready for stirring into creamy batter, cookie jars waiting to be filled—that's Christmas. And to spark that holiday spirit in you, here's a collection of delectable cookie recipes, great for nibbling and for sharing with friends.

Candied cherries and a coating of chopped walnuts give Swedish Christmas Cookies that special holiday touch. Flavored with a hint of nutmeg, Rolled Sugar Cookies can be cut into festive shapes with a cookie cutter—something the youngsters would love to help with.

Old favorites include Gumdrop Cookies and Fruitcake Cookies.

Swedish Christmas Cookies are rolled in chopped walnuts and topped with candied cherry halves.

FROSTED OATMEAL-RAISIN COOKIES

2 cups all-purpose flour
1 teaspoon soda
¼ teaspoon salt
1 teaspoon ground cinnamon
½ teaspoon ground cloves
¼ teaspoon ground nutmeg
1 cup firmly packed dark brown sugar
½ cup shortening
2 eggs
1 teaspoon vanilla extract
⅓ cup cold coffee
¼ cup whipping cream
1 cup quick-cooking oats, uncooked
1 cup raisins
Spiced Coffee Frosting

Combine first 6 ingredients; set aside. Combine sugar and shortening, creaming until light and fluffy. Add eggs, and beat well; stir in vanilla. Combine coffee and whipping cream; add to creamed mixture alternately with dry ingredients. Stir in oats and raisins.

Drop dough by heaping teaspoonfuls onto lightly greased baking sheets. Bake at 350° for 12 minutes or until lightly browned. Place on racks to cool. Frost lightly with Spiced Coffee Frosting. Yield: about 6 dozen.

Spiced Coffee Frosting:

1 cup powdered sugar
3 tablespoons butter or margarine, softened
1 tablespoon hot coffee
1 teaspoon vanilla extract
½ teaspoon ground cinnamon

Combine all ingredients; beat until light and fluffy. Yield: ⅔ cup.
Mrs. Virginia L. Weber,
Morgantown, West Virginia.

SWEDISH CHRISTMAS COOKIES

½ cup butter or margarine, softened
¼ cup sugar
1 egg, separated
1 tablespoon grated orange rind
1 tablespoon lemon juice
2 teaspoons vanilla extract
⅛ teaspoon salt
1 cup cake flour
1 cup chopped walnuts
18 candied cherries, halved

Combine butter and sugar, creaming until light and fluffy; add egg yolk, and beat 1 minute. Add orange rind, lemon juice, vanilla, and salt; beat thoroughly. Add flour, mixing well. Chill dough 2 hours.

Beat egg white slightly. Shape dough into ¾-inch balls; dip each in egg white, and roll each in walnuts. Place 2 inches apart on greased cookie sheets, and slightly flatten each. Place cherry half on each cookie, and bake at 325° for 20 minutes. Yield: about 3 dozen.
Barbara McGlothter,
Nashville, Tennessee.

SLICE-OF-SPICE COOKIES

½ cup butter or margarine, softened
½ cup shortening
2 cups firmly packed brown sugar
2 eggs
1 teaspoon vanilla extract
3 cups all-purpose flour
1 teaspoon soda
1 teaspoon cream of tartar
½ teaspoon salt
1 cup quick-cooking oats, uncooked
½ cup sugar
1 tablespoon plus 1 teaspoon ground cinnamon

Combine butter, shortening, and brown sugar; cream until light and fluffy. Add eggs, beating well; stir in vanilla.

Combine next 4 ingredients; add to creamed mixture, mixing well. Stir in oats. Chill dough 1 hour.

Divide dough into 3 portions, and shape each into a 12-inch roll. Carefully wrap each roll in waxed paper, and place on a cookie sheet. Chill 4 to 5 hours.

Combine sugar and cinnamon, mixing well. Unwrap rolls, and cut into ¼-inch slices. Dip each slice in cinnamon mixture, and place on greased cookie sheets. Bake at 350° for 10 minutes. Yield: about 8 dozen.
Mrs. W. P. Chambers,
Louisville, Kentucky.

TWICE-BAKED PECAN SQUARES

½ cup butter or margarine, softened
½ cup firmly packed dark brown sugar
1 cup all-purpose flour
2 eggs
1 cup firmly packed light brown sugar
1 cup coarsely chopped pecans
½ cup flaked coconut
2 tablespoons all-purpose flour
1 teaspoon vanilla extract
Pinch of salt
Powdered sugar

Combine butter and dark brown sugar, creaming until light and fluffy. Add 1 cup flour, and mix well. Press mixture evenly into a greased 13- x 9- x 2-inch baking pan. Bake at 350° for 20 minutes.

Beat eggs until frothy; gradually add light brown sugar, beating until smooth and thickened. Combine pecans, coconut, and 2 tablespoons flour; stir well. Combine egg mixture, nut mixture, vanilla, and salt; mix well, and spread over crust.

Bake at 350° for 20 minutes or until golden brown; let cool. Sprinkle lightly with powdered sugar, and cut into squares. Yield: 3 to 4 dozen.

Mrs. H. S. Wright,
Leesville, South Carolina.

ROLLED SUGAR COOKIES

3 cups all-purpose flour
2 teaspoons baking powder
¾ teaspoon soda
½ teaspoon ground nutmeg
1 cup shortening
2 eggs, beaten
1 cup sugar
¼ cup milk
1 teaspoon vanilla extract

Combine flour, baking powder, soda, and nutmeg; cut in shortening with a pastry blender until mixture resembles coarse crumbs.

Combine eggs, sugar, milk, and vanilla; mix well, and pour into crumb mixture. Stir with a fork until all dry ingredients are moistened. Shape into a ball, and chill 1 to 2 hours.

Work with half of dough at a time; store remainder in refrigerator. Roll dough out on a lightly floured board to ⅛-inch thickness; cut with shaped cookie cutters. Place on lightly greased cookie sheets; bake at 375° for 10 minutes or until edges are lightly browned. Yield: about 4½ dozen.

Mrs. Robert Collins,
Fairfax, Missouri.

NUGGET COOKIES

¾ cup sugar
¾ cup firmly packed brown sugar
1 cup butter, softened
2 eggs
2½ cups all-purpose flour
1 teaspoon soda
1 teaspoon salt
2 teaspoons vanilla extract
1 (6-ounce) package semisweet chocolate morsels
1 cup chopped pecans
2 cups seedless raisins

Combine sugar and butter, creaming until light and fluffy. Add eggs, one at a time, beating after each addition. Combine flour, soda, and salt; add to creamed mixture, beating 1 minute. Stir in vanilla, chocolate morsels, pecans, and raisins.

Drop dough by teaspoonfuls onto lightly greased cookie sheets. Bake at 375° for 10 to 12 minutes or until golden brown. Yield: about 2½ dozen.

M. J. Victory,
Goodlettsville, Tennessee.

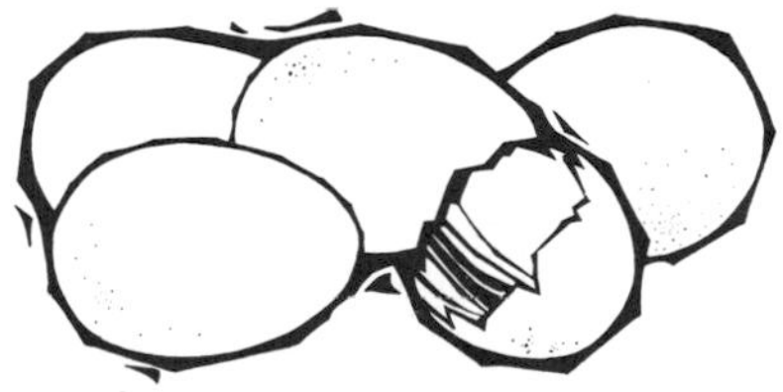

FRUITCAKE COOKIES

1 cup melted butter or margarine
1 cup firmly packed brown sugar
3 eggs
3 cups all-purpose flour
1 teaspoon soda
1 teaspoon ground cinnamon
½ cup milk
2 tablespoons cream sherry (optional)
6 slices candied pineapple, finely chopped
1 cup candied red cherries, finely chopped
1 cup candied green cherries, finely chopped
2 cups chopped dates
1 (15-ounce) package white raisins
7 cups chopped nuts

Combine butter and sugar, mixing well. Add eggs, and beat well. Combine dry ingredients; add to butter mixture alternately with milk, mixing well after each addition. Stir in sherry, if desired. Add fruit and nuts to dough, mixing well.

Drop dough by heaping teaspoonfuls onto greased cookie sheets. Bake at 300° about 20 minutes. Yield: about 16 dozen.

Linda Thompson,
High Point, North Carolina.

CREAM CHEESE FRILLS

1 cup butter, softened
1 teaspoon vanilla extract
2 cups all-purpose flour
½ teaspoon salt
1 cup uncooked regular oats
1 (8-ounce) package cream cheese, softened
Preserves or jelly

Combine butter and vanilla, creaming until smooth. Add flour, salt, and oats; mix well. Add cream cheese, and beat until smooth. Shape into a ball, and chill 1 to 2 hours.

Roll dough out on a lightly floured board to ¼-inch thickness. Cut into 2-inch squares, and spoon about ½ teaspoon preserves onto center of each. Fold in half diagonally, pressing edges together to seal.

Place cookies on ungreased baking sheets; bake at 425° for 10 to 12 minutes. Yield: about 3½ dozen.

Marlene Beasley,
San Antonio, Texas.

APPLE BUTTER SPICE COOKIES

2½ cups all-purpose flour
1 teaspoon baking powder
1 teaspoon soda
1 teaspoon salt
½ teaspoon ground cinnamon
1 cup sugar
½ cup shortening
1 egg
1 cup apple butter
½ cup raisins
½ cup chopped nuts

Combine first 5 ingredients, and set aside. Combine sugar and shortening, creaming until light and fluffy. Beat in egg, and stir in apple butter. Add dry ingredients, mixing well; stir in raisins and nuts.

Drop dough by heaping teaspoonfuls onto lightly greased baking sheets. Bake at 375° for 10 minutes. Remove to racks to cool. Yield: about 8 dozen.

Mrs. Brenda Arehart,
Fairfield, Virginia.

Tip: To get maximum volume when beating egg whites, have them at room temperature and beat in a deep glass or metal bowl—not plastic. Tip the bowl to determine if whites have reached the proper consistency. The whites will not slide when they have reached the "stiff but not dry" stage called for in many recipes.

CHOCO-CRUMBLE BARS

1½ cups all-purpose flour
¾ cup firmly packed light brown sugar
¼ teaspoon salt
½ cup butter, softened
1 (6-ounce) package semisweet chocolate morsels
1 cup peanut butter

Combine flour, sugar, and salt; cut in butter with a pastry blender until mixture resembles coarse crumbs. Pat mixture into an ungreased 13- x 9- x 2-inch baking pan. Bake at 375° for 10 minutes. Cool slightly.

Combine chocolate morsels and peanut butter in a small saucepan; place over low heat, stirring constantly, until chocolate melts. Spread over crust; chill until firm. Cut into bars. Yield: 2 to 3 dozen.   *Dorsella Utter,*
Columbia, Missouri.

COCONUT-CHERRY COOKIES

2 cups all-purpose flour
½ teaspoon soda
½ teaspoon salt
1 cup firmly packed brown sugar
¾ cup butter or margarine, softened
1 egg
2 tablespoons milk
1 teaspoon vanilla extract
½ cup chopped pecans
½ cup flaked coconut
½ cup chopped maraschino cherries

Sift together flour, soda, and salt; set aside.

Combine brown sugar and butter, creaming until light and fluffy. Add egg, milk, and vanilla; mix well. Add dry ingredients, mixing well. Stir in pecans, coconut, and cherries.

Drop batter by heaping teaspoonfuls onto lightly greased baking sheets. Bake at 375° for 9 to 10 minutes or until lightly browned. Place on rack to cool. Yield: about 6½ dozen.
Mrs. Gay Bridges,
Oneida, Tennessee.

GUMDROP COOKIES

1 cup melted margarine
1 cup firmly packed brown sugar
1 egg, slightly beaten
1 teaspoon vanilla extract
1¾ cups all-purpose flour
½ teaspoon baking powder
½ teaspoon soda
½ teaspoon salt
1 cup uncooked regular oats
1 cup gumdrops, cut into ¼-inch pieces
½ cup chopped pecans or walnuts

Combine margarine, sugar, egg, and vanilla in a large mixing bowl; mix well. Add next 5 ingredients, mixing only until blended; stir in gumdrops and pecans.

Drop dough by rounded tablespoonfuls onto ungreased cookie sheets. Bake at 375° for 10 to 12 minutes. Yield: about 3 dozen.
Mrs. John L. Faulkenberry,
Lancaster, South Carolina.

Serve Chutney On The Side

A colorful, sweet chutney is frequently the perfect accompaniment to holiday meat dishes. Mrs. Carl E. Smith of Melbourne, Florida, combines apples, oranges, cranberries, raisins, and nuts to make her Orange-Cranberry Chutney. Mrs. Smith says she enjoys preparing large batches to serve for special occasions.

Be sure to store this tasty condiment in the refrigerator.

CRANBERRY-ORANGE CHUTNEY

1 cup fresh orange sections
¼ cup orange juice
4 cups cranberries
2 cups sugar
1 cup chopped, unpeeled apple
½ cup raisins
¼ cup chopped walnuts
1 tablespoon vinegar
½ teaspoon ground ginger
½ teaspoon ground cinnamon

Combine all ingredients in a large saucepan, and bring to a boil. Reduce heat and simmer 5 minutes or until berries begin to burst. Chill until serving time. Yield: 5½ cups.

These Cornish Hens Are Brandied

When Mrs. James Bright of Anniston, Alabama, serves Cornish hens, she stuffs the tiny birds with a cornbread dressing enhanced with brandy and pecans. Brandy also flavors the butter sauce used to baste the hens during baking.

BRANDY-BUTTERED CORNISH HENS

6 (1- to 1½-pound) Cornish hens
Salt and pepper
Pecan Stuffing
½ cup melted butter or margarine
¼ cup apricot-, peach-, or plum-flavored brandy

Remove giblets from hens; reserve for another use. Rinse hens with cold water, and pat dry. Sprinkle cavity of each with salt and pepper. Secure neck skin to back with toothpick; lift wingtips up and over back so they are tucked under hen.

Lightly stuff cavity of hens with Pecan Stuffing; close cavity, and secure with toothpicks. Tie leg ends to tail with cord or string. Brush hens with butter, and sprinkle generously with pepper. Combine remaining butter with brandy.

Place hens, breast side up, in a large shallow baking pan. Bake at 350° for 1 to 1½ hours, depending on size of hens; baste every 10 minutes with brandy mixture. Yield: 6 servings.

Pecan Stuffing:

1 cup unsweetened apple juice
¼ cup apricot-, peach-, or plum-flavored brandy
¼ cup butter or margarine
1 (8-ounce) package cornbread stuffing mix
¾ cup chopped pecans

Combine apple juice, brandy, and butter in a large saucepan; cook over medium heat, stirring occasionally, until butter melts. Add stuffing mix and pecans, stirring lightly. Yield: enough stuffing for 6 Cornish hens.

Note: Stuffing may be used to stuff a 6- to 7-pound baking hen.

Tip: After removing a roast from the oven, let it rest at least 15 minutes for easier carving.

Flame A Coffee For Dessert

For a dramatic finale to a special dinner, serve a flaming dessert coffee. We suggest Flaming Irish Coffee, flavored with Irish Mist liqueur, or Flaming Cappuccino, which calls for Galliano and chocolate syrup.

Both recipes are favorites of George E. Jackson, Jr., of Fort Stewart, Georgia, who enjoys serving flaming coffee to his guests.

To serve it with a flair, use an Irish coffee burner or alcohol burner to flame the coffee as your guests watch. If you prefer, simply warm the liqueur in a saucepan, ignite, and assemble in the kitchen. As an extra precaution against breakage, pour the hot coffee down a metal spoon placed in the glass.

FLAMING CAPPUCCINO

Lemon juice
Sugar
¾ cup Galliano liqueur, divided
6 cups hot coffee, divided
2 tablespoons chocolate syrup, divided
1 cup whipping cream, whipped
6 cinnamon sticks

Rinse glass with hot water; dry. Dip rim of glass in lemon juice, then in sugar, making a ½-inch band around top. Rotate glass over flame of Irish coffee burner or alcohol burner until sugar crystallizes.

Pour 2 tablespoons Galliano in glass. Rotate over flame until liqueur ignites. Fill with coffee to bottom of sugar rim; stir in 1 teaspoon chocolate syrup. Top with whipped cream; garnish with a cinnamon stick. Repeat for remaining servings. Yield: 6 servings.

FLAMING IRISH COFFEE

¾ cup Irish Mist liqueur, divided
6 cups hot coffee, divided
2 tablespoons sugar, divided
1 cup whipping cream, whipped
Ground nutmeg

Rinse glass with hot water; dry. Pour 2 tablespoons Irish Mist into glass. Rotate glass over flame of Irish coffee burner or alcohol burner until liqueur ignites. Fill with coffee to within 1 inch of rim; stir in 1 teaspoon sugar. Top with whipped cream; sprinkle lightly with nutmeg. Repeat for remaining servings. Yield: 6 servings.

Ladle Up Lamb Stew

When cold winter days call for something hot and hearty, Doris Garton of Shenandoah, Virginia, serves lamb stew. Thyme, garlic, bay leaf, and tomato puree flavor the lamb and vegetables while they simmer slowly in the oven.

LAMB STEW

1 (2-pound) boneless shoulder of lamb, cut into 1½-inch cubes
¼ cup plus 2 tablespoons vegetable oil
½ teaspoon sugar
2 tablespoons all-purpose flour
½ cup tomato puree
1 teaspoon dried thyme
1 teaspoon parsley flakes
1 clove garlic, crushed
1 small bay leaf
6 cups water
8 small potatoes, peeled
12 baby carrots, peeled
1 cup frozen English peas

Sauté lamb in oil until brown; drain off excess drippings. Combine sugar and flour; sprinkle over meat, stirring to coat meat. Cook over medium heat 2 minutes.

Combine tomato puree, thyme, parsley, garlic, and bay leaf; pour over meat, and stir well. Stir water into meat mixture; boil 10 minutes, skimming excess fat from top as it cooks.

Transfer meat mixture to a 3½-quart casserole; cover and bake at 350° for 1 hour. Drain liquid from stew into a saucepan; boil until reduced by a third, skimming excess fat from top as it cooks.

Strain reduced liquid; combine with lamb and vegetables in casserole. Cover and bake an additional 45 minutes. Yield: 4 to 6 servings.

Sample Hickory-Smoked Turkey

For a delightful alternative to the traditional roast turkey, try preparing the holiday bird in a smoker this year. During the slow cooking process, the turkey takes on a distinctive hickory-smoked flavor.

Leftover smoked turkey is delicious served hot or cold. Slice chilled meat into julienne strips, and toss with lettuce, Swiss cheese, cucumbers, and tomato wedges for a hearty chef's salad. For an elegant appetizer, slice the turkey thin and serve on party rye bread spread with cream cheese.

Offer pan-fried turkey slices in place of bacon for a special breakfast treat. The sliced meat can be fried in a non-stick skillet without adding oil.

Turkey sandwiches are always welcome after the holiday feast. Serve chilled turkey with the traditional sandwich trimmings, and add a scoop of potato salad on the side. For hot sandwiches, prepare gravy with turkey broth and reheat the sliced meat in the sauce. Serve open-face on toasted bread.

To prevent the meat from drying, add moisture before reheating turkey slices in the oven. Place slices in a shallow pan, and sprinkle lightly with water or broth. Cover tightly, and bake at 425° until thoroughly heated, about 10 to 12 minutes.

SMOKED TURKEY

1 (8- to 12-pound) turkey
Seasoned salt
Vegetable oil

Rinse turkey, and pat dry; rub with seasoned salt and vegetable oil.

Prepare charcoal fire in smoker, and let burn 10 to 15 minutes; add 6 to 8 pieces of hickory to fire. Place water pan in smoker, and fill with water.

Place turkey on grill, and cover with lid. Allow turkey to cook 8 to 10 hours (do not open smoker). Turkey is done when drumsticks move easily in joint. Yield: 16 to 20 servings.

Tip: Use the following timetable for roasting your holiday turkey. Times are based on an oven temperature of 325°. The turkey will be done when a meat thermometer inserted in the thickest part of the thigh registers 185°.

Ready-To-Cook Weight	Approximate Roasting Time*
6 to 8 pounds	*3 to 3½ hours*
8 to 12 pounds	*3½ to 4½ hours*
12 to 16 pounds	*4½ to 5½ hours*

*Add ½ hour to total roasting time if turkey is stuffed.

Add a festive touch to your party by serving the dip from a wreath of fresh vegetables. Guests can pluck out the vegetables and use as dippers.

Dip Into A Vegetable Wreath

For those savory dips that call for crisp, fresh vegetables as dippers, we have a suggestion for the holiday season: Arrange the vegetables into a colorful wreath.

Though spectacular, a vegetable wreath is easy to fashion. All you need is a circle of plastic foam, toothpicks, enough parsley to cover the circle, a stapler, and an assortment of fresh vegetables. Then assemble the wreath according to the procedure illustrated in the step-by-step photographs, and refer to the tips that follow.

—Be sure to include a variety of colors and textures of vegetables in the wreath. And don't forget to add touches of holiday red with cherry tomatoes or pimiento-stuffed olives.

—Carrot sticks, celery and green onion fans or sticks, and radish roses can be prepared a day in advance. Place each vegetable in a separate container, cover with ice water, and refrigerate.

—After they are thoroughly washed, cut broccoli and cauliflower into flowerets; then refrigerate until needed.

—The vegetable wreath is at its best when prepared just before the party, but it can be assembled several hours ahead. Just cover it with damp paper towels and aluminum foil, and store in the refrigerator.

Step 1—*For the vegetable wreath, you'll need a 12-inch diameter plastic-foam circle (about 2 inches deep) with an 8-inch opening in the center, a 6-inch-diameter bowl for the dip, a round platter to set the wreath on, a stapler, sturdy wooden toothpicks, prepared vegetables, and enough parsley to cover the foam circle.*

Step 2—*After thoroughly washing and trimming the parsley, staple it to the plastic-foam circle, overlapping the sprigs to ensure complete coverage.*

Step 3—*Skewer vegetables with toothpicks, and stick them into the wreath. Olives and tomatoes are easier to attach by inserting the toothpick in the wreath first, then sticking the vegetable onto the end of the pick.*

You're Prepared With These Appetizers

Be prepared for guests with appetizers that can be served in minutes. A handful of Spiced Pecans will keep your guests satisfied while you have time to slice and bake Asparagus Rolls. Cucumber Spread is also handy to keep in the refrigerator, ready to be served with assorted fresh vegetables or crackers.

SURPRISE CHEESE PUFFS

1 cup (¼ pound) shredded Cheddar
  cheese
½ cup all-purpose flour
¼ cup butter or margarine, softened
½ teaspoon paprika
¼ teaspoon salt
About 3 dozen pimiento-stuffed olives

Combine first 5 ingredients; mix well with a fork.

Drain olives well on paper towels. Shape a thin layer of cheese mixture around each olive; place on an ungreased cookie sheet. Bake at 425° for 8 to 10 minutes or until lightly browned. Yield: about 3 dozen.

Note: Cocktail onions may be substituted for olives. *Lilly S. Bradley,
Salem, Virginia.*

Step 4—*At serving time, place the bowl of dip in the center of the wreath.*

CUCUMBER SPREAD

2 cucumbers, unpeeled and grated
1 small onion, grated
1 (8-ounce) package cream cheese,
  softened
2 tablespoons salad dressing or
  mayonnaise
½ teaspoon seasoned salt
¼ teaspoon lemon juice (optional)

Place cucumber and onion on paper towels, and squeeze out moisture.

Beat cream cheese until smooth, and stir in vegetables, salad dressing, and salt; add lemon juice, if desired. Serve spread with fresh vegetables or crackers. Yield: about 2 cups.
  *Varniece Warren,
Hermitage, Arkansas.*

CHEESE BISCUITS

2 cups (½ pound) shredded sharp
   Cheddar cheese
2¼ cups all-purpose flour
1 cup butter or margarine, softened
1 cup chopped pecans
1 teaspoon Worcestershire sauce
½ teaspoon salt
½ teaspoon red pepper

Combine all ingredients, mixing well.
Drop by heaping teaspoonfuls onto ungreased baking sheets. Bake at 425° for
12 to 15 minutes. Yield: about 6
dozen.
Clara McWillie,
Tulsa, Oklahoma.

ASPARAGUS ROLLS

20 slices white bread, crusts removed
3 ounces blue cheese
1 (8-ounce) package cream cheese,
   softened
1 egg, beaten
1 (14½-ounce) can asparagus spears,
   drained
1 cup melted butter or margarine

Use a rolling pin to flatten each slice
of bread. Combine blue cheese, cream
cheese, and egg in a small mixing bowl,
mixing well. Spread evenly on bread,
covering to edges.

Place 1 asparagus spear on each slice
of bread; roll up, and secure with 3
toothpicks. Dip in melted butter. Place
on a baking sheet and freeze.

Partially thaw asparagus rolls, and
slice each into 3 equal pieces. Bake at
375° for 15 minutes. Yield: 60 appetizer
servings.
Mrs. James Petty,
Columbia, South Carolina.

SPICED PECANS

1 cup sugar
1 to 2 teaspoons ground cinnamon
1 teaspoon salt
½ teaspoon ground nutmeg
¼ teaspoon ground cloves
¼ cup water
2 cups pecan halves

Combine first 6 ingredients in a large
saucepan; stir well. Place over medium
heat, stirring constantly until sugar dissolves; then cook to soft ball stage
(about 232°). Remove from heat; add
pecans, stirring until well coated.

Spread pecans on waxed paper, and
separate nuts with a fork. Cool. Yield:
2 cups.
Mrs. Ed Lee Niles,
Marshall, North Carolina.

Three Easy Ways With Dressing

These three dressing recipes each
take a different approach to the traditional holiday accompaniment. Corn-
bread-Biscuit Dressing is for stuffing the
turkey or baking separately as a side
dish. But Easy Turkey and Dressing
calls for the cornbread dressing to be
combined with chopped turkey for an
appealing entrée—a great way to use
those holiday leftovers.

If chicken is your preference, enjoy
Baked Chicken and Dressing: chicken
pieces arranged around a mound of savory dressing and baked in a creamy
sauce.

EASY TURKEY AND DRESSING

1 (10¾-ounce) can cream of chicken soup,
   undiluted
1 cup water
1 teaspoon poultry seasoning
½ cup shredded carrots
⅓ cup chopped onion
½ cup melted butter or margarine
1 (8-ounce) package cornbread stuffing
   mix
2 cups chopped cooked turkey
2 tablespoons chopped fresh parsley

Combine soup, water, and poultry
seasoning in a small bowl; mix well, and
set aside.

Sauté carrots and onion in butter
until tender. Stir in stuffing mix, turkey,
and soup mixture. Cook over medium
heat 8 to 10 minutes, stirring often.
Spoon into serving dish, and sprinkle
with parsley. Yield: 4 to 5 servings.
Charlotte Pierce,
Greensburg, Kentucky.

CORNBREAD-BISCUIT DRESSING

1 medium onion, chopped
1 cup diced celery
¼ cup melted butter or margarine
4 cups cornbread crumbs
2 cups dry biscuit crumbs
½ cup milk
2 cups warm turkey broth
1 egg, slightly beaten
1 teaspoon salt
1 teaspoon poultry seasoning

Sauté onion and celery in butter until
tender; combine all ingredients. Stuff
bird with dressing; or spoon into a
greased 9-inch square pan, and bake at
375° for 20 to 25 minutes. Yield: 8
servings.
Margaret Farley,
Columbia, South Carolina.

BAKED CHICKEN AND DRESSING

¼ cup all-purpose flour
1 teaspoon salt
¼ teaspoon pepper
1 (2½- to 3-pound) broiler-fryer, cut up
¼ cup melted shortening
10 slices bread, cut into 1-inch cubes
2 tablespoons minced onion
½ cup melted margarine
1 (10¾-ounce) can cream of chicken soup,
   undiluted
1 teaspoon salt
½ teaspoon pepper
1½ teaspoons rubbed sage
3 tablespoons all-purpose flour

Combine first 3 ingredients; dredge
chicken in seasoned flour. Fry in shortening until browned on all sides; drain
on paper towels, reserving drippings in
skillet.

Combine bread, onion, margarine, 1
cup soup, and remaining seasonings;
mix well, and spoon into the center of a
greased 2-quart shallow casserole. Place
chicken around dressing, and set aside.

Add enough water to remaining soup
to make 2 cups; mix well, and set aside.

Add 3 tablespoons flour to drippings
in skillet, stirring until smooth. Cook 1
minute, stirring constantly. Gradually
stir in soup mixture; cook over medium
heat, stirring constantly, until thickened
and bubbly. Pour over chicken and
dressing; cover and bake at 350° for 1
hour or until chicken is tender. Yield: 4
servings.
Mrs. Henry Horn,
Deltona, Florida.

Appendices

EQUIVALENT WEIGHTS AND MEASURES

Food	Weight Or Count	Measure Or Yield
Apples	1 pound (3 medium)	3 cups sliced
Bacon	8 slices cooked	½ cup crumbled
Bananas	1 pound (3 medium)	2½ cups sliced, or about 2 cups mashed
Bread	1 pound	12 to 16 slices
Bread	About 1½ slices	1 cup soft crumbs
Butter or margarine	1 pound	2 cups
Butter or margarine	¼ - pound stick	½ cup
Butter or margarine	Size of an egg	About ¼ cup
Cabbage	1 pound head	4½ cups shredded
Candied fruit or peels	½ pound	1¼ cups cut
Carrots	1 pound	3 cups shredded
Cheese, American or Cheddar	1 pound	About 4 cups shredded
cottage	1 pound	2 cups
cream	3 - ounce package	6 tablespoons
Chocolate morsels	6 - ounce package	1 cup
Cocoa	1 pound	4 cups
Coconut, flaked or shredded	1 pound	5 cups
Coffee	1 pound	80 tablespoons (40 cups perked)
Corn	2 medium ears	1 cup kernels
Cornmeal	1 pound	3 cups
Crab, in shell	1 pound	¾ to 1 cup flaked
Crackers		
chocolate wafers	19 wafers	1 cup crumbs
graham crackers	14 squares	1 cup fine crumbs
saltine crackers	28 crackers	1 cup finely crushed
vanilla wafers	22 wafers	1 cup finely crushed
Cream, whipping	1 cup (½ pint)	2 cups whipped
Dates, pitted	1 pound	3 cups chopped
Dates, pitted	8 - ounce package	1½ cups chopped
Eggs	5 large	1 cup
whites	8 to 11	1 cup
yolks	12 to 14	1 cup
Flour		
all-purpose	1 pound	4 cups sifted
cake	1 pound	4¾ to 5 cups sifted
whole wheat	1 pound	3½ cups unsifted
Green pepper	1 large	1 cup diced
Lemon	1 medium	2 to 3 tablespoons juice and 2 teaspoons grated rind
Lettuce	1 pound head	6¼ cups torn
Lime	1 medium	1½ to 2 tablespoons juice
Macaroni	4 ounces (1 cup)	2¼ cups cooked

Food	Weight Or Count	Measure Or Yield
Milk		
evaporated	5.33 - ounce can	⅔ cup
evaporated	13 - ounce can	1⅝ cups
sweetened condensed	14 - ounce can	1¼ cups
sweetened condensed	15 - ounce can	1⅓ cups
Miniature marshmallows	½ pound	4½ cups
Mushrooms	3 cups raw (8 ounces)	1 cup sliced cooked
Nuts		
almonds	1 pound	1 to 1¾ cups nutmeats
	1 pound shelled	3½ cups nutmeats
peanuts	1 pound	2¼ cups nutmeats
	1 pound shelled	3 cups
pecans	1 pound	2¼ cups nutmeats
	1 pound shelled	4 cups
walnuts	1 pound	1⅔ cups nutmeats
	1 pound shelled	4 cups
Oats, quick-cooking	1 cup	1¾ cups cooked
Onion	1 medium	½ cup chopped
Orange	1 medium	⅓ cup juice and 2 tablespoons grated rind
Peaches	4 medium	2 cups sliced
Pears	4 medium	2 cups sliced
Potatoes, white	3 medium	2 cups cubed cooked or 1¾ cups mashed
sweet	3 medium	3 cups sliced
Raisins, seedless	1 pound	3 cups
Rice, long-grain	1 cup	3 to 4 cups cooked
pre-cooked	1 cup	2 cups cooked
Shrimp, raw in shell	1 pound	2 cups (¾ pound) cleaned, cooked
Spaghetti	7 ounces	About 4 cups cooked
Strawberries	1 quart	4 cups sliced
Sugar		
brown	1 pound	2¼ cups firmly packed
powdered	1 pound	3½ cups unsifted
granulated	1 pound	2 cups
Whipping cream	1 cup	2 cups whipped

EQUIVALENT MEASUREMENTS

Use standard measuring cups (both dry and liquid measure) and measuring spoons when measuring ingredients. All measurements given below are level.

3 teaspoons	1 tablespoon
4 tablespoons	¼ cup
5⅓ tablespoons	⅓ cup
8 tablespoons	½ cup
16 tablespoons	1 cup
2 tablespoons (liquid)	1 ounce
1 cup	8 fluid ounces
2 cups	1 pint (16 fluid ounces)
4 cups	1 quart
4 quarts	1 gallon
⅛ cup	2 tablespoons
⅓ cup	5 tablespoons plus 1 teaspoon
⅔ cup	10 tablespoons plus 2 teaspoons
¾ cup	12 tablespoons
Few grains (or dash)	Less than ⅛ teaspoon
Pinch	As much as can be taken between tip of finger and thumb

CANNED FOOD GUIDE

Can Size	Number of Cups	Number of Servings	Foods
8-ounce	1 cup	2 servings	Fruits, Vegetables
10½- to 12-ounce (picnic)	1¼ cups	3 servings	Condensed Soups, Fruits and Vegetables, Meats and Fish, Specialties
12-ounce (vacuum)	1½ cups	3 to 4 servings	Vacuum-Packed Corn
14- to 16-ounce (No. 300)	1¾ cups	3 to 4 servings	Pork and Beans, Meat Products, Cranberry Sauce
16- to 17-ounce (No. 303)	2 cups	4 servings	Principal Size for Fruits and Vegetables, Some Meat Products
1 pound, 4 ounce (No. 2)	2½ cups	5 servings	Juices, Pineapple, Apple Slices
27- to 29-ounce (No. 2½)	3½ cups	7 servings	Fruits, Some Vegetables (Pumpkin, Sauerkraut, Greens, Tomatoes)
46-ounce (No. 3 cyl.)	5¾ cups	10 to 12 servings	Fruit and Vegetable Juices
6½-pound (No. 10)	12 to 13 cups	25 servings	Institutional Size for Fruits and Vegetables

HANDY SUBSTITUTIONS

Even the best of cooks occasionally runs out of an ingredient she needs and is unable to stop what she is doing to go to the store. At times like those, sometimes another ingredient or combination of ingredients can be used. Here is a list of substitutions and equivalents that yield satisfactory results in most cases.

Ingredient Called For	Substitution
1 cup self-rising flour	1 cup all-purpose flour plus 1 teaspoon baking powder and ½ teaspoon salt
1 cup cake flour	1 cup sifted all-purpose flour minus 2 tablespoons
1 cup all-purpose flour	1 cup cake flour plus 2 tablespoons
1 teaspoon baking powder	½ teaspoon cream of tartar plus ¼ teaspoon soda
1 tablespoon cornstarch or arrowroot	2 tablespoons all-purpose flour
1 tablespoon tapioca	1½ tablespoons all-purpose flour
2 large eggs	3 small eggs
1 egg	2 egg yolks (for custard)
1 egg	2 egg yolks plus 1 tablespoon water (for cookies)
1 cup commercial sour cream	1 tablespoon lemon juice plus evaporated milk to equal 1 cup; or 3 tablespoons butter plus ⅞ cup sour milk
1 cup yogurt	1 cup buttermilk or sour milk
1 cup sour milk or buttermilk	1 tablespoon vinegar or lemon juice plus sweet milk to equal 1 cup
1 cup fresh milk	½ cup evaporated milk plus ½ cup water
1 cup fresh milk	3 to 5 tablespoons nonfat dry milk solids in 1 cup water
1 cup honey	1¼ cups sugar plus ¼ cup liquid
1 square (1-ounce) unsweetened chocolate	3 tablespoons cocoa plus 1 tablespoon butter or margarine
1 clove fresh garlic	1 teaspoon garlic salt or ⅛ teaspoon garlic powder
1 teaspoon onion powder	2 teaspoons minced onion
1 tablespoon fresh herbs	1 teaspoon dried herbs or ¼ teaspoon powdered herbs
¼ cup chopped fresh parsley	1 tablespoon dehydrated parsley
1 teaspoon dry mustard	1 tablespoon prepared mustard
1 pound fresh mushrooms	6 ounces canned mushrooms

METRIC MEASURES

Approximate Conversion to Metric Measures

When You Know . . .	Multiply by . . .	To Find . . .	Symbol
Mass (weight)			
ounces	28	grams	g
pounds	0.45	kilograms	kg
Volume			
teaspoons	5	milliliters	ml
tablespoons	15	milliliters	ml
fluid ounces	30	milliliters	ml
cups	0.24	liters	l
pints	0.47	liters	l
quarts	0.95	liters	l
gallons	3.8	liters	l

COOKING MEASURE EQUIVALENTS

Metric Cup	Volume (Liquid)	Liquid Solids (Butter)	Fine Powder (Flour)	Granular (Sugar)	Grain (Rice)
1	250 ml	200 g	140 g	190 g	150 g
¾	188 ml	150 g	105 g	143 g	113 g
⅔	167 ml	133 g	93 g	127 g	100 g
½	125 ml	100 g	70 g	95 g	75 g
⅓	83 ml	67 g	47 g	63 g	50 g
¼	63 ml	50 g	35 g	48 g	38 g
⅛	31 ml	25 g	18 g	24 g	19 g

APPROXIMATE TEMPERATURE CONVERSIONS—FAHRENHEIT TO CELSIUS

	Fahrenheit (°F)	Celsius (°C)
Freezer		
coldest area	-10°	-23°
overall	0°	-17°
Water		
freezes	32°	0°
simmers	115°	46°
scalds	130°	55°
boils (sea level)	212°	100°
Soft Ball	234° to 240°	112° to 115°
Firm Ball	242° to 248°	116° to 120°
Hard Ball	250° to 268°	121° to 131°
Slow Oven	275° to 300°	135° to 148°

APPROXIMATE TEMPERATURE CONVERSIONS—FAHRENHEIT TO CELSIUS (*continued*)

	Fahrenheit (°F)	Celsius (°C)
Moderate Oven	350°	177°
Hot Oven	425° to 475°	218° to 246°
Deep Fat	375° to 400°	190° to 204°
Broil	550°	288°

To convert Fahrenheit to Celsius:
    subtract 32
    multiply by 5
    divide by 9

To convert Celsius to Fahrenheit:
    multiply by 9
    divide by 5
    add 32

TIMETABLE FOR ROASTING BEEF AND LAMB

Kind and Cut	Approximate Weight	Internal Temperature	Approximate Total Cooking Times at 325°F.
	pounds		hours
Beef			
Standing ribs* (10-inch ribs)	4	140°F. (rare)	1¾
		160°F. (medium)	2
		170°F. (well done)	2½
	6	140°F. (rare)	2
		160°F. (medium)	2½
		170°F. (well done)	3½
	8	140°F. (rare)	2½
		160°F. (medium)	3
		170°F. (well done)	4½
Rolled ribs	4	140°F. (rare)	2
		160°F. (medium)	2½
		170°F. (well done)	3
	6	140°F. (rare)	3
		160°F. (medium)	3¼
		170°F. (well done)	4
Rolled rump	5	140°F. (rare)	2¼
		160°F. (medium)	3
		170°F. (well done)	3¼
Sirloin tip	3	140°F. (rare)	1½
		160°F. (medium)	2
		170°F. (well done)	2¼
Lamb			
Leg	6 to 7	180°F. (well done)	3¾
Leg (half)	3 to 4	180°F. (well done)	2½ to 3
Cushion shoulder	5	180°F. (well done)	3
Rolled shoulder	3	180°F. (well done)	2½
	5	180°F. (well done)	3

*Standing ribs (8-inch ribs) allow 30 minutes longer.

TIMETABLE FOR ROASTING STUFFED CHILLED POULTRY

Kind of Poultry	Ready-To-Cook Weight	Approximate Amount of Stuffing	Approximate Roasting Time at 325°F.
	pounds	quarts	hours
Chicken			
Broilers or fryers...	1½ to 2½	¼ to ½	1¼ to 2*
Roasters...	2½ to 4½	½ to 1¼	2 to 3½†
Capons and caponettes	4 to 8	1¼ to 1¾	3 to 5
Duck	3 to 5	½ to 1	2½ to 3
Goose	4 to 8	¾ to 1½	2¾ to 3½
	8 to 14	1½ to 2½	3½ to 5
Turkey			
Fryers or roasters (very young birds)	4 to 8	1 to 2	3 to 4½
Roasters (fully grown young birds)	6 to 12	1½ to 3	3½ to 5
	12 to 16	3 to 4	5 to 6
	16 to 20	4 to 5	6 to 7½
	20 to 24	5 to 6	7½ to 9
Halves, quarters, and half breasts	3½ to 5	1 to 1½	3 to 3½
	5 to 8	1½ to 2	3½ to 4
	8 to 12	2 to 3	4 to 5

*Or roast unstuffed at 400°F. for ¾ to 1½ hours
†Or roast unstuffed at 400°F. for 1½ to 2¾ hours

TIMETABLE FOR COOKING FISH AND SHELLFISH

Method of Cooking	Product	Market Form	Approximate Weight or Thickness	Cooking Temperature	Approximate Total Cooking Time
Baking	Fish	Dressed	3 to 4 lbs.	350°F.	40 to 60 min.
		Pan-dressed	½ to 1 lb.	350°F.	25 to 30 min.
		Steaks	½ to 1 in.	350°F.	25 to 35 min.
		Fillets		350°F.	25 to 35 min.
	Clams	Live		450°F.	15 min.
	Lobster	Live	¾ to 1 lb.	400°F.	15 to 20 min.
			1 to ½ lb.	400°F.	20 to 25 min.
	Oysters	Live		450°F.	15 min.
		Shucked		400°F.	10 min.
	Scallops	Shucked		350°F.	25 to 30 min.
	Shrimp	Headless		350°F.	20 to 25 min.
	Spiny lobster	Headless	4 oz.	450°F.	20 to 25 min.
	tails		8 oz.	450°F.	25 to 30 min.
Broiling	Fish	Pan-dressed	½ to 1 lb.		10 to 15 min.
		Steaks	½ to 1 in.		10 to 15 min.
		Fillets			10 to 15 min.
	Clams	Live			5 to 8 min.
	Lobster	Live	¾ to 1 lb.		10 to 12 min.
			1 to 1½ lbs.		12 to 15 min.
	Oysters	Live			5 min.
		Shucked			5 min.
	Scallops	Shucked			8 to 10 min.
	Shrimp	Headless			8 to 10 min.
	Spiny lobster	Headless	4 oz.		8 to 10 min.
	tails		8 oz.		10 to 12 min.

Method of Cooking	Product	Market Form	Approximate Weight or Thickness	Cooking Temperature	Approximate Total Cooking Time
Cooking in water	Fish	Pan-dressed	½ to 1 lb.	Simmer	10 min.
		Steaks	½ to 1 in.	Simmer	10 min.
		Fillets		Simmer	10 min.
	Crabs	Live		Simmer	15 min.
	Lobster	Live	¾ to 1 lb.	Simmer	10 to 15 min.
			1 to 1½ lbs.	Simmer	15 to 20 min.
	Scallops	Shucked		Simmer	4 to 5 min.
	Shrimp	Headless		Simmer	5 min.
	Spiny lobster	Headless	4 oz.	Simmer	10 min.
	tails		8 oz.	Simmer	15 min.
Deep-fat frying	Fish	Pan-dressed	½ to 1 lb.	375°F.	2 to 4 min.
		Steaks	½ to 1 in.	375°F.	2 to 4 min.
		Fillets		375°F.	1 to 4 min.
	Clams	Shucked		375°F.	2 to 3 min.
	Crabs	Soft-shell	¼ lb.	375°F.	3 to 4 min.
	Lobster	Live	¾ to 1 lb.	350°F.	3 to 4 min.
			1 to 1½ lbs.	350°F.	4 to 5 min.
	Oysters	Shucked		375°F.	2 min.
	Scallops	Shucked		350°F.	3 to 4 min.
	Shrimp	Headless		350°F.	2 to 3 min.
	Spiny lobster	Headless	4 oz.	350°F.	3 to 4 min.
	tails		8 oz.	350°F.	4 to 5 min.

TIMETABLE FOR ROASTING FRESH PORK

Cut	Approximate Weight	Internal Temperature	Approximate Cooking Times at 325°F.
	pounds		minutes per lb.
Loin			
Center	3 to 5	170°F.	30 to 35
Half	5 to 7	170°F.	35 to 40
End	3 to 4	170°F.	40 to 45
Roll	3 to 5	170°F.	35 to 40
Boneless top	2 to 4	170°F.	30 to 35
Crown	4 to 6	170°F.	35 to 40
Picnic shoulder			
Bone-in	5 to 8	170°F.	30 to 35
Rolled	3 to 5	170°F.	35 to 40
Boston shoulder	4 to 6	170°F.	40 to 45
Leg (fresh ham)			
Whole (bone-in)	12 to 16	170°F.	22 to 26
Whole (boneless)	10 to 14	170°F.	24 to 28
Half (bone-in)	5 to 8	170°F.	35 to 40
Tenderloin	½ to 1	170°F.	45 to 60
Back ribs		cooked well done	1½ to 2½ hours
Country-style ribs		cooked well done	1½ to 2½ hours
Spareribs		cooked well done	1½ to 2½ hours
Pork Loaf		cooked well done	1¾ hours

TIMETABLE FOR ROASTING SMOKED PORK

Cut	Approximate Weight	Internal Temperature	Approximate Cooking Times at 325°F.
	pounds		minutes per lb.
Ham (cook-before-eating)			
Whole...	10 to 14	160°F.	18 to 20
Half...	5 to 7	160°F.	22 to 25
Shank portion	3 to 4	160°F.	35 to 40
Butt portion................................	3 to 4	160°F.	35 to 40
Ham (fully cooked)			
Whole...	10 to 12	140°F.	15 to 18
Half...	5 to 7	140°F.	18 to 24
Loin	3 to 5	160°F.	25 to 30
Picnic shoulder (cook-before-eating)	5 to 8	170°F.	30 to 35
Picnic shoulder (fully cooked).....................	5 to 8	140°F.	25 to 30
Shoulder roll (butt)................................	2 to 4	170°F.	35 to 40
Canadian-style bacon................................	2 to 4	160°F.	35 to 40

CHEESE SELECTION GUIDE

Cheese	Flavor and Texture	Used For	Goes With
Bel Paese (Italy)	Spongy, mild, creamy yellow interior	Dessert Use as is	Fresh fruit Crusty French bread
Brie (France)	Soft, edible crust, sharper than Camembert, creamy	Dessert Use as is	Fresh fruit
Blue (France)	Marbled, blue veined, creamy white, semi-soft, piquant, spicy	Dessert Use as is in dips, salads, appetizers, cheese trays	Fresh fruit Bland crackers
Brick (United States)	Semi-soft, mild, cream-colored to orange	Use as is in sandwiches, appetizers, cheese trays	Crackers Bread
Camembert (France)	Edible crust, creamy yellow, mild to pungent	Dessert Use as is	Especially good with tart apple slices
Cheddar (England) (American)	Mild to sharp, cream-colored to orange	Dessert As an ingredient in cooking, sandwiches, salads, appetizers, cheese trays	Especially good with apples or pears
Cottage Cheese (United States)	Soft, moist, mild, white, large or small curd	Fruit salads, use as is, as an ingredient in cooking, appetizers	Canned or fresh fruit
Cream Cheese (United States)	White, soft, smooth, buttery, mild	Dessert Use as is in sandwiches, salads, as an ingredient in cooking	Jelly and crackers

Cheese	Flavor and Texture	Used For	Goes With
Edam (Holland)	Firm, mild, red wax coated	Dessert Appetizer, cheese tray (cut off top and scoop out)	Fresh fruit
Feta (Greece)	Snow white, salty, crumbly, but sliceable	Use as is, as an ingredient in cooking	Usually Greek salad
Gorgonzola (Italy)	Semi-soft, blue veined, less moist than blue, piquant, spicy	Dessert Use as is in salads, appetizers, cheese trays	Fresh fruit Squares of crusty French bread
Gouda (Holland)	Softer than Edam, mild, nut-like, with or without red wax coating	Dessert Use as is in appetizers, cheese tray	Fresh fruit Crackers
Gruyere (Switzerland)	Nutty blandness, similar to Swiss, firm, tiny holes	Dessert Use as is in appetizers, as an ingredient in fondue	Fresh fruit
Liederkranz (United States)	Edible light orange crust, texture of heavy honey, soft, robust	Dessert Use as is	Fresh fruit, Matzo, Pumpernickle, Sour rye, Thin slice onion
Limburger (Belgium)	Soft, smooth, robust, aromatic, creamy white	Dessert	Fresh fruit, Dark bread, Bland crackers
Mozzarella (Italy)	Semi-soft, delicate, mild, creamy white	As an ingredient in cooking Use as is in pizza	Italian foods
Muenster (Germany)	Semi-soft, mild to mellow	Use as is in sandwiches, cheese trays	Crackers Bread
Parmesan (Italy)	Hard, brittle body, light yellow, sharp, piquant	Use as is, grated as an ingredient in cooking, table use (use young cheese, not aged)	Italian foods Combine with Swiss for sauces
Pineapple Cheese (United States)	Pineapple-shaped, firm, sharp	Dessert (serve whole and scoop out) Appetizers, salads Use as is	Fresh fruit
Port Salut (France)	Fresh buttery flavor, semi-soft	Dessert Use as is, appetizers, cheese trays	Fresh fruit Crackers
Provolone (Italy)	Usually smoked, salty, hard, yellowish-white interior, mild to sharp	Appetizers Use as is, as an ingredient in cooking Dessert	Italian foods
Ricotta (Italy)	Soft, white and creamy, bland but semi-sweet	Use as is, as an ingredient in main dishes, filling for pastries	
Roquefort (France)	Semi-soft, sometimes crumbly, sharp, blue veined	Use as is in dips, salads, appetizers Dessert	Bland crackers Fresh fruit Demitasse
Stilton (England)	Semi-soft, blue veined, slightly more crumbly than blue	Use as is in dips, salads Dessert Cheese trays	Fresh fruit Bland crackers
Swiss (Switzerland)	Sweetish, nut-like with large holes, pale yellow	Use as is, as an ingredient in cooking, salads, sandwiches, appetizers Dessert Cheese trays	Fresh fruit Squares of crusty French bread

WINE SELECTION GUIDE

Type of Wine	Specific Wine	Serve With	Temperature	When to Serve
Appetizer	Sherry (dry), Vermouth (dry), Port	Appetizers, nuts, cheese	Chilled, room temperature, over ice	Before dinner
Table Wines (white)	Rhine, Chablis, Sauterne, Light Muscat, Sauterne, Riesling, White Chianti	Fish, seafood, poultry, cheese, lamb, veal, eggs, lighter foods, pork (except ham)	Chilled	With dinner, any time, with or without food
Table Wines (red)	Rosé	Curry, patio parties, Chinese food, any food	Slightly chilled	With dinner, any time, with or without food
	Claret	Game, Italian food, beef, Hawaiian food	Slightly chilled	With dinner
	Chianti	Red meat, cheese, Roasts, game, Italian food	Slightly chilled	With dinner
	Burgundy	Cheese, Italian food, game, ham, heartier foods, roasts, steaks	Slightly chilled	With dinner, any time, with or without food
Sparkling Wines	Champagne, dry	Appetizers, fish, seafood, poultry, main courses, desserts, cheese, any festive meal	Chilled	Any time, with or without food
	Sparkling Burgundy	Appetizers, main courses, roasts, game, desserts	Chilled	Any time
Dessert Wines	Port, Muscatel, Tokay, Champagne (sweet), Sherry (cream), Madeira (sweet), Sauterne, Marsala, Malaga	Desserts, fruit, nuts, cheeses, cakes, pastries	Cool room temperature	After dinner With dessert

WINE BUYING GUIDE

The following size bottles give you approximate servings based on 3- to 3½-ounce servings for dinner wines and champagne; 2- to 2½-ounce servings for appetizer and dessert wines.

Size	Ounces	Dinner Wines and Champagne	Appetizer and Dessert Wines
Fifth (4/5 qt.)	25.6	8 servings	8 to 12 servings
Tenth (4/5 pt.)	12.8	4 servings	4 to 6 servings
Split (2/5 pt.)	6.4	2 servings	2 servings
Quart	32.0	10 servings	10 to 14 servings
Pint	16.0	5 servings	5 to 7 servings
½ Gallon	64.0	20 servings	20 to 30 servings
Gallon	128.0	40 servings	40 to 60 servings
Magnum	52.0	16 servings	

COOKING HINTS

Baking	Unless otherwise specified, always preheat the oven at least 20 minutes before baking.
Browning	For best results in browning food in a skillet, dry the food first on paper towels.
Measuring	Always measure accurately. Level dry ingredients with top of a cup or a knife edge or a spoon handle. Measure liquids in a cup so that the fluid is level with the top of the measuring line. Measure solid shortening by packing it firmly in a graduated measuring cup.
Storing	Milk cartons make splendid freezing containers for stocks, soups, etc. They also serve well for freezing fish or shrimp, foods that should be frozen in water.
Baking Powder	Always use double-acting baking powder.
Breads and Cakes	To test for doneness in baking a butter or margarine cake, insert a straw or wire cake tester into the center of the cake in at least two places. The tester should come out clean if the cake is done. The cake should be lightly browned and should be beginning to shrink from the pan's sides. If the cake is pressed with a finger in the center, it should come back into shape at once. If cake tests done, remove from oven, invert cakepan for 5 minutes (or time specified in the instructions); then loosen the cake from the sides and bottom of the pan. Invert it onto a plate or cake rack and turn it right side up on another cake rack so that air may circulate around it. This prevents sogginess. A sponge cake should be tested for doneness in the same manner as a butter cake, but keep the sponge cake inverted until it is thoroughly cold. Then run a knife around the sides and across the bottom and remove from pan. Trim off any hard edges. To test bread made with fruit or nuts, thump the crust and if it sounds hollow, remove the bread from the oven and cool on a wire rack. Bread cooked with fruit or nuts should be tested with a straw in the center. The straw should come out perfectly clean if the bread is done.
Butter	When a recipe says "greased pan," grease the pan with solid shortening or an oil, unless butter is specified. Do not use commercial whipped margarine in place of butter unless the recipe calls for melting the butter.
Candies	The weather is a big factor in candymaking. On a hot, humid day it is advisable to cook candy 2° higher than in cold, dry weather.
Eggs	Unused or extra egg whites may be frozen and used as needed. Make meringues or angel pies with the whites later. Egg whites freeze well and do not need to be defrosted. When boiling eggs, add 1 teaspoon salt to the water. This prevents a cracked egg from draining into the water.
Fruit	A whole lemon heated in hot water for 5 minutes will yield 1 or 2 tablespoons more juice than an unheated lemon.
Sauces	When a sauce curdles, remove pan from heat and plunge into a pan of cold water to stop cooking process. Beat sauce vigorously or pour into a blender and beat. When making a cream or white sauce, melt butter, add flour, and blend well. Remove from heat before adding warmed milk. It should never lump.
Seafood	For improved texture and flavor when using canned shrimp, soak shrimp for 1 hour in ice water and drain. One pound raw shrimp yields about 2 cups cooked and peeled shrimp.
Vegetables	Cooking such vegetables as green peppers and cucumbers briefly in boiling water makes them more digestible than raw vegetables. All strings can be easily removed from string beans after washing if they are plunged into boiling water for 5 minutes. Drain in colander and string. New potatoes should be cooked in boiling water. Old potatoes should start in cold water and be brought to a boil. When vegetables or other foods scorch in cooking, immediately remove the pan's cover and the contents and plunge the saucepan into cold water for 20 to 30 minutes. Wash saucepan and return contents and resume cooking. When cooking cabbage, shrimp, or other foods that cause unpleasant odors, put a dozen cloves in a small pan of boiling water and let simmer. The odor of the cloves will counteract the unpleasant odor with a delightful fragrance. (It's cheaper than commercial deodorant sprays.) Rub hands with parsley to remove any odor.

HERB CHART

For:	Appetizers & Garnishes	Soups	Fish	Eggs or Cheese	Meats	Poultry & Game	Vegetables	Salads	Sauces
Basil	Tomato Juice Seafood Cocktail	Tomato Chowders Spinach Minestrone	Shrimp Broiled Fish	Scrambled Eggs Cream Cheese Welsh Rarebit	Liver Lamb Sausage	Vension Duck	Eggplant Squash Tomatoes Onions	Tomato Seafood Chicken	Tomato Spaghetti Orange (for Game) Butter (for Fish)
Bay Leaves	Tomato Juice Aspic	Stock Bean	Court Boullion Poached Halibut, Salmon		Stews Pot Roast Shish Kabob Tripe	Chicken Fricassee Stews	Tomatoes	Aspic Marinades	All Marinades Espagnole Champagne
Dillweed	Cheese Dips Seafood Spreads Pickles	Borscht Tomato Chicken	Halibut Shrimp Sole	Omelet Cottage Cheese	Beef Sweetbreads Veal Lamb	Chicken Pie Creamed Chicken	Cabbage Beets Beans Celery	Coleslaw Cucumber Potato	White (for Fish) Tartar
Fines Herbs			Baked or Broiled Cod or Halibut	Omelet Scrambled Eggs Cheese Sauce Soufflés	Broiled Liver and Kidneys Roast Pork Pot Roast, Stews Meat Loaf Hamburgers	Dressings Broiled Chicken	Peas Mushrooms Tomatoes		
Marjoram	Liver Pâté Stuffed Mushrooms Butters	Spinach Clam Mock Turtle Onion	Crab Tuna Clams Halibut Salmon	Omelet Scrambled Eggs	Pot Roast Pork Beef Veal	Creamed Chicken Dressings Goose	Carrots Zucchini Peas	Chicken Mixed Green	White Brown Sour Cream
Oregano	Guacamole Tomato	Tomato Bean Minestrone	Shrimp Clams Lobster	Huevos Rancheros	Sausage Lamb Meat Loaf	Marinades Dressings Pheasant Guinea Hen	Tomatoes Cabbage Lentils Broccoli	Vegetable Bean Tomato	Spaghetti Tomato

Herb	Appetizers	Soups	Fish	Eggs/Cheese	Meats	Poultry	Vegetables	Salads	Sauces
Peppermint*	Fruit Cup Melon Balls Cranberry Juice	Pea	Garnish for Broiled Shrimp, Prawns	Cream Cheese	Lamb Veal		Carrots New Potatoes Spinach Zucchini	Fruit Coleslaw Orange Pear	Mint
Rosemary	Fruit Cup	Turtle, Pea Spinach Chicken	Salmon Halibut	Omelet Scrambled Eggs	Lamb Veal Beef Ham Loaf	Partridge Capon, Duck Rabbit	Peas Spinach Potatoes	Fruit	White Barbecue Tomato
Saffron		Bouillabaisse Chicken Turkey	Halibut Sole	Cream Cheese Scrambled Eggs	Veal	Chicken Rabbit	Risotto Rice	Seafood Chicken	Fish Sauce
Sage	Sharp Cheese Spreads	Chicken Chowders	Halibut Salmon	Cheddar Cottage	Stews Pork Sausage	Goose Turkey Rabbit Dressings	Lima Beans Eggplant Onions Tomatoes		
Salad Herbs	Fruit Cup Vegetable and Tomato Juices Seafood Cocktail Sauce		All Fish		Meat Loaf			All Salads	
Savory	Vegetable Juice Cocktail	Lentil Bean Vegetable	Crab Salmon	Scrambled or Deviled Eggs	Pork Veal	Chicken Dressings	Beans Rice Lentils Sauerkraut	Mixed Green String Bean Potato	Horseradish Fish Sauce
Tarragon	Tomato Juice Cheese Spreads Liver Pâtés	Chicken Mushroom Tomato Pea	All Fish	All Egg Dishes	Veal Sweetbreads Yorkshire Pudding	Chicken Squab Duck	Salsify Celery Root Mushrooms	Mixed Green Chicken Fruit Seafood	Bearnaise Tartar Verte Mustard
Thyme	Tomato Juice Fish Spreads Cocktails	Borscht Gumbo, Pea Clam Chowder Vegetable	Tuna Scallops Crab Sole	Shirred Eggs Cottage Cheese	Mutton Meat Loaf Veal Liver	Dressings Venison Fricassee Pheasant	Onions Carrots Beets	Beet Tomato Aspics	Creole Espagnole Herb Bouquets

*Use ½ teaspoon for 6 servings

Courtesy of Spice Islands

SPICE CHART

For:	Appetizers & Garnishes	Fish	Eggs or Cheese	Meats	Poultry & Game	Vegetables	Sauces	Desserts & Beverages
Allspice		*Marinades		Pot Roast Stew Braised Veal Pork, Lamb	*Marinades (for Game)	*Pickling Liquids for All Vegetables	Chili, Catsup Barbecue Spaghetti Brown	Fruit and Spice Cakes Mincemeat	Apple Pie Pumpkin Pie
Cardamom				Spareribs Ham Pork			Barbecue	Coffee Cakes Breads Fruitcake Cookies	Hot Fruit Punches *Mulled Wines
Chili Con Carne Seasoning	Cheese Dips Spreads		Welsh Rarebit Soufflés Baked or Scrambled Eggs	Marinades for Pork Lamb Beef	*Marinades for Chicken	Corn Rice Kidney Red or Lima Beans	Barbecue Cheese		
Cinnamon	Cranberry Sauce Pickled or Spiced Fruits Broiled Grapefruit *Pickles *Chutney Catsup	*Court Bouillon for All Fish and Shellfish		Ham Lamb Pork Chops Beef Stew *Stock for Pickled or Smoked Meats	Dressing for Goose			All Milk Drinks Custard, Fruit, or Rice Puddings Pumpkin, Apple, Peach, Cream, or Custard Pies	*Mulled Wine *Hot Tea *Coffee *Chocolate *Spiced and Pickled Fruits
Cloves		*Court Bouillon Baked Fish	Scrambled or Creamed Eggs	*Marinades for Beef, Pork Lamb, Veal *Stock for Boiling	*Marinades for Game *Stock for Boiling Poultry	Harvard Beets Sweet Potatoes Tomatoes	Spaghetti Chili Wine Barbecue	*Hot or Cold Fruit Punches *Mulled Wines	All Spice Cakes, Cookies, Puddings
Curry Powder	Dips	Broiled Baked	Deviled Eggs Egg Salad Cheese Spreads	Lamb Pork Beef	Chicken	Cooked Vegetables	Marinades for Lamb, Beef, Chicken, Fish, Game White Sauce		
Ginger	*Pickled or Spiced Fruits *Preserves Jams Jellies	Broiled Baked		Pot Roast Steak Lamb *Marinades for Beef, Lamb	Dressing for Poultry *Marinades for Chicken, Turkey	Candied Sweet Potatoes Glazed Carrots or Onions Winter Squash	For: Pork Veal Fish	Canned Fruit Gingerbread Gingersnaps Ginger Cookies	Steamed Puddings Bread or Rice Puddings

Spice								
Mace	Pickles Fruit Preserves Jellies	Trout Scalloped Fish	Welsh Rarebit	Lamb Chops Sausage		Buttered Carrots Cauliflower Squash Swiss Chard Spinach Mashed or Creamed Potatoes	Fish Veal Chicken	Cooked Apples Cherries Prunes Apricots Pancakes Chocolate Pudding	Fruit Cottage or Custard Puddings
Mustard (Hot)	Butter for Vegetables Seafood Cocktail	Crab		Stew Pot Roast Ham Pork	Fried Chicken	Creamed Asparagus Broccoli Brussels Sprouts Cabbage Celery Green Beans Pickled Beets	French Dressing Mustard Sauce Gravies Cheese and Newburg Sauces		
Mustard (Mild)		Fried Broiled		Beef Stew Swiss Steak		Scalloped & au Gratin Potatoes Steamed Cabbage Brussels Sprouts Asparagus Broccoli	French Dressing Cooked Salad Dressing Mayonnaise Raisin, White Sauces		
Nutmeg	Garnish for Milk, Chocolate, and Spiced Drinks	Baked Croquettes Broiled	Welsh Rarebit	Swedish Meatballs Meat Loaf Meat Pie	Chicken	Glazed Carrots Cauliflower Squash Swiss Chard Spinach	White Sauce for Chicken Seafood Veal	Ice Cream Cakes	Cookies Puddings
Paprika	Pâtés Canapes Hors D'oeuvres		All Cheese Mixtures	Ground Beef Dipping Mixture for Pork Chops Veal Cutlets	Dipping Mixture for Fried Chicken	Baked Potatoes	Cooked French Sour Cream Salad Dressings White Sauce		
Tumeric	Marinades for Broiled Salmon, Lobster, or Shrimp		Scrambled or Creamed Eggs	Curried Beef or Lamb	Marinades for Chicken		White Mustard		

Courtesy of Spice Islands

Note: All spices are ground except those indicated by an asterisk (*), which indicates whole spice

Glossary

au Gratin—A food served crusted with breadcrumbs or shredded cheese

au Jus—Meat served in its own juice

à la King—Food prepared in a creamy white sauce containing mushrooms and red and/or green peppers

à la Mode—Food served with ice cream

Al dente—The point in the cooking of pasta at which it is still fairly firm to the tooth; that is, very slightly undercooked

Aspic—A jellied meat juice or a liquid held together with gelatin

Bake—To cook food in an oven by dry heat

Barbecue—To roast meat slowly over coals on a spit or framework, or in an oven, basting intermittently with a special sauce

Baste—To spoon pan liquid over meats while they are roasting to prevent surface from drying

Beat—To mix vigorously with a brisk motion with spoon, fork, egg beater, or electric mixer

Béchamel—White sauce of butter, flour, cream (not milk), and seasonings

Bisque—A thick, creamy soup usually of shellfish, but sometimes made of pureed vegetables

Blanch—To dip briefly into boiling water

Blend—To stir 2 or more ingredients together until well mixed

Blintz—A cooked crêpe stuffed with cheese or other filling

Boil—To cook food in boiling water or liquid that is mostly water (at 212°) in which bubbles constantly rise to the surface and burst

Boiling-water-bath canning method—Used for processing acid foods, such as fruits, tomatoes (with high-acid content), pickled vegetables, and sauerkraut. These acid foods are canned safely at boiling temperatures in a water-bath canner.

Borscht—Soup containing beets and other vegetables, usually with a meat stock base

Bouillabaisse—A highly seasoned fish soup or chowder containing two or more kinds of fish

Bouillon—Clear soup made by boiling meat in water

Bouquet Garni—Herbs tied in cheesecloth which are cooked in a mixture and removed before serving

Bourguignon—Name applied to dishes containing Burgundy and often braised onions and mushrooms

Braise—To cook slowly with liquid or steam in a covered utensil. Less-tender cuts of meat may be browned slowly on all sides in a small amount of shortening, seasoned, and water added.

Bread, to—To coat with crumbs, usually in combination with egg or other binder

Broil—To cook by direct heat, either under the heat of a broiler, over hot coals, or between two hot surfaces

Broth—A thin soup, or a liquid in which meat, fish, or vegetables have been boiled

Capers—Buds from a Mediterranean plant, usually packed in brine and used as a condiment in dressings or sauces

Caramelize—To cook white sugar in a skillet over medium heat, stirring constantly, until sugar forms a golden-brown syrup

Casserole—An ovenproof baking dish, usually with a cover; also the food cooked in it

Charlotte—A molded dessert containing gelatin, usually formed in a glass dish or a pan that is lined with ladyfingers or pieces of cake

Chill—To cool by placing on ice or in a refrigerator

Chop—A cut of meat usually attached to a rib

Chop, to—To cut into pieces, usually with a sharp knife or kitchen shears

Clarified butter—Butter that has been melted and chilled. The solid is then lifted away from the liquid and discarded. Clarification heightens the smoke point of butter. Clarified butter will stay fresh in the refrigerator for at least 2 months.

Coat—To cover completely, as in "coat with flour"

Cocktail—An appetizer; either a beverage or a light, highly seasoned food, served before a meal

Compote—Mixed fruit, raw or cooked, usually served in "compote" dishes

Condiments—Seasonings that enhance the flavor of foods with which they are served

Consommé—Clear broth made from meat

Cool—To let food stand at room temperature until not warm to the touch

Court Bouillon—A highly seasoned broth made with water and meat, fish or vegetables, and seasonings

Cream, to—To blend together, as sugar and butter, until mixture takes on a smooth, cream-like texture

Cream, whipped—Cream that has been whipped until it is stiff

Crème de Cacao—Chocolate-flavored liqueur

Crème de Café—A Coffee-flavored liqueur

Crêpes—Very thin pancakes

Croquette—Minced food, shaped like a ball, patty, cone, or log, bound with a heavy sauce, breaded and fried

Croutons—Cubes of bread, toasted or fried, served with soups, salads, or other foods

Cruller—A doughnut of twisted shape, very light in texture

Cube, to—To cut into cube-shaped pieces

Curaçao—Orange-flavored liqueur

Cut in, to—To incorporate by cutting or chopping motions, as in cutting shortening into flour for pastry

Demitasse—A small cup of coffee served after dinner

Devil, to—To prepare with hot seasoning or sauce

Dice—To cut into small cubes

Dissolve—To mix a dry substance with liquid until the dry substance becomes a part of the solution

Dot—To scatter small bits of butter over top of a food

Dredge—To coat with something, usually flour or sugar

Filé—Powder made of sassafras leaves used to season and thicken foods

Fillet—Boneless piece of meat or fish

Flambé—To flame, as in Crêpes Suzette or in some meat cookery, using alcohol as the burning agent; flame causes caramelization, enhancing flavor

Flan—In France, a filled pastry; in Spain, a custard

Florentine—A food containing, or placed upon, spinach

Flour, to—To coat with flour

Fold—To add a whipped ingredient, such as cream or egg white to another ingredient by gentle over and under movement

Frappé—A drink whipped with ice to make a thick, frosty consistency

Fricassee—A stew, usually of poultry or veal

Fritter—Vegetable or fruit dipped into, or combined with, batter and fried

Fry—To cook in hot shortening

Garnish—A decoration for a food or drink; for example, a sprig of parsley

Glaze (To make a shiny surface)—In meat preparation, a jelled broth applied to meat surface; in breads and pastries, a wash of egg or syrup; for doughnuts and cakes, a sugar preparation coating

Grate—To obtain small particles of food by rubbing on a grater or shredder

Grill—To broil under or over a source of direct heat, such as charcoal

Grits—Coarsely ground dried corn, served boiled, or boiled and then fried

Gumbo—Soup or stew made with okra

Herb—Aromatic plant used for seasoning and garnishing foods

Hollandaise—A sauce made of butter, egg, and lemon juice or vinegar

Hominy—Whole corn grains from which hull and germ are removed

Jardiniere—Vegetables in a savory sauce or soup

Julienne—Vegetables cut into long thin strips or a soup containing such vegetables

Kahlúa—A coffee-flavored liqueur

Kirsch—A cherry-flavored liqueur

Knead—To work a food (usually dough) with the hands, using a folding-back and pressing-forward motion

Marinade—A seasoned liquid in which food is soaked

Marinate, to—To soak food in a seasoned liquid

Meringue—A whole family of egg white-sugar preparations including pie topping, poached meringue used to top custard, crisp meringue dessert shells, and divinity candy

Mince—To chop into very fine pieces

Mornay—White sauce with egg, cream, and cheese added

Mousse—A molded dish based on meat or sweet whipped cream stiffened with egg white and/or gelatin (if mousse contains ice cream, it is called bombe)

Panbroil—To cook over direct heat in an uncovered skillet containing little or no shortening

Panfry—To cook in an uncovered skillet in shallow amount of shortening

Parboil—To partially cook in boiling water before final cooking

Pasta—A large family of flour paste products, such as spaghetti, macaroni, and noodles

Pâté (French for paste)—A paste made of liver or meat

Petit Four—A small cake, which has been frosted and decorated

Pilau or pilaf—A dish of the Middle East consisting of rice and meat or vegetables in a seasoned stock

Poach—To cook in liquid held below the boiling point

Pot Liquor—The liquid in which vegetables have been boiled

Pot Roast—A larger cut of meat cooked with liquid added

Preheat—To turn on oven so that desired temperature will be reached before food is inserted for baking

Puree—A thick sauce or paste made by forcing cooked food through a sieve

Reduce—To boil down, evaporating liquid from a cooked dish

Remoulade—A rich mayonnaise-based sauce containing anchovy paste, capers, herbs, and mustard

Render—To melt fat away from surrounding meat

Rind—Outer shell or peel of melon or fruit

Roast, to—To cook in oven by dry heat (usually applied to meats)

Roux—A mixture of butter and flour used to thicken gravies and sauces; it may be white or brown, if mixture is browned before liquid is added

Sangría—A beverage based on dry red wine and flavored with various fruit juices or brandy; served cold

Sauté—To fry food lightly over fairly high heat in a small amount of fat in a shallow, open pan

Scald—(1) To heat milk just below the boiling point (2) To dip certain foods into boiling water before freezing them (also called blanching)

Scallop—A bivalve mollusk of which only the muscle hinge is eaten; also to bake a food in a sauce topped with crumbs

Score—To cut shallow gashes on surface of food, as in scoring fat on ham before glazing

Sear—To brown surface of meat over high heat to seal in juices

Set—Term used to describe gelatin when it has jelled enough to unmold

Shred—Break into thread-like or stringy pieces, usually by rubbing over the surface of a vegetable shredder

Simmer—To cook gently at a temperature below boiling point

Singe—To touch lightly with flame

Skewer—To fasten with wooden or metal pins or skewers

Sliver—A fine thin slice

Soak—To immerse in water for a period of time

Soufflé—A spongy hot dish, made from a sweet or savory mixture (often milk or cheese), lightened by stiffly beaten egg whites

Steam—To cook food with steam either in a pressure cooker, on a platform in a covered pan, or in a special steamer

Steam-pressure canning method—Used for processing low-acid foods, such as meats, fish, poultry, and most vegetables. A temperature higher than boiling is required to can these foods safely. The food is processed in a steam-pressure canner at 10 pounds' pressure (240°) to ensure that all spoilage micro-organisms are destroyed.

Steep—To let food stand in not quite boiling water until flavor is extracted

Stew—A mixture of meat or fish and vegetables cooked by simmering in its own juices and liquid, such as water and/or wine

Stir—To mix with a steady, circular motion with a spoon, whisk, or beater

Stir-fry—To cook quickly in oil over high heat, using light tossing and stirring motions to preserve shape of food

Stock—The broth in which meat, poultry, fish, or vegetables has been cooked

Syrupy—Thickened to about the consistency of egg white

Toast, to—To brown by direct heat, as in a toaster or under broiler

Torte—A round cake, sometimes made with breadcrumbs instead of flour, which may contain dried fruits and nuts

Tortilla—A Mexican flat bread made of corn or wheat flour

Toss—To mix together with light tossing motions, in order not to bruise delicate food, such as salad greens

Triple Sec—Orange-flavored liqueur

Veal—Flesh of a milk-fed calf up to 14 weeks of age

Velouté—White sauce made of flour, butter, and a chicken or veal stock, instead of milk

Vinaigrette—A cold sauce of oil and vinegar flavored with parsley, finely chopped onions and other seasonings; served with cold meats or vegetables

Whip—To beat rapidly to increase air and increase volume

Wok—A round bowl-shaped metal cooking utensil of Chinese origin used for stir-frying and steaming (with rack inserted) of foods

Recipe Title Index

The Recipe Title Index lists alphabetically every recipe by the exact title as it appeared in Southern Living. *Refer to the Month-by-Month Index, page 321, for an alphabetical listing of every food article and accompanying recipes that appeared each month in* Southern Living. *Refer to the General Recipe Index, page 329, for a listing of recipes according to category and/or major ingredient.*

Month-by-Month Index

The Month-by-Month Index lists alphabetically within the month each food article and accompanying recipes as they appeared in Southern Living. Refer to the Recipe Title Index, page 314, for an alphabetical listing of every recipe by exact title. Refer to the General Recipe Index, page 329, for a listing of recipes according to category and/or major ingredient.

General Recipe Index

The General Recipe Index lists every recipe that appears in this cookbook by food category and/or major ingredient. Refer to the Recipe Title Index, page 314, for an alphabetical listing of every recipe by exact title. Refer to the Month-by-Month Index, page 321, for an alphabetical listing of every food article and accompanying recipes that appeared each month in Southern Living.

A

Favorite Recipes

Record your favorite recipes below for quick and handy reference.

Recipes A-C	Source/Page	Remarks

Recipes D-F	Source/Page	Remarks

Recipes G-J	Source/Page	Remarks

Recipes K-M   Source/Page   Remarks

_____

_____

_____

_____

_____

_____

Recipes N-Q   Source/Page   Remarks

_____

_____

_____

_____

_____

_____

_____

Recipes R-T   Source/Page   Remarks

_____

_____

_____

_____

_____

_____

_____

Recipes U-Z   Source/Page   Remarks

_____

_____

_____

_____

_____

_____

_____